(1987 reprint 40°)

ABRAM S. HEWITT: *With Some Account of* PETER COOPER

ABRAM S. HEWITT

ABRAM S. HEWITT

With Some Account

of

PETER COOPER

By

ALLAN NEVINS

Author of "GROVER CLEVELAND, A Study in Courage"
"HENRY WHITE, Thirty Years of Diplomacy," *Etc.*

HARPER & BROTHERS, *Publishers*

New York · MCMXXXV · London

ABRAM S. HEWITT

CONTENTS

v

Preface

HENRY ADAMS, writing from Washington on January 18, 1904, gave Abram S. Hewitt's second daughter, Sarah, his counsel upon biography and biographers. "My dear Miss Hewitt," he wrote: "After talking with Hay, we agree in advising you to consult old John Bigelow, if you've not already done so. If you have relations with Whitelaw Reid, ask his advice too. You want a New York man, more or less connected with the press, and not by any means of the professorial class. At the same time, in my opinion, you will have to do at least half the work yourself, and had better do it all. Of course, certain moments of the story will require help, but still you had better keep the control in your own hands. You will never be satisfied with anyone else's treatment of the subject. You may look through every biography which has been written about contemporaries for the last generation, and you will not find one which will satisfy you. In fact, you will probably not find one which has not injured the subject of it. Except Hay's Lincoln, every distinguished man has been a victim of or at least has not been benefited by his Life. For that reason I have always refused to undertake the Life of my own father. He stands better on his public record. . . . You are intellectually incompetent, you say; and no doubt we are all intellectually incompetent, but we have to do our work all the same. You will learn as you go. Authorship is anyway at so low an ebb, in an artistic point of view, that we are all practically amateurs. I prefer the amateur to the newspaper man. On the whole I think I feel rather more confidence in the female taste than in the male. The great point is to let the facts state themselves, and to assert nothing outside. Let your father tell his own life, with as little foreign aid as possible."

The essence of this letter is that it would be deplorable to choose a newspaper man while an amateur was available, and that on no account should such a task be entrusted to a member of the professorial class. Henry Adams would doubtless have regarded it as

a signal piece of ill luck that the work should finally fall to one
who has been a newspaper man and is a professor! And he would
doubtless have been right. After all, from Boswell on, the best
biographers *have* been diligent and gifted amateurs. And Mr. Hewitt's life should have been written in his own time by someone
who knew him well.

Yet the author begs to make certain excuses for a book which he
realizes could better have been done by an earlier hand. The subject was suggested to him by President Nicholas Murray Butler,
who, conscious of the great debt which Columbia University owed
to Mr. Hewitt, felt it a matter of regret that no biography had ever
been written. The task was cordially confided to him by the present
head of the family, Mr. Erskine Hewitt, who placed at his disposal materials which Miss Sarah Hewitt had been at much pains
and expense to collect. The theme had self-evident attractions. It
is strange that none but the briefest record has heretofore been
made of the careers of Abram S. Hewitt and Peter Cooper, two
of the most powerful and picturesque personalities in New York's
history; and it is time that this gap were partially filled. The author
is aware that his attempt at a history, a portraiture, and a critical
appraisal often falls short of the mark. A fire destroyed many family
papers; all of Peter Cooper's contemporaries and most of Mr.
Hewitt's are gone, taking their memories with them. Yet the task
has been fascinating in its variety, its contrasts, and the color
drawn from a century of history, and the author has at least given
it no little measure of enthusiasm. A one-volume collection of Mr.
Hewitt's principal writings, shortly to be published, should help
do justice to the liberalism of the ironmaster's ideas. And it is to
be hoped that before long somebody will give separate and fuller
treatment to the work of Peter Cooper.

Thanks are due to many who have assisted in the preparation of
the volume. Mr. Erskine Hewitt has been unsparing in aid, his
advice has been invaluable at every stage, and he has encouraged
rather than discouraged a critical attitude. President Butler has
also given much advice. Judge Morgan J. O'Brien has written a
helpful memorandum upon his relations with Mr. Hewitt. Among
others who have supplied anecdotes and facts have been Miss
Caroline Duer, Mrs. Cadwalader Jones, Mr. Elihu Root, General
Charles H. Sherrill, Mr. Burton J. Hendrick, Mr. Norvin H. Green,

and the late John C. Van Dyke. The officers of Cooper Union have furnished important data. Mr. Edward Ringwood Hewitt has corrected parts of the manuscript and furnished valuable notes. For assistance in research the author is indebted to Mr. Philip Foner, Mr. Jack Foner, Mr. Harry Baehr, Mr. Richard Emery, and Mrs. Walter Campbell. Parts of the manuscript have been read by Mr. Harry Omer of the National Steel Company, Professor Henry Steele Commager, Dr. Alexander C. Flick, Mr. Frank E. Hill, and Mr. Simeon Strunsky. To many others, for the list is far too long to give in full, the author makes grateful acknowledgments.

and the late John C. Van Dyke. The officers of Cooper Union have furnished important data. Mr. Edward Ringwood Hewitt has corrected parts of the manuscript and furnished valuable notes. For assistance in research the author is indebted to Mr. Philip Foner, Mr. Jack Foner, Mr. Harry Beebe, Mr. Richard Emory, and Mrs. Walter Campbell. Parts of the manuscript have been read by Mr. Harry Omer of the National Steel Company, Professor Henry Steele Commager, Dr. Alexander C. Flick, Mr. Frank E. Hill, and Mr. Simeon Strunsky. To many others, for the list is far too long to give in full, the author makes grateful acknowledgments.

ILLUSTRATIONS

ABRAM S. HEWITT: *With Some Account of* PETER COOPER

CHAPTER I

A Craftsman of Old New York

IT SOMETIMES happened during the bustling years of the later
forties, when Polk was President, when the republic was being
pushed to the Pacific, and fuel was being laid for the conflagration of civil war, that on Broadway the citizens of New York saw
Abram S. Hewitt and his father walking arm in arm. The city then
had but a half million people, and many knew the two by sight.
They were a striking pair. The young man, short, alert, resolute of
manner, in his careful Sunday attire of blue cutaway coat, black
satin waistcoat, and tight doeskin trousers, attracted attention by
his high forehead, stern bearing, and keen glance. His father, now
seventy years of age, gray and prematurely enfeebled, walked with
trembling gait, but his eyes still sparkled with benignant vivacity.
He also was short, and life had bent him. But he was still handsome
—with regular features, ruddy complexion, and a look of innate generosity and warmth. Not a few who recognized this pair were aware
of their history. They knew that the keen, quick, brusque-looking
young man, though out of Columbia College only a few years, was
already highly esteemed by the leading business men of the city, was
regarded by Peter Cooper almost as a son, and was universally pronounced to have a brilliant career before him. They knew that the
venerable man with the dignified English aspect was one of the
elders of the city, who well remembered when Alexander Hamilton
had spoken against Thomas Jefferson, when Aaron Burr had practised law and politics downtown, and when John Jay had been
saluted in the streets as governor; and who himself had passed
through a checkered and unfortunate life.

This book is concerned less with a single individual than with a
family; a family of two branches, each distinguished, the Coopers

and the Hewitts; a family which spans American life from 1791, when Peter Cooper was born, until 1903, when Abram S. Hewitt died, and which touched this life at many points. Of the two dominant figures, that of Hewitt will bulk larger, for he was the more versatile and intellectual, and his energy produced weighty achievements in three successive fields. He left his imprint in business, for he was one of the first great American ironmasters; in national politics, for he served five terms in Congress and became a leader of the Democratic party; and in municipal reform, for his work as mayor of New York City is still visible and influential. Hewitt would unquestionably have placed a more conspicuous mark upon American life had he concentrated his energies upon a single objective. He might have rivalled Andrew Carnegie had he not turned away from iron and steel when he had won a fortune; he might have risen to higher Federal office if he had entered politics in early manhood instead of middle life; he might have been a more commanding figure in New York's history had he given that city more of his time. But if he had limited his activities in this way his life would have been less interesting, less a reflection of the important forces of American society, and less useful. Nor did he spend his years in outward action alone. Unlike most of our busy men, he had an inner life; and his thought, reading and ideology bore a vital relation to the work he did in the world.

But this narrative will be only less concerned with the picturesque genius of Peter Cooper, inventor, industrialist, and idealist. It was his daughter whom Abram S. Hewitt married, and he was Hewitt's partner in business, education, and philanthropy for forty years. America has produced few more striking figures. An unwearied adventurer in industry, builder of the first American locomotive, accumulator of a fortune in glue and gelatine, Cyrus W. Field's chief associate in laying the Atlantic cable, Peter Cooper was also one of the rarest spirits this country has known. His mechanical talent, his business shrewdness, his zeal to better himself and others, his pragmatic conception of philanthropy, made him as distinctively an American type as Benjamin Franklin, and one as quickly taken to the American heart. But he had a shining simplicity and a high idealism that Franklin never possessed. He was our first rich man to preach year after year that wealth is a trust, carrying paramount duties and obligations; he was a lifelong egalitarian. However naïve in some ways, he was one of the most courageous of all the thinkers upon social issues whom the agrarian society of the early nineteenth century bequeathed to the overgrown capitalism of the period following the Civil War; and the immense concourse which followed him to his grave in 1883 honored not only the founder of Cooper Union but a brave fighter for the poor man's rights against plutocratic aggression. We shall give some attention also to lesser personages—to Peter Cooper's son Edward, an inventive business leader and able mayor of New York; and to Peter Cooper Hewitt, Abram's son, the inventor of the mercury vapor lamp and many other devices.

But first we must turn back to the tottering, bright-eyed old gentleman who walked on Abram's arm in New York of the forties, and from whom he derived some of his finest qualities of brain and heart —John Hewitt, the English mechanic, cabinet-maker, business failure, and artist who planted the Hewitt family in America.

Early in 1796, when Jay's treaty with England had thrown American opinion into a ferment, there beat up Delaware Bay the sailing vessel which bore John Hewitt from Liverpool to Philadelphia.[1] He told his shipmates that he was nearly nineteen years of age, that he had been born at Penkridge in Staffordshire, during the American Revolution (January 8, 1777) and reared in the village of Cannock hard by, and that he was coming over as a machinist. He was, in fact, part of a migration only less important than that represented by the *Mayflower*—the migration of skilled English workmen who did so much to transplant the industrial revolution to American soil. He had been trained at the great Soho engine-works of Boulton & Watt at Soho near Birmingham.[2] The export of engines was then rigidly forbidden by the British government, but that of engineers could not be so easily controlled; and a place was awaiting the youth in the employ of one of the first Americans interested in steam machinery, Nicholas J. Roosevelt of New York and New Jersey. We can imagine John Hewitt, always talkative, expatiating on the Soho shops, on the types of steam-engines made there, and on his acquaintance with Matthew Boulton, chief builder of the establishment, and James Watt, one of the most eminent inventors

[1] Some uncertain family records state that he landed January 12, 1796; Hewitt Papers.
[2] A good account of these works, and of the Birmingham area, may be found in Charles Pye, *A Description of Modern Birmingham* (1820), and J. A. Langford, *A Century of Birmingham Life, 1741-1841* (1868).

of all time.[1] He had originally been reared in his father's trade of cabinet-maker. But Cannock, a quiet village enlivened only by its annual fair or "wake," was but fourteen miles from Birmingham. He was distantly related to Matthew Boulton, and he had entered the Boulton & Watt works to learn engine-making and engine-design. An apt pupil, he was soon a proficient draughtsman and pattern-maker.

With John Hewitt on his ship was another machinist named Smallman. Indeed, it appears that a considerable group of English engine-workers came to America together, or at least not far apart. Another was Charles Stoudenger, who later became Robert Fulton's capable engineering foreman. There was also one Rhode, or Rhodé, who became the preceptor of James P. Allaire.[2] Many of the country's engines early in the nineteenth century came from the Allaire ironworks. Whether these men emigrated together or not, they were soon all hard at work at the Schuyler Foundry on Second River— that is, at the town now called Belleville, on the Passaic. The plant which Nicholas J. Roosevelt established here was at once renamed Soho in honor of the Boulton & Watt works. Roosevelt, a manufacturer and inventor, believed that with the imported workmen he could turn out serviceable steam engines. It was he who some years later built and navigated the *New Orleans*, the first steamboat to descend the Ohio and Mississippi from Pittsburgh to New Orleans.

For several years John Hewitt was busy at Belleville upon undertakings novel to America. Family tradition and other records show that he assisted in constructing the two powerful engines which pumped the water for the new Philadelphia water-system. Nicholas J. Roosevelt received the contract for them, one on the Schuylkill and one at Centre Square, and they were built and installed in 1799-1800. It is probable that Hewitt helped to construct other machinery. By 1803 the country had five steam-engines; four made at home, one—that of Aaron Burr's Manhattan Water Company in New York—brought from the Boulton & Watt shops.

And it is certain that at Belleville in 1798 John Hewitt made a momentary appearance upon the page of history. That sharp-eyed,

[1] See Samuel Smiles, *Lives of the Engineers*, especially Vol. 3, *The Steam Engine* (1874).
[2] See the article by Abram S. Hewitt in *The Stevens (Institute) Indicator*, Vol. XIV, No. 2, 107ff., which gives some of his father's reminiscences of the Belleville days.

thick-set, indomitable pioneer of American engineering, Colonel
John Stevens of Hoboken, had become well acquainted with the
experiments of John Fitch in steamboat-building. Indeed, he knew
the visionary but heroic Fitch himself; he had seen his curious craft,
crawling noisily down the Delaware with steam-driven oars. Stevens
about 1796 caught the then prevalent "steamboat fever" and resolved on experimentation. Together with Nicholas J. Roosevelt,
who controlled the foundry and workmen, and Chancellor Robert
R. Livingston, who had the influence to obtain a legislative charter
for a company, in 1798 he set about constructing a steamboat. Livingston insisted that the boat and engine should follow his own
decidedly impractical designs. Stoudenger, who was put in charge of
the construction, said he would use them: "But don't blame me if
it doesn't work!" John Hewitt and Smallman then assisted in making and installing the first non-condensing, double-acting steam engine made in this country, and attached it to a water-wheel hung
horizontally under the stern—for this was the Chancellor's queer
idea. When the wheel proved a failure, Stevens designed a set of
elliptical paddles instead![1]

All was ready in June, 1799. On the trial trip from Belleville
down the Passaic to New York and back, Hewitt accompanied the
half-grumbling, half-triumphant Colonel Stevens. An array of notables watched the boat, among them the Spanish Minister. He estimated its speed at five miles an hour, but Stevens thought it did no
better than three and a half. Moreover, the engine shook until the
craft, with pipes leaking and seams opening, was almost racked to
pieces. This experiment took place eight years before the historic
day when Fulton's *Clermont*, spouting smoke and steam before delighted crowds, began its regular service between New York and
Albany. Fulton's vessel, it may be noted, contained the third steam-
engine which the British authorities permitted the Boulton & Watt
works to export.[2] The second had gone to France for the pumping-
station at Chantilly.

There is pathos in a bundle of yellowed letters, still surviving,

[1] Archibald Douglas Turnbull, *John Stevens: An American Record,* 129ff.

[2] See Robert H. Thurston, *History of the Growth of the Steam Engine,* 49ff.,
and Mrs. A. C. Sutcliffe, *Robert Fulton and The Clermont, passim.* The exclusive
right which Robert R. Livingston had obtained in 1798 to navigate the waters
of New York State with steamboats was changed in 1803 to a joint grant to
Fulton and Livingston.

which John Hewitt's parents and other relatives sent him from Staffordshire during these early years. He had originally intended to remain in America but a short time. His father wrote him in 1796 how at night, after he left, the thought of the wild waves had kept his mother awake—"she used to be almost frightened out of her wits when the wind was violent"—and how eagerly they looked forward to his return. The family, a close-knit and affectionate circle, repeatedly implored him to come back. "We all have a wish to see you in your native place," wrote his brother-in-law, Joseph Lees, in February, 1799; "since you find the trade and health of the country is so precarious, we cannot help but think you may live comfortabler among your friends, if you don't get so much money." A month later his brother Robert, also a cabinet-maker, pleaded in stronger terms: "Come back this spring, for what purpose will it answer you to stay, when there is no likeliwards of we coming to you?" He offered to take John into partnership on his return. Twice the family made arrangements with British shipowners to furnish John his return passage if he were in need and unable to pay his way. Gradually a plaintive note crept into his parents' letters. The father wrote that the mother was aging and ailing, and the mother described the father's increasing feebleness, each with a wistful note of longing for the boy.[1]

But John Hewitt never saw them again. Once, in midsummer of 1801, he hesitated and wrote of coming home; but soon afterward, in the spring of 1802, word reached England that he had married. His father, sending wishes "for all the comforts the world can afford," wrote that much as he would like to see the young people in his own country, "I think it is not a desirable one at present, for it has been very much oppressed on account of the war." With the Napoleonic conflict spreading its dark cloud over Europe, and a wife to keep, Hewitt remained in America. Of this first wife we know only that she was named Phoebe Tiemann, of a prosperous family which a half-century later gave New York City a mayor; that she bore him two sons, John and James, who died in infancy and are buried in Bloomfield, N. J.; and that she did not long survive them.[2] Either just before or after his marriage, Hewitt left the foundry and turned to his original occupation as cabinet-maker.

[1] John Hewitt Papers, in the possession of Mr. Erskine Hewitt.
[2] Hewitt Papers.

In his business beginnings we can discern some of the bold enter-prise that later characterized his son. To organize a workshop and make furniture was not difficult, but to find markets was in those days a perplexing problem. The South, where planters appreciated shining mahogany and where the recently-invented cotton-gin was diffusing a golden prosperity, offered an attractive field. Early in 1802, therefore, Hewitt was in Savannah, energetically establishing a branch business which he entrusted to a partner named Benjamin Ansley. Furniture was shipped from his Belleville shop by sea to Savannah, and thence distributed to the sea-islands, to South Caro-lina planters, and to the uplands about Augusta. Georgia alone now counted more than one hundred thousand people, steadily increas-ing, and the demand was strong. Hewitt shortly removed from Belleville to New York, where at the beginning of 1805 he was the owner of a busy establishment at 191 Water Street, with a number of journeymen and apprentices. His work was of high quality. The Museum of the City of New York, at its opening in 1932, exhibited a pair of his tables as specimens of the finest cabinet work of the period.[1]

But the conditions under which his business had to be carried on were exasperating and perilous. To obtain Southern sales, Hewitt obligingly took orders from planters or retailers in Georgia for gen-eral merchandise, shipping it from Savannah or New York. The planters and merchants usually paid in notes, which proved diffi-cult to collect. Frequently an account was settled by a shipment of cotton or rice, which the creditor had to dispose of as best he could. Furniture and other wares, when sent by sea, were often damaged and sometimes lost altogether. A mass of Hewitt's business papers, methodically filed away, leaves one dominant impression: that of a man of scrupulous integrity, proud of his handiwork and over-sanguine of returns, struggling against a sea of difficulties to obtain hard money for his wares, and repeatedly betrayed by misfortune, other men's delays, and their dishonesty.

During the first two years Hewitt's fortunes were especially pre-carious. In 1802-03 he and his partner Ansley ventured too deeply

---

[1] John Hewitt's work as a cabinet-maker has received occasional references in the magazine *Antiques*, and his pieces have been represented in exhibits at the Metropolitan Museum.

in the South, supplying customers with general goods and taking their unsecured notes. When these fell due they were not paid. A heavy epidemic of yellow fever in 1802 drove nearly everybody out of Savannah and made the town "a terror to the country people"; the cotton crop that year was a failure; and a craze for negroes was sweeping over the State and devouring what little ready money the planters possessed. In February, 1803, Hewitt and his bride of a year were in actual want, and only by importunate demands did he obtain enough from his debtors to tide himself over. He tried feverishly to build up a Northern trade, and gradually sold more and more pieces in New York itself.

After 1803 his business became more prosperous, and till the approach of the War of 1812 grew steadily larger. With competition keen and men of less artistry able to undersell him, he labored continuously to widen his market. He began sending cargoes of furniture to foreign ports, and disposed of stock in Madeira, Havana, Curaçao, and even England. This was attended with some risk, for his commission agents occasionally proved dishonest. He found customers in New Haven, Bridgeport, Boston, and other parts of New England. Meanwhile in Savannah he held an incontestable supremacy, and though a few buyers complained of his prices, others would have nothing but his work. On paper, John Hewitt became a man of substantial means. Most of his assets were in long-term notes, but his business seemed on an ever-firmer footing, and if times had continued good he could have collected most of the money due him. In 1810 he was elected a member of the General Society of Mechanics and Tradesmen; he was becoming a man of position. He was known also as an ardent musician, with a voice of remarkable range and quality.

In these years of comparative prosperity, his first wife having died, he remarried. His choice fell on Ann Gurnee, daughter of a small farmer near Haverstraw, N. Y., and descendant of a French Huguenot, Isaac Garnier, who had landed at New York in the first half of the seventeenth century. The Garniers had been people of importance in La Rochelle, France, and tradition states that the progenitor of the American family had escaped to sea during the religious wars in a wine-cask. Much English blood had been mingled with the French strain in America, and the name had become

Anglicized.[1] John Hewitt and Ann were married on October 31, 1808, when she was twenty-three years of age. A portrait painted in later life shows that she was a sweet-faced, attractive woman. But family tradition always laid greater emphasis upon her courage, cheeriness, and resourcefulness in caring for a large household under grinding hardship.

For unfortunately, times again became bad. Jefferson's embargo, bitterly unpopular in New York, interfered with Hewitt's shipments of "fine cabinet furniture" to the West Indies, Curaçao, and other foreign markets. Letters came from England warning him that war was possible and shipping would be unsafe in any event. And then in 1811 there burst upon his head the first of a series of misfortunes which in the end prostrated him. Three years earlier he had given up his partnership in Savannah, and had begun doing business there through a commission agent. His revenues had been much reduced. Now Ansley died. When his estate was settled it was found that during 1806 and 1807, without Hewitt's knowledge, he had borrowed $6,000 from the banks and private lenders on notes to which he had signed the firm name of Hewitt & Ansley. Judgments were immediately taken holding Hewitt responsible. Some furniture which he had sent to Savannah on commission was temporarily attached. For more than two years he was harassed by these debts, and his letters show how bitterly he felt over their injustice. In the end Ansley's widow paid most of the outstanding notes, but Hewitt did not escape without some loss.

And immediately afterward the War of 1812, doubly tragic to the large number of American citizens born in England, began. While there is no evidence in John Hewitt's papers as to his feeling upon the matter, he would simply have been in agreement with most New Yorkers and New Englanders if he had condemned it. Business was instantly prostrated. He had been warned in time to have no goods on the high seas, where they might be seized by British cruisers. But word came from Savannah that no more wares could be sold there—that crops were poor, prices low, men talking of stay-laws. By the fall of 1812 all was confusion and bank-

[1] The population of Haverstraw was primarily British and Dutch. Till 1873 the village was locally called both Warren and Haverstraw, and in 1854 was incorporated as Warren. See F. B. Green, *History of Rockland County* (1886).

ruptcy in the South. His agent in St. Mary's, Ga., a place with which he had steadily traded, sent him late that year an anguished account of the confusion following the attempted seizure of East Florida by American adventurers, and the restiveness of the Indians:[1]

> I could say a good deal on the Distresses of this Community from the Revolution in East Florida, from where we formerly derived our greatest benefit in a commercial point of view, which now from the Depredations and Murders already committed by the Indians, has not only stopped all Trade, but has occasioned a general Evacuation of all Inhabitants from St. John's River to this country, while Buildings on their plantations are Burnt, Crops destroy'd, Negroes carried off, and many have only escaped with their Lives and a small remnant of Property. Consequently my Receivals for large Demands on many of them are this season nothing, and some have commenced taking refuge under the Act of Insolvency. However, under all difficulties from disappointment, I shall make arrangement to meet your Acceptance in favor of Sadler & Sands for the balance of Acct. if possible.

The American seaboard during 1813-14 was inexorably blockaded by the British, and even coastwise shipments of furniture became impossible. All staple American exports were unsalable, and the buying power of the people sank to a low ebb. The defective banking machinery of the nation broke down, specie was drained from the rest of the country into New England, and the South was left almost without a medium of exchange. Hewitt, on learning that many firms had failed in Savannah and that the survivors were tottering, realized that it would be long years, if ever, before he could collect the money owed him in the South. New England was the one section which, its manufactories stimulated by the war, retained a considerable prosperity, and he strove valiantly to make the most of trade in that area. An agent was established in Hartford. Another was sent up the Hudson with boatloads of furniture, pine lumber, and mahogany. But the returns were so meagre that he feared he would be forced out of business. It is eloquent of the wretched conditions of this whole period that, even in time of peace, when he sold large lots of furniture in New England he

[1] John Hewitt Papers.

often had to allow six years for full payment, while his Southern customers rarely finished paying their larger bills in less than ten years.

When in 1815 the treaty of peace restored the hungry markets of Europe to America and brought a transient burst of prosperity, John Hewitt seemed likely to share in it. For a time he did— until fresh misfortunes smote him in rapid succession. In the last days of 1816 his shop and warerooms at 191 Water Street, with all the furniture, business equipment, and lumber, were destroyed by one of the frequent fires of the time. Though letters from friends show that the loss was regarded as a terrible disaster, it was by no means irreparable. He had not only the good will of his business, but a number of accounts from which payments were now hopefully trickling in. After a brief period of discouragement, in which he thought of settling in Savannah, he rented smaller quarters in New York and returned to his calling. He eked out his income by odd carpentering, and even resorted to his old trade of engineer, manufacturing wheels and cotton-gin parts for Southern buyers. He dealt in hardware, particularly the fine brasses then so largely imported from England. He also acted as jobber, receiving consignments of various kinds, particularly lumber, to sell on commission. In short, he was rapidly regaining his feet when he sustained a series of fresh losses at the South, and before he could repair them, was utterly ruined by the treachery of a friend whose notes he had signed.

The involved story of his new Southern losses need not be told in any detail. It is sufficient to say that in the autumn of 1817, he sent another agent, William Scott, to reopen the branch office in Savannah; that Scott, an energetic young journeyman with more loyalty and enthusiasm than business experience, made a contract with the principal furniture dealers of Savannah, Faries & Miller, by which they agreed to accept almost Hewitt's entire output, paying by notes due in four months; and that in the next half-year Hewitt shipped more than $4,000 worth of furniture to them— only to learn that they could not or would not pay. They gave the excuse that the summer of 1818 had brought a new epidemic of yellow fever, and that all the people with money had fled to the country. It may have been a valid excuse. It may be that, urged on by the exuberant William Scott, they had ordered wares too rashly, and that the hard times which again afflicted the whole nation in 1818 were the true reason for their default.

At any rate, poor John Hewitt, wringing his hands at 242 Water Street, was loser of a sum that he simply could not afford. In paper assets he was still far from a poor man, but he possessed so little cash that he was again in actual want. Desperate efforts were required to carry his family through the winter. A cargo of his best wares was hastily gotten together and despatched to New Orleans for disposal at almost any price. The reports he received from his commission agent in Louisiana were depressing in the extreme: the South was glutted with British and Northern goods of all kinds, New Orleans was crowded with merchants already half ruined by the cost of hauling their goods from market to market, and daily auctions of all kinds of wares took place at appalling sacrifices. Among the losers was Hewitt's famous New York competitor, Duncan Phyfe, who after selling at vendue "Extencible tables for $30, Sideboards at $40, Bureaus for almost nothing," was reported out of pocket by $2,500. Part of Hewitt's consignment went to country plantations on long credit. But fortunately, the rest brought in sufficient cash for his immediate needs.

Yet immediately after this came the *coup de grace*, for it proved no less, in the defalcation of a trusted friend. "What the fire started," John Hewitt wrote despairingly in 1819, "man has finished." When the close of the Napoleonic Wars threw thousands of British veterans into industry, the factories strained every sinew to find buyers for their increased production. In the United States a new tariff was hastily thrown up in 1816 to prevent British dumping. But the English exporter found an ingenious method of nullifying its *ad valorem* rates. He would send two agents to New York, Boston, or Philadelphia, and to one, kept in ignorance of the real value of the goods, would consign a cargo at an absurdly low price. The invoice setting forth this false-price statement was presented to the American consul at the port of shipment, endorsed by him, and used as a basis for computing duties at our port of entry. Thus the tariff was largely evaded. But once the goods were inside the United States, the first agent promptly sold them to the second. The latter had a true bill of costs, and placed them on the market at their real value.[1] It appears that Hewitt, always guileless, was entrapped by one of the men engaged in this disreputable game.

This plausible fellow, one Robbins, represented himself as the partner and American representative of an English hardware company. He called at Hewitt's shop and the two in time became friends. When the suspicious custom-house required Robbins to post bonds for $20,000 to guarantee the accuracy of an invoice, Hewitt furnished the security. Shortly afterwards, when Robbins became financially embarrassed and was threatened with a debtor's prison, Hewitt, in an almost incredible burst of generosity, endorsed notes for him to another heavy total—one of his letters says $83,000. Finally, in 1819, Robbins and his clerk were convicted of conspiring to defraud the government, and Hewitt went bail for his fellow-countryman in the sum of $5,000. Thereupon, having gained his freedom, Robbins promptly fled to Canada. Hewitt's bond at the custom-house and his bail-money in the courts were forfeited, while holders of the notes which he had endorsed descended upon him for payment.

This time his ruin was complete, stunning, irrevocable. After so many years of buffeting the waves, after struggling out of one financial slough after another, John Hewitt was exhausted. Everything had to be sold—his stock, his business, his tools, and even his personal belongings. Now forty-two years old, with a family of four growing children to support,[2] he had to begin life anew without money, materials, or helping friends. We might almost add without hope, for it is evident that from this time he was a changed man. His faith in humanity, a corollary of his own simple-hearted honor and integrity, was quenched; his faith in himself was also largely gone. His papers show that some inner spring now snapped. The pride of his life had been the repute of his little manufactory, and his sense that the name John Hewitt on a piece of cabinet-work was a sterling-mark. The loss of money would have been endurable had he been left with means to satisfy his love of craftsmanship in his own bustling shop, with journeymen busy on

[1] For an extended account of these practises, see John Bach McMaster, *History of the People of the United States*, IV, 321-342.

[2] These children were Francis, born in 1809; Sarah, born in 1811; Thomas, born in 1813; and John, born in 1817. John Hewitt Papers.

pieces he had designed, and carters carrying forth some carefully-crated highboy for a Southern mansion or a fine New England house. But like Othello, his occupation was gone. From this time onward we find all his letters written in a trembling hand, totally unlike his previous firm penmanship.

When the blow fell he immediately assigned all his unrealized assets to a friend. Dazed and distraught, he wrote letter after letter to his debtors, frantically urging them to pay him what they could at the earliest possible moment. The next few months were spent in trying to realize something from his possessions and accounts. While matters were at their worst his wife's brother drove in from Haverstraw to see what aid he could give the family. The children were all small; at the close of 1819, Francis was ten years old, Sarah was eight, Thomas was six, and John was only two. They had to be clothed and fed, and there was not even money for the rent. The brother-in-law, seeing them without prospects, bundled them and their household goods into his wagon, and transported them to the small farm owned by Mrs. Hewitt—the only salvage from the wreck—near Haverstraw. Here, in a miserable log cabin, they settled down in the spring of 1820. Some ten acres of tillable ground lay near the house, on which John Hewitt planted a crop, while they had a larger wood-lot. In this spot they passed the next four years; and here, at midnight on July 31, 1822, the fifth child, Abram Stevens Hewitt, was born.

The rise and fall of John Hewitt has been narrated at this length not only because it is a poignant story, interesting in itself, but because it furnishes a background which helps us to understand the traits and outlook of Abram S. Hewitt. He came of parents who had striven much, suffered much, and borne disaster courageously. He was reared in a house almost bare of furnishings, where his fare was usually limited to unsweetened porridge of oatmeal or Indian corn and milk. As he later recalled, his family seldom ate meat except at Christmas and other holidays; he often broke the ice in the horse-trough to wash his face; and worst of all, he was dressed in makeshift garments. A kindly Haverstraw neighbor named Abram Stevens had been helpful, and the boy was named after him. He once brought a bolt of cheap greenish-yellow baize as a gift, and for several years little Abram was dressed in it—the other boys calling him "Baizy." About him, as he played before the cabin door, stretched the rocky, unfertile fields of their Haverstraw farm, mortgaged to obtain money for a cow, a pig or two, some crude implements, and an old nag for plowing. Their social life was as poor as their home; acquaintances were few, and friends still fewer.

Yet back of this family stretched a tradition of enterprise and achievement. A dozen years earlier they had lived in one of the better houses in New York; John Hewitt had counted himself one of the principal furniture-makers of the country; a friend had written that he was glad to learn that he was "filling his coffers as well as his cradle pretty often." The family had dispensed a hospitality which more than one traveller from the South and from old England had acknowledged in glowing terms. For example, an English trader who had come out to make an examination of business prospects in America wrote John Hewitt before his departure that the cabinet-maker had shown him more courtesy and assistance than anybody else. And now, despite poverty, the family still maintained a certain amplitude of outlook. They made a practise of dressing in their better clothes for dinner as well as Sunday.

John Hewitt, after recovering a little money from his Southern debtors, established himself in New York in the spring of 1824 as a baker, with his shop at 5 Laight Street, where his family soon joined him. The next year he reverted to the lumber business, acting as a jobber or factor for a shipper of mahogany and other fine woods from Santo Domingo, and opening an office at the corner of Jay and Washington Streets. A little later still, and he had returned to the bakery. We find him writing a merchant of Augusta, Ga., who owed him money, that the baking business was precarious, "and I assure you that this small amount would be of great use to me." Meanwhile he clung to the farm to help him eke out his living. A tenant there, struggling with the briers and rocks, contrived to send him some produce. In 1827 John Hewitt acquired the patent for a folding bedstead with superior springs and such tight joints as to exclude insects or bedbugs. He opened a manufactory at 20 Hudson Street, between Reed and Duane, where he also lived, and where he called himself a "Patent Bedstead Manufacturer." A few years later he took his son Francis, now a capable joiner, into partnership, and began to make considerable shipments of furniture to the South and to New England again.

But the family still had a hard struggle. It was a larger family; after Abram had come Charles, born near the close of 1824, and Anna, born in 1828, making seven in all. Every member of the household had to share in its burdens and responsibilities.

From these circumstances a boy might well derive strength of character. Abram S. Hewitt inherited from his father his fine rectitude, his driving energy, and some of his altruistic impulses. Of what he inherited from his mother we can say little, for she is a more shadowy figure. Family history, as we have said, credited her with great common sense, industry, power of loyal endurance, and a French wit and humor. From the iron hardships of his youth Abram obviously drew an iron decision and determination. A stern practicality of outlook, a realistic grimness toward both men and institutions, always distinguished him from the father who had lost so much through his naïve faith in others. From his earliest years he knew life as a constant struggle, and was trained to intense application and hard fighting. He often said later that he had made up his mind as a small boy to succeed early so that his mother would never again know the dire straits and anxieties which he had helplessly watched her endure.

CHAPTER II

Columbia College in the Forties

BRAM could have remembered little of the first harsh years on the Haverstraw farm. The stony acres were soon consigned to a tenant, who made a bare living for himself. In 1830 a Haverstraw neighbor wrote John Hewitt that the place was badly cared for. "I suffer to see years passing away without any improvements on your place," he lamented.[1] "Contrary, it falls to destruction and total Wilderness particular about the Buildings. I dont blame the present occupant, in fact he with his teame are in Seasons Laboriously employed to plough among the immensities of loose Stones big Solide in the ground round about rocks and since several years heaps of large Stones. The lotts containing 10 acres round about the buildings, are so handsome situated the soil good No Interruptions of Ridges or holes. . . . I belief that you got as good a tenant as you ever had before, and I can assure you with very little Benefit for their hard laborrs which seems at intervals very discouraging to them. It is no wonder; when the year has passed he has nothing left but just a Hard living. To be sure he has six in familie, but you nor anybody else could or would live as they do." This letter (the neighbor added, "excuse for the freeness I take") indicates what sort of life the Hewitts themselves must have lived in Haverstraw. John Hewitt, always kindly, made a three-year lease to Cooper on more generous terms, and bound him to make yearly improvements.

With his workshop reëstablished at 20 Hudson Street, John Hewitt by 1830 again knew a measure of prosperity. We once more find

[1] John Sutter to John Hewitt, Haverstraw, November 22, 1830; John Hewitt Papers. Abram S. Hewitt used to say that of eight boys he played with in Haverstraw, four later become mayors of their cities—one being his kinsman, Mayor Walter S. Gurnee of Chicago.

him shipping his furniture to all parts of the South, and into New England; he took special pride in the patent bedstead. It is evident that his workmanship was no longer of the highest quality. A letter from one Colonel B. B. Lamar, of Montgomery, Ala., in 1834, complains that "the cradle you sent me is a poor concern; every time the weather is damp it will not work," and that "the tables are poor, coarse, common wood." He had trouble in meeting regional tastes. A New Orleans dealer in 1829 explained that the patent bed would sell slowly there because it lacked the canopy-top which well-to-do Southerners still considered essential. Nevertheless, the family had adequate though narrow means. The eldest son Francis, though lame from birth, made a capable assistant to his father. At a later date he took over the shop entirely, and maintained a profitable clientele in the Southern States. The Hewitt family was able to resume the old friendships in the city, and John Hewitt again became active in the General Society of Mechanics and Tradesmen.

A few of Abram's memories reached vividly back to his third or fourth year. He recalled several early trips between Haverstraw and New York by sailing sloop, the only water conveyance, for steamboats did not stop short of Newburgh. On one occasion the boat was becalmed, and it took three days to accomplish the forty-five miles. He recalled the warm interest of his elders in 1825-26 in the newly-opened Erie Canal. He remembered his mother taking up the newspaper one day in 1828 and exclaiming, "The Governor is dead!"—De Witt Clinton had died. He remembered the talk about wages among his father's workmen, and that $1.50 was considered a very good day's pay for a mason, carpenter, or furniture-maker.[1] Though he was a very shy lad—he later said that till well-grown he always blushed when spoken to—he was precocious and highly observant.

Best of all he recalled a trip to Hoboken, at the age of six or seven, to be introduced to the great engineer John Stevens. One day, walking down to the Jay Street wharf with his father, he had seen a fine steamboat, with four straight slender smoke-stacks, churning rapidly up the Hudson, and had asked about it. His father told him there were two, the best in the world, built by

[1] *New York Railroad Man*, February, 1891, pp. 76-85; address by Abram S. Hewitt, January 13, 1891, to railwaymen.

the Stevens family. "Do you know the Stevens family?" demanded
Abram; and his father finally promised to take him to visit the
Hoboken workshops and to "see the greatest engineer in the world."
They found John Stevens, though bent and grayed by his eighty-
three years, still keen-eyed, strong-jawed, and in possession of all
his faculties.[1] He was delighted to see his old friend, and when
Hewitt said, "This is my son—I want him to see and know you,"
he was keenly interested in the little boy. He called the elder
Hewitt "John"; he patted Abram on the head. They talked of
Smallman and Rhode, of low and high-pressure engines, and of the
famous trip from Belleville to New York and back. "John," said
Stevens reminiscently, "that was a fine engine you helped to build.
There was only one screw, but it had power. Our great mistake
was in not putting the wheels at the side instead of the stern."
And Hewitt, thinking of the new Hudson steamers, agreed.[2]

At six Abram entered school a few blocks away, most if not all
of his elementary education being obtained at Public School No.
10, in Duane Street. We know nothing of his teachers, but he later
recorded a conviction that he had been most efficiently instructed.
Books were so few that most of the lessons were read to the children; and the course was limited to the three R's, with a little composition and some ancient, English, and American history. The
room was hung with mottoes, some of which never left Hewitt's
memory, and made their impress upon his character. "For example," he wrote a friend sixty years later, " 'Order is heaven's first
law,' has been the key to the work which I have tried to do in
public life." The monitorial or Lancasterian system, then in use,
was profitable to at least the brighter pupils. A conspicuously brilliant lad, Abram was regularly a monitor, and in clearing up his
own knowledge before he imparted it to others learned much that
would otherwise have escaped him.

In hours of leisure, the quick youngster saw much of the city.
With chums like "Billy" Riker, later well known as founder of
the greatest drug business in the country, he scoured every part of
it. Long afterward he recalled the quaint sights—the chains stretched
across the streets in front of churches during Sunday services; the
roaming hogs; the Park Theatre, where Kean played; the skating

---

[1] Turnbull, *Life of Stevens*, 135, 136.
[2] *The Stevens (Institute) Indicator*, Vol. XIV, No. 2, 109, 110.

on Sunfish Pond; the interest whenever one of the richer citizens, a Howland, Varick, or De Lancey, bought a new carriage, for carriages were few. In 1835 he watched the great fire which, breaking out on a bitter December night, laid in ashes nearly seven hundred buildings about Pearl, Exchange, and Wall Streets, the richest part of the city. He and a schoolmate named William H. Armstrong walked down to the Battery to see the two steamships, *Sirius* and *Great Western*, as they lay there after their arrival from England; the first steam vessels to cross the Atlantic westward to New York, and the inaugurators of the regular transatlantic service of the Cunard Line. He remembered Thomas Addis Emmett, the Irish patriot exiled the year before the execution of his more famous brother Robert in Dublin, who had risen to be attorney-general of New York and an eminent lawyer. Emmett, who lived on Hudson Street, often stopped at John Hewitt's shop door for a friendly word. Just past sixty, a man of powerful frame and large square head, he exhaled an air of dignity, vigor, and cheeriness. Abram eyed him and his green bag with curiosity, for he had heard schoolmates spout "The Death Speech of Robert Emmett." Late in 1827, Emmett dropped dead while conducting a case in the Federal circuit court; and Abram always recalled the excitement in Hudson Street and the concourse of admirers at the funeral.

The boy took a precocious delight in books. When he was eleven his father led him to the library which the General Society of Mechanics and Tradesmen had recently opened in connection with its school for apprentices in Crosby Street. His opportunities for reading had been limited, for the family owned few volumes. But in Crosby Street he was confronted with one of the richest collections in the city. He felt a hungry desire to possess himself of these treasures, and said to his father, "I am your apprentice, so I can have some of these books." The librarian mentioned Shakespeare; he began with *The Tempest*, and did not stop till he had read every play. Thereafter half his spare hours were spent in Crosby Street.[1]

The next summer he turned his reading to account. His father knew the wealthy commission merchant Jonathan Goodhue, who

[1] Hewitt's address, *Centennial Celebration of the General Society of Mechanics and Tradesmen*, 1885; Published Proceedings. The original library and school had been in Chambers Street.

had a large store in South Street, where he acted for Salem ship-owners, and sold imported commodities, chiefly drygoods.[1] Goodhue was a Salem man himself, prominent in civic affairs, and possessed of some culture. One of his children was recovering from a long illness, and the youngster's eyesight being weak, Abram was engaged to read to him several hours daily—sometimes five or six. They read the histories of Gibbon and Hume; Locke, Addison, and Dr. Johnson; and translations of ancient classics. Abram stored in his mind part of what he did not understand, to be made useful later. He always recalled with some resentment that Goodhue failed to pay him what the service was worth—that after weeks of reading, he tendered the boy $10, and when tears sprang into his eyes, increased the compensation only $5; for Abram had counted on enough to buy his mother a new dress. But the reading repaid itself.

At thirteen Abram entered as a free pupil the Grammar School of Columbia College, of which the "rector" was Charles Anthon, LL.B., professor of Latin and Greek in Columbia. Its connection with the college having become nominal, it was at this time really a private enterprise; but it was one of the most efficient preparatory schools in America.[2] Courses were given in the classics; in French, German, Italian, and Spanish; in mathematics, bookkeeping, declamation, composition, and mythology; in trigonometry, natural philosophy, and chemistry; and for those who paid a dollar extra every quarter, in vocal music. Each quarter lasted twelve weeks and vacations were short. Students might choose a full English and mathematical course without Latin and Greek (fee $10 a quarter), or with them (fee $12.50). Abram elected the classics, in which he obtained a thorough grounding. The college library of some 7,000 volumes was open to pupils. For three years Abram studied hard in the substantial school building which had been erected in 1829 on Murray Street, just behind the college; and he kept at the head of his class, taking every prize open to him. Then in 1838 he was graduated.

---

[1] Cf. Walter Barrett, *The Old Merchants of New York*, I, 112.

[2] The Grammar School had been founded in 1784 by William Cochran, a graduate of Trinity College, Dublin, who was Anthon's predecessor as professor of the classics in Columbia College. In 1828, after a period of eclipse, it was revived or recreated, and Anthon took charge in 1830. Cf. Brander Matthews, et aliis, *A History of Columbia University*, 1754-1904, 62, 109-110.

Another financial panic had just devastated the land; money in the Hewitt family was as scarce as ever. But Columbia College offered some free scholarships, of which two were assigned to the New York Public School Society. Abram entered the competitive examination held by this organization and easily secured one, thus escaping the tuition charge of $90 a year. The achievement was a turning-point in his career. His father had planned to train him for a trade; but, impressed by Abram's brilliancy and fondness for books, he now approved a larger ambition. "If you want an education," he said, "you want a good one; go ahead, and I'll help you all I can."

The youth might well feel elated by his opportunity. Columbia College, to be sure, was still a small institution, financially weak, narrow even for that day in its emphasis on the classics, and of lower reputation than Harvard, Yale, or the University of Pennsylvania. Dissatisfaction with its shortcomings had led a few years earlier to the establishment of New York University. The student-body numbered between one hundred and one hundred and twenty-five, and the annual income fell short of $25,000. Nevertheless, the college had claims to distinction. The roll of alumni included such names as Alexander Hamilton, John Jay, Robert R. Livingston, Gouverneur Morris, John Stevens, De Witt Clinton, and Daniel D. Tompkins—names that had made New York great. The wealthiest and most aristocratic families in the city took pride in the institution, even if they seldom loosed their purse-strings for it. The faculty under President William A. Duer, though small and paid only $2,500 a year each, was able, scholarly, and devoted, and made up a group not surpassed even in Cambridge or New Haven. The students and teachers formed a closely unified body—veritably a large family—and a promising youngster received careful personal attention.[1]

The college, to which Abram could walk from his home in five minutes, was happily situated. It occupied a plot in what had lately been the most fashionable part of the city, bounded by Church and Murray Streets and College Place, directly west of the site of the

---

[1] *Ibid.*, 112-123. Hewitt had attracted some attention by taking a mathematical prize. He said later he placed an example on the blackboard; sat down; saw an error in the work; erased the problem and did it over again, still finishing first.

present-day Woolworth Building. Business had only lately begun
to press heavily about it. There was a single massive brick building
of three stories, covered with light brown stucco and trimmed with
gray freestone, which faced southward over a large grassy lawn,
bordered by spreading sycamores. At the eastern and western ex-
tremities two pleasant houses, occupied by faculty members, projected beyond the central structure, and helped to shelter the green.

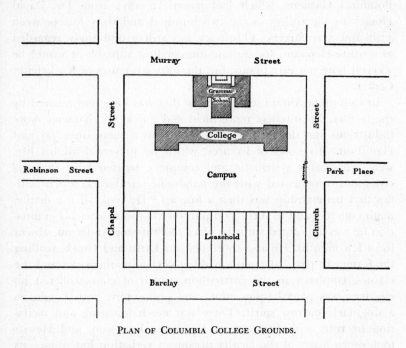

PLAN OF COLUMBIA COLLEGE GROUNDS.

Broad steps led up to the white-painted doors. Here the fiery-
spirited Hamilton had trod the flags; here that elegant scholar and
witty man of society, President Myles Cooper, had faced the Revolutionary mob in 1775; here young De Witt Clinton and long,
lanky John Randolph of Roanoke had sauntered and studied. With
its air of dignity and seclusion, the building looked a veritable seat
of learning; and alumni have recorded that in summer, with the
shadow of the broad leaves shimmering on the brown walls and
white walks, it was a delightful spot. On the first floor was the
chapel, flanked by classrooms, and on the second were more class-

rooms and the library. The structure was surmounted by a tall cupola, from which the college bell rang sonorously to chapel at nine each morning, and by a few emphatic clangs marked the close of each recitation hour. It is a pity that this green campus, with its trees planted when George II ruled the Province, should not have been preserved down to our own day as a park.

Far uptown, in a district which few penetrated, lay the Elgin Botanical Gardens, which had passed in 1812 from Dr. David Hosack to the college—some two hundred and sixty lots between 47th and 51st Streets. This tract was still grumblingly regarded as a white elephant, for no one foresaw how valuable it would be when it bore not rare plants, but the lofty structures of Rockefeller Center.

In Columbia Abram made a mark that was long remembered by the faculty. No intellect more lucid and quick, no character more industrious and determined, had been known there since Jay and Hamilton. His notes of lectures, which he preserved all his life, were remarkably systematic and complete, written with care for style, and ornamented with the handsome scroll-work which testifies that penmanship was then a fine art.[1] He took all the mathematics offered, and to such good purpose that soon after his graduation he was appointed tutor in place of Professor Anderson, absent for a few months. He also continued his Latin and Greek, reading the former in particular with avidity. Next to mathematics and the classics, emphasis in the curriculum, which of course offered no electives, was placed upon ethics and philosophy, both taught in a singularly narrow spirit. There was much lecturing and recitation by rote, with little or no classroom discussion, and Hewitt took down many of the faculty discourses verbatim; but numerous written essays gave some scope for originality. During his four years, Abram not only led his class, but excelled in forensic and literary competitions; and in doing so he gained a certain reputation in a city where most educated people took an interest in the college.

Several of the faculty exercised a strong influence upon Hewitt. Not least of these was President William A. Duer, a distinguished jurist, who took personal charge of the Freshman course in com-

---

[1] These notebooks, with his undergraduate papers, are now in the collection of Columbiana belonging to Columbia University.

position, and lectured to Seniors on constitutional jurisprudence. Now past sixty and in failing health, Duer was nevertheless a man of robust personality. He had been born in New York while the Revolutionary War was still raging, had graduated from Columbia College, studied law, and then impetuously enlisted as a midshipman against France, serving on the same ship with Stephen Decatur. Becoming a law-partner of Edward Livingston when the latter was mayor, he had followed him to New Orleans. After his return he was appointed a judge of the supreme court of New York. He had resigned this post in 1829 in order to liberalize and invigorate his struggling alma mater. At Columbia he introduced courses in science and modern languages, bent a careful eye on the teaching, and proved in general a wise, efficient administrator. Of medium height, portly, with high bald brow and piercing eyes, he had a commanding presence. Hewitt always delighted to relate how he once quelled a nocturnal student riot in the college yard. He emerged on the top steps, candle in hand; the expression of intense shock on his face sobered the boys; and he said quietly, "The ringleaders of this disturbance will present themselves at my office tomorrow morning." They did.[1]

Several other faculty-members were decidedly picturesque; for example, the fussy, self-important, versatile Dr. McVickar, who not only taught logic, ethics, philosophy, and rhetoric, but was one of the earliest scholars in the country to lecture upon political economy. McVickar was a tall, spare, handsome man, quick in his movements, irascible, and above all aristocratic. He was proud of his family connections, of his learning and professorial dignity, of his importance in Episcopal and Whig circles. With chin in air, quick strut, and martinet ways, he was disliked by many, but everyone recognized his usefulness. His talks upon English writers were particularly interesting, for during his travels in Europe he had visited Wordsworth at Rydal Bank, Scott at Abbotsford, Southey, James Mill, and other notables. His publications, ranging from a devotional manual to a pamphlet advocating a national bank, showed a versatile mind.[2] Equally sharp-cut was the individuality of

---

[1] For President Duer, see the article by his descendant William A. Duer in *Columbia University Quarterly*, March, 1902.

[2] Cf. Joseph Dorfman and Rexford Guy Tugwell, "The Rev. John McVickar," *Columbia University Quarterly*, December, 1931. McVickar liked to impress

Charles Anthon, the Jay Professor of Greek and Latin—"Bull Anthon," as the students called him in tribute to his obvious force. He was physically the biggest man on the faculty; heavy-limbed, broad-shouldered, with massive head, black deeply-set eyes, and a strong jaw. His father had been a German surgeon who, captured by an English privateer while serving in the Dutch West Indies trade, had entered the British army before the Revolution and after Pontiac's rebellion had been stationed at Detroit. From him Anthon had inherited a military sternness. He had other peculiarities. Though a brilliant conversationalist, he avoided society; he never married, devoting himself to his sisters; and he took even his walks in the college grounds after dark. The best classicist in America, he had a broad literary bent to which Poe did justice in a brief critical essay.[1] From his private library, one of the largest in the country, he sent out an endless series of textbooks and editions of classical authors, executed with a keen perception of method and a wealth of accurate erudition; while from time to time he produced a more ambitious compilation. Hewitt, who had gotten behind his sternness in the grammar-school, profited by his learned talk. So he did also from his friendship with Anthon's junior lieutenant, Henry Drisler, who had many eccentricities, including a hatred of walking sticks and tobacco, but who was a rugged, honest classicist.[2]

With the professor of natural philosophy, James Renwick, Hewitt had a quarrel. He not only taught physics and chemistry but was a distinguished engineer, assisting the city in the construction of the Croton Aqueduct, and the Federal Government in survey-

---

upon such young men as Hewitt the value of application, pointing to himself as one in whom perseverance had hardened a feeble constitution, made a treacherous memory retentive, and created a large fund of scholarship. Hewitt took his course in rhetoric, and his notebook shows how systematic was the instruction.

[1] *Poe's Works,* Putnam Edition, 1902, VIII, 349-352. As Hewitt was intimate with Anthon, it is worth noting that Poe wrote: "His address in general is bold, frank, cordial, full of *bonhomie.* His whole air is *distingué* in the best understanding of the term; that is to say, he would impress anyone at first sight with the idea of his being no ordinary man."

[2] This was a lifelong friendship; Drisler, after twice being acting-President of Columbia, and teaching for more than fifty years, died in 1897. See Evert A. and George L. Duyckinck, *Cyclopaedia of American Literature,* I, 400, 402; and articles on Drisler in *Harper's Weekly,* June 9, 1894, December 11, 1897.

ing the disputed Maine-New Brunswick boundary. But his temper
was difficult, and so already was Hewitt's. Hence a letter of Renwick's, December 13, 1841, to John Hewitt: "Your son, a member
of the Senior class of this institution, holding too the highest rank,
addressed to me during the past week language unbecoming the
relative positions in which we stand, and which should I pass it
unnoticed would be subversive of all discipline. I ascribed this to
a temporary irritation, and instead of taking immediate steps for
bringing him to the punishment which the statutes of the college
would probably require to be inflicted in such a case, I excluded
him from the room. . . . On meeting him on the college green this
morning he coolly and deliberately repeated the offence, and
coupled with it a threat of appeal to a higher authority." Renwick
wanted an immediate apology, or he would summon Abram before
the trustees; as this would cut him off from further honors, the professor begged John Hewitt to save the youth from his "folly and
self-conceit." But the breach was healed, for Abram remained at the
head of his class.

Students in those days made little use of the college library, which
was all too carefully guarded. Borrowing was allowed only between
12 and 3 on Saturdays, was restricted in general to the three highest
classes, and was discouraged by a librarian who felt happiest when
the books were all safe on their shelves. The only catalogue was
one in manuscript by Professor Moore. A ledger in which outgoing
books were charged shows that many students got through college
without more than a healthy month's reading.[1] But Hewitt, especially in his last two years, almost set a record for borrowings.
In history he took home the *Anglo-Saxon Chronicle*, Hallam's
Middle Ages, Froissart's *Chronicles*, Hume's *History of England*,
Hallam's *Constitutional History*, Heron's *Scotland*, and various
American histories and biographies. In pure literature his selections
ranged from Burton's *Anatomy* and Milton's prose to Charles
Lamb. He read a good deal of science—Cuvier, Humphrey Davy,
and works on mathematics and mineralogy—and a list of books
on criminology. Much of this reading was distilled into essays,
rather laboriously modelled after the papers in the heavy British
and American reviews of the day, and carefully tinged by the Epis-
copalianism cultivated at Columbia. A study of "The Mission of

[1] This ledger is in the Columbiana Room of Columbia University.

the Roman Empire," for example, ended in some resounding religious maxims. A paper on "England's Three Revolutions," which begins with a sonorous quotation from Burke, is full of ringing democratic pronouncements and sympathy with the Chartists. An essay on "The Rise and Fall of the Spanish and Portuguese Colonies" likewise mingles reflections upon the superiority of Anglo-Saxon freedom and Protestant ideals with poetical quotations from Shakespeare and Sir Walter Scott.

He not only won four times in succession the gold medal that the college awarded for scholarship and character, but received various special marks of faculty esteem. He did research and clerical work for President Duer and Dr. Anthon, and in his papers are their letters thanking him for assistance. He was a member of the Philolexian, a literary society founded in 1802, and, in the absence of organized athletics, a leading centre of student interest. Each year in May it held an anniversary meeting. Hewitt spoke at that of 1842, which took place in a church at the corner of Greene and Broome Streets, and received mention in the press. When President Duer's resignation was announced to the students this year, it was by a letter addressed to Hewitt as head of the graduating class. It was Hewitt who, taking charge of a small fund raised for the purpose, commissioned Henry Inman to paint Duer's portrait.[1]

Yet while making this sturdy record he had to pay his own way entirely. His tuition was free and he of course lived with his parents, now established at 160 Duane Street. But he clothed himself, bought his own books, and paid all incidental expenses. It is evidence of his ambition that he dressed not only neatly but with attention to fashion; for his tailors' bills show a strikingly large outlay for broadcloth, satin waistcoats, and the best boots. He had ingenious ways of making money. Thus at one time he familiarized himself with the book market, frequented the wholesale book-auctions regularly held uptown, bought volumes there at bargain rates, and hurried downtown to sell them to the retail stores. Such transactions, as old bills of sale still show, sometimes paid him several dollars. He did copying, and odd jobs for merchants.

[1] Hewitt also won a special award for a long Latin essay upon the career of George Washington, offered by a friend of Columbia College; and in later life he sometimes spoke amusingly of the locutions he used in order to express modern facts in the ancient tongue—"leaden hail," for example, serving for bullets.

His principal resource, however, was tutoring. In this he had practice at home, for throughout his college years he drilled his younger brother Charles at night in what he himself had learned by day. Laggards in his classes came to him for paid lessons, while he also taught youngsters preparing for college. One of his pupils was a grandson of the aged Albert Gallatin, then closing his cosmopolitan career at 57 Bleecker Street, and when he gave the boy his first algebra lesson, Gallatin came into the room to listen. His strongly-marked features and austere manner disconcerted Abram. But at the close the old statesman remarked emphatically, "Young man, that is the clearest mathematical exposition I have ever heard!"—no slight praise from a former Secretary of the Treasury. Under date of October 27, 1841, a merchant named F. Cottenet paid Abram $40 for instruction given his sons.

But it was not all work and no play during these Columbia years. Hewitt used to join his classmates in playing rounders on the college green. They often batted the ball out of bounds and into the rear of a fine house fronting on Barclay Street. On one occasion the boys exhausted their stock of balls, and found they did not have money for a new one. Hewitt was deputed to ring at the Barclay Street house and ask for the ball that had last disappeared into its yard. The door was opened by a kindly-faced woman, of whom he asked permission to go in and pick up the ball. She hesitated, and at that moment a gentleman appeared from the study adjoining the hallway. He was tall and handsome, with rich brown locks shading a sunny, benevolent face. Hewitt did not know that he was Robert L. Stevens, one of the greatest mechanical and naval engineers produced by the United States during the nineteenth century.

"So you want a ball," he said genially. "Will you be satisfied with one ball?" In great embarrassment, Hewitt replied, "Yes, sir." The gentleman smiled. "Margaret," he said, "go and get the basket." A few minutes later she reappeared with a basket in which were piled fifteen or twenty balls. "Are all these yours?" demanded Mr. Stevens with a twinkle. "I suppose they must be," stammered Hewitt. "Well, nearly every one of them has broken a window in my music room." "But," protested the boy, "we didn't do it on purpose." "No," Stevens replied, "I know that. I was a boy myself once, and I have no doubt that I have broken dozens of windows in my time."

He added: "Take them, go back, enjoy yourselves, and when you have broken all the windows in my music room, go over to Hoboken and I will give you a fair field in which you can play without breaking any window."

The boys continued to play ball and to break the windows of the eminent engineer.[1]

Commencement exercises in those years were held in the autumn. They were an important event, celebrated with pomp and dignity; President Washington and the houses of Congress had attended those of 1789. In 1842 they took place on October 4, in the Middle Dutch Church on Cedar Street, for Trinity, their usual scene, was closed for repairs; and Abram was Greek salutatorian, that being the position of greatest honor.[2] At 9:30 in the morning a procession moved to the church which included Governor William H. Seward, the lieutenant-governor, members of the legislature, the mayors of New York and Brooklyn, and other dignitaries. The outgoing class numbered thirty. Before the graduation ceremonies began, Dr. Nathaniel F. Moore was installed as president of the college, and addresses were made by him and Peter A. Jay, chairman of the board of trustees. Abram then rose to speak. We may imagine the thrill of pride felt by John Hewitt as, after all his years of toil and sorrow, the English mechanic saw his handsome son standing before the wealth and fashion of the city as the most brilliant student of the college.

[1] *The Stevens (Institute) Indicator, ut supra.*
[2] New York *Tribune, Evening Post,* October 5, 1842. Of the thirty graduates three were absent on leave; twelve besides Hewitt were given parts in the programme. An "Honorary Testimonial" was conferred upon Edward Cooper and E. V. Clark, "late members of the highest class of the Literary and Scientific Course"; that is, members of the graduating class who had dropped out because of illness.

CHAPTER III

European Tour: 1844

BURKE, whom Hewitt frequently quoted in his college essays,
had written in his *Speech on Conciliation with America* that
a capital source of the fierce spirit of liberty which characterized the colonists was their widespread interest in legal knowledge. "In no country perhaps in the world," he asserted, "is the
law so general a study." At that time it was the principal avenue
to public distinction; it so remained during the Revolution and
afterwards; and when in 1842 Hewitt faced the world, it was still
the best means of gaining public office and influence. From the
beginning of his career Hewitt wished to play a part in governmental affairs, and even when most immersed in the iron business
he subconsciously felt it a deviation from his true path. President
Duer's lectures and repute as a jurist had perhaps touched a responsive chord, while he has told us what a spell was thrown over
him in college by the fame of James Kent. Though Kent did no
teaching and received no salary after 1826, he nominally remained
professor of law in Columbia College until his death in 1847, his
name giving lustre to the faculty register. Hewitt often saw him at
college gatherings. He knew something of Kent's *Commentaries*,
which, he later tersely stated, "have had a deeper and more lasting
influence in the formation of national character than any other
secular book of the century."

We do not know in what law office Hewitt studied during
1842-43—perhaps it was in several. It was impossible to pursue law
in Columbia College; for not until Theodore Dwight was appointed
professor of law in 1857 did it offer a regular course.[1] At that time

[1] F. M. Burdick in Brander Matthews *et aliis*, *A History of Columbia University 1754-1904*, 77, 80, 335-353.

requirements for the bar were low, and, with some supervision from an attorney, Hewitt probably did most of his studying at home. We do know that in a year and a half he went through some of the standard books, Blackstone, Coke upon Littleton, Kent's *Commentaries*, and the like, and did some practise work in a law office.[1] But meanwhile he had to labor almost incessantly to support himself and help support his family. He took just one vacation in these years. In August, 1842, he went on a ten-day excursion with Dr. Moore up the Hudson, across by the Erie Canal to Niagara Falls, and on to Toronto; giving up for this a fishing excursion which he had planned with Lorenzo Shepard.

Most of his work was as a teacher in the grammar school of Columbia College, where Dr. Anthon and Henry Drisler, the rector and sub-rector, had immediately offered him a place. The school was the best of its kind in the city. Divided into four departments, the English, classical, commercial-mathematical, and collegiate-mathematical, it really offered a wider range of electives than the college itself.[2] For a year and a half Hewitt was principal of the collegiate-mathematical department. The grammar school had a staff of some twelve or fourteen, and he soon obtained a place for his brother Charles as "principal of the junior department"—that is, in charge of pupils from five to nine years old. At the same time Abram continued his private tutoring. Since he was warmly recommended by the Columbia faculty, there was plenty of remunerative work; one pupil, Charles Swan, even paid him $150 a term. At first he was occupied from 9 to 3 with the grammar school and private pupils, giving the late afternoon and evening to law study. But after a time he even tutored between 7 and 9 in the morning. One of his pupils was Peter Cooper's son Edward, not quite two years his junior, who had been his classmate at Columbia but had fallen behind through sickness.[3] This tuition was given chiefly at Peter Cooper's house, with which Abram was already familiar.

[1] Most published sketches of Hewitt incorrectly state that he was admitted to the New York bar. For extensive researches proving that he was not the author is indebted to Dr. Miles O. Price, librarian of the Columbia University Law School, and Mr. H. B. Closson of Parsons, Closson, & McIlvaine.

[2] Annual announcements of the Grammar-School, 1843, 1844, in Hewitt Papers.

[3] Edward Cooper was born October 26, 1824; see the "Biographical Notice" of him in *Transactions of the American Institute of Mining and Metallurgical Engineers*, Vol. XXXVII, 349-356, by Rossiter W. Raymond.

2. Mr. John Hewitt

1. Mrs. John Hewitt

4. MR. PETER COOPER

3. MRS. PETER COOPER

5. BED AND CABINET MADE BY PETER COOPER

6. Mantelpiece carved by Peter Cooper

7. Chair and table made by John Hewitt, now in Ringwood

8. Dressing-table and Sideboard made by
John Hewitt, now in Ringwood

9. COLUMBIA COLLEGE IN 1828

LECTURE FIFTH

New Testament
Genuineness — Historic Proof

Ques I Contents.

It consists of 27 books — Five narrative — 21 are letters
or Epistles. One is prophetic. There are only eight authors.
Five are Apostles. One called to be such by miracle.
and Two companions of the Apostles, viz Mark and
Luke, and wrote their books under the guidence of
St Peter and St Paul.

Dates 1. Earliest that of St Matthew. A.D. 38. The language was in Hebrew, but afterward in Greek.

2. The latest was St John, to supply deficiencies
in the others. A.D. 96 or 98.

Ques II Genuineness how proved?

1. As a practical question, it is received on the authority
of the Christian Church. But every one may examine
the question according to his ability.

2. Critical. To be proved in the same manner as any
other ancient Manuscript.

Tests. 1. The external proof — to contemporary writers to see
if there were such a work.

10. SPECIMEN PAGE FROM HEWITT'S NOTEBOOK IN COLUMBIA COLLEGE

During the spring of 1843 the professor of mathematics at Columbia, Henry J. Anderson, a versatile man who had once helped Bryant edit the *Evening Post*, was ill; and Hewitt, as we have seen, took his place with the title of tutor. In June Anderson resigned. He wrote Hewitt to acknowledge his "promptness and skill" in the work, and added:[1] "You have also my thanks for the great extent to which you have lightened my college labours by your admirable training of your private pupils. I have never found classes of young men brought forward so rapidly, so efficiently, and so uniformly as I have under your tuition. . . . I cannot conclude without a personal acknowledgement of the fidelity, punctuality, and good management of any business entrusted to you." Hard-pressed as he was, Hewitt refused all salary for the tutorship, for he felt that he owed Columbia a recompense for his free tuition.

But the triple burden of law study, grammar school, and tutoring proved too much for him. In the autumn of 1843, his eyes failed. It was not the first such difficulty—in college he had once been incapacitated in the same way; but this time it was serious. For a few weeks he struggled on with his work, but at Christmas the doctor intervened and ordered a complete rest.

Edward Cooper, who had just graduated at Columbia, was eager for a European tour. Hewitt had saved not far from a thousand dollars; and it was arranged that the two should go abroad for ten months. To eke out his savings, Hewitt tried to obtain some foreign employment. He made a trip to Washington in February in the hope of being commissioned by the State Department to take dispatches abroad. Professor Anthon asked Thomas R. Dew of William and Mary College to recommend Hewitt to President Tyler, and this Dew cordially did.[2] Dr. Wainwright, the Episcopal minister who had officiated at Daniel Webster's second marriage in 1829, wrote that statesman that if he could help Hewitt "you will serve a most deserving young man, and one who is in danger of becoming a martyr to the cause of learning." Hewitt was acquainted with Samuel J. Tilden, rising young lawyer of thirty, who gave him a letter to Senator Silas Wright. The trip to Washington was fruit-

[1] Dr. Henry James Anderson to Hewitt; Hewitt Papers.
[2] Dew to Anthon, February 5, 1844; Hewitt Papers. Among others who gave Hewitt recommendations were Hiram Ketchum, William Ward, Samuel Ward, and President Nathaniel F. Moore of Columbia College.

less. But Hewitt did make arrangements to supply correspondence to a New York newspaper, and on March 6, 1844, he and Edward Cooper sailed. Among those who waved goodbye were Peter Cooper and his charming daughter Amelia, John Hewitt, and a group of college mates. The passage was smooth, and twenty days later the two young men were dining at the Hotel Mersey in Liverpool.

"At Cannock, four miles from Penkridge," John Hewitt had written in a trembling hand,[1] "you will find the House my Mother left me and my Sisters Sarah and Martha share and share alike. They married two brothers, Samuel and Joseph Beach of Bloxwich, six miles from Cannock. The House was formerly called the Roebuck, and was occupied by a Mr. Lewis. It is the last house on the right, as you go from Cannock to Stafford, and perhaps the Person who lives in it may have purchased it without my third. I have enclosed two Letters from my nephew Frederick Beach (son of my sister Sarah) , who states in one of his Letters that he believes I have money from his Mother. But I never had one shilling from her. . . . You will learn from some of my relatives whether my Brother Robert is living, if so whereabouts." He included some other directions: there was an old friend in Birmingham to whom he would like to be recalled; he had relatives at Knutsford and Stafford; while at Penkridge were the graves of his parents, and some surviving friends of the family. He concluded: "I pray the *Lord* will protect you, *my dear son,* and send you safe back to your Loving parents—adieu, adieu." The journey meant much to poor John Hewitt.

Realizing this, Abram sent home the fullest possible letters. Writing from Penkridge on April 1, he informed his family that the voyage had been delightful.[2] "Here I am, and in my father's native village," he wrote, "with the scenes which he knew when young and full of hopes all blooming around me, without scarcely a particle of change. Here are the houses where lived his friends; here the streets in which he followed his youthful sports, and here the noble church in which he was taught to reverence that Providence who had given him every joy." After describing the voyage and a short excursion into Wales, Abram went on:

[1] Undated memorandum in Hewitt Papers.
[2] Hewitt Papers. While Abram went down to Penkridge, Edward Cooper remained in Liverpool to hear a speech by Daniel O'Connell.

On my return to Liverpool, March 30, we immediately left on
the railroad for Penkridge, where we arrived about nine o'clock
at night; and after a walk of about 2,000 yards, passing the
church, we came to the Littleton Arms, where we got as good a
supper as ever was eaten, and a bed as good as the supper. The
next morning I hunted the whole churchyard through to find
the tombs of my grandfather and grandmother, but although
there were plenty of Tomlinsons and Merseys I could not find
them. We then went into the church, which with its chancel is
certainly the finest I have ever seen. I must not omit to state how
beautifully the bells chimed, but for particulars you must await
my return. I then ascertained that there was an old man of the
name of Boulton, on whom I called after lunch, and found him
to be the same mentioned in my grandmother's letter. He married the only child of your uncle Joseph Tomlinson, of Penkridge,
and his children are of course my second cousins. He recollects
you well. He is very rich—the richest man in fact in Penkridge
—and his daughter is a very intelligent ladylike woman. They
live in a fine house, and in capital style. He and his daughter
send their respects.

The George Inn has been pulled down and a teashop erected
in its place, so that I did not have the gratification of beholding
your birthplace. We then walked to Cannock, over the road that
you have traversed a thousand times—by the Common and along
the ledges that are so regular and beautiful.

He related how he finally found the graves of his grandfather and
grandmother, with a handsome monument, in Penkridge, and ascertained from the parish register that the former had died July
26, 1803, the latter November 6, 1806. He also learned that his
grandmother had left John Hewitt, in lieu of a third interest in her
house, the sum of £50 "in gross." Being able to collect £15 of this
he sent it to his father. On April 2 he went south by coach to
Wolverhampton, already noted for its iron works, and from here
wrote again:[1]

This is the most wonderful country you can possibly conceive
of. It is like one continuous town, so populous is it. Thousands
and thousands of furnaces are everywhere casting forth their
black and blackening smoke, so that it is impossible to keep the
face clean one hour; while the fire streaming from the tall tops

[1] Hewitt to his parents, Wolverhampton, April 2, 1844; Hewitt Papers.

of the chimneys realizes the story of Agamemnon's fire beacons from Troy. I counted twelve in sight from one spot, and as for Wolverhampton, it is only one vast smithy. If it had existed in the time of the ancients, they never would have placed Vulcan at Lemnos. Turn where you will the word "license" meets your eye —to brew and to sell ale, to hire horses, to sell tea, coffee, sugar, and tobacco. "Tax" is the great secret of the misery to be met with everywhere here, and beautiful as the country is, I would not exchange the happiness of our land for all the beauty and wealth of England.

There are only the very rich and the very poor, and if there is splendor and comfort in one case, there is poverty and degradation in the other, such as we never see. But volumes would not tell the story which every face here proclaims. . . . I think of you all continually. My eyes are about the same. But I think they will improve now. Give my best respects to Mr. and Mrs. Cooper and Amelia. Anna must get to be a smart girl. Your loving son, dear Papa and Mamma, A. S. Hewitt.

A week later he was full of wonderment over London. It is difficult today to realize just how provincial any citizen of New York felt in 1844 upon entering the British capital. Abram reached it after a train journey through "the most beautiful country the sun ever shone upon":

You may conceive what my sensations were on reaching this wonderful city, the queen of the world—wonderful for its wealth and its misery, wonderful for its size and splendor, its public institutions, its everything that can make a place desirable as a residence. You may imagine how lonely I felt when I reflected that I was but one of two millions of people and that among them all there was but one soul that knew and cared for me. I felt like a lost one. As I passed through its crooked streets, with the tall, smoked black houses on either side, and a black cloud of smoke above my head, with every highway and by-way filled with a countless mass of human beings, I gained a conception of what a wondrous thing humanity is.

Take Broadway at its most crowded hour and imagine every side street as full of people as it is, and the large ones almost blocked up with them, and carts, and stages, and carriages, and every possible contrivance you can suggest; imagine every third or fourth man a soldier, a footman, or a porter, with bright scarlet trimmings and gold lace sprinkled upon him as if London were in the immediate vicinity of the Mexican mines; imagine all these people intent upon themselves alone, without one look or thought for a stranger, even though he were a Turk, a Chinese, or an Indian, and there are plenty such; imagine the omnibuses with eight or ten persons outside and fifteen inside, with a driver who could navigate his way through Scylla and Charybdis with perfect safety, and a guard who yells away as if he had nine tongues and a throat of brass: "Charing Cross, Piccadilly, Pall Mall, Holborn, Tottenham Court Road, Bank, St. Paul's, Cornhill," and a thousand other cries; imagine all this and everything else you can conceive of put into one vast cauldron, nine miles long and six broad, kept boiling by the fires of the lower world and stirred by the devil and all his imps, and you will have some idea of what a place London is. . . .

He and Edward Cooper took a parlor and two bedrooms on Fitzroy Square, paying only a pound a week. Their letters of introduction shortly brought a number of dinner invitations, and Hewitt found much to praise in English courtesy to American visitors. He was delighted by the sights—St. Paul's, the Tower, the palaces, and even Greenwich Fair. But the contrast between wealth and poverty, between the fashion of Birdcage Walk and the misery of Tottenham Court Road, depressed him. It would be sickening, he wrote,[1] to set down the details of London's squalor. He went to Parliament, where he heard Sir Robert Peel, Lord John Russell, John A. Roebuck, and other distinguished orators. He saw the Queen, Prince Albert, and the Duke of Wellington; he visited the courts of law and heard some of the great lawyers; and he even inspected the Hoxton Lunatic Asylum. Visits were paid to Oxford and other interesting spots. He found in England "more beauty and more deformity, more wealth and more poverty than my eyes have rested upon during the whole course of my life"; and he discovered a spirit of social discontent that in his opinion needed only a strong cementing organization to become irresistible. Chartism was not a sufficiently broad movement; but if radical reforms were not granted, the Anti-Corn-Law League might prove fulcrum enough to bring about a revolution. Meanwhile, he thought that "no matter what the strength of England abroad, she is weak at

[1] Hewitt to his parents, London, April 17, 1844; Hewitt Papers.

home from the fact that nine-tenths of her subjects never acquire a penny beyond their actual expenses."

In all his English letters he sent affectionate greetings to his brothers and sisters, and wished to be remembered to "Billy" Riker and "Lorry" Shepard. It is an indication of his natural generosity that, having ascertained that his uncle, Robert Hewitt, was living in Cheshire in "reduced circumstances," he sent from his slender means a present of £5.

Late in April Edward Cooper and he shook off the soot of London for Paris. They took two rooms at l'Hôtel des Pyramides, 286 Rue St. Honoré, for a month, paying 25 francs apiece. "You would laugh very much to hear me talk French," Hewitt wrote, "and as Cooper can't speak a word, I have it all to do." They met Professor Anderson of Columbia in Paris; he had been on the point of writing to Hewitt in New York to come travel with him and aid him in his calculations—but Hewitt's eyes still forbade such labor.[1] While seeing the sights Hewitt took time to write an article for the New York *Democrat* on "English Affairs," a fairly shrewd production for a young man of twenty-two. In two columns of fine print he argued that the chief sources of suffering in England were the immense public debt and the excessive population. Peel had carried his income tax in 1842, and in Hewitt's opinion that would rapidly take care of the debt. As for the over-population, abolition of the corn laws would do much to lessen its evils. This would lower the cost of foodstuffs and bring about a general fall of rents. But there would still be a surplus of labor:[2]

> To provide for the surplus, an extended scheme of colonization, like that adopted by the states of ancient Greece under precisely similar circumstances, must be adopted. The government must provide the means of departure, must encourage emigration by bounties of land and implements of agriculture—must, in fact, adopt a liberal and enlightened policy in all its dealings with the emigrant; and then, and then alone, will she be able to see the cheerful firesides and the happy homes which the early ballads tell us were the toast of "Merrie England."

And here every philanthropist and every well-wisher of Eng-

[1] Hewitt to his parents, Paris, July 18, 1844; Ibid.
[2] New York *Democrat*, July 18, 1844.

land will put the question, Will these remedies be adopted? There is no alternative but a popular revolution. . . . I speak the words of soberness and reflection, that the English government must either work a radical revolution in the whole system, or the English people, I mean the masses, will work it for themselves.

He mentioned with approbation the humane labor legislation introduced by Shaftesbury (then Lord Ashley), and discussed the relation between tariffs and export markets. Obviously, the trip was opening his mind to economic and political problems which he had never before noticed.

The rest of the tour contained some adventurous episodes. He and Edward Cooper, after seeing northern France, travelled into Germany. Here his funds ran so low that in desperation he meditated leaving Cooper, going to the coast, and working his way home as a sailor before the mast. But at Baden-Baden he wandered into the Casino, watched the *rouge-et-noir*, and decided that since his money was too little to be of use he would risk his few remaining florins. He won, divided his winnings in half, won again, and kept on playing until he had several hundred thalers. When he rushed off to tell young Cooper, the latter could hardly be restrained from trying his own fortune.[1] Thus enriched, Hewitt went on with Edward to the Tyrol, where they walked for some days with a delightful young German priest, conversing as best they could in Latin. As the summer ended they pushed into Italy, visiting Venice, Florence, and Rome. In October, reaching Leghorn, they took passage for New York on a ship laden with Tuscan marble, straw goods, and silks. They little guessed that they were about to sail into the jaws of death.

The ship was the four-master *Alabamian*, Captain Hitchcock. The cargo was heavy, the boat rode low, and when it encountered a stiff gale in the western Mediterranean Hewitt noticed that it rolled ominously. On October 29 it cleared the Straits of Gibraltar. Sixteen days later, off the Azores, it met one of the worst storms

---

[1] So Hewitt often told his children; Erskine Hewitt to author, June 11, 1932; Edward Hewitt to author, September 12, 1934. The young men were in an adventurous mood. As Hewitt later said, when he was too poor to give waitresses a tip he made up for it by kissing them.

ever witnessed by any person on board. The ship seemed to be at
the focus of two tremendous gales, one from the northwest and the
other from the north-northeast, which howled past in blinding
fury. The uproar of the screaming wind, groaning timbers, and
breaking waves was deafening; sheets of spray swept the deck; it
was impossible to keep any canvas on the masts except the mizzen
staysail. To add to the distress of the crew and passengers, a leak
which had existed since they left port grew worse, and the pumps
had to be put into action. Only the staunchness of the vessel saved
her. Several sailors were in manifest terror, and when Hewitt
looked at the storm-lashed waters he shared their fears.[1]

After two days the gale died away, but the ship was still in peril.
It was tossed about by heavy seas which, like the previous winds,
seemed to come from two points at once. The captain headed it
northwest, and thus while one sea struck it on the bows, the other
fell with the force of a huge trip-hammer upon its counter. Moreover, the marble in the lower hold had worked loose, and the ship
rolled from side to side almost to the water's edge; there were
moments when it appeared certain to go completely over. Fortunately the mate had succeeded in partly stopping the leak, but the
pumps were still kept going a third of the time. The seas seemed
to rise even after the wind fell, so that the bulwarks were partially
staved in and the bowsprit demolished. Thus they lay for several
days. Then the ocean finally moderated, a fair wind came from
behind, and they made rapid progress across the Atlantic. From
the moment this auspicious change occurred until they were within
one hundred and twenty miles of New York, they enjoyed the most
delightful weather. Although the ship was now weak and the pumps
were in motion much of the time, they hoped for a speedy arrival
home. But at the last moment fell the heaviest blow of all.

On the morning of December 10 the sky looked favorable and
the wind was still good. They were close enough to Delaware Bay
to pick up a pilot, who predicted fair weather. But at noon, to their
intense disappointment, the wind suddenly veered to the northwest.
Captain Hitchcock made every effort to get within Delaware Break-

---

[1] The story of this voyage was related at length by Hewitt in a graphic
pamphlet, called *"The Shipwreck of the Alabamian, December 12, 1844."* Copies
are in the Hewitt Papers. This is a reprint of an article in some New York
newspaper of December, 1844, which the author has been unable to trace.

water, but it was impossible. That evening the wind grew fiercer, shifted to the north and northeast, and turned into a gale. During the night and all day of the 11th it blew with what Hewitt later called inconceivable violence. The ocean seemed a vast succession of water volcanoes, spouting volumes of foam. The pumps were worked continuously, and finally all hands were called to them. Before dawn on the morning of the 11th the upper part of the mainmast went overboard with the topsail, and at seven o'clock the mizzen staysail followed it. The incessant gale and the heavy blows of the waves were manifestly racking the ship to pieces. From this point the story may best be told in Hewitt's own words:

Nature seemed thundering forth a doleful requiem, and we soon lost all hopes of keeping the ship long afloat. So mighty was the power of the sea, that one blow in the bows threw the men from the pumps, and caused the ship to quiver like a leaf in the wind. The whole stern of the ship and the cabin were working as if they would go to pieces, while the dead-lights were ground about as in a mill. At eight o'clock at night the double pump-break was rigged, and passengers and crew betook themselves to pumping; but still the water gained rapidly. At this time the water was above the keelson; at twelve o'clock our only hope was to keep her afloat till morning. Would that we could do justice to the efforts of the crew to save the ship, and the perfect cheerfulness which reigned among them! Slowly passed the hours till daylight dawned. A lifetime seemed to be contained in a minute. Part of the crew now got the boats ready for launching: the one a surf-boat which might live in almost any sea, the other the long-boat, which had been used for a pig-pen for ten years, was full of holes in the bottom, and in such a state of decay that no person was allowed to tread upon the planks lest the bottom should fall out. At this time the sea was still breaking with fearful violence, although the wind had somewhat subsided. At length morning dawned, and to our great joy a brig was discerned about three or four miles to the windward. We made signals of distress, but no attention was paid to them.

Not a murmur was heard from the crew, and the only exclamation came from the Captain, who, as he saw our chance of deliverance running away from us, said: "God grant that he may never need that aid which he now refuses to afford!" At seven o'clock A.M. on the 12th inst. the crew prepared to launch the boats, while the passengers worked the pumps. The ship was now fast settling by the head. Captain Hitchcock in the noblest manner gave the mate, Mr. Benson, the choice of boats, although he knew that in one there was almost certain life, and in the other almost certain death. Indeed, it would be impossible to do justice to the coolness, intrepidity and generosity of Captain Hitchcock during the whole of this trying occasion. Mr. Benson chose the surf-boat, and to that we owe our preservation. The passengers resolved to accompany the Captain in the long-boat; but such was its rottenness that we did not dare to save one particle of clothing beyond what was on our backs. At eight o'clock the long-boat, or rather pig-pen, was launched; and as the sea was still running fearfully high, the greatest care was observed to prevent her from being dashed to pieces against the ship. We were afraid to jump in, for fear of staving the bottom; but as Providence would have it, a wave brought her alongside, so we all got in safely; and were soon clear of the ship.

God alone knows what our feelings were when we thus committed ourselves to the mercy of the raging sea, in perhaps the frailest boat that ever floated with twelve men on the Atlantic. After seeing the mate safely clear, we lay for more than an hour within one hundred and fifty yards of the ship, expecting every instant to see her sink; for when we left her she had ten feet of water forward and seven aft, and was very much down by the head. No refuge but that of death was now before our eyes; and, cast away as we were in lat. 36° 40′, long. 74°, in a spot where no vessel would be likely to traverse, unless driven thither by stress of weather; in the Gulf Stream, where storms and the sea rage with accumulated power; in a boat that we could not press our weight upon, through dread that all that separated us from eternity would stave out beneath our feet, and leaking so badly that continual bailing alone kept her afloat; chilled with the water that had dashed over us while on board of the ship, we looked upon death not only as certain, but as a kind of relief from worse evils. We had no sails, but with the aid of the drag she drifted with the current away from the ship, so that at three o'clock we were perhaps five miles distant. The sea ran so high that the ship was hid from view more than half the time.

At this time the men, wearied with their toilsome labors, for the last three days, ate some bread; and after a solemn invocation to Him who rules the storm, either to grant us rescue or to smooth our path to that world in which we soon expected to appear, all but the Captain and one passenger reclined as well as they could to sleep. The same thoughts of home and friends and family were passing through the minds of these two, and unbidden tears came from the eyes of both, for the first time during the whole of this awful scene, when suddenly, as if in answer to our prayer, the Captain exclaimed, "Sail ho!" The crew started as if struck by an electric shock; and all with joy that knew no bounds saw a ship at the distance of ten miles. We pass over the fearful anxiety of the two hours, during which we knew not whether she would see us or not, when every minute seemed an age, till about half-past five o'clock we were safely on board the ship *Atlanta*, Captain George B. Raymond, of New York, where to our great joy we found the mate with the five men who had accompanied him. Indeed, to the exertions of Mr. Benson and his men, under Providence, we owe our deliverance, for in little more than two hours they had pulled more than twenty miles from the ship, so as to board another ship which was not in the horizon of the *Alabamian*.

Mr. Benson, the night before, had been unable to leave his berth from a severe fever; but in the morning excitement gave him strength to accomplish this remarkable feat. To Captain Raymond we never can be sufficiently grateful, and we trust that God will reward the generous conduct of this noble man, who stood from his course, although he had a fair wind. Mariners who know how little southerly wind we have on the coast in winter, can appreciate the sacrifice he thus made. He had resolved, if he had not found us, to proceed to the *Alabamian* (which Providence seemed to have wonderfully kept above water as a guide for him), heave to, and set a light at his masthead so that we might pull to him before morning. Captain Raymond, his officers and crew, did everything to render the eighteen human beings whom they had preserved comfortable; and in one hundred and ten hours we were landed safely in New York, but destitute in everything save thankfulness to God, that He in His great mercy had seen fit to preserve us from the awful fate which had impended over us.

The *Alabamian* was never seen again. Hewitt, like his shipmates, lost all his baggage. He had nothing left in the world save two dollars in his pockets. But as a mark of their gratitude, he and Edward Cooper gave a handsome silver vase to the Captain, thus inscribed:

Presented to
George B. Raymond
Master of the Ship Atlanta of New York
for having nobly rescued
The Officers, Passengers, and Crew (18 souls in all)
Of the Ship Alabamian
Which Foundered at Sea Dec. 12th, 1844
by
His Grateful Passengers
Edward Cooper
Abram S. Hewitt[1]

He had gone away a boy, and came back a man. The varied
sights he had seen, the magnificence and squalor he had passed in
review, the strange people he had met, the English dinner-tables at
which he had talked, his adventures on European roads, had opened
a new world to him. He could never again be satisfied with the
narrow ideas, the limited talk and reading, and the complacent
indifference to social problems to which he had been used. Columbia College, the friendship with McVickar, so scornful of petty aims,
the association with Anthon, so steeped in ancient culture, his opportunity of proving that he could teach mathematics as well as
Professor Anderson, his acquaintance with such leaders as Albert
Gallatin and Peter Cooper—this had been a preparatory process.
The tour of Europe was an awakening experience. Henceforth
there were memories—the crowds of Pall Mall, the monuments of
Westminster Abbey, the glitter of the Champs Elysées, the sweep of
the Rhine from Ehrenbreitstein—which, whenever he looked up
from his desk, gave him a wider range of feelings and ambitions.
But most important in maturing him was the final shock of his shipwreck. For hours amid those icy December seas he had faced death.
As he labored at the pumps under the smoky lanterns with water
swirling over his feet, he had gained a new sense of the solemnity
of existence.

Thereafter, he often said to his intimates, he felt that his life had
been given him by God in trust; that it was his by a special dispen-
sation, to be employed not for his own pleasure or gain, but for
the good of others.

---

[1] This vase, retrieved a long generation later from an antique dealer, is now
in the possession of Mr. Erskine Hewitt.

CHAPTER IV

The Rise of Peter Cooper

IN OUR admiration for the venturesome wilderness hunter in fringed buckskin and the heroic frontier farmer in homespun, we are wont to forget the pioneer industrialist. He too could be adventurous and heroic. The change he wrought was as picturesque as anything in American life. The housewife at her spinning-wheel vanished like a dream before the gaunt mill-ranges at Lowell and Fall River, with the swaying rows of girls at their buzzing rollers and flashing spindles. The village cooper or wheelwright who made carts, barrels, cheese-presses, and splint brooms gave way first to the local shop and then to the great city manufactory. The rural family which sent its calfskins to the tanner to be made into leather, and kept the evil-smelling rolls till an itinerant shoemaker came with bench, lapstone, and awls, learned first to buy its footgear from a neighborhood cobbler, and then from the village store. The travelling tailor who "whipped the cat" through the countryside was driven out of existence by machine-made clothing. Busy smithies which once supplied a whole township with tools were reduced by the hardware manufactories to mere shops for horse-shoeing and emergency repairs. The household economy under which country families were so long self-sufficient—making their own soap and candles, boiling their own maple-sugar, dressing their own flax and spinning their own thread, looming their own rag carpets, baking their own rye-and-Indian-meal bread—yielded to the complex modern order. Our industrial age began, and a thousand shrewd, speculative, aggressive men pushed it forward with astonishing rapidity.

Among them all—among men like Samuel Slater, who made a success of the Pawtucket cotton mill, Francis Lowell, who put the power loom into operation at Waltham, Frederick Geissenhainer, who smelted iron ore with anthracite coal, Eli Whitney, of cotton-gin fame, who at his arms factory in Connecticut first made inter-changeable machine parts, Oliver Evans, who invented the high-pressure steam engine, and John Ryle, who established the silk industry at Paterson—none was more typical than Peter Cooper.[1] He was not, of course, at all typical of industry in the form it took after the Civil War, still less of the industrialist of today. He was typical of the pioneering or experimental age in American indus-try; of the period when new devices, new processes, new combina-tions were being worked out by trial and error; of a time of wild hopes, ludicrous miscalculations, blank uncertainties; of an alter-nation of incredible advances with interludes like 1815-18 when the United States seemed fated to remain permanently a rural na-tion, of dazzling gains and ghastly losses. In this period industry needed most of all the adventurer and the versatile experimenter.

In Peter Cooper it found such a man, and much more. His en-dowment included a genius for invention, a rich philanthropic instinct, and an unflagging interest in the common man. His ad-venturousness never made him ruthless; his talent for organization never made him heedless of the human unit. In youth a painstaking workman, he always remained essentially a master craftsman as Thorstein Veblen has since used the term, and to him the ideal society was one of capable, independent farmers and craftsmen. In brief, he united certain characteristics of the old rural age with other characteristics of the new industrial era. He became the head of great undertakings, a multi-millionaire, a national power; yet even in later years the tall, keen-eyed, long-jawed gentleman at 17 Burling Slip, immaculate in white chin-whiskers, black stock, and frock coat, gave the impression of being ready at any moment to drive a bolt, put a belt on a pulley, or correct a blue-print. Like Horace Greeley, he kept the tang of the rural atmosphere in which he had been reared. To be sure, he had been born in New York City. But that was when it had fewer than 35,000 people; and his

[1] No adequate biography of Peter Cooper has yet been written. The fullest book is Thomas Hughes's *Life and Times of Peter Cooper* (London, 1886), highly eulogistic in tone and lamentably inaccurate; it was suppressed by the family. The best short sketch is Rossiter W. Raymond's *Peter Cooper* (Boston, 1901), in the Riverside Biographical Series. This chapter is based largely on the papers of Peter Cooper and Abram S. Hewitt.

youth was passed largely in the country above Peekskill, so wild that his father once grappled with a she-bear there in the Hudson thickets and slew her.

If some traits of Peter Cooper are explainable by early environment, others are clearly referable to heredity. His mother's father, John Campbell, was a man of remarkable enterprise and ingenuity. Before the Revolution he had owned profitable pottery works in Duane Street, and a number of houses near the junction of Duane and Broadway. He was an alderman, and during the Revolution became a deputy quartermaster-general of the patriot forces, in which office he sacrificed a considerable fortune.[1] Peter's father, John Cooper, was also a bold spirit, though he seems to have lacked worldly judgment. When the war began he was a hatmaker at Fishkill; he was one of the first to enlist, and helped to throw up entrenchments on Governor's Island before the arrival of the British forces from Boston. Becoming a lieutenant in the Dutchess County militia,[2] he served under George Clinton, and later in the forces which protected the upper Hudson Valley from the depredations of the Westchester cowboys and "skinners." During the conflict he met John Campbell's daughter Margaret. Against the angry opposition of her father, the two were married at Fishkill on December 21, 1779. Family tradition speaks of Mrs. John Cooper's remarkable beauty, and great placidity and poise. John Cooper himself, a wayward, roving man, had extraordinary strength; it was said that he could lift a barrel of cider from the ground unaided, and that once, being attacked by a savage bull, he seized the animal by the nose with one hand, and battered its head with a stone till it was glad to fly.

After the war John Cooper and his wife returned to New York City, where he resumed his trade of hatter; and here in Little Dock

---

[1] J. C. Zachos, *The Political and Financial Opinions of Peter Cooper, With an Autobiography of his Early Life*, p. 3, 4. Zachos was long curator of the reading room and library of Cooper Union. This "autobiography" was given Zachos in conversations before 1877, and is to be distinguished from the "reminiscences" that Peter Cooper dictated in 1881-83. The latter, though used by both Thomas Hughes and Rossiter W. Raymond, are in manuscript form, and held by the family. They show that John Campbell's father, Hugh Campbell, had emigrated from Scotland, but John had broken from the Presbyterian faith to become a Moravian. Duane Street till after the Revolution was called Barley

[2] James A. Roberts, *New York in the Revolution as Colony and State*, p. 135.

Street (now South Street between Whitehall and Old Slip) the boy
Peter was born on February 12, 1791. He was the fifth of nine children. As he liked to recall in later years, he was given his name in
consequence of a dream. His father, feeling a curious premonition
that the child would attain eminence, bestowed much thought upon
the subject; and one night it seemed to him that he was walking in
Broadway and a voice spoke distinctly, "Call him Peter!" The family fortunes were prosperous. John Cooper's hat-shop was not far
from the fur-store of John Jacob Astor. An old ledger, still preserved, shows that he sold groceries as well as headgear. "This,"
writes a great-granddaughter, "is easily explained, for while he made
excellent beaver, castor, and felt hats, and found a ready market for
them, the lack of money at that time was such that many resorted to
primitive methods of barter and exchange; and instead of receiving
cash for his hats, John Cooper found himself the recipient of payment in kind—of hay, buggy-hire, bricks, firewood, tobacco, wool,
sugar, flour, honey, old sheepskins, casks of rum, three days' work
of a negro, and so on." Having sheared the fur from his skins for
hats, he sometimes resold the "bare skins" to John Jacob Astor.
Not because he was unprosperous and inefficient, but because he
could do well anywhere and turn his hand to anything, John Cooper
was always trying some new venture.

Tiring of city life, soon after Peter's birth he bought some land
near Peekskill, with which town his family had been associated for
more than a century.[1] There he built a store, and first there and
later at the town of Hudson gained his livelihood from a combination of callings. He was storekeeper, hatter, shoemaker, brewer, and
farmer, sometimes all at once; and to eke out the limited return
from these callings he would scour the woods on off days for wild
honey and fur, which he sold. He also netted wild pigeons. Peter
sometimes assisted him in these diversions, and learned to trace bees
to their hollow trees by burning honey to attract them, flouring
their backs, and following or triangulating their lines as they started

---

[1] Peter Cooper writes in his MS reminiscences: "Originally there were three
brothers by the name of Cooper who came from England about 1662. One of
them settled in Fishkill, another in New Jersey, and the remaining brother
on the east end of Long Island. The son of the Cooper who settled in Fishkill,
from whom my father descended, tradition reports was the fourth man child
born of white parents in Dutchess County." Fishkill and Peekskill are but
eighteen miles apart and there are numerous graves of Coopers in both.

homeward. As the family grew, its means became pinched, and Peter, between early ill-health and hard work at home, got almost no education. He later wrote:[1] "My only recollection of being at school was at Peekskill, where I attended three or four quarters, a part of the time (probably half of it) being half-day school." He adds, "The reason why I was the only one of my father's family who had so poor a chance was that he moved into the country when I was only three years old."

But he picked up a practical training in a hundred ways. His father was a religious man, the principal builder of a Methodist church near Peekskill, and Peter had much religious instruction. The boy drank in all that his elders told him. In rare trips to New York he saw something of his grandfather, the quartermaster-general, who survived till the lad was seven; he remembered riding with him through the streets in a gig. When the grandfather died in May, 1798, from the effects of an earlier seizure of yellow fever, he left some valid and indeed officially accepted claims against the government, upon which Peter Cooper long afterwards collected $7800 in Washington.[2] Peter always liked to speak of the old hero. He would tell how John Campbell had ridden throughout the war a white stallion imported from England, for which he had been offered $3000, and how in the hardest kind of service this finely-bred animal never once failed him. He would retail small anecdotes. "My grandfather on one occasion during the war had to carry $500,000 in Continental money, to pay the troops. Having to ride with it a considerable distance in time of great danger, he wrapped this large sum around the body of my little uncle Samuel and took him on horseback, believing that no one would think of looking for

---

[1] Hughes, *Peter Cooper*, 41. Other children in the family were better educated.

[2] This was after Peter Cooper was grown and married. His mother spoke to him about the claim, and he asked an aunt regarding it. "She said there was an old trunk full of papers upstairs in the garret. She went up with me to the garret, where she found a bundle of old papers, which she gave me. I . . . found that the accounts had been critically examined by the government and a balance found due to my grandfather of $7800, as I recollect it now. Finding it a plain case, I got a power of attorney from mother and her sisters, authorizing me to collect if I could. I went to Washington and had the claim presented. It was immediately acted upon . . ." As no dates are given, there seems no way of verifying this story.

For an interesting obituary notice of John Campbell see New York *Weekly Museum*, May 26, 1798. He was buried in the Moravian churchyard then in John Street.

money on the person of so small a child." His grandfather's career plainly appealed to his imagination.

His Grandmother Campbell, who survived much longer, could tell even more of the past, for her parents' memories extended almost to the infancy of British New York. They had told her of seeing guard mounted on the Wall Street fortifications erected to keep the Indians out, and of the stir and excitement when Sir Edmund Andros assumed viceregal authority in New York in 1688. They remembered when the East River waves lapped Pearl Street, so called from its heaps of oyster shells. She herself could recall the cheering when the redcoats marched through the town to fight in King George's War. She had seen a succession of royal governors move in and out of the stone mansion which Dongan called Whitehall, a succession of commanders marshal the troops at Fort George on the site of the present Battery Park. She could describe the Bowery Lane when it was really a lane, and the country houses on it few and scattered; the riots of the Liberty Boys, the demolition of leaden George III to make bullets, and the look and talk of Washington. For that matter, Peter Cooper's own father could tell some interesting stories of social changes. Even after the Revolution, he had seen a gang of black slaves landed from a slave-ship and driven through the streets, so famished that they fought for corn thrown to them by compassionate onlookers.

Peter Cooper himself saw some curious scenes. When he was eight or nine his restless father returned to Brooklyn for a year or two, and the boy thus witnessed George Washington's mock-funeral procession in 1799—the empty boots placed in the stirrups of Washington's horse particularly striking him. He watched a man hanged in Potter's Field, where Washington Square now is, and was sickened by the limp head falling to one side as the neck was broken. His father once took him to call on an insolvent friend in the jail in City Hall Park, and he saw that it was "literally filled with persons confined there because they could not pay their debts." He writes also in his MS reminiscences of seeing as a small boy a white man and a negro flogged at the Whipping Post near the jail. "After the whipping the white man's back from his shoulders to his hips resembled one great blood-blister, and his screams will always remain in my memory. They were perfectly frightful to hear. He would scream, 'Oh! a little lower down,' 'A little higher up,' as though he could not have the lash touch him on the same spot again, each stroke being beyond his endurance." It is clear that Peter was a tender-hearted and highly impressionable lad. Indeed, he describes how shocked he was in early years by seeing a sheep slaughtered—it made him physically ill.

Naturally his practical training was varied. His father's versatility insured that, if it insured nothing else. Sharing all the labors of the multifariously busy household, Peter early displayed great manual dexterity and an extraordinary aptitude for mechanics. One of his first occupations was helping to make hats by pulling the hair out of rabbit-skins, when his head was just above the table. Before long he knew how to make every part of a hat. He also assisted his mother at an early age with the family washing. They placed the soiled clothes in a half-barrel of soapsuds, and he pounded them with a long-handled wooden club. It was tiresome work, and he soon devised a crude washing-machine. "I constructed a wheel about half the size of the diameter of the barrel," he later wrote. "On each side of this wheel I attached a handle for a pounder—resembling two handles to a pump—by which I could keep the pounder in operation. To work them more conveniently, I made a double lever, as it might be called, fastened by a wheel on each side of it. A post in the top of this wheel, connected with this double lever, enabled me to take hold of a handle with its opposite end fastened to the wheel in the pounding barrel, and thus work both pounders at once; and by means of a ratchet attachment I caused them to strike in a new place every time. This was about the first improvement I ever attempted on anything with success." The boy also made a little wagon which was so attractive that a friend of his father's gave him six dollars for it. His curiosity being aroused by shoes, he carefully dissected an old boot, made a last, and persuaded his mother to buy leather, awls, and shoe-thread. Then he set to work making shoes and slippers for the family, and especially for his little sister; and his work compared favorably with that of trained cobblers.

Clearly, the boy was a mechanical genius. And he had also a daring temperament which betrayed itself in all kinds of curious misadventures. We have spoken of his year or two in Brooklyn about 1798-1800. Once, crossing from Manhattan to Brooklyn in the old-fashioned horse-ferry, he was thrown overboard by a sudden collision with a schooner, but fortunately caught hold of the stern.

At another time he barely escaped drowning while crossing the frozen Hudson with horse and sleigh. He and other boys sometimes played dangerously on the big log rafts which came down the Hudson, and were moored along shore opposite the Trinity Church and Washington Market. When his father returned to Peekskill about 1800, and entered or reëntered the brewery business, Peter had the job of delivering kegs of ale about the countryside. His horse was addicted to running away, and again he was more than once in peril. Early in the century he grew to be a preternaturally tall, lanky, powerful lad, and when his father built a malthouse at Newburgh he did most of the work. "I carted the stone for the foundation of that building for more than a mile, a neighbor having given us all the stone we required from his land. I picked up those stones, many of them being all I could possibly lift."

Besides his astonishing mechanical talent and his adventurous nature, he had an endowment of shrewd, hard sense that led him to look far ahead. It is impossible, even were it worth the while, to trace all his father's protean little business undertakings in Peekskill, Hudson, and Newburgh. What is certain is that Peter, so energetic, ingenious, and self-reliant, soon tired of the little brewery, its limited returns, and the provincial spirit of the sleepy Hudson River towns. The people were painfully limited. When a Peekskill lawyer who had made a little money put a carpet on the stairs of his house, and his wife caught her toe at the top, fell headlong, and broke her neck, the neighbors held that it was a terrible but righteous judgment on his extravagance. As Peter Cooper subsequently wrote, they thought themselves well enough off if they had clean floors covered with Rockaway sand, ornamented in different figures with a broom. No doubt he also despaired of ever making a success under the guidance of such an unstable jack of all trades as his father. At seventeen, therefore—that is, in 1808, when Jefferson was ending his second term, and New York City had perhaps 80,000 people, he descended upon the little metropolis. After some search for a place, he apprenticed himself for four years to John Woodward, of Burtis & Woodward, the leading coach-builders, whose shop was well uptown at the northeast corner of Broadway and Chambers Street, on part of the ground later occupied by A. T. Stewart's store, and now by the New York *Sun*. He received his board and $25 a year, and lodged with his Grandmother Campbell on Duane Street, doubtless in one of the houses built by the quartermaster-general.

New York, of which Peter Cooper was soon to become so prominent a figure, was then what Washington Irving called a handy city.[1] Everyone knew everybody else. The leafy, ill-paved highways, the swine that basked in Broadway and Wall Street, the single theatre on John Street, the reliance on pumps for water, the high piles of hickory cordwood in the back yards, the universal pride in Trinity Church, the leather-capped watchmen who nightly called the hours in the streets, the general use of the Battery as a summer promenade, the interest in the Boston, Albany, and Philadelphia stage-coaches which, with much horn-blowing, rolled once daily to and from the City Hotel, the curiosity whenever some rich merchant bought a new carriage, the concern over the number of country traders who came in every spring and fall—all this proclaimed the place but an overgrown town. Many merchants in Pearl Street lived yet, and for years to come, over their shops; John, Fulton, Beekman and Cliff Streets were filled with private houses; on the Hudson River side the buildings hardly yet extended above Chambers Street, though on the East River they were stretching up toward Rutgers. The most fashionable residences were about the Battery, and on Broadway and Greenwich as far north as Cortlandt. At night the town was practically dark, a few smoky oil lamps shedding faint circles of illumination; no public street-cleaners existed, every property-owner being responsible for the space in front of his premises to the middle of the street; and in most of the streets open gutters took the place of sewers. The postoffice was in the lower half of the house of Theodorus Bailey at what is now Exchange Place, and thither everyone went for letters—which, in consequence of the steep postage charges, were few. Every few years a pestilence of yellow fever would revisit the city, people would flee by thousands, and till the autumn frosts New York would appear half dead. In short, it was a quaint, inconvenient, unsanitary, very crude, and very delightful little city.

Peter Cooper soon mastered the town. Like other apprentices, he

[1] Peter Cooper's MS reminiscences contain many glimpses of old New York, which are amplified by a manuscript of family history written by Miss Eleanor Hewitt and now in the Hewitt Papers. Cf. the lecture on "Old New York" by Cooper's friend and contemporary William E. Dodge, printed in Carlos E. Martyn's *William E. Dodge,* 33-50.

had to be up at daybreak. He swept and dusted Woodward's office, fetched water from the nearest pump, sprinkled the sidewalk and street, and pushed the rubbish into a heap at the curb for the dirt cart to remove. In winter he carried in wood and made fires. He went on errands—to the Hudson waterfront for lumber, to the auction stores downtown between Wall and Pine for upholstery, to the Fly Market at Pearl Street and Maiden Lane for food. His physical endurance was prodigious, and he could work sixteen hours without fatigue. He soon knew by sight the principal men in the town: politicians like De Witt Clinton, the efficient and popular mayor when Peter arrived, savants like Dr. Samuel Latham Mitchill, editors like William Coleman of the *Evening Post*, merchants like Robert Lenox, Gideon Lee, the Howlands, and the Aspinwalls. He accompanied Woodward to talk with out-of-town customers at the City Hotel near Trinity, or the Pearl Street House near Coenties Slip. Above all, he became expert at his craft.[1] The coach and cart business was not so large or lucrative as might be supposed. The city being compact, with very few pleasant drives outside—even the Bloomingdale Road, chiefly used for this purpose, was dusty in summer—few families kept a two-horse carriage. Such vehicles were chiefly in demand by gentlemen who had summer homes along the two rivers. Nor were there many carts. Porters with large handcarts or wheelbarrows stood at many corners ready to take loads, each wearing a heavy leather strap over his shoulders and a brass plate with a license number on his breast; and they charged only twelve and a half cents for any distance below Chambers Street, eighteen and three-quarters cents above. What horse-carts did exist were of a clumsy two-wheel kind. But as Peter Cooper wrote later, he "thoroughly learned the business" of carriage-making. His employer voluntarily paid him $50 at the end of the third year, and $75 for the fourth.

But he learned much more than carriage-making, for he was the very type of Hogarth's Industrious Apprentice.[2] New York offered

---

[1] George W. W. Houghton, *The Coaches of Colonial New York*, describes the trade as practised to 1800.

[2] He used to say in later life that the best investment he had ever made was $10 which he put when an apprentice into a lottery ticket. He lost it, and the experience taught him never to gamble. Wm. F. Beller, *Peter Cooper: A Tribute in Commemoration of the Hundredth Anniversary of His Birth*, 10; a book which also contains biographical material taken from Cooper's lips.

ample means of dissipation; in 1810 there were 3500 licensed drinking places, and it was estimated that of the city's twelve or fifteen thousand families, two thousand gained a livelihood through the sale of liquor; while disorderly houses were numerous. Instead of spending his time with the other apprentices "who were in the habit of going out nights to indulge in sports of all kinds," writes Peter Cooper, "I made it a practise to go to a little room furnished by my Grandmother Campbell in one of the buildings she had on Broadway at the time and there I employed myself in various things." In this garret, buying candle-butts for light, he practised ornamental woodcarving, and sold his pieces to Woodward and other coach-builders. Ashamed of his lack of education, he read and re-read the Bible, Pope's *Essay on Man*, Burns, and a few other British authors from whose pages he always showed great facility in quoting; indeed, when ninety years of age he repeated the *Essay on Man* entire.[1] Naturally, he gave rein to his genius for mechanics. His first device was a machine for mortising the hubs of carriages, theretofore done by hand, which had so much merit that Woodward bought it from him. He could write in 1879: "That method is still mortising all the hubs in the country."

He showed himself, in fact, a born inventor. "I was always fussing and contriving, and was never satisfied unless I was doing something difficult—something that had never been done before, if possible." He put his heart into a preposterous scheme for deriving power from the swift East River tides by using them to compress air into large reservoirs on the docks, in quantity sufficient to propel ferries from bank to bank. An ingenious system of waterwheels, cogs, trannel-head, and gearing was to force the air into a receptacle; the ferry-boats were to contain huge metal cylinders, tightly-sealed, supporting the decks; every time the boat entered the dock to receive and discharge passengers and freight it would be supplied with compressed air through flexible tubes from the dock-reservoir to the boat-cylinders; and the air would drive the paddle-wheels. Robert Fulton came to see the model that Peter built. Under the apprentice's eager gaze the great engineer examined it carefully, and walked away without comment. The smart of this rebuff rankled with Peter Cooper throughout life, and he carried

[1] So family tradition; but to quote the first two Epistles of the *Essay*, nearly 600 lines, would be as much as any audience could stand.

the model from one home to another. He liked to tell of the occasion when Fulton dined the leading men of New York (among them now Peter Cooper) on his new steamboat the *Chancellor Livingston*. After dinner Fulton remarked triumphantly, "Gentlemen, this vessel presents to the world the perfection of steamboats." The merchant John Watts spoke up jocularly: "Mr. Fulton, I shouldn't wonder if some Yankee would make some little improvement even in this boat." And Fulton, offended, replied, "Sir, that is all you know about it!"[1]

His apprenticeship ended, Peter Cooper shrewdly rejected John Woodward's offer to set him up in business. An incident had confirmed his doubts about the trade. "Mr. Woodward had just completed one of the finest coaches that had ever been built in New York. The gentleman for whom it was made was supposed to be one of the richest men in the city. But a day or two before the coach was to be delivered the gentleman died intestate. This made me hesitate." Visions of heavy obligations in equipping his shop, accidental reverses, bankruptcy, and imprisonment for debt floated through the young man's imagination, and he declined. Instead, visiting a brother in Hempstead, L. I., he became acquainted with a man who was making machines for shearing the nap from cloth, and accepted employment as a mechanic at the then generous wage of $1.50 a day. He was anxious to increase his capital. Before three years elapsed he had saved enough money to buy the rights for New York State of an improved cloth-shearing machine devised by a Quaker named Mulnex; and he commenced its manufacture on his own account. His first sale was to Matthew Vassar of Poughkeepsie, who not only took a machine, but bought the agency-rights for Dutchess County. With about $500 in his pocket, Peter Cooper made the error of stopping off on his return at Newburgh, where his father promptly "borrowed" nearly all his money. He was seldom able to resist a plea for financial help.

As soon as he was fairly on his feet, he began to aid his hardpressed family. A letter of his dated Hempstead, May 24, 1812, survives, and (with spelling corrected) reads: "Dear Mother,—We are all well, and hope that you enjoy the same blessing, and wish you would write to me before you go home. Dear Mother, I wish you to make yourself as contented as you can, and if father should

[1] Hughes, *Peter Cooper*, 59.

fail in Newburgh, I shall strive to have a home for you and the family. Give my love to the girls, and tell them not to despair, for I hope to be so situated before a great while as to have them come and live with me, and what I have they shall have with pleasure. I think that it will be best to have as many of your things as you can spare stored for fear of the worst. I will write no more, but ever remain, your affectionate son, Peter Cooper." Within a few years he was providing for "the girls"—two older sisters—who came to live with him, and who both died many years later under his roof. He also made increasing provision for his parents.

For some years his business remained profitable. To be sure, the War of 1812 broke out just as he was getting well launched, and for a few weeks he drilled in Brooklyn; but finding it "very tedious," he paid for a substitute and gladly went back to his little manufactory.[1] Imports of foreign cloth were cut off by the war, textile manufacturing boomed in New England and the Middle States, and till 1815 he found a ready sale for his machines—in which, it is unnecessary to say, he soon made numerous improvements. As money flowed in he saved it. By the close of 1813 (December 18) he felt safe in marrying Sarah Bedell of Hempstead, a young woman of half English, half Huguenot descent, educated by the Moravians of Pennsylvania.[2] He now had a new outlet for his inventiveness— the home:

> Shortly after our marriage I bought me a house there [in Hempstead], and in the course of a year we had our first son. We did not keep servants then as we do nowadays, so that when I went home from my work nightly I often found my wife rocking the cradle. I always took that work out of her hands and did it myself. I soon concluded that I could find an easier way of having the cradle rocked. I went to my shop and got up a pendulous cradle that not only kept going, but by an attachment, I gave it a musical instrument that would sing the child to sleep. It had a still further advantage, for by placing a cloth on the frame, its swinging motion would keep the flies off the little one. One day a Yankee pedler came along, and seeing the invention, for which

---

[1] He enlisted in the 22d brigade of militia infantry (Kings and Queens Counties) under General Jeremiah Johnson of Brooklyn. Cf. R. S. Guernsey, *New York City and Vicinity During the War of 1812*, I, 102.

[2] The name is sometimes spelled (incorrectly) Bedel; cf. Zachos, *Peter Cooper*, 19.

I had a patent, insisted on my selling him the right to make them in, and for, the State of Connecticut. I asked him how much he would offer. "I'll give you my horse and wagon and all there is in it." On that we concluded the bargain. Among its contents was a hurdy-gurdy. I had heard one played before on a steamboat trip, and I thought it the sweetest music I had ever heard.

The government records show that this musical fly-chasing cradle was patented March 27, 1815.[1]

The peace of 1815, which did so much to ruin John Hewitt, likewise overthrew Peter Cooper's little machinery business, for many textile factories were forced to the wall by British competition; but he showed far greater skill than Hewitt in regaining his feet. His first step was to turn his Hempstead machine factory into a furniture shop. His second, since the shop paid badly, was to sell it and his house for what he could get, remove to New York, and despite total inexperience, set up as a grocer.[2] This was with some member of his wife's family under the firm name of Bedell & Cooper, at the corner of Stuyvesant Street and the Bowery. He remained there three years, becoming sole owner; and he then bought an unexpired lease for nineteen years of the ground (six or eight lots) and two buildings where the American Bible House now stands at Fourth Avenue and Eighth Street, just opposite the site of Cooper Union. His grocery was on the corner, and he erected four frame houses to be rented. He and his thrifty wife let no source of income escape. She baked what Peter called "the best bread in New York" for the grocery, and looked after his home with a zeal to which he later ascribed much of his success. In the morning a breakfast plentiful and hot was on the table at six; her washing or other work was well begun as soon as her husband opened the store; her housework was finished before lunch, and she had the afternoon for her oven.[3] The city was fast growing northward, particularly along the line of the old Boston Postroad—that is, the Bowery and Third

[1] *Patent Office Reports,* 1815.

[2] There was a brief interlude at some other occupation. He is listed in *Longworth's New-York Almanac for the year of our Lord 1816* (p. 171) as "mechanist 95 Elm." Subsequent editions of *Longworth's American Almanac, New-York Register and City Directory* list the grocery firm.

[3] "Mrs. Cooper often said later that she used to think at the time, if her arms would ever stop aching and she did not have to get up at three o'clock in the morning, it would be Paradise." Miss Eleanor G. Hewitt's MS. family history.

Avenue. Money flowed in steadily, and Peter Cooper was ready for his great opportunity.

One day in 1827 John Vreeland, well known as a hardware dealer at Broadway and Ann Street, of whom Cooper had bought tools when an apprentice in the carriage factory, asked him why he did not take over the glue factory on the Old Middle Road. This was at Fourth Avenue and Thirty-third Street, where the Park Avenue Hotel was later built. The establishment, though large and well equipped, had been mismanaged, and Peter Cooper purchased it for only $2,000. Now thirty-six years of age, he had followed half a dozen callings in as many different places, and had seemed in danger of becoming a rolling stone; but here at last he found his field. There was need for a good American glue. All thus far manufactured was of poor quality; that imported from the British Isles and France was costly; and Cooper saw the possibility of a large market. "I determined to make the best glue that could be produced, and found out every method and ingredient to that end." He tried experiments, took out patents, and by 1830 had equalled the best imported glues. Not only that, but by patient labor he learned how to test glue and produce it in a wide range of standard and unvarying qualities. No other manufacturer could do this; seventy years later a grandson trained in the University of Berlin examined his method, which is still a trade secret, and found that he had solved a difficult problem in organic chemistry without an iota of chemical knowledge![1] From glue he turned to isinglass. The American market was largely supplied by Russia at $4 a pound, but Peter Cooper manufactured a fair quality at seventy-five cents. Finally, some years later, he began making the first table gelatine to be sold in packages. Mrs. Cooper wrote the recipes printed on the packets, and housewives were soon buying it in large quantities.

The humble glue factory that stood where the Metropolitan Life now throws its late afternoon shadow proved the Pactolian stream of Peter Cooper's fortune. For many years in the twenties and thirties he gave it incessant labor.[2] At first he had no manager, no agent, no salesman, no bookkeeper—nothing but a force of work-

[1] Edward Hewitt to author, March 18, 1934.

[2] The factory remained twenty-one years on this site before its removal to Maspeth Avenue, Brooklyn; city directories. For many years other glues in America had—in general—to be sold as equal in strength to one specified grade of Peter Cooper's glue, giving the latter a standard position.

men. Soon after dawn he would be at the factory lighting fires and preparing for work. In the afternoon he drove to the city and made his sales; at home in the evening he wrote letters and held business conferences. His bookkeeping was rudimentary, and at the end of the year he used to drive about town settling balances in gold. All this was characteristic of the pioneering age in American industry, as was the fact that he was his own technologist and research-expert. His most successful patent, dated April 29, 1830, and signed by President Jackson, was for an "improvement in the art of making Glue, by evaporating the water commonly called the foot-water, or the liquor after boiling the bones of all kinds of animals, to a proper consistence for cutting, drying, and making into Glue, by means of a double-floored evaporating basin."[1] This double-boiler made possible a more even evaporation and hence a more consistent product. Glue was increasingly needed for furniture-making, pianos, and other fine cabinet work, for the inking-rolls used in printing, for book-binding, the leather-trade, and household uses. Isinglass was in demand for clarifying wines and spirits, making jelly, ice-cream, and candy, giving lustre to textiles, and manufacturing ink, courtplaster, and household cement. For every housewife who had made her own calvesfoot jelly, a hundred shortly learned to use Peter Cooper's gelatine. He was soon growing rich, but his family continued to live in the plainest style, with one maid, one stableman, and a one-horse chaise instead of a carriage.

He encountered a hundred problems. Glue- and gelatine-making, based on the prolonged boiling of hooves, hides, bones, pates, horn-piths, and sinews, had its fascinating difficulties. What bones were best for glue-making: that is, fullest of fatty and nitrogenous elements? How could the fats best be separated—the bones "de-greased"? He treated them with steam under pressure; but men later learned that solvents, especially petroleum, were invaluable. How should glue-liquor, collected at the foot of an upright cylindrical boiler fitted with a false bottom, be concentrated to the proper strength? It was here that Peter Cooper's patent of 1830 entered; for evaporating the foot-water in vacuum pans placed over a basin of boiling water yielded a clearer, finer-grained product than open boiling. After concentration, the liquor was run out into troughs or moulds,

[1] *Patent Office Reports,* 1830.

left to congeal, and neatly sliced into viscid cakes. But the "desiccation" of the glue, almost the final process, was itself a prolonged and delicate operation, much affected by weather conditions. Again, if skins were used—cowskins, sheepskins, rabbit-skins, tan-yard parings, old gloves—entirely different difficulties had to be conquered. Ingenuity, expertness, and vigilance were ceaselessly demanded.

Even the making of isinglass involved a complex art. From ancient times it had been derived from the bladders of various fish, especially sturgeon. It was produced chiefly on the shores of the Volga, the Caspian, and the Black Sea; but some came from Brazil and some from the Orient. While no boiling was required, the cleaning, trimming, and drying of the bladders demanded great pains, and different types of isinglass called for different treatments. Peter Cooper found that he could make a good quality from cod, hake, and other ordinary American fish, and he sold it widely. As for gelatine, his product became standard.

There were questions of supply for his raw materials; there were vexatious problems in marketing the finished product. Peter Cooper's success with glue was built less upon preëminence of quality than cheapness of materials, for New York until after the Civil War was one of the greatest meat-slaughtering centres of the country. Daniel Drew, whose Bull's Head Tavern at Third Avenue and Twenty-fourth Street was headquarters for drovers, made a fortune in the twenties and thirties by bringing herds from upper New York and the Middle West. His yards, which held 1500 cattle, were conveniently near the slaughterhouse and glue-factory. Hooves of bullocks when Peter Cooper began his business sold for a cent apiece.[1] He drove up the price to twelve cents, and took all the city could supply. Henry Astor, brother of John Jacob Astor, was for years the city's largest slaughterer, and every morning Peter Cooper's carts could be seen standing at his establishment.[2] In selling, Cooper advertised but little. His method was to canvass the wholesalers

[1] Peter Cooper's daughter Amelia wrote of her childhood in these years: "Just below us, where is now the Madison Square Garden, were the cattle sheds where the Harlem railroad ran in the cattle for market when the road was first put through; the cattle cars would often be left all right on the tracks in front of our house, and the lowing of the animals disturbed my father." Autobiographical fragment in the Hewitt Papers.

[2] Bouck White, *The Book of Daniel Drew*, 27 ff.; Walter Barrett, *The Old Merchants of New York*, I, 286.

and jobbers personally, and give generous credit-terms on orders for the Southern and Western trade.

Thus, as Adams gave way to Jackson, and Jackson to Van Buren; as men first heard of Longfellow, Poe, and Emerson; as the nation's population rose above the thirteen millions of 1830; as Chicago grew from a frontier fort to a town, Detroit from a town to a city; as men became familiar with railroads, national conventions, illuminating gas, penny newspapers, and Abolitionists, Peter Cooper rose to be one of the important American capitalists. There had been something of the lanky, headlong Ichabod Crane about him, but as he acquired wealth and station he became more dignified. He grew the throat-whiskers which set off his face like a ruff, wore his hair long with flaring bangs over the ears, donned gold-rimmed spectacles with four octagonal lenses, one beside each eye as well as in front of it, and dressed with careful neatness. His face was curiously longitudinal. With his high forehead, keen eyes, ascetic lantern jaw, and enough chin for two ordinary men, he had the look of a Puritan deacon or Yankee schoolmaster; but no one who dealt with him for five minutes ever forgot his business vision and breadth of view. In some ways he was still ignorant, even illiterate. His correspondence was ungrammatical and ill-spelled, his speech incorrect, his manner, though courteous, a bit uncouth; but he was manifestly growing. He was a prominent Unitarian, he was active in civic movements, and his warm human sympathy and practical benevolence were becoming widely known.

His inventive faculty was as eccentrically fecund as ever. Sometimes it expressed a mere tinkering instinct, and he knocked together curious devices without quite understanding their possibilities. While he was manufacturing his cloth-shearing machine, for example, an Episcopal clergyman of Hempstead saw that its principle could be applied to grass-cutting and asked him to make a mower for his yard. Peter Cooper constructed one which, with flat reciprocating bar geared to the wheels, numerous sharp blades fastened to this bar, and finger-guards through which the blades flashed back and forth, anticipated (so he later asserted) the commercial mower. Had he improved and pushed it, he might have received the patent that was granted to William Manning of New Jersey in 1831. A much less practical device was his torpedo constructed to aid the Greeks in their war for liberation from the

Turks. Their revolt in 1824, followed by a burst of sympathy in Western Europe and the romantic departure of Lord Byron and others for the scene, aroused warm emotion in the United States. Peter Cooper had heard of the torpedo with which David Bushnell during the Revolution proposed to blow up the British warships in New York harbor. Fired by a speech which he heard Henry Clay deliver at the City Hotel, he set to work and made a steam-propelled "torpedo vessel," to be guided by two steel wires unreeled from the controlling ship—a torpedo which he believed he could send across at least six miles of water to explode by contact against an enemy warship.[1] But before he could demonstrate the practicability of the invention, the ship taking American supplies to the struggling Greeks sailed away!

He patented "an improvement in the construction of steam boilers"; an improvement in the art of grinding marble tops for tables and glass and metal surfaces "to perfect and polished planes"; a new method of salt-making; and a method "of effecting the rotary motion directly from the alternate rectilinear motion of the steam piston," this last being a curious and impractical device for replacing the crank, which he considered a power-wasting implement.[2] He was regarded with mingled admiration and suspicion in technological circles. The *Journal of the Franklin Institute* at one time accused him, not at all sportively, of seeking to patent a plan for the cheap transportation of salt by pouring it in at one end of a canal and extracting it from the brine at the other! One abortive invention which nevertheless did him genuine credit was his endless chain for hauling boats on the Erie Canal, patented January 24, 1820. It is best described in a newspaper interview which he gave a reporter many years later:[3]

> Fifty-three years ago, a year before the water was let into the Erie Canal, it occurred to me that canal boats might be propelled

[1] After the "torpedo vessel" did its work six miles away, it would come back again! Cooper writes: "The torpedo being placed on a bent piece of iron projecting far from the bow of my boat, when it struck the enemy the shock would explode the torpedo and bend the piece of iron, and by a proper contrivance reverse the action of the engine, and send the boat back again, guided and directed by the wires." Zachos, *Peter Cooper*, 18.

[2] The files of the *Journal of the Franklin Institute* offer the best guide to Peter Cooper's inventions, there being one almost every year.

[3] Hughes, *Peter Cooper*, 67-70.

by the force of water drawn from a higher level, and made to move a series of endless chains along the course of the canal. So I made experiments, and after a little built a flat-bottomed scow, took a couple of men, and choosing that part of the East River which lies between what is now the foot of Eighth Street and Bellevue Hospital—a distance of one mile—I drove posts into the mud 200 feet apart. On these posts I fastened grooved rollers made of block-tin and zinc, on which my endless chain could run. There were two on each post, one above the other, so that the chain would run up one roller and back on the other. Then I made two miles of chain . . . of four-horse-power. I tested it. I then arranged a water-wheel to run the chain. This prepara-tion took a deal of time, for I did most of the work myself. When it was completed, I took a small boat, fastened my tow line to the chain, started my wheel, and found that the experiment was a success.

I invited Governor Clinton and a few other gentlemen to make a trip. We ran the two miles up and back in eleven minutes. The Governor was so well pleased that he gave me $800 for the first chance to purchase the privilege of using the patent on the canal.

But it was never used, and for this reason: Governor Clinton had great difficulty in getting the farmers on the line of the canal to give him the right of way, and in order to induce them to grant it had held out to them the great advantages that would arise to them of selling their oats, corn, hay, and other produce to the canal men for the use of the horses. If the endless chain was used, these promises would be broken, as there would be no horses to feed. So Governor Clinton gave up the scheme. I ran the chain on the river for ten days, during which time hundreds of people made the trip. . . . A few years ago Mr. Welch, the president of the Camden & Amboy Canal Company, hit upon the endless chain plan for getting his boats through the locks. He tried it and it worked well. So he went to Washington and found, on searching the records, that I had taken out a patent on the very same invention fifty years before.

Peter Cooper, with this exuberant, expansive, contriving tempera-ment, was full of faith in the nation's future, and ready to embark with enthusiasm on any hopeful speculation. In 1828 he began an adventure which gave him national renown. On July 4 that year, on an estate just outside Baltimore called Mount Clare, the ven-erable Charles Carroll of Carrollton, with impressive ceremonies, lifted the sod for the first stone of the Baltimore & Ohio Railroad. It was Maryland's challenge to the Erie Canal. Bands, flags, a huge parade of soldiers, tradesmen, and school-children, picturesque floats, carriages with Revolutionary veterans, governors, and Congressmen, and evening fireworks, all helped make the event memorable. An orator hailed the approaching moment when the railroad "will have surmounted and reduced the height of the Alleghenies." The company had been launched the previous year, shares snapped up like hot cakes, and surveys made. Some important questions remained to be settled—just where the terminal should be, whether steam-power, horse-power, or (as some proposed) sail-power should be used, and so on; but Baltimore felt that as the eastern extremity of a line from the Ohio Valley her future was assured. A land boom was on. Peter Cooper went headlong into it with two New York acquaintances who, just before Charles Carroll turned the sod, asked him to join in buying 3,000 acres within the city limits, including a long shore-front, for $105,000. The merchant Gideon Lee advised Cooper that the investment was good, whether the Baltimore & Ohio was ever finished or not. The tract lay to the south and east of the town in the Fells Point section, a district later devoted to shipbuilding and manufacturing; and after a single visit, Cooper took a one-third share and paid $20,000 down—presently finding that he had to pay for his partners as well.

The purchase proved a source of endless worries. Construction of the Baltimore & Ohio was far costlier than had been expected, the average charge for grading and masonry alone on the first dozen miles reaching about $17,000 a mile.[1] A foolish attempt at a deep cut just outside Baltimore threatened to wreck the whole enterprise. It had been planned to lay a practically level line all the way southwest to Point of Rocks on the Potomac, and much time and money were lost before the engineers admitted that this was impossible. Enthusiasm died, and the real estate boom collapsed. Not until October, 1829, were the first sections of permanent track laid. Peter Cooper, disturbed by the situation, went down to look at them. He saw an extraordinary sight. Some of the rails, which were simply long metal straps, had been bolted down upon wooden stringers placed on wooden cross-ties. Most of them, however, were placed on blocks of the fine granite which abounded near Ellicotts

---

[1] Edward Hungerford, *Story of the Baltimore & Ohio*, I, 52ff.

Mills. Some 16,000 blocks had been cut, fourteen inches square, and laid in continuous lines, with diagonally opposite corners touching; the rails, held by metal "chairs," ran diagonally across their faces; and the effect resembled an old-fashioned tessellated marble floor!

Taxes, special assessments, and other costs soon forced Peter Cooper's two almost penniless associates, whom he called scamps, out of the undertaking, leaving him alone with what resembled a white elephant. He examined the tract more carefully. There was timber on it, and iron ore was easily obtainable. His ingenuity extended to business as well as to mechanics; and to raise a revenue he built kilns for burning the wood into charcoal, a furnace for smelting iron, and a small rolling mill. Evidently he hoped to sell rails to the Baltimore & Ohio. Much of the work he supervised himself, and once nearly lost his life. Having burned the wood in one of the great kilns—twenty feet in diameter, and twelve feet high, hooped around with iron bands—and, as he thought, smothered the fire out, he and his workmen began removing the charcoal. "But when we had got it about halfway out," relates Peter Cooper, "the coal itself took fire, and the men, after carrying water for some time to extinguish it, gave up in despair. I then went myself to the door of the kiln to see if anything more could be done, and just as I entered the door the gas took fire and enveloped me in a sheet of flame. I had to run some ten feet to get out, and in doing so my eyebrows and whiskers were burned, and my fur hat was scorched down to the body of the fur. How I escaped I know not. I seemed to be literally blown out by the explosion, and I narrowly escaped with my life." He succeeded in making iron. But he could not turn out metal good enough for the main track of the Baltimore & Ohio, whose managers found that English mills could lay down excellent iron rails at the Baltimore wharf for only $54.50 a ton, duty included. American furnaces had quoted them at $90 a ton.[1] Cooper had to be content with selling cheap cast-iron rails for branches and sidings, and met so many other "difficulties" that he resolved to dispose of the property at the first opportunity.

While he was struggling with his unwieldy tract the permanent line of the Baltimore & Ohio was slowly moving westward from Mount Clare to Ellicotts Mills and eastward to the city waterfront.

[1] Ibid., I, 72ff.

Passenger cars were built—curious two-decked coaches, boatshaped fore and aft, on queer wheels heavily flanged to hold them to the track. Horses were hitched to them, and it was found that a party of twenty-four could be conveyed (to quote the Baltimore *American*) "at the extraordinary rate of fifteen miles an hour!" The question of an engine arose. In New York the diarist Philip Hone, whom both Peter Cooper and John Hewitt knew, had helped in 1829 to import a heavy English locomotive, the *Stourbridge Lion*, to be used on the crude tracks of the Delaware & Hudson Canal Company at Honesdale, Pa.—the first locomotive operated in America.[1] Three agents or commissioners of the Baltimore & Ohio, one an army officer who became the father of James McNeil Whistler, spent the winter of 1828-29 in England inspecting railways and locomotives, and returned with augmented confidence in their enterprise. Builders of other American lines were inclined, like ex-Mayor Hone, to import English engines; particularly after the astonishing success of Robert Stephenson's *Rocket* at the great trials on the Liverpool & Manchester Railway in the fall of 1829. The Mohawk & Hudson, the Camden & Amboy, the Boston & Lowell, and other railways did so. But when Peter Cooper proposed to the heads of the Baltimore & Ohio to construct an experimental locomotive at their shop, assuring them he could beat the English makers, they gladly gave him the opportunity. They may even have invited the application, for their road was radically different from those of Great Britain. In England the lines were remarkably straight, with slight grades and no curves except of wide radius; the rougher American landscape demanded curves with as short a radius as two hundred feet.

Peter Cooper set to work in the new railroad shop at Mount Clare in the fall of 1829. Always self-confident, he was positive that when finished his locomotive would pull cars around a curve of only 150 feet in radius; positive also that he could show English manufacturers that the crank with which they applied power to the wheels could be replaced by a more efficient device. As he writes in another scrap of autobiography:[2]

I came back to New York for a little bit of a brass engine of

[1] *Diary of Philip Hone* (edited by Allan Nevins), I, xvi.
[2] Hughes, *Peter Cooper*, 97ff.

mine—about one-horse-power—it had a three and a half inch cylinder and fourteen inch stroke—and carried it back to Baltimore. I got some boiler iron and made a boiler about as high as an ordinary wash-boiler, and then how to connect the boiler to the engine I didn't know.

I couldn't find any iron pipes. The fact is that there were none for sale in this country. So I took two muskets and broke off the wood part, and used the barrels for tubing to the boiler, using one on one side and the other on the other. I went into a coachmaker's shop and made this locomotive, which I called the *Tom Thumb* because it was so insignificant. I didn't intend it for actual service but only to show the directors what could be made; and secondly, that I could get rotary motion without the use of a crank. I effected both of these things very nicely. I changed the movement from a reciprocating to a rotary motion.

I got steam up one Saturday night. The president of the road and two or three gentlemen were standing by, and we got on the truck and went out two or three miles. All were very much delighted, for it opened new possibilites for the road. I put the locomotive up for the night in a shed. All were invited to ride on Monday—a ride to Ellicotts Mills. Monday morning what was my grief and chagrin to find that some scamp had been there and chopped off all the copper from the engine and carried it off— doubtless to sell to some junk dealer! The copper pipes that conveyed the steam to the piston were gone.

It took me a week or more to repair it, when someone got in and broke a piece out of the wheel in experimenting with it. Then two wheels, one after another, were cast, which were damaged by the carelessness of the turner. I was thoroughly disgusted and discouraged, but was determined I would not be balked entirely, and I so changed the engine that the power could be used with the ordinary shacklebar connected with the crank. At last all was ready, and—on a Monday it was—we started, six on the engine, and thirty-six on the car which I took in tow. It was a great occasion. . . . We went up an average grade of eighteen feet to the mile, and made the passage, thirteen miles, to Ellicotts Mills in an hour and twelve minutes. We came back in fifty-seven minutes. Ross Winans, the president of the road, and the editor of the Baltimore *Gazette*, made an estimate of the passengers carried and the coal and water used, and reported that we did better than any English road did for four years after that.

The boiler of the *Tom Thumb* was about as thick as a large-sized kitchen water-heater of the present day, but only two-thirds as high. It was placed upright on a small car; the lower part served as the firebox, and the upper part contained the vertical tubes which Cooper improvised from musket barrels. To force air through the wood-burning firebox, he devised a blower, driven by a drum fastened to one of the car-wheels, over which passed a cord attached by a pulley to the blower-shaft. It was ingenious but cumbersome, and shortly cost Peter Cooper one of the sorest mortifications of his life. The *Tom Thumb* had but a single cylinder, which as he states was less than four inches in diameter. The wonder was not that it ran well, but that it ran at all. On the successful trip which he describes, in the early summer of 1830, he was himself the engineer, and the attached car contained a number of directors. Grades were taken with ease, the speed hardly slackened on even the shortest curves, and the party exhibited great excitement when a pace of eighteen miles an hour was attained. According to John H. B. Latrobe, some of the gentlemen pulled out memorandum books and wrote connected sentences just to show that such a feat was humanly possible![1]

But we have mentioned Peter Cooper's mortification. The leading stage proprietors of Baltimore, Stockton & Stokes, challenged him to a race; and, hitching a gallant gray of beauty and speed to another car on the second track, met the engine one day at the Relay House on its return trip from Ellicotts Mills. At this point the race began, with a fair field and no favor; away went horse and engine, the snort of one and the puff of the other keeping time and tune. At first the gray led, for he started with an instant bound, while the locomotive did not get under speedy way till the rotation of the wheels gave the blower a strong draft. Writes Mr. Latrobe:[2]

> The horse was perhaps a quarter of a mile ahead when the safety-valve of the engine lifted and the thin blue vapor issuing from it showed an excess of steam. The blower whistled, the steam blew off in vapory clouds, the pace increased, the passengers shouted, soon it lapped him—the silk was plied—the race

---

[1] John H. B. Latrobe, *Lecture Before the Maryland Institute*, 1868; Latrobe was for many years attorney for the railroad.
[2] Ibid.

was neck and neck, nose and nose—then the engine passed the horse, and a great hurrah hailed the victory. But it was not repeated; for just at this time, when the gray's master was about giving up, the band which drove the pulley which drove the blower slipped from the drum, the safety valve ceased to scream, and the engine for want of breath began to wheeze and pant. In vain Mr. Cooper, who was his own engineman and fireman, lacerated his hands in attempting to replace the band upon the wheel; in vain he tried to urge the fire with light wood; the horse gained on the machine, and passed it; and although the band was presently replaced, and steam again did its best, the horse was too far ahead to be overtaken and came in the winner of the race. But the real victor was Mr. Cooper notwithstanding.

Peter Cooper, we may be sure, made an improvement in the fan belt which rendered a repetition of the accident impossible. Next day the *Tom Thumb* was hauling passengers and freight again, but the horse was out of competition with the railroad forever; for while the race is to the swift, a single day does not prove swiftness. Later this summer the *Tom Thumb* drew the president and directors to the Oliver Viaduct, three massive stone arches over the Frederick Turnpike. With twenty-six passengers jammed into an open car in front and a tender piled high with wood behind, the little one-cylindered locomotive propelled a burden of between four and four-and-a-half tons, and did it magnificently. The return trip of thirteen miles was done in sixty-one minutes, including four lost in taking water; and one mile was run in the gratifying time of three minutes and fifty seconds. In September the locomotive hauled a festive company of Baltimore gentlemen home from a dinner at Doughoregan Manor, where they had celebrated the ninety-third birthday of Charles Carroll. Peter Cooper might well feel proud.[1]

Thereafter he was well known to the American public. It was

[1] A full and scholarly account of Peter Cooper's work as locomotive-builder is given in W. S. Wright, "The Romance of American Railroads," Part III, *Railroad Man's Magazine*, October, 1912 (Vol. 19, No. 1). See also W. H. Brown, *History of the First Locomotives in America* (1871); and Hewitt to W. K. Ackerman, December 26, 1882, in Hewitt Papers. The true father of locomotive construction in the United States was Horatio Allen, who built an efficient and durable locomotive for the South Carolina Railroad in 1831 at the West Point Foundry on the Hudson River, and later produced other locomotives there. Hewitt knew him, 1845-65, as part owner of the Novelty Iron Works in New York City; *Cassier's Magazine*, October, 1896.

far easier then to earn fame than now. Our list of exploits in invention and industry, like our achievements in most other lines, was so slender that any unusual feat was amply celebrated. The man who wrote a *Sketch-Book*, who defeated the Indians in a skirmish at Tippecanoe, who built our first locomotive, was instantly conspicuous. Peter Cooper knew that at best the *Tom Thumb* was only an experiment, and told the directors of the railway so. He did not repeat the experiment, and when the Baltimore & Ohio advertised in 1831 that it would pay $4,000 for the "most approved engine" delivered for trial in the next six months, declined to enter the competition. The palm went to the *York*, built at the Pennsylvania town of that name. Content to leave locomotive-building to the Baldwin and Norris plants, founded in 1832 and 1834 respectively in Philadelphia, and to other works, he returned to his glue-factory in New York. But first he sold out his tract of land in Baltimore. The purchasers were two Bostonians, Amos Binney and Edmund Monroe, who formed the Canton Company, and gave him much of his pay in stock at $44 a share, its par value being $100. Luck always attended Peter Cooper; the stock soon appreciated, and kept on rising until he was able to sell the last of his holdings at $225 a share. Meanwhile, he disposed of his iron mill in Baltimore to a Mr. Abbott, whom—in the tense days of the Civil War—we shall meet later in our story. Altogether, he landed, as usual, squarely on his feet, and felt as he closed the Baltimore chapter of his life that he had gained in both money and reputation.

He had gained more, for he had acquired experience; he put his practical knowledge of railroading to use in the next thirty years in making some shrewd investments, and he never lost his interest in real estate. Most important of all, for our narrative, was his new interest in iron manufacture. He shrewdly perceived that in a world rapidly being conquered by railways and machinery, iron would be king, and before many years he acted upon that perception.

After his permanent return to New York he built an iron foundry in Thirty-third Street near Third Avenue.[1] It was an exten-

---

[1] The metropolitan field was not overcrowded. James Hardie, in his *Description of the City of New York* (1827) lists only three iron companies as having any importance. They were the Peru Iron Co. of 32 South Street, the New York Steel Manufacturing Co. of 84 Washington Street, and the Sterling Iron Co.

sive establishment, and as he was otherwise occupied, he leased it
to a man who failed within two years. Taking it over, Peter Cooper
then turned it into a rolling mill where he manufactured rails and
bars and drew wire. His management was signalized by one notable
innovation; he was among the first in America to use anthracite coal
in smelting iron-ore. The effective use of anthracite for smelting was
hit upon almost simultaneously by a number of men, the chief being
David Thomas of Wales and Frederic W. Geissenhainer in America,
both in the thirties. Thomas's was the more practical and complete
demonstration. Making iron on the edge of the Welsh anthracite
deposits, he found that ability to employ them instead of the more
expensive coke which had now displaced charcoal everywhere would
mean the difference between ruin and success. All previous attempts
had failed because of the difficulty of using the blast with anthracite
in a way to produce complete combustion at very high temperatures
at the base of the furnace. Repeatedly the furnaces chilled. In 1835
it occurred to Thomas that if he used a hot blast instead of cold
blast, as had already been done in Scottish coke furnaces, he might
obtain the high temperature needed to melt the reduced metal,
and at the same time economize fuel. He introduced the air through
a coil of iron pipe embedded in hot fuel, and the result was marvelous. Thomas (later affectionately called Father Thomas) was
brought to America and started a furnace for the Crane Iron Company at Catasauqua on the Lehigh in 1839. His method at once
revived iron smelting east of the Alleghanies, especially in Pennsylvania and the parts of New York and New Jersey reached by
canal. Nicholas Biddle and Peter Cooper were pioneers in using it,
and on Twenty-third Street it stimulated a doubtful business.
Cooper immediately began thinking of removing his mill nearer the
source of fuel—to Trenton or Philadelphia.

By the beginning of the forties, when Abram S. Hewitt fell in
with Edward Cooper at Columbia, Peter Cooper was wealthy,
famous, and endlessly busy. Though the glue factory took most of
his time, he was increasingly interested in his iron business.[1] His
quaint brown notebook shows that in 1833 he had estimated his

---

[1] Besides glue, isinglass, and gelatin, he manufactured oil, Paris white, and
prepared chalk, ground white lead, and did some fulling of buckskins for buck-
skin-leather. Zachos, *Peter Cooper*, 7.

possessions at \$123,459; in 1846 at \$385,500.[1] As his fortune accumulated, he had begun to elaborate a plan long in his mind for a great popular educational institution to be planted in the heart of New York—now a city of more than 300,000 people. He was not only admired but loved, and many anecdotes were current of his kindliness, simplicity, and guilelessness. His goodness, as David Dudley Field said later, amounted to greatness. Shrewd, rugged, methodical, always decisive and at times stern; having his own ideas about religion, all definitely theistical; decidedly radical in his views on labor and the poor man's rights; still ill-read, untravelled, and by bookish standards ignorant, but practically well-informed and determined to think for himself; passionately fond of work and experiment; stubbornly averse to litigation or dispute—altogether he was a picturesque and powerful character. Fifty years old in 1841, he knew he would soon be past his prime and wished to enlist his only surviving son Edward behind the many ideas which aroused his enthusiasm. The businesses must be carried on, the great philanthropic dream which he had at heart must be realized. He needed the assistance which a young college-trained man, full of energy and broadly grounded in knowledge, could give him. But he was more fortunate than he knew; he was about to find two such aides instead of one.

[1] This is a blank-book with a paper label, "Committee on Arts and Sciences"; Peter Cooper Papers. For details, see Appendix II.

CHAPTER V

Iron on the Delaware

BY 1840 John Hewitt and Peter Cooper had been acquainted for many years, for both were loyal members of the General Society of Mechanics and Tradesmen, which had some of the characteristics of a social club.[1] And they had occasionally met elsewhere. As an apprentice to Burtis & Woodward, young Peter Cooper knew Hewitt's little furniture business and bought lumber from him. When a little later Cooper himself made furniture, he competed with Hewitt, who after all his disasters had reëntered the trade. Doubtless Hewitt watched with a certain envy the dexterity with which Peter Cooper made money out of everything—textile machinery, glue, groceries, and iron. As Abram grew up he often heard Cooper mentioned as a remarkable inventor and rising manufacturer, and sometimes saw him. In 1838 Cooper was chosen a trustee of the Public School Society, and took some interest in the free scholarship which that body awarded to Abram. Then in college days Abram became half a chum, half a mentor of Edward Cooper, and the two families were drawn into intimacy. Edward often came to the Hudson Street household, which the growing children kept full of merriment and activity; he knew the quick, ingenious Charlie, the attractive Anna, the lame Francis, whose manual dexterity made up for his crooked back, nearly as well as he did Abram. The two youths felt the attraction of contrasting natures. Abram was brisk, decisive, boundlessly energetic, highstrung, and quick-tempered; Edward was deliberate, indecisive, shrewd rather than brilliant, full of practical sagacity, and with his father's kindly ability to make friends with everybody. They sup-

[1] Cf. Thomas Earle and Charles T. Congdon, *Annals of the General Society of Mechanics and Tradesmen, 1785-1880* (1882).

plemented each other. Particularly after 1843, the year in which Abram tutored Edward, the friendship of the Cooper and Hewitt families began to be commented upon.

Abram found the Cooper home singularly attractive. Soon after acquiring the glue factory, Peter Cooper had purchased a quaint two-story wooden house built by one of the early Stuyvesants on the East River near Fourteenth Street. Being strongly pinned together with wooden pegs instead of nails, it was easily moved to the vicinity of the glue factory; that is, to Fourth Avenue and Twenty-eighth Street, just northeast of the crossing of the Boston Post-Road and the Bloomingdale Road. Greatly altered, it stood there until 1909—the ground floor in its last years being used as a dairy lunch-room under the alluring title of the "Peter Cooper Homestead." Cooper enlarged the original structure with wings, painted it white, and planted fruit trees and shrubs, among which it loomed up as a handsome if unsymmetrical house in the Dutch Colonial style. He likewise inserted new windows, widened the stairs, and built in a good deal of carved and ornamental woodwork from his own workshop—made after the best Adam designs. The upstairs guestrooms, for example, had wooden mantelpieces which he himself made and carved gracefully, one with a figure of Diana as huntress, accompanied by her dog, with suitable trophies at the sides, the other with slender pilasters, a shield, and garlands of roses; and these really striking evidences of skill in wood-carving are still preserved at Ringwood, N. J. The kitchen and dining-room were in the basement, and the first floor was given over to living rooms. A commodious entrance hall on the north led to an ample stairway, with steps of broad low tread and curved mahogany handrail. There were large parlors on both sides of these stairs, each of which had two windows looking out upon the roads, with their two northerly forks, one leading to Albany, the other to Boston. Both parlors also had marble fireplaces, in which Peter Cooper liked to see a fire gleaming on the polished furniture. For heating the upstairs rooms he made a characteristically ingenious device, a large drum fitted upon the stovepipe.

Surrounding the house was a large garden, which extended nearly through the block from Twenty-seventh to Twenty-eighth Street. The two rear piazzas, one for each story, looked out into a veritable thicket of peach, plum, pear, and apple trees. In the immediate vicinity there was at first little but open fields and rail fences, though a few wooden cottages had been built on the low hill which intercepted the southward view down Fourth Avenue. Peter Cooper used to stride across these fields to and from his glue factory. "I remember," he writes, "how my little boy Peter waited and watched for me as I returned home; peeping through the gate panels, as pleased to see me as I was happy to view his joyous face." For getting downtown he kept a gig, and there were stables back of the house.

When Abram first knew this house there were but two children. Six in all had been born to Peter Cooper, but four had died in infancy, leaving only the son Edward and daughter Amelia.[1] Edward was eighteen in 1842, and Amelia only twelve, a rosy girl in pigtails, who went through the fields to attend a public school at what is now Twenty-seventh Street, just east of Third Avenue. At that age probably both Abram and Edward regarded her as a nuisance. The parents, and especially Peter, were strict disciplinarians. "You must teach children to mind before they can walk," he used to say. Edward was drilled in handicrafts—for Peter believed that his children, and later his grandchildren, should each learn a trade so that if they lost everything they would have it as a resource; Amelia was taught housekeeping, and could wash, cook, and sew with the best. The painter Thomas Snell recalled going as a small boy to Peter Cooper's house with a message from his father. He entered with muddy shoes. Cooper surveyed his tracks disapprovingly. "Son, you must always be more careful of other people's property than of your own," he remarked sternly; and took him out and set him to weeding cabbages as a lesson! Snell remembered that later Mrs. Cooper consoled him with a piece of cake.[2] But for all Peter's strictness, he and his wife were hospitable. They liked to see boys from the college flinging their books and bats about, and

---

[1] The children were, in order, John Campbell Cooper, Benjamin Bedell Cooper, Sarah Amanda Cooper, Peter William Cooper, Edward Cooper, and Amelia Cooper; see the family Bible preserved in the Hewitt Papers. In his "reminiscences" Peter Cooper gives a harrowing history of the first four children. Three died of croup or acute bronchitis; one of concussion of the brain after falling from a chair. One, though given the best of medical attention, suffered agonies from an operation on the eye.

[2] Memorandum by Thomas Snell for the author, June 11, 1932.

going over to the glue factory to investigate its strange sights and smells.

Indeed, a great variety of people came in to talk with Peter Cooper, for he was interested in everybody, young or old. On some evenings, in an improving mood, he would read his family and visitors a sermon from the celebrated eighteenth century divines, Ebenezer and Ralph Erskine, of Stirling and Dunfermline in Scotland, whose Calvinism he deplored but whose ethics he admired. More frequently he would talk of business, of his battle with the Catholics over the public school question, or of family history. It did not escape the observant Hewitt that he was in many respects still a son of the frontier; there remained much in his talk, manners, and outlook of the rough, self-reliant Peekskill days. His love of experiment, his impatience of everything academic, his admiration for finished craftsmanship, his shrewdness, belonged to that environment. So did his office methods, for he kept few records, knew only the simplest single-entry bookkeeping, and carried most accounts in his tenacious memory. His business maxims were few and simple. He used to impress on his children and grandchildren one strict injunction: "Never endorse anybody's note; *give* a man money, if you want to, but don't endorse his paper." He liked to repeat frontier aphorisms, and sometimes cautioned young people against ever building a house too close to the woods—they would make it damp, and then there was the danger of forest-fires![1] He had, in fact, one great defect, a total lack of humor. This emphasized his naive simplicity of mind, though nobody ever doubted his quickness and grasp.

But his career was now entering upon a new phase, a public phase, and he was destined to become a much broader, worldlier, and more urbane figure. The year 1842 witnessed the completion of the first public labor in which he engaged. Elected assistant alderman in 1828 for the fourth ward, he became a member of the committee on the urgent problem of water supply—for the city still depended on the springs and wells of Manhattan. He persuaded the committee to inspect the Schuylkill system in Philadelphia, after which it examined the Croton and Bronx Rivers to ascertain their flow. Fearing that these sources would prove inadequate, Peter Cooper also visited the streams of Northern New Jersey. They

[1] Miss Eleanor G. Hewitt's MS. family history.

were generally regarded as unavailable, but he held that it would be quite unnecessary to build a high aqueduct, Roman style over the Hudson—that heavy pipes sunk in the bed of the river by dredging would be perfectly safe, and much cheaper. Time has proved him right, at least in principle, but the engineers then believed that the only course was to go north of the Harlem River, spanning it with the "high bridge" aqueduct. He and the other committeemen finally constructed an experimental dam of wooden planks on the Croton to measure the water. It was a dry season; the quantity was so small that they began to despair of a sufficient supply; and they ultimately determined that the only feasible course was to impound water from a wider drainage area. To do this it was necessary to construct a 40-foot dam to form Croton Lake, holding more than a half-billion gallons. The committee, with Cooper now chairman, drew up plans, submitted them in 1835 to popular vote, and set to work. In June, 1842, the aqueduct was so nearly complete that water could be turned into the reservoir at Yorkville, which is now part of Central Park. That fall occurred the spectacular Croton Water Celebration, with a seven-mile procession reviewed by Governor Seward and Mayor Lawrence, and a banquet at which Peter Cooper was one of the principal figures.

As the aqueduct reached completion, a new and heavier burden fell upon him. He accepted the responsibility of finding for the city the best and cheapest distributing pipes available. The chief foundries of New York besieged him with applications and bids. However, he knew Stephen Colwell of Philadelphia, who had made the iron pipes for that city, and obtained estimates from him by which the city saved several hundred thousand dollars. As fast as the pipes arrived he tested each section exhaustively. He closed the ends, applied hydraulic pressure of three hundred pounds to the square inch, and made the slightest flaw a ground for rejection. At the same time he dealt with other water problems. "The next great difficulty we had to contend with," he writes, "was to secure a process by which all the hydrants should be so constructed that they could be conveniently drained of water, so that when wanted they would not be found frozen in winter. Various projects were offered, but it was some time before we could find one free from all kinds of objections."

As assistant alderman, and beginning in 1840 alderman, he was also interested in establishing a well-organized and uniformed police force, a movement crowned with success during the mayorality of the publisher James Harper in 1844. The mayor told Peter Cooper that, as evidence of his own disinterestedness, he meant to appoint a political opponent head of the police department, and Cooper was much impressed. He was proportionately disappointed when he discovered soon afterward that the department was becoming a political machine. To meet the evil, he suggested a remedy which illustrates his incorrigible naïveté. "I proposed," he writes, "that a law should be obtained which should authorize the police to be elected to serve for and during good behavior, and that the Common Council, after having fixed their regular pay, should declare that, as a reward for reducing the losses and damages by fire and the property stolen, in each period of five years below the average, when such difference had been arrived at, the whole amount should be equally divided and paid over to the men who formed the police and fire departments."

But what interested him most in the early forties was the city's educational system. Since De Witt Clinton had founded the Free School Society in 1805 it had been the foster-parent and vigilant guardian of the New York public schools. Funds were supplied by the legislature and local authorities, and under the so-called "unsectarian principle" were strictly denied to all parochial schools. No one believed more earnestly in this principle than Peter Cooper. Soon after he was chosen a trustee of the Free School Society in 1838, the Roman Catholic leaders laid claim to part of the money collected for public education. They were encouraged by William H. Seward, Governor in 1839-42. In his first annual message Seward, urging that pains be taken to extend public education to "the children of foreigners, found in great numbers in our populous cities and towns," added: "I do not hesitate to recommend the establishment of schools in which they may be instructed by teachers speaking the same language with themselves, and professing the same faith." This was a dangerous piece of folly. It would have undermined the ideal of non-sectarian education, and the equally important ideal of public education in the English tongue alone.[1]

[1] Cf. Frederic Bancroft, *Life of W. H. Seward*, I, 96ff.; T. K. Lothrop, *Seward*, 23ff. See also William Oland Bourne, *History of the Public School Society of New York* (1873).

The Catholic leaders redoubled their efforts, and in 1840 Bishop John Hughes petitioned the New York aldermen to supply funds for eight parochial schools in the city. Peter Cooper sprang to the defense. A committee of which he, Lindley Murray, and Robert C. Cornell were leading spirits was at once appointed by the Free School Society to vindicate the two great principles just named.

It is needless to say that the principles were maintained. In September, 1840, two great debates took place in City Hall, various clergymen and the attorneys of the Public School Society, Theodore Sedgwick and Hiram Ketchum, battling with Bishop Hughes. In January, 1841, the aldermen rejected Hughes's petition. The legislature later sustained them; public funds continued, as Peter Cooper wished, to be withheld from all church schools, and English continued to be the sole language of instruction. In 1894 a provision was written into the State Constitution forbidding public support of any ecclesiastical school whatever. To this extent Peter Cooper triumphed, and Bishop John Hughes and the Catholics were defeated; the mischievous doctrine to which Seward had rashly committed himself was repelled. At the same time, the Catholics did have one genuine grievance, and Governor Seward deserves no little credit for bringing about a reform. Until his administration New York had been divided for educational purposes into two areas. Up-State, where almost the whole population was Protestant and imbued with New England ideas, education was in the hands of school districts with represented local feeling. In New York City, with its growing Catholic element, it was in the hands of the Public School Society; that is, of a centralized Protestant control quite divorced from the popular vote, and in some areas from popular feeling. The Catholics complained of the use of the King James Bible and of biassed textbooks, and demanded a full voice in the educational system. In 1842, therefore, the legislature extended to New York City the general law on public schools, and set up a local board of education. While explicitly forbidding the use of public money for sectarian schools, the statute gave all faiths their due voice in public education. Both Bishop Hughes and Peter Cooper were discontented, but it was a sound result.[1]

For eleven years longer the Public School Society continued ac-

---

[1] Lives of the Most Rev. John Hughes, by J. R. G. Hassard (1866) and Henry Brann (1892) do justice to the courageous activities of this Catholic leader.

11. FROM LEFT TO RIGHT: AMELIA COOPER, PETER COOPER,
EDWARD COOPER, MRS. COOPER

Exciting Trial of Speed between Mr. Peter Cooper's Locomotive, "Tom Thumb," and one of Stockton & Stokes' Horse-Cars.

The trial took place on the Baltimore and Ohio Rail-Road, on the 28th August, 1830. The sketch represents the moment the Engine overtook and passed the Horse-Car, the passengers filled with excitement,

12. Race of "Tom Thumb" and the Stage-Coach, 1830

13. Peter Cooper's "Tom Thumb": The first American Locomotive

14. Birthplace of Abram S. Hewitt

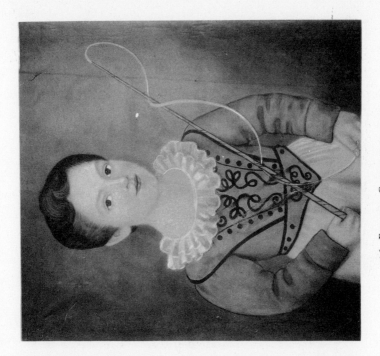

16. EDWARD COOPER AS A BOY

15. ROBERT LIVINGSTON STEVENS

18. Silas Wright

New York Feby 1 1844

Hon Silas Wright, &c

My Dear Sir,

I take pleasure
in introducing to you Mr Abram S.
Hewitt of this city : a gentleman of
very superior talents and literary acquirements
and of much personal worth, in whose eyes
I have been made industry
He is now on a visit to your city, and I
commend him to your friendly office.

Truly Yr Frien

Samuel J. Tilden

17. Letter of Samuel J. Tilden introducing Hewitt
to Silas Wright

19. HEWITT BEFORE MARRIAGE

20. Garden at Ringwood: Gates of Middle Dutch Reformed
Church through which Hewitt walked to Columbia
graduating exercises

tive, with Peter Cooper for a time vice-president and always its most energetic member. He was assiduous in attending meetings, inspecting schools, scrutinizing curricula, and writing reports. Catching up the doctrine which Horace Mann was then vigorously propagating, he helped to establish normal schools for the training of teachers. When in 1853 the Society and the Board of Education were by common consent amalgamated under a new law, he delivered a valedictory address. After commenting on the recent convulsions in the Old World, he hurled a last shot at Catholicism by asking whether free government and freedom of worship were safe, and declaring: "I tremble for the answer when I see the combined influences of pride, of selfishness, of bigotry and superstition, all uniting to undermine the virtues and misdirect the energies and intelligence of our people." For two years more, 1853-55, he acted as vice-president of the Board of Education.

But meanwhile his plans for the establishment of a new educational institution had slowly taken shape. Sensitively aware of the gaps in his knowledge, he often declared that he hoped no one would ever have to go through his own hard struggle to get a training. He had early resolved that when he obtained the means he would smooth the educational path of other poor and ambitious young men. While assistant-alderman in the thirties, he talked with a fellow-member who had studied the polytechnic institutions of Europe. This man described in detail the industrial schools of Bavaria, and more particularly the École Martinière at Lyons, founded to give poor boys gratuitous instruction in drawing, modelling, chemistry, physics, mechanics, wood and iron working, and German and English. Students at the École visited factories with their masters, obtained practical training whenever possible, and on graduation easily found places in the many factories, shops, and commercial houses of Lyons. Peter Cooper knew also of the admirable Birkbeck Institute in London, and the Rensselaer Polytechnic Institute at Troy, founded the same year that the Erie Canal was opened; while Stephen Colwell, a benefactor of the University of Pennsylvania, showed him its engineering and scientific departments. Its large museums of minerals and fossils particularly delighted him. New winds were blowing through the educational sphere in the thirties; coeducational, co-racial Oberlin was being founded, Girard College was being launched under rules which rigorously excluded the clergy, foundations of several State universities were being laid in the West, education everywhere was being democratized. As a manufacturer, Peter Cooper knew that the system of teaching technical work by apprenticeship instead of professional schools was becoming a wasteful anachronism. His ideas slowly grew into a vague plan for a great democratic polytechnic institute in the heart of New York.

With all this, with the glue factory expanding, with his railway investments and very shortly an active interest in the telegraph industry as well, Peter Cooper's hands were full. Yet by 1845 he realized that he must transplant his rolling mill nearer the sources of pig-iron and anthracite, or have his investment in it wiped out. To compete with other American ironmasters and with British imports he must obtain cheaper raw materials. Anthracite was reaching New York in quantity by the Delaware and Hudson Canal, but the costs of transportation were high, and for Adirondack or New Jersey ore still higher. Had he been second-sighted instead of merely farsighted, he would have established his furnaces and mills at Pittsburgh. But at the time the banks of the Delaware seemed to offer more advantages. This river, with its main branch the Lehigh, penetrated the heart of the anthracite region. The Morris Canal, which traced a crooked path across northern New Jersey from the Passaic on the east to the Delaware at Phillipsburg on the west, traversed the best ore fields of the State—by the standards of the time, really rich ore fields. Somewhere on the Delaware seemed the best spot.

Edward Cooper and Abram S. Hewitt landed from their shipwreck in the last days of 1844 to face certain exigent demands. Abram was penniless and had to turn to the law, or something equally good, at once; Edward's father thought that he had given enough time to his education and should accept hard work and responsibilities without more delay. Edward possessed conspicuous talents of an inventive and mechanical nature, while he promised to make capable superintendent of workmen. He had all his father's geniality, kindness, and bluff ability to extract loyal effort from employees, while he grasped practical problems instantly. His father proposed to transfer the mill to Trenton and put him in charge of it.

But Edward knew his own business deficiencies, and at once insisted that Abram join him in the undertaking. There was affection in this; there was also a realization that Abram's resourcefulness and brilliancy, his incisiveness and determination, would make him an invaluable business partner. Men later repeated amusing stories of how many half-written telegraph blanks Edward Cooper would tear up before dispatching a decision; but Hewitt's initiative and decision were unfailing. Peter Cooper had an ingrained fear of partnerships, and at first refused. Somewhere in his early career a business associate had betrayed him, while he had seen too often the fate of men who, like John Hewitt, trusted distant partners and went on plausible notes. "During his long life," Hewitt wrote in 1883, "Mr. Cooper never had a partner in any business transaction whatever. So careful was he on this point that even his own children were never admitted to partnership with him." But when Edward insisted, he finally yielded, stipulating only that the two young men should set up a corporation of their own, for which he would supply most of the initial capital, and that he should have no financial responsibility for their operations save what he deliberately incurred. This arrangement was duly completed early in 1845.

"I don't know," Peter Cooper told Hewitt, "that you can get books far enough out of your head to let even a little business in, but if you'd like to try, here's a chance."[1]

Trenton for several reasons offered the best site on the Delaware for the iron mill. For one, waterpower had been developed there by the Trenton Waterpower Company, which had diverted part of the river into a seven-mile canal falling through and past the town. For another, labor was abundant. But most important of all, transportation facilities were excellent. The Camden & Amboy Railroad (which today is long since part of the Pennsylvania system) had been built in 1830-32 to connect New York and Philadelphia by rail, and of course ran through Trenton. Shipping ventured up the shoal waters of the Delaware to the town, while two artificial waterways, the Morris Canal and the Delaware & Raritan Canal, furnished access to the interior. There would be no difficulty in getting rails, bars, wire, and other products to both Eastern and Western markets. At first the partners would buy

[1] Hewitt quoted this remark to a reporter shortly before his death; N. Y. *Sun,* January 19, 1903.

their pig-iron in the open market; later they would purchase mines and set up their own furnaces in or near Trenton. Peter Cooper would be president of the company, and Hewitt secretary. The plan seemed simple and highly practicable. The initial operations would be cautious, Peter Cooper would furnish the necessary cash, some credit could be obtained elsewhere, and after two or three years the mills might be expanded. Edward's task would be to super-intend the mechanical operations, Hewitt's to manage the business. But to realize even these simple plans required Herculean planning and effort, and most of the burden fell upon Hewitt's youthful shoulders.

By the spring of 1845 Edward and he were hard at work over-seeing the erection of wire and bar mills at the foot of Warren Street in Trenton, building puddling furnaces, installing ma-chinery, hiring workmen, and seeking orders. A rolling mill was to go up later in South Trenton. Peter Cooper came over frequently from New York to assist them. Most of the Hewitt family was to come and live in Trenton. It was an adventure with boundless possibilities.

Hewitt found Trenton an attractive brick-and-stone town of about nine thousand people. In spite of its dignity as the State capital it was in many ways still a village, its business men long since resigned to seeing New York and Philadelphia suck away all the trade and vitality from it. The Delaware wound about it like a blue ribbon, to vanish noiselessly under the graceful arches of the stone bridge that led southwestward. The business district was made up of three-storied brick structures, slate-roofed, with wooden canopies to shelter the sidewalk loafers. A few blocks were paved. The remainder were dusty in droughts, deep in mud after rains, and badly lighted at all times. Across the river lay the prosperous Pennsylvania farms of Bucks County, and in the rear stretched the Jersey homesteads of Mercer County; most of the trade was simply that of a country market town.

"I remember well," Hewitt wrote fifty years later, "in first walk-ing from the Trenton House to the site selected for our works on the Delaware, that Warren Street seemed like Sunday during church hours. I met neither a vehicle nor a person during this walk of a mile in length, but the sun was shining and full of prom-ise which has since been realized." The iron mill was welcomed with enthusiasm. Another hopeful firm was establishing a yarn factory, the Badger Mills, and still another a wire mill, but Peter Cooper's name carried a special magic. Everyone anticipated that the Cooper and Hewitt establishment would prove invaluable; and as a matter of fact, from the outset its policy of paying workmen in cash and meeting every obligation promptly at maturity added enormously to the prosperity of Trenton.

The site of the South Trenton Iron Company, as the establishment was at first called, united three lines of transportation, the Delaware River, the Delaware & Raritan Canal, and the Camden & Amboy Railroad. A large wire and rod mill went up first, and a rolling-mill for rails immediately afterward. Machinery came by boat from New York, and engineers connected it with the water-power of the canal company. Of this company, which supplied power to various other factories, Peter Cooper promptly took control by purchasing nine-tenths of its $100,000 of stock. It was already profitable, and might have been made more so but that the Trenton fishermen successfully opposed the erection of the dam needed to ensure a full supply of water in midsummer. A number of houses for workmen were erected on "Helper's Row," and a company store was stocked for selling at cost. Meanwhile, Peter Cooper and Hewitt strove to obtain orders for iron.[1]

During the summer Hewitt brought his mother and the youngest children to Trenton. His brother Charles, who possessed a marked talent for mathematics and engineering, helped him and Edward Cooper to get the mills in order. When operations began Charles served as cashier, but soon became deputy-superintendent of the works, with direct charge of the puddling furnaces, and authority to act as superintendent when Edward Cooper was absent. His initial salary was only $500, but he had free use of "the Sarton house," which Abram and the family shared with him. We find Abram writing his father, still in New York, on November 6, 1845, to send some furniture to Trenton by one of Peter Cooper's water-shipments. "We are getting settled and will have our house aright sometime next week, and would be very comfortable if you were

---

[1] See the admirable *History of Trenton, 1679-1929*, published in two volumes under the auspices of the Trenton Historical Society. In Vol. II, Ch. 10, John H. Sines presents a wealth of detail on "Industries of Trenton." The author has also searched newspaper files 1845-55 in the New Jersey State Historical Library.

only with us," Abram affectionately added. "We expect you very soon, and at any rate write us on the receipt of this how you are getting on, as we feel anxious to hear from you." By Thanksgiving the family were all safely transplanted and happy in their new home.

The erection and starting of the mills tested Hewitt and Edward Cooper to the utmost. Both were amateurs in business; but Hewitt had the advantage of his legal training and his work in his father's establishment, and took practical charge with extraordinary rapidity. From the outset he showed resourcefulness, thoroughness, and a stern sense for discipline. Peter Cooper made a number of flying trips from New York, but their correspondence shows that he tended more and more to leave matters in Hewitt's hands. The latter submitted sketches for improvements in the building-plans; he decided how many men should be hired; he bought raw materials. Throughout the summer and fall he was in a dozen places at once to see that not a minute was lost. He made himself fully acquainted with the market for all forms of iron. Peter Cooper of course decided the most important questions, choosing the mill sites, fixing terms of contracts, and laying down general policies. But when the works got fairly under way, we find Hewitt giving oversight to a multitude of details—the purchase of platform-scales to weigh the puddlers' heats, the building of workmen's houses, the repair of broken machinery, and the quality of the charcoal iron and the puddled blooms. We find him keeping a keen outlook for bargains—advising Peter Cooper not to sell his iron too low, and to buy an adjoining lot that he expected to come up at auction for a bargain.

Rods, wire, and bars were all being manufactured in the new Trenton establishment by early fall, and before Christmas of 1845 the first rails were being rolled. Immediately after New Year's the partners had a golden stroke of luck. Peter Cooper had advertised widely the high quality of the rails they were rolling. Just as the mill was ready for full production, Robert L. Stevens and Edwin A. Stevens of Hoboken, sons of the John Stevens who had employed John Hewitt on the Passaic, sent for Abram. They were replacing the tracks of the Camden & Amboy, of which they had been the principal builders. Dissatisfied with the English rails they had received, and anxious to keep their gangs of men busy, Edwin

L. Stevens, who was in charge of construction, offered to pay Hewitt the exact cost of the English product, $90 a ton, for two thousand tons of rails weighing 65 pounds to the yard. No doubt the Stevens brothers were cannily willing to assist an iron-mill which, if successful, would provide the Camden & Amboy with large quantities of freight. Of course Hewitt and Edward Cooper leaped at the contract. Robert L. Stevens was the inventor of the T-rail, which could be fastened to the ties by spikes without the use of the chairs employed in Europe. With its special flange, this rail was difficult to make, but the Trenton mills delivered the supply in time. The payment of $180,000 in cash gave the new enterprise a flying start.[1]

A happy result of the transaction was the establishment of cordial relations between the iron company and the powerful Camden & Amboy, which within a short time was ruling New Jersey. Hewitt soon knew the Stevens brothers and other officers well. Edwin L. Stevens was a man of force and shrewdness, who in a family marked by genius had already distinguished himself as a balance-wheel— an organizer, financier, and stabilizer. He had begun his career in 1825 as superintendent of the Union Stage and Union Steamboat lines, managing them from a huge brick and mortar building in Trenton which served both as residence and office, and which later passed into Hewitt's possession. The Union Stage Line had once been highly prosperous. Just before the railroad was built thirty or forty of the Stevens coaches might sometimes be seen starting from New Brunswick on the arrival of the New York steamboat there, and with horses at a spanking trot and side-panels gleaming in the sun, crossing to Trenton where another boat lay with steam up. It was Edwin A. Stevens who did most to organize the Camden & Amboy in 1830. It was he also who did most to keep the family fortune intact, and who founded the Stevens Institute of Technology, which opened its doors in 1871. He became a lifelong friend of Hewitt's.[2]

[1] Annual reports of the Trenton Iron Company, written with great care by Hewitt as its secretary, were published until 1864. A copy of the minutes of the directors of the company is preserved in a special volume in the Hewitt papers. The above paragraphs are based on these documents, and on the letterbooks of the company.

[2] Archibald Douglas Turnbull, *John Stevens, An American Record*, contains much material on the sons of John Stevens; see especially chs. XX, XXI, and XXII.

So also did his brother John Cox Stevens, one of the great American sportsmen—the founder of the New York Yacht Club, and the leader in the capture of the *America's* cup in 1851. And so, above all, did the most gifted and famous of the brothers, Robert L. Stevens. This distinguished engineer, inventor of the modern ferry-slip, the walking-beam, the first marine tubular boiler, and one of the first effective percussion shells, and builder of the floating ironclad called the Stevens Battery, was now near the height of his reputation. Until Stevens's death in 1856, Hewitt was a frequent visitor at the spacious Castle Point mansion in Hoboken, where he learned to admire the man whose windows he had once broken. He often held Stevens's little daughter on his knee. "I never was made to feel that there was any difference either in social standing or in wealth, in years or even ability," he testified long afterward. Stevens loved literature and art, entertained many notable men at his house, and liked to talk with Hewitt of the new books and of his greatest enthusiasm, music.

Hewitt and Edward Cooper soon realized that they had launched their business at an auspicious moment. The nation early in the forties had begun to recover from the panic of 1837, and by 1846 was again on the floodtide of prosperity. The pioneer advance swept forward with the speed of a prairie fire; a great railroad boom sprang up; and shortly lines were not merely lacing the Atlantic seaboard, but spreading into the Middle West. Before 1852 a total of more than ten thousand miles had been built. During 1846 the iron mill had more orders for rails than it could meet. By the close of that year the works were employing almost five hundred men, and with a payroll of more than $5,000 weekly gave support to at least a thousand people. Bars, rods, wire, and rails were manufactured in growing quantities; the daily production was forty tons, and would soon be fifty. The company had attracted large numbers of workers, English, Irish, Germans, and Yankees, to South Trenton, where fifty new dwellings were built or building. An Episcopal Church, St. Paul's, had been founded there, and John Hewitt was present as warden every Sunday in well-brushed broadcloth to welcome the parishioners. Young Hewitt had become an important figure, to whom workmen touched their hats as he hurried to the "steam depot" for business in New York or Philadelphia.

In March of 1846, he was sending Peter Cooper news of a formidable flood on the Delaware which at first threatened to sweep away the wire-and-bar mill. "It is now within two feet of the great freshet of 1841," he stated, "and thousands of acres of ice mixed with timber enough to build a city have been and are sweeping by with fearful rapidity." April found him in Boston drumming up orders for rails, and writing Peter Cooper that the mill must be hard at work by the middle of May; "you will have half the superintendents in New England at Trenton to see the operation." During the summer he toured upper New York from Albany to Buffalo for new customers, with encouraging results. Everywhere he assured the railway heads that the Trenton mills would sell rails as cheap and good as English iron. He left no stone unturned, and was pleased to report that one executive would give Peter Cooper his order "for certain reasons (political) which I will mention on my return."

The continued railroad boom yielded a series of profitable orders in 1847. In November that year Hewitt obtained a contract with the Hudson River Railroad for 5,000 tons of rails to be delivered in 1848, with a provisional agreement for 7,000 tons more to be delivered thereafter. In return, the Trenton firm took $20,000 in shares of the railroad, paying partly in cash, partly in rails. The Trenton mill also sold rails in quantity to the New York & Harlem, the Camden & Amboy, and the Rutland & Burlington. By the opening of 1848 the total net earnings exceeded $67,500; and that year a dividend of 20 per cent was declared, followed by one of 18 per cent in 1850. In the latter year the capital was increased to $500,-000. At the same time the first step was taken toward a profit-sharing arrangement. The directors' minutes, kept by Hewitt as secretary,[1] record:

> Resolved, that the secretary be directed to report a plan by which the workmen employed in the rolling-mill may be made to have a more immediate interest in the profits of the business than the payment of current wages secures.

As the mills were thus called upon for increasing quantities of rails and wire, Edward Cooper and Hewitt strove constantly to improve the quality—for they knew there was room. Whenever

---

[1] Now in the Hewitt Papers.

rails were rejected as crooked or brittle they felt a keen mortification. A special employee was retained in 1848 to have charge of the
puddlers on each turn, watch every heat squeezed, and report "what
the quality, the number of bad balls, and the reason why the iron
was bad." In the intervals of managing the business, Hewitt travelled over northern New Jersey to search for better grades of ore.
It was a fascinating occupation. All the hilly, forested upper
counties, Hunterdon, Warren, Sussex, Morris, and Passaic, were
full of old mine-shafts, forges, furnaces, and other old iron-works.
He felt that they might hold out possibilities. While rail-making
the world over was still a rudimentary art, Americans rails in particular were subject to one great defect—the top surfaces soon wore
out, splintered, and became dangerous. The Trenton force tried
re-heating the metal, but something more was needed to make the
surface, as Hewitt put it, "close-grained and tenacious." Searching
for better material, he finally came upon iron bars made at the
old Andover mine in Sussex County during the Revolution, and
tested them. They produced, as he later wrote, "the chief requisites for a good rail in the greatest perfection." He at once inquired
about the mine.

The result was a stroke of business far more important than
even the Camden & Amboy contract. The Andover mine, long
disused, was for sale cheap, and by astute bargaining Hewitt obtained it early in 1847 for just under $9,500. It was one of the
most historic mines in America, being part of a tract long in the
possession of the Penn family, but which about the time George III
ascended the throne had passed to Allen & Turner, the most prominent ironmasters of the day in British North America. These men
had opened the mine, built a furnace, and commenced making bar-
iron in 1763. From that date until the Revolution the furnace
was in blast every year, and the iron soon earned a higher reputation than any other made in the colonies. Much of it was sold in
Philadelphia, but some was taken to England, where the records
of the Woolwich Dockyard contain references to its special value.
When the Revolution came, its owners adhered to the royalist side.
The Continental Board of War knew the reputation of the metal,
and Richard Peters, its chairman, urged the Continental Congress
to authorize him to take possession of the works; but before it did
so the New Jersey authorities seized them. Colonel Whitehead

Humphries then took charge of the shafts, which were worked intensively, and much of the cast-iron and nearly all the wrought-iron used by the Continental army was manufactured there. At the close of the war the works reverted to private management, and their history became chequered and unfortunate. By the year 1840 they were idle and the furnace was in ruins, a fact which explains the absurdly low price.

The Andover hillsides had two main shafts, one producing red hematite and the other blue magnetite ore. When mixed, the two made an unusually tough iron. Since railroad builders had become extremely irritated by the brittleness of American rails, the special value of the Andover ores was plain, and a keen demand was rapidly built up by Hewitt's skillful advertising. It was easy to get the ore to the Phillipsburg furnaces, for the mine was only seven miles by cartroad from the Morris Canal. Production rose steadily. During 1851-53 inclusive Andover yielded a monthly average of 3,000 tons of ore—more, as Hewitt boasted, than had previously been obtained from any single iron mine in the United States; and until 1854 the Trenton mills found this mine and the small continued shipments of metal from other sources ample for their needs.

With the success of the Trenton venture assured, the time had come to place it upon a permanent basis and to give Hewitt and Edward Cooper a firmer position in its control. At the outset everyone had regarded the establishment as Peter Cooper's iron company, and the two young men as hired officers who were managing and enlarging it. But the beginnings were past. Hewitt had won Peter Cooper's full confidence, and three important steps could now be taken.

The first was the creation of a better and more stable organization under the name of the Trenton Iron Company. With much lobbying, wire-pulling, and newspaper puffing, an act of incorporation was gotten through the New Jersey legislature and signed by the governor on February 16, 1847. It gave Peter and Edward Cooper, Abram S. Hewitt, James Hall, and their associates and successors power to manufacture and sell iron, and all articles of which it forms a part. Capitalization was at first limited to $500,-000, but the company was authorized to issue 2,500 shares of stock with a par value of $100 each. Peter Cooper was president, Hall treasurer, and Hewitt secretary, a list of officers which remained unchanged till just before the Civil War. Of these three Hall alone received a salary, $2,000 a year; but Edward Cooper was paid $2,000 annually as superintendent. Little effort was made to sell the stock, which for some years remained in the hands of the Cooper family, Hewitt, and a few others. In fact, of the original issue of $300,000 in stock, $151,000 was held by Peter Cooper and $149,000 by Cooper & Hewitt, a firm which we shall describe in a moment. In order to pay for their shares, the two young men obtained a loan of $50,000 from the Mechanics and Manufacturers' Bank of Trenton. The bank was reluctant, in view of their lack of reputation, to grant it, and secretly asked Peter Cooper for a guarantee, which he furnished —saying nothing to them.

The second step lay in the erection of furnaces on the upper Delaware, and the general expansion of the works. After the purchase of the Andover Mine there was obviously every reason why the company should make its own pig-iron. In the spring of 1847 Hewitt bought forty acres of land at Phillipsburg, N. J., just across the river from Easton, Pa. Here ores transported from Andover and other points in Northern New Jersey by the Morris Canal met the Pennsylvania anthracite brought down the Delaware and Lehigh, and smelting would be as cheap as anywhere in the country. Two furnaces—the Cooper furnaces, the largest in America—were at once erected. The pig-iron turned out here could be taken down to Trenton on the lower half of the Morris Canal, which paralleled the Delaware. To facilitate deliveries at the Trenton works, Hewitt during 1847 purchased the Morrisville Basin, which offered a short cut, and boats carrying pig-iron were thereafter saved several miles each way, with an economy of twenty cents a ton. The plant in Trenton was also enlarged. Two new buildings for the rolling-mill were pushed to completion by the fall of 1847; and additional machinery, including the latest devices for fabricating spikes, wire, rivets, and other hardware was installed. By the beginning of 1848 the partners could pride themselves upon the best-rounded iron-works in the land.[1]

---

[1] See Hewitt's article, *The Stevens Indicator*, Vol. XIV, No. 2, with reminiscences of all the Stevens brothers. Edwin A. Stevens in the later fifties became a considerable stockholder in the Trenton Iron Company.

The Trenton press made much of these improvements, for Peter Cooper and his two aides were putting the city on the industrial map. Throughout the early part of 1847 the Mexican War was raging; Hewitt was perhaps in the crowd before Kay's Hotel on the April morning when Captain Yard's company assembled, heard a short speech on Commodore Stockton's recent victory in California, and marched off; but if so, he thought little of it. He was intent on solving financial problems, keeping the construction gangs busy, and drumming up orders for bars, wire, and rails.

The third and most interesting step was the creation of a managing company, of which Hewitt was the real head, to take charge of the iron business. That is, Edward Cooper and he formed a partnership under the name of Cooper & Hewitt, to act as agents for the Trenton Iron Company. All purchases of ore, coal, and other raw materials, and all sales of finished iron, were put into their hands, subject only to general decisions by the Trenton Company's directors. They also supplied credit for current operations, accepting company drafts and making any necessary cash advances. This enabled Hewitt and Edward Cooper to be virtual managers of the Trenton Iron Company while Peter Cooper remained president and nominal head, and yet avoided the partnership which Peter Cooper so disliked. At the same time, since Cooper & Hewitt asked only $25,000 a year for their services, the arrangement was distinctly advantageous to the Trenton Company; it got its notes discounted, and all its purchases and sales made, at a much lower cost than ordinary commissions.

The year 1849 opened with the prosperity of the Trenton Company still growing. The country, emerging from the war with California and New Mexico, and selling wheat in large quantities to Great Britain now that the corn laws were repealed, seemed full of money. Railroads had come of age, unmistakably outdistancing canals as a means of communication. The Camden & Amboy continued its orders, paying $80 a ton for rails made out of Andover ores, partly puddled and partly reheated. Commodore Vanderbilt's Hudson River Railroad made good its contract for 7,000 more tons, and several Western lines became customers. The company now advertised that it was rolling a thousand tons of rails a month, and was prepared to furnish them in any pattern and at all seasons.

By the close of 1849 its total production had reached almost 30,000 tons. With the election of Zachary Taylor by the Whigs, who were expected to furnish better tariff protection for the iron trade, and with the discovery of gold in California, the outlook for all branches of industry seemed bright.

CHAPTER VI

Growth of the Trenton Mills, 1848-1854

THE consumption of iron," Hewitt once wrote, "is the social barometer by which to estimate the relative height of civilization among nations."[1] It is certain that nothing better exhibits the distance which industry has traversed since Polk was President than the advances made in the manufacture of iron and steel. When the mill at Trenton was launched, men thought of iron alone—a fact in itself indicative of the difference between two ages. Present-day civilization is built upon steel. We ride in steel ships and steel automobiles, on steel railroads or in steel subways; we live and work in steel buildings; steel implements till our fields, steel machines make half the articles we use; we are served everywhere by steel appliances, from needles to dynamos. But in 1848 steel was made in considerable quantities in only two spots on the globe, Sheffield in England and Essen in the Prussian Rhineland. The world at large regarded it as rare, costly, and rather unnecessary.

In 1848 it could still be said that "iron, cold iron, is master of them all." Hewitt often repeated John Locke's phrase, that "he who first made known the uses of iron may be truly styled the father of the arts and the author of plenty." The identity of that first discoverer is lost in the dim murk of prehistoric happenings, ages before Tubal Cain walked the earth. Some skin-clad savage, no doubt, happening one day to build his hottest fire upon some pieces of iron ore, found a lump of redly-glowing metal in the coals, and by a brilliant inspiration pounded the soft mass into a rude axe-head or spear-point. His tribe recognized in this first smith

[1] A. S. Hewitt, "Statistics and Geography of the Production of Iron," address before the American Geographical and Statistical Society, 1856.

an almost miraculous power, such as was later imputed to Vulcan and Thor; and a legend of awesome magic was carried down to the tales of the supernatural forging of great swords, like Arthur's Excalibur or Siegfried's Balmung. From the Hittites the Assyrians learned the uses of iron. The charcoal furnace and the forge in ancient times spread around the Mediterranean, and in the middle ages over all western Europe. But at the dawn of modern times the highest output of a furnace was only four or five tons of iron a week, and it was thought a marvelous feat when in the sixteenth century the iron works of Sussex began making cannon of three tons' weight. The era of extensive iron manufacture did not open until the eighteenth century.

England led the way. In 1715 Abraham Darby of Coalbrookdale first made practical use of coke for smelting iron ore, and charcoal began to wane. Furnaces at once became larger and more efficient; the industry rapidly shifted from Sussex to northern England. Just before and during the American Revolution such engine-works as that in which John Hewitt was trained began to demand iron parts made with more precision and with better metal; and steady improvements were effected in the working of malleable iron and the conversion of cast iron into wrought iron. The engineer John Wilkinson, a friend of John Watt, showed how to produce stronger iron tools and to bore iron cylinders. In 1776 he drilled a cylinder of which Boulton wrote admiringly that "it does not err the thickness of an old shilling in any part." (A cylinder that erred by more than one ten-thousandth of an inch would today be rejected in any automobile factory.) The introduction of the steam engine naturally did much to enlarge and improve iron manufacture; for example, steam power was at once used to furnish the air-blast for the furnaces. In 1783 Henry Cort patented the grooved roll, which is the basis of the modern rolling-mill and which made rails, rods, and other elongated shapes far more efficiently than any hammer could do; and a year later he patented the puddling-furnace. The inventor Neilson introduced in 1828 the hot-air blast instead of the cold-air blast, an innovation of immense value. In 1842 Nasmyth patented his steam hammer, which, followed by steam stamps of various kinds, made it possible to shape iron far more quickly and accurately than before.[1]

[1] Cf. H. D. Traill and J. S. Mann, *Social England*, V, 416-420; 631-638; 813ff.

When the Trenton mills were set in operation in 1845, the American iron industry had behind it a rather rudimentary record of more than a century, roughly paralleling but always following the development which had taken place in Great Britain. Iron had been smelted at many points between the Adirondacks and Carolinas, but nowhere more energetically or successfully than in the region between the Hudson and the Delaware. New Jersey has two distinct ranges of mountains or rather hills, the Kittatinny Range in the northwest and the Highland Range, which includes the Orange and Ramapo Mountains and many isolated ridges like Copperas and Schooley's. In these highlands the early settlers found abundant iron ore, and hastened to make use of it.

Hewitt, in searching for the best ores for his Trenton mills, steeped himself in the lore of the old Jersey mines, furnaces, and forges. He formed the habit of spending two or three days, when he could spare them, in excursions into the hills of the four northwestern counties, Hunterdon, Warren, Morris, and above all, Sussex. The woods—beech, oak, maple, and birch below, pine and spruce on the crests—were still deep; they were filled with the melody of waters, dashing over the gneiss and limestone rocks. In these forest recesses, following half-faded paths, he would sometimes come upon remains that seemed to speak of an older race of men. Shafts, with rusting bars and chains at the top, would suddenly open into the rocky hillsides. Heavy walls of crumbling masonry, enclosing a dilapidated water-wheel, would rise beside some brawling stream, whose waters had been diverted into a deep pit-like basis. Or some stark donjon of stone and brick, overgrown with vines and moss, with a gaping iron maw at the bottom, would close the end of a deeply rutted road, where slag lay mixed with clay and gravel—the ruins of an old furnace.

The first users of iron in these hills had been the Indians, mingling the powdered ores with other substances to make war-paints. The early settlers had set up charcoal furnaces and rude forges to work the metal into kettles, wheels, fire-backs, and other household articles, and had occasionally built a bloomery to manufacture iron blooms or rods. These workshops sprang up wherever streams, forests, and ores coincided, the water being required for power. Sometimes they were found even in the lowlands, where the ebb and flow of iron-impregnated water in swamps and half-stagnant streams had left thick beds of bog-ore at the sides. Even a small furnace required at least twenty thousand acres of timber to ensure a constant supply of charcoal, a thousand acres being cut each year.[1]

As he explored the region, Hewitt found furnaces that had been built with admirable skill and ingenuity. A few rose twenty-five feet in air; others twenty. They were usually square at the base, built like stone bastions near the side of a hill, with the heavy walls occasionally caught together with iron braces or tie-rods. At the base on three sides were arched recesses for the introduction of the blast, and on the fourth a larger opening for taking out cinders and tapping the molten pig-iron. The lining was usually of fire-brick, for which New Jersey offered excellent clays. Some of the old forges and bloomeries were equally striking. A cluster of iron spikes and decayed beams would show where tilt-hammers had been con-structed to batter impurities out of the pigs as they were brought glowing from the furnace, and beat them into the desired shape. These hammers, weighing even six hundred pounds, were raised by cams on the rim of a drum turned slowly by a waterwheel; and as they dropped, rose, and dropped again, their noise had once boomed through the quiet valleys for miles.

The first forge or bloomery in Morris County was erected in 1710 near the present town of Whippany. At Ringwood in Passaic County a small forge had been built as early as 1739, and a fur-nace in 1742. Thereafter others had rapidly been sown across the Province. Hewitt in his peregrinations learned their names—the Charlotteburg Forges, Andover Furnace, Bloomingdale Furnace, Mount Hope Furnace, Boonton Forge, Cumberland Furnace, Frank-lin Furnace, and many more. Shortly after the Revolution it was said that a man could not ride across the State in any direction without stumbling upon at least two of these old works; and in Morris County alone there were nearly a hundred iron forges in operation by the year 1777.[2]

To Hewitt the study of these ruins was business, but he felt their romance none the less. They evoked the romance of woodland adventure; men had pushed into rough mountain wastes, into

[1] The admirable book by Charles S. Boyer, *Early Forges and Furnaces in New Jersey*, contains brief essays on the principal iron-works.

[2] Cf. Miriam R. Waxberg, "Money in Morris County," New Jersey Historical Society *Proceedings*, Vol. 53, 20ff.

swamps and tangled forests, fighting the Indians and panthers as they went, not merely to take furs or clear farms, but to lay the foundations of mining and industry. Their names called up the romance of business risk; the "London Company" which built the works at Ringwood, Long Pond, and Charlotteburg in Colonial days had spent more than £54,000 before any tangible returns appeared. And there was the romance of invention. These early iron-masters had to sell their wares in the form of stoves, farm implements, kitchen utensils, hardware, and arms, and they exercised great ingenuity in devising new iron commodities. As he looked at some rusty pig with the name Hanover or Speedwell stamped upon its battered side, Hewitt could imagine the scene when that bit of iron had been produced: the furnace, built into the slope of a hill in the primeval forest, blazing with heat; negro slaves stoking the charcoal fires and adjusting the huge bellows of the blast; indentured English or German servants noisily drawing off the slag from an upper outlet, while others tapped the molten iron below and ran it through long gutters in the sand into "sow" and "pig" moulds; the water-wheels which furnished power for the blast turning with a continuous splash; and from the bloomery near by the regular rise and fall, with ear-shattering noise, of the trip-hammer.

The iron plant at Trenton was the inheritor of all this and of the inventions made with increasing rapidity in English mills during the previous century. The ores which Cooper & Hewitt used came in the main from the Jersey hills, though some were also brought from Pennsylvania. They went to Phillipsburg, where the three tall blast furnaces—for a third was built in 1852-53—were able to smelt at least 25,000 tons of iron annually. Hewitt could boast that these furnaces, 55 feet high and 20 feet in diameter at the "boshes," were the largest in America; that the engine equipment, made at the Allaire works, was unexcelled; and that the establishment, as a whole, "is without a rival for completeness, substantiality, and good work." Thence the pig-iron travelled, for a time by canal and after 1850 by the Trenton & Belvidere-Delaware Railroad, to the Trenton mills. These mills would seem quaint and small by present-day standards, but in the middle fifties they were the largest in the country.

They consisted of puddling furnaces, heating furnaces, rolling

mill, and wire mill, equipped with machinery that was partly
American and partly English. The double puddling furnaces, which
steadily increased in number until by 1854 there were twenty-two,
converted molten pig-iron, under constant stirring by skilled workmen, into wrought iron or at least a better quality of cast iron. The
double heating furnaces, of which there were six in the year named,
heated the pigs or ingots for the first rolls—those which crushed
them into flat blooms or billets. These billets, taken up white-hot,
were then shot forward through a series of other rolls adjusted to
turn them into rails, beams, or rods, as desired. As the smaller
pieces went forward, hissing wherever they touched any moisture,
they rapidly took on the aspect of fiery writhing snakes, struggling
in the murky gloom to escape workmen who caught them with
pincers and thrust them back and forth with incredible quickness.
When the larger rails were ready for final shaping, vises seized them
and laborers hammered away deafeningly. As they finished, the rail
was pushed under sharp steel saws which cut it to the precise length
required. It then passed to a cooling-bed, and when quite cold was
thrust into powerful presses, which straightened out bends or other
irregularities. There were also foundries and pattern-shops for the
production of special castings, and blacksmith shops and machine
shops. "No pains or expense have been spared," Hewitt wrote in
1854, "to make the mill perfect in its arrangements."

Power was derived partly from the before-mentioned race of the
Trenton Waterpower Company, with three great wheels serving
the mills, and partly from steam, for two engines were operated by
the waste heat of the furnaces. Anthracite was of course used at
both Phillipsburg and Trenton. The whole plant had a capacity
by 1854 of more than 35,000 tons of finished iron annually—a
spoonful to the gargantuan production of after years, for Hewitt
lived to see a single American corporation formed with an annual
capacity of 8,000,000 tons of finished steel; but a very satisfactory
figure in the early fifties.

Hewitt took pride in the economy and effectiveness of every
branch of the establishment. He declared in 1853 that if the Andover ores only continued abundant, the Phillipsburg furnaces
could undersell all other American makers of pig-iron. They had
proved it:

We have made iron at various prices, ranging in cost from $11 to $16 per ton, according to the running of the furnaces. Judging from our present rate, I consider the following to be a fair estimate of the cost of the Andover Iron:—

2½ tons,	Ore, at $1.50	....	$3.30
2 "	Coal, at $3	....	6.00
¼ "	Limestone, at 25¢	....	0.06¼
Labor and Incidentals		....	4.00

$13.36¼

We have made iron much cheaper than this, but I consider it to be a fair average statement. It costs, to deliver the iron at Philadelphia, $1.37½ per ton, and at Elizabethport, at $1.50 per ton. In other words, $15 per ton will cover cost of the iron in market, with a liberal allowance for incidental expenses. We have never sold it for less than $25 per ton, and now are refusing orders, which would absorb the whole product, at $35 per ton. Some, which we sold, was re-sold last week at $40 per ton. At $35 the profit will be $20 per ton, which, on 25,000 tons, would yield $500,000 per annum. I have always estimated that the three furnaces, under all contingencies on the average of years, may be safely set down to yield a profit of $200,000 per annum.

Pig-iron cooled in the morning at Phillipsburg could be delivered that night at the Trenton Mill for 94 cents a ton; for the Trenton & Belvidere-Delaware Railroad connected the two plants so directly as to obviate rehandling or cartage. Once delivered at the mill, it could be manufactured into a wide variety of pieces. "The machinery," Hewitt wrote in 1853, "is adapted for railroad iron, railroad axles, and railroad chairs, forging bars, faggotting iron, wire rods, brasiers' rods, and bar iron"; while that year they were erecting a new mill "for the manufacture of wrought-iron beams, shop iron, and other heavy iron, of a class that no mill in the world can now make."

The prominence which the Trenton establishment at once assumed was attributable to several factors; to Peter Cooper's prestige, his generous expenditure, the patronage of the Camden & Amboy, and above all to the energy which Hewitt immediately gave its operations. There were plenty of other iron manufactories in the United States in 1850; the census listed 377 makers of pig-iron, 1,391 makers of castings, and 552 makers of wrought iron. But most of these were small local establishments which, like the Myrtle Forge that Hergesheimer describes in *The Three Black Pennys*, like the historic furnace that Thaddeus Stevens set up near Chambersburg, Pa., were unknown outside their own communities. The republic in 1854 possessed only a half dozen rolling mills with an annual capacity of ten thousand tons or more of rails. The largest, the Montour Works at Danville, Pa., could roll only 16,000 tons of rails, in quality vastly inferior to those made in Trenton. Tiny iron works everywhere, but particularly in Pennsylvania, with poor equipment and an uneconomic force of men, passed rapidly from birth to death; they rose, fluttered, and fell like May-flies.[1] Mills which, like the Trenton works, were built on broad and durable foundations, became nationally famous; and the most vital part of the equipment at Trenton was not the capital of the establishment, or its contracts, or Peter Cooper's name, but the busy, ingenious brain of Hewitt.

It was a remarkable feat that Cooper & Hewitt accomplished in creating the principal iron establishment of the nation in a seaboard city at precisely the time when iron manufacture was moving rapidly westward. By 1850 Pittsburgh had already become the Birmingham of the United States. Her smoking mills were consuming some 150,000 tons of pig-iron annually. The production of that dirty giant between the Monongahela and Allegheny spurted forward when in 1852 indirect rail communication was opened with Philadelphia, and again when 1854 brought direct rail communication. Ohio by 1850 was manufacturing twice as much pig-iron as New Jersey and more than twice as much as New York, while large rolling mills were soon to be established in Chicago and St. Louis. High up in the new State of Michigan, where the rugged northeastern peninsula juts out between the waters of Lakes Michigan and Superior, the solitudes had been broken in the middle forties by prospectors who were astonished by the rich ores they discovered.[2] One, a Connecticut Yankee named Philo M. Everett, located a claim, later the famous Jackson mine, on what he called "a moun-

---

[1] See Census of 1850; the survey in British Parliamentary Reports, 1854, Vol. XXXVI; B. F. French, *Rise and Progress of the Iron Trade of the United States, 1621-1857* (1858), this last being very full on the years 1840-55.

[2] Cf. Frederick Morley, *Michigan and Its Resources* (1882).

tain of solid iron ore, 150 feet high," and boasted: "The ore looks as bright as a bar of iron just broken." The first bloomery in the peninsula was set up in 1848. A year later there was an "iron rush" thither which in some ways resembled the contemporaneous gold rush to California, and the boom town of Marquette sprang up on Lake Superior. By 1855 three more bloomeries were in operation. The completion of the Sault Ste. Marie Canal that year by the Federal Government, carrying steamships past the tempestuous rapids which divide Lakes Superior and Michigan, made it easy to bring the raw ore down to Cleveland and Buffalo. No one could foresee that a few decades later the greatest centres of iron-ore production in the world would lie farther northwest still, in the incredibly rich Mesabi and Vermilion ranges of Minnesota. But everyone perceived that the iron industry was moving inexorably westward, and was doing so for reasons which already placed a coastal mill at a disadvantage.

Success at Trenton was hence conquered against many difficulties, and there were periods when even this energetically managed and conservatively financed company faced disaster. The establishment of a great iron manufactory required both a wide range of staples and unsleeping resourcefulness in the development of markets. A small manufacturer might do well with one specialty. In Trenton one little mill prospered for a time by making anvils. But as the two Coopers and Abram S. Hewitt meant to be among the largest manufacturers, they found they could not succeed simply as makers of excellent rails. They must turn out many products; when British competition became too spirited in one field, they must whip alertly to another; if railroad construction flagged, they must find a market among bridge-builders, telegraph-promoters, and building contractors. They must keep a keen eye not only upon older competitors like the Phoenix Works, but upon the new ones that began to spring up formidably—the Cambria Iron Works, established at Johnstown, Pa., in 1853; Jones & Laughlin's, Ltd., at Pittsburgh in the same year; and the Bethlehem Iron Company at Bethlehem in 1860. They must look forward, invent, and be as responsive as weathercocks to every shifting economic wind.[1]

Hewitt learned his hard initial lesson in the necessity of having several arrows in his quiver during the first year of cutthroat British

[1] Annual Reports, Trenton Iron Company; Cooper & Hewitt Letterbooks.

competition, 1848-49. Rails of Andover iron, still expensive to mine, smelt, and temper, cost the mill $70 a ton to manufacture, and he had been selling them at $80. But as a result of the low Tariff of 1846 and the rapid development of new English processes, the price of British rails delivered in New York shortly fell to $40 a ton. Though not as good as Andover rails, they were good enough for most American lines, and Cooper & Hewitt were threatened with the loss of their whole market. Moreover, as railroad construction boomed in the United States, many British ironmasters shrewdly sold rails in exchange for railroad bonds, and on this basis drove a flourishing business. A few figures tell the story. Between 1847 and 1849 imports of British pig-iron into this country rose from 557,000 cwt. to 2,113,000; imports of British bar iron from 841,000 cwt. to 2,298,000; imports of British railroad iron from 271,000 cwt. to 1,383,000. And the British shipments of railroad iron continued increasing by steady bounds—to nearly four, nearly five, and nearly six million cwt. in the years 1851, 1852, and 1853 respectively.

What could Hewitt do? He could make rails of ordinary iron, surfaced with Andover metal, at $52.50 a ton, and trust to its superiority for a certain sale. As costs declined, by the spring of 1852 he was even able to sell these rails at $47.50 a ton, and obtained orders from a few railway contractors. At the same time he joined in the vigorous outcry for higher tariffs. But a new staple was necessary, and he turned to wire-making.

Peter Cooper had made wire in New York City, and it had continued a minor product when the mill was removed to Trenton. Now chance made a sudden expansion possible. In the middle forties a struggling corporation—the Delaware Manufacturing Company—had established a wire mill in Trenton, which in 1849 went on the rocks. The Trenton Iron Company at once took over the plant at cost, $75,000, paying the debts and assuming the stocks and bonds at par. In the next six years these securities were all retired, partly out of profits and partly by an issue of Trenton Iron Company stock. Cooper & Hewitt meanwhile enlarged their new acquisition, which Hewitt termed in 1853 "the largest and best wire mill in the United States." They advertised that they were ready to supply telegraph wire, bridge wire, wire fence, rivets, and railroad spikes, all made from the Andover ore. In 1851 Hewitt exhibited his wire at the Crystal Palace Exhibition in London, the first world's

fair, and even secured an English order. In the Eastern States and
Canada sales were made in unexpected volume.

This was because telegraphs were now being spread over the
country in a fast-widening network. In 1844 Silas Wright had received and declined the Democratic nomination for Vice President
by telegraph; by the fall of 1846 Mexican War news was being
flashed over twelve hundred miles of wire; and early in the fifties
the system reached nearly every important city and town. The first
telegraph millionaire, Ezra Cornell, soon appeared. A thick wire of
galvanized iron was then used. In 1852 Hewitt stated that his company had made nearly all the telegraph wire strung in the preceding two years, and it continued to hold its primacy for some
time. Wire fencing was a less important product, which he called
"an amateur business, undertaken rather with the purpose of drawing attention to the matter than with any object of doing more ourselves than sell materials." Yet during the decade 1850-60 the Trenton fencing was sold in large quantities to enclose rights-of-way
along railroads; it spread to the Pacific Coast, where Frémont and
Commodore Stockton used it on their ranches; and some was even
sold in Europe.

Among the customers to whom the wire mill made extensive sales
was John A. Roebling, a pushing industrialist whom Hewitt used
later to say he had brought to Trenton. And here we touch not only
the most famous sister-industry of the New Jersey capital, but one
of the important friendships of his early life. Roebling, a gifted
Prussian-American whose long, thoughtful face, baldish brow, chin-
whiskers, and brilliant eyes made him look a little like the
familiar picture of Charles Dickens, established his mill for making
wire rope in Trenton in 1848, and the next year took up his residence there. Till his death of overwork while building the Brooklyn
Bridge, he and Hewitt were on the most cordial terms.

They had much in common besides their mutual interest in ironmaking, wire, and engineering. Roebling came from the ancient
walled town of Mülhausen, close to the historic cities of Jena, Erfürt, and Weimar. The son of a substantial tobacco manufacturer,
he had been thoroughly educated, first in the town gymnasium,
then privately by a former professor of Erfürt, and finally at the
Polytechnic Institute in Berlin. He also attended lectures by Hegel
at the University of Berlin, becoming his passionate disciple. Em-

ployed by the Prussian Government in roadbuilding in Westphalia, he grew interested in bridges. A visit to an ingenious structure suspended by chains over the River Regnitz, known as the "miracle bridge," filled him with enthusiasm. But as he found his proposals and promotion blocked in every direction by red tape, inertia, and jealousy, he finally turned to America as the land where a young man really had a chance. In 1831 he was in Pennsylvania, much impressed by his first view of our bustling young democracy.[1] "Nowhere does one see a person in rags; all, even the common workmen, go very neatly and cleanly dressed." "The removal of the hat and frequent greetings, which are so burdensome in Germany, do not exist here." "The Americans set to quickly, eat even more quickly, and leave the table without having said a single word."

For some years he was occupied by a half-successful attempt to found a German community, Saxonburg, some twenty-five miles from Pittsburgh, and by farming and house-building. Late in the thirties, having been appointed a State engineer to help build canal dams and locks, he hit upon the innovation that was to make him famous. In their anxiety to compete with the Erie Canal, the Pennsylvanians had built canals and dredged river channels to the two sides of the central Allegheny ridge, and had then bridged the crest between Johnstown and Hollidaysburg, 2300 feet high, by inclined planes. Puffing stationary engines, well braced, pulled cars up one side of these planes and cautiously lowered them down the other. Huge hawsers of Kentucky hemp, nine inches in circumference, were used. They were cumbrous, expensive, and easily frayed. Roebling had read in a foreign scientific journal of the invention of wire rope in Germany; and it was easy to persuade the State Board of Public Works to give it a trial. Success led him to begin manufacturing it in quantity at a shop in Saxonburg. It was an inevitable third step for him to devise new uses for the wire rope, first in building a suspension aqueduct for a canal across the Allegheny River, and then, during 1846, in throwing a suspension bridge across the Monongahela to Pittsburgh.[2] By this time the Saxonburg shop was far too small, while Roebling had become

[1] Cf. John A. Roebling, *Diary of my Journey from Mülhausen to the United States, 1831*, translated by Edward Underhill (1931).

[2] Hamilton Schuyler, *The Roeblings: A Century of Engineers, Bridge-Builders, and Industrialists.*

worried by the high cost of transporting wire to the east, there still being no railroad from Pittsburgh to Philadelphia. He therefore wrote to Peter Cooper on December 23, 1847, that he wished to establish a wire-rope manufactory near Trenton, and would like to know if five or ten acres of dry level ground could be obtained near the railway and canal.

Peter Cooper found him a site; and Hewitt that summer gave him much practical assistance in establishing his factory in Trenton.

Roebling had imagination as well as enterprise, and an authentic vein of philosophy and poetry. With the versatility of a Da Vinci he combined the industry of an Edison. He attended trade conventions, wrote for scientific journals, played the flute and piano, studied history, invented tools and machinery, designed bridges, canals, and portage railroads, made his own drawings for the patent office, and supervised a large business. Yet each night before retiring he wrote up his journal and notebooks in great detail, and in a lucid English style; and following his Hegelian bent, at his death left a manuscript volume of several thousand pages entitled *Roebling's Theory of the Universe*. A man of strict integrity, he always exacted his full rights from others. He made a fetish of punctuality, and if anyone who had an appointment with him was five minutes late he postponed the conference. Once during the Civil War General Frémont in St. Louis sent for him and kept him waiting in the anteroom. Roebling took a card and scribbled on it: "Sir, you are keeping me waiting. John Roebling has not the leisure to wait upon any man." Hewitt, equally a student, equally tireless, and equally punctilious, found him a neighbor after his own heart; and he admired his son Washington and the latter's remarkable wife, Emily Warren Roebling.

In the first crisis of the Trenton Iron Company the Roebling Company also made an invaluable customer. For some years it bought nearly all its wire from Cooper & Hewitt. The first great bridge employing this wire was that over the Niagara gorge. Here in 1847 a contract had been let to Charles Ellet for a suspension bridge of 800 feet, but Ellet had never finished it. Hewitt had supplied him with wire and had visited the uncompleted structure. "I remember even now with a thrill of anxiety," he wrote fifty years later, "the feeling which I had in crossing the river on foot over a plank about one foot in width. Shortly afterwards I saw a woman

with a basket of eggs on her arm coolly walk over the same plank."
Roebling took over the structure in 1850, contracted for new supplies of wire from Cooper & Hewitt, and despite many obstacles,
including a virulent cholera epidemic, finished it. The test train
that passed over it in March, 1855, weighing 340 tons and drawn
by a 28-ton engine, was sustained by Andover wire. When Roebling
later began turning out his own wire, he bought from Cooper &
Hewitt the rods from which much of it was made.[1]

Another product which furnished the Trenton company much
business and some profit was the "chairs" then used on many American railways, as they still are on some European lines: that is,
cast-iron sockets which, fastened to the ties, supported the rails in
an upright position. Cooper & Hewitt purchased for $10,000 the
chair patent of E. S. Remick, granted in the fall of 1850, and when
the initial models proved unsatisfactory, Abram and his brother
Charles devised an improved pattern. A machine was installed
which turned out 3,000 a day, and soon more than paid for the
patent and the experimentation.

Thus with Andover rails, wire, chairs, and other products, and
a steady backlog in the sale of Phillipsburg pig-iron, the Trenton
mill defeated the first great threat to its existence. There followed
a brief but golden prosperity.

Early in 1852 a marked rise in the price of rails began. The flood
of gold from California and Australia had stimulated business
throughout the world, and railway building spread from the United
States and England all over western Europe, to Russia, to India,
and to South America. During May, 1852, the price of British rails
in our Eastern seaports rose from $34 a ton to $38, and a month
later they sold at $50. On the basis of his London advices, for
Cooper & Hewitt sometimes imported English rails for customers,
Hewitt predicted still higher rates the next year. The British manufacturers, he explained, had been engaged in a fierce competition,
and for three years had been making metal at a loss. The weaker
firms having now been crushed out of existence, the comparatively
strong survivors had finally combined, as more than once in the
past, to raise their prices. His predictions proved sound. By October
Hewitt was refusing offers of $55 a ton and selling only at $60,

[1] John A. Roebling published an interesting monograph, *Long and Short Span
Railway Bridges* (1869).

while as 1853 opened he wrote that the prospects of the iron business had never been so satisfactory. In the following spring rails were steady at $70 a ton, and the Trenton mill was being pushed to capacity.

This refreshing prosperity, felt in every department of the Trenton works, continued for about two years. In 1852 all the rolling mills of the globe, Hewitt estimated, could have produced enough good iron for only six thousand miles of railroad. The world needed far more rapid construction than that. In the United States alone a total of more than 13,000 miles had then been built, and at least an equal amount was planned for immediate completion. In fact, during the two years 1853-54 almost 8,000 miles were laid. Most of this trackage necessarily consisted of cheap and inferior British rails, which wore out so rapidly that Hewitt believed renewals would have to be made at the rate of 2,000 miles annually. Translating this into dollars, he estimated that each mile of railroad would require in its first ten years at least $10,000 worth of iron for replacements, or an average of $1,000 a year. An American system of 26,000 miles would thus need $26,000,000 worth of iron annually for mere upkeep.

The general rise in prices also assisted the wire mill, which was now driven to capacity. Hewitt had arrived at a price-fixing agreement with his chief competitor, Henry S. Washburne of Worcester, Mass., and during 1851-53 they exchanged many letters upon rates. "We must be careful," Hewitt wrote, "not to encourage too much competition"; but he was eager for a large return while the market was "bare of wire." Early in 1853, besieged by orders, he and Washburne advanced their prices from 40 to 45 per cent. Meanwhile the Trenton foundry had obtained large orders for wrought iron from the Corliss Engine Works. Such was the efflorescent national prosperity on which Franklin Pierce rode into the Presidency, and which enabled Hewitt to write in March, 1853, that after eight years of hard work large returns were in sight. On a cost basis the establishment he had done so much to build up was then valued at $625,000; but he reminded the stockholders that this sum included nothing for experience, skill, or good will:[1]

You must remember that everything is in effective operation,

[1] Annual Report, Trenton Iron Company, 1853.

with experienced workmen, reputation established, and business connections formed. You must remember at what sacrifice of time, money, and labor this has been done;—how much it has cost to teach each man his business; and that in doing this, the legitimate profits of five years have been consumed. We now see large profits. Before, we knew we ought to get them, but did not. We have reduced the cost of making rails from $80 to $40 per ton; of wire rods from $120 to $60. In doing this, the whole time and ability of Mr. Cooper and myself have been consumed for eight years, and that not one dollar has ever been charged for all this to construction account; I believe that it is a low estimate to value this experience, skill, and business connection, at 50 per cent of the whole cost of the property, and I am quite sure that no company of gentlemen could start to build new works at the magnitude of ours, without having $300,000 less money at the end of eight years, than they would have had, if our works had been purchased.

CHAPTER VII

Beams and Bessemer

THE great half-empty nation over whose destinies, in 1850, slavery and free-soil politicians were squabbling in Washington, a nation still partly unexplored and largely undeveloped, seemed hungry for iron. As its youth stiffened into manhood it needed ferric strength. There was hardly an iron building in the land. Iron bridges were still a curiosity, iron machinery was rare. Railroad maps showed a sparse irregular patchwork of lines along the Atlantic Coast, and almost nothing else. The New York traveller who packed his gayly-flowered carpetbag to travel northward could not yet reach Albany by rail without making a wide detour into New England. He could ride as far south as Washington on "the cars," but not to Richmond. If he were going west he could not yet travel as far by rail as Pittsburgh; he might take the Erie, which was building bravely across southern New York, but it stopped short three-quarters of the way to Dunkirk on the lake. There were not yet three hundred miles of railway in Illinois, and if Lincoln had wished to go from Springfield to Chicago on the north, or Indianapolis on the east, he would have had to traverse the entire distance by horse. Not a rail had been dropped in Wisconsin; not a spike had been hammered home beyond the Mississippi. All this was fast being changed by the "railroad fever"; twenty-one hundred miles of railway were built in 1851 and twenty-three hundred in 1852; but the change must be fed by the rumble and smoke of busy iron-mills.

And yet the familiar sequence of scarcity, expansion, glut, and depression, the unfailing cycle of capitalism, made itself felt then as later, and in the iron trade as in older and less booming industries. In the flush days of 1850-53 Hewitt had been distrustful of the future. He read the omens aright, for high demand brought the inevitable over-production. Both in Great Britain and the United States new streams of iron were rapidly tapped and old ones were expanded, a plethora ensued, and prices crashed ruinously. In the last days of 1854 Hewitt addressed Senator Richard Brodhead of Pennsylvania a gloomy letter:

> If, when I talked to you, the delusion still prevailed in my mind that Great Britain could not supply all the iron required by the world at the present time, recent occurrences must have dispelled it. Stocks of iron are accumulating in every market in the world, and the impossibility of selling at the cost of production has closed nearly all the American mills, and would have closed the English works but for the possession of the large capitals which enable them to run and to pile up stocks. At this time, there are 25,000 tons of rails (Welsh) at the Atlantic Dock at this port, waiting for purchasers, and yet the shipments keep up, on the idea that somebody will be able to buy. If that would happen, it would only tend to ship out of this country a portion of that fund which is now paid to the citizens who are at work, and thus add to the number who have no work. The productive power of Great Britain in 1853-54 was taxed to the utmost for existing works, and the product reached 2,700,000 tons. This was too much. The world could not use it. The United States, her best customer, has bought so much that her own laborers are idle, must be fed, and consequently we can buy no more. Stocks therefore accumulate. And yet, so long as prices could be kept up by the inflation of bank credits, preferred stock, income bonds, and the numberless issues by which the bubble was inflated, the work of increasing production abroad was continued.

As Hewitt explained, two years earlier it had been supposed that every available district for ironmaking in Great Britain had been scarred over with pits and workshops. But geologists had found extensive bodies of ore in the Cleveland Hills in Yorkshire, and fifty or sixty furnaces sprang up there. Scottish pig-iron in New York fell in one year from $40 a ton to $27, British rails from $70 to $50, and bar iron to a song. Throughout the broad State of Pennsylvania furnaces were banked and forges silent. "The ability of Great Britain to supply the world," wrote Hewitt, "has been demonstrated by an actual increase of production of seven hundred thousand tons in a single year (1853). If her efforts to dispose of such an enormous yield do not paralyze the industry of the world, and reduce our own labor to a starving condition, we certainly cannot compete against her great capital. The iron business has, for many years, failed to produce a satisfactory return of profit for the ironmasters of this country, and were it not for public-spirited motives, many of them would have abandoned it long since. We ourselves have a pride in the business and want to continue it if we can."

Some new source of income had to be found; and under this fresh spur of necessity the Trenton Iron Company embarked upon one of its chief contributions to American technology.

Up to this time three methods of erecting semi-fireproof structures had been used in our large cities. One was the Old World method of piling up heavy walls of stone, which consumed space, gave the interior rooms a cell-like appearance, and usually resulted in a damp, cold, and gloomy edifice. Another, which had lately gained in favor, was the combination of masonry with cast-iron beams. James Bogardus of New York, beginning in 1850, even erected a large number of buildings whose entire framework was cast-iron, but these were small. In larger cast-iron structures the beams were laid in close array from wall to wall, and short segmental arches of brick between them supported the flooring. But they had to be made so thick and heavy that they were costly and inconvenient, while even then they tended, under continuous strains, to sag or buckle. As a third method, men were experimenting with wrought-iron, which they found stronger, safer, and more economical of space; Robert Stephenson built the great Menai bridge of wrought tubular beams in 1849; but nobody had yet rolled solid wrought-iron beams of sufficient length and depth for large buildings. Several short beams could be welded together, but the process was costly and untrustworthy.

In 1852 Peter Cooper at last decided to begin erecting Cooper Union, for which he had so long made plans and accumulated funds. His golden dream was about to take on substantiality. He often related how, when he first began to derive considerable profits from his grocery store and his rented houses at Fourth Avenue and Astor Place, he had fixed his eyes upon the plot opposite, in the triangle where Third and Fourth avenues join, as a desirable site for his workingmen's institute. He bought his first lot there in 1825, and from time to time purchased adjoining strips, until he now owned the entire block. It seemed an ideal site, in the very center of a district that was rapidly being devoted to letters, art, and music. A stone's throw away on Lafayette Place was rising the Astor Library, incorporated in 1849 by John Jacob Astor, and opened to the public in 1854. Likewise within a stone's throw was the Astor Place Opera House, scene of the bloody Forrest-Macready riots of 1849. The Academy of Music was built in 1854 on Irving Place, only a half-dozen blocks to the north; a few blocks westward, at 109 University Place, the new building of the New York Society Library in 1856. Fine residences were scattered about, and people of note had lived in the immediate vicinity; hard by Peter Cooper's site, for example, stood Colonnade Row (now upper Lafayette Street) in which Washington Irving and palsied old John Jacob Astor had occupied houses, and from which Julia Gardiner had been married to President John Tyler.

Peter Cooper had envisaged a monumental structure. He had gathered several hundred thousand dollars in liquid funds over and above the capital invested in his glue and iron businesses. It was not enough for an institute whose initial cost proved more than $600,000; but it was enough for a beginning, and he remarked, "If the Lord wants me to build it, He will provide the money—if He doesn't, He will withhold it!" He wished a spacious, handsome, and enduring edifice of at least six stories, but at the same time he wanted to avoid the preposterous expense of a stone structure like the Custom House, with massive pillars, piers, and arches. The government could afford such a building; he could not. Recently Princeton College had bought Trenton rails for the structural work in building Old North hall. He now decided to use wrought-iron beams, and directed the force at Trenton to begin experiments based upon rail-making. These rails were four and a half inches deep; why not beams nearly twice as heavy?

The foreman, a capable Englishman named William Barrow, set to work upon new machinery, for none existed which would roll flanged beams seven inches in horizontal section. His designs promised success, but he died before completing them, and was succeeded by Charles Hewitt, who spent a year in carrying forward the effort. Abram and he installed the heavy new machinery. After a total outlay of about $150,000, including a general enlargement of the rolling-mill, the object was achieved. For those interested in technical details, Hewitt's subsequent description may be quoted. He writes that the main feature was "a three-high mill placed vertically instead of horizontally," and that "additional horizontal rolls were provided to operate where thè vertical rolls came together at the top." In other words, the machinery was substantially "what is known as the universal mill, now in use for rolling plates and shapes. It was so far as I know the first universal mill that was ever built." It was necessary to put in lifting tables for handling the heavy piles, and driven rollers. No patents were taken out, though most of the machinery was subsequently patented by John Fritz and other men who seemed to be ignorant of what had been done at Trenton.

This machinery could be used to produce both structural beams and heavier rails; and in his annual report of 1853 Hewitt wrote that if it proved as effective as he anticipated, the entire output of the rolling mill should be salable at much higher prices. That year beams were rolled twenty feet in length and seven inches deep which met every test, and a few months later, beams twenty-five feet long.

Early in 1854 Peter Cooper laid the cornerstone of his institute.[1] He placed in it a scroll with a characteristic inscription, stating that his great object was "to open the avenues of scientific knowledge to the youth of our city and country, and so unfold the volume of nature that the young may see the beauties of creation, enjoy its blessings, and learn to love the Author" of all good. His architect, one Peterson, permitted bad foundations to be put in, which later had to be replaced at great expense. Each story was to be built of iron, stone, and brick, without the use of wood. The first horizontal rows of Trenton beams were soon in place; and they constituted the earliest fabric in America in which a rolled wrought-iron grid was used to support the flooring of a large and

[1] Peter Cooper and Hewitt had frequently talked of the institute or union. "It was a matter of serious discussion between Mr. Cooper and his family," said Hewitt later, "whether the endowment which he proposed to make for the education of the working classes of that city should not be given to the General Society of Mechanics and Tradesmen. He very much desired that the Society should be the administrator of his bounty. The only reason why he concluded to not carry out his first intention was the fact that there was a limitation in the Society's charter confining the benefits to the apprentices of mechanics and tradesmen." Peter Cooper wished his institution to have a broader scope altogether. *Centennial Celebration of the General Society of Mechanics and Tradesmen, 1885*, p. 20.

heavy structure. When the outer walls had risen sufficiently, the second floor was likewise laid.

But meanwhile the new beams had received an additional advertisement. In December, 1853, the combined manufactory, warehouse, and offices of Harper & Brothers, the greatest publishers in the country, spectacularly burned down. The partners at once laid plans to rebuild on Cliff Street and Franklin Square, in the part of town then still called "the swamp." Hewitt called James Harper's attention to the wrought-iron beams, and the firm adopted them. Cooper Union could wait—indeed, Peter Cooper was glad to have time to make a little more money. Beam-making for it stopped, and the new machinery was temporarily devoted to materials for the Harper building. The result was its construction within a few months, a feat of unparalleled rapidity. It covered more than half an acre, was seven stories high, and as the first large fireproof building for commercial purposes in the country attracted wide attention.[1]

At this juncture the Federal Government decided to build an Assay Office in New York. Hewitt proposed his beams to the Treasury Department, they were adopted, and again Cooper Union was held up while the required number were rolled. However, during 1854-55 the last beams for the Union were turned out, and by Christmas in 1856 the building was almost complete. The Lord had provided! In fact, Peter Cooper's brown notebook shows that on July 10, 1856, he estimated his wealth at $1,106,000.

Every important builder in the country soon heard of the new materials—how they had met the government tests, how they easily sustained Harpers' heavy presses, how they made Cooper Union light, airy, and strong. The result was an active demand for beams at nearly double the price of rails. At the very moment that the depression in the iron industry threatened grave consequences, Cooper & Hewitt were placed in a position to exploit a most profitable new market. The superintendent of architecture for the Treasury, Captain A. H. Bowman, shortly decided to use Trenton beams and girders for all public buildings constructed under his supervision; and initial government orders for six thousand tons of iron were filled during the winter of 1855-56 and the following

---

[1] Cf. J. Henry Harper, *The House of Harper*, 104-106. This building was used till after the World War by the publishing house and gave the completest satisfaction.

summer. One order was particularly memorable. In Washington on July 4, 1851, with fitting ceremonies and an oration by Daniel Webster, the cornerstone had been laid for an extension of the Capitol, two wings of pure marble on each side of the familiar central edifice. Symmetry demanded that the old cupola, squat and ugly, now be replaced by a nobler and loftier dome. Plans were drawn, and great was the exultation of Cooper & Hewitt when the Treasury Department ordered their beams for the roofs and the crowning framework. Trenton beams likewise went into the new mint in Philadelphia, the new general postoffice in Washington, and a succession of other Federal structures.

Altogether, by the end of 1855 the new enterprise had proved a dazzling success. Structural iron had then been ordered for more than a hundred Federal buildings, and many States had adopted them. Indeed, nearly every important public edifice constructed in America in the five years after 1854 was equipped with Trenton iron. When the Vermont State House at Montpelier proved shaky and dangerous, Hewitt pointed out with gratification that this was one of the few structures for which his firm had not supplied material. And private orders had been numerous. The machinery at Trenton was steadily improved, and when horizontal rolls were substituted for vertical rolls it was much enlarged; so that beams were shortly being fabricated thirty feet in length, and twelve, sixteen, and even twenty inches in depth.[1]

Whenever a disastrous fire occurred in some American city, and such fires were incessant, Hewitt pointed out to prospective customers the advantages of his materials. It was easy, by using his beams, to render structures highly fire-resistant if not fireproof. Outer walls might be made of brick, masonry, or stone; the floors might be either terra-cotta tiles or brick arched between the beams and levelled off with cement. Hewitt offered prominent contractors a commission of five per cent for introducing his materials. "The insurance companies here," he wrote one, "have already reduced their rates one-fourth for first-class risks for buildings built in this manner, and for the merchandise in them." Selling iron at five cents

[1] In August, 1859, Hewitt wrote to government officers: "We are now rolling beams with great success, and are prepared to execute orders for six-inch by nine-inch beams of any length up to forty feet at $4\frac{1}{2}$ cents per pound." Hewitt Papers.

a pound to ordinary customers, four and a half to the government, the mill was reaping large profits.

It is clear that this structural business saved the Trenton company from the second threat of disaster just as the wire business had saved it from the first. Several years later Hewitt acknowledged to Pierce's Secretary of the Treasury, James Guthrie, that the government contracts had been invaluable. "At a time when business was prostrated, and ruin seemed to be impending over us, you . . . enabled us to meet our obligations and to keep our workmen employed. It is true that you consulted the interest of the government by the large orders which you gave us, but this consideration does not lessen our gratitude a particle." The winter of 1854-55 had indeed brought bitter hardship to ironmasters. Hewitt offered to sell rails at bare cost to procure work for his men, whom he pronounced in danger of "starving." He instructed the superintendent of the blast furnaces at Phillipsburg to cut down expenses "to the lowest point consistent with running the furnaces at all. . . . It is a matter of life and death." Laborers there and at Trenton were "crying for food, they ask no money." Ascribing the depression to the fierce competition of foreign iron, he declared that he was "oppressed in feeling by an overpowering sense of the distress which now is crushing out the industry of the country." But he and the two Coopers, by pitting against the British ironmasters an ingenuity equal to their own and providing the United States with a valuable new commodity, had kept their company in a strong position.

Rising corporate income enabled the firm to carry forward a policy of steady expansion. It was the ambition of both Hewitt and Peter Cooper to build up a self-sufficient plant—one with rich mines, machinery to crush the ore, blast furnaces to smelt it, and rolling mills and foundries to convert the pig-iron into a long array of articles, from rails to bolts. Up to the Civil War pig-iron production was for the most part a distinct business from the manufacture of castings and wrought iron. In the early fifties only five American establishments, besides the Trenton company, combined the whole process of smelting, puddling, and shaping iron, these being at Phoenixville, Safe Harbor, and Danville, Pa., at Boonton, N. J., and at Mt. Savage, Md. The Trenton works were easily the best. An expert sent by the British Government in 1853 to inspect the

Crystal Palace Exhibition in New York reported as much:[1] "In New Jersey the largest works are at Trenton, belonging to the Trenton Iron Company. This may be looked upon as the leading establishment of the United States, not only in regard to its production but also in regard to its working arrangements."

After the spring of 1855 business improved rapidly. There was much excitement when a group of Russian officers appeared in Trenton to test the Andover rails, possible contracts for tens of millions of dollars worth of iron spreading an aura about their heads. This unfortunately fell through. Nor did anything come of Charles Hewitt's invention of an improved car-wheel, with wrought-iron centre and cast-iron hub and rim, which Abram called "the best in the country." It cost too much to manufacture.[2] But late in 1856 another important deputation came to Trenton. The general superintendent of the Boston & Maine, Thomas Wilson, had reported to New England railwaymen that the Trenton rails were better than those generally used in their section. Three railroad presidents arrived to verify this statement, and the result was the more general use of the Cooper & Hewitt rails in New England. The profits for the fiscal year 1855-56 were $173,800, a goodly return on an investment of one million dollars—for to this sum the capital had now climbed. The three main supports of the Trenton company, pig iron, rails, and beams and girders, were all selling at favorable rates. The mines, furnaces, rolling mills, wire mill, and other holdings impressed visitors, Hewitt wrote, with a sense of "exhaustless resources."[3]

Little by little, in fact, every element necessary to a great ironworking establishment was acquired. By 1855 the company was drawing 36,000 tons of ore annually from the Andover mine. Since such a draft on a single mine was unprecedented, and exhaustion was feared, it paid $22,775 in 1854 for five hundred acres of the ore-range at Rosehill, N. J., with the mineral rights on two hundred additional acres. These Rosehill ores lay only five miles from the Morris Canal, were mined from large veins at low cost, and made excellent bar iron. Soon afterwards the Dell mines, also in Sussex County, were acquired, while negotiations were opened for

[1] John Wilson, *Special Report on the New York Industrial Exhibition, British Parliamentary Reports,* 1854, Vol. XXXVI, 42, 43.
[2] Charles Hewitt also invented and patented a wire sash-bar, which sold well.
[3] *Annual Report,* 1857, p. 9.

the Mount Hope mines, not far from the Andover tract in Morris County. The company was trying to build up adequate ore-reserves.

But the most important purchase in these years, in ultimate though not in immediate results, was the huge Ringwood estate of 22,000 acres in northeastern New Jersey. In all his land purchases Hewitt was actuated by one apprehension and one hope. His luckiest stroke had been the purchase of the Andover deposit, with its very superior ore—but no one knew when the shafts might come to an end. The Phillipsburg furnaces by 1856 needed 50,000 tons of ore a year, and the possibility that they might run short haunted his pillow. If only he could find another property like Andover! In 1853 Ringwood, the most celebrated iron-ore property in all the East, with a history that ran back for a century and a half, came upon the market. Peter Cooper, as an act of kindness to the hard-pressed Ryerson family, had first taken over a mortgage which the griping Peter Townsend held upon the property, and had then paid the Ryersons its fair appraised value. Ringwood lay in what is now Passaic County, just southwest of the present-day towns of Tuxedo and Suffern, and was easily reached from New York; while a glance at the map showed that it could easily be connected with the new Erie Railroad. At the beginning of April, 1853, Hewitt sent the company's mine expert, P. R. George, to inspect it. George was enthusiastic. Hewitt thereupon made a visit himself, and at once wrote a friend that the prospects were "the best I have ever seen."

The result was that after brisk but complicated negotiations with Peter Cooper, the Ringwood estate was bought for $100,000, of which $60,000 was paid in cash, and the remaining $40,000 in five-year bonds of the company.[1] In order to make the cash payment, the company sold additional stock to Robert J. Walker of New York, who had been Polk's Secretary of the Treasury, and to Edwin Post, the New Jersey ironmaster who had first smelted the magnetite ores of the State with anthracite, and had first reduced the refractory Franklinite ore, with its heavy zinc content.

Ringwood might well be called the birthplace of the American iron industry. Lying astride the New York-New Jersey line about twenty miles west of the Hudson, most of it in New Jersey, the tract was originally rough, broken, heavily wooded, and difficult of

[1] The purchase was nominally from Martin J. Ryerson, though Peter Cooper was the real owner; minutes of the directors, August 19, 1853.

access. Soon after 1700 iron ore was discovered. An enterprising
settler under George II, Cornelius Board, built a small forge on
the banks of the Wanaque or Ringwood River. Shortly afterward
several members of the Ogden family which played so large a role

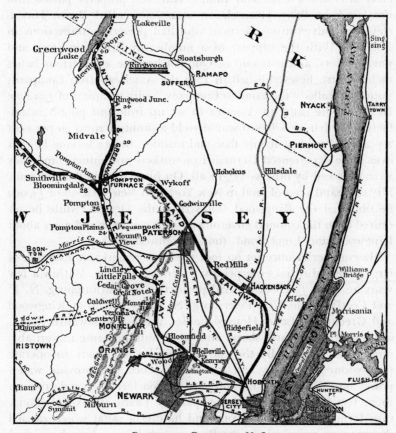

POSITION OF RINGWOOD, N. J.

in the early history of Newark—Colonel Josiah Ogden, David
Ogden, Sr., and others—formed the Ringwood Company, and in
1742 erected a furnace. Their original purchase of land was only
sixteen acres about the old forge, for £63, but they later made examinations along numerous streams in northern Morris and Passaic
Counties, and took up many tracts, a great part of the Pequannock

and Wanaque Rivers, with their waterpower, thus falling into their hands. The works prospered, making "share moulds," and bar iron which was advertised as "very fit for Ship Building and County Work, and esteem'd equal to the best of Swedish Iron." Immediately after the French and Indian War, the property passed into the hands of Peter Hasenclever, sometimes called Baron Hasenclever, an adventurous German who had powerful connections in England. With the support of a number of British military and naval officers, and it is said of Queen Charlotte and various ladies of her court, he established in 1763 the American Iron Company, popularly called "the London Company," with a capital of £21,000. Next year he came to America to set up iron and potash manufactures which he believed would yield a profit of 20 to 30 per cent a year, and to grow hemp, flax, and madder. Before leaving he sent over some experienced German iron-workers and miners, and they were followed by others—535 in all. On his arrival he bought some fifty thousand acres of land in New York and New Jersey. For £5,000 he obtained the Ringwood works from the Ogdens, while he acquired from the colonial government some ten thousand acres about Ringwood and Long Pond (now Greenwood Lake).

Hasenclever at once set on foot the most remarkable example of large-scale industrial enterprise yet seen in America. Within a few years he spent £54,600. He had properties at Charlotteburg, N. J., and Cortland and New Petersburg, N. Y., as well as at Ringwood and Greenwood Lake. Houses, stables, grist-mills, sawmills, blacksmith shops, carpenter shops, and other buildings rose in veritable mushroom villages. By the end of 1766 he was ready to operate twenty-four forge fires and furnaces at once. To provide waterpower near Ringwood, he built a dam 860 feet long and from 12 to 22 feet high across the lower part of Taxito (Tuxedo) Pond, thus forming a huge reservoir; and he dug a canal which carried the water to points along the Pequannock River where he wished to place his forges and mills. The Ringwood furnace had a capacity of fully twenty tons a week. Clustered about it were forges, hammers, and a stamping mill which could make the whole product into bars and other shapes. Here he had also built seven frame houses, and thirty-seven log houses. Near the centre of the property, on the southern side of a hill overlooking the road to the Passaic River and Hackensack, the Ogdens had left a commodious residence of early Georgian architecture. Tradition states that "Baron" Hasenclever lived here in state, with gold and silver plate, musicians playing every night at dinner, and a retinue of household slaves.[1]

What is certain is that he was accused of waste and mismanagement, and recalled to London in 1769. He had spent money in anticipation of profits which never came in; he had left no margin for the inevitable accidents. In 1770 he was declared bankrupt, and the property of his company became a bone of litigation for years. Hasenclever had suffered the fate of most too-enthusiastic entrepreneurs. But several ideas which he introduced, notably those for the recovery of iron from old cinder-banks and for the lining of furnaces with slate, were copied and continued by other ironmasters in America. And the pamphlet which he wrote in his defence, *The Remarkable Case of Peter Hasenclever, Merchant,* is one of the most interesting colonial documents of the time.

He was succeeded by a man of very different stamp and an even more important figure, Robert Erskine. He was a shrewd, well-educated, energetic Scot, already well known as an inventor of hydraulic machinery and a fellow of the Royal Society (where he had been proposed by Benjamin Franklin), when the London Company sent him over in 1771.[2] He brought his attractive wife. Finding the works badly disorganized, he soon placed them on the road to prosperity. Some of the early shafts had played out, but he made the most of a new mine, the Hope, discovered in 1767. He invented the first magnetic ore-separator in the country—an oak drum, driven full of magnets, over whose revolving surface the crushed ore was poured; this apparatus survived at Ringwood within the memory of living men. But as troubles between the mother country and the colonies thickened, and as Erskine called upon the stockholders for funds to make improvements, his British backers grew discouraged. They tried vainly in 1772 to sell the works, and soon afterward left him to shift for himself.

[1] The printed material upon Ringwood is voluminous. There are a number of papers in the *Proceedings* of the New Jersey Historical Society touching its history; see New Series, IV, and Second Series, XI. The best brief sketch is in C. S. Boyer, *Early Forges and Furnaces in New Jersey,* 17-25. Hasenclever's *Case* is available in a number of American libraries.

[2] See the sketch of Erskine in *Dictionary of American Biography,* VI, 180, 181, and Albert H. Heusser, *The Forgotten General.* His papers were still at Ringwood when Hewitt occupied it, and Hewitt gave them to the New Jersey Historical Society.

He resourcefully continued operations. When the Revolution began he took the side of the colonists, raised a company of iron workers, and was commissioned a captain in the Bergen County militia by the Provincial Congress. His main object was to keep the men together, prevent their being drafted into other units, and thus maintain the iron works. Exempted from military duty except in the event of local invasion, they manufactured various products for the Continental authorities; shot, wagon-tires, camp-ovens, and according to some writers, part of one of the great iron chains stretched across the Hudson. In 1779 advantage was taken of the isolation of the tract to establish a supply base at Ringwood. But long before this Erskine's knowledge of engineering had attracted Washington's attention. In the summer of 1777, at one of the darkest hours of the war, just before Brandywine and Valley Forge, he was appointed geographer and surveyor-general in the Continental army, and for a time was Washington's chief engineer and mapmaker. While in the field the fall of 1779 he caught cold, and died the same day that André was executed.

Today Erskine lies on the Ringwood estate, with a Scottish clerk buried beside him. A tombstone records that he was born at Dunfermline in 1735, the son of the Rev. Ralph Erskine, whose sermons Peter Cooper used to read with so much relish; and beside the grave long grew an oak tree which Washington was said to have planted on the day of the funeral.

After the Revolution Ringwood passed through further interesting vicissitudes. Erskine's influence had saved it from confiscation, and the British stockholders still held title. His widow Margaret managed it for a time, and the London Company finally sold it to James Old, noted as an early ironmaster of Pennsylvania. In 1807 it was acquired by Martin J. Ryerson of Pompton, for almost half a century the most prominent iron manufacturer in New Jersey. The War of 1812 sent iron prices rocketing, and Ryerson, with a keen eye for money (his enemies said that he smuggled cannonballs out to British warships), realized a small fortune from the tract. His sons continued it with less success, and it was they who had become indebted by heavy mortgages to Peter Townsend; though later in Chicago the Ryersons built up a new fortune. One by one since 1763 a dozen highly productive mines had been opened; the Blue, the Little Blue, the London, the Cannon, the Peters, which Erskine considered the best, the St. George, and others. When Hewitt bought the place, from 300,000 to 500,000 tons of ore had been taken out, but enormous quantities were still in the ground; and he breathed easier. At first, to be sure, it was little more than an idle reserve. For a number of years the company worked only two old-fashioned forges, which earned interest on the cost of the tract; for to put up blast furnaces or build a railway connection would have cost too much money. But in the end the purchase proved valuable.

Thus far Hewitt, from the time he entered Columbia Grammar-School onward, had played all his cards with wisdom and skill. Tireless, aggressive, high-strung, nervously alert to every opportunity, he had leaped every obstacle. No other manager in the iron industry was so highly regarded; none was shrewder, none worked with such incessant energy. But in 1856-57, less through his own fault than the backward state of the American industry, he did miss a striking opportunity; the opportunity to institute the Bessemer process in America almost a decade before it was actually applied.

Hewitt had heard in 1855, with momentary curiosity, that Gilbert Martien of Newark, N. J., had obtained an English patent for the partial purification of cast iron by passing a stream of air "through and amongst the melted metal as it flows from a blast furnace." He had read in British trade journals of experiments at Ebbw Vale in Wales in forcing air through molten crude iron or remelted pig-iron to improve the metal. But he and the rest of the world were taken by surprise when in August, 1856, Henry Bessemer appeared at the Cheltenham meeting of the British Association for the Advancement of Science, a body which for twenty-five years had furnished England with a scientific and technological parliament, to announce an epochal discovery in steel manufacture. Bessemer was a wealthy but little-known manufacturer of London, forty-three years old, whose chief product was bronze powder and bronze paint. He had turned his attention in the Crimean War to the improvement of artillery by introducing rifled projectiles, and had learned with dismay that this was impossible till cannon could be cast of stronger metal. Krupp was already making magnificent steel ordnance in Germany. But no one in England or France could do it, and Bessemer set up a small ironworks at his establishment in the

St. Pancras quarter, called Baxter House, where he began experiments. After two years of labor he lighted, partly by accident, partly by careful planning, upon his great discovery—a discovery which he described under the bold title "The Manufacture of Iron Without Fuel."[1]

His discovery was as simple as it was marvelous. He found that if men force a blast of cold air through a retort or converter filled with molten pig-iron, the oxygen in the air unites with the carbon, silicon, and sulphur in the iron, burns them out in a stream of fiery gas, and—*if all the conditions are right*—converts the residue into an incandescent liquid which, when cooled in moulds, is steel. It was one of the most momentous of modern discoveries. Bessemer tells us in his autobiography that when he tested his first steel ingot in the privacy of Baxter House, he was absolutely overcome by its magnitude. "What all this meant, what a perfect revolution it threatened in every ironmaking district in the world, was fully grasped by the mind as I gazed motionless at that glowing ingot, the mere contemplation of which almost overwhelmed me for the time." When he read his paper at Cheltenham, ironmasters were at first incredulous. And as his assertions reached widening circles, iron men everywhere realized that if they were confirmed a new industrial world would instantly spring into being.

In his original patent, granted October 17, 1855, Bessemer claimed that he had found a method of converting pig iron or refined iron into cast steel. And so, on the basis of his first experiments, he had. He had built a converter, a pear-shaped furnace which could be tilted up and down on axes. He had filled it with molten pig-iron, and then, amid the protests of an assistant who thought him insane, had begun to blow cold air through the bottom of the converter. The result was spectacular. At first a few fiery sparks from the top of the converter; then a dull glare of red light, gradually growing brighter till it pained the eyes; then a terrific turmoil inside the converter, a shrieking roar as of a thousand imprisoned fiends, and a blaze of flame that threatened to blow the roof off Baxter House; then a slow subsidence of the deafening noise, the flame becoming intensely white and hotter than ever; and finally a sudden extinguishment! Bessemer knew what had happened. The oxygen had

[1] Sir Henry Bessemer wrote his *Autobiography*, with a full history of his invention; it was published with a concluding chapter by his son in 1905. See also R. F. Mushet, *The Bessemer-Mushet Process* (1883).

united first with the silicon and then the carbon, burning them all
away. The pig-iron had become as liquid as water. When he tipped
the converter it flowed like a stream of blinding white fire into the
moulds. As it cooled, Bessemer seized an axe and struck sharply on
the edge of the ingot. Had it been iron, red-hot pieces would have

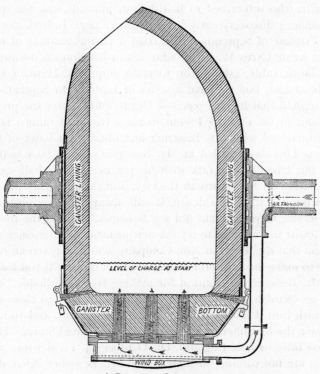

A BESSEMER CONVERTER.

flown in all directions. Instead, his axe simply sank into a fiery
sponge. It was steel!

Yet as a matter of fact, the Bessemer process in its first form was
rather one for the production of wrought iron than cast steel. When,
after the Cheltenham meeting, he continued his experiments, and
other men began to apply his method, the result proved disappoint-
ing in the extreme. He quickly learned that a lucky accident had
contributed to the making of steel that fateful day in his Baxter
House laboratory. The product had been steel because his pig-iron,

made from ores in a certain district of Wales, happened to contain
little phosphorus, and was in other respects precisely suitable. When
other irons were used, the process failed. Not until the Bessemer
method was supplemented by the formula of the inventive Scot,
Robert F. Mushet, could steel be counted upon.[1] The experimentation had to be continued.

Hewitt, who subscribed to British iron journals, saw the reports
of Bessemer's discovery early in September, 1856. Indeed, the New
York *Tribune* of September 16 carried a partial account of it. He
at once wrote Cyrus W. Field, who was in London on business for
the Atlantic cable, asking him to make inquiries. Hewitt's letters
have been lost, but we have a series of replies. On September 29
Field replied that he had received Hewitt's first letter the previous
day, "and in the evening I went to see a friend of mine who was
well acquainted with Mr. Bessemer and obtained a letter of introduction. This day I called at Mr. Bessemer's office; he was out of
town, but I had a long talk with his partner, and I shall see him
immediately on his return to the city, and do all in my power to
obtain for you what you desire. It will always give me pleasure to
be of service to you." Field did see Bessemer. He told the inventor
that Hewitt was anxious to try the new process, and Bessemer promised him that the Trenton Iron Company would be given an opportunity to make the first bid for the American rights. "If you feel sure
that Mr. Bessemer's invention for making iron is valuable," wrote
Field on October 9, "you had better come out here to close a contract with him. I have said and done all that I can, and your firm
will have the first offer of his patent for the United States." Hewitt
was too busy to visit England. On October 14, Field wrote again:
"If you are not coming out here to see Mr. Bessemer, what shall I
say to him that you are willing to do about his patents in the
United States?"

Meanwhile Bessemer's agent had reached the United States on
the *Persia* to file application for patents in Washington. Hewitt
talked with him. As a result word was sent the superintendent of
the blast furnaces at Phillipsburg, Joseph C. Kent, to make ready
for a trial of the Bessemer process so that the iron company might
know what terms to offer. On October 27 Hewitt wrote a Boston

[1] David Dale, Presidential Address, in *Journal of the British Iron and Steel
Institute*, 1895; Mushet, *op. cit.*, 16-34.

friend that "I have received a piece of Bessemer iron. It looks well." By this time a converter had been set up in one of the Phillipsburg furnaces. "We have all the arrangements completed for trying the Bessemer process," Hewitt informed the same friend on November 15. "We had deferred the experiment for reasons which were controlling in the matter. We shall not try it out yet for some days. We should like extremely to see Dr. Hayes. The writer is coming to Boston this month and will let you know in advance. We do not believe that Bessemer has got the only plan for cheapening the cost of wrought iron, and we have some doubt whether he has the best plan. We have samples of his iron, and they are very good indeed—but to make the product on a large scale is another affair."

Hewitt's experiment took place early in December, 1856. It was unsuccessful, but he decided that the blast might have been insufficient. A more careful trial was therefore made late in January, 1857. This was also unsatisfactory. At the same time unfavorable news came from England. Five firms there had immediately applied for licenses under the Bessemer patents, and several had gone to great expense in erecting converters, but all had met with failure. Bessemer himself, bewildered by the gloomy reports, visited several converters, scrupulously supervised every detail of his process, and was aghast when the experiments ended disastrously. The metal produced was even less malleable than the pigs which had gone into the tops. The English press rang with the failures; Bessemer was branded a cheat and a charlatan. Like everyone else—except Bessemer—Hewitt gave up the experiments.

For Bessemer, after meeting general rebuffs when he tried to persuade English ironmasters to go on using his system, was compelled to retrieve his own reputation. He continued his experiments; within two years he was able to show a product not at all inferior to that of the crucible-steel works; and he again tried to persuade makers to take up his system. When they refused, he erected steel-works in Sheffield and kept doggedly on. Friends assisted him. He was soon able to sell steel by the ton where makers of crucible-steel were selling it by the hundredweight, and his firm, Henry Bessemer & Company, underpriced older traders by £20 a ton. They perforce fell into line and bought the franchises they had recently despised. The inventor had vindicated his discovery and made himself the true father of the modern age of steel.

Even so, and without detraction from Bessemer's great fame, it should be noted that the process which finally proved successful and was adopted by the world was really a combination-process of two parts. The first part was the Bessemer discovery, its essential feature being the conversion of pig iron into wrought iron by forcing cold air through the molten mass to burn out the carbon; the second part, due to Robert Mushet, consisted in the transformation of the molten wrought iron, thus obtained, into steel by mixing with it a suitable quantity of fused carbonized iron containing manganese in the form of spiegeleisen or ferro-manganese.[1] Bessemer's method alone would make steel if the pig-iron were of precisely the right quality, and if the blowing were stopped at the precise moment to produce the required degree of carbonization, but not otherwise. In Sweden and at Seraing in Belgium, where pig-iron initially rich in manganese was available, the pure Bessemer process was successfully developed, but it was hardly known elsewhere. Nor was this process, when taken alone, satisfactory even in producing wrought iron. If the blast continued a shade too long, the product was "burnt iron," a brittle metal full of oxide, while if it ended a shade too soon the iron was too hard and steel-like. Bessemer had hit upon a great discovery—but it needed supplementing by lesser discoveries.

All this is said to explain why Hewitt did not push the Bessemer process. Possibly he talked with Joseph Henry, director of the Smithsonian Institution, who was one of the first to furnish an exact chemical explanation of the limitations of the Bessemer method. Moreover, a conflict of patents arose in the United States. In 1847 a Pittsburgher named William Kelly, who with his brother owned the Suwanee Iron Works near Eddyville, Ky., and made large

---

[1] Bessemer may be said to have made two discoveries, not one: (1) that the sending of a blast of air through molten cast-iron raised its temperature above the melting-point of low-carbon steel, or what is now called Bessemer steel; and (2) that this low-carbon steel is a much more valuable product than men had supposed. The Bessemer process has also been called the "pneumatic" and the "fuel-less" process. It ultimately developed along two different lines. The original line was the "acid" Bessemer process, thus called because the converter was lined with quartz, clay, and other materials rich in silicic acid. The line later pointed out by Sidney Gilchrist Thomas, an English metallurgical chemist, was the "basic" Bessemer process, thus called because the converter is lined with dolomite and other materials rich in lime. Ores with a high phosphorus content, like those of the Southern States, can be made into Bessemer steel only by the basic process.

kettles for boiling molasses down to sugar, had hit upon the same principle as Bessemer. He used it in a small way; turned out a number of steamboat boilers by what he called the "pneumatic process"; and when customers objected to the "new-fangled" plan of making iron, and compelled him to go back to the old methods, nevertheless continued his experiments in a backwoods hiding-place, where he built seven converters in succession—though none was as good as Bessemer's. When in 1856 he heard that Bessemer had taken out a patent in Washington, he filed a claim to priority and substantiated it. The American government therefore refused Bessemer a patent on the main idea involved, and granted it to Kelly.[1] Yet Bessemer did take out other valuable patents, notably upon his beautifully devised machinery. It was impossible for any American to make large quantities of steel without combining the rival patents, and this was not done until after the Civil War.

For the next half dozen years Hewitt remained skeptical of Bessemer metal. When he visited England during the Civil War he talked with many ironmasters and found most of them equally doubtful. His opinion on the subject was then summed up in a letter he wrote our Navy Department on March 6, 1863:

> You are probably aware that Bessemer designed his process for the manufacture of iron, but it was not until he abandoned this idea and made steel the object that he had any practical success. The difficulty which he was entirely unable to overcome in the manufacture of iron was the impossibility of making two successive heats of the same quality. A second more or less in the duration of the blast changes the whole character of the result. The process was, therefore, a failure until he conceived the idea of recharging the mass of melted metal by the addition of some highly carbonated pig-iron. He thus produced steel. Occasionally the quality of the steel is good, but as a general rule, it is of inferior quality, and its use is limited to a very narrow circle of objects. The only really practical purpose to which it has been applied is the manufacture of rails, and Mr. Brown told me himself that he had utterly failed in his attempts to make reliable common piston rods, or other good work.

Had Hewitt persevered with his trials of the Bessemer method,

---

[1] See J. N. Boucher, *William Kelly: A True History of the Bessemer Process* (1924), *passim*. Kelly's total receipts from his invention were about $450,000; Bessemer's about $10,000,000.

had he taken the purest ores and conducted endless experiments, had he obtained franchises under both the Kelly and Bessemer patents, had he spent large sums which he did not possess, he might possibly have placed steel-making on a firm basis in the United States by 1861. That is, he might have matched the work of the Swedish ironmaster Göranssen, who in these years successfully applied the Bessemer process to the pure charcoal iron of his country. If so, the history of our steel industry, our railways, even of our Civil War, might have been different. But the chances are he would have failed, for he lacked the manganiferous ores which Göranssen used; and he showed wisdom in sticking to established methods.

For the Trenton Company in 1855-56 and the first half of 1857, despite the fall in prices, despite growing competition, was signally prosperous.[1] Thanks to the Andover metal, it was rolling rails for a long list of roads—the Illinois Central, the Philadelphia & Reading, the Vermont Central, the Boston & Maine, the Pensacola & Georgia, the New York & Harlem, and so on. Thanks to the fame of its beams and girders, it was supplying them for more than a score of custom houses, for Forts Proctor and Sumter, for Watervliet Arsenal, for the branch mint at New Orleans, for marine hospitals at Burlington, Vt., and Detroit, and other Federal structures, and for State buildings and business houses. There was only one cloud on the horizon. Year by year it became clearer that the iron industry was moving westward, that fuel and ore could be united more cheaply at Pittsburgh, Johnstown, and Cleveland than at Trenton, and that the Trenton mill worked at a disadvantage. Hewitt was aware that the company should at least secure some Pennsylvania mines, as the following letter to his agent at Easton shows:

> The securing of hematite ore has been too much neglected, and must now be attended to. The North Pennsylvania Railroad

[1] Hewitt felt justified, in his annual report for 1857, in stating: "This meeting (Aug. 26, 1857) closes the tenth year of the existence of the company. In that period, from an inconsiderable beginning it has built up a great business, erected extensive works, acquired a valuable mining property, extended its operations into six counties in this State, till it even employs over 2,000 men in the various departments of its business. During all this time, and under the most discouraging circumstances, every obligation of the company has been met at maturity. Its capital has been procured without paying usurious rates of interest, and the officers employed have all been honest and faithful. The dividends actually made amount to 108 per cent, and there is a surplus on hand of 8½ per cent."

(Lehigh), which strikes the Lehigh River at Freemansburgh, passes through a very rich ore region in the Saucon Valley. Already the Crane, Thomas, and Allentown Iron Companies have secured leads and leases, and they inform us that there is plenty of unappropriated deposits in that valley. The other railroad which the Crane and Thomas companies are building also opens up a very fine region. The former railroad is, however, most advantageous to us, because it is nearer. You are therefore instructed to examine in person, or cause to be examined, the region through which the North Pennsylvania Railroad passes, and see if you cannot secure leases. The best kind of lease is one which gives the right to take ore without the obligation to do so. It will be well also to see what can be got on the Foglesville Railroad.

In order to post you up fully, there is another railroad projected from Allentown to Reading. These roads both pass through a good ore region and will be built. We have a man named Lee securing leases on them. But as the North Pennsylvania Railroad will be open in October next, it is evident that for the present your main, and perhaps only, efforts ought to be devoted to securing leases on its line and we hope no time will be lost. If you succeed, ore can be got out next winter.[1]

But meanwhile the company was paying large dividends, its stockholders were content, and Hewitt had work that drove him at times sixteen hours out of the twenty-four. Moreover, within a few months the panic of 1857 burst with a violence which thrust such matters as Bessemer steel and Lehigh ore-beds into the background.

[1] To Joseph C. Kent, August 19, 1856; Hewitt Papers.

CHAPTER VIII

An Ironmaster's Wife

WE ARE permitted singularly few glimpses of Hewitt's personal life in this period. If he wrote letters to such friends as "Lorry" Shepard and "Billy" Riker, they have not been preserved; he kept no diary; and while his business correspondence was large, he seldom allowed an intimate flash to light it up. Yet it is not hard to capture a clear image of the young man. From beginning to end of his career a striking dualism stamped his personality—the dualism of a natural student converted into a man of affairs. Short, wiry, electric, decisive of speech, with a quick laugh and a way of letting exuberant bursts of talk break through his customary reticence, he had a captivating presence. And one reason for its captivating quality was that it constantly gave hints of a hidden depth. Everyone could see the outward Hewitt, the tireless, resourceful young business man, radiating energy, full of plans and enthusiasm, always hurried and always getting his job done. Acute observers could also see another Hewitt; a man who hungered for larger and more fundamental aims, and in the end was to abandon business for public life.

Stern necessity, in the fifteen years before the Civil War which witnessed the rise of the Trenton iron mills to American primacy, forced him to devote to business a more exclusive attention than he would have liked. Intense and nervous, his anxieties and toils inevitably produced changes in his outer aspect and traits. He was still always frank, witty, patently honest of mind and heart, and remarkably unselfish; but his temper became uncertain. Few men worked as hard. On December 27, 1850, he wrote the superintendent at Phillipsburg: "Our merry Christmas was spent all day at the store, at hard work and no dinner at all. We trust you were better off." His letter-books show that he never took a real vacation until overwork during the Civil War forced one upon him. He complained in 1853 that every minute of his time was mortgaged, and he had not an instant to himself. He rose with the dawn, he travelled on "owl" trains to reach customers, he hurried from office to office. Now he would be at Andover, watching the teams strain at the traces to get the ore over the wet roads, now at Phillipsburg as the grim gray furnace disgorged a dazzling stream of molten metal, now in New York to confer with Commodore Vanderbilt, or in Philadelphia with J. Edgar Thomson, upon a rail contract. Iron workers are used to rough language, but he developed sharpness and irritability beyond most bosses.

This is not strange, for the risks, uncertainties, and toils were often grueling. Prices had to be watched with eagle eye, the credit of customers scrutinized with severity, the quality of the output guarded against a thousand possible variations. Ores were constantly changing in quality, and the Andover or Rosehill manager had to be reprimanded if hematite and magnetite were not properly mixed. The specifications of the railways, the Treasury Department, and other contractors had to be studied minutely. Flying trips had to be made on short notice to head off competitors. Accidents sometimes drove Hewitt frantic. "For heaven's sake," he wrote a customer who complained of delays, "do not talk about nervousness. The very sight of a letter or telegraph boy puts us into a cold tremor all over. We have never had such work, and if there was anything else left to break down, or give out, we should expect never to meet our promises." He had to be quick to note the slightest threat to the business. Once when he was sick in New York a petition was circulated in Trenton for superfluous street improvements which would have meant a heavy bill. His eye caught the newspaper paragraph, and he at once took steps to defeat the movement. Whenever the consumption of coal or other materials rose he protested. "The waste should not be tolerated a day," he wrote on one such occasion, "and the puddlers who make it should have notice that their services will not be required if they cannot do better." Actually he seldom discharged a man, and then only upon repeated provocation.

Strewn through the letters are allusions to his bursts of irascibility, usually followed, very engagingly, by bursts of contrition. He would fly out at some employee in a sudden access of wrath, and next day would ruefully apologize. Late in 1855, when he had arranged for a railroad barge to enter the canal at the Trenton works and take a load of rails, the men in charge through some misunderstanding ordered the boat off. "The officers of the company are very indignant," wrote Hewitt, "and I am sorry to say that I had a very disagreeable scene with my old personal friend Mr. Johnston." Once the superintendent at Phillipsburg resented Hewitt's tart letters by threatening to resign. Hewitt hastened to mollify him. "If the writer has used strong language you will, under the circumstances, know how to make allowance for it. You may be assured of the warm friendship we have for you personally. The writer may be a little rough, but he has never felt anything but the kindest interest in your welfare, and he hopes he is numbered among your friends."

And for all his brusque hurry and hatred of inefficiency, he could display warm generosity, while he and Peter Cooper agreed perfectly in detesting controversy. Once some negligent workmen at Trenton caused the company a grievous loss. In most mills they would have been discharged forthwith. Hewitt wrote the superintendent that "no money will pay for our mortification in the matter," that "we confess we have scarcely patience to write about it"—but he merely imposed a trifling fine. Sometimes a customer disputed a bill. It was his practise on such occasions to pay the charge in full, concluding with the formula: "You will please send us whatever you see fit, and we will send a receipt in full." In all his papers there is but one threat of court action. That was addressed to the president of the Long Island Railroad in 1856, and was preceded by these conciliatory words: "We dislike controversy. We have never yet sued anybody. We have asked you to send us what is justly due us by your own admission. We are still ready to take old rails in payment, and we will do what any fair-minded man will say we ought to do." His letters seldom showed severity, though he occasionally indulged in cutting sarcasm, as when he wrote a Rochester debtor in 1851:

> It seems as if no indulgence can make any impression on your torpid sense of justice. May we ask the favor of a line from you by return mail stating what you propose to do? If you want anything less than a receipt in full, we presume that our previous concessions will make a good precedent for frankly stating it.

There is no evidence that in his tireless labor and reckless expenditure of nervous energy he cared greatly about money-making. He wrote Peter Cooper quite honestly in 1849: "For myself, I am willing to do any amount of labor or feel any amount of anxiety that may be necessary to attain a successful issue in this great enterprise —and not because I desire to avail myself personally of the results. You will bear me witness that I have from the beginning refused to take any more than a bare support for myself and those who are dependent upon me." He was actuated far more by the zest of competitive activity, by the pleasure it gave him to be a leader in the development of American resources; while he gave no little thought to the broad public objects which such a leadership might subserve. In 1854 he quoted to Senator Brodhead of Pennsylvania the passage in Locke's *Essay on the Human Understanding* which referred the wealth of Great Britain primarily to her iron manufactures, and by contrast ascribed the poverty of the American Indians to the fact that they had not entered the iron age. A flourishing iron industry, he believed, was indispensable to American greatness, and would be our chief sinew in both war and peace. It could not be strengthened too rapidly.

We have said that a part of the exhilaration he felt in his work rested upon his studious interest in inventions and improvements. As a matter of fact, he cared a great deal more about quality than quantity; like the older American industrialists in general, he took pride in good workmanship. When in 1850 he sent a varied exhibit to the Crystal Palace Exhibition in London, including puddled bars, re-heated iron, finished wrought iron, and wire, he was delighted that it won a prize. He took pride in the Andover iron because it made the most durable rails in the world. When in 1853 his Andover rails sold at the high price of $65 a ton, he asserted that they were as superior to ordinary American iron as the best English rails were superior to ordinary Welsh products. "On the Hudson River Railroad," he informed the head of the Baltimore & Ohio, "the wear has been so remarkable in competition with English rails as to call forth the remarks of the leading English journals." He was pleased when the New Orleans & Carrollton Railroad assured him in 1858 that Trenton rails laid in 1849 were still giving excellent service. "There has been so much bad iron made, both English and American, that our rails begin to form the only exception to the rule that rails will not last over four or five years," he commented exultantly. It was criminal to use rails which endangered life, he protested, and still more criminal to re-roll the old metal for precarious further service. The tragic wrecks on the Erie Railroad in the late fifties, which aroused a fierce outcry against Daniel Drew, led Hewitt to propose a Federal inspection of rails as stiff as that of steamboat boilers; and he proudly asserted that his own iron had never yet cost a single life.

Hewitt made a point of reading upon mining and ironmaking. He bought the principal treatises on metallurgy, became familiar with Karsten, Petiet, and Flachat,[1] and kept a file of the *Annales des Mines*. In 1852 he promised a young Philadelphian who proposed translating Karsten that he would purchase five copies at $20 apiece. He took a great interest throughout the decade in efforts, which were finally successful, to reorganize the geological survey of New Jersey. There are evidences in his letters that he was constantly thinking on economic problems. He had a shrewd prevision, for example, of the social benefits to be derived from the rapid development of machinery. "The world is now realizing," he wrote a Boston friend in 1853, "for the first time since the discovery and development of the great mechanical agents—printing, steam, railroads, and telegraphs—the enormous increase in physical output and production which results from labor all profitably employed instead of being squandered in warlike enterprises consuming the entire surplus energies and produce of the world."

In these years, also, he produced his first brochure. In 1856 he made an address before the American Geographical and Statistical Society,[2] which was printed by it and reprinted in *De Bow's Review*; an essay on "The Statistics and Geography of the Production of Iron." Besides a lucid summary of the iron manufacturing of the world, it argued at some length the thesis that the growth of iron manufacture and the rise of modern civilization were in direct

---

[1] That is, Karl Johann Bernhard Karsten, author of *Handbuch der Eisenhüttenkunde* (1841), etc., and Jules-Alexandre Petiet and Eugéne Flachat, authors of *Traité de la fabrication de la fonte et du fer* (1842-46), etc.

[2] This society was incorporated in New York in 1852; among its first trustees were George Bancroft, John Jay, Joshua Leavitt, Hiram Barney, and Edwards Pierrepont. By 1856 there were some two hundred members, including Peter and Edward Cooper. It held regular monthly meetings in New York City at which papers, later printed in a *Bulletin*, were read.

ratio. It also ventured upon statistical predictions which then seemed reckless. Hewitt declared, for example, that by 1875 the world's production of iron would reach fourteen million tons annually, a figure that in actual fact proved too low. He also predicted that by 1956 the world would require a hundred million tons of iron and steel annually, and that half that amount would be produced between central Pennsylvania and the Missouri River. The pamphlet, which was illustrated by a graph of iron consumption and prices,[1] showed both hard study and vision.

But his studious bent appeared most clearly in his constant attention to technological processes. They interested him quite as much as they did his brother Charles. He was largely responsible for Edward Cooper's tour in 1849-50 to study the best British and Continental processes, and deluged him while abroad with letters of advice. There was much need for study and research. With mineralogy and metallurgy then in their infancy, with industrial chemistry all but unknown, with ironmasters the world over combining their ores in hit-or-miss fashion and guessing blindly at the amount of phosphorus, manganese, zinc, and other impurities that the pig-iron would contain, he might well feel eager for more certainty in the mill's operations. "For twelve months," he wrote a customer in the fall of 1851, "we did not make a ton of iron that was not superior to any other iron we have ever seen. Now the reverse is true. It occurred once before, under similar circumstances, and afterwards the iron recovered its regular quality. We have no doubt that this will now be the case." A year later he lamented that for almost three months he had not been able to make a ton of iron rods that would meet his standards, and had remelted the metal. In 1853 he obtained an order for the shaft of a new Fall River steamboat, the largest in the world. This was a triumph. But, he warned his associates, "to have the shaft break would be an irreparable disgrace, and would be crowed over in all directions. Now if the iron you have made is not very tough when cold, and sufficiently free from redshortness to forge well, do not attempt to use it." He and Charles tried elaborate experiments in puddling iron. Once they used asphalt; at another time carburetted hydrogen. In manufactur-

---

[1] Hewitt used to say later that he had worked out the idea of statistical graphs for himself, having gotten the idea from a fever chart. But they had been known among economists since the eighteenth century.

ing wire they likewise experimented with the zinc-bearing ore from the Franklin Furnace called franklinite. The product was roughly equivalent to galvanized wire, resisted rust, and sold largely.

One problem was particularly baffling. In the manufacture of rails he and Charles exerted themselves to the utmost to avoid lamination or splitting. All rails in America were then rolled out of pig-iron in successive horizontal layers. As the rails decayed, especially if made of poor iron, the layers tended to loosen and those on top to split off. If this occurred at the end of the rail, a spearhead or "snakehead" sometimes entered the car floor, maiming passengers and even wrecking trains. At first Hewitt hoped that by using only the best materials they could avoid lamination. In 1851 he examined the Auburn & Rochester Railroad, where twenty-six miles had been laid the year before with his toughest iron and the remainder with British rails. Not a yard of his metal had failed or laminated, while all of the British iron was rapidly decaying. But as time passed he found that it was insufficient to roll the tops of his rails from Andover iron. Railway traffic was increasing, heavier engines were being used, and it was more and more difficult to make the rails really durable. He concluded that the chief weakness arose from the method of rolling them in a succession of thin layers.

Charles and he therefore tried hammering several puddled balls into a heavy mass of homogeneous iron, and then rolling this into a rail-top in which no laminae existed. The improved process involved extra costs, and a heavy steam hammer had to be purchased. But when production fairly began in the winter of 1859-60 the new rails proved eminently successful, and gave him hopes of a large market.

It is not surprising that within a short time after the founding of the Trenton company this short, slight young man with the snapping gray eyes, quick mind, and self-reliant ways was Peter Cooper's principal adviser. He not only shouldered the main burden of the iron business, but together with Edward Cooper helped the unsystematic but ever-adventurous philanthropist to look after other affairs as well. For this purpose he often left Trenton, where he shared a comfortable house with Charles and his parents, and took lodgings in New York for weeks at a time. (He has recorded only that this was with an elderly lady belonging to one of the best families, who let neat rooms for a moderate price, and furnished him a breakfast of coffee or tea, bread, butter, and boiled eggs for twenty-five cents. Sometimes in town he stayed with Lorenzo Shepard, now a rising young attorney who had the most brilliant mind Hewitt ever knew, or at Peter Cooper's house.) Soon there was a distinct new object of interest at the Coopers'. Just when he formed a sentimental attachment for Amelia we cannot say, but he must have been in love as early as 1849.

So close were his relations with Edward that he was already almost a member of the family; and Peter Cooper now leaned upon him heavily for counsel. Business letters are seldom very readable. It would be tiresome to print many of those which he constantly sent to Cooper. But we may mention one, dated August 13, 1849, which shows how carefully he kept all Peter Cooper's varied interests in mind. The capitalist had betaken himself, his wife, and Amelia to Schooley's Mountain, N. J., to escape the heat of midsummer. Hewitt, forgetful of the temperature, had been scurrying busily between New York and Trenton on business. While engaged in selling some bonds of the Rutland Railroad, taken in payment for rails, he had met George B. Smith, the agent of the richest of all New Workers, William B. Astor. They had fallen into conversation. Smith had confided to Hewitt that Astor then had $300,000 lying idle, because he could not put it out on real estate mortgages at 7 per cent and would not take less. It at once flashed upon Hewitt that here might be a chance for Peter Cooper to borrow money for his great educational experiment. He inquired if Astor would lend $60,000 or $70,000 on Cooper's Astor Place property? "Yes," said Smith, "at 7 per cent, but not at 6." "Well," replied Hewitt, "would Mr. Astor be willing to make a loan for ten years, five years at 7 per cent and five at 6?" "That is possible," said Smith; "but at 7 per cent I am certain. I will ask Mr. Astor."

"Now," wrote Hewitt to Peter Cooper, "I want to urge you to make this loan, at 7 per cent if you can do no better, and in order to show you the propriety of it let me make a brief statement of our position." He explained that the iron company had a total of $195,000 in debts outstanding. It had means at hand to pay off all but $72,000. But if times became hard that $72,000 might become very bothersome. It was possible "that we should be subjected to that kind of anxiety and dependence on banks which would be very painful to you." And Hewitt went on:

"You would do well to borrow the money on the security of your square. You could first pay off the other mortgages, which would reduce the amount left to about $50,000. With this we could pay off the notes so that next spring we should have a large stock of pig-iron on hand, and but few notes to pay. This iron we could either work or sell, and I can show you that we can do either with great profit. You could then withdraw the money necessary to put up your building, and thus carry out the project to which I know you are more attracted than any other. Mrs. Cooper will feel no objection to making a loan which is to be expended in the improvement of the iron property, and the advantage of making the loan now, when money is easy, will be obvious to her." He added: "You know that I have always made our calculations well in advance, and have never been mistaken or deceived you about the results to be reached."

The advice offered in this letter was not followed. But its frankness is as striking as its boldness; here is a youth of twenty-seven giving financial counsel to one of the most experienced and successful business men of the country. Parts which we have no room to quote show close familiarity with the money-market and a desire to lay plans far in advance as well as characteristic resourcefulness. In other letters Hewitt demonstrated that he would never wait for Peter Cooper to furnish leadership. In one transaction he proved that he could make money as Cooper had often made it. Just after new Lehigh anthracite fields were opened he hurried to the district. He saw that while the coal operators had bought only the areas which showed outcroppings, the upper slopes must also contain seams; he obtained options on promising land; and he was soon able to sell at a large profit.

Amelia Cooper was not without a vein of coquetry, and knew enough to keep Hewitt in suspense. In fact, she used to tell her children later that she never was quite certain she would marry him till she walked up to the altar! A number of the young man's letters this summer of 1849 contain revealing references to her. In one, addressed to Peter Cooper on the mountain, he writes: "Isaac says they are all well at the house. Please say to Amelia that I send up by Mr. Bishop a pair of slippers for the prettiest pair of feet at the mountain, and that Mr. Hough says they will fit to a charm. Give my affectionate regards to Mrs. Cooper and Amelia, and tell them not to forget, very affectionately yours, Abram S. Hewitt."

In still another letter he speaks of sleeping the previous night at Mr. Cooper's house, and finding Amelia's aged Aunt Martha there in good health. "She goes all about the house and says she began to get well the moment you left, and means to cheat you all yet by getting entirely well." He concludes, "Give my kindest regards to all—Edward, Mrs. Cooper, and Amelia—affectionately yours, Abram." And with a stroke too fine to be seen by Peter Cooper's near-sighted eyes, but perfectly visible to the daughter, a line connects the names Amelia and Abram.

When Edward Cooper went to Europe, Hewitt sent him warmly affectionate letters. That winter he divided his time almost evenly between Trenton and New York; he was selling a good deal of iron in exchange for railroad bonds, and retailing the bonds as fast as possible. He worked daily in the Burling Slip office which Peter Cooper had first taken in 1844, and which they retained—enlarging the quarters from time to time—till long after Cooper's death. At night he would stroll over to Broadway, full from curb to curb with a Niagara roar of buses and other vehicles, and go up to Cooper's house. "I am still staying at your father's as you desired—although somewhat against my conscience—all the time; but it is very hard to resist one's inclinations, especially when an excuse is easily framed." So he wrote Edward on February 5, 1850. He sent full news of the iron business; of politics, with Clay's great compromise holding the national stage; and of the brilliant Lorenzo B. Shepard, who was rising steadily in the local Democratic organization, and in the fall of 1848 was elected corporation counsel. Hewitt urged "Neddy" to obtain all the information about new processes that he could. "Look out for the pickings and *steelings*, so as to bring home as much as you can."

But he took transparent pleasure in writing of the family circle, and particularly of the twenty-year-old daughter who sparkled in it. There are constant references to "your mother, father, and Amelia." The Cooper family always sent their love, "so fond and pure that my black ink refuses to record all its fervor." He found suitors dis-tressingly numerous. "Amelia says she will send her own love, as soon as she gets a letter from you all for herself. Plenty of beaus as usual. Bowley was there both Saturday and Sunday (six hours), but don't be frightened—she understands what she is about. It amuses me to see the manner in which your father receives Mr. Bowley, in a way so foreign to his kindly nature. You know how hospitable and habitually friendly he is to everybody. And his stiffness to Bowley is therefore the more comical." A cousin had temporarily joined the household; in fact, Peter Cooper's house was always full of relatives. "Amelia and Julia go regularly to Miss Kirkland, and are working away very faithfully. The mysteries of logic are rapidly being converted into no mysteries, and I am giving them mathematical lessons. Every moment of time is consumed that the beaus leave at their disposal—and they have a little more time than they had a while ago." Later Hewitt could add: "Amelia and Julia are really doing very well—and will be a credit to all concerned if they 'persevere unto the end.' "

The house in which he tutored Amelia was no longer the somewhat isolated mansion near the glue factory on Twenty-eighth Street; for in 1845 the factory had been transferred to Maspeth Avenue in Brooklyn, and three years later Peter Cooper removed to a large house which he himself erected at No. 9 Lexington Avenue, a few paces above Gramercy Park. He thought for a time of building at Fifth Avenue and Twenty-sixth Street, but S. B. Ruggles, the founder of Gramercy Park, offered him the other site at the same price, and promised that the lot between him and the park would be maintained as a rose-garden; while he feared that Fifth Avenue would be too fashionable.[1] Cooper was now too busy to give more than general oversight to the glue factory. Daily supervision was entrusted to his younger brother William, a rolling stone who had been captain of a brick schooner on the Hudson and was glad to come to rest so lucratively. Peter stepped in only in time of crisis.

[1] John B. Pine, *The Story of Gramercy Park*, 24-28. As to Cooper's dislike of fashion, Miss Eleanor Hewitt's MS. family history states:

"Peter Cooper's republican principles would never permit him to wear a dress coat, which he considered the livery of fashion, though he always had a fine broadcloth frock coat and high black satin stock for evening wear. So, when he was made chairman for the ball given in New York to the Prince of Wales, afterwards King Edward VII, and by common consent of the community his was the only name on the card of invitation, it was with great difficulty that he was persuaded to wear a dress suit. The argument which finally made him yield was that he would not be honoring the Queen of England and she would be annoyed. He said that he would never do anything to displease a lady, and ordered a suit, but that was the one and only time he wore it."

Soon after the removal the factory suddenly burnt down without insurance; he left the fire still burning, went down to Wall Street, and without collateral, obtained money to rebuild it. Coming home, he told the story of the fire to Mrs. Cooper, and concluded: "The lumber will be on the ground in the morning." This was typical of his bold decision.

The new Lexington Avenue home was a square, roomy, comfortable structure of brick, with a high stoop in front where, in Gramercy Park fashion, the family chatted with neighbors on warm evenings, and with stables and greenhouses behind. There were trees in the yard, and from the front windows, past Cyrus W. Fields's neighboring house, they had a pleasant view of the park. Though the city was rapidly covering all central Manhattan, this particular neighborhood was still leafy and restful. As the house was built on the bank of a little stream which, originating somewhere about Twenty-third Street and Fourth Avenue, meandered down to the East River, it was placed on heavy piles.[1] The move had brought Peter Cooper much nearer the fashionable part of town as well as the site of his Union. It also placed Amelia and her cousins closer to the best schools and amusements. For a time she had attended the select classes of Mrs. Meer, at Tenth and Broadway, and while there watched the erection of Grace Church over the way. Occasionally she had been sent down to Howard Street to take dancing lessons of Ferrero, an Italian patriot who had fled his country after the revolt of 1838. In 1850, a tall, statuesque young woman, she was finishing her education at Miss Kirkland's.

Years later she used to tell her children of old New York as she knew it then or a little earlier.[2] She sometimes went shopping with her mother at William Constable's in Canal Street, or A. T. Stewart's in Chambers Street; while more frequently she would take long northward excursions on foot, for abounding health made her a good deal of a tomboy. She would pass the two great elms which made a landmark on the Boston Post-Road near Thirtieth Street, and turning east, stroll down to the East River house of General Horatio Gates; or farther northwest, visit the reservoir just constructed at Fifth Avenue and Forty-second Street. She was familiar

[1] This stream was Cedar Creek; F. B. Kelley, *Historical Guide to the City of New York,* 110.

[2] Miss Eleanor G. Hewitt's MS. family history.

with the stockyards near the site of Madison Square Garden, whose nightly uproar had helped persuade Peter Cooper to remove to the neighborhood of Gramercy Park. When she went to Bushwick to see her cousins, daughters of William Cooper, they caught crabs on the shores of the bay, carried them to the glue factory, and cooked them by plugging one of the hot exhaust pipes. Her father had been persuaded, for her mother's sake, to purchase a small chaise called a clarence,[1] and on Saturday afternoons she sometimes drove with her parents to the wilder parts of Manhattan—say to Seventieth Street, or to see the Tiemann's at Manhattanville.

Just when Hewitt and Amelia Cooper became engaged we do not know, but it must have been in 1850 or soon afterward. The letters quoted above show that it could not have been earlier, and Hewitt always said that she made him wait five years before they were married; but perhaps it only seemed five years. From the moment of the engagement he became virtually Peter Cooper's second son. Financially, however, he was now completely independent. This is proved by a mass of evidence, of which it is sufficient to quote a single letter:

(Hewitt to Peter Cooper, New York, June 4, 1853)
My dear sir:

By my understanding with you, I was to have all that the New Jersey property might realize over $500,000, with interest from 1st January last. One half of the stock of the Trenton Iron Company having been disposed of for $300,000, I am entitled to the other half of that stock, the farm and mules at Andover, the stock and bonds of the Sussex Railroad Company, the North River mine, and a bond and mortgage for $10,000, received for part of the basin property at Trenton; on paying to you $200,000, or securing this amount to you to your satisfaction. I have reason to believe that I could make this property bring the following amounts, if I have a reasonable time to accomplish it.

---

[1]"Mr. Cooper, who was a thorough believer in simplicity, and knew from long experience the willingness of his wife to do without all luxury, still thought as she grew older she should have a carriage, so she and his daughter purchased a landau which would do for every season and which all the family could enjoy. But when it came home he thought it entirely too fashionable, and exchanged it for an old-fashioned clarence with a glass front, which he thought more in keeping with his democratic ideas. He had to pay the dealer a large bonus to take the other one back." Miss Eleanor G. Hewitt's MS. family history.

Half the Trenton Iron Company stock	$300,000
Farm and mules at Andover	10,000
Sussex R.R. stock and bonds	75,000
Bond and mortgage	10,000
say total	$395,000

Deduct from this cost of Sussex Railroad over and above the bonds, and for real estate in Sussex, leaving $375,000.

After paying you $200,000, I should have $175,000 over. I think that it would be perfectly certain to calculate on $150,000.

What I proposed to you and Edward was to put in this property against one hundred thousand dollars in cash, and then Edward and myself would jointly own the above described property, subject to a debt to you of $200,000. For this I proposed that we should give our bond bearing interest from 1st January last, payable annually, the principal to become due in five years, or before if we have the means to discharge it. As security for the payment of the bond, we leave with you as collateral the $300,000 of stock of the Trenton Iron Company, reserving the right to sell the whole or part of the stock if we see fit, paying the proceeds to you on the bond. . . .

Yours truly,
Abram S. Hewitt

This single letter makes it clear that Hewitt was by 1853 the acknowledged executive head of the business, that eight years after he had landed penniless from the shipwreck of the *Alabamian* he was worth at least $175,000, and that he stood firmly on his own feet.

His marriage to Amelia Cooper took place Monday, April 6, 1855, at the Lexington Avenue house, the Rev. Dr. Henry Bellows of All Souls' Unitarian Church, where the Coopers worshipped, performing the ceremony. He immediately took his wife to Trenton, where they lived the next winter, and where their first daughter was born February 28, 1856. The following spring Hewitt changed his legal residence to Ringwood, for Mrs. Hewitt, going to see it, had fallen in love with the place. Actually, they spent only the summers there, for Peter Cooper wished him and Amelia constantly at hand at 9 Lexington Avenue, and in some ways depended upon him more and more. The house was fitted up for two families,

Hewitt occupying the northern half, and Peter Cooper the southern, while all the inmates took their meals together.

For summer use the Ringwood house was easily made into a commodious and convenient residence. Martin Ryerson had erected it near the site of "Baron" Hasenclever's mansion; a really fine house for the time. It stood three stories and a garret high, of wood and brick, with fireplaces built on strong stone arches. At a later date Mrs. Hewitt covered the walls with whitened cement. The windows had lattices in the colonial style, and the heavy eight-panelled front door was adorned with a ponderous knocker and lock of English brass. Ryerson had brought the interior woodwork of finely carved mahogany from New York City, while the tiles for the handsome fireplaces came from Europe. In front a wide avenue ran down to the main road, lined with magnificent trees; planted, it was said, by Mrs. Ryerson to celebrate the Peace of Ghent. The house lent itself to the additions which Mrs. Hewitt took in hand, and to the gardens which she laid out, all of which within a few decades transformed it into one of the most interesting places near New York.

About it stood many objects of historical interest. There was an Indian burial ground, and an old Indian camping-place. The colonial road, dating from the seventeenth century, joined one which General Greene had laid out to connect Morristown with West Point and by which Ringwood iron was carried to the Hudson. A Revolutionary magazine still stood in the grounds, and the mossy tombstone of Erskine. Hewitt added steadily to the historical objects, one of his proudest acquisitions being a section of one of the immense iron chains, supposedly of Ringwood metal, with which the patriots had tried to close the Hudson against British ships.[1] He had it placed on the stone terrace in front of the house. Each link, three feet wide and nine inches long, weighed 280 pounds; the chain had failed, in fact, because despite its log buoys it sank so far that the enemy sailed carelessly over it! The anvil upon which it had traditionally been forged was placed on the terrace in front of the

[1] Most if not all of the great chain used at West Point was made of iron from the Stirling and Long mines in Orange County, and manufactured by Peter Townshend at the Stirling Iron Works in the same county. But two other iron chains were stretched across the Hudson during the war, one at Murderer's Creek, the other at Fort Montgomery. Benson J. Lossing, *Field Book of the Revolution*, I, 705, 732.

house, and beside it the water-power wheel which had raised the great hammer. Another acquisition was four stone mortars, found on the place, in which the Lenni Lenape had pounded their corn.

The situation of the house was beautiful. Whaleback and Hope Mountain on the west and the Ramapos on the east sheltered it; Greenwood Lake and Tuxedo Lake were within easy driving distance; virgin forests stretched all about, and dashing streams were numerous. The gardens were soon landscaped, and in time a brook was impounded to form a broad lake just in front of the house. Flower and vegetable gardens were planted at the back, where a steep ridge gave protection from the bleak north winds, and orchards were laid out. Mrs. Hewitt's flowers became locally famous. She used to say that she could not paint a picture, but she could make one—and every year she did. Robert Erskine had sunk a well forty feet in the solid rock, and near it Hewitt built an ice-house and greenhouses. The old sorting and crushing mills were converted into a large stable. Altogether, Ringwood made an ideal summer residence for a young couple with growing children and a large circle of friends.

The note of the household from the beginning was liveliness. Both Hewitt and his wife loved to entertain. Since she was all placidity, kindliness, and practical common sense, while he was all fire and energy, they attracted different types of people. Her tastes were quietly artistic, with emphasis on painting, music, and gardening, while his were for talk and activity. They soon made Ringwood and the city house they shared with the Coopers notable for hospitality. Then, too, the family grew steadily. Amelia Bowman Hewitt was born in the spring of 1856, Sarah Cooper Hewitt in the fall of 1858, Peter Cooper Hewitt in the spring of 1861, and Eleanor Gurnee Hewitt in the summer of 1864, to mention only the first four. By the last-named year the dooryard seemed full of young children. Peter Cooper and his wife were frequent visitors at Ringwood. John Hewitt died on May 30, 1857, at Trenton, and was perhaps never there. But Abram's mother, who lived until 1873, often came out for long stays. Altogether, it was a full household in which Hewitt lived, and his guests saw that it was merry and spirited.

Busy as he was, he cared little to go outside his home circle; he was no more inclined to consistent dining-out than to fishing, hunt-

ing, or theatre-going. He liked the talk of men prominent in politics and finance, and such professional men as Peter Cooper's minister, Dr. Henry Bellows. Though he saw much of Tilden, his most
intimate friend continued to be "Lorry" Shepard, whose keenness
and high-mindedness had long since won his affection. Shepard was
married shortly before Hewitt, and his son, Edward Morse, who
was to play a prominent role in New York affairs, was born in 1856.
It was a stunning blow when in 1857 Shepard suddenly died.
Hewitt always believed that the country and the Democratic Party
lost in him a leader who would have proved more a statesman than
Tilden. Occasionally Mrs. Hewitt carried her unwilling husband
to a party or reception. For example, she was one of the most admired of the young matrons at the grand ball for the Prince of
Wales in 1859, her gown being still preserved by the New York
Historical Society. In 1857 Hewitt was elected to the Century Club.
A small group of friends went in at the same time—Clarkson N.
Potter, a brilliant and handsome young lawyer; William B. Ogden,
a keen, hardheaded man of business; William E. Dodge, Jr., son
of the eminent merchant; and Edward Cooper. Hewitt was seldom
at his best with strangers or in large gatherings. But the Century
was a very congenial club indeed, containing the most distinguished
men of the city from Bryant down; and he liked the special Saturday evening gatherings at its quarters on East Fifteenth Street, a
few minutes' walk from Peter Cooper's house.

At Trenton there were few men with whom he felt inclined to
any warm friendship. The most striking exception was Charles
Russell Lowell, the poet's nephew, who was there in 1853-54. He
came to the iron company at twenty, a tall, active, well-read graduate of Harvard, treading the gallant way that ended when at twenty-
nine, already a brigadier-general of Union troops, he died at the
battle of Cedar Creek; one, as his uncle the poet wrote in the
Commemoration Ode, of

The sacred dead
Who went, and who return not—say not so![1]

The young ironmaster would have gained in elasticity and breadth

[1] Edward Waldo Emerson, *Life and Letters of Charles Russell Lowell*, contains material on his work at Trenton.

of mind had he allowed himself a wider margin of leisure in these years. But that was not his way, for he preferred incessant activity. If it shut him from a deeper and broader development, he was nevertheless happy in it, and especially after his marriage to Amelia Cooper gave him the compensating and varied satisfactions of a happy home.

CHAPTER IX

Western Rails and Atlantic Cables

FOR the younger generation of Americans, the eventful decade 1850-60 was at once a period of steadily expanding boundaries and of a steadily-approaching catastrophe. Material progress, it seemed, had never before been so rapid: railways were conquering the West, telegraphs were annihilating the distances of mountain and plain, steamships were being perfected, cables were permitting continent to talk with continent. Science, in this decade of Lyell and Darwin, was opening up a new world. Old philosophies and old religious views, in these years of Renan's essays and *In Memoriam*, were dissolving and fresh vistas were appearing. But all the while, in the United States, the steady throb of a great drum —the drum of sectional passion—beat out its warning of approaching war. Blow followed blow: the Fugitive Slave Act, the Kansas-Nebraska Act, the assault on Sumner, the Kansas War, the Dred Scott decision, John Brown's raid. At one moment, to sanguine young men like Hewitt, any achievement seemed possible in this lusty young republic; at another, these bright vistas paled under the lowering cloud of civil conflict.

Yet our competitive industrialists, hoping that war could be averted, pressed on with an optimism that no political apprehensions could chill. Stimulated by the spirit of the time, the opportunities of the country, and personal ambition, Hewitt expended his energies in a dozen diverse fields. Iron led to an interest in mines, railroads, telegraphs, and land; his association with Peter Cooper led to a share in the latter's business and philanthropic activities; and his concern with tariffs involved him in politics.[1] With

[1] Hewitt also gave no little attention to Columbia College, being active in alumni movements for its betterment. On April 7, 1856, he and John Jacob

his keen ambition and zest for action he was in danger of frittering away his energies upon a variety of unrelated enterprises; but in the end the panic of 1857 brought him back with a jerk from this unwise expansion—amounting to dissipation—of his interests.

By natural inclination Hewitt was a Democrat. He grew up in a period when Jacksonian principles appealed to most young men; he was bred among New York mechanics who for the most part favored Democracy; he came of age when the Democrats were identified with westward expansion, a movement which attracted the rising generation. His best friends, including Shepard, Tilden, Robert J. Walker, and Edward Cooper, were Democrats. Yet, casting his first vote in a Presidential election in 1848, he voted for Zachary Taylor and the Whig ticket. The reasons for this were simple. The Democratic tariff of 1846—the Walker Tariff under Polk—was highly unsatisfactory to ironmasters. Previously, from 1818 to 1846, rolled bar-iron, such as was made in large quantities at Trenton, had been protected by a tariff of almost 100 per cent; now the duty was suddenly lowered to 30 per cent. The duty on hammered bar-iron was likewise reduced. Thanks to the widening use of hot-blast anthracite furnaces in place of the old charcoal furnaces, the American production of pig-iron had risen from about 300,000 tons in 1840-41 to about 650,000 or 700,000 tons in 1846-47; and upon this a large business in fabricated iron had been built. The Walker Tariff fell upon this business like a chilling frost. Hewitt had resented it; and the day after Taylor's election he warmly congratulated the cashier of the Trenton Company on the prospect of higher tariff barriers against English iron, and better times for American iron mills.

Thereafter for ten years, in spite of his youth, he was as prominent as any ironmaster in laboring first to obtain higher rates, and when that became hopeless, to defeat any reduction. For a brief period he worked with the Whigs. But he soon turned back to the Democratic Party, for after the election of 1850 he foresaw its continued dominance, and he thought it more profitable as well as agreeable to work inside its ranks than outside. In this he was well advised; even in Zachary Taylor's first two years the House was

---

Astor, Jr., were nominated as trustees, but neither was elected till later—Astor in 1859, Hewitt in 1901. Minutes, Columbia College Board of Trustees.

strongly Democratic, and then came two Democratic Presidents, Pierce and Buchanan.

We cannot deal with Hewitt's tariff activities in any detail. It is sufficient to say that from beginning to end in this period when tariffs were very low and all ironmasters thought they should be higher, he held moderate views; that he labored to restrain the extremists; that he used every legitimate agency in bringing pressure upon Congress; and that he and his associates failed utterly. No tariff increases were obtained, and in the end the tariff of 1857 actually made new reductions. Yet, placing himself at the head of the New Jersey iron-mills, he fought a good fight. In 1849 he helped to arrange for two State conventions of ironmasters, one in New York and one in New Jersey, which began the contest. At the former, which met in Trenton on November 14, he was made chairman of the committee on petitions and correspondence. He drafted a memorial to Congress and an address to the public; he published a long argumentative letter in the New York *Evening Post*; he visited Washington and labored with members of Congress. In 1850 he helped the principal ironmasters of the East to raise a fund for the contest, Cooper & Hewitt contributing $500. With this a professional lobbyist, John L. Hayes, was sent to Washington.[1] A year later, in trying to get the Democratic caucus to act in favor of higher duties, he repeatedly visited Washington and became acquainted with all the leaders.

He early learned that local conventions of ironmasters were useless. The Democratic leaders told him that money, lobbyists, and newspaper pressure were what counted; and that if the ironmasters wished results, they must show that they had political strength. If they could prove that they controlled 60,000 votes in New York, New Jersey, and Pennsylvania, they would be treated respectfully. Hewitt in 1851 besought the ironmasters to contribute to a still larger chest. "I can name half a dozen politicians," he wrote, "who can do us more good than one thousand ironmasters, but they must be paid. Last year we were very deficient in means, and this year

---

[1] Hayes later became secretary of the National Association of Wool Manufacturers, and one of the best-known high-tariff lobbyists in the country; while in 1883 he was chairman of the Tariff Commission. Cf. Edward Stanwood, *American Tariff Controversies in the Nineteenth Century*, II, 147-156, 204; and H. K. Beale, "The Tariff and Reconstruction," *American Historical Review*, January, 1930.

we will fail beyond a doubt unless every man sends in his quota."
In 1852 he renewed these appeals for money, and also urged the
iron interests to show moderation. After a visit to Washington, he
wrote a friend on March 16 that he was convinced of two facts: " (1)
No Tariff bill can be passed without Southern and Western votes;
(2) These votes cannot be secured unless a concession is made on
railroad iron." That is, the newer parts of the country wanted railroads more than they wanted anything else, and the Pennsylvania
ironmasters would simply have to let the new roads get at least their
first tracks free of duty.

Within a short time, after Pierce's inauguration, he and other
iron men were fighting on the defensive. Henry Clay had justly
said in 1848 that "large portions of the Northern population . . .
feel and believe that their manufacturing interests have been sacrificed by Southern domination." Yet by 1853 the iron interests were
asked to make further sacrifices. The great cry of the day was for
the rapid development of the country, and cheap iron was essential
to such development. Moreover, another factor had come into play.
The Walker Tariff had fixed ad valorem duties on iron. As we
have seen, the years 1852-53 witnessed a marked rise in world prices,
and particularly in those of iron. As levels went up, the ad valorem
tariff went up with them. British rails at the beginning of 1853 sold
in our seaboard cities at about $70 a ton, of which approximately
$12 represented the duty paid to our government. Among the pow-
erful groups interested in the building of railways—the promoters,
bankers, realty speculators, shippers, and farmers—there arose a deafening clamor for the repeal of this duty and the saving of the $12 a
ton. They declared that the existing tariff was a disastrous brake
upon our national growth. Thus Hewitt and his associates had to
give up their struggle for higher duties in a determined effort to
avert marked reductions!

The demand for tariff reductions took various forms. There were
advocates of a direct cut. In the spring of 1853 an amendment for
cancelling the tariff on iron rails was attached to an appropriation
bill, and was with difficulty defeated. Hewitt regarded it indignantly
as a scheme to benefit the new Southern and Western railroads at
the expense of the Eastern iron-mills, and to take a large part of
the public revenues and put them in the pockets of a small group
of railroad contractors. Early in 1854 a well-heeled railway lobby

was busy again in Washington for tariff-reduction, and was being accused by the iron trade of bribery and corruption. It offered a new plan—a proposal for remitting to the railways the tariff paid on railroad iron, thus making sure that the benefits would pass into American and not British hands. Hewitt wrote Senator John R. Thompson of New Jersey that this also was an outrage.[1] He had ascertained that the total duties thus far paid by the Illinois Central on imported rails amounted to $750,000, which that richly endowed road could well afford; and he declared that the whole of such sums "would now be taken from the Treasury to be transferred to the pockets of a few wealthy capitalists." Fortunately, President Pierce was opposed to the rebate plan, and it also failed.

Yet despite his anxiety over the Democratic tariff policy, Hewitt easily resisted in 1856 the temptation to turn to the new Republican Party, which was supposed to be friendly to tariff increases. Like many other Northern business men, he believed that national peace and safety required the election of the conservative Buchanan. He was genuinely fearful of Southern secession if Frémont won, while he had several reassuring conversations with Stephen A. Douglas. On November 6 he wrote: "Buchanan being elected, I now feel as if our investment both in the Illinois Central Railway Company and the Trenton Iron Company were worth a good deal more than if Frémont had succeeded."

I

This mention of the Illinois Central brings us to another of Hewitt's engrossing activities in this period, his interest in railroad expansion, particularly in the Middle West. The railroad of that day was a curious affair; rough wooden cars heated by stoves, wood-burning locomotives with big-bellied smokestacks and drive-wheels still often at the front instead of the back, hand brakes, uneven couplings, and bumpy tracks. But since every step in its development meant much to the iron trade,[2] Hewitt followed its progress

[1] May 12, 1854; Hewitt Papers. These papers show that he influenced William Cullen Bryant to attack the tariff-rebate scheme in the *Evening Post*.
[2] His papers leave no doubt of the connection. On February 18, 1854, Hewitt wrote the Hon. Charles Skelton in Washington that he presumed there would be a reduction in the duty levied on iron, and he would not object to a moderate cut. He added that there was a better way to sustain the iron business than by the tariff; it was by the building of railroads. Some 5,000 miles

alertly and little by little was drawn into association with the railroad builders.

His first venture was of minor importance. Early in the fifties he played the principal part in building the Sussex Railroad, for the carriage of ore from various mines in northern New Jersey down to the Morris & Essex Railroad at Stanhope. Several corporations were interested in it—the Franklinite Company, the Sussex Iron Company, the Passaic Company, and the Natural Paint Company; but Cooper & Hewitt assumed the whole financial responsibility. Though the road had a distinct value to the iron company in cheapening the cost of Andover ore, in itself it was never profitable. Hewitt tried hard from year to year to pump vitality into it by planning extensions and drumming up traffic, but it was always in difficulties. Within a few years Cooper & Hewitt were fruitlessly trying to "give" it to the Morris & Essex on condition that the latter assume its debts, amounting to a little over $210,000. It was only gradually and with much trouble that they succeeded, just before the Civil War, in getting rid of the property by turning the stock over to a new management, and selling the bonds in various quarters.

The Sussex Railroad was a mere appendage of the iron business; but larger fields beckoned to Hewitt, and he found it easy to enter them. His marriage to Peter Cooper's daughter had given him added prestige; he had capital of his own to invest, and knew where to find more; and his judgment and executive ability had become widely known. Among the capitalists and entrepreneurs who valued his friendship was William H. Osborn, who in 1855 became president of the Illinois Central. As early as 1852 the Trenton Iron Company had formed a business connection with the Illinois Central, selling rails to it in exchange for bonds which it then disposed

---

were awaiting only the means of completion. "The land grants afford the only means of pushing them through. It seems to me that these grants can be made without pecuniary loss to the government, and at the same time greatly enrich the country. The example of the Illinois Central Railroad you know, and you will observe how favorably the Governor of Illinois speaks of the enterprise in his message. The great object is to get the public land settled. The readiest mode of doing this is to build railroads, and the settler can better afford $6 per acre where there is a railroad than $1.25 where there is none." If 5,000 miles of railroad were built, the iron interests would have to supply 500,000 tons of rails, and as much more metal for cars, engines, spikes, and so on. Hewitt Papers.

of in Europe. Hewitt was gradually drawn into close association with the line. It had unusual resources, and he believed that it would soon become one of the great railroads of the world. He acquired a considerable amount of bonds and stock, was elected a director in 1854, and next year became a member of the executive committee of the board. Osborn, a man of indomitable will, sometimes visited him in New York, and valued his advice. None of the road's affairs, from the displacement of the old "wood-burners" by coal-burning locomotives to the details of dividend-payment and bond-renewals, escaped his eye.

Hewitt made repeated trips to Chicago, and acquired land along the route, including an entire section near Urbana. He urged Eastern capitalists like Mark Healey of Boston to invest, and kept such Congressional friends as Representative Phoenix and Senators Brodhead and Stockton informed upon the legislative interests of the road. In the fall of 1856, a vice-president being needed, he suggested Captain George B. McClellan, who was about to resign from the army and wished to find a business post. "He is an A1 man and I wanted to get him before," Hewitt wrote his associates. "He is a gentleman of lengthened education, and for mental and physical endurance has no rival in the army. He is about thirty-five years old, and in my judgment the best man to be secured in the country. He has just returned from the Crimea, being one of the three officers sent out by our government." McClellan, duly chosen, made a brilliant record as traffic manager and engineer.[1]

Even before the Illinois Central was completed in 1856, the longest railroad yet projected in the United States, men had begun to discuss tributaries to tap the great Western plains. In addition to the project for a grand transcontinental line, the project that had brought Northern and Southern ambitions into conflict and done so much to produce Douglas's rash Kansas-Nebraska Bill, there were various lesser plans. Hewitt, now enthusiastic over the prospective wealth of the Middle West, placed himself at the head of one such undertaking. "I have decided," he wrote Mark Healey on November 6, 1856, "to take up the Dubuque & Pacific Railroad, being an extension of the Illinois Central west to the Missouri River. I shall have two million dollars of stock to be subscribed

[1] Cf. Paul Wallace Gates, *The Illinois Central Railroad and its Colonization Work*, 77ff., 177, 236.

at five per cent paid up. I will send you the particulars. I want you to take one hundred thousand dollars of the stock. It will be a better thing than the Illinois Central. Osborn, Sanford, and other directors join me. If you have any friends in Boston who want an interest, I shall be pleased to have them take hold." Congress was expected to make a land-grant equal to that to the Illinois Central, and Hewitt assured John G. Stevens of Hoboken that the undertaking would be so valuable that "I do not doubt that ten million might be made out of it."

Though Iowa had now been a State for ten years and its population was growing so fast that in 1860 it almost reached 700,000 people, its fertile plains were virtually without railways. The single short line yet built ran well to the southward of that which Hewitt now undertook to finance. The Dubuque & Pacific had been planned several years earlier to connect with the Illinois Central at the Mississippi and run westward. A small amount of money had been raised locally. At the beginning of 1855 the county and city of Dubuque stood pledged to subscribe $300,000 in capital, and citizens of the town $150,000 more, while a ten-acre site had been granted for a depot; but it was necessary to enlist Eastern and European capital.[1] The line, as Hewitt now laid plans for it, was to extend west-northwest across the whole State, following the general route of the western branch of the Illinois Central today. Its length would be about 300 miles. Since northern Iowa fairly cried out for settlers, there seemed a certainty of a profitable freight and passenger business. With the support of both Western and Eastern friends, Hewitt assumed principal charge of the scheme. In the winter of 1856-57 he had bills introduced in the Illinois and Iowa legislatures to authorize the construction of a Mississippi River bridge at Dubuque. He made inquiries as to the possibilities of a bond-flotation in Europe, and prepared to go to London if necessary. McClellan, with the consent of the Illinois Central, devoted much of his time to drafting the engineering plans. So enthusiastically did Hewitt labor that Osborn suggested in one of his letters that he ought to be president of the new line. "I am not making a place for myself," Hewitt responded somewhat indignantly.[2] "I do not want any more interest than the other trustees. I propose to attend to it more, but

[1] Franklin T. Oldt, *History of Dubuque County, Ia.,* 243ff.
[2] To Osborn, November 13, 1856; Hewitt Papers.

to give the salary to someone who will act for the trustees. As for myself I have enough, and want no more than I now receive. I want this road built because it will help the Illinois Central."

For a time all went well. Assurances were received from Senator Douglas that a Federal land grant could be obtained without difficulty; and late in 1856 Hewitt, with advice from Osborn, drew up a detailed scheme for financing the line. He proposed an issue of $12,000,000 in bonds and $1,000,000 in stock, the stock to be sold immediately at par in order to start the construction. This would furnish a capital of $13,000,000 in all—or, after making various discounts, perhaps $35,000 a mile—for building the road; while land could be disposed of to settlers for providing equipment and meeting interest payments. The bonds were to be sold partly in the East and partly in Europe; the stock partly to the city and county of Dubuque, and partly to private interests. "I hope there will be no coquetting by these Dubuque people," Hewitt wrote a leading citizen of that town.[1] "I have made up the best party I have ever known here, but the terms must be complied with."

By the spring of 1857 all was in readiness. Congress had passed the land grant bill, giving a total of 1,306,605 acres for completion of the line, and President Pierce signed it. Plans had been made to market the securities in London. In March Hewitt wrote Congressman Bernhard Henn that "if practicable, the road should be built from both ends, provided the bonds can be realized on with sufficient rapidity." Already bonds had been engraved, and a contract signed with R. B. Mason & Company for construction from Dubuque to Fort Dodge. J. P. Farley had been chosen president of the road, and Hewitt wrote him in high spirits:[2] "I feel sure now that with prudence and good management here and in Iowa, the whole enterprise will result in a great success."

A great success indeed seemed within his grasp. Robert J. Walker, whose advice Hewitt repeatedly sought in these years, was confident that $6,000,000 worth of bonds could be sold in the British market. In April, 1857, Robert Benson & Company of London[3] were authorized to receive British subscriptions on a basis which was expected to net the builders of the new line $850 or more for each

[1] December 8, 1856; Hewitt Papers.
[2] March 23, 1857; Hewitt Papers.
[3] They had done much to sell Illinois Central bonds in Great Britain; cf. Gates, *Illinois Central*, 70ff.

$1000 bond. In a letter to this firm Hewitt compared the position of the Dubuque & Western with that which the now highly successful Illinois Central had held when first launched.

(Hewitt to Robert Benson & Co., New York, June 9, 1857)

If any comparison be instituted between the Illinois Central Railroad and the Dubuque & Western as *new* projects, the conclusions are all in favor of the Dubuque & Western Railroad.

(1) As to capital—we have $1,000,000 full paid in actual cash— They had only $200,000 actually paid in, when the construction bonds were issued and sold.

(2) We have 30 miles of road done and open for business. They had none.

(3) *They* lost the title to their lands unless the road was completed in four years. We get the lands for every 20 miles previous to building it, and if we do not complete the road by 1865, do not forfeit any of the lands appropriated to aid what is done.

(4) The very results achieved by the Illinois Central Railroad in the way of business and land sales, give a certainty to our plans, which in their case at the *outset* was only a matter of conjecture, and speculation.

(5) The preference of emigrants for Iowa is perfectly understood here, and will enable us to sell the lands on shorter credits, and at a better rate of interest than have attached to the Illinois Central sales.

(6) The law of east and west business which characterizes all our railroads, attaches directly to the Dubuque & Western Railroad, and when the road gets out 75 or 100 miles, it will be found to be self-sustaining, and will probably contribute very largely to the means required for its extension. The only real profitable part of the Illinois Central Railroad is the very line from Freeport to Salena, of which the Dubuque & Western Railroad is a continuation.

A British financial agent, William Ferguson,[1] came over to investigate the company. And then, as the American supporters of the company waited, dark clouds suddenly arose on the financial horizon. Hewitt, informed by his English adviser that they might rapidly thicken, warned President Farley to go slow with his construction.

[1] Ferguson wrote a graphic volume of travels, *America by River and Rail; or, Notes by the Way on the New World and its People* (London, 1856).

"He (Ferguson) says *distinctly*," wrote Hewitt, "that the *immediate* success of the negotiations depends entirely on the state of the money market when the bonds reach London. The news by the steamship just arrived is very discouraging as to the state of money matters in London. . . . Under all circumstances, I feel that you ought to restrain your actions in every engagement, until we have heard from London that at least $500,000 of the bonds are placed. Please remember that your character and mine are both at stake in this matter. Do not let us get into deep water. . . ."

II

It was a wise word, uttered in the nick of time. A few days more and financial affairs looked ominous; a few days later still they were darkly threatening. The great panic of 1857 was about to burst, and the Dubuque & Pacific enterprise came to an abrupt stop.

While busiest with his railroad interests in Illinois and Iowa, Hewitt was called upon to lend no little assistance to Peter Cooper in a far-distant project—the affairs of the Atlantic cable. Doubtless one of the few facts which every schoolboy really knows is that Cyrus W. Field was the principal American figure in that grandiose undertaking. But for him, it might easily have been an all-British achievement. But it ought not to be forgotten that on the American side Peter Cooper stood a close second. At the meeting which marked the real inception of the American effort—the meeting of a few New York capitalists at the Clarendon Hotel in March, 1854, when it was agreed to form the New York, Newfoundland & London Telegraph Company—Peter Cooper took the chair, and for twenty years thereafter was president of this particular company. Naturally he soon enlisted his son-in-law.

Cable-laying was one of the distinctive new enterprises of the time. Submarine telegraphy had not become practicable until gutta-percha was introduced for insulating purposes, Dr. Werner Siemens in England being one of the first to invent machinery for applying it to wire. Before the forties closed a daring English company laid a cable from Dover to Calais. It carried several messages, and the London *Times* remarked, in the words of Shakespeare, that "the jest of yesterday has become the fact of today." But the cable was feeble, and when a Boulogne fisherman hooked up the line, "mistaking it for a new kind of sea-weed," it was abandoned. In 1851 another Dover-Calais cable proved a success, and in 1853 Charles Bright—one of the most brilliant figures in this field—laid a permanently successful line from England to Ireland.[1] Soon afterward deep-sea soundings were made in the North Atlantic by the British and American navies. They showed that between Ireland and Canada lay a gently undulating plateau, at an average depth of two and a half miles, with no precipitous breaks, and with no disturbing currents at the bottom. All this was encouraging.

Some enterprising Britons, led by the engineer F. N. Gisborne, had already conceived of carrying a telegraph line from St. John's, Newfoundland, across the island to Cape Ray, whence it might be connected with the Canadian mainland. With this it was natural to link the plan of a cable from Ireland to St. John's. When the projectors failed to obtain sufficient funds in England and Canada to complete the Newfoundland line, Gisborne sought the aid of Cyrus W. Field in New York. Field, the son of a poor Connecticut clergyman, who had made a fortune as merchant and paper-manufacturer, was not actively engaged in business, and was easily won over. He summoned to the Clarendon Hotel the famous little knot of men, Peter Cooper, Marshall O. Roberts, Moses Taylor, and Chandler White, who gave the initial Newfoundland-Canadian project a substantial backing. In the next few weeks the party held repeated meetings in Field's comfortable parlor overlooking Gramercy Park from the north, just around the corner from Peter Cooper's house. Five abler capitalists could not then have been found in the city.[2] Hunt was a merchant, and Roberts a merchant and shipper; both conservative, broad-minded, and highly successful. Moses Taylor was one of the most farsighted bankers in the country.

Experts were called in—David Dudley Field on legal questions, and Samuel F. B. Morse as electrician. The group of five furnished $22,000 in ready money, for initial expenses. Field and Chandler White obtained a better concession from the government of Newfoundland. Poles were cut, and a route was cleared across the

---

[1] See Charles Bright, *Life Story of Sir C. T. Bright.*

[2] Daniel Huntington's fine painting of the Atlantic Cable projectors was presented to the Chamber of Commerce of the State of New York on May 23, 1895. It shows Peter Cooper presiding while Cyrus W. Field calls attention to Trinity Bay, Newfoundland, on a chart. A booklet prepared under the supervision of Morris K. Jesup, Abram S. Hewitt, and William E. Dodge contains addresses on the presentation, and interesting historical data.

stony wilds of the island. While Field handled business affairs, Peter Cooper, the most famous, experienced, and inventive member of the group, looked after much of the practical work. His enthusiasm had been aroused by the undertaking, which he characteristically welcomed as "the consummation of that great prophecy, that 'knowledge shall cover the earth, as waters cover the deep.'" But the difficulties encountered at every step were almost incredible. During the spring and summer of 1856 Hewitt supplied the company with telegraph wire, a typical shipment being "eighteen tons best quality annealed charcoal iron telegraph wire No. 7, put up in bundles of 100 pounds each and boiled in oil, as before." He also helped Peter Cooper arrange for the vessels needed. Cooper then went to Newfoundland to supervise the completion of the line across its southern littoral. It traversed a wild country of tangled scrub alternating with barren rock, "so hard that we could not set the poles by digging, but had to support them by a stone embankment round each pole"; but at last the wind sang in the wires for the whole land distance.

There remained the more delicate task of laying the line across the Gulf of St. Lawrence to the Canadian mainland. The requisite amount of cable, about 85 miles in length, was shipped over by English makers. But the company had not obtained a suitable vessel of large size, and therefore resorted to the awkward device of using two ships, one with the cable and reel, the other to tow it. This was dangerous in high seas. Moreover, the captain of the tow-steamer quarreled with the electricians, took offence at some fancied slight, and determined that he would rule or ruin the enterprise. After the leaders had fastened the cable on the Cape Breton shore, they ordered him to tow the cable-ship across. Cooper writes:

> In starting he managed to run into the ship, carrying away her shroud and quarter-rail, and almost making a wreck, so that we had to lay up. Again . . . he started and again had the misfortune to get the larger line entangled with the wheel of his vessel. In the confusion that followed the ship that had the cable by his orders parted her anchor; the line was cut, and she drifted toward a reef of rocks. We entreated the captain to get hold of her as quickly as possible, but before he did so she was almost on the reef. It was then found necessary to go back and have the

machinery fixed, which took several days before we were ready
to start again. At length one beautiful day we got off.

Before starting our engineer, who had charge of laying the
cable, gave the captain instructions to keep constantly in view a
flag placed upon the telegraph-house and bring it in range with
a white rock upon the mountain, which would give him the exact
lines upon which to steer. As soon, however, as we got off, I saw
the captain was going out of the way, and as president of the
board I told him so. The answer was, "I know how to steer my
ship, I steer by my compass." I said, "your instructions were to
steer by the flag and the rock on the mountain." "I steer by my
compass," was all I could get out of him. He went on steering
in that manner until I found he was going so far out of the way
that I told him I would hold him responsible for all loss. This
had no effect. I then got a lawyer who was on board to draw up
a paper warning the captain that if he did not change his course
we should hold him responsible for the loss of the cable. He then
turned his course and went as far out of the way in the other direction. We soon after encountered a gale and had to discontinue.

The first cable, or much of it, was finally abandoned to sea-weed
and fishes, and Cooper thought it fortunate that the storm which
drove them to port did not swallow the two vessels as well. But
undaunted by the loss of some $350,000, his associates subscribed
for a second line. This was successfully laid next year by an Englishman, Mr. (later Sir) Samuel Canning. They could now turn to
their battle with the Atlantic.

Most of the credit for financing and laying the deep-sea cable
must clearly go to Englishmen. In London on September 29, 1856,
Field, John W. Brett, and Charles Bright pledged themselves to
form a company to establish a line between Ireland and Newfoundland, E. O. Whitehouse soon afterward joining them. The Atlantic
Telegraph Company was duly registered on October 20, 1856, with
William Thomson, later Lord Kelvin, as one of the directors. The
total capital was to be £350,000. Three-fourths of the shares were
eagerly taken in England; Field thought the other fourth would
be snapped up in America. But it was only after much trouble that
American subscribers were obtained for about $135,000 worth of
shares, or less than one-twelfth the capital. Next to Field himself
Peter Cooper was the largest American investor. Bright was appointed engineer-in-chief, Whitehouse electrician, and the making

of the cable was placed in the hands of two capable British firms. Efforts were then made to obtain financial and naval aid from both the American and British governments.[1]

It was here that Hewitt gave his principal assistance. Congress was asked to assure a minimum sum ($70,000 a year was finally fixed upon) for the transmission of government messages. Hewitt's growing acquaintance with public men was too valuable to be left unused. By visits to Washington and letters he enlisted the influence of Howell Cobb, at this time the principal Democratic leader in the House, and others. As he wrote Cobb, most mercantile men were convinced that the cable was essential to the growth of good feeling between America and Britain, that it would promote trade, and that it offered the only practicable means of controlling speculation in American staples; and it would be very mortifying if, after we had taken the initiative, the glory of completing the task should be seized by Great Britain. He used vehement arguments with Representative George Vail of New Jersey[2] and others.

During 1857 two warships, the *Niagara* and the *Agamemnon*, were lent by the American and British governments. Hewitt had done much to get the requisite bill through Congress, bombarding Senators Douglas, Brodhead, Thompson, and others with letters.[3] Since the *Niagara*, the largest and finest man-of-war yet built, was not quite completed when the bill passed, he ascertained that the contractors, Pease & Murphy, would be glad to have it tested by the cable-laying trip, and so informed the Secretary of the Navy. With great ceremony, the start was made from the Irish coast on August 7, 1857. Unfortunately, early on the fourth day the cable parted and disappeared in the depths. It was a heavy blow. Hewitt had just written that "Mr. Cooper and his immediate circle of friends are made poor by the Atlantic telegraph—" and here was a huge fresh expense. Still undaunted, Bright, Field, and their associates prepared for another attempt. Again Hewitt conducted much corre-

[1] See Charles Bright, *The Story of the Atlantic Cable;* articles in the Dictionary of National Biography on Sir John Pender, Sir William Thomson (Lord Kelvin), and Sir Charles Bright; the *Electrician*, Vol. XXXVII, 334ff.

[2] Hewitt to George Vail, February 9, 1857; Hewitt Papers.

[3] He wrote Douglas and Brodhead simultaneously on February 18, 1857, declaring that "we want the vessel got ready at once, as the cable is nearly done." Hewitt Papers.

spondence about vessels. His papers contain a letter of thanks from the head of the enterprise:

May 14th, 1858

My dear Sir,

Your esteemed letter of the 27th ultimo with enclosure was duly received.

Many thanks for all the trouble you have taken to obtain a paddle-wheel steamer from the Government of the United States to attend upon the *Niagara*.

I wish you would try to have the Secretary of the Navy order a screw or paddle-wheel steamer, to be stationed off the entrance of Trinity Bay, to meet us on our arrival there. Such a vessel might be of great service to us, in case of fog or bad weather, and should be there by the 25th of June. . . .

Very truly your friend,

Cyrus W. Field.

In the summer of 1858, despite icebergs and sportive whales, the cable was finally laid, and on August 5 Newfoundland and Ireland were at last connected.

"The success of the cable agreeably disappointed me," Hewitt wrote on August 12.[1] "I regarded the investment of so much money in a doubtful enterprise as a piece of folly. I am forced to acknowledge the superior wisdom of Mr. Cooper." He was in New York when President Buchanan and Queen Victoria exchanged messages. With amused interest he witnessed the ensuing celebration; a hundred guns, a grand procession, a brilliant public dinner, fireworks and illuminations, all ending in the partial conflagration of City Hall! But there was already reason for uneasiness about the line. "I hope," he wrote near the end of August, "the cable will get up speed enough to pay." Instead it grew slower and slower. The insulation was ruined by the high-potential currents which were first mistakenly used, and at last, on October 20, 1858, communication failed altogether.

The indomitable Peter Cooper retained his faith in the undertaking, but eight more years were to pass before it was successfully completed. Yet in the end Hewitt still acknowledged Cooper's superior wisdom. A new corporation, the Anglo-American Telegraph Company, was organized. The old gentleman put more money than

[1] To J. C. Neilson; Hewitt Papers.

ever into it.[1] He also acquired a large part of the bonds of the New York, Newfoundland & London Company at about half their face value, and a great block of the stock; for he retained faith in it when nearly everyone else was disheartened. When the cable proved a success in 1866, the bonds of this Newfoundland Company went to par, and he sold his stock at 90; so that his eventual profits were sufficient to reimburse him for the whole construction of Cooper Union.[2]

But the opening of Cooper Union has not yet been related; nor the disaster which preceded it, the panic of 1857, or the greater disaster which followed, the outbreak of Civil War.

[1] Cooper later stated: "We succeeded in getting another cable, but when we had got it about half-way over, we lost that as well. Then the question seemed hopeless. The matter rested some two years before anything more was done. My friend Mr. Wilson G. Hunt used to talk to me often about it; for we had brought him into the Board some two or three years before. He said he did not feel much interest in it, but he felt concerned about spending so much money; and he remarked that he was not sure, as we had spent so much money already about the telegraph line, but we had better spend a little more. So we sent Mr. Field out again. We had spent so much money already, it was like pulling teeth out of Roberts and Taylor to get more money from them; but we got up the sum necessary to send Mr. Field out." Zachos, *Peter Cooper*, 11-13; Thomas Hughes, *Peter Cooper*, 219, 220.

[2] A second cable had to be laid across the Gulf of St. Lawrence by the Newfoundland Company, and Cooper, Moses Taylor, Marshall O. Roberts, and Cyrus W. Field met the whole expense just when the skies were darkest.

CHAPTER X

The Birth of Cooper Union

WHEN the first gusts of the panic of 1857 burst upon business, even well-informed men, as in so many other financial storms, anticipated only a brief disturbance. Hewitt had taken note in April of ominous signs. The security markets in London and New York were disturbed, railway bonds were fluctuating violently, prices were falling, and banks contracting their loans. Iron had dropped during 1856 and as consumption declined early in the following year, it continued sinking. In June he shrewdly wrote Captain Bowman of the Treasury Department: "I am afraid there is going to be financial difficulty. The outflow of specie is terrific. I am trying to get under close-reefed topsails." But few realized how topheavy a structure had been reared in America by exuberant over-expansion and rash speculation. Particularly in the West, premature railroads had built up premature cities, bustling with premature trade for a premature population.

August brought the first heavy thunderclap, the failure of the Ohio Life Insurance Company of Cincinnati for seven millions. A succession of bankruptcies instantly toppled a dozen rows of dominoes—one cascading row of banks, one of mercantile houses, one of railroads, one of factories. A long and heavy row, alas, was represented by the iron mills. Early in the year a new and "non-partisan" tariff had at last lowered duties again, and had hit some iron interests hard. Hewitt's Dubuque & Pacific Railroad, which had hardly begun, could easily be stopped. But the largest iron manufactory in the country simply had to go on; and for a time the struggle to maintain it was desperate.

The first result of the panic was an unprecedented pressure for money. "The feeling here," Hewitt wrote from New York on

August 27, "is such that people who have money are holding on to it, and people who have none cannot get it." Hoarding had instantly commenced. "No one," he commented next day, "knows whether he will be able to pay his butcher's bill, so great is the panic." He shortly added: "No one appears to have money but those who get five cents at a time." The construction of railroads, fireproof buildings, and telegraphs ceased, and the sound of hammers died away in the shipyards. Cooper Union was the last edifice of really large size built in New York for some years. No one bought iron, and half the former customers of the Trenton Company were bankrupt. The usual crop of defalcations and other breaches of business trust was appearing, creating the usual indignation and apprehension. By September 6 Hewitt was writing: "The condition of the money market here is frightful beyond anything we have ever known." Though he offered two and a half per cent a month for funds, he could obtain no ready cash. In October the New York banks, fairly mobbed by their depositors, suspended specie payments, and other banking houses throughout the nation followed. The wages of common labor dropped to 80 cents a day, and multitudes were left penniless as cold weather came on.

The Trenton company had to strain every nerve to collect and husband its resources. Hewitt asked Major P. G. T. Beauregard, in charge of the new custom house in New Orleans, to expedite payment for the iron beams going up there, and he called on all his debtors to pay their bills. Unfortunately, even his strongest customers seemed helpless. Colwell & Company of Philadelphia suspended; Stillman, Allen & Co., also largely in debt to the firm, went under entirely. When Reeves, Buck & Co., who owed some $25,000 for iron, failed in September, he wrote in bitter terms of their conduct. "You cannot imagine how much these people have injured us without benefiting themselves; and I think it has never entered into the heart of man to conceive the inestimable meanness with which they have treated us. We shall endeavor to repay them in a Christian spirit." Early in October he reported that the company had failed in efforts to collect some $50,000 that was overdue, and providence alone knew how long they could withstand such disasters. "We are as powerless as children," he added on October 10. "No imagination can properly estimate the chaos which reigns here. It is terrific."

Yet the firm never for a moment considered suspension or shutting down. Indeed, Hewitt knew that it simply could not afford to suspend. Its chief resource at the moment lay in government contracts; if it stopped payments, the government would lose faith in it; and with no more contracts, all would be lost. By one expedient or another, Edward Cooper and he gradually collected sufficient funds. At the height of the crisis he instructed his Boston agent to sell their notes at any discount within reason. Peter Cooper, throwing some of his best stocks on the London market, had the proceeds remitted in gold, and so managed to lend the company $20,000. The Treasury Department, through the kindness of Secretary Howell Cobb, made unusually prompt payments for structural iron. Though most of the firm's efforts to borrow were unavailing, two or three banks which held short-term notes of the Trenton company agreed to extend them. Thus the Newark Banking and Insurance Company considerately suggested that it be paid in instalments. At the same time, Hewitt refused to honor any draft an hour become it came due. He wrote a Philadelphia creditor on October 2 that "the rate for the best paper is 6 per cent a month, and we cannot get money at all."

That autumn more than half the furnaces and ironmills in the country shut down, those of Pennsylvania being especially hard hit; and Hewitt had to reduce his operations to a minimum. On September 4 he wrote his mine superintendent, Philip R. George, to stop work at all but three shafts, and to discharge the superfluous hands. Early in October, with large stocks of ore on hand, even these three were temporarily closed. He ordered the vice-president, Timothy Abbott, to dismiss every dispensable man at Trenton and cut off every possible expense. "Remember that this is the only course now. *Do not let your sympathies interfere with your judgment.*"[1] At Phillipsburg the manager was directed to operate the blast furnaces until the ore on hand was reduced to the needs of one, and then blow out the other two.

"I am sorry for the hands," wrote Hewitt as hundreds thus lost their jobs, "but any other course will lead to inevitable ruin." As the worst of the crisis passed, however, he began re-hiring workmen. During the fall and winter he sent letters to every possible cus-

[1] September 19, 1857; Hewitt Papers. The Trenton Iron Company, as Hewitt frequently pointed out, always suffered from inadequate floating capital.

tomer, offering to make iron without profit simply in order to provide work; for example, he proposed to furnish a Massachusetts railroad a thousand tons of rails for the bare cost of wages and materials, without charging for capital or overhead.[1] This was to "get the cash required to buy food for our men. If you have any order to give out, we shall be glad to see you about it, as we feel a great responsibility resting on us to provide for our helpless workmen if we can." He instructed his Boston agent to take any order for iron "that Christians could give," and wrote Abbott[2] that "the great object and *duty* is to keep the men in work, or the framework of society will go to pieces."

Moreover, the company adopted various expedients to soften the disaster to its workmen. Hewitt asked the superintendents to keep all family men on the rolls and discharge bachelors, while he reduced wages with the explanation that more men could thus be retained. "My idea is that it is better to knock off 25 per cent all around at once, and pay in food at wholesale prices. Starvation at least will thus be prevented." For a short time after the banks suspended specie payments, the men were necessarily paid in food and clothing—that is, in orders on the stores of Trenton, Phillipsburg, and Andover, the shopkeepers being given four-month notes. Payments were later made partly in cash, and partly in provisions which the company distributed at wholesale cost. The firm purchased not less than five hundred barrels of flour, two hundred and fifty barrels of pork, and two hundred and fifty barrels of salt fish. "Tell the men we have no choice," Hewitt wrote his subordinates. "In New England and New York it has already come to this." When the mines and forges at Andover and Ringwood shut down, the men were allowed to remain in the company-owned houses rent-free, and to take the necessaries of life from the company stores without payment.

By the spring of 1858 the panic was over, money was again procurable, business was slowly reviving, and it was possible to survey the damage wrought. The country felt the blow for years, particularly in the industrial sections. While the North struggled slowly

[1] To Williams & Page, October 21, 1857, Hewitt Papers.
[2] October 13, 1857; Hewitt Papers. It will be noted that these attempts to provide for re-hiring men came within a few weeks after the forced discharges. Edward Cooper and Hewitt were alike anxious to take care of their workingmen.

to its feet, the agricultural South boasted that the sale of 1,600,000 bales of cotton to Europe at comparatively high prices had saved the nation. Yet the injury to the Trenton Iron Company proved surprisingly slight. It is true that its surplus had been almost wiped out, that the losses through bad debts had reached almost $50,000, that the fiscal year (August, 1857, to August, 1858) showed no profits, and that there were large losses on inventory, the value of materials on hand falling by almost $70,000. But the capital was intact, while in a period of unparalleled stringency every obligation had been promptly and honorably met, and not a single bill was left unpaid—an astonishing record. Indeed, some of its liabilities had been materially reduced; no less than $63,000 in bonds had been paid off, and $13,612.78 in current accounts. The company's reputation was higher than ever, and the loyalty of its workmen stronger.[1]

One change had been effected during the panic (December, 1857) on Hewitt's own initiative. The agency held by Cooper & Hewitt was abolished in order to save expense to the company at a time when orders were few and earnings small. "We attend to the business as before, have and retain the same control, but do not take pay," Hewitt explained to the stockholders. Although the annual compensation of Cooper & Hewitt, $25,000, had amounted to a very small percentage on sales and acceptances, in hard times it seemed a severe drain upon the establishment. The Trenton Company gladly entered a new arrangement by which Cooper & Hewitt continued to manage sales and purchases and furnish advances of money and credit, and were paid only one per cent every four months on these advances. Commissions were dropped entirely. Since in the first half of 1858 the amount of interest thus paid was but $3,657, the stockholders who otherwise would have paid $12,500 had reason to be grateful.

The capital stock of the Trenton Company was still restricted to one million dollars, and the bonds outstanding amounted to only $286,700. Against these liabilities stood assets which, on the basis of original investment, were now computed at $1,550,000, and beyond question were really worth well over two millions. By the end of 1858 some two thousand men were once more on the pay-

[1] The Annual Report, August, 1858, written by Hewitt, contains a full summary.

roll. In its first ten years the company, despite all its troubles, had
distributed dividends amounting to 108 per cent, and its outlook
seemed brighter than ever.[1]

But for Hewitt personally the years 1857-58 had been harassing
in the extreme. The iron company had fared far better than his
railroad enterprises. The Illinois Central trembled dangerously
under the first shocks of the panic, and before the close of August
assessed its stockholders $10 a share to meet its immediate obliga-
tions. There was a heavy floating debt, the road could not sell its
notes, and it possessed little ready cash. During September its position became worse, and in October, along with the Erie and the
Michigan Central, it confessed insolvency. This, wrote Hewitt, "was
unavoidable, and absolutely necessary to protect the interests of all
parties. I believe that the property will be worth more than if we
had spent a million in sacrifices." Its bonds were then selling at 50.
Meanwhile, the golden bubble of the Dubuque & Pacific had been
pricked. Hewitt's losses in it were heavy, and though he continued
to hold his Illinois Central securities, which in the end yielded
large profits, his interest in transportation was permanently chilled.
He never turned back to the railway field.

The Trenton Company was soon in a strong position again, for
with its varied output it was prepared to make the most of national recovery. By the fall of 1858 the mills were pushed to capacity

---

[1] A summary may here be interesting. The Trenton Iron Company had
originally been a family corporation. Of the first issue of stock, $300,000, Peter
Cooper held $151,000 and Cooper & Hewitt $149,000. In August, 1850, the capitalization was increased to $500,000, and so remained until August, 1853. A
stock dividend then, however, brought the capital up to $825,000. By 1854 there
was a considerable list of stockholders. In the course of that year $175,000 addi-
tional stock was issued, and the capital thus raised to $1,000,000. Large holdings
were now in the hands of Robert J. Walker, former secretary of the Treasury,
and Edwin Post, the New Jersey ironmaster and capitalist. These men were
regarded with suspicion in financial circles. Late in 1854 Hewitt was informed
by the principal bank of Easton, Pa., that it would no longer honor the drafts
of the Trenton Iron Company on Cooper & Hewitt, for while they had felt the
fullest confidence in the company while Peter Cooper was in control, they distrusted Post, and more particularly Walker, who was "regarded as a schemer."
Hewitt replied that of the 8,250 shares of stock, Peter Cooper still owned 3,798,
and he held 600 more, giving them more than a majority control. By the middle
of 1857 the Trenton Iron Company had more than a hundred stockholders.
They included Spofford & Tileston in New York, Thomas McElrath of the
same city, and Mark Healey of Boston. In 1859 Edwin A. Stevens of Hoboken
was listed as owner of 294 shares.

and refusing orders for rails; and Hewitt, having sold pig-iron in large quantities at a price that would assure $5 a ton profit, was prodding the furnaces at Phillipsburg to increase their production. Among the railroads which bought iron were the Baltimore & Ohio, the Vermont Central, and the chief New York and New Jersey lines; while the Trenton beams were going into the almshouse in Washington, the Chicago waterworks, the arsenal at Fortress Monroe, and other public buildings. Telegraph wire, chairs, and rods were all selling well. The three furnaces at Phillipsburg could, when running at capacity, turn out ten thousand tons of pig-iron each, and in 1859-60 all excess iron above the needs of the Trenton mills was salable at an average profit of about $3 a ton. Both in 1859 and 1860 the company declared semi-annual dividends of 3½ per cent, and in September of the latter year had an undivided surplus of about $85,000. Improvements were steadily being made. Besides the heavy steam hammer already mentioned, new blooming rolls were installed, and in 1860 one of the Phillipsburg furnaces was greatly enlarged. But for the threat of civil war which followed hard on the panic, all would have been bright.

I

It was at the very period when the panic was most mercilessly devastating the land that the undaunted Peter Cooper, aided by Edward Cooper and Hewitt, was perfecting the plans for his workingmen's institute and setting it in operation. Nothing ever better illustrated his courage and strength of purpose. The Act to "enable Peter Cooper to found a Scientific Institution in the City of New York" was passed at Albany on February 17, 1857. During 1858 the building which he wished to call simply The Union of Science and Art, but which the public at once named Cooper Union, was completed. The total cost was $630,000, and the founder gave $30,000 more for equipment and the expenses of beginning instruction. In the spring of 1859 the legislature passed an amendment to the enabling law, and in it specified the six original trustees: Peter Cooper, Edward Cooper, Abram S. Hewitt, Daniel F. Tiemann, John E. Parsons, and Wilson G. Hunt. They were all to hold office for life, and the board was to be self-perpetuating with an ultimate strength of five. A few days later, on April 29, 1859, Peter Cooper and his wife executed a deed of trust covering the title to the property. By that date instructors were being hired and preparations made for an early opening.[1]

The enabling legislation, which Hewitt and the lawyer John E. Parsons helped Peter Cooper to draft, specified the five main objects of the new institution. It was to give regular free night courses in applied science, in social and political science (these always to have preëminence), and in other branches of knowledge designed to "improve and elevate the working classes of the city." It was to offer a free reading room, art galleries, and scientific collections. It was to maintain a school "for the instruction of respectable females in the arts of design" and other useful arts. As soon as funds allowed, it was to provide "a thorough polytechnic school." And lastly, it was to maintain rooms for a society to be called "The Associates of the Cooper Union for the Advancement of Science and Art." It was emphatically not to be a trade school—a school for instruction in ordinary mechanic employments, for Peter Cooper had higher aims than that. All of the five objects were sound, and all but one were in due time realized; the plan for an affiliated academy or society of "Associates" somehow never came to anything.

In a letter to the trustees accompanying the deed of trust Peter Cooper expressed some characteristic and in part exceedingly curious views.[2] After emphasizing the fact that no religious tests whatever were to be permitted, he nevertheless gave a full statement of his own religious convictions. He wrote that he established the Union "in the hope that unnumbered youth will here receive the inspiration of truth in all its native power and glory." He stated that he wished editors of the press, whose influence he thought immeasurable, to be invited to become Associates. He wanted an office maintained in the building where people from all over the country might apply for the services of young men and woman of character and training. He requested that the students be permitted once each year to suggest their own rules of discipline. He wished them to have one of the large halls for a monthly lecture to be delivered by one of their own number, and another hall for debate. In the former room there should be full-length likenesses of Washington,

---

[1] In all the early reports of Cooper Union the legislation which established it, and the deed of trust by Peter and Sarah Cooper, are printed in full.

[2] This letter also is printed in the early reports, of which there is an almost complete file in the library of Cooper Union.

21. Hewitt's Associates in the Illinois Central: McClellan, Osborn, and Stephen A. Douglas

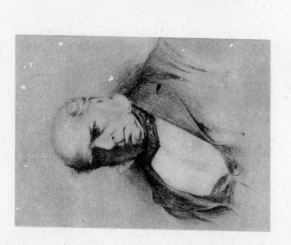

22. THREE BRITISH INVENTORS IN STEEL: SIR HENRY BESSEMER, SIDNEY
GILCHRIST THOMAS, AND SIR WILLIAM SIEMENS

23. Charles E. Hewitt, Charles Hewitt, and Edward Cooper:
Three of Abram S. Hewitt's Associates

24. Peter Cooper hitching his horse to a lamp post at the
South side of Cooper Union about 1860

25. MAYOR DANIEL F. TIEMANN, ONE OF THE ORIGINAL TRUSTEES
of COOPER UNION

26. Cooper Union, South Face, Today

27. Hewitt Building, Cooper Union, when completed
Only two stories have been finished.

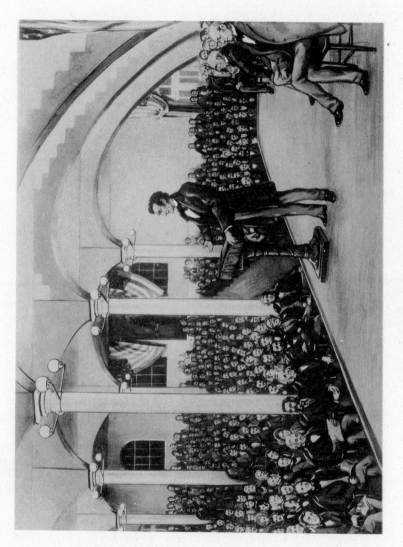

28. Lincoln's Cooper Union Address

Copyright 1935 by Hudson Historical Bureau

29. PETER COOPER'S CHAIR, USED BY HIM AND LINCOLN
AT COOPER UNION

Franklin, and Lafayette; and he wished students to remember that "notwithstanding they are dead, they yet speak the language of truth and soberness." He wrote that he hoped the windows of the third-floor reading-room would eventually be equipped with "such cosmoramic and other views as will exhibit in the clearest and most forcible light the true philosophy of life." This philosophy, he added, should always show "an inseparable connection between a course of vice and the misery that must inevitably follow."

The letter as a whole was a remarkable mixture of shrewd practicality and naive idealism, of genuine vision and of moralistic rigidity; a mixture that completely expressed Peter Cooper's personality. It showed that his views on the work of the Union were still but half-matured. But with all its eccentricities, it was a better letter than his friends expected. For as a matter of fact, Peter Cooper's original ideas for his institute had been very naive and impractical in most details, and as late as 1856 had been the despair of his son and Hewitt.[1] They were based upon his own experience as a young mechanic. In his youth ambitious young men had worked such long hours that they could not pursue regular courses of instruction even had any been offered; and in his first plans he thought little of such courses. They should be given, but should hold a subordinate place. He himself had profited greatly as a lad from the famous collection of curiosities called Scudder's Museum, later succeeded by Barnum's Museum. Its wax-works, stuffed animals, historical relics, and mechanical devices had stimulated his mind and awakened his imagination. At first, therefore, he wanted a large museum in his Union. On the upper floor of Scudder's Museum had also been a cosmorama: a collection of pictures of foreign scenes, historical events, and eminent personages, brilliantly illuminated and surveyed through peepholes. This likewise had once delighted him, and he wished a similar cosmorama in his Union. Since in early manhood he had listened eagerly to lectures, and the fifties were the heydey of the lyceum, he planned a large lecture-room. He had always learned much, in Yankee fashion, from conversation and debate with practical men as keen as himself. He therefore believed that his Union should contain a number of rooms where young men

[1] These ideas are admirably outlined in Rossiter W. Raymond, *Peter Cooper*, 64-74.

of the same pursuits or trades could meet regularly and engage in free discussion.

The building of the Union embodied all his original ideas, good and bad. In some respects it was strikingly well-planned. The great lecture hall was on the basement floor, easy of access, protected from all the noises of the street, and utilizing space that might otherwise have been lost. The two first floors above were to be occupied by stores and offices, whose annual rent would pay the operating expenses of the Union. Since it was in the very heart of the city, the Union would easily find tenants. On the third floor was a spacious room intended for the museum; while on the story above was another large room to contain the cosmorama. A large part of the remainder of the building was divided into small meeting-rooms for the "discussion groups" or informal debating societies. The broad flat roof was to be enclosed with a balustrade and converted into a roof-garden, where on warm days or evenings crowds of people might listen to music from a band and buy inexpensive refreshments. Pains were taken to supply ample safety-exits. The studio was furnished with double-paned skylights to prevent draughts. Mechanical ventilation by means of a large fan, run by steam-power, was provided. Edward Cooper designed this fan, and did it so capably that when long years afterward the system had to be remodelled, it was the marvel of the ventilating engineers who were called in.[1] In one feature Peter Cooper looked far ahead. No really excellent elevator had yet been invented, though the Crystal Palace in London had exhibited one of some merit. But Peter Cooper knew that elevators were coming. He therefore left an oval space from top to bottom—as he said, an oval space offers

---

[1] Edward Ringwood Hewitt to author, September 18, 1933. An anecdote in Miss Eleanor G. Hewitt's family history illustrates the efficiency of the ventilation in the lecture hall. A speaker one evening broke a large glass retort in which he was demonstrating the combustion of phosphorous. "The white fumes of phosphoric acid gas floated out into the air toward the ventilation outlets at the sides and rear. To one who knew the irritating nature of these fumes, it seemed inevitable that the hall must be emptied of its crowded audience in a few minutes. Already coughing had begun on the front seats when Mr. Hewitt, who was seated on the platform, quickly rose, and pulling a cord, reversed the currents of ventilation and opened a new outlet into the street, behind and above the platform. The curling clouds of vapor paused, wheeled, and retreated, and in another minute the air was perfectly pure."

more room than a square—in which one might later be installed. Today elevators move up and down in that space!

But as the building was completed, and as definite and detailed plans were first made for its use, Peter Cooper's advisers had persuaded him to modify and enlarge his ideas. Foremost among these advisers was Hewitt. The final charter of the Union, as the legislature adopted it by its amendatory act of April 13, 1859, was drafted in his handwriting. Edward Cooper did only less. John E. Parsons, who for the next forty years performed all the legal work of the Union free of charge, made important contributions. The plans were broadened to be worthy of Peter Cooper's generous expenditures and high ideals. The proposed museum gave way to a great free reading room. A huge stuffed whale which Peter Cooper had already bought for it was given to the Museum of Natural History! The room designed for the cosmorama became a laboratory; the discussion rooms for the various trades became classrooms; the roof was left unused. Systematic courses of instruction by expert teachers were made the principal care and labor of the institution, and its organization was based on well-drilled classes. If Peter Cooper sometimes showed reluctance, he was won over to these changes—and to others which followed—by the proof that they worked and that they pleased the groups he meant to reach. Now and then he may have sighed. Once, years later, a friend who stood with the old man on the roof heard him, as he looked over the area where he had once pictured happy crowds under the spell of a fine orchestra, exclaim wistfully, "Sometimes I think my first plan was the best!"[1] But for the most part he agreed cordially that the later plans were the wiser. He had always been willing to learn, and his one wish was to make the Union the most efficient agency for social betterment possible.

The opening ceremonies of the Union were held on July 1, 1859. Dr. John W. Draper of New York University delivered an oration which later made part of his famous book, *The History of the Conflict Between Religion and Science*. The founder spoke in his simple, fervent way. The institution they were launching, he said, had scarcely been absent from his thought a single day for thirty years; he had labored for it "with an intensity of desire that can never be explained"; and he hoped soon to see the building

[1]Rossiter W. Raymond, *Peter Cooper*, 75, 76.

thronged by thousands in the eager pursuit of knowledge. "I trust that the time will come when the knowledge and application of science and art will elevate the hearts of men above the tinselled toys and grovelling pursuits that now so effectually engross their thoughts."[1]

Instruction began that fall. From the first day it was evident that the Union met an immense need. Hewitt conducted the registration. It had been announced that all who wished to enroll should give a week's notice. "The scene was beyond belief," he later wrote. "There was a mob assembled so large and eager that the efforts to register students almost resulted in a riot. It was incredible that there should be such a passion for learning among the toilers. Every class was filled in one night, and from that day there was never a vacancy in the Cooper Union classes." What was shortly called a "free night college for the working classes" was organized. It at first gave a three-year course in technology (pure and applied mathematics, chemistry, physics, theoretical and applied mechanics, architectural drafting, and mechanical and free-hand drawing); later a five-year course. There already existed in the city a school of design for women, which had been established by some public-spirited ladies, but had languished for want of means; Cooper Union at once absorbed it, and the ladies, who included Mrs. Hewitt, Mrs. G. W. Curtis, and Mrs. Hamilton Fish, became an advisory council. The reading-room soon had four thousand volumes on the shelves and nearly three hundred magazines and newspapers. A temporary picture gallery, with several hundred paintings on loan, was opened. At the beginning of the second year, 1,167 students had registered in the various classes, and by 1864 there were nearly 1,500. The first students completed the five-year course in May, 1864—two clerks, an engraver, a machinist, and a coachmaker—and were given not only diplomas but medals. Most students of course took only part-courses, but they were given certificates for any year they completed.[2]

In the work of planning the curriculum, hiring instructors, and overseeing the tuition, Hewitt necessarily played a leading part. While Peter Cooper was president of the board of trustees, he was

[1] Cf. New York *Evening Post, Times,* July 2, 1859; the *Tribune* did not mention the occasion.

[2] No history of Cooper Union has yet been written; but the annual reports furnish ample material, supplemented by the Hewitt and Peter Cooper papers.

secretary; and the secretary was the chief administrative officer. Under the by-laws he was to have "the general oversight of the various departments of the Union, and manage the scholastic operations and correspondence"; while he was also to be "the organ of communication with the community." Before many years had passed a subordinate officer, Fitzgerald Tisdall, Jr., was made director of the evening schools. But it was Hewitt who, within the broad lines of policy determined by Peter Cooper and the other trustees, really managed the Union. For the remainder of his life, save for some intervals when he deputed his duties to others, he held a position roughly equivalent to the presidency of a small college. It cost quite as much time and labor. Voluminous papers show that he wrote the important letters, interviewed prospective teachers, planned courses, and oversaw discipline. It was he who, familiar with the work of the Lowell Institute in Boston, advised Peter Cooper to emphasize the free evening lectures. He more than any other built up the library.

Thus was the vision of Peter Cooper, who called himself in the legal papers of the Union "a mechanic of New York," converted into substantiality. It was an inspiring achievement. We must remember that the founder was at this time in many ways still a grievously ill-educated man. A letter which he wrote to Hewitt in 1860 will illustrate his vagaries of spelling:

Dear Abram
    Purchas the stock as you request.
    Mr. Stephens I thought scemed anchious to setel his acount by the sale of the horses.
    If you like the horses after seeing them driven I think you had beter pay him the $350 dollars for me and get a setelment with him by two notes at 3 & 5 months interest aded. If I am not mistaken we will find it difficult to get as good a teem as they appear to be.
                                        Yours, &c, Peter Cooper.
    Joseph will give you his acount.

But this ill-educated philanthropist had raised in the metropolis its first great instrumentality for giving higher education to young men and women on a truly democratic basis. Throughout his later years Peter Cooper talked much of the responsibilities of wealth. He was wont to say that a man who made a fortune was entitled

to a "reasonable usufruct" during life from it; he was entitled also
to bequeath his children enough to maintain them in life; but the
remainder he should devote to public uses. He had done this. He
had also carried out his oft-expressed wish to see that the poor
young men of New York need not undergo such a severe struggle
for education as he had done. From this time he gave more and
more of his working hours to the school he had labored so hard
to create.

At first his purpose was not always appreciated. One day, riding
up the Bowery in a horse-car, he heard two men talking in the seat
across from him. "There is Peter Cooper's building," said one.
"That man is a snake in the grass. See the stores on the ground
floor. It is a commercial building, and he is trying to evade tax-
payments by calling it an educational institution." Peter Cooper
stopped them and introduced himself. "Alight, gentlemen," he said,
"and come in with me. You have maligned me. Let me show you
the building and explain it." He took them over it, showed them
that it was unfortunately necessary to lease the ground floor to provide revenues for instruction, and described its aims. They were
contrite, and one of them afterward made a small gift. But the city
in general quickly appreciated the usefulness of the Union, and
working youths flocked to it.

II

While Peter Cooper was launching the Union, and while the
Trenton Iron Company was recovering from the shock of the panic,
the nation was steadily approaching civil war. The party conventions of 1860, following hard upon John Brown's raid, shook men
wide awake to the dread crisis before them.

To none was this shock more appalling than to the conservative
business men whom Hewitt fairly typified. Throughout these years
he had remained a loyal Democrat. In 1856 he had attended the
Democratic National Convention in Cincinnati as a delegate from
New Jersey, and had won the approving notice of Horatio Seymour
there by some assistance which he lent to the "soft-shell" or anti-
slavery delegation from New York.[1] Alarmed by the possibility that
if Frémont were elected by the Republicans, the Lower South

[1] This assistance was in making hasty tabulations and calculations to be used
in a speech by Seymour; Hewitt's quickness with figures was always astonishing.

would secede, he had labored energetically in the campaign of that year to help carry New Jersey for Buchanan. After the contest Buchanan paid him the compliment of consulting him about his Cabinet, asking him to ascertain the opinion of New York and New Jersey business men upon the best appointees to the State and Treasury Department. Hewitt recommended Howell Cobb of Georgia and Robert J. Walker of Pennsylvania, and was much gratified when the former was actually selected for the Treasury. During the Buchanan Administration the Trenton mills continued to supply the Treasury Department with structural iron despite the competition of the Phoenix Iron Company.[1] With Secretary Cobb, Hewitt's relations were always highly cordial.

But with another member of the Buchanan Administration he came into sharp conflict. In the closing months of Buchanan's single feeble term, Hewitt had a bitter quarrel with the Secretary of War, John B. Floyd of Virginia, which throws some light upon a man whose character is still the subject of controversy. Floyd was the weakest member of a weak Cabinet; prejudiced, erratic, dilatory, and incompetent, he was despised by the army and disliked by the whole North. The charge that when secession approached, he attempted to distribute an excessive share of government arms among the Southern arsenals, has not been proved; but there is no question whatever that he was dishonest. In December, 1860, Buchanan learned that he had paid large sums to government contractors in anticipation of their services, and requested his resignation. Long before this Hewitt had made up his mind that he was a corrupt trickster. In 1856 Hewitt had proposed to the War Department the construction of an experimental iron gun-carriage for its heavy ordnance; and with the assistance of Colonel H. K. Craig of the Bureau of Ordnance and two subordinates, Captains Dyer and Benton, the Trenton works had built the carriage. It proved satisfactory. During the next few years the Trenton mill supplied wrought-iron parts for other carriages, which gave good service at Fortress Monroe. In the spring of 1860, a large appropriation being available, the Ordnance Bureau prepared to order

---

[1] The Phoenix Iron Company had been founded in Trenton within a few years after Peter Cooper's rolling mill was transplanted there. It failed in the panic of 1857, but was revived, and after the war did much business in structural beams.

iron for a still larger number; but at this point Floyd stepped in. Refusing to publish advertisements, solicit competitive bids, or even to notify the Trenton Iron Company, he let an order, over the indignant protest of Colonel Craig, for $50,000 worth of gun-carriage iron to a favored contractor named Reed, who was neither owner nor part-owner of any iron works.[1]

Hewitt, angered by the news, went to Washington to interview Floyd, but the latter refused to see him. He also refused, by letter, to state the price he had paid Reed, and insulted Hewitt by writing that the latter would probably now lie about his own rates on iron. Thereupon the ironmaster took steps to bring about a Congressional investigation, and on April 10, 1860, laid the whole correspondence before President Buchanan. In a covering letter he pointed out that Floyd had failed to call for competitive bids; that he had let the order without public notice; and that he had given it to Reed against the specific advice of the head of the Ordnance Bureau. "It is a notorious fact," continued Hewitt, "that there are in this country but two makers of the difficult shapes required for gun-carriages, both of whom could have been reached by mail from Washington within twelve hours. It is equally true that the Bureau of Ordnance were fully advised of the address and ability of these two establishments—that neither of them was applied to by the Secretary of War, but that the order was given to an individual who has not the means of making a single pound of the wrought iron, but has been compelled to purchase it from one of the very parties to whom the Secretary ought to have applied for a bid. . . ."

The Senate at once passed a resolution directing Floyd to state whether he had ever given a preference to favored individuals in letting contracts or making purchases. Other men were making complaints. The Secretary's reply was unsatisfactory to the press, to Congress, and to the President; while Hewitt was particularly angered by one misstatement which did him a serious injustice. Floyd informed the Senate that his department had been experimenting with iron for gun-carriages, and that at first the Ordnance Bureau had purchased it without consulting him. "The prices thus paid amounted to $17\frac{1}{8}$ cents per pound, as I found from the bill paid the Trenton Iron Works. The prices for this character of iron

---

[1] In a letter of May 7, 1861, to Col. J. W. Ripley of the Ordnance Bureau, Hewitt reviews the whole transaction; Hewitt Papers.

became continually lower, and I ordered the Colonel of Ordnance to purchase a supply of the same iron from the New York Architectural Works at prices averaging from four to eight cents a pound, which proved of the best quality, and is in the process of manufacture into gun carriages." This was false. Hewitt pointed out, with the support of Colonel Craig, that the price paid the Trenton Iron Works had always been five cents a pound, not 17⅛. In actual fact, Floyd's strange order had compelled the Ordnance Bureau to purchase a large quantity of iron at distinctly higher rates than it had been paying for small quantities.

In August, 1860, Hewitt met Jefferson Davis, chairman of the Senate Committee on Military Affairs, at West Point. The ironmaster brought with him Major Robert Anderson, who, as he wrote Davis, "knows most of the facts which prove conclusively the bad faith of the War Department, and the disgraceful statements of the Secretary in his letter to the Senate." He hoped to persuade Davis to ask for a new Congressional inquiry. But when Congress met again in December the cotton States were seceding, and there was no time for investigations. Hewitt had to be satisfied with Floyd's virtual dismissal by Buchanan, and his retreat from the capital a disgraced man.

Meanwhile, Hewitt, like Peter Cooper, like most Northern business men, had been an apprehensive spectator of the events which ushered in the campaign of 1860. Some authors of *tendenz* history have written as if the Civil War were a conscious struggle between the industrial North and agrarian South, and as if many leaders of these economic elements, in their antagonism to each other, had courted the conflict. But the facts are otherwise. The two economic elements were complementary and not antagonistic. A host of Northern industrialists and merchants strove to the last to avert a war which was caused primarily by political, social, and moral, not economic, forces. Peter Cooper and Hewitt were among the host, for both believed that war was needless and insane. Peter Cooper, indeed, like Lincoln a little later, advocated the extinction of the grand cause of discord by the Federal purchase and liberation of all slaves. He worked out his scheme in some detail, proposing a Federal Convention to agree upon a fair price and a practical method of manumission, and the raising of two to four billion dollars for the purpose by the sale of Federal bonds. As war came nearer, he threw his influence behind various other proposals, notably the Crittenden Compromise, for conciliation and peace. Hewitt, for his part, was anxious to restrain the Democratic Party from contributing to a breach.

On a rainy night early in 1860—February 27—he went to Cooper Union to hear Abraham Lincoln of Illinois give the third lecture in a series arranged by the Young Men's Central Republican Union of New York. The fame of the Westerner had preceded him. Since the Lincoln-Douglas debates nearly two years earlier his name had been frequently mentioned in the press; and though the *Times*, a jealous Seward organ spoke of him simply as "a lawyer who has some local reputation in Illinois," the *Evening Post* had praised him and predicted that he would furnish "a powerful assault upon the principles and policy of the pro-slavery party."[1] Many were curious to hear the prairie giant who was already mentioned for the Presidency. The hall was crowded; people stood in the aisles. William Cullen Bryant presided in the great underground room— the platform then being at the south end of the hall, and not as now at the west side. David Dudley Field escorted the speaker to the platform; and among the distinguished men present were Horace Greeley, John A. King, Charles C. Nott, and Peter Cooper. As the *Tribune* said, no one since the days of Clay and Webster had spoken to a larger body of the city's culture and intellect. When Lincoln walked forward with ungainly gait in a blue suit with brass buttons, too short at the ankles and wrists, and wrinkled from packing in his small bag, an audible titter rose from some parts of the room. He began speaking in a harsh raucous voice, so hard to understand that cries of "Louder, louder!" came from the rear, and his first gestures were labored and uncouth. But as he warmed to his theme his voice became soft and mellow, his movements quicker and more polished. From the beginning he held the closest attention of the house. In his entire address there was not an anecdote, a witticism, or a rhetorical passage; yet the audience, impressed by his intense earnestness, found a growing interest in his closely-reasoned exposition. As the *Tribune* said next day, "the tones, the gestures, the kindling eye, and the mirth-provoking look"

[1] Nicolay and Hay, *Lincoln,* II, ch. XII; memorandum for the author by Mr. Erskine Hewitt; memorandum by Mr. Thomas Snell, who was present at the speech.

moved the hearers till "the vast assemblage frequently rang with cheers and shouts of applause."

Hewitt, who had come to this Republican meeting in a distrustful mood, was carried away like the rest. "Before Lincoln had spoken five minutes people thought only of what he was saying," he later told his children. "I became convinced that I was listening to the greatest intellect with which I had ever come into contact."[1]

When the Democratic National Convention met in Charleston on May 23, 1860, Edward Cooper was present as a Douglas delegate and Hewitt as a spectator.[2] Both had feared in advance that it would result in a schism between the radical Southerners and the supporters of Douglas and popular sovereignty. Early in March Hewitt had urged Joel Parker of New Jersey to go as a delegate, "for we want conservative men there." His hope was that James Guthrie of Kentucky, the moderate ex-Secretary of the Treasury, would be nominated as a compromise candidate. As the Charleston Convention opened it was evident that Stephen A. Douglas was easily in the lead. But it was also evident that the radical slavery men of the lower South would not consent to a platform embodying Douglas's views upon slavery in the Territories. The schism which Hewitt had dreaded swiftly followed. When the Southern extremists were defeated on the convention floor they withdrew in an angry block, and the Democratic Party was left hopelessly divided in the face of a powerful and confident enemy.

Neither Edward Cooper nor Hewitt was present when the regular Democrats, meeting in an adjourned session in Baltimore, defiantly nominated Douglas. The representatives of the Calhoun-Jefferson Davis wing of the democracy at once selected Breckinridge. With Democratic defeat now virtually certain, Hewitt feared the temper of the lower South when that defeat came.

At first, to be sure, like other Northerners, he was inclined to take the oft-repeated threats of secession lightly. But this time his customers below the Potomac assured him the threats were genuine. "Affairs in the South look very bad," he wrote the Trenton office

---

[1] Mr. Erskine Hewitt and Mr. Edward Hewitt to the author.

[2] No complete list of delegates at Charleston exists, and Hewitt may possibly even have been a delegate, though his name appears on no printed list. He wrote April 9 to a Southern railwayman: "I shall be at Charleston if no accident occurs. . . . I am very anxious for a Conservative nomination." Hewitt Papers.

on October 26. "If Lincoln is elected, secession is certain. I hope you all appreciate the terrible responsibility which rests upon the Middle States to save the Union from dissolution. We hope to beat Lincoln in this State [New York], and New Jersey ought to be on the right side in such a contest. If I did not feel an insuperable repugnance to public speaking, I should go into every manufacturing town in New Jersey and proclaim the dangers which threaten to destroy the industry of the State." Other letters were equally gloomy. "There is no chance of the election of Breckinridge," he wrote a Baltimore firm. "Lincoln will be the next President, and in my opinion business will be in a very depressed condition for a year at least."

Within a few weeks after Lincoln's victory it became clear that the lower South was about to secede and was making preparations for a conflict. "Do not run the puddling mill after next week," Hewitt instructed the Trenton force on December 15, "no matter how little puddled iron you have, until you receive orders from here. I believe the government is already breaking up." Ten days later Peter Cooper returned from a visit to Washington with dispiriting intelligence. On hearing of South Carolina's secession, the Chamber of Commerce had sent thirty leading citizens down to ascertain President Buchanan's plans for the crisis. They obtained a White House appointment. Buchanan entered in his soft, infirm way a few minutes late, and sat down without saying a word. Abiel Low was chairman. After an embarrassing pause, Low eloquently and vigorously stated the object of the mission. "I have no power in the matter," sadly replied Buchanan. "I have no power in the matter." He added that his time had been so heavily occupied that he had only been able to read the penny newspaper of the day to see what was going on at the South! "This," said Cooper, "was about all we succeeded in getting out of him." The anxious delegation then called upon Senator Seward to learn whether he had any remedy to propose.[1]

The year 1861 began amid a growing paralysis of business. No one could undertake any new enterprise, confidence fled, and the banks were reluctant to lend even small sums. Several Southern railroads which had bought rails of the Trenton Company cancelled their orders and defaulted on their notes. Hewitt wrote a

[1] Cooper's MS. reminiscences; Hughes, *Cooper*, 180, 181.

director on January 2 that the iron trade was approaching a stand-still. "The Big Mill is standing idle. The wire mill is running, and I hope to keep it in motion. There is no sale for rails, pig, or bar iron. We are running two furnaces, and I intend to run them until our money gives out, so as to get the coal and ore into a marketable shape. Of course without sales we cannot make money or dividends. . . . We have two pretty large items in the South amounting to $90,000 in the aggregate, which the times have put into suspense. . . . We are well secured, however, if the securities are not rendered valueless by civil war."

Major P. G. T. Beauregard, who came to New York on government contract work, assured him this month that the Union was irreparably broken and that the North should accept the fact resignedly. But Hewitt was confident that Northerns would fight for the Union. As Georgia hesitated, he wrote James A. Gardner of Augusta in warning terms.[1] "I made a speech at Tammany Hall the other night. The Union feeling here is tremendous. Secession has no friends—but justice to the South is stronger than ever. When you leave us without your support, you do neither justice to us (who have fought your battles, and will win them yet) nor to yourselves. For heaven's sake do not secede! You are sure of your cause in the Union. The prospect outside is, to me, one of impenetrable gloom. The Union cannot be peaceably dissolved, if I know the present temper of the North." At the same time he was trying to induce Seward and other Republican leaders to consider some compromise. "I have worked very hard to secure concessions from the Republicans," he wrote Mark Healey on January 2, "and I know that they will make them sooner or later, but I fear that they will come too late to prevent the saddest spectacle of political ruin that modern history records."

During January five Southern States followed South Carolina into secession, and on February 4 a convention met at Montgomery to form the Southern Confederacy. Meanwhile, Hewitt kept bombarding his Southern customers with letters of expostulation. "If we are to wait for payment until the country is reunited," he wrote a Georgia debtor on January 28,[2] "I fear that our embarrassment will be great, for, unwilling as the Northern people have always

[1] January 10, 1861; Hewitt Papers.
[2] To Col. E. Houstoun, February 4, 1861; Hewitt Papers.

been to break up our government, I think that there will be found
but little disposition ever to reconstruct it." A week later he warned
a Tallahassee correspondent against violence. "All my political
friends are using every effort to induce the public mind to give up
the idea of coercion, and to take to that of a peaceable separation.
If our Southern friends will only refrain from attacking the forts
we shall succeed, but if a collision is precipitated, I fear a civil
war which will be equally disastrous to both sections of the country." Pleading with Southerners to come back to the Union, he insisted that the recent election had implied no hostility to their
section. "Is there no possibility that the disastrous complications
of government can be settled?" he demanded of a Savannah banker.
"There is, and always has been, a predominating conservative element in the North, ready and desirous to secure to the South whatever it may demand, but in the late election it was temporarily
overborne by the general disgust at the corruption of the Administration, and the determination of Pennsylvania to get the tariff
modified. The manufacturing interests in Pennsylvania have suffered since 1846 beyond belief, the sheriff having been most of the
time in possession of the large majority of the works, and the ruin
which has devastated the State really decided the election; the 'everlasting nigger' having literally nothing to do with the result."

Early in the year he had given strict orders that no iron which
might be used for war purposes should be shipped to the South.
But to the end he hoped for a reconciliation. "It seems incredible,"
he wrote the head of the New Orleans & Columbus Railroad on
February 16, "that there can be two nations where there is so much
good feeling personally, and I still hope for a solution . . ." After
Lincoln's inauguration he repeated: "I do not see any light, but I
hope that there will be good sense enough in the country to bring
about a settlement of our political differences."

The answer was the firing on Fort Sumter. Never had Hewitt
seen such excitement in New York. He could feel with Walt
Whitman:

> Forty years had I in my city seen soldiers parading,
> Forty years as a pageant, till unawares the lady of this teeming
>   and turbulent city,
> Sleepless amid her ships, her houses, her incalculable wealth,
> With her million children around her, suddenly,

At dead of night, at news from the south,
Incens'd struck with clinch'd hand the pavement.

The mails that morning, as soldiers fell in to the drum-tap,
brought news that another Southern railroad had defaulted on its
debt. "It fills me with sorrow," Hewitt wrote the president of the
line, "but my regret is slight when compared with the profound
despair with which I regard the impending conflict between North
and South, so long united in fraternal bonds, but now about to
engage in fratricidal strife." And he wrote the managers at Trenton:

"If you have a flag, hoist it over the works, and let it fly there
until this contest is ended. If you have no flag, *get one,* and let it
float in the breeze as soon as you can. If you cannot fly a flag ready-
made, you can do as some of my people are doing, *make one.*"

CHAPTER XI

Gun-Metal and Mortar-Beds

NOT all the victories of the North during the Civil War were achieved on the battlefield. Some were won in the industrial areas far behind the lines. And of all the industries which contributed to the war effort on both sides, the iron mills unquestionably deserve to be ranked first. What made the defence of Richmond most important to the Confederates was the fact that it contained the great Tredegar Iron Works, which supplied the gray armies with so much of their material; what made Sherman's march to the sea so heavy a disaster to the South was above all his destruction of furnaces, forges, rolling mills, and carshops throughout Georgia. Industrially, the North possessed immense advantages over the South, and in nothing was this more evident than in metals and machinery. The iron mills of New York, New Jersey, and Pennsylvania poured forth an overwhelming weight of metal for the Northern thrusts.

First among these mills stood the Trenton Iron Company, and its contributions to the war had a more dramatic quality than those of any other establishment. This was because Hewitt quickly perceived one of the gravest weaknesses of the North, its dependence for gun-metal upon half-hostile England; because he realized that if Great Britain intervened upon the side of the Confederacy the North must oppose inferior arms to her troops in Canada, and to the rifles with which she would equip the South; and because by a brilliant stroke he learned the British secret and supplied the deficiency.

When the first shots were fired Hewitt felt confident that the war would be fought to a victorious conclusion, and that if it lasted for several years—as he expected—the Trenton mills would have an opportunity to help wage it. "The issue is certain," he wrote his London agent, Osgood Field, on April 26. "The power of the general government will be asserted, and rebellion crushed once and forever, if it takes every man and dollar in the Northern States." Immediately after the capture of Fort Sumter he was asked by the New York State authorities to be ready to go to England for arms, and replied that he could leave on twenty-four hours' notice.[1] He also visited Washington, where he offered the services of the Trenton Works to the Secretary of War, called the attention of the new chief of the Ordnance Bureau, Colonel J. W. Ripley, to his facilities for making iron gun-carriages, and informed Secretary Welles that he was now making "indestructible" iron deck-beams, the first in America, of a type well suited for warships.

All was confusion at the capital and particularly in the War Department, where the flustered and inept Simon Cameron hardly knew what to do, and where Hewitt was disgusted by the scramble for contracts. "There is too much noise and too little system in public affairs, as at present conducted, to suit my taste," he wrote. He was indignant to discover that Cameron was permitting gross laxity in contracts and manifesting open favoritism to Pennsylvania friends. Secretary Welles showed no interest in the deck-beams, and the ironmaster returned to New York, where there was more to do. Some Democratic friends had responded to the first call for troops by raising a volunteer regiment, its colonel being the grand sachem of Tammany Hall, William D. Kennedy, and Hewitt secured a lieutenancy in it for one of his nephews. During these hectic days he gave no little assistance to Samuel J. Tilden, who was energetically rallying the Democrats of the metropolis to support Lincoln.

Some one inquired whether Cooper & Hewitt were with the Union. "I do not see how any incorporated company can be wanting in 'loyalty'—individuals may be," wrote Hewitt.[2] "But inasmuch as all the owners and officers of this company are sacrificing time, money, and effort for the country, I should think there could not be much doubt as to the company."

Obviously large supplies of munitions would be needed: artillery, rifles, bayonets, naval armor, and a hundred other varieties of iron, but above all, good rifles and artillery. Abundant means, public

[1] To William M. Evarts, April 23, 1861.
[2] To Vice-President Abbott, April 23, 1861; Hewitt Papers.

and private, existed for manufacturing small arms. Hewitt had no intention of competing with the Springfield armory, which was immediately expanded to huge proportions, or with Remington, Whitney, and other well-established makers of firearms. But these manufacturers needed the best wrought iron for their barrels, while the introduction of better artillery would require either steel or a very superior quality of iron. The Trenton Company had long been proud of its Andover metal. Hewitt resolved that he would now produce the best gun-metal that America had yet seen, and—if the government encouraged him—devote the Trenton Mills to its fabrication in large quantities. In April he informed the Whitney factory in Connecticut that he could supply gun-metal in the qualities and quantities needed, and on May 15 sent a more explicit letter to Colonel J. W. Ripley, head of the Ordnance Bureau of the War Department:

> We have for some time been making cast steel bars, with a view to supplying a good material for rifle barrels, and rifled cannon. We believe that we have succeeded in procuring a perfectly reliable article. The difficulty has been to make the steel "mild" enough to bore easily, and we think that we have a result that will compare favorably for sound texture and mild quality with anything made by Krupp.
>
> The object of this letter is to ask if we may send you some small samples for examination, and whether the bars can be tried at Springfield. We do not see any limit as to our means of supply, as we have the raw material in superabundant quality, and we have only to add melting furnaces, which we can do in one month. . . . Our manager has already made one ingot for experiment, weighing over four hundred pounds, and is now ready to make one weighing a ton if desired. We have a seven-ton steam hammer. . . .

The Ordnance Bureau at once requested an experimental sample for the Springfield Armory. Hewitt was elated. The first shock of the conflict had half-paralyzed general business. He had been compelled to make a personal canvass to drum up small orders for rails, while few beams were being sold. If the gun-metal were carefully made, he wrote his subordinates at Trenton, "I think it will give us the business of making gun iron, and the result will be to make the company a profitable concern."

His reference to the manufacture of cast-steel bars at Trenton points to an interesting innovation which Edward Cooper and he hoped to carry much farther. He had been impressed between the panic and the war by the rapid increase of steel production at Sheffield, England, the successful use of the Bessemer process in Sweden, and the rise of the great Krupp Works at Essen; and he perceived that steel must shortly replace wrought iron for most industrial purposes. Charles Hewitt's visit to the chief British works in 1859 had resulted in important mechanical and technological changes at Trenton, designed to furnish better iron rails under the new British methods. But Hewitt wished to go a long step further. He had been revolving the subject when Lincoln was elected.

"You are aware," he had written Charles in November, 1860, "that Krupp at Essen, in Prussia has, during the last few years, built up an establishment much larger than ours for the manufacture of cast steel. He makes all his steel by the melting, and not the cementing process. His product is chiefly used for railroad work. I enclose all the circulars I have been able to get hold of in regard to his business. You will see that his axles cannot be sold here for less than 24 cents a pound. . . . Now I cannot get it out of my head that we can gradually get into the steel business on a scale that will absorb our capacity. I believe that every pound of Ringwood iron can be used to advantage in this way. As to puddled steel, it doubtless has its uses and advantages, but for the best work I do not see how the homogeneous character of cast steel can ever be dispensed with. I am so much impressed with this matter that I would like to go to Europe and get all the facts, and I certainly will go if I can. Krupp was a poor man twenty years ago. Today he has the largest steel works in Europe, and is very rich. Somebody will do this thing in this country." He referred to what is known as the Bell-Krupp process, invented independently by Krupp in Prussia and Sir Lowthian Bell in England. In this process, molten iron oxide was rapidly stirred into molten pig-iron in a saucer-shaped furnace revolving on its axis, at a temperature slightly above the melting point. The phosphorus and silicon were thus removed rapidly, without greatly affecting the carbon-content, and the result was a form of cast-iron so extremely pure that it might be called steel.

He might well wish to become the Alfred Krupp of America. Krupp, born in poverty, had inherited only his father's simple water-driven forges in Essen. But against many trials he had built up the works, specializing at first in crucible steel, until they became famous throughout the world. He made his first steel gun in 1847; four years later he created a sensation by exhibiting at the Crystal Palace in London a flawless steel ingot weighing two tons. In the ensuing decade he made steel rails, steel locomotive tires, and steel artillery that were the envy of the rest of the industrial world. He and his aides gradually perfected new methods of producing fine steels. Others clung to the old, slow, and costly crucible process; some adopted the "cementation" process; still others embraced the Bessemer process. But Krupp learned to make steel by new methods of fluxing bar or scrap iron with powdered charcoal and manganese oxide or spiegeleisen; that is, by the Bell-Krupp process just described. By the sixties he was employing not far from ten thousand men, and by 1866 making more than 60,000 tons of steel a year—some of it in shapes that no one else could match. Hewitt hoped in 1860 to develop some new fluxing process for making steel from Andover and Ringwood ores. His letters early next year contain numerous references to experiments and tests at Trenton.

With this experimentation he now wished to combine war-work; and such services as the Trenton plant might offer the Union were urgently needed. The Federal Government when the war began had barely enough muskets and rifles to equip half a million men; 400,000 would be a fairer estimate. And such arms! More than nine-tenths were smooth-bore muskets; more than half of these had originally been flintlock guns, and had only recently been altered to percussion.[1] Many thousands were utterly useless, and thousands more of the rifled muskets were so light and weak that their barrels sprung after a dozen shots. One officer said it would be a masterstroke of policy to let the Confederates steal all the guns served to his battalion, for they "kicked farther than they would shoot." It was necessary to obtain not only enough firearms, but better firearms; partly by purchase abroad, partly by manufacture at home. But actually most of the firearms that were purchased in large quantities in Europe during the first two years of the war were poor

[1] The best treatment of arms in the Civil War is in Fred A. Shannon, *Organization and Administration of the Union Army, 1861-65*, I, 107-151; see also Annual Reports of the Secretary of War, 1861-64, and the Official Records, *passim*.

stuff. Up to January 30, 1862, nearly 740,000 muskets, rifles, and carbines had been bought; of these 116,740 were Enfields, probably the best rifle in Europe, 48,108 were of the French official type, and the rest were "a nondescript conglomeration." As for home manufacture, one great difficulty was at once encountered. Springfield rifles of the latest model were equal to any muzzle-loaders in the world—even the Enfield, though many American soldiers preferred the latter. But no first-class gun-metal was available in the United States. The supply of such metal had to be imported at high cost from Europe. A little came from Scandinavia, but most of it from Great Britain; the bulk of the British shipments being from the famous Monway Iron Works of Marshall & Mills at Wednesbury in south Staffordshire.

When men realized how excellent the Enfield rifles were, how much the English gun-metal surpassed ours, the thought of British intervention took on redoubled grimness. Such intervention had seemed imminent after the Mason-Slidell affair in 1861; throughout 1862 the threat still hung over the future like a lowering cloud. Hewitt had good reason for his undertaking.

Yet even with the Andover ores, his first experiments were discouraging. The manufacture of a sterling gun-metal was far more difficult than he had expected; far more difficult than we can imagine today unless we comprehend the then universal ignorance of metallurgical science, or most of it. Hewitt's initial efforts for the Springfield Arsenal proved a humiliating failure. The first samples tested were good enough, to be sure, to warrant a government order for seven tons, while orders began coming in from private manufacturers. Extensive changes were made in the Trenton mills. Foremen and mechanics labored feverishly; machinery was installed to enable the company to manufacture a thousand gun-barrels weekly by the end of 1861, and much more immediately afterward; Alfred Jenks & Son contracted for 50,000 barrels at a high price. But Hewitt's principal hope was that Washington would give him large contracts, for Colonel Ripley had told him the government would pay $200 a ton. And in the summer of 1861 came heartbreaking news. The seven tons sent to Springfield had proved utterly unsatisfactory, and officers at the armory demanded far better material before they would place a second order.

A fresh trial must be made, and in repeated letters to the men in charge at Trenton Hewitt implored them to improve their methods. One of the two bar mills was now devoted exclusively to a gun-barrel iron, a costly stake to throw upon their hopes. Cooper and he temporarily gave up all thought of steel and concentrated upon producing a tough wrought iron similar to the famous "Marshall iron."

Yet the butterfly success still fluttered out of reach. The metal turned out in the autumn of 1861 was as poor as ever. Early in January, 1862, Major Dyer of the Springfield Armory held a conference with Hewitt in New York.[1] He explained a method that was thought hopeful by the Massachusetts wire manufacturer Washburn, in which the gun-metal was "piled," and offered to teach it to two of Hewitt's men; he also asked for fresh samples from Trenton. Hewitt exhorted the managers: "Be careful that the metal is reliable, for if we fail this time, our chance is gone." A week later he scolded Charles because some of the specimen gun-barrels were excessively uneven in external appearance. They were good enough for private manufacturers, for whom the mills were by this time turning out some two thousand rough barrels a week, but not for the government. When finished, the new samples again proved unsuitable. The Trenton experiments went on; Hewitt sent advice, Edward Cooper sent advice, Charles Hewitt labored incessantly. But the metal remained defective, the government continued to reject it, and during months when the British attitude became more and more alarming, the United States remained dependent upon Marshall & Mills. The British ironmasters had the formula; the Americans did not.

Till a formula could be obtained, Hewitt's great plant was as helpless to assist in the production of rifles and other new-style arms as a turtle on its back, its feet waving in air. All its ponderous machinery, its furnaces, its ore, its workmen, were useless for want of a few sentences written on a sheet of paper. More and more he brooded upon the means of obtaining these few sentences, this priceless bit of information.[2] To add to his discouragement, the

---

[1] Hewitt to the Trenton Works, January 8, 1862; Hewitt Papers.

[2] Some of his experiments were crude enough. His London agent reported in 1861 that tungsten prices had soared. "This confirms me," he wrote Charles, "in my idea that tungsten is the material which enables Krupp and the other steelmakers to cast sound ingots of great size. There is another matter which

Andover mine, so long one of the mainstays of the Trenton works, now showed signs of imminent exhaustion. Its yield during the winter of 1861-62 steadily slackened. There dawned upon him the possibility, later shown to be a fact, that it was a great pocket of ore rather than a true shaft, and that its deposits had been nearly all scooped out. Since the company had recently bought the Dell and Roseville mines, and leased the Hibernia, the Allen, and other shafts in northern New Jersey, no shortage of ore was to be feared; but the Andover metal had been prized for wrought iron of unsurpassed quality.

Altogether, the year 1862 began for Hewitt, as for the nation, amid clouds of gloom. With good gun-metal still a mere dream, during 1861 only one furnace at Phillipsburg had been kept in blast; dividends had been out of the question. Anxiety had tormented Hewitt until it visibly impaired his health. The previous autumn he had written of "my efforts to save the company from ruin," and had said that for ready money he was nearly "reduced to buttons." As he informed Mark Healey, his chief worry was for his fellow-stockholders;[1] "For myself, I have cared nothing, but I have not been able to endure the thought of failure for the company." As proof of this statement, Cooper, Hewitt & Co., during 1861 refused any compensation whatever for managing the business.

I

But at this moment, Hewitt performed an incidental service to the government of which he always remained proud, and which brought him into personal relationship with Lincoln.

Late in 1861, Cooper, Hewitt & Company had received from the Navy Department an order for twenty-one mortar-beds, or gun-carriages of the type required for mortars, to be furnished with all possible speed. These carriages were extremely difficult to build. The shot from a heavy mortar was fired at an angle which often reached 45 degrees; the recoil was of devastating strength—suffi-

we can easily try. It is becoming apparent that the nitrogenous compounds of hydrogen have a very important influence in changing iron into steel. Ammonia exists in large quantities in guano. I have an idea that if guano were mixed in the heat in the puddling furnaces, or possibly in the melting-pots afterward, it would produce startling results—but whether good or bad I do not know." Hewitt Papers.

[1] February 24, 1862; Hewitt Papers.

cient to shatter an ordinary earthwork or concrete foundation, and
to break through the iron deck of an ordinary vessel or even sink
a light craft. The mortar-bed had to be built of several tons of
interlacing iron and wood-work, including roller-rings, recoil-buffer,
and slide-frame, in such fashion as to show great elasticity and
absorb the shock before it reached the foundation. Hewitt had
taken personal supervision of the contract, which came to him
through a government agent named Charles Knap. He had enlisted
three other establishments, H. Abbott & Son of Baltimore, the Cornell Company of New York, and the Phoenix Iron Company, to
assist him; had pushed the work energetically; and had been pleased
to complete it in the first days of 1862. He wrote Lieutenant Henry
A. Wise of the Navy Department on January 6: "We have now delivered fifteen of the mortar-beds, and the remaining six beds will
be completed this week." When the Cornell Company tried to gouge
the government by an overcharge, he successfully demanded a reduction. A bill for $15,194 was sent the navy, and paid with thanks
for his promptness.[1] His zeal, quickness, and fairness (he made no
charge for his personal services) were all remembered when an
emergency arose requiring still greater celerity.

    This emergency occurred in the West. Late in 1861 General
Grant had seized Paducah, Ky., and collected troops there for an
early forward movement, while a force of river gunboats, protected
at the bows with iron plating and bearing cannon of various types
was rapidly assembled to aid him. The Confederate line in the West
ran from Columbus on the Mississippi River eastward through Fort
Henry on the Tennessee, and Fort Donelson on the Cumberland,
the two rivers at this point being only eleven miles apart. If these
forts could be captured, two highways into the heart of the Confederacy would be opened. Grant asked that he be permitted to
move against them, in this request he was joined by Foote of the
navy, and before January ended the order was given. Lincoln, eager
to save the loyalists of Kentucky and Tennessee, took the keenest
interest in the movement. On the Confederate side, Albert Sidney
Johnston was prepared to defend the posts to the last. Fort Donelson seemed especially formidable. High on a bluff above the Cumberland, it had a large garrison, elaborate earthworks, numerous

----

[1] Full materials on this episode are found in Book No. 21, abstracts of Cooper,
Hewitt & Co. files; Hewitt Papers.

field-pieces, and seventeen heavy cannon so placed as to command the winding reaches of the river. On February 2 Grant started from Cairo with 15,000 men on transports, protected by Foote's seven gunboats.[1] For this campaign the War Department wanted additional mortar-beds in a hurry.

On January 23, General J. W. Ripley of the Ordnance Bureau telegraphed Hewitt for thirty mortar-beds to be delivered as quickly as possible. Hewitt wrote some three decades later that Lincoln also telegraphed him "substantially as follows:[2] 'I am told that you can do things which other men declare to be impossible. General Grant is at Cairo, ready to start on his movement to capture Fort Henry and Fort Donelson. He has the necessary troops and equipment, including thirty mortars, but the mortar-beds are lacking. The Chief of Ordnance informs me that nine months will be required to build the mortar-beds, which must be very heavy in order to carry 13-inch mortars now used for the first time. I appeal to you to have these mortar-beds built within thirty days, because otherwise the waters will fall and the expedition cannot proceed. Telegraph what you can do. A. Lincoln.'" No other evidence of such a telegram exists. Hewitt's narrative of the episode continues:

It was Sunday night when this dispatch was received. From my connection with the Ordnance Bureau I knew that a model mortar-bed had been under construction at Watertown Arsenal, where General Rodman was in command. I happened also to be president of the American Telegraph Company, and was therefore able to be put in communication with General Rodman on Sunday night. In fact, we talked over the wire. I learned that the model mortar-bed had just been completed and could be shipped at once. I requested him to send it by the Fall River Line on the next day, Monday, and as a matter of fact it was received on the wharf in New York on Tuesday morning. General Rodman took my word in lieu of any order, which subsequently, at my request, was sent to him. On Monday, I arranged with the leading machine shops in New York to have workmen on the wharf on the delivery of the model mortar-bed. Its weight was about one ton and a half.

As soon as it was transferred to the wharf I had it carried to the Novelty Works, where it was taken apart and templets made

---

[1] J. F. Rhodes, *History of the United States*, III, 581-598.
[2] Hewitt to the Bureau of Ordnance, October 27, 1896; Hewitt Papers.

of the several parts. These templets were distributed among four shops, with the request that each one should make thirty sets. I furnished all the material required except the chassis rails, which could only be got from the Phoenix Iron Works at Phoenix-ville, Pa., because the rolls had been made there especially for the purpose. I therefore telegraphed the owner of the works to put the rolls in and deliver the rails within one week. He replied that he could not possibly deliver them under four weeks, because he was engaged upon other pressing work. I therefore telegraphed to the President to send an officer to take charge of the works and received a reply, stating that the officer had been dispatched.

He had indeed acted with instant dispatch. Within the first few hours he had made arrangements with the other shops concerned. Abbott & Son were to supply the plates; the Phoenix Iron Company the chassis rails and chord bars; and the Cornell Company was to assemble the parts.[1] On January 24, the day after the order came, he telegraphed Ripley: "The arrangements for building the mortar-beds will be completed today. One bed per day can be turned out after two weeks required for getting the materials in hand." By letter he explained that he could supply each bed for about $100 less than he had charged the navy, his experience saving that much. "As in the case of the Navy Department, we will decline all compensation or profit in this business, being glad that our knowledge and position can in any way be turned to account in the present crisis of our national existence." On January 28 his confidential clerk was standing at the rolls in the Abbott mill to hurry the plates; and on January 29 he appealed to Assistant Secretary of War Watson to stop the delays in the Phoenix mill. He advanced money to the several shops to secure unstinted coöperation. Even so, the government implored more speed. On January 28 Charles Knap arrived from Washington. "The President has just sent a special messenger to us," Hewitt wrote the Abbott mill, "directing that every human agency shall be employed on the mortar-beds, as the safety of one of our great expeditions may depend upon a delay of even one day. We therefore entreat you to roll and ship all the plates this week and send them all by rail; we will pay whatever extra expense may be incurred. . . . We are doing what we do as patriots and not merchants." The next day he assured the War Department

[1] Materials on this are also in Book No. 21, abstracts of Cooper, Hewitt & Co. files; Hewitt Papers.

that he could deliver four beds a day as soon as his materials arrived, and could have the whole thirty done by February 15. His anxiety vibrated in every letter he wrote. For example, he informed the Trenton Works on January 29:

> You are aware that under the *special orders of the President of the United States* we are making 30 mortar-beds. The plates come from Abbott & Son by rail. Some were shipped yesterday, but they are not here yet. *As the safety of our great army in the West depends* upon the prompt receipt of these plates, I want you to arrange with the C. & A. R.R. Co. for their *instantaneous* delivery here; that is, not to let them rest an hour in Philadelphia or on the way. They will come daily for the next eight days. If *ever a R.R. Co. was called upon to be patriotic, this is such a case.* We are directed to spare nothing to accomplish the end, and if we were permitted to divulge the facts, the Co. would send them by a lightning line. You may judge when I say that his omission to provide the beds in time has cost General Ripley his place at the head of the Ordnance Bureau.

On Janary 31 the first plates arrived from Baltimore, but chord-bars were still lacking. On February 3 only six chord-bars had arrived. No others came until February 6, and Hewitt chafed angrily. But the moment they arrived his workmen fell upon them frantically, and on February 7 he telegraphed the War Department: "We will ship four mortar-beds tomorrow and four a day afterwards." He had meanwhile taken steps, with the same driving energy, to ensure rapid delivery in the West. In fact, he had sent urgent directions to the War Department in the matter. Four mortar-beds would make a car-load; a freight car could be attached to the Jersey Central express daily, and delivered at Harrisburg, from which it could be sent without change to Chicago by way of the Pennsylvania Central and the Pittsburgh, Fort Wayne, & Chicago; thence going to Cairo by the Illinois Central. The time, if the daily car were hitched to passenger trains, would be 44 hours to Chicago and 16 hours to Cairo. But a military order, Hewitt twice reminded the War Department, would be necessary. "Excuse our suggestions, but we desire that no precious time may be lost."

On February 8 the first car with four mortar-beds went west. On the 10th, 11th, and 12th four more beds went each day. On the 14th five more were shipped, and the remaining nine were ready

to follow at once. Hewitt painted on each car in glaring black letters against a white background: "U. S. Grant, Cairo. Not to be
switched under penalty of death."

He thus executed the order for the thirty mortar-beds in precisely three weeks from the time it was received. In this brief period
every piece of material used, plates, bars, and springs, had been
fabricated, the parts fitted, the whole finished off, and shipment
made. He sent an employe to follow the shipments through to Chicago and telegraph Washington if any hitch occurred. "No effort
has been spared," he wrote the military authorities, "and as usual
when people are in earnest, the work has been accomplished." The
total cost, $21,000, had all been advanced by Cooper, Hewitt & Co.
When he sent the bill to the War Department he indulged in a
pardonable expression of pride. "This," he wrote Assistant Secretary Watson,[1] "brings to a close the most remarkable mechanical
achievement, so far as time is concerned, that we have ever witnessed. . . . To serve the country in its time of trial is the dearest
wish of our hearts, and we hope that the Department will avail itself of our services at any and all times when we can be useful, and
we can promise fidelity, industry, and honesty in the execution of
its behests." Secretary Stanton had already, on February 3, written
to express his "high appreciation of your energy and promptness as
business men, and your public spirit and patriotism as citizens."

Nine days after the first mortars were shipped, and three days
after the last were ready—that is, on February 17—Hewitt heard
that Fort Donelson had been captured the previous day with nearly
all its garrison. "If that is so," he exuberantly wrote a friend, "the
backbone of the rebellion is broken." Fort Henry had fallen ten
days earlier. The former Secretary of War, Floyd, had scuttled out
of Donelson just before the surrender; he had his own reasons for
not wishing to be taken North a prisoner. None of Hewitt's mortar-
beds was required for the victory. But they would have been at hand
had a prolonged siege of Donelson been required; and two of them
shortly served the army well in capturing Island No. 10, and thus
opening the whole Mississippi as far as Vicksburg. Long after the
war Hewitt bought one of the mortars thus used from the War
Department, and set it up on the terrace at Ringwood.

An interesting sequel of this service was Lincoln's personal in-

[1] Hewitt to P. H. Watson, February 27, 1862; Hewitt Papers.

tervention to obtain the payment of Hewitt's bill. Since Cooper, Hewitt & Co. could ill spare the $21,000 they had advanced, Hewitt wrote General Ripley on February 14 asking that they be reimbursed as soon as possible. A fortnight passed without payment. Then a gentleman called at the Burling Slip office to say that a friend named Brown in Washington had heard that Cooper, Hewitt & Co. had filed a claim which, for a small fee, he could expedite. Hewitt was indignant to find men thus speculating upon the debts of the government to private individuals, and suspected that somebody in the War Department was purposely delaying claims in order to feed such cormorants. He waited with rising impatience. At last, early in March, the Second Auditor of the Treasury advised him that the bill had been audited and a requisition made for $21,000, and that this sum would be remitted when the Secretary of War signed the warrant. But he also learned that the Secretary might delay it indefinitely. Stanton was just bringing order out of the chaos of waste and corruption which Simon Cameron had left, and was wisely investigating everything before he signed. On March 12 Hewitt sent General Ripley an urgent letter. When no answer came he caught a train to interview the President.

"I was received, on sending in my card," he writes, "in advance of a large number of persons who were waiting admission. The President had never seen me before, although I had heard him deliver his Cooper Institute speech and therefore knew him by sight. He received me with great cordiality, and at once expressed his astonishment that 'so small a man could do so great a work in so short a time.' I explained to him the object of my visit. He expressed surprise that the money had not been refunded, and asked me whether any profit had been charged, to which I of course replied that I had only charged the actual disbursements . . ." Lincoln remarked that it was outrageous that while speculators who made enormous profits from the government were paid instantly, honest men performing services at cost had to wait. He sent for Stanton, who knew Hewitt well. With a touch of the irony in which he excelled, Lincoln remarked, "Do you suppose that if I should write on that bill, *'Pay this bill now,'* the Treasury would make settlement?" Stanton shrugged his shoulders. Nevertheless, the warrant was sent for, and Lincoln wrote at the bottom, "Pay this bill now. A. Lincoln." Not content with this, he added, "Now, Mr. Stanton,

I want you to do me a service. I am going to trouble you to go to the Treasury Department with Mr. Hewitt and see this bill sent through the proper channels for immediate payment." Stanton did so, and on March 24 Hewitt wrote the Second Auditor that he had duly received a draft for $21,000.[1]

II

From this digression we must return to the history of the effort to make good gun-metal at Trenton. In the middle of March, 1862, Hewitt suddenly decided to visit England. He had long gone without rest and was half ill. "The doctor," he wrote Mark Healey, "thinks that three months' rest will restore me, and that the same time devoted to work will kill me. I believe that it is for the best interest of the company that I should go away, especially if I come back restored to health." The mills were at last fully restored to prosperity, for government contracts and greenback inflation had produced the inevitable wartime boom. The market for pig-iron was rising. The firm was again selling large orders of rails to the Erie, the Illinois Central, the Jersey Central, and Vanderbilt's lines, and was supplying the government with increasing quantities of beams, rails, telegraph wire, and spikes. Moreover, Cooper, Hewitt & Co. had at last induced Secretary Welles to purchase iron deck-beams for government vessels. A nasty corner had been turned and the outlook was bright.

But above all, he wished to discover in England just how Marshall & Mills made their tough, durable, and highly polishable gun-metal. Though experiments were still being assiduously continued at Trenton, no light had yet dawned on the horizon. Somehow, somewhere, the method by which such superior iron was made in large quantities must be found, and he felt that it could not be found save on British soil. Ordinarily he would have respected any trade secret scrupulously, but these were far from ordinary

[1] Hewitt's letters show that the picturesque story which George Haven Putnam made from this episode in his *Memories of a Publisher*, 417-425, contains nearly as many errors as lines. His own story is in the letter to the Ordnance Bureau, October 27, 1896. Hewitt told his children that when he entered Lincoln's office the President paused, slowly surveyed him from head to foot, and said quizzically: "Why, you're not such a big fellow after all." "What did you expect to see?" said Hewitt. "From what they told me," said Lincoln, "I expected to see a man at least six feet tall"—a joke the short Hewitt greatly enjoyed.

times; war might begin abruptly with Britain and France, and the information would then be of vital importance to our national safety. To facilitate his undertaking, he obtained from the Ordnance Bureau letters to various British iron works, including Marshall & Mills, while he was empowered to let an additional government contract for gun-metal to this firm. Secretary Welles also commissioned him to examine the principal iron establishments of Great Britain "with a view especially to the processes of making armor plate for ships of war," and asked him to submit a formal report. "I would particularly suggest that any results you may obtain in reference to the relative merits of the single thick armor plate, and an equal thickness formed of thin plates, be communicated to us at the earliest opportunity . . ."[1] While Hewitt took this request with great seriousness, the subject which most engrossed him in England was gun-metal. He sailed on March 26.

Though he rested sufficiently on the voyage to arrive in improved health, his trip was characteristically crowded. In the north of England he was entertained by various ironmasters; he visited the Laird shipyards where the Confederate cruisers were built; he talked with the managers of the Birkenhead Iron Works about armor plate; and he spent some active days in Sheffield. Once more he stood on the ancestral green at Cannock, reflecting, no doubt, upon the change in his fortunes since he was there eighteen years earlier. In London his agent, the banker Osgood Field, squired him about town; he was entertained by Richard Cobden, and impressed his views of the war on the great Liberal leader. From May 6 to May 23 he took the hydropathic cure at Tudor House in Great Malvern. Then, making a hasty trip to Belgium and France, he inspected the fortifications at Liége, and called in Paris upon Minister Dayton, an old New Jersey acquaintance, who gave him a confidential message upon the sinister designs of Napoleon III to be carried back to Minister Adams—a message apparently only of general purport. Another busy week in London ended on June 10, when he returned to Staffordshire for purposes of his own. After some eventful days there he made a short trip into Scotland before sailing home from Liverpool. But most of the tour he devoted with intense industry to his inquiries.

The study of armor plate was easy, but when he tried to ascer-

[1] Navy Department, General Letter-Book, No. 67, p. 445.

tain the British method of making gun-metal he found all formulas carefully guarded. The War Department had authorized him to buy four hundred more tons of Marshall iron as a special order for the Springfield Armory. He paid two visits to the London office of Marshall & Mills for this purpose, making payment to the firm by drafts through George Peabody & Co. upon J. Pierpont Morgan in New York. He also arranged with the Whitworth Ordnance Company of Manchester to make an experimental 70-pounder gun for the navy. But naturally neither Marshall & Mills nor the Whitworths allowed him to learn just how they produced their superior metals; he must gain his knowledge by indirection—if at all.[1]

Nevertheless, he did make certain open efforts to gain a general understanding of the Marshall & Mills secret. He talked in London with one of the two partners, Mills, a shrewd practical mechanic who seemed to him rather ignorant and limited in his views. He had hit on his formula by trial and error. Though reticent, he told Hewitt a few facts—that he bought pig-iron, puddled it, then broke it up, and himself selected the pieces to be remelted for gun-barrels. He also said that two and a half tons of pig entered his works for every ton of gun-metal that emerged. Hewitt pondered these statements. "My idea is," he wrote his brother Charles a little later,[2] "that he must have discovered that pig-iron heated in some peculiar way in the puddling furnace produced a very clear metal, probably identical with very high puddled steel. I think that he is not able to handle all the iron in the furnace so as to produce this grade of metal, either because he is ignorant of the true process or because his pig metal is not thoroughly adapted to it. Hence he is compelled to select the very highest portion, which is done by breaking up the puddled bar so as to show the grain. Having got his raw material clean by nature, and having cleaned off the scale, he next proceeds to temper it down to the welding degree." But here Hewitt was brought to a pause. How did he temper it down for welding?

On June 10, as we have said, he set off for Staffordshire—for Wednesbury, where the Marshall & Mills works lay. At this point we come to a partial mystery. He went to Wednesbury with some

[1] Numerous letters on this English visit are given in Book No. 22, abstracts of Cooper, Hewitt & Co. files; Hewitt Papers.

[2] To Charles Hewitt, October 27, 1862; Hewitt Papers.

essential elements in the making of Marshall iron still eluding him; he came away with most of the secret in his grasp—that much is certain. But just how did he master it? The explanation might lie in money, or in astute detective work about the mill, or in what he could learn by conversing with workmen; it might lie in all three combined. Our most direct evidence is a letter which he wrote his brother Charles before leaving England. In this he speaks of questioning a workingman whom he identifies only as "Hawkins's man." This man told him that the metal was tempered by bushelling it on an ordinary cinder bottom. Hewitt believed that this might be erroneous—that it might be tempered in an ordinary sinking charcoal fire; and he wrote Charles that he felt sure at any rate that the sinking-fire process would succeed even if the bushelling method proved a failure. It is clear that "Hawkins's man" did not give him very much help—that he had to have supplementary information. How did he get it? Nearly thirty years later he was reported in a newspaper interview as saying: "I entered an iron foundry in disguise, learned how iron for gun-barrels was made, telegraphed the information to our Secretary of War, and in twelve days the United States Government was making gun-barrels." But there was no time for disguise, no discoverable telegram was sent the Secretary, and the "twelve days" is absurd.

The fairest clue to what happened is offered by family tradition. Hewitt told his children that before leaving London he had sounded Marshall & Mills on much larger shipments to America, found them chilly, and warned them that he would get the secret if he could. In Wednesbury he went to one of the pubs, and during several evenings became well acquainted with some of the honest, hard-headed workingmen who frequented it. They at first refused to answer his questions. But he told them of his father's boyhood in Cannock hard by; he explained the issues of the war; and one evening he mounted the bar and made a set speech which he thought the very best of his life. He eloquently described the great issues at stake— the fate of slavery, the survival or destruction of the Union, the vindication or abasement of democracy in the sight of the world. This part of England was already for the North. The men knew that the British working classes, struggling against entrenched aristocracy and privilege, had a heavy stake in the conflict. Two of them—one a Scotsman—declared that if he would prove that he had tried to buy Marshall & Mills iron in large quantities and failed, they would tell him the secret. He had the proofs in his pocket, and they thereupon furnished the information. Such, at least, is the family tradition.[1]

One part of the rather complex formula was curious. "While puddling," they told him, "we take a wooden bar and stir it in the molten metal. The charcoal gives the required amount of carbon."

At any rate, he left Wednesbury with nearly all, though not quite all, of the information he wanted; he boarded ship at Liverpool with an exultant confidence that he could quickly storm the last secrets of good gun-metal. Back in New York at the beginning of July, he at once set the experimenters at Trenton to work on his new suggestions. His brother Charles was in charge, and was promised a new house if he succeeded. A protracted series of trials followed, and slowly grew more and more promising. During August the mills began turning out a gun-metal made according to Hewitt's formula for what he called "decarbonized puddled steel" and though an army expert, Major Hagner, condemned the process, he was certain it was right. The barrels were given severe tests at Springfield, and word shortly came that they were better than any previous lot.

Difficulties were still encountered. No British formula could be of more than limited service, for great adaptations had to be made to American ores and working conditions. On September 4, after a visit to the Springfield Armory, Hewitt sent new instructions to Charles. Victory was now within their grasp. In Trenton a few days later Hewitt found that an inspector sent by Major Hagner had just tested the latest specimens of metal and was very nearly satisfied. On September 9 he wrote Assistant-Secretary Watson in jubilation, saying he was now certain that he could meet all the demands of the War Department.

His success had come in the nick of time. The War Department had just decided to send him to Europe again to obtain much larger supplies of Marshall iron. He had made preliminary preparations for sailing. The trip seemed necessary because the English firm continued to take an arrogant attitude with regard to government contracts. "Marshall & Mills," Hewitt shortly wrote Major Dyer of the Springfield Arsenal,[2] "have not yet replied to our letters in regard

[1] Erskine Hewitt to author.
[2] October 7, 1862; Hewitt Papers.

to an additional supply of iron, for the reason that Mr. Marshall
has been getting married and is away on his wedding tour. A friend
of ours has, however, seen Mills, who told him that the U. S. Government desired to procure an additional supply which would neces-
sitate the erection of new works, and that he would only consent to
put up such works on receiving an order for 5,000 tons, delivered
at the rate of 20 tons per week for five years; that he would require
an advance of £5 or £6 per ton on the whole quantity to bind the
contract and enable him to erect the works, and that the price must
be greater than the present rate, as he had to inspect every piece,
and was getting old and was already rich enough for his desires."
Hewitt's orders for the trip were now cancelled, and Cooper, Hewitt
& Cô. received instead a letter from Secretary Stanton:[1]

Gentlemen:

This Department deems it highly important to procure a supply of gun-barrel iron of American manufacture possessing the
essential qualities of sufficient tenacity, evenness of texture, easy
welding, the proper hardness and density, in as high a degree as
the Marshall iron, now imported from England, and hitherto
used exclusively at the National Armory. You state that you
have ascertained that you can produce at your manufactory in
New Jersey an adequate supply of barrel iron, which possesses
the above-named essential requisites, only wanting the ornamental qualities of freedom from specks and high silvery lustre
which characterize the Marshall iron, and you offer to manufacture and sell to the United States 2,000 tons of such iron of the
standard shape and size now in use at the National Armory, at
eight cents a pound, delivered in New York. I hereby request
you to make 2,000 tons of iron of the quality before mentioned,
and deliver the same as far as the public service may require, it
being understood that you are not to receive any pay for any iron
not fully equal to the standard of quality before described, nor
for any excess of waste or defective iron beyond the proportion
which has resulted in working the Marshall iron. It is further
understood that if you shall succeed in producing any portion
of the 2,000 tons of iron with the essential qualities before named,
and in addition as free from specks and as high in silvery lustre,
and capable of as fine finish as the Marshall iron, for such portion

---

[1] September 10, 1862; Hewitt Papers.

of the 2,000 tons you shall receive the same price as paid for the Marshall iron.

The object of this Department in giving this order is to hold out to you as a known responsible party with great experience, enterprise, science, and means, an adequate inducement to undertake the production, if possible, of a domestic supply in sufficient quantity of a quality of iron indispensable to the public service, so as to render this country independent of the supply from abroad, which at any moment might be interrupted.

Very respectfully, your obedient servant,

Edwin M. Stanton.

The War Department at the same time informed Major Dyer of the new arrangement. Assistant Secretary Watson wrote him that on learning of Hewitt's proposed return to Europe, Stanton had called the ironmaster to Washington. The two had discussed the problem fully, and Stanton had decided to transfer his orders from Marshall & Mills to the Trenton firm. "If a supply of iron can be had in this country which is equal in all essential particulars to the Marshall iron, and inferior only in freedom from specks and a high silvery lustre when polished," Watson enjoined Dyer, "we may well dispense with these mere ornamental qualities for the sake of rendering independent of foreign nations for the supply of an article so important as gun-barrel iron." He concluded with a compliment to Hewitt's firm that was particularly gratifying because it was purely spontaneous. "The Secretary of War is the more desirous that a full trial should now be made of the Trenton iron because he is convinced that the daily increasing experience of Cooper, Hewitt & Co., their liberal expenditure of means, and the enterprise, science, and skill which they command, stimulated by their high public spirit and patriotism, will soon overcome every obstacle to the production of American gun-barrel iron of a quality equal, if not superior, to any now made by any foreign nation."

Hewitt, grateful for this first order of two thousand tons, knew that others would follow it. But he never expected to make large profits on the manufacture of gun-metal. In the effort to produce an effective iron for rifles he had disarranged half of the Trenton establishment for almost two years. He subsequently estimated that he had spent about $250,000 in the venture. While this is doubtless excessive, if we add to the direct cost of his experiment the loss which resulted from the reduced production of rails, beams, and wire, the total sum must have been large; and as government contracts practically ended with the war, the net profits on the whole undertaking were inconsiderable. Doubtless he would have felt uncomfortable had he pocketed large gains from a process wrenched, in part, from the trade secrets of a foreign competitor; he knew that war alone could justify his action. A little later Marshall & Mills sent him a letter of reproach and expostulation; and for once in his life he replied evasively. But he was proud to have employed the best iron manufactory of the country in such telling service to the Union. "Fully appreciating the difficulties of the task," he wrote Secretary Stanton on September 15, "and deeply sensible of the confidence reposed in us . . . , we shall devote whatever of skill, energy, and resources we may possess to the undertaking, in which we expect to be able to report a successful issue at an early day."

Indeed, there was now no question of success. It was virtually attained. A few small troubles remained to be cleared up. In coping with them, the Trenton mills were assisted by additional information upon the Marshall & Mills formula which reached Hewitt from England in December.[1] Of its origin we know only that it came "by the *Scotia* in a letter from Mr. Benzon." The next month Hewitt received a laconic telegraph from Major Dyer: "Tell Charles Hewitt to build his house. Success certain." The new Trenton metal proved even better than that from abroad.[2]

These were days of flame and shock. When Hewitt received his contract from Stanton the armies of Lee and McClellan were about to grapple bloodily at Antietam; Lincoln was about to read his Cabinet the draft of the Emancipation Proclamation. The workers in the mills were as patriotically engaged as the soldiers in the

[1] It reached him December 20; the full formula may be found in Book No. 24, transcript of Cooper, Hewitt & Co. files; Hewitt Papers.

[2] Secretary Stanton wrote in 1863: "The efforts made during the war to extend and improve the manufacture of arms and munitions have resulted in discoveries of great importance to the country in peace as well as in war. Among the arts thus improved is the manufacture of wrought iron, now rivalling the finest qualities of the iron of Sweden, Norway, and England, so highly prized in the arts. This country, until the present year, has relied upon those countries for material to make gun-barrels, bridle-bits, car-wheel tires, and other articles requiring iron of finest quality. The iron of our own production is now superior to that obtained abroad for all these purposes." *Annual Report*, December 5, 1863, pp. 10, 11.

ranks. The thick black smoke rolling from the chimneys at Trenton, the flames that spat into the night from the blast furnaces at Phillipsburg, the clank and hammering of shops and forges now running at full speed with three thousand men, were one response to the crash of gunfire and the tramp of armies on Southern battle-fields. Hewitt had won his victory as much as any officer on the battlefield. His feat in making the mortar-beds was a mere spectacular incident. He long remembered it because of the sleepless nights which that crisis had cost him, and because it had brought him into contact with Lincoln. But as he began to supply the armories with the first large quantities of fine gun-metal yet produced in the United States, he performed a far larger service for the country. The best piece a soldier could carry was soon termed the Trenton-Springfield rifle. Before Gettysburg was fought he was able to write an arms manufacturer: "We are making gun-barrels for the armory at Springfield and for nearly all the private contractors." The troops who pushed south under Grant and Sherman bore Hewitt's metal in their hands.

CHAPTER XII

Big Guns and Armor

WHILE Hewitt was thus devoting his best energies to the manufacture of a really good American gun-metal, he was giving no little attention to certain of our naval needs. He was one of the growing number of Americans who realized that while our guns and armor were good enough to fight the Confederacy, they would fare badly in an encounter with Great Britain and France. In this field he accomplished a good deal less than in helping to equip our troops. Nor did it greatly matter; by skill and luck our navy achieved a brilliant record with second-rate equipment, and it was not called upon to encounter European armaments. But the history of his efforts throws a corrective light upon some of the frequent misstatements regarding the immense strength of our Civil War Navy.

In March, 1862, while Hewitt was preparing for his trip to England, the dramatic sortie of the *Virginia* (formerly the *Merrimac*) first awakened most Americans to the fact that a revolution had occurred in warship design. The Confederates had taken possession of this 40-gun frigate at the Norfolk navy-yard, cut her down to the water's edge, placed on the hull a casemate covered with four-inch iron plates, and fastened an iron ram to her prow. On March 8, 1862, the ship, which embodied every one of the five great naval revolutions of the century—steam power, shell guns, screw propeller, rifled ordnance, and armor[1]—moved into Hampton Roads and began a wholesale demolition of the Federal blockading squadron, whose shots were as ineffective as pebbles. At nightfall she

[1] A thorough treatment of the rise of the new navies, and of the position in which American fleets were left by the rapid development of British and French ironclads, is given by James Phinney Baxter in *Introduction of the Ironclad Warship* (1933).

retired, but everyone knew she would be back the next morning to complete her work.

The news of this blow struck consternation to the Federal Government. No one at the North knew the real weaknesses of the *Virginia*—that she drew twenty-two feet, that her engines were wretchedly poor, that her best speed in calm waters was only five knots, that she steered so badly that it took thirty to forty minutes to turn her great length, that she had a green crew; everyone thought of her as both invulnerable and efficient. A Cabinet meeting called by Lincoln was pervaded by the deepest gloom. "The *Merrimac*," solemnly declared Stanton, "will change the whole character of the war; she will destroy seriatim every naval vessel; she will lay all the cities on the seaboard under contribution. I shall immediately recall Burnside; Port Royal must be abandoned. I will notify the governors and municipal authorities in the North to take instant measures to protect their harbors." His alarm was shared by the whole War Department.[1]

Early on March 9 Hewitt was called to the door at 9 Lexington Avenue by his neighbor Henry B. Renwick, one of the most noted engineers and architects of the country. Renwick bore a telegram which he had just received and which has never before been published:

> War Department, March 9, 1862.
> Henry B. Renwick, Esq.,
> 21 Fifth Avenue, New York
>   The *Merrimac*, an armor-clad vessel belonging to the rebels, issued from Norfolk yesterday, and captured several of the United States blockading vessels, and threatens to sweep our whole flotilla from Chesapeake Bay. Under the circumstances it is of the last importance to capture or destroy the *Merrimac*, and the whole wealth and power of the United States will be at command for that purpose. As this movement was anticipated and the subject of a discussion between you and myself last December, you have no doubt thought of various modes by which it could be met and overcome most promptly. The Secretary of War desires you to quietly call a meeting of from three to nine persons, at your discretion, of the best judgment in naval engineering and warfare, to meet immediately at your father's house or some other convenient and suitable place, and to sit as a com-

[1] See *Diary of Gideon Welles*, I, 61-67.

mittee to devise the best plan of speedily accomplishing the capture or destruction of the *Merrimac*. I would suggest the name of Abram S. Hewitt as a member of the committee. You will bear in mind that every hour's delay to destroy the *Merrimac* may result in incalculable damage to the United States, and that the plan or plans for her destruction shall be submitted at the earliest hour practicable for the approval of this department, to the end that their execution may not be unnecessarily delayed a moment. To enable you to communicate hourly with this Department, the telegraphic company is directed to transmit all messages from you at the expense of the Government.

Acknowledge this dispatch the moment you receive it. Spare no pains or expense to get the committee together immediately. Act with the utmost energy. You and each member of the committee will consider this whole matter confidential.

> P. H. Watson,
> Asst. Sec. of War.

Hewitt hurried into an overcoat and in half an hour he, Renwick, and several other leading citizens were conferring at the house of Mayor George Opdyke. Fuller particulars were now available. The frigate *Cumberland* had been sunk with many of her crew, the *Congress* had been set afire and destroyed, and the *Minnesota* had been helplessly driven aground. The discussion centred upon two questions: first, how to destroy the Confederate iron clad, and second, how to save New York City if she came up the coast. Upon the first question the verdict was unanimous. All hope depended upon Captain John Ericsson's little *Monitor*, which, after being launched in Brooklyn on January 30 and commissioned on February 25, had started in tow of the tugboat *Seth Low* for Hampton Roads on March 6. Hewitt knew all about this strange craft, for he had furnished iron rails, specially bevelled, for its armor. This was done by contract with Griswold & Winslow of Troy, N. Y., who were associated with Ericsson and C. S. Bushnell as partners in constructing it. There seemed a chance that the *Monitor* might check the Confederate warship.

For saving New York if the *Virginia* came north, many had the panicky idea that the best hope lay in blocking the Narrows by sinking loaded coal barges. Nobody knew how much time was left. Stanton had said at the Cabinet meeting early that day that he felt no doubt the monster was already on her way to Washington;

and looking out of the window toward the Potomac had despondently remarked, "Not unlikely, we shall have a shell or cannonball from one of her guns in the White House before we leave this room." New Yorkers felt an equal fear that she was on her way north. Messengers hurried through the wintry streets, barges were collected, and preparations made for the temporary ruin of New York harbor! But while the city leaders were busiest, a telegram arrived from Washington. The *Monitor* had reached Hampton Roads the previous night, had confronted the *Virginia* at dawn like David facing Goliath, and in an all-morning battle had fought her to a standstill. In effect it was a victory, for the *Monitor* had proved the faster, more manageable, and less vulnerable.

Henceforth our wooden ships were as obsolete for the new conditions of naval warfare as Jefferson's gunboats. Had the Confederacy not been virtually without a navy (the *Virginia* was blown up in May, when Norfolk was abandoned, and other projected ironclads could not be built in time), the United States might have rued deeply this sudden obsolescence of its entire fleet. Even so, it behooved the naval authorities to lose no time in applying to our warships the newest discoveries in armor, ordnance, and naval design. Hewitt, the year before, had pondered the possibility of manufacturing armor plate at Trenton, and this had been one of the reasons why he had thought of imitating Krupp and making crucible steel upon a large scale. It was for this purpose that he had experimented with the addition of tungsten to iron ore.

Congress and the Navy Department were somewhat less indifferent to ironclad warships than has often been supposed. Two besides the *Monitor* were being built, and the Bureau of Construction and Repair had proposed building twenty more. Even before the duel of the *Merrimac* and *Monitor* the Senate Naval Committee had reported in favor of appropriating $500,000 for a forge and rolling-mill at the Washington Navy Yard to furnish heavy iron plates for warships. Hewitt had immediately protested to Senator Thompson of New York, arguing that it would be ruinous to private enterprise if the government went into the iron business, and that it would be cheaper to order armor from responsible steelmakers; at most, he thought the government should merely erect its own armor-plate mill as an adjunct to some large private ironworks. Actually the government did nothing at all. But discussion continued in Washington and among ironmakers, and armor and heavy guns were much in Hewitt's mind when he went to England in March, 1862.

Secretary Welles had asked him to ascertain why European naval authorities covered their new warships with heavy one-layer plating instead of several thin plates bolted together. Hewitt inspected the principal British armor-plate mills—the John Brown & Company works, the Park Gate works, and the Thomas Works, all at Sheffield; while he talked at Birkenhead and Portsmouth with shipbuilders and naval officers. The armoring of warships was still a novelty even in Europe. During the Crimean War both the British and French had sent some floating ironclad batteries to the Black Sea. In 1859 the French had converted a wooden frigate of 5600 tons on the stocks into a battleship armored from prow to stern with 4¾ inches of iron, making the name *La Gloire* forever famous. A year later the British had launched the *Warrior*, a 9200-ton ship with its centre armored by 4½ inches of iron, but the bow and stern unprotected. After these first great experiments progress was rapid.

France, with six seagoing ironclads built or building, began work on ten more in the fall of 1860. In Great Britain three ironclads immediately followed the *Warrior*, one, the *Black Prince*, being a sister-ship. In 1862 eleven more armored ships were ordered, five being converted from wooden ships on the stocks, and six built entirely new. Hewitt found them all under way when he arrived the next spring, and realized that they could easily blow the American navy out of the water. Three, the *Minotaur, Agincourt,* and *Northumberland*, were being encased from end to end with steel (not iron) armor five and a half inches thick, and weighed 10,690 tons each. The clumsy *Merrimac* weighed only 3500 tons, and had seemed a giant compared with the tiny *Monitor*! Moreover, these British vessels were thoroughly seaworthy, while neither of the first two American ironclads was safe in a gale; the *Monitor* actually sank in a storm off Cape Hatteras in December, 1862.

And while the American naval heads still favored the use of thin plates riveted together, British experts had developed a superior technique in armor manufacture. When Hewitt explained Secretary Welles's hesitation between solid plates and "built-up" plates, the officers at Portsmouth threw up their hands. They explained that the British and French Governments, after elaborate experiments, had abandoned the idea of using anything but solid plates, and that the numerous ships under way for the two governments were all so armored. Warships on the stocks for Russia, Spain, Italy, Austria, and Belgium were likewise being covered with solid plating 4½ to 5½ inches thick. Admiral Gray showed Hewitt several targets at Portsmouth. Whitworth and Armstrong rifled guns at 200 yards had put heavy shots squarely through eight inches of "built-up" armor every time, but had merely dented and cracked the 4½ inch plates of solid armor, without penetration. Obviously, our Navy Department was in danger of a costly mistake.

The best British works impressed Hewitt. Government inspection was severe. Since it was impossible to produce good armor by hammering and rolling separately, the two operations had been combined, the hammer being used freely in the preparatory stages with the rolls, and the plates being finished in the rolls exclusively. Only the three Sheffield establishments just named had machinery for this combined process. Altogether, Hewitt became convinced that the making of good armor was a much more complex, delicate, and difficult operation than the authorities in Washington yet realized; and he also concluded, as he read European newspapers and listened to European talk, that it was high time the United States took steps to protect itself.

"I fear that the importance of this matter is underrated," he wrote Secretary Welles immediately after landing.[1] "During my visit in England I mingled with all classes from the lowest to the highest, and with a few honorable exceptions, I found no sincere friends of the American Union. If not positively hostile there is a selfish indifference in the public mind which bodes no good to us, if accident or design should give rise to a serious disagreement between the two nations. Immediate and adequate preparation is the best way to avoid the dangers of a warlike collision, and in nothing are we so deficient as in iron-plated ships; for I can assure you that the vessels built up of riveted layers would be pierced by every fair and square shot from the British 68-pound guns."

The proposals of his formal report were radical and far-reaching. He had gone to England bitterly opposed to the government fabri-

---

[1] July 10, 1862; Hewitt Papers.

cation of armor. Before leaving he had rashly expressed his readiness to contract with the Navy Department for the manufacture of satisfactory armor plates on an advance of only $250,000 for the necessary machinery. But he now saw that his views on government manufacture and his offer had alike been founded upon ignorance of the actual requirements; he was certain that the only way to obtain an immediate supply of good armor-plate was to establish a government mill under the best experts procurable, and equally certain that the cost would be much higher than he had supposed. A complete plant would require nearly or quite a million dollars. The leading British works, those of John Brown & Company, had spent £180,000 for facilities to produce sixteen steel plates daily, each 3½ feet wide, 15 feet long, and 5 inches thick; and any American mill ought to have a similar capacity.

How could the Navy Department provide a quick and satisfactory supply of armor? The government, declared Hewitt, ought to meet the emergency by taking over one of the great iron plants on or near our seaboard; one of those in Boston, Troy, Trenton, or Phoenixville, Pa. Here they would obtain not only the equipment for supplying iron or steel plates, but seasoned workmen and expert managers. "So far as our own works are concerned," he wrote, "I am quite sure that it has cost more to educate the managers and men than the entire outlay on the works themselves." In his opinion, almost any of the major establishments—the Bay State works, the Phoenix Iron Company, the works of Griswold & Winslow at Troy, where excellent crucible steel was made—could be brought or leased. But the government should make a cautious selection. The best pig-iron and coal must be available at cheap rates. The workmen must possess long experience in the fabrication of heavy iron or steel pieces. The works should be readily accessible to the navy yards of New York and Philadelphia, and yet far enough from the sea to lie beyond the reach of foreign fleets.

Clearly, the Trenton works best fitted Hewitt's description. They were the largest in the country and the most efficiently managed, had quick communication with the Atlantic ports, were close to ore and anthracite, and for years had been making heavy rails and beams, so that the employees could easily turn to heavy plates. Hewitt proposed to Secretary Welles that the government take over the Trenton mills at once. As he pointed out, he stood to lose by this sequestration of a mill which was in highly profitable operation; "but in my judgment all private interests should in this crisis yield to the public welfare." He believed that the owners would give up the mills "either for an annual rent, or sell them at cost, or at a valuation of impartial referees, or upon any terms which the Department should deem right under the circumstances." Moreover, he and Edward Cooper would cheerfully furnish their services without pay.

But Welles refused to take such action. Our government was not averse to commandeering private property for the prosecution of the war, and it actually ran a rolling-mill at Chattanooga. The sum Hewitt had mentioned as the cost of complete armor-plate works, a million dollars, was but a drop in the bucket of war costs. For another year the danger of war with England and France remained grave. In the summer of 1863 Minister Adams was making persistent but at first fruitless efforts to get the British Government to detain two powerful armored rams, superior to any American warships, which were nearing completion for the Confederacy at Birkenhead; and on September 5, 1863, he sent Earl Russell his famous ultimatum: "It would be superfluous in me to point out to your lordship that this is war." Had war occurred—even had the two rams escaped—our lack of properly armored seagoing vessels might have had the most disastrous consequences. But Secretary Welles was content with a programme by which, in the summer of 1862, we had twenty-seven coast-defence ironclads under construction, and he paid little attention to the need for a strong cruising fleet. We did not have such a fleet or really good armor till a generation later. In fact, in 1866 a French officer found that we had only two seagoing ironclads.

During 1862-63 Hewitt repeatedly urged the government to keep the United States up to the mark in heavy artillery, a subject into which he had also inquired while in England. The United States has done well in the invention of modern light-calibre weapons; the Gardner, Lowell, Hotchkiss, and Maxim guns, and the best magazine rifles, are all of American origin. Dr. Richard Gatling of Indiana patented his famous light field-gun in 1862, though it was given no actual service of importance until the Franco-Prussian War. But in heavy artillery the story is different. At this period the United States, still largely dependent on old-fashioned smooth-bore cannon of cast iron, had fallen far behind Europe in rifled guns; and Hewitt felt that the deficiency might prove as costly as our lack of good armor.

During the autumn of 1862 he pointed out to the War and Navy Departments that the only really fine gun in the country was the Whitworth steel rifle which he had ordered for the navy in Sheffield, and suggested that he be given an experimental contract for ordnance made from his new gun-barrel iron. He thought that he could make guns as good as either Armstrong or Whitworth in England. Within a short time he was writing the authorities at Washington in more emphatic terms. On March 13, 1863 for example, he impressed upon Gustavus Fox, the Assistant Secretary of the Navy, three facts:

First. In a war with England or France we are in a defenceless condition, because we have no guns which can penetrate their ironclads, and our ironclads are so constructed that they cannot resist the shots from the improved ordnance now in general use in Europe.

Second. This improved ordnance is produced by the use of wrought iron and steel in lieu of cast iron for heavy guns, and the reason for the superiority of their ironclads is to be found in the use of $4\frac{1}{2}$ to $5\frac{1}{2}$ solid plates in lieu of layers of one-inch plates melted together. When we have used the heavy $4\frac{1}{2}$-inch plates the quality is inferior, and hence such vessels as the *Ironsides* and *Roanoke* would be no match for the *Warrior* and *La Gloire*.

Third. The ability to use wrought iron and steel for ordnance depends upon the possession of hammers to work them properly into the required form. We have no hammers in this country of sufficient weight for this purpose, and there is no use for such hammers in the peaceful arts. These tools must therefore be provided by the Government . . .

To trifle with this question is mere folly. We are today at the mercy of England and France, or either of them, and the ruling classes hate us and desire our destruction. If the danger is appreciated at Washington I have not been able to see the evidence of it, and I feel relieved to think that there is one man who is willing to listen.

And six weeks later he sent the following letter to Assistant Secretary Watson of the War Department:

In accordance with your request I now submit for official action the substance of my examinations in regard to the purchase and production of heavy guns. . . .

1. Whatever may be the merit and advantages of our 12″ and 15″ wrought cast iron guns, I believe it to be conceded that they cannot safely be loaded with a charge of quick-burning powder proportioned to the weight of the missile which they discharge. As the effective range of guns is pretty nearly proportioned to the charge of the powder, it is evident that a gun which is loaded with 50 lbs. of powder will be able to do effective work at a greater distance than one which burns only half the charge. This perhaps will explain some of the phenomena of the attack of Charleston. The rifled guns of the rebels, although of smaller calibre, were really more effective than our 12″ and 15″ guns. But whether the 12″ and 15″ guns be better for attack or not, we need heavy guns for defence, and to oppose a gun that can pierce an iron plate at a distance of 800 yards, we must have a gun that will do the same thing, or else the English and French ironclads with wrought iron and steel 10″ guns can enter our harbors, attack and destroy our forts with impunity at a safe range, and then destroy our cities. . . .

2. The experience of England, France, and Germany during the last three years has demonstrated that 10″ guns can be made of steel and of iron which can be safely fired with fifty pounds of quick-burning powder, 1,000 rounds or more, without bursting, and that the destructive power of these guns far exceeds all the old ideas on the subject, and that shells can be pierced through 5½ inches of solid (not built-up) iron plates at a distance of 800 yards. There is considerable controversy as to the best form of guns.

3. These improved guns are now being made in considerable numbers in Europe, and Whitworth has completed arrangements by which he will be able to make a largely increased product of 7″ and 11″ guns. If these guns are not secured to us, the Rebels will get them. By buying these guns we disarm the Rebels.

4. In addition to buying guns, it is the plain duty of the government, first, to decide what is the best mode of building steel guns; and secondly, to make arrangements for their production in this country, for it will not do to be dependent on foreign countries for a supply of ordnance and munitions of war, on which the safety of the country may rest.

He recommended that an investigating commission, to include Major Dyer of the Springfield Armory, be sent to Europe, and offered to serve on it without recompense.

Through the competitive activity of Europeans a revolution had, in fact, taken place in the design of ordnance. While our army and navy for the most part continued the use of smooth-bore cast-iron guns of 12, 15, and even 20 inches, new guns of wrought-iron and steel, rifled to send projectiles at far higher velocities, were being made abroad. The British had used rifled guns at Sebastopol, and a few years later had adopted the Armstrong breech-loading rifle. Sir William Armstrong had been the first to manufacture successfully a "built-up" gun of wrought-iron coils shrunk over one another in such a fashion as to give great strength. Krupp, who was furnishing rifles to half of Europe, bored a solid piece of steel.[1] Sir Joseph Whitworth manufactured heavy guns by forcing massive layers of steel tubing over a central cylinder by intense hydraulic pressure. Nor were the French far behind. It seemed absurd for the United States to remain content with old-fashioned ordnance simply because the Confederacy had nothing better.

Our armed forces in the spring of 1863, the darkest hour of the war, just after Burnside's bloody disaster at Fredericksburg and just before Hooker's defeat at Chancellorsville, had plenty of heavy artillery. But our 12 and 15-inch smooth-bores were far inferior to England's 7-inch Armstrong steel rifles. They could not safely be loaded with a quick-burning powder proportionate to the weight of their projectiles. The result was that either their fire fell short, or they burst and killed their crews. Moreover, their accuracy was low. It was for these reasons that at the naval attack on Charleston, as Hewitt wrote, the small rifled guns of the Confederates proved

[1] Hewitt learned in England in 1862 that Krupp had made at Essen several hundred steel cannon of various calibres for the French, Belgian, and Prussian governments. The largest was of 10½ inches bore. It had been forged from a solid ingot of cast steel under a sixty-ton hammer, and Hewitt did not believe that it could be burst by any charge of powder whatever. He urged the government to buy at least one Krupp gun of the largest calibre, and an English steam-hammer of at least 25 tons weight. "There is no possible chance," he wrote Assistant-Secretary Fox, "of our being on an equality with Great Britain or France until we substitute either cast steel or wrought iron for our cast-iron ordnance in all cases where high charges of powder are required . . . I think it is a national shame that we are doing so little to improve our ordnance." March 12, 1863; Hewitt Papers.

deadlier than the biggest cast-iron pieces of the Union warships. Our coast-defence forts, he believed, would be helpless against the 11-inch rifles of the British and French navies, which could be fired with remarkable precision and rapidity, and which had tremendous velocity and penetration.

He continued to urge the government to face the problem and to call the attention of the Navy Department in especial to its errors. When the Ordnance Bureau requested proposals for wrought-iron guns of 100-pounder calibre, he disgustedly wrote Assistant Secretary Fox that a good gun of that size simply could not be made in the United States until a much larger steam-hammer was built or imported. He urged the Department to place somebody who understood the properties and manufacture of iron in a position where he could prevent the use of poor materials in our ordnance; for neglect of this precaution had ruined the Wiard guns. He wrote Fox again that "it would relieve my anxiety if I could see proper tools at work in this country turning out such guns as now daily reinforce the armaments of England and the continental nations of Europe." He forwarded Secretary Welles letters from the chief British gun-makers—Firth, Whitworth, and Vickers. He argued that the Navy Department should at least import a supply of rough steel forgings, and a heavy steam hammer. He even made tentative arrangements, hoping for Welles's approval, to import a set of Whitworth tools for rifling cannon.[1]

But in July, 1863, Gettysburg and Vicksburg dispelled the menace of European intervention, and the Navy Department ceased to worry about European guns or armor—if it had ever really worried. It had doubtless been wise after all. If Britain and France had declared war our navy would have been hopelessly inferior anyway; no amount of emergency effort could have saved us from retreating within our coast defences and seeing the Southern blockade lifted; and under the circumstances it was best to save our money and trust to luck. The North had better ships and guns than the South, and that was enough. Napoleon III and Lord Palmerston would not be frightened off by a mere armor-plate mill and steam-hammer, and the important object was to keep up the plain old-fashioned slugging below Mason and Dixon's line. Hewitt did induce the War Department to send 70,000 pounds of his

[1] Hewitt to Major Dyer, October 7, 1862; Hewitt Papers.

gun-metal to the Danvers Works in 1864 to be made into a twenty-one-foot gun; but the piece was never finished.[1] As for the navy, it did not pay serious attention to modern rifled ordnance until the brilliant William C. Whitney became Secretary twenty years later.

Meanwhile the Trenton mills, pushed to capacity with gun-metal and other contracts, had become indispensable to the government. In March, 1863, they were producing ten tons of the metal daily, and the head of the Springfield Armory declared it unsurpassed abroad. As the British gun-metal had cost about ten cents a pound in gold delivered at Springfield, Hewitt charged an equal sum. In October, 1863, the government order on the English manufacturers was completely cancelled. Late that year the head of the Ordnance Bureau approved a contract for 3,000 additional tons of gun-metal, making 5,000 long tons in all.[2] Both the Watertown and Springfield armories now bought all or nearly all their iron from Trenton. It was shipped for the most part in bundles of "gun-flats," though the mills supplied private makers with welded barrels. Large consignments were also being sent to the Spencer Repeating Rifle Company, Alfred Jenks & Sons, the Remington Works, and others. Since ten pounds of iron made one barrel, 5,000 long tons meant not fewer than 1,000,000 rifles and muskets. When we consider the large shipments to private companies, we can see how much the Cooper, Hewitt establishment did to supply the army.

Yet the chief profits were in other branches of its work. In 1864 it was making iron for gun-sockets, gun-carriages, and entrenching-tools, and selling the government rails, wires, and pig-iron. After its losses at the beginning of the war, the company exhibited steadily improving returns; yet its war profits were far from bloated. The books show that for the last half of 1863 they were $45,427; for the first half of 1864, $223,571; and for the second half of 1864, $235,000. In a summary of operations for the directors on June 30, 1864, Hewitt wrote that the manufacture of gun-metal had been of far more advantage to the country than to the mills.[3]

[1] Hewitt to General D. Ramsey, February 8, 1864; Hewitt Papers.
[2] Hewitt to H. A. Whittaker, December 11, 1865; Hewitt Papers.
[3] It was a heavy business risk that Hewitt took in turning to gun-metal. The costs of new equipment and of disarranging half the mill were formidable. The head of the Ordnance Bureau suggested that he might now charge enough for his gun-metal to make up the loss. Hewitt refused. "But," he added, "if I could

"It has been found extremely difficult to produce a grade of iron which will uniformly stand the inspection for cleanliness in force at the United States Armories. There has been no difficulty in producing iron of sufficient strength, but the rejections for lack of cleanliness have thus far been far too great to admit of any profit in this branch of the business." He believed, however, that the company had gained some valuable experience.

When Lee surrendered, Hewitt could feel that the iron mills had done their part in sustaining the government. Years later his son Erskine hung in the house at Ringwood a statement which Secretary Stanton had written on War Department stationery. "It is the purpose of this Department," it ran,[1] "to acknowledge and place in its archives a memorial of all loyal and patriotic services that may be rendered to the country as well in the workshop and manufactory as upon the field. To that end the patriotic services of Cooper, Hewitt & Company of New York are publicly acknowledged. On the sudden call of the Department, and at no small sacrifice of their own interests, the energies of their establishment were devoted to the construction of mortar-carriages for the Western gunboats, which, completed within a time unexampled in mechanical history, enabled the government to shell the rebels in their stronghold at Fort Donelson. They and the mechanics in their employment have well served their country." Beside this letter might be placed a speech which Assistant Secretary Watson made at Ashtabula, O., on September 23, 1876, paying tribute to the company for its provision of gun-metal.[2] In supplying this, said Watson, "they stopped other highly remunerative work, thereby sacrificing hundreds of thousands of dollars," and performed a service of the greatest moment. In this service, he added, the essential factor was "the matchless executive skill of Abram S. Hewitt, who organized and directed the work."

consistently with my sense of right to the public have got enough money to have made good the actual loss to the Trenton Iron Company, you cannot appreciate the load of anxiety which would have been removed from my shoulders. The past year has been most painful to me, because by my action in this gun-barrel business the interests of my associates have suffered." While the company evidently did make a profit in the end, it was modest. Hewitt to head of Ordnance Bureau, November 10, 1863; Hewitt Papers.

[1] This testimonial is still at Ringwood.

[2] This speech, published in pamphlet form as a campaign document in 1876, is in numerous libraries.

CHAPTER XIII

The Coming of Open-Hearth Steel

WHEN the Civil War closed, and Americans could look soberly about them once more, the whole world was in a state of rapid fermentation and change. Within half a dozen years after Appomattox occurred the unification of Germany, the liberation of Italy, the confederation of Canada; the Suez Canal was completed, the first American transcontinental railroad was built, and, as Stanley found Livingstone, the rapid opening up of Africa began. Men beheld the passage of the second great reform bill in England, the downfall of the Second Empire in France, the completion of Reconstruction in America. Unprecedented aggregations of capital were arising. But among these varied changes, political and economic, we are probably safe in asserting that one was of transcendent importance to all Western society. The age of iron was just fully giving way to the age of steel, and no modern revolution has been more momentous or far-reaching.

The production of iron and steel, but particularly steel, was now multiplied again and again, prodigiously stimulating machine labor and machine transportation, and cheapening the cost of living the world over. At first this was largely the work of the Bessemer process, still in its pristine success in the sixties; but within a few years the open-hearth process was overtaking it. Far larger establishments, with far costlier and better machinery, sprang up in Europe and America to exploit both of the new processes. They were fed by new stores of ore in Lorraine, in Spain, in Africa, and above all in the very heart of North America, where beds rich beyond any previous dreams of mankind were laid bare west of Lake Superior. The steel rail, making possible heavy steel locomotives, fast expresses, and huge freight trains, covered half the globe. It was swiftly followed by the steel ship, and that even more swiftly by the steel skyscraper. Within a generation the British leadership in iron and steel was first disputed and then overthrown by America. In this country, the tidewater production of these metals was swept into insignificance by the development of huge mills in the Pittsburgh district and along the Great Lakes.

Nobody just after the war divined better than Hewitt the nature of the great changes then impending. Realizing that the Southern Appalachians would become the seat of a rich iron industry, he headed a Northern group which bought the rolling mill that John Fritz had built for the government at Chattanooga. He resumed his arguments with Peter Cooper for a piecemeal removal of the Trenton works to the westward, but without success. In various public utterances he sketched in bold terms the future lying before iron and steel. Between 1865 and 1870 he repeatedly declared that America would soon wrest the leadership in production from Great Britain. In 1876, making the presidential address to the American Institute of Mining Engineers,[1] he pointed out that the consumption of iron had risen in England to 200 pounds, in America to 150 pounds, and in the whole world to 30 pounds a head. "It is not possible," he said, "to convey a more striking idea of the progress of the world." He predicted that the next seventeen years would double the annual production of iron, bringing it to 28,000,-000 tons a year; "and I feel quite safe in asserting that the beginning of the twentieth century, which some among you may hope to see, will witness an annual production of over 40,000,000 tons."

He himself lived to see the new century, and to find that in 1900 the United States, Great Britain, and Germany alone were producing more than 50,000,000 long tons of iron and steel.

In this same address he also explained why America would soon outstrip England. The supply of raw material and labor in Great Britain was limited; in the United States, population was increasing by bounds, and our natural resources seemed almost illimitable. The modern world would continue hungry for supplies of iron and

---

[1] Hewitt was elected head of the Institute, a position previously held by David Thomas, Rossiter W. Raymond, and Alexander L. Holley, because the Centennial Exposition had brought many eminent visitors to America and he was desired to receive them. His address was published as a pamphlet, "A Century of Mining and Metallurgy in the United States."

steel, and the American mills would inevitably become exporters on a large scale. He felt little doubt that before the close of the century the United States would be manufacturing fifteen million tons of iron and steel, and in order to do this would be producing forty million tons of iron ore and a hundred million tons of coal annually. This would require an investment of not less than a half billion dollars, and more probably a billion. "New York is already the financial centre of the American continent, and is destined to be the main distributor of capital for the world. This vast sum of money will, therefore, be drawn from the accumulations of capital controlled in New York." These statements were received with natural incredulity. Yet the United States actually outdistanced Great Britain by 1890 instead of 1900; and in the latter year it was making almost twenty-four million long tons of iron and steel instead of the fifteen million which he had predicted. It was then making, in fact, not far from twice as much as the United Kingdom.

Hewitt likewise prophesied the coming supremacy of steel. Indeed, by 1865 it was evident to far duller perceptions than his that steel would build the coming world. He realized that iron rails, iron machine-parts, and even iron girders were becoming anachronisms. He knew that ore in the Marquette district of the Michigan peninsula, brought through the Soo Canal, was free from excessive phosphorus and thus admirably fitted for the Bessemer process. He had read of the rush of European ironmasters to adopt the process; and he was aware that a Bessemer all-steel rail laid in 1862 in the Camden freight-yards of the London & Northwestern Railroad had lasted on and on while iron rails beside it were repeatedly replaced. He knew that in 1865 the Lehigh Valley Railroad imported some Bessemer rails from England.[1] He learned in 1866 that the holders of Bessemer's American patents—Winslow, Griswold, & Holley, who had a small experimental plant at Troy, N. Y.—had pooled their rights with the holders of William Kelly's patents,[2] and that the road was therefore clear for the rapid application of both in the United States.

[1] John Fritz, *Autobiography*, 152.

[2] This was under the leadership of Alexander L. Holley, who, like Hewitt, had gone to England during the war to study materials for armaments, and had become a friend of Bessemer. He obtained the exclusive right to Bessemer's process in the United States, and on his return built a Bessemer converter at the Albany Iron Works in Troy. But the Kelly rights, with which a group of

Though Hewitt remained interested in steel, his scheme for manufacturing it had encountered various impediments. One was the
concentration upon wrought iron which necessarily accompanied
his partial conversion of the mill into a gun-metal manufactory.
During 1862-63 Edward Cooper and he made changes in order to
utilize tough varieties of iron in many ways—for wrought iron
beams, locomotive tires, merchant-bar iron, braziers' rods, wire rods,
and wire. By the close of 1863 the company had four steam hammers at work. Hewitt took marked pride in some of his new products. "If we succeed in producing locomotive tires equal in quality
to the best Yorkshire tires," he wrote, "we shall have taken another
and profitable step in the emancipation of this country from its
dependence on Great Britain." Thus for a time little attention was
paid to rails.

Another impediment lay in the failure of the Andover mine and
the continued difficulty of getting iron out of Ringwood. In the
emergency new sources of ore had to be found. During the war the
Hibernia, Allen, Hurd, and Lindsley mines, all in New Jersey, had
been leased to supplement the Dell and Roseville beds. On April
2, 1864, the famous Durham Iron Works in Bucks County, Pa., just
across the Delaware River southeast of Phillipsburg, including
mines and blast furnaces, were purchased. This was another historic site, for as early as 1726, when it was owned by William
Penn's secretary, James Logan, a company had been formed to
erect ironworks there.[1] The latest owner had built two large blast
furnaces, but Cooper & Hewitt were interested primarily in the
mines. During the fiscal year 1864-65 the Trenton company required
more than 50,000 tons of ore, and of this only 5,000 tons came from
the old Andover pits. The Hibernia mine furnished approximately
15,000 tons, the Dell 10,000, and Ringwood 5,000, while the remainder came from various sources. This dependence upon new

---

American capitalists had joined the Mushet rights, stood in his way. Burton J.
Hendrick, *Life of Andrew Carnegie*, I, 164-169. A biography of Alexander Holley
is much needed.

[1] The Durham Works lay in the exceptionally beautiful Durham Valley,
bounded by high hills, and intersecting the Delaware near some of its finest
cliffs. For the history of the district and its mines, see Herbert C. Bell, *Durham
Township* (1887), and B. F. Fackenthal, *The Durham Iron Works* (1922), two
scholarly pamphlets. The latter contains sketches of Edward Cooper and Abram
S. Hewitt.

and largely untested material greatly hampered any experimentation. Moreover, the Ringwood ore proved full of phosphorus; Hewitt wrote that "when we charge more than one-quarter of Ringwood iron we get bad iron."

Nevertheless, experiments were made. In the fall of 1864 Hewitt made blooms from the Ringwood pig-iron in the refining fires, and sent them to Trenton to be tested. Other blooms were made by thrusting the pig-iron directly into the forge fires. Both, but especially the latter, proved well adapted to those methods of steelmaking which depended upon a careful mixture at high temperatures of malleable iron and carbonized iron. "We believe that they are the best stock yet made in this country for steel," Hewitt wrote on February 11, 1865, "but we may be mistaken." An increasing number of ironmasters were now manufacturing small quantities of steel according to the plan known in England for years as the Mushet-Heath process; that is, by fusing wrought iron and special types of carbonized iron in a furnace. Ringwood blooms, rich in carbon, could be sold to such manufacturers. Hewitt, writing Thomas S. Blair of Pittsburgh about the hard times that temporarily followed the end of the war, recommended them for not only the Mushet-Heath but the Bessemer furnaces.[1]

But while selling these carbonizing blooms, the Trenton Company itself also began making steel. Steel manufacture in these years was like a mountain stream which, fed near its source by innumerable tributaries, becomes at once a rushing river. In every nation, but particularly in Great Britain, Germany, and the United States, new formulae were being tried, new methods devised, and new improvements on old methods introduced. Some used the original Bessemer principle, some the Bessemer-Mushet principle; some a method founded on Heath's fusion of malleable and carbonized iron, patented as long before as 1845; some the Krupp process; some a puddling process; and so on endlessly. Alexander L. Holley, after bringing about the Bessemer-Kelly combination, was undertaking numerous improvements of his own in the construction and arrangement of blast furnaces and machinery. In Great Britain G. J. Snelus was making the trials which led within a few years, in 1872, to his patent for the use of lime or limestone as a lining for the converter, the foundation of the "basic" process, and another

[1] April 11, 1865; Hewitt Papers.

epochal step forward. In England Siemens, and in France the Martin brothers, were busy with far-reaching innovations. Bessemer looms up as the greatest figure among those who unlocked the gates of the new steel age, but a hundred other men, some scarcely less important, stood beside him.

I

Hewitt in 1865-66, during the brief business recession which preceded the great post-war boom, thought of making steel both at Trenton and in the South. Many years later he wrote Adolph S. Ochs of his plans at this period. "I may be pardoned," he stated,[1] "for recalling the fact that I was the purchaser of the rolling-mill at Chattanooga from the government at the close of the war, and put it in operation for the purpose of showing that the iron business could be successfully carried on in the Southern States. From the outset I was aware of the difficulty in the way of making steel due to the presence of phosphorus in your ores, and hence I watched the progress of the basic process with the greatest possible interest, and so long ago as 1862 I was aware of the experiments made by Mr. Snelus which served to show that lime could be used to neutralize phosphorus in pig-iron. Messrs. Thomas and Gilchrist, however, first made a successful application of this principle, and I had always intended if the works had remained under my control to establish the manufacture of basic steel at Chattanooga." Unfortunately it proved impossible to carry out his plans either at Chattanooga or on the site of Birmingham, where he had owned a tract since 1859. He soon found it necessary to confine himself to Trenton, and at Trenton began making steel in quantity.

The method used was an adaptation of the Mushet-Heath process; that is, a fusion of wrought iron and special Ringwood blooms rich in carbon, effected in a high-temperature furnace. The details have been lost. We do not know the proportions of metal used or the exact nature of the furnace. We do know that by the beginning of 1866 steel in small quantities but of high quality was being produced, and that Hewitt relied upon it and his gun-metal as the two pillars of the business.

Proud of the gun-metal, he found an increasing number of uses for it, the most interesting being the locomotive tires already men-

[1] February 27, 1891; Hewitt Papers.

tioned. "We have driven every pound of English iron out of the armories," he wrote on December 11, 1865, "and even the Norway iron heretofore used for the component parts of the locks has been superseded by our iron. We use the same quality and the same process of manufacture for the tires as we employ for gun-barrels, and we shall probably name the material gun-metal. It is dense and hard but of such strength that the barrels never burst under powder-proof." Tires made for the Long Island Railroad were, after five months of hard use, as good as new and "as clean as silver." But he became even prouder of the Trenton steel.

There was a peal of elation in his announcement to customers early in 1866. "We have succeeded in making steel-headed rails," he wrote Ashbel Welch on March 1. "They have the great advantage over Bessemer or cast-steel rails in that, when worn out, they can be re-rolled, and also that they cost one-half more than iron rails, instead of double." By steel-headed he of course meant steel-topped. He assured another customer that the rails were more uniform in quality than Bessemer rails, and cost but $135 a ton (in greenbacks) as against $170 charged for all-steel Bessemer rails. "The saving thus made is sufficient, out of the interest, to re-roll the steel-headed rails forever, whereas when the Bessemer rail is worn out, a new set of rails must be got at the original high cost." Cheapness was important, for iron and steel prices during and just after the war were very high.

Orders for steel-topped rails soon began to pour in. The first important lot went to J. Edgar Thomson, president of the Pennsylvania Railroad, for trial. Beginning in 1866 considerable quantities were purchased by the New York Central, Illinois Central, and other lines. By the autumn of 1869 the Trenton Iron Company was rolling rails at the rate of 24,000 tons a year. The price had then been brought down to $100 a ton, at which the company made $10 a ton profit. Though a long list of railroads had gradually become customers, the Erie, dominated by Jay Gould, was then the largest single purchaser. To an ironmaster of Middlebow-on-Tees, England, who doubted whether a good weld could be obtained between the steel and iron, Hewitt wrote that his rails—"we use both puddled steel and Siemens-Martin steel"—were completely successful.[1]

[1] To Edward Williams, October 27, 1869; Hewitt Papers.

Steel-topped rails were to prove a mere temporary bridge from the iron rail to the all-steel rail; but they were a useful bridge, and the Trenton mills attained an easy leadership in their American manufacture. Indeed, they became one of the principal manufacturers of this peculiar product in the world, for the similar rails from England and Westphalia were not so good. Users of the Trenton rails bore testimony to their durability, cheapness, and safety. Various historians have written as though the all-steel rail made a swift and easy conquest of our important railroads after the war, but in reality the part-steel rails were an important factor in the situation. When, in 1866, an American named Hart applied for a patent on the steel-topping process, Hewitt and his brother Charles easily proved that they had been the first to employ it.

But the most important feat of these years was Hewitt's adoption—as the letter above notes—of the Siemens-Martin process. The equipping of the Trenton mills to turn out 2,000 tons of steel-topped rails monthly was not the work of a few weeks or months; it was effected only by much labor and inquiry; and though Cooper & Hewitt were never to be important steelmakers, his introduction of the Siemens-Martin or open-hearth method was of great service to others. The European industry, led by Bessemer, Heath, Krupp, Siemens, and the Martin brothers, had pushed far in advance of the American industry; in this transaction of 1867-68 Hewitt assisted the United States to catch up.

The general plan of the open-hearth furnace for steel-making had been laid down by Josiah Marshall Heath under the before-mentioned patent of 1845. His apparatus bore certain resemblances to the puddling furnace devised long before. This puddling furnace was essentially a reverberatory furnace with a firebox at one end, a chimney at the other, and between them a basin or "hearth" for pig-iron. The fierce flame in the firebox, roaring past the molten pigs to escape by the chimney, heated them into an incandescent liquid which boiled on the "hearth." In this liquid the puddler stirred iron oxide with a long hook or "rabble." The object was to oxidize the carbon, silicon, and phosphorus in the molten pig-iron, and when this had been done the result was either wrought-iron or steel, according to controllable circumstances. The puddler, as the carbon and other impurities burned away, gradually molded the metal into balls of seventy or eighty pounds, which were later worked up under a steam hammer. Heath's rudimentary form of the open-hearth furnace added new principles to this general scheme of the puddling furnace. Once more a reverberatory furnace was built. Once more it had a shallow basin-like bottom or "hearth," made of dolomite or other heat-resisting material. Once more a flame roared from a firebox over the metal materials on the hearth, and out the chimney. But Heath did not puddle the molten metal or stir oxide into it.

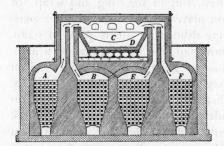

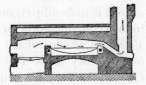

Open-hearth furnace. *A*, *B*, Air and gas heated by passing over hot bricks. *C*, Steel in process of making. *D*, Hearth lining. *E*, *F*, Bricks heated by gaseous products. These are later made inlets to warm the entering air and gas.

Reverberatory furnace.

His patent provided for placing pig-iron in the hearth of the roaring furnace—preferably first melting this pig-iron in a separate cupola; then introducing malleable iron (instead of iron oxide) into the molten pig-iron in such fashion that, melting as it gradually pushed forward, it fused with the carbonized pig-iron; and maintaining a fierce heat for hours, till the impurities were burned out and steel resulted. Unfortunately, Heath did not know how to furnish the intense heat required; but the subsequent invention of the regenerative furnace made this easy. Later inventors also found that excellent results could be obtained by charging the furnace, along with the fuel and pig-iron, with waste pieces of steel and wrought-iron—that is, "scrap"—and with iron ore.

The conversion of metal into steel, in the perfected open-hearth process, was effected by two parallel steps. In the first place, the impurities, such as carbon, silicon, and phosphorus, were burned out of the raw materials by the heat of the furnace, aided by the

oxygen and carbon in the iron-ore and pig-iron. This oxidation of
the foreign elements was slow. In the Bessemer process they were
burnt out by a terrific blast lasting but a few minutes and passing
through the pig-iron. In the open-hearth process hours were consumed while the flames passed *over* the materials. The second step
in reducing the foreign elements lay in "diluting" them with scrap
steel and wrought iron. In the "pig and ore" process devised by
Siemens little reliance was placed upon dilution, and oxidation
was almost exclusively employed. But in the "pig and scrap" or
Siemens-Martin process dilution played a much heavier role; sometimes ten parts of pig-iron were diluted by ninety parts of scrap.

Sir William Siemens, a Hanoverian who in 1859 became a naturalized British subject, made his first great contribution to the iron
industry of the world in his regenerative furnace of 1856—that is,
a furnace which utilized the heat of combustion ordinarily lost in
hot chimney gases. For decades one of the sights of the Black
Country in England had been the flames shooting at night from
the furnace tops, far and wide over the district—the flames that
Hewitt noticed on his first visit; but now year by year they faded
away. The first regenerative furnaces used anthracite, but in 1861
a much hotter regenerative gas furnace was placed in operation in
a Birmingham glass factory. Siemens found that the new furnaces
made Heath's principle really effective for steel-making. Then several Frenchmen lent their hands to perfecting the process. Le
Chatêlier took it up; and in 1864 the brothers Martin, at Sireuil,
made the first completely successful open-hearth furnace in the
world. Hewitt was eager to learn of these innovations.

The greatest international exhibition the world had yet seen
was held on the Champs de Mars in Paris in 1867. Here Napoleon
III received Europe with characteristic pomp. His troops had been
turned out of Mexico; he had watched jealously the triumph of
Prussia at Sadowa; across the channel the material and cultural
achievements of Victorian England were as solid and durable as
the pomp of the Second Empire was flimsy and unsubstantial. But
he could still boast the preëminence of France in art and taste; he
could still receive the sovereigns of Europe with glittering military
splendor. A great circular building looking like an enormous
gasometer had been erected. Scattered outside its walls were speci-

mens of every style of modern architecture, from Turkish mosque and Swiss chalet to British lighthouses. Inside the gasometer were arranged some forty-three thousand exhibits. A great outer ring was devoted to machinery; a series of inner rings showed the development of civilization from the old stone age to Napoleon III.

On April 16 Hewitt sailed for Paris as one of the American Commissioners to the exhibition. On arriving he hastened to inspect the great fair; he then went to London to visit friends and transact Atlantic cable business for Peter Cooper. A royal commission was holding an inquiry into labor unions, and at its request he gave testimony on the labor problem in the United States.[1] But his primary attention while abroad was devoted to iron and steel, upon which he wrote an elaborate report for the American Government. To gain material he visited all the great European establishments, made observations, and took notes which he embodied in voluminous letters to Edward Cooper.

His study of the iron and steel section at the Exhibition confirmed his impression that Europe was far ahead of the United States. Both British and Continental manufacturers were grappling with undertakings from which American works would shrink. For example, Petin Gaudet & Co. of France exhibited a wrought-iron beam a foot in width and 32 feet long. They made intermediate sizes in all shapes for buildings. Even more remarkable were the specimens of steel plates. John Brown & Co. of Sheffield had sent over a great slab which weighed twenty tons—thirteen feet long, six feet wide, and thirteen and a half inches thick. The Krupp Works showed a cast steel ingot weighing forty tons; steel locomotive-tires, axles, and boiler-rings of the largest sizes; and a steel crankshaft for a steamer weighing more than nine tons. They also showed the hostile French crowds a breechloading steel rifle of fifty tons, throwing a half-ton shell (1080 lbs.). What seemed to Hewitt still more wonderful, Krupp had a cast-steel rail fifty feet long which had been bent double, cold, in the middle, without a fracture. Borsig, of Berlin, presented a wrought-iron piston, without a weld, of almost 1200 pounds. An English manufacturer exhibited a 281-pound coil of wire, 1590 feet long, rolled from a

[1] This Commission was headed by Sir William Erle; its most active member was Frederic Harrison; and it included Thomas Hughes, with whom Hewitt formed a friendship that lasted as long as Hughes lived.

single billet, and a 200-pound coil, also rolled from a single piece, which was 2,700 feet in length!

When Hewitt began visiting the chief mills and furnaces in Europe his astonishment increased. In England, France, and Germany alike he perceived a science, a skill, and an inventiveness which far outstripped America's. "The more I see and hear," he wrote Edward Cooper from England on July 12, "the more I am satisfied that you ought to come over as soon as I return, and examine all these new things." He wished his partner to inspect the new Bessemer machinery, the Siemens gas-furnace, and the Martin open-hearth process. "They beat us to death in France. They roll one-inch round iron in lengths of 100 feet . . . But I cannot begin to make you see the progress. You must come for yourself."[1]

The size and completeness of the principal works excited his admiration. Krupp's plant at Essen covered 450 acres, employed 10,000 men, and in 1866 had produced some 61,000 tons of cast steel, worth more than $10,000,000. Hewitt wrote of this establishment as "by far the most extensive ever produced by the energy of man," and of Krupp's processes as "the most difficult ever attempted by human ingenuity." At Le Creusôt, the Schneider works covered 300 acres, employed 9,950 men, and turned out annually 240,000 tons of wrought and cast iron, worth about $7,000,000 in gold. In England a number of works approached the capacity of Le Creusôt—some in South Wales, some in the Cleveland region, and others at Sheffield.

But the most eloquent praises of the American visitor were reserved for the quality of the European products. Their best plants made not one variety of iron or steel, but many. At Le Creusôt, for example, seven different grades of merchant bars were sold, each having its own well-recognized market. And European consumers, he found, realized that in general it paid to use a high quality of

[1] Hewitt observed everything with a view to improvements at home. He was much impressed by a furnace—Westman's Furnace—used by the Swedish iron-masters, and ordered a duplicate for Ringwood. After visiting some works in South Wales, he wrote Edward Cooper that puddling was better understood there than anywhere else. "Hence I was very glad to be able to get a copy of a little book by a man named Baylis, who was a practical puddler and is now the manager of a tin works. . . . This book I send you . . . In the same package will be found a cost sheet of the rails made at Swindon by the Great Western Railway Company, which will be valuable on many accounts, but especially as a model for a cost sheet." Hewitt to Cooper, May 18, 1867; Hewitt Papers.

30. The House at Ringwood

31. Mr. Erskine Hewitt, Governor A. Harry Moore of New Jersey, and the old Hammer, Anvil, and Hudson River Chain, 1932

32. Garden at Ringwood: Former Newel Posts of Lafayette Place, known as Colonnade Row

33. Home of Peter Cooper and Abram S. Hewitt at 9 Lexington Avenue before alteration in 1883 from a high stoop to a basement entrance house.

34. Daniel Huntington's Picture of The Atlantic Cable Projectors

35. Mortars for which the carriages were made by Hewitt

36. The Trenton Iron Company just after the Civil War

38. Offices at 17 Burling Slip

37. New Jersey Steel and Iron Company
about 1880

metal. In visiting the gigantic establishments which had grown up in the mountains of Wales, Hewitt was humiliated to find that the vilest trash which could be dignified by the name of iron was called "the American rail." This was because American contractors and railways had for years bought the lowest-priced iron available. The managers of European railroads knew better. They purchased rails guaranteed to last from five to seven years, according to traffic; and for this guarantee they willingly paid from thirty to fifty per cent over ordinary prices. But American users continued their stupid insistence upon cheap iron; and to this cause more than any other, declared Hewitt, was attributable the necessity for almost annual renewals of rails in the United States, with all the consequent financial troubles of the owners.

Everywhere in Europe the Bessemer process was making steady progress. Hewitt gave it little attention in his report, but a brilliant young mechanical engineer whom he employed as assistant, Frederick J. Slade, prepared a supplementary paper on the subject under his direction. They found Bessemer steel being made in all the principal nations; expert chemistry had rendered its quality far more certain than a few years earlier, and it was particularly useful for rails, tires, and plates. In Sweden it was used in making razors, cutlery, hand-mirrors, and other small objects of the highest finish. Even in England Hewitt saw specimens that would meet any test. "It has been spun into ornamental vessels of shapes such as would bring the most severe strain upon the metal without exhibiting any sign of cracking, or bent into the most crucial shapes with equal evidence of its toughness." Before going to Europe he would not have believed that Bessemer metal could equal the best crucible steel; now he saw that it did. He also saw the facilities for its production expanding with enormous rapidity. Already Europe had more converters than it needed, and "contrary to all experience, the inventor and the public at large seem to have profited by its introduction at the expense of the manufacturers." It was making steel too cheap!

Five years later Andrew Carnegie, visiting England, stood awe-struck as he watched the dazzling brilliance of a Bessemer converter in full blast, a sheaf of white fire rising from its mouth, and rushed to the first steamer to transfer his American establishments to the Bessemer system. Hewitt felt differently. He had already taken the first steps toward the open-hearth process in his own works at Trenton. Now, as he looked about Europe, he became convinced that despite all the rapid conquests made by the Bessemer system, the open-hearth was better. In the first place, most of the pig-iron produced in the world was not good enough for the Bessemer furnaces, which required a metal almost completely free from sulphur and phosphorus. Such pig-iron could be made into good steel only by the open-hearth or crucible methods. Again, the usefulness of the Bessemer process was still limited by the uncertain quality of each flow or "cast." No manufacturer could be sure that his product on any particular day was good enough for locomotive tires, rails, or machine-parts unless he made severe tests by the steam punch or other methods. But the quality of open-hearth steel could be rigidly controlled during manufacture, and the mill-superintendent knew without subsequent tests just how much it would endure. Within a few weeks Hewitt felt that he must at all costs lay hold of the American rights to this new process. As early as May 9 he wrote Edward Cooper outlining the lessons the exhibition had already taught him:

1. The thorough roasting of the magnetic ores in Sweden is the main element of the superior quality of the iron. There is a model of Westman's furnace, and Akerman has written to him to have a duplicate made and sent to us. The young Swede engaged by us, Syöberg, also will bring drawings. I consider this furnace indispensable at Ringwood. It is used at Dannemora and at all the works where Bessemer steel is made with success. . . .

2. Swedish pig-iron, and also Styrian pig-iron, made with charcoal from magnetic ores, thoroughly roasted, and in furnaces managed with great care, produce pig-iron so good, that by the Bessemer process steel of the very best quality, fully equal to cast steel, is produced, and used in the highest quality of cutlery, dies, etc. Iron is also produced which makes the finest wire I have ever seen. . . . The apparatus used in Sweden is stationary and cheap, and Syöberg will bring drawings—and I also will send a copy. . . .

3. In rolling wire rods I observe that all the makers here roll the rods to No. 9 before they begin to draw. I am sure that there is room for progress in the United States in this respect.

4. There are many specimens of deep-rolled beams in the

Exposition, made mostly in France. I have not got any price lists yet, but will do so. There are some four feet deep and rolled. . . .

    5. Steel-headed rails are evidently a large business on the Continent. About 9 per cent of the heads come off in one year. The rest stand. They use mostly puddled steel, and do not roll it down as we do. The general impression seems to be, however, that the Bessemer rails are cheaper in the end—my own idea is that for the United States steel-headed rails are the thing, and I have no doubt that if our mill were moved to Chicago, and Lake Superior iron used, we could make a success in this business.

American ironmasters were dilatory in making use of expert metallurgists, partly because experts were rare. Andrew Carnegie boasts in his autobiography[1] that a German chemist employed at his Lucy Furnace in 1870 was the first worker of the kind in the United States, and that his special knowledge found a way to make the cheap Pilot Knob ores of Missouri, long despised though actually very rich, available for the Carnegie mills. But as this letter shows Hewitt sent a Swedish chemist to Ringwood in 1867. Syöberg proved exceedingly useful both there and in Trenton. The Swedish roasting-furnace at Ringwood, the first of its kind in the United States, was employed primarily to roast phosphorus out of the ore.

It will be noted that in this initial letter Hewitt does not speak of the Siemens-Martin process. His eye at first caught nothing connected with it at the Exhibition. In England he observed a number of important innovations. They included various types of steel-headed rails; Enfield rifles with steel barrels; admirable new processes for making wire rods at the works of Hill & Company near Newport; locomotive tires of Bessemer steel, which the foreman of the Blaemar works thought would soon supplant his own puddled-steel tires; and devices for mechanical puddling. Then returning to Paris in June, he paid another visit to the Exhibition. As he walked down the long circle devoted to iron and steel, his attention was caught by some bright ingots marked "Sireuil." He made inquiries and found that it was Martin steel. As a result he wrote Edward Cooper:

    There is a French process, I find, called that of Pierre Martin, who makes steel in the reverberating furnace, from pig-iron, equal to the best cast steel. I have seen the specimens in the Ex-

[1] *Autobiography of Andrew Carnegie*, 182, 183, 223.

hibition but have not yet got a description of the process. It has been in practical operation, however, for over two years, and is said to be carried on on a large scale. I will endeavor to get the facts.

On June 23, in another letter from Paris, he makes his first mention of the Siemens furnace—adding a message to Samuel J. Tilden:

. . . I shall have a good deal to tell you about making steel when I return, but from what I have seen I believe that a ton of steel an hour can be made in a reverberating furnace, direct from pig-iron, and that the quality can be regulated with perfect certainty.

The Siemens furnace is the essential feature in the process. I have not seen it yet, but I expect to do so this week. This is better than Bessemer, and the arrangements far cheaper. Ringwood is the place for this business, and also Lake Superior. Tell Tilden that the manganese ores on the Iron Cliffs property are its most valuable feature.

He resolved immediately to investigate the Siemens-Martin process in detail. At that season a trip to the beautiful department of Saône-et-Loire was a pleasant experience. Here, in a basin rich in coal and iron, nestled Le Creusôt, a town of about twenty thousand people, where Adolphe and Eugène Schneider had established their iron mills in 1816.

Since my last letter I have visited the great works at Creusôt of Schneider & Cie., where there are fifteen blast furnaces and a rolling mill 1400 feet long, of recent and uniform construction, with three high rolls and all the modern improvements. They have not put up the Bessemer apparatus, but have just erected a gas furnace on the Siemens plan, for heating, and one puddling furnace—the object being to use up the fine coal, slack, etc. . . .

Mr. Schneider told me that he now expects to try the Martin process for making steel and homogeneous iron, for which the Siemens furnace is essential. He thinks that the Martin process is a success. It consists in using pig-iron of first-rate quality, melting it down slowly, mixing it with puddled steel, wrought iron, and iron ore at proper stages and in suitable quantities to produce the grade of steel required. The time is six hours, and the quantity produced is six tons, which is one ton per hour. No work is required, and just one man to watch the process and make the charges. There is no doubt that Martin is making one hundred tons per month at his works.

On my return to Paris I arranged with Martin, who is rich and a highly respectable man, to visit his works, but I find that I must travel several hundred miles to do it, and I do not feel well enough. I will therefore arrange for Slade to go there, and stay there long enough to learn how to erect the furnace and conduct the process, so that we can put it up at Trenton. . . .

Today I have made the following arrangement with Martin. We will take out his patent in America at our expense. We will grant licenses to all who may want them, retaining for ourselves the exclusive use of the patent for gun-barrel iron, and any other things for which we will undertake to supply the demand, especially tyres. The royalty is to be the same as the Bessemer royalties, from which is to be deducted the royalty paid for the use of the Siemens furnace. After we are refunded the cost of taking out the patents we are to divide the royalties equally with Martin, we paying our royalty into the common fund, the same as any other parties.

This, added Hewitt, was a fair arrangement. It promised the Martin brothers a large income from America; it gave the Trenton mills control of the only practical method of large-scale steel-making besides the Bessemer method—and in his opinion a better method. "Siemens seems inclined to abandon his crucible process and try this, but I will see him in London and ascertain his views." In fact, the more he thought of the open-hearth process the greater became his enthusiasm. The apparatus was cheaper than the great Bessemer converters; it would produce steel of a definite quality, day after day, and month after month, eliminating rejections for defects; and it would make use of materials that the Bessemer system could not employ. Moreover, the growing accumulation of cut-off ends of Bessemer rails could be used in lieu of the puddled iron required by the process.

It was a happy day for Hewitt when he signed the legal papers, and he wrote Edward Cooper jubilantly on July 8:

I have closed my contract for the Martin process, we agreeing only to take out the patent and divide the royalties. This is subject to the report of Mr. Slade, whom I have requested to go to the works and remain there long enough to satisfy himself. . . .

Meanwhile, the drawings and descriptions are being prepared

to be sent to us. These I have examined. The furnace is a modification of the puddling furnace, but a sand bottom is used. The
gas is generated in a Siemens furnace, which must be used in order
to produce a sufficiently high heat. The process of operation is
simple enough. The very best kind of pig-iron is used, as in the
Bessemer process. It is melted down in the bottom of the furnace,
and is kept there at a high heat for about twenty minutes. To
1200 pounds of melted pig about 150 pounds of puddled steel or
wrought iron in scrap is then added. This soon melts in the bath
of pig-iron, and then another charge of wrought iron is added,
and so on until the regular proportion of carbonization is produced in the mass. . . .

In a final inspection of English works before he sailed, he made
additional observations. At Sheffield he saw a twelve-ton ingot,
made of steel poured from crucibles each containing about fifty
pounds, cast for a Woolwich gun; a beautiful example of precise
and rapid work, for it was indispensable that the metal be poured
continuously into the mold at high temperatures. He was impressed by the economy of large-size furnaces, for these recently
erected in England were bigger than any in the United States, and
a furnace ninety feet high could easily undersell one sixty feet high.
Nearly all the blasts in England were pre-heated to 1300 or 1400
degrees. And, he wrote Edward, "the new rolling mills beat us to
death by the use of hydraulic cranes everywhere to lift and carry
the iron. They do not employ half the men we do for the same
work." The whole tour abroad must have been somewhat painful;
for the European industry was ten years in advance of America.

II

On December 10, 1868, Hewitt sent a triumphant announcement
to Pierre and Emile Martin. "We beg leave," he wrote them, "to
state that we made our first ingot of steel yesterday at Trenton,
and that the furnace worked well in all respects, except that the
bottom was too porous to hold the melted steel well, and a considerable portion of the charge was lost. The quality of the steel,
however, appears to be good, and we are now making a new bottom
of more fusible sand than we used at first. The heat in the furnace
appears to be all that could be desired. We have a demand for all
the steel that the furnace will produce, and as soon as the product

is regular, we shall license other parties who are waiting to see the result of our operations."

It had taken fifteen months to put the Siemens-Martin process into successful operation at Trenton, for many obstacles had been met. To begin with, it had by no means been easy to carry through the necessary agreement with Siemens for the use of his furnace. The patent was controlled in the United States by Tuttle, Garfield, & Company of Boston, and a protracted three-cornered correspondence had to be carried on before the Trenton Iron Company could obtain a license. Finally, in the spring of 1868, Hewitt began to erect two Siemens furnaces, agreeing to pay a royalty of $3 a ton on all steel they turned out. Other furnaces, if needed, could later be added for $5 a ton. But material suitable for the hearths could not be found in America, and bricks and cement were finally brought from Hirwain, Wales. Meanwhile, he had to fortify the Martin patents, for his attorney advised him that as first granted they were not proof against attack in the American courts. He therefore insisted that the Martin brothers petition for a reissue of the patents, and took care that this was effected on grounds which clearly distinguished the Martin process from all others.

Late in 1868 the first shipments of open-hearth steel in the United States were ready; and as 1869 began, Hewitt was prepared not only to make limited quantities himself (the furnaces being small) but to teach other American mill-owners to make it. His *Report on the Production of Iron and Steel in Its Economic and Social Relations* had been published in an edition of 8,000 copies by the government.[1] It discussed not only the iron and steel exhibits in Paris, but the recent advances in metal-working all over Europe; and it helped direct general attention to the experiment he was now making at Trenton. There was great curiosity regarding the Siemens-Martin process, and general gratification when his trial of it succeeded.

During 1869 the successful production continued; the steel turned out at Trenton was excellent, and only one difficulty clouded the

[1] It was also republished in pamphlet form in New York in 1870, together with Hewitt's testimony before the Parliamentary Commission on Labor Unions. Though it contains fewer than a hundred pages, it is one of the most useful works on the nineteenth century development of steel manufacture in print. A number of pages in the report proper deal with the position of labor in England and France.

outlook. This was the annoying slowness of the process. Partly because of the small size of the furnaces, not more than two and a half tons of material could be successfully treated at a heat. In 1869 Hewitt made another flying trip to Europe. While he took time to look through some of the British and German mills, his primary object was to visit France, talk with the men in charge at Sireuil and Le Creusôt, and find out how they worked the process so much more rapidly than he could. John Fritz, a rough Pennsylvania-German genius, the most practical iron-mill superintendent of his day, accompanied him on much of his tour. Hewitt learned just the lessons he needed; for example, he wrote Edward Cooper from Lyons on July 22:

> From Styria we went to Creusôt. Here they are erecting immense Bessemer works. They will be the largest and finest in the world. The pig is made from Algiers ore, which is absolutely free from phosphorus, and makes a stronger steel than the Cumberland hermatite. They have two Martin furnaces at work, and are building four more, making six in all. The process is a perfect success. They run two charges per day regularly in each furnace, of five tons each, so that each furnace produces ten tons and the product is twenty tons per day. The steel is splendid in quality, and there are few or no bad ingots. They are used for rails, and for parts of machinery where the strongest and best material is required. Their success is so great that they do not allow anyone to see the process, but of course I was admitted with Fritz. His last doubt disappeared here, and he is decided in favor of the process, and will put up a furnace as soon as he returns. They make about 75 meltings, that is, nearly 400 tons, without repairing the furnace. The conditions of success are, 1st, a bath of gray pig-iron, containing no phosphorus, and 2nd, wrought iron or steel for the charges, free also from phosphorus. Unless the steel has a fine grain it is rejected, and I want here to give you and Mr. Slade the most emphatic caution not to allow any coarse-grained ingots to be used for rails, as the material will undoubtedly fail. You must have the right quality or nothing. . . .

> We next went to Terre Noire, near St. Etienne, where we saw altogether the most interesting and instructive operations we have yet seen. There are two blast furnaces, making each about 25 tons per day from Algiers ore, of dead gray iron which is tapped into large ladles and transferred directly to the Bessemer

converters, of which there are four in number. The converters make twenty charges per day of $3\frac{1}{2}$ tons each, that is, seventy tons of ingots per day. The ingots are all, or nearly all, good— and the whole process goes on like clockwork, and far more easily than a puddling mill. They make rails only, and the ingots weigh about 500 pounds each.

Alongside are four Martin furnaces, making each seven tons per day, so that the united product is about 100 tons of ingot per day. The Martin ingots look as well and no better than the Bessemer, and the manager told me that he could see no difference in the quality. The Bessemer scrap and rail ends are used for the charges, with a ball of pig-iron made from the Algiers ore. Pieces of rails four and five feet long are melted down without trouble, and the regularity of both the Bessemer and the Martin processes was admirable to see.

In Paris Hewitt once more talked with Pierre Martin and received detailed advice; while on his return he wrote the Schneiders asking if they would not give him equally careful instructions based on their practise at Le Creusôt, and received instructive answers.[1]

By 1870 virtually all the difficulties, many and various, had been conquered. Though the Trenton mills were producing both puddled and open-hearth steel for rails, most railroads preferred the latter. Their principal customer, the Erie Railroad, had contracted to send large quantities of old rails to be re-rolled with steel heads; and early in 1870 some 12,000 tons, or enough for its whole eastern section, had thus been treated. Edward Cooper and Hewitt also searched hard for other customers. During the next few years they supplied the Illinois Central, the Long Island Railroad, the Atlantic & Great Western, the Michigan Central, and minor lines, while they rolled rails for the street railways in New York City after designs made by Hewitt himself. Meanwhile, they still furnished gun-metal to the Federal armories, and remained the principal American manufacturers of wrought-iron beams and girders.

Year by year the centre of the iron and steel trade of the nation moved farther west. Larger and larger establishments were rising to supply the appetite of our hungry industries; the Bessemer process was gaining a firmer and firmer hold. W. W. Durfee and

[1] Constantine Peipers, C. E., published in 1869 an eight-page pamphlet, *Martin's Process of Making Cast Steel,* which remains the best brief treatment of the subject.

Robert W. Hunt were making Bethlehem steel in a small converter at Wyandotte, Mich., in 1864, and Bessemer rails were being rolled in Chicago in 1865.[1] In 1868-69 the redoubtable John Fritz, as superintendent and chief engineer of the Bethlehem Iron Company, built—with many misgivings—our first really large Bessemer steel plant, with four eight-ton converters. Its success at once belied his fears.[2] Bethlehem, Pa., became a great steel centre; so did Johnstown, Pa., where Daniel J. Morrell established the Cambria Works in 1871; and so did Braddock, a dozen miles from Pittsburgh, where in 1872 Carnegie began raising on the banks of the Monongahela the majestic structure of the Edgar Thomson Steel Works.[3] Meanwhile, the Trenton mills remained in the quiet town on the Delaware where they had been planted nearly thirty years earlier. Yet despite the growing disadvantages of their position, Hewitt's vision and energy temporarily enabled them to retain an important place in iron and steel manufacture; and his adoption of the open-hearth process in 1867 was a stroke which many a rival was soon glad to imitate, and which in the end meant more to the American steel industry than the Bessemer process itself.

[1] Cf. Waldemar B. Kaempffert, *Popular History of American Invention*, II, 3-46; James M. Swank, *The Manufacture of Iron in All Ages*; H. N. Casson, *The Romance of Steel: The Story of a Thousand Millionaires*; *Census Reports*, 1870, 1880.

[2] John Fritz, *Autobiography*, 153ff.

[3] Burton J. Hendrick, *Andrew Carnegie*, I, 178-200.

CHAPTER XIV

Expanding Horizons

I AM happy to say that I do not do everything," Hewitt responded in 1864 to an inquiry whether he made railway cars, "but I do a great deal more than is good for me personally." Of his own accord or at the solicitation of others, he was constantly pushing into enterprises which needed his energy but which placed fresh burdens upon an overtaxed body and brain. His letters from 1857 to 1870 are full of complaints of tired nerves, headaches, impaired eyesight, and insomnia. After the panic of 1857 he had been confined to his house for several weeks with nervous exhaustion, writing that he was "too ill even to talk," "able to come to the office for one hour at a time, but any attempt to think results in a nervous headache which it takes twenty-four hours to allay." Though he knew he should retrench, in the decade after the war he entered a multiplicity of fresh undertakings, and advanced to a quasi-public position in New York.

Apart from his natural restlessness and strenuosity, a groping dissatisfaction prompted these activities. He was increasingly discontented with the sphere that business afforded. While he might fairly be called the leading American ironmaster, that did not satisfy him. He wished something else—just what he did not know, but something not connected with moneymaking. The hope of a public career that he had cherished while studying law now revived. As he surveyed the yeasty social life of Reconstruction days, the political corruption, the business dishonesty, the rapid growth of the West, the disorderly recovery of the South, he saw many avenues for service; but for a time he did not know which to choose.

He now helped to supervise fully a dozen businesses. To the iron properties at Trenton, Phillipsburg, and Ringwood had been added the important works at Durham, Pa.; and, though for a time they were operated and partly owned by a manufacturer of iron safes, in 1870 Edward Cooper and he took them over. Here Cooper introduced several valuable inventions, notably the Durham hot-blast stoves which came to be used at many American furnaces. Hewitt remained active in the Morris & Essex Railroad, and was a conscientious director of the Illinois Central till 1872, when he resigned in protest against the sharp business practises of its president, William B. Ogden. Together with Samuel J. Tilden and others he owned the Franklin Coal Company, which operated mines near White Haven, Pa. He was likewise associated with Tilden, William H. Barnum (later Democratic National Chairman), and other capitalists in managing the Iron Cliffs Company, which owned rich iron mines in the Marquette district of Michigan.[1] The ore was smelted here in charcoal furnaces and shipped east through the Soo Canal. Still another venture in which he and Tilden had been partners was the Phoenix Park Coal Company, of which Asa Packer, founder of Lehigh University, was the controlling spirit, but they sold their shares in 1864.[2] In 1863 Edward Cooper and he acquired part-ownership of the Balliet Furnace on the Lehigh River, which shipped pig-iron to Trenton, and they later took full title.

The most interesting of his minor ventures in this busy period was his investment in the principal iron works at Chattanooga, Tenn. When the war closed the government rolling-mill, built here by John Fritz in 1864, was for sale at a low price. Rich beds of fossiliferous red hematite ore lay near Chattanooga, in close proximity to coal that was easily convertible into coke, and to large deposits of limestone. Within a few months after Appomattox, Hewitt organized a New York group which paid the War Department $175,000 for the mill, $25,000 for cars and engines, and nearly $60,000 for old rails; besides subscribing $40,000 more to carry on the business, a total of $300,000. Of this, one-fifth came from

[1] This corporation became one of the constituents of the present Cleveland-Cliffs Iron Company, with mines at Ishpeming and Negaunee, Marquette County, Mich., some twelve or fifteen miles from Lake Superior at Marquette. See the voluminous treatment in Volume I of the *Geological Survey of Michigan* (1873). The author is indebted to Mr. Joseph E. Jopling of the Marquette County (Michigan) Historical Society for additional information.

[2] Cf. Hewitt to Asa Packer, October 10, 1864; Hewitt Papers.

Hewitt's pocket. A former Confederate who owned the land on which the mill had been built soon afterward made a claim for damages, and though the government had guaranteed the company peaceable possession for four years, it generously bought the Southerner out.[1]

Hewitt had several motives in organizing this purchase. He wished, he said, to set Northerners an example of prompt and liberal investment in Southern enterprises to help set the stricken section on its feet. He wished to do something to restore the fraternal feeling which had existed before the war; and he took pains to draw Southerners into the company, prominent among them being President W. B. Johnson of the Georgia Central Railroad. Finally, he believed that the mill would prove profitable—as it did. The Southwestern Iron Company, as the new corporation was first named, sold its large stock of rails on hand at high prices. "The profits," Hewitt wrote, "are larger than we had expected." For several years they remained satisfactory. The Southern railroads had to be rebuilt, and they paid as much as $90 a ton for rails; labor was plentiful, and shipping facilities over the Chattanooga & Louisville were good. General Gustavus W. Smith, a former Confederate officer, was sent to Chattanooga in 1866 as a very efficient general manager. In 1868, with business dull, the corporation was reorganized under the name of the Roane Iron Company, but Hewitt remained the largest single owner. He never had any reason to regret his venture, which paid moderate returns and made his name well known below the Mason and Dixon line.

As Peter Cooper grew old (he was seventy-four when the war ended), he relinquished more and more of his business affairs to his son and son-in-law; so that Hewitt found it necessary to pay much attention even to the glue factory, now more profitable than ever. Early in the war he spent many hours over a plan for a branch factory in England, where Cooper's glue was sold in large quantities, but it came to nothing. On each of his three visits to Europe in the sixties Hewitt transacted business for Peter Cooper relating to the Atlantic cable. In 1865 Cooper & Hewitt, in answer to an insistent demand from English interests, began buying and exporting petroleum, on which they made handsome profits for

[1] Cf. Edmund Kirke, "The Southern Gateway of the Alleghenies," *Harper's Magazine*, April, 1887.

several years. Even as a landowner Hewitt had large responsibilities. Just after the war he owned a half dozen large properties—600 acres near Whitehall, N. J.; 400 near Roseville, N. J.; 700, containing coal, in Sullivan County, Pa.; 640, together with W. H. Osborn, near Urbana, Illinois; 400, together with General McClellan, near Chatsworth, Ill.; and a tract in Iowa. This was in addition to the old farmstead at Haverstraw, which he had acquired, and the great estate at Ringwood. During most of the war he shared Ringwood with one of the leading stockholders in the Trenton property, Edmund H. Miller, but in 1868 he purchased the latter's portion for $100,000.

If we add to these cares his share in the direction of Cooper Union, we can realize why he often felt harassed beyond endurance. He wrote in 1862 that "my health has been in a very precarious condition for months"; in 1863 that "it seems as if my eye were required everywhere, and I am so nearly exhausted in body and mind that I feel more like lying down in the ditch than anything else"; and in 1864 that he was "suffering from nervous prostration." Yet he always seemed ready to accept new burdens and opportunities for service. In the same letter in 1864 in which he spoke of nervous prostration, for example, he expressed willingness to accept a Democratic nomination for State Senator in New Jersey. This was simply because the Senate at Trenton had fallen under the sway of a greedy ring representing the Camden & Amboy, which held a monopolistic grip upon the principal means of transportation in the State and was employing bribery and business blackmail to maintain it. Despite his other cares and his precarious health, he was ready to enter the legislature with the object of breaking down this arrogant monopoly.

In the years just after the war the Trenton properties passed completely into the hands of the Cooper-Hewitt families. This was by a series of steps. In 1865-66 the serious post-war slump cost the Trenton Iron Company heavy losses. A group of the more important directors and stockholders, Samuel J. Tilden, E. H. Miller, and Mark Healey, agreed with Hewitt that it was desirable to relieve the company from the business of rolling iron and confine it to the manufacture of pig-iron. They believed also that it was important to reduce the bonded debt of the company. The deficit for the second half of 1865, as Hewitt wrote Thaddeus Stevens, was about $33,000; it had been necessary to draw upon capital to pay the heavy internal revenue taxes; and if a long depression set in, the business would go down in ruin. Obviously, the proper course was to sell the rolling-mill for enough to pay off most of the bonds, and keep only the more promising half of the business. But it proved impossible to dispose of the mill for anything like its real worth. Thereupon Hewitt, emphasizing the fact that his motives were quite unselfish—that he was indeed making a heavy sacrifice —offered in behalf of the family to buy the rolling-mill at its valuation in the latest inventory. He would pay the $500,000 required, more or less, in bonds and stocks of the company. This would at once wipe out the debt, and leave the company free to make the most of its favorable position for manufacturing pig-iron. Such manufacture had been highly profitable for the past twenty years, and there was every reason to believe that it would remain so.

By action of the board on April 12, 1866, this generous offer was accepted. Hewitt, aided by Peter and Edward Cooper, took sole ownership of the rolling-mill; the Trenton Iron Company remained in possession of the mines, furnaces, and wire mill. A new company, a family possession of which Hewitt was principal owner, was at once incorporated under the name of the New Jersey Steel & Iron Company, the precedence given to steel in the title being significant. Peter Cooper thought that his son-in-law was acting quixotically. He believed that Hewitt was acquiring a white elephant, and that the stocks and bonds they paid over would be a total loss; but he also was willing to make the sacrifice. Several trusted men, including Charles Hewitt, Timothy Abbott, and later F. J. Slade, put their shoulders to the wheel to help make the new corporation a success. And within a short time the steel-headed rails were rendering it moderately profitable.

But the Trenton Iron Company did not long continue an independent establishment. The Cooper and Hewitt families had remained considerable stockholders in it. In May, 1866, James Hall was elected president, and under him the company pursued a fairly prosperous course. But a majority of the stockholders were anxious, in the troubled years after the war, to sell the property. Early in 1867, therefore, Cooper & Hewitt agreed with two-thirds of these stockholders to buy their shares at $70 each, plus an undetermined sum, estimated in advance at $13.33 a share, for the Southern debts owing to the company. Late that summer the remaining stock-holders were notified that they must enter the agreement at once. Before the year closed this company had also become completely a family possession, and Charles Hewitt was elected its president. Thus within two and a half years after the end of the war all the mills, mines, furnaces, and other holdings at Trenton, Phillipsburg, and Ringwood were in the hands of the founders of the business.

It was Hewitt's hope that while they kept the pig-iron business at Phillipsburg and the wire-and-rod mill at Trenton, he might re-move the New Jersey Steel & Iron Company to a far more advan-tageous locality, and there develop the open-hearth process on a scale comparable with that of the great French mills. For a time this hope burned brightly. The minor depression of 1868 made a transfer westward seem more urgent than ever. He argued with Peter Cooper that the rolling-mill simply must be shifted; that it was too far distant from good coke and cheap iron ore. It could never again pay large profits on rail-making unless by some lucky chance abundant new ore-beds of high quality were found in the Schuylkill or Lehigh Valleys; and from his knowledge of the geology of these regions he believed any such discovery impossible. In the spring of 1868 he made a trip to western Pennsylvania and the Central West in search of suitable sites. "Generally I incline to the valley of the Ohio River, somewhere between Wheeling and Cairo," he wrote a friend; but he also gave a careful examination to the southern shores of the Great Lakes as far west as Chicago. He re-turned convinced that a number of good positions were available.

His discontent with Trenton was accentuated by the heavy charges which the Camden & Amboy levied upon freight. Year after year he grumbled over them, as Andrew Carnegie a little later grum-bled at the Pennsylvania for its excessive freight charges out of Pittsburgh. He and Charles Hewitt made indignant personal repre-sentations to the railroad. "Your rates," he wrote the officers in 1868, "make it impossible for us to conduct our business in Trenton in competition with other iron works situated on the Lehigh or the Schuylkill"; for the latter could ship to both New York and Philadelphia more cheaply. The rates on bar iron from Trenton to Jersey City ought not to be more than $1.50 a long ton, and to Amboy more than $1. "Unless something can be done to rectify the injustice under which we have so long suffered," he complained, "we must either close the works or remove them to a locality where business is permitted to live." But the road made few and slight concessions.

If the Cooper-Hewitt families were to remain in the forefront of the iron and steel business of America, a removal westward was really imperative. But there was one insuperable obstacle. Cooper Union was in New York; Peter Cooper, who thought they had money enough, had to remain with his beloved Union; and Mrs. Hewitt had to remain with her father. For that matter, it was important that Hewitt also stay near the Union. The existing business in Trenton could be managed from New York. Had he set up a great new steel business in Pittsburgh or Cleveland, he and his family would have had to make their homes there. As Mrs. Hewitt repeatedly said in later years, Hewitt "sacrificed himself for Mr. Cooper and me." Moreover, he could not have acted independently had he wished (which he emphatically did not), without heavy borrowing. When the mills were hard pressed financially in 1868, only Peter Cooper's generous aid averted serious embarrassments.

Hewitt simply had to make the best of the situation at Trenton; and Edward Cooper and he did so by a variety of expedients, of which the introduction of the open-hearth process was only the foremost. A steady reorganization was carried on during the years 1868-73. By foreclosure of a mortgage, the partial ownership of the Durham works was made complete, and both mines and furnaces there were worked with new energy. The Balliet or Lehigh furnace, near Allentown, was made highly productive. It thus became possible to sell the furnaces at Phillipsburg, which were now out of date. At Ringwood, Hewitt began operating two large furnaces at full capacity, and speeded up the mines; he built four miles of railroad, arranged with the Erie to ship large quantities of pig-iron and ore to Piermont on the Hudson, and in general began using the property on a considerable scale. The charcoal for fuel cost only eight and a half cents a bushel, and pig-iron could be loaded on the cars at $35 a ton, a profitable figure.

I

The demand for steel rails was rising tremendously. Traffic was doubling and trebling as the crops of the now populous West were hauled to the seaboard and merchandise was sent back; locomotives and cars were growing heavier; ordinary iron rails simply could not withstand the wear and tear. "It is now quite evident," Hewitt wrote a London firm in the spring of 1868, "that all our leading lines of railway will lay down either steel rails, or iron rails with steel heads." Later that year he added: "There is plainly going to be a very large business both in steel and iron rails next year, because the promise of the crops is bountiful, every small town wants a railroad, and the wealth of the agricultural classes in ready money is something wonderful. . . . If we had the ordinary motives of business men to secure a share of this business, we can scarcely see a limit to it." His first important contracts were with the Erie Railroad.

Jay Gould and James Fisk, Jr., then respectively the adroitest and the most impudent of American financiers, took control in July, 1868, of this still important trunk line, which Daniel Drew had all but wrecked. For a time Gould showed a sincere desire to rehabilitate it. His first marked success in life had been the reorganization of two little broken-down railways, the Rensselaer & Saratoga and the Rutland & Washington, from which he had realized large profits. Now, between the impulse to rebuild the Erie and the impulse to use it in disreputable stock-market operations, he at first inclined uncertainly to the former. The directorate included some public-spirited men. J. C. Bancroft Davis, later Assistant Secretary of State, was a director in 1867-69, while Dorman B. Eaton, destined to fame as a civil service reformer, served as counsel. For a time men hoped that the courts would evince sufficient integrity to throw out the looters, that honest directors would assume control, and that the line would be saved. The imperative need was for good rails, the roadbed having become appallingly dangerous. Jay Gould turned to the Trenton mills. What useful work he did for the Erie—almost the only useful work of his career —was in conjunction with Hewitt.

The two men had met just after the war. One summer afternoon in 1865 or 1866 Hewitt had travelled to Ringwood by the Erie when the train broke down just below Sloatsburg. The only other passenger in the car was a dark, dapper, shrewd-faced man who introduced himself as Jay Gould. As there was no other place to stay Hewitt took him to Ringwood for the night. While the iron-master would never have asked Jim Fisk to his house, Gould was a gentleman. He chatted interestingly after dinner; he was quiet, carefully dressed, and of cultivated speech. But after he had gone upstairs to bed Mrs. Hewitt gave a shiver of repugnance. "I hope you will have nothing to do with that man, Abram," she cried. "He has a snake's eye and I don't like his feet"—for while conversing Gould kept nervously twisting his feet as Uriah Heep twisted his hands.

But Hewitt did have something to do with Gould. One bright day in 1868 he stepped aboard a special car provided by the Erie. He had been asked to examine the line all the way from Jersey City and Piermont to Dunkirk, on Lake Erie. Accompanied by experienced trackmen, he rolled westward through the pretty scenery of the "southern tier," and at various points halted that he might walk over sections of the track. He was amazed by its wretched condition—rails flaking to bits, sinking into rotten ties, weaving under the wheels. The iron laid in recent years under Drew and Fisk was particularly worthless. There were stretches where cheap rails bought from an Elmira mill only a few months earlier were already breaking down, and every train was in peril of derailment. But Hewitt was also struck by the bright prospects which the road offered any enterprising and honest manager. Southern New York, full of agricultural wealth, Pennsylvania, with its coal, oil, and iron, and the huge Great Lakes trade, promised a rich freight revenue. Already traffic on the line, the most direct and the easiest route between ocean and lakes, was heavy.

Assuming that Gould was honest, he addressed himself earnestly to the new president. Even a double-tracked road might be crowded to capacity if the freight were properly developed, and Gould could then defy the New York Central and Pennsylvania. In coal alone he had "an unlimited business for all time to come." But the poor trackage must first be replaced. "Steel rails offer an obvious remedy, but they cost too much, and even on the main roads in Europe, where the traffic is almost unlimited, they are laid only in small quantities near the stations and other exposed positions. It is a mistake to suppose that the day for iron rails has passed away, unless the supply of iron of *good quality* has also passed away." It had not passed away, for the best wrought iron rails laid by the Erie a dozen years earlier were still giving good service. Gould need only make sure of *good* iron, declared Hewitt—topped with steel; and the best way to do this was to acquire his own mill:

> We have just completed the reconstruction of the Trenton mill, and it is now capable of producing about 1500 tons of rails per month, and our existing orders will all be executed by the first of November, after which the mill can be devoted exclusively to your work. About half the product can be made into steel heads, of which the Martin-Siemens steel could perhaps be one-fourth, and the remainder could be made of puddled steel of the kind we are now producing with so much success. Of the quality of the puddled steel heads, and the certainty of the weld, the enclosed letters will afford the most conclusive evidence. . . .
>
> The result of my careful consideration is as follows: First, that the Erie Railroad Company shall purchase our works at Trenton for the sum of $500,000, payable in bonds, secured by a mortgage on the property, bearing seven per cent interest. . . . Second, the Erie Railroad Company shall at its leisure select a site on the line of its road for the removal of the Trenton machinery, and erect the buildings and put up the furnaces and trains. . . . Third, when the removal is effected, the real estate, including the railroads, water-wheels, and buildings at Trenton, are to revert to us. . . . Fourth, we will run the works at Trenton as your agents, and make the plans and put up the new works without any charge for our personal services.

This was a reasonable offer. It would have given the Erie Railroad one of the best-planned rail mills in the country for only $500,000 plus the cost of new structures and equipment, with skilled workmen, and with temporary use of all the experience of Cooper & Hewitt. But Jay Gould did not wish an iron mill, and did not have the money for one. He insisted on making another arrangement. In October, 1868, the New Jersey Steel & Iron Company signed a contract with him by which it agreed to re-roll, with steel heads, all the rails required by the Erie in the next ten years. The open-hearth process, if successful, was to be used in making the steel. It was also agreed that the Erie Railroad might buy at will one-half of the stock. A price was fixed for the rails which would assure a fair profit. On this basis the mills were set to work, and for more than a year ran at full capacity. The Ringwood, Durham, and Lehigh furnaces produced an ample supply of pig-iron, and F. J. Slade operated the open-hearth furnace at its utmost speed. Not until the winter of 1869-70 did the requirements of the Erie slacken, and then the Illinois Central stepped in with heavy orders.

It is possible that in making this arrangement the designing Gould temporarily hoped to obtain a majority of the shares of the New Jersey Steel & Iron, and to squeeze out Hewitt and Edward Cooper on his own terms. In the spring of 1869 he resumed negotiations for a complete sale, but soon dropped them. Cooper and Hewitt, however, knew that for two reasons they were perfectly safe from Gould's control. They intended to hold a full half of the stock at all costs; and the mills were utterly worthless without the expert management which they supplied. Had he squeezed them out he would have destroyed the only factor which made them valuable. And after all, Gould's larger interests lay elsewhere. During 1867-68 he was carrying on the "Erie War" with Commodore Vanderbilt; the year 1869 saw him engaged in the dastardly operations which culminated in Black Friday. He found it easier— and far more profitable—to deal with men like President Grant than with Hewitt. In 1869 he withdrew entirely.

During this period of close relations with the Erie, Edwin F. Bedell, secretary of the New Jersey Steel & Iron, was accustomed to go every week to "Jim" Fisk's offices to collect payment for rails and transact other business. The offices were in Pike's Opera House on Twenty-third Street, which Fisk owned and managed in his swaggering way, and where he maintained a troupe of brazen beauties. He was "driving the four-in-hand of his riches, packed with courtesans," as William M. Evarts remarked. Bedell, a handsome man, was austere and strait-laced, and one of the pillars of his Methodist congregation. Fisk took delight when he appeared in calling in a bevy of half-clad chorus girls of the Black Crook company. He would offer poor Bedell a ten-day note for $10,000 to kiss one of them; they touseled the unhappy man's hair, poured champagne for him to drink, and snatched the check from his hands, while Fisk roared and the quiet, self-restrained Gould, reclining on a sofa, kicked his heels and chuckled. Finally Bedell told Hewitt that he simply could not go back to the iniquitous place.

Hewitt's willingness to sell the steel mill indicated his realization that the iron industry of the Delaware Valley had entered upon an irretrievable decline. During 1869-70 the open-hearth furnace was inspected by visitors from all parts of the Union. The company was producing 400 to 500 tons of steel-topped rails a week, or more than 20,000 tons a year, part of the steel being open-hearth but most of it puddled. Unfortunately, the small open-hearth furnace, with its capacity of only eight tons at a heat, was uneconomic, and within a few years the Bessemer mills far outstripped such limited production. The cost of the Siemens-Martin metal was much higher than that of Bessemer steel, and so remained until the Englishman Gilchrist and his cousin Gilchrist Thomas perfected the basic open-hearth process.

In or about 1900, President Butler of Columbia University was present at a dinner which Hewitt gave for Andrew Carnegie shortly after the latter had presented $600,000 to Cooper Union. Hewitt fell into a reminiscent mood. He related that following the Civil War he and Edward Cooper had asked Peter Cooper to consent to removing the steel mill westward. Peter Cooper emphatically declined. After giving various reasons connected with the necessity of keeping the family near Cooper Union, he added a clincher: "You young men lose so much money in the iron mill now that it takes all I make from the glue factory to pay your deficits!" The mills stayed where they were. "And," President Butler heard Hewitt, his eyes flashing, remark, "I give you my word, gentlemen, that in the thirty-five years since then the entire net profit of the Trenton mills has not aggregated the $600,000 that Mr. Carnegie has just given to the Union!"

Fastened to the seaboard, Edward Cooper and Hewitt could have installed the Bessemer process at Trenton by transporting the proper ores from Spain and Algiers to mix with their own. Had it not been for the tariff, such ores could have been brought in cheaply as ballast for vessels laden with wine and fruit. He protested vigorously to influential Congressmen against the high duties. "The miners of iron ore," he wrote James Brooks of New York, "among whom we are to be classed, desire no protection, but on the contrary greatly prefer that any foreign ores which can be advantageously mixed with their own ores shall be admitted duty free." But the barrier proved immovable. The iron manufacturing interests to the westward, especially in Pennsylvania, profited heavily by it and

were unwilling to reduce duties a cent. They wished to crush out
the coastal iron and steel mills as the Michigan copper interests,
by a duty on foreign ores, crushed out the tidewater copper plants
in these same years.

And unhappily for the Trenton mill, early in the seventies the
business of welding steel tops to iron rails was completely exhausted. All-steel products became much too cheap. Early in 1872
the Erie decided to lay only all-steel rails thereafter; the Atlantic &
Great Western, the company's next largest customer, had already
done so; and the Illinois Central followed suit. A mere driblet
of orders came from the Long Island Railroad and other lines. It
was necessary to cast about for a substitute business. The company
could have rolled all-steel rails, but this would have meant a costly
outlay for new machinery, and would not have fitted in with the
manufacture of wrought-iron beams and girders, which was too
valuable to drop; while competition with the Bessemer mills was
soon impossible. In the spring of 1872 Hewitt therefore suggested
that the mills begin making car and locomotive axles from puddled
steel and Martin steel. He warned Slade a little testily that "we
must decide on something new, because you will come to next
winter without work unless you look out for it now. Nothing but
my personal influence has saved you this summer, and I cannot do
it again."[1]

Large orders were soon received for these axles, while the sale
of structural beams continued on an extensive scale until the panic
of 1873. But the fact could not be disguised that, in spite of Hewitt's
incessant exertions, in spite of the open-hearth process, the New
Jersey Steel & Iron Company had dropped out of the race—that it
would play but a minor part in supplying the vast quantities of
metal that America needed.

Hewitt continued to look wistfully to the West, and sometimes
even to the South. As he acquired a knowledge of the immense
mineral resources of Alabama and Tennessee, the vision of leadership in a vast industrial development there sometimes rose in his
mind. Some man or men, some day, would make the South the
seat of a magnificent iron trade; why not himself? Now and then
he spoke to others of the aspiration. In 1872, writing to the ironmaster John A. Jones of Middlesbrough, England, he burst out

[1] Hewitt to F. J. Slade, May 1, 1872; Hewitt Papers.

with his vision. "What would you say to making up a party to buy five hundred thousand acres of the coal and iron land you saw in Alabama for the sum of $1,500,000 on credit, at seven per cent interest, from the State of Alabama, and then putting up furnaces enough to meet the interest, extending them from time to time, and selling land when it reaches something like its value? To me it seems the most magnificent estate in the world. Of course, you and I ought to make a good thing out of it. I can get the property at $3 an acre; we ought to sell it for $5 to the company, and then they will have the cheapest and best property in America." But he knew when he wrote these lines that the plan was far too grandiose, too much a Col. Mulberry Sellers scheme, for realization. Alabama did not have the public land, and her hour had not struck.

II

Cut off as he was from industrial leadership, it was natural for Hewitt to turn to a field whose boundaries he had once or twice cautiously approached—the field of politics. It would doubtless be erroneous to say that he made any conscious choice. Some of the greatest decisions of life overcome men like a summer cloud. They find themselves drifting away from one shore and toward another, and before they know it their barks are on a new sea. So it was with Hewitt. In 1873 the great panic reëmphasized the fact that business could no longer consume all his energies. Once more he found it necessary to restrict all his operations. The operations at Trenton, Ringwood, Durham, and Balliet were greatly reduced in scope. Strenuous efforts were made to maintain employment, nearly 2,000 men were kept on the payrolls, and during the next four years a huge mass of surplus iron was simply stored away until markets should reappear. But after the first emergency steps Hewitt found his hands freer than ever before; the mills were running smoothly, while new enterprises were out of the question. He was placed at liberty to enter political life, and at this very moment politics presented itself more attractively than ever before. The Democratic sun, after its long eclipse, began to emerge from the clouds. In wholesome disgust with the abuses of the Grant Administration, and irritation with the hardships of the depression, the voters began in 1873-74 to turn back in hosts to the Democratic Party.

Since the Civil War Hewitt had taken a minor part in the Democratic councils of New York State. He now knew Horatio Seymour fairly well. They had been jointly interested in a business venture, the Fox & Wisconsin Canal, and Seymour had jocularly told him when he entered the undertaking that he had "given up ambition for avarice." With Tilden, the ironmaster had become increasingly intimate. During the war Tilden had bought fifty shares in the Trenton Iron Company, and in 1863 was elected a director. He gave much advice in the management of the company, and became so closely identified with it that he made the principal address in 1865 at memorial services for its secretary, J. W. Pullman. Intellectually he and Hewitt had much in common; both possessed quick and subtle minds, both were widely read, and both were lovers of good talk. Temperamentally they presented a sharp contrast, Tilden being conservative, dilatory, and secretive, while Hewitt was liberal, decisive, and frank; but that fact perhaps increased the attraction between them. They lived on opposite sides of Gramercy Park within three minutes' walk of each other. We find Tilden repeatedly inviting Hewitt to his house—for example, asking him and a friend to "a family dinner," and adding that however unappreciative they might be of good railroad investments, "paying large incomes," he hoped they would share his taste for good wine. Hewitt in return often had Tilden at 9 Lexington Avenue when he entertained distinguished men. It was natural for Seymour and Tilden to draw Hewitt into political affairs.

In the campaign of 1868 Hewitt knew much about the Democratic movements, even though he played no part in them. With Grant certain to be the nominee of the Republicans, the Democrats had perhaps a slender chance to defeat him by nominating either Chief Justice Chase or General Hancock; but they threw it away. "I remember perfectly well," Hewitt wrote later,[1] "the scenes which resulted in Seymour's nomination for President. The night before, Mr. Tilden, John Kelly, Governor Seymour, and myself dined together at the Manhattan Club, and there was a unanimous agreement that Chief Justice Chase was to receive the nomination the next day. None the less the convention was carried off its feet, and Governor Seymour, who was presiding, was nominated in spite of all his efforts to prevent this action. He was greatly distressed, and it required all

[1] Hewitt to George L. Miller, December 8, 1898.

the persuasion of his intimate friends to prevent a refusal of the nomination then and there. His reluctance was slowly overcome."

Many a political discussion Hewitt held with Tilden in the fine panelled dining-room of the latter's Gramercy Park house, over one of the bottles of Johannisberger which Tilden prized, or in his library with its full shelves and beautiful pictures. And when 1871-72 brought the dramatic uprising against the Tweed Ring, he was glad to be one of Tilden's aides in the overthrow of Tammany. Edward Cooper and he lent what help they could. The *Times* published the "secret accounts" of the Ring in July, 1871; Tilden took command of the movement for inquiry and prosecution in early August; and in September a Committee of Seventy was created. Both Edward Cooper and Hewitt were members. Edward Cooper's family always declared that it was he who suggested to Tilden the unearthing in the Broadway Bank of full judicial proof of the frauds, and this is doubtless true. When, in the fall of 1871, a Democratic Reform organization had to be hastily extemporized to fight Tammany at the State Convention, Edward Cooper was the leading agent in raising the ten thousand dollars necessary, and was publicly thanked by Tilden. Hewitt contributed liberally. Next year both men assisted in the establishment of a new and temporarily honest Tammany Hall, of which they became members. While John Kelly and the pugilist John Morrissey made the reformed Hall acceptable to Irish voters, such men as Tilden, Cooper, Hewitt, and Francis Kernan gave it dignity and character.

Tilden's exploit in destroying the Ring earned him the reward of the governorship. Up-State and in the metropolis the reform forces of the party rallied behind him. When the Democrats held their State Convention in 1874 he was nominated with a triumphant shout. Already the eyes of the whole nation were turning toward him as the most impressive figure in Democratic affairs since the death of Stephen A. Douglas. New forces were stirring in the Democratic party, and new men were wanted. It was not hard to predict that Hewitt would be one of these men. The smoke and rumble of the iron mills faded from his active life; they became part of his remembrance of things past; and new scenes opened before him —party conventions, campaign rallies, the hustings, the hall of the House.

CHAPTER XV

Peter Cooper: Embattled Age

DURING these years of multiplying activities, Hewitt and his family continued to occupy, for at least half of each year, the same house with Peter Cooper at 9 Lexington Avenue, a block above Gramercy Park. Across the street, where the Russell Sage Foundation now stands, Edward Cooper built a residence—the first air-cooled house in New York, with an ice-chamber in the basement and cold-air ducts leading above. He had married Cornelia Redmond in 1863, and they soon had young children to play with Hewitt's. For Hewitt's family grew steadily; after the three daughters and one son already mentioned, Edward Ringwood Hewitt was born in 1866, and Erskine Hewitt in 1871. When their father entered Congress in 1874, the six children ranged in age from Amy and Sarah, then nineteen and seventeen respectively, to Erskine, only four. Peter Cooper that same year was eighty-four, but hale and alert as ever. Two such varied households would have been exceptionally lively and interesting even had their members been people of ordinary note. But they were not; their doors were constantly admitting the most distinguished figures of the city; eminent foreign visitors were frequent; and Peter Cooper, his son, and Hewitt talked at the family meals of affairs of far-reaching importance.

The aged philanthropist, now at the height of his fame, was entering upon a third lustrum of his long career. In the first he had made a fortune, in the second he had set up his long-planned educational institution, and now, while carrying it on, he had embarked upon a trenchant crusade in behalf of social, industrial, and political reform. During the war he spoke, wrote, and published with the energy of a young man. He was one of the early advocates of emancipation, addressing arguments on the subject to Lincoln and to Governor Seymour, both issued in pamphlet form. Still a believer, on the ground of his own experience and the theories of Henry C. Carey and Friedrich List, in the protective tariff, he published a number of pamphlets and letters on that subject. He advocated "wise discriminating duties" for the benefit of labor. In 1865, when the misgovernment of New York City became intolerable, he became president of the Citizens' Association, a reform organization which enlisted virtually every business and professional leader in the city. He did much to direct its activities in the next ten years, when it struggled to reduce waste and corruption, to improve sanitation, to make a beginning in housing reform, and to throw off the coils of the Tweed Ring. In the end it was betrayed by its secretary, who sold himself to Tammany and sorely deceived the too-confiding reform leaders in the interests of the Tweed Ring. But, before this betrayal came, Peter Cooper wrote a number of vigorous pamphlets—on the city's need for more "home rule," on the evils of political manipulation of tax-levies, and on the importance of more attention to public health. And while doing all this, he gave more and more time to the discussion of national financial and political questions; above all, to the currency.

At a time when most men think their education over, Peter Cooper really began his. Unable in 1850 to write a letter without ludicrous errors in grammar and spelling, woefully ignorant on many subjects, he trained himself in the next fifteen years to be a remarkably forcible and effective pamphleteer on public questions. He had earlier absorbed the doctrines of Albert Gallatin and Henry C. Carey; he now studied such younger writers as Eleazer Lord, Wendell Phillips, Richard Cobden, and John Stuart Mill. But as he had always insisted on independence in business, so now he insisted on independent thinking and hammered out many of his own ideas. For a rich man, he was singularly successful in avoiding the preconceptions of his own moneyed group. Amid the confusion, waste, and graft of the Gilded Age he stood erect to do battle for the Jeffersonian and Jacksonian principles that he had breathed in with the air of his young manhood. This New York millionaire was able to write a few years after Appomattox: "I consider the persistent class legislation of Congress since the war, a worse despotism than that of Great Britain before the Revolution, because it reduces the laboring classes to periodic distress and starvation, that are worse than any despotism ever was; for monopolizing corporations, whether in the shape of banks or railroads, have no soul."[1]

To New Yorkers he was still chiefly identified with the Union, and to it he always gave most of his time. As he had turned over the glue business to his brother William, so he resigned the iron business to his son and son-in-law. Every day he breakfasted early, and at 9:30 his brougham might be seen near the Seventh Street entrance of the Union. He spent long hours at the office inside, talking with the staff or transacting business. But his chief delight was mingling with the students in the corridors, visiting the third-floor reading room, or slipping into a classroom to hear the instruction. His cheerful, kindly, sagacious face, framed in long white hair, his tall, angular, slightly stooping form clad in black broadcloth, the air cushion like a small life-preserver which he or a servant carried, were familiar to everyone. The old-fashioned stock had given way to a black string tie, but he still wore the four-lensed glasses. He liked to bring visitors to the Union, and took pride in ushering little groups of friends about. He moved so noiselessly that often it was only when his silvery head was seen retreating in the distance that the students knew he had been there; but sometimes he paused to throw out a pithy, moralizing remark. Once he noted how diversely the young women in a drawing-class sketched the same person seen from varying angles. "Such a sight," he told the pupils, "should be a lesson in charity, when we perceive how the same person may look so different to different people."[2]

His mere presence, so simple, benign, and radiant with enthusiasm for the school, was an inspiration to its staff. Sometimes he conducted a great public figure through the doors: the Prince of Wales, later Edward VII, the Empress of Brazil, Count de Lesseps, Dean Stanley, and Thomas Huxley. He seldom missed the free Saturday evening lectures which became a feature of the Cooper Union programme in and after 1868. "Many an eloquent person," writes Thomas Hughes, "when Peter chanced to be a minute or two late,

---

[1] Letter to Representative A. A. Hardenberg, June, 1882. He said repeatedly in these years: "There is fast forming in this country an aristocracy of wealth—the worst form of aristocracy that can curse the prosperity of any country." *Ideas for a Science of Good Government*, 167.

[2] Hughes, *Peter Cooper*, 153-170.

has been astonished at an outburst of unlooked-for applause in the midst of his exordium, due to the usual recognition of the old founder, stealing in, air cushion in hand, and taking his seat quietly on the platform . . . Often, if interested in the subject, he would make a few remarks at the end of the lecture; and, even if bored, would keep an unfailing smile and pleasant word for the lecturer to carry away." He often spoke to students in the great basement hall. These little addresses were naïve in their homiletic quality, and usually contained a quotation from Pope's *Essay on Man*, but, delivered with his characteristically rapt expression, they moved many auditors. He never interfered with the methods of an instructor, never asked a special favor, never requested the suspension of a rule. If he made a suggestion to an instructor, he always added with hasty emphasis: "But on no account do this unless you really think it best."[1]

He was the true head of the Union, and also its informing heart; but because of his age, the gaps in his education, and his natural incapacity for exact and minute attention to business, he needed much assistance in its management. Year after year, decade after decade, Cooper Union was administered by a president (first Cooper and then his son Edward), a treasurer (Wilson G. Hunt), and a secretary (Abram S. Hewitt). Till Peter Cooper's death these men, with John G. Parsons and ex-Mayor Daniel F. Tiemann, made up the board of trustees. In fact, no other trustee save R. Fulton Cutting was chosen until the century ended. But, then as now, the principal executive officer was the secretary.

Cooper Union in the generation after the Civil War was really three institutions in one. It was the first great experiment in adult education in the country. From the beginning its night classes in science, mechanical drawing, art, and technology attracted a large registration. As early as 1867 some 2,000 men and youths were enrolled, and the number grew until by 1888 there were almost 3,100. It was also the first great trade-school for women in America. Its day classes in art and design, telegraphy, photography, shorthand, and other subjects enlisted increasing numbers; more than 200 in 1873, more than 400 by 1888. And finally, the Union was an institution for broad popular culture. For decades, until the construc-

[1] Cf. Mrs. Susan Carter, "Recollections of Peter Cooper," *Century Magazine*, December, 1885.

tion of the New York Public Library, it offered the most attractive reading room and free library in the city, open day and night. A handsomely-designed apartment, 125 feet long and 80 wide, with deep alcoves all along one side, made available some 20,000 well-selected books, some 150 magazines, and more than 400 newspapers. During the seventies more than a thousand visitors came to this room daily; in the eighties the number grew to two thousand. The popular lectures every Saturday night in the "great hall," open to everybody, were well planned. And the same hall was for a half century the most popular centre for public meetings in the city, being available to all, without respect to race, creed, or political tenet, who would pay the modest fee.

It might be added that the Union was also one of our first important experiments in coeducation. The night classes in science drew men and women alike, and Hewitt's own daughters attended them. Not a single complaint was ever heard. "On the contrary," Hewitt testified as early as 1865, "we believe that both sexes are the gainers by learning together. Of course there will be found evil-minded people everywhere, even in churches, but in six years we have not had a single case of scandal in Cooper Union, and we should as soon think of excluding the young men as the young women." The only difficulty encountered throws an interesting light on the period. Hewitt, in 1884, asked the city to restore a detail of police to the Union. The building, he wrote, was used by four or five thousand persons daily, and nearly 500 women came to the day classes in art, telegraphy, and typewriting. "The policemen were originally assigned because well-founded complaints were made that evil-minded men took the opportunity afforded by the privileges of the Institution to make it very uncomfortable for the young ladies, and in many cases gross insults were offered them. It has required the greatest possible watchfulness on the part of the officers to remove this reproach from the civilization of the city, and the trustees know from experience that it is impracticable to carry on the female art school and the reading room without the protection of special policemen."

Of course the institution was not developed without discouragements and false steps. Funds were always meagre. In 1872, for example, though Peter Cooper had provided a cash endowment of $150,-000, receipts were about $37,000 against expenditures of $56,000.

The founder always made up the annual deficit. Hewitt's letters contain numerous efforts to persuade instructors who were worth $3,000 a term to teach for $2,000. During all these years only the two upper floors could be used for instruction, it being necessary to rent the two lower floors for revenue. The hope that wealthy citizens would contribute to the Union was illusive, for till long after Peter Cooper's death the only money came from him and his family. Great ingenuity had to be expended by the trustees upon making every dollar stretch as far as possible.[1]

The curriculum was necessarily the subject of much experimentation. At first the trustees had expected to give emphasis to popular lectures for working people. But they soon found that while these were pleasant, entertaining, and mildly instructive, they did not meet the true need. Thereafter the instruction was carefully systematized, recitations and examinations were required, and disciplinary rules were strictly enforced. By 1866 the night classes for men had been arranged in a five-year technological course, though students were given certificates at the completion of each year. This course began with algebra, geometry, physics, and elementary chemistry, and passed through higher mathematics and mechanical drawing to applied mechanics and analytical chemistry. Graduates of Cooper Union soon took their places with the best-trained mechanical engineers, chemists, and metallurgists of the country, and some won high distinction.

"The night classes in science and art have been a wonderful success," Hewitt wrote Reverdy Johnson when the latter was helping establish Peabody Institute in Baltimore just after the war. "During my recent visit to Europe I have seen nothing equal to them, in any of the institutions for popular instruction."

The main tendency of the school from the beginning was utilitarian. It trained men and women in the practical arts in order to increase their income and usefulness, and lift them in the world. Cultural subjects, except drawing and painting, were of necessity left in the background. Peter Cooper's deed of trust, to be sure, had required that instruction in political and social science should have preëminence over every other branch; and in accordance with

---

[1] Annual Reports, trustees of Cooper Union; these were all written by or under the direction of Hewitt as secretary.

this clause, classes were opened in the late sixties in political economy and sociology. But pupils were few, the teaching was unsuccessful, and such topics were soon left to general lecturers. Hewitt devoted much time to a search for the most authoritative and interesting speakers. For several years he arranged with the Social Science Association, of which the able Henry Villard was secretary, for a number of discourses. He also drew steadily from Columbia, Princeton, and Yale; but as college professors often spoke badly he found it wise to go outside their ranks. In 1878, a typical year, he obtained lectures by Horace White of the *Evening Post*, David A. Wells the economist, J. W. Hyatt the inventor of celluloid, Dorman B. Eaton the civil service reformer, and George Haven Putnam. Two popular lecturers were Francis A. Walker and Dr. Benjamin Silliman. Considering that the Union could in general pay only travelling expenses, this part of its work was maintained at a remarkably high level.

British speakers, too, occasionally appeared. On December 19, 1872, the great cave-like hall was jammed as Hewitt stepped forward to introduce John Tyndall, whom he had persuaded to come from England to give the *Lectures on Light* which Tyndall published in book form in 1873. With his electric light (itself a novelty), his screen to show prismatic hues, his machines for experiments, and his ready, clear, vehement exposition, Tyndall made a deep impression on audiences which were exceptionally representative of the culture and intelligence of the city.

Nothing was nearer to the desire of Peter Cooper, his son Edward, or Hewitt, than the expansion of opportunities for women, still narrowly limited, in the fields of teaching, design, secretarial work, and business. As yet wages were low, hours long, and working conditions usually hard and cheerless, while the opportunities to rise were few. Both the founder and Hewitt felt that Cooper Union could do nothing more useful than help women gain a fairer footing in American industry and business. Whenever a hopeful new occupation appeared, Hewitt sought to furnish training for it. Thus in 1865, after photography had been taught successfully for some years, he added an instructor to teach the coloring of photographs as an additional calling. A year later he approved of perhaps the first systematic course of lectures on culinary art in any American institution. "Your offer," he wrote Professor P. Blot, who volunteered his services,[1] "was fully discussed, and although it is rather a novel idea to include cooking under the head of 'social and political science,' the trustees agree with you that it is a social art, and accept with thanks your offer to deliver free of charge a course of lectures on the subject in the great hall of Cooper Institute." Every year the Union boasted of the large sums earned by women in the classes of drawing and design.

Beginning in 1869-70, the Union maintained a free school for teaching young women telegraphy. At first it was highly successful; during the first four years it sent out 307 operators. But after a decade the trustees found that railroads preferred men, and that despite the helpful policy of the Western Union they were supplying more telegraphers than could find places. The school of wood engraving also encountered a glutted market. It was necessary to open other fields of employment. When Christopher Sholes invented the typewriter early in the seventies, Peter Cooper had been quick to see its possibilities. Typewriting was light and easy, it would soon be indispensable in business offices, and it should emancipate thousands of women from household drudgery. A typist was hired at the Burling Slip office in 1879—Peter, always fearful of women, putting her into a room with glass walls! He told his associates that "if life and strength can last till I get a typewriting class started here in the building, I shall be very glad." Difficulties and delays arose, but in 1880 Hewitt learned that a good many places were open down town for women trained as stenographers, and in the spring of 1881 he made arrangements for teaching shorthand. The next step was to teach women to use machines. On July 20 of that year he requested the Remington Company to furnish practice typewriters and an instructor—pointing to the market waiting to be opened up—and that fall a course in typing went on the curriculum.

But it was the art courses of which the Union felt proudest. They included free-hand drawing, architectural drawing, mechanical drawing, painting, engraving, and clay-modelling. The organizer and first head of the School of Design for Women was the gifted English-born painter T. A. Richards, a romanticist whose work

[1] January 9, 1866; Hewitt Papers.

belongs to the Hudson River school, and who was for forty years the influential secretary of the National Academy of Design. He stayed but two years. His first important successor was William Rimmer,[1] also English-born, a sculptor, painter, and physician who worked furiously, lavished his extraordinary talents all too widely, and by his inspiring personality and profound knowledge laid a deep impress upon students. With tossing hair he would stand at the board and by admirable quick sketches vivify his meaning. He was more than worth the $4,000 a year which the school paid him from 1866 to 1870. There was a distinguished staff which numbered, in the early years, such notable figures as J. Alden Weir, Jervis Mc-Entee, Wyatt Eaton, Swayne Gifford, and Douglas Volk. Men were instructed both by day and night, while the women's art school, which came finally under Susan N. Carter, was open from 9 to 1. At Peter Cooper's death nearly 3,000 students, about one-third of them women, were annually enrolled in the various art courses, and the earnings of women students the previous year had been nearly $30,000.

Poor lads of parts were, as the founder hoped, quickly drawn to the Union. In 1861 a French cobbler who had a shop on Third Avenue came in one day with his thirteen-year-old son. He had a roll of brown wrapping paper in his hand, and unfolded it to show some striking pictures the boy had drawn. The youngster caught up a pencil and made some additional sketches to prove his gift. Hewitt, impressed, admitted him in spite of the rules as to age. His name was Augustus Saint-Gaudens, and his statue of Peter Cooper stands in front of the Union today. In 1874 the Serbian lad Michael Pupin, having sold his yellow sheepskin coat and black sheepskin cap to gain the money, arrived by steerage in New York. That winter he was living in a hall-room in Norfolk Street, on the East Side, chosen so as to be near Cooper Union and its library. "The Union," he wrote later, "was my spiritual refuge when things looked black and desolate." There he read the stories of inventors, and resolved to become one himself; there he joined several evening classes. One day he saw Peter Cooper enter the room. He was so awed that decades afterward the vision of the old gentleman, with

[1] Sketches of both Richards and Rimmer are given in the *Dictionary of American Biography*.

his snowy locks, pure rosy complexion, and luminous blue eyes, rose before him as freshly as ever.[1]

For many years after the founding of the Union Hewitt hoped that a connection might be formed between it and Columbia College. As a loyal alumnus of the latter, he was disturbed by its narrow and unprogressive character. At this time it occupied restricted quarters in the rather dilapidated building once used by the Deaf and Dumb Asylum at Madison Avenue and Fiftieth Street; its faculty was small and inert, and its curriculum still predominantly classical; while several trustees were reactionary in their conservatism. The venerable institution needed waking up. When, in 1864, the excessively cautious Charles King was succeeded by the energetic Frederick A. P. Barnard, alumni plucked up hope. Barnard was not quite such a practical statesman of education as Charles W. Eliot of Harvard, but he had new ideas and a progressive temper. Hewitt, perceiving that Columbia needed to have its work enlarged by more practical studies, thought that a union with Cooper Institute would best effect this result.

When Peter Cooper's deed of trust was drawn up, Hewitt had shrewdly inserted a clause looking toward a future amalgamation with Columbia. That is, he included a provision that until the funds at the disposal of the trustees sufficed to erect a polytechnic school "equal to the best technological schools now established, or hereafter to be established," the board might assign the use of its building and equipment to "any college or university," or any individual, or the city, for the maintenance of such a school. When he made this provision he had in mind the Andersonian School of Glasgow, which was founded by Dr. Anderson but carried on by the University as a school of practical science, with classes for workmen at night. Soon after the Union was opened he had suggested to the Columbia trustees that the two institutions would be far more effective if united. But President King was indifferent, and the board rejected the proposal with a galling asperity.

Early in 1868, however, President Barnard wrote that he would like to reopen the discussion. Hewitt was delighted. "I am very glad indeed," he replied,[2] "that you have initiated the reconsidera-

[1] Royal Cortissoz, *Augustus Saint-Gaudens;* Pupin, *From Immigrant to Inventor,* 64-66; 75-77.
[2] March 10, 1868; Hewitt Papers.

tion of a plan which always had my sympathy, but which it was not possible for me ever to revive, under the peculiar circumstances of its *death* at the hands of the trustees of Columbia College. But there are less difficulties in the way of its resurrection than you might imagine, because there are no personal grievances on the part of the trustees to be removed. We have been and are superior to such considerations."

With Peter Cooper's full approval, he proposed a simple plan to Dr. Barnard. Cooper Union had six trustees. Two would retire, and their places be filled by two trustees of Columbia College. The college and the Union would then fill all future vacancies in either board out of the other, and in a short time the six trustees of the Union would also be trustees of Columbia. A practical amalgamation would thus be effected, although the legal title to the property of each institution would always be vested in its own board. Columbia College, working through the Union as a subordinate institution, could thus at once add to its former resources an excellent school of mechanical engineering and an art school. It would also have to maintain a free reading room at Cooper Union and the free night courses in science and art, but such alterations could be made in these as the standards of the college seemed to require. Hewitt, it is clear, had a vision of raising in New York City a university as broad in aim and spirit as Cornell University, which was just being opened on Lake Cayuga—a university where the classics, the social sciences, engineering, and art would all be taught together. He wrote Dr. Barnard:

> One good effect of the union I can plainly see, and that is the sympathy which will naturally be created between the working classes of this city, and its men of science and learning. And it seems to me that out of this new relation would arise a better social organization and government of the great city which is destined to be the commercial centre of the world. I can scarcely estimate the good which would flow both to the rich and the poor from such a union of effort in the extension of knowledge in a community *now devoted solely to business, avarice, and greed.* But I forbear to follow out this line of thought.

> My trouble is that I do not believe that the trustees of Columbia College will ever take the view of this subject which is so

evident to you and me. They must have changed greatly if they will ever listen to you.

Against stubborn opposition, Dr. Barnard backed the proposal in his board of trustees with such energy that he finally brought about the appointment of a committee to meet a similar committee of Cooper Union trustees and discuss the details of amalgamation. The two groups met, and Hewitt read an exhaustive argument in behalf of the project. On December 7, 1869, President Barnard sent him a letter outlining a tentative basis for unification. Unfortunately, at this point insurmountable obstacles appeared. The opposition of one Columbia trustee, in particular, stiffened. At the same time, it became evident that Cooper Union could not be converted into a scientific and technological school, suited to form part of a new Columbia University, without the installation of large laboratories and shops. This would mean remodelling a great part of the building; and to any reconstruction whatever old Peter Cooper was rigidly opposed. "The trouble is," Hewitt finally wrote President Barnard, "that we can do nothing for the Scientific School that would be satisfactory to you and the faculty *if we have any regard for the comfort and probably the life of Mr. Cooper.* I have given the whole week to a careful and patient examination of the question. There is absolutely no room in the building suitable to the laboratories." Full room, it was true, might be made by drastic alterations. But "these we cannot undertake *now, while Mr. Cooper is averse to alterations.*"

Hewitt deeply regretted this difficulty. He might have felt like trying to convert Peter Cooper had it not been that at this juncture Mrs. Cooper died; and it was not a time to grieve or cross the old gentleman. "I have been brought to the conclusion," Hewitt wrote sadly in closing the matter, "that we cannot provide suitable accommodations for the School of Science at present, in the Cooper Building. We are quite ready to surrender $10,000 a year in rents for this purpose, but we do not see our way clear to reconstruction of the building, and without such reconstruction the school would be a failure." In this failure of the plan the conservative trustees of Columbia rejoiced. Yet if the proposal could have been carried through, if Columbia College could have been converted in the sixties into a true university with a great engineering and scientific department and the benefit of Peter Cooper's endowment, it might have been immensely to the advantage both of Columbia and of New York City.

The regrettable feature of such a result would have been the extinction of Cooper Union as an independent institution; for in these years it was becoming an unquestioned success. The decade 1859-69 was the period of its novitiate. The trustees then brought into existence all the departments contemplated in the original plan; won the confidence of the wage-earners of the metropolis and their children; and proved that they could train hundreds of young men and women every year for a higher walk of life. In this labor Peter Cooper furnished the inspiring force, Hewitt most of the practical planning. The latter told the British Royal Commission on Trade Unions that he devoted nearly all his evenings to the work of the Union. He watched its curriculum, its staff, its investments, its interests great and small, with incessant care. When the Third Avenue Elevated was opened past the building in 1878 the noise was so appalling that a dozen recitation rooms had to be transferred to the Fourth Avenue side. This cost $540, and Hewitt coolly sent the bill to his friend Cyrus W. Field, president of the Elevated. As he wrote, it was unfair of the railroad to cut down, for its own profit, the funds available for educating the poor boys and girls of the Union. And Field paid the bill.

The death of Peter Cooper's wife took place December 20, 1869, on the fifty-sixth anniversary of their wedding day. Dr. Bellows, minister of the Unitarian Church to which Peter Cooper belonged, said in his funeral discourse that it was fitting she should be buried on December 22, the day the Pilgrims had landed, for she had inherited their qualities as well as their blood. "Here is what is left of a frame that has used every nerve and tissue in human service, household cares, diligent and painstaking duty to husband, children, and dependents. Here are the ashes of a woman of the Puritan and Huguenot spirit—one who knew nothing about the modern discontent with woman's sphere; nothing about the weariness of leisure and the lack of adequate occupation; nothing about the inequality of her woman's lot, or the monotony and oppression of a wife's and mother's duties. She found the place Providence gave her large enough for all her gifts . . . and she did her full part in making, keeping, and spending her husband's fortune." It was a heavy blow to Peter Cooper, and rendered him more dependent upon Mrs. Hewitt than ever, more eager to be diverted by his grandchildren. He wrote in his characteristically simple fashion:

> Not only do I think of my wife during my waking moments, but she often comes to me in my dreams, sometimes once a week, sometimes once in two weeks, and sometimes it will be at longer intervals. It is one of the greatest pleasures of my life that I can believe that she has been and is now my guardian angel, and it is one of my happiest hopes that I shall see that this our world is but the bud of a being that is to ripen and bear its choicest fruit in a brighter and better world.

It is easy to understand why the city which made such increasing use of Cooper Union regarded the founder, prominent as he was in so many good causes, with something like veneration. No one, not even William Cullen Bryant, was so well known, and no one so much beloved. His face was unmistakable. Wherever his plain carriage appeared, traffic stopped until he had passed. The fashionable coachman and the Irishman on a dray alike gave him the road. When his vehicle drew up at the curb, men leaped to open the door. Hats came off as he walked down the street. His annual receptions in Cooper Union, when on two evenings in May he greeted students, alumni, and friends, were memorable occasions. "I can see him now," writes one observer, "with his smiling face and interested look, and his soft white hair waving over his shoulders, amid flowers, lights, and the cheerful music, while his presence brooded like a benediction over the swaying and surging crowd." He was as true a democrat as the country held. "I still feel somewhat in debt to the world," was one of his last sayings. Even those who unjustly regarded his financial ideas as absurd respected him deeply. His ingenuity, versatility, practical shrewdness, and idealism all touched a responsive chord in American hearts.[1]

To these traits we should add an open-hearted generosity which had become proverbial. Mendicants of every type had marked him as an easy prey. Once, walking with his grandson Edward, he gave a beggar a quarter. "Sonny," he said as they went on, "never do that. Don't give men money—that hurts them. The proper course is to aid them to aid themselves." "Then why did you do it,

[1] Cf. Lloyd Bryce's excellent essay on Peter Cooper, *North American Review*, Vol. 152, p. 401ff (April, 1891).

grandpa?" demanded Edward. "Because I can't help it," said Cooper. But he did aid men to aid themselves. The same grandson was once with him in Philadelphia when suddenly a shopkeeper rushed out and drew him into a commodious store. Years before Cooper had given him help which enabled him to start in business; he had made a small fortune; and now he insisted that Cooper select a complete set of dishes—the old gentleman of course choosing one in atrocious taste.[1]

His interest in invention remained keen to the last—in his ninety-second year he described in writing an improvement which he believed would double the value of the elevated railroad to the public. This interest touched the readiest spring of his generosity, for he was always ready to listen to a fellow-inventor. When nearly ninety he spent $10,000 to give a trial at Ringwood to a patent turbine water-wheel and pump which some plausible engineer had brought to him. Hewitt's brawny manager at Ringwood, a Cornishman named P. R. George, was invited to the test. He at once declared that "This wheel will never do the work," and when Peter Cooper asked why, gripped the moving shaft in his hands and stopped the whole machine. After Cooper's death worthless securities were found in bundles in his desk. But more than simplicity entered into his speculative investments. He believed, as he once wrote, that money should be used for promising innovations even at the risk of safety. "Hence I have been ready to engage in all new enterprises, and, without incurring debt, to risk the means which I have acquired in their promotion, provided they seemed to me calculated to promote the general good."

The rugged fighting aspect of Peter Cooper comes out more clearly in his financial theories, his opposition to plutocracy, than in any other phase of his long career. Hewitt and Edward Cooper did not share his ideas, but they respected his spirit and aims. The self-reliant patriarch, whose recollection reached back to the time when "unmarried white men could be sold for debt in the State of Connecticut," had always distrusted banks and money power. In Jacksonian days he had enlisted with the President against "Nick Biddle's monster."[2] Believing vehemently in early life in the Benton-

[1] Edward R. Hewitt to author, October 11, 1934.

[2] Much before this time his resentment had been excited by the contraction of credit practised by the Second Bank of the United States in its early years.

Jackson doctrine of hard money, and hating debt, high interest rates, and note-juggling, he early determined, as he writes in his reminiscences, "to be wholly independent of banks." For some time, while his businesses were small, he was his own banker. When they had grown large, in the thirties and early forties, he resorted to an ingenious device to meet his needs and still keep clear of bankers. His friend and adviser, Gideon Lee, accepted his deposits of cash every Saturday, and kept them until he needed money. "From the first," writes Cooper, "I paid every outstanding bill and got a receipt by the Saturday before Christmas. This mode of doing business enabled me to go through fifty years of business without once taking stock. When I had paid everybody I was satisfied with what I had left. All crises have been advantageous to me, as I was most easy in money matters when others were in the greatest distress." When Edward Cooper and Hewitt took charge of the iron business, they used ordinary banking facilities. But he clung to the last to a set of beliefs upon the proper relations between finance and industry which curiously anticipated the independent views and practices of Henry Ford a long generation later.

It is remarkable that no adequate history has yet been written of the greenback movement. It had numerous phases and aspects, and nothing could be more erroneous than to identify Peter Cooper's careful and largely practical theories with the radical inflationism of certain Western elements. His initial ideas were largely derived from Edward Kellogg, whom he had long known.[1] Kellogg, a native of Norwalk, Conn., had established in 1820 a drygoods house in New York City which soon grew prosperous. The panic of 1837 struck his flourishing business, he could not make collections, and though his assets were ample he had to suspend. Thus painfully educated in the evils of the existing monetary system, he began studies which convinced him that money, being a medium of public exchange, should be controlled completely by the government and not by banking corporations. He inveighed with particular eloquence against the extortion of usurers, and manipulation

---

It is possible that Peter Cooper himself suffered heavily in this contraction, which he frequently mentioned with indignation; see his letter in the New York *Tribune*, November 21, 1874, as an example.

[1] See C. M. Destler, "The Influence of Edward Kellogg upon American Radicalism 1865-1896," *Journal of Political Economy*, Vol. XL (1932), pp. 338-365.

of credit and currency. Greeley and the *Tribune* in 1843 helped
him to circulate his treatise, *Currency, the Evil and the Remedy.*
Peter Cooper read this and his subsequent book, *Labor and Other
Capital,* and their influence is manifest in Cooper's writings. The
philanthropist also read such theorists as Silas Moore Stilwell.[1] The
Civil War resulted in an enormous inflation of the currency, and
the legal tender paper currency or greenbacks partially answered
one of the chief demands of Kellogg and Stilwell. When the next
few years brought a rapid deflation of the currency, falling commodity prices, and an enrichment of bondholders by the payment
of interest on the national debt in gold, the discontent of farmers
and workingmen resulted in the great revolt called the greenback
movement. Peter Cooper always thought for himself. He had by
this time developed views which, plainly stemming from Kellogg's
theories, differed in many details from them and from the doctrines
of Wendell Phillips, Judge Alexander Campbell of Illinois, W. D.
Kelley of Pennsylvania, George H. Pendleton of Ohio, and others
loosely classified as "greenbackers." He began to expound them in
a notable series of articles and pamphlets.

Gradually he built up a complete theory regarding finance, labor,
and trade; a theory inspired not only by his reading but by his long
experience in industry and his observations during repeated alternations of boom and panic, and one fitting the status of the United
States as a fast-developing debtor nation. In brief, it called for what
we now call a managed currency. He saw that under our haphazard
currency system, subject to a vast deal of selfish manipulation,
periods of inflation and easy credit, encouraging speculation, were
followed by periods of deflation, total stoppage of credit, and general bankruptcy. At the height of the cycle we had a fatal facility
for running in debt to Europe and to each other; then some shock
caused a drain of gold abroad, or hoarding at home; and the result
was panic, cessation of industry, and terrible distress among the

[1] In *Ideas for a Science of Good Government,* 3ff, he pays tribute to Stilwell.
This merchant (1800-1881) was an alderman of New York after 1835, serving
with Peter Cooper and becoming chairman of the board. He lost his fortune
in the panic of 1837. Later he declined a position in Harrison's Cabinet because
he was busy retrieving it. He contributed much toward shaping the banking
and bankruptcy legislation of New York State. He was the author of numerous
essays on finance, the first of which, "A System of Credit for a Republic . . .,"
was published in 1837.

poor. He recalled what had happened in 1837 and 1857. He even recalled what had happened when Langdon Cheves tried in 1818 to save the Bank of the United States by a drastic contraction of its loans. He rescued it, but at the same time "literally ruined all who were in debt by the shrinkage of all values throughout the country to less than one-half the amount" they were worth during the previous period of prosperity.

What could be done? In his opinion the primary remedy was the establishment of a purely domestic currency, insulated as far as possible from European influences, controlled by the government alone, and managed in such a way as to be constantly adequate to the needs of the country. There should be enough currency in a nation to put all the useful labor it contained to work, and keep it working. History had proved that this was impossible with a gold and silver currency supplemented by bank-notes good and bad. But the government could make anything it pleased money, and it should make its own paper, with *due safeguards and full security*, the only legal tender—as it actually came to do in 1933.

Nothing disgusted Peter Cooper more than the charge that he wished the government to issue greenbacks as the French had issued assignats and the Continental Congress its paper bills; for he wished nothing of the kind. He explained the depreciation of the assignats as due to insufficient security, to the menaces of internal and external enemies of France, and to the flood of counterfeits, while the Continental bills had no basis whatever for redemption. But he would make the new American currency convertible at the will of the holder into Federal bonds. He insisted also upon limiting the currency according to population and trade. The new currency (there was no reason for calling it greenbacks) would thus be a mortgage upon the whole wealth of the nation; excessive issues would mean higher taxation, and taxpayers would resist them. The government would hold at once the position of debtor and creditor; it would pay for all the service and labor it needed by its own paper, and would redeem that paper by taxes. Peter Cooper believed that under this managed currency there would be no panics, with their attendant misery, because contraction of the currency would be impossible, and curtailment of credit could easily be stopped. Under the Banking Act, bankers had power to inflate the currency to within about ten per cent of the entire bonded debt, and then contract it as they chose; that power would be destroyed. He held that the new currency would be a permanent and unfluctuating standard of values; would automatically hold a fixed level in proportion to the national population and wealth; and would be placed above sinister interference by moneyed interests at home or in Europe. Such interference, he wrote, was all too easy as matters stood, for the moneyed class wished scarce money and high interest rates. Gold and silver, according to his original theory, need not be demonetized; but they would fall into a subordinate position, their chief value being in making purchases abroad and settling balances with foreign nations.

Incidentally, according to Peter Cooper, the national debt would no longer be a means by which the rich bondholder doubled and trebled his wealth (as he unquestionably did just after the Civil War) ; it would become the poor man's saving bank. The successive Government measures by which the value of Civil War bonds was enormously increased for the benefit of men who had bought them in depreciated money, while at the same time the currency was steadily contracted, aroused Cooper to anger. He wrote in 1877 in his open letter to President Hayes:[1]

> This country had, up to the year 1865, issued in different forms of currency and Treasury notes, current in money among the people, $2,192,395,527. This vast sum had, on the first of November, 1867, shrunk to $631,488,676. In the year 1865 there was in the hands of the people, as a currency, $58 per head; in 1875 the currency of all kinds was only a little more than $17 per head.
>
> You may call this currency a vast debt of the people, as it was incurred by the Government to save the life of the nation. But it was *money—every dollar of it*. It was paid by the Government "for value received"; it was used by the people to pay their debts, to measure the value of their property, and as your present Secretary of the Treasury said in his seat in the Senate, "every citizen of the United States had conformed his business to the legal tender clause."
>
> This currency was also the creature of the law, and under the entire control of the government, but held in trust for the benefit of the people, as are all its functions. Was it either just or humane to allow $1,100,000,000 of this currency, a large part bearing no interest, but paying labor, and fructifying every human enterprise,

[1] In *Ideas for a Science of Good Government*, 117ff.

to be absorbed into bonds in the space of eight years, bearing a heavy interest, of which the bondholder bore no share? The Government seemed to administer this vast currency as if there were but one interest in the nation to be promoted, and that the profit of those who desired to fund their money with the *greatest security*, and to make money scarce and of high rate of interest! This is the issue of the hour; this is the battle of the people.

In other words, Peter Cooper held that every dollar of the two billions issued during the war was paid out for labor or service of some kind in putting down the rebellion; that being thus the price of the nation's life, it became the money of the people who had earned and paid for every dollar of it; and that the people had a right to keep it and use it for industry and agriculture. He believed that they needed it all. The government should have made this proportional amount of currency sacred and kept it as the permanent measure of all values, not to be increased or diminished except as population and exchanges rose or fell. Instead, the government had altered the measure of value drastically, and in a way which injured the farmer and workingman while benefiting the rich man.

Peter Cooper began his public labors on the financial question by a petition to Congress on December 14, 1862, asking it to take sole control of the issuance and valuation of currency in the United States. He warmly commended Secretary Chase's action in emitting legal-tender Treasury notes convertible on demand into interest-bearing bonds; in fact, he believed that his friend Silas M. Stilwell, whose writings had been nearly as influential as Kellogg's, had persuaded Chase to take this step.[1] Later he pointed out that these Treasury notes, unlike the non-convertible greenbacks, always maintained their parity with gold. After the war he kept up a steady stream of petitions, pamphlets, and articles. Their invariable burden was that the Federal Government should take over the whole function of issuing money; that Congress should declare that the legal-tender currency in circulation (Treasury notes and greenbacks) should not be contracted, but rather increased as population rose; and that the greenbacks should be brought to parity with gold, made full legal-tender, and given the feature of con-

[1] Stilwell himself made this claim; see the article upon him in Appleton's *Cyclopaedia of American Biography*.

vertibility into interest-bearing bonds. The interest on such bonds should be low to avoid interference with the flow of money into industrial development; not more than 3.65 per cent. When Congress declined to follow the path he desired, he attacked it as representing one economic group alone. A recent session, he declared in 1871, had shown 120 bankers in Congress, 99 lawyers, 14 merchants, 13 manufacturers, 7 doctors, 4 mechanics, and not a single farmer or laborer.

Beyond these financial theories, he expounded a set of highly liberal and advanced political doctrines. He insisted that it was high time for the nation to take steps to halt the concentration of wealth and preserve "equal rights to all"—political, social, and economic. He was appalled by the buccaneering which marked the era of Jay Gould, Jim Fisk, Collis P. Huntington, the Credit Mobilier, the Whiskey Ring, the more extortionate pools, the anthracite combination, and the endless stock-watering of the Gilded Age. He was shocked by the tenderness of the government for big business and its harshness toward the farmer and workingman. "I have always been, am, and ever shall be with the poor toilers and producers," he wrote in his ninety-second year; "therefore I desire Congress to legislate for the poor as well as the rich, who can take care of themselves." He was one of the few prominent men who thought that the great strike of 200,000 desperate railroad workers in 1877 required something more than denunciation of the "lawless" laborers. It arose, he wrote very justly, from a "further reduction in their wages already reduced to the living point," and it demanded a constructive remedy. As he looked at the workers who, in 1877, were glad to get a dollar a day, and at the farmers of the mortgage-ridden West, his heart filled with resentment. He contrasted their lot with that of the moneyed men who endured the long depression happily because "they know that money is appreciating in value all the time!" He quoted John Sherman himself as saying in 1869 that currency-appreciation meant "the sorest distress to every person except a capitalist out of debt, or a salaried officer, or an annuitant." The struggle for freedom, he proclaimed, had not ended with Appomattox; it only began there:

The danger to our free institutions now is only less than in the inception of the rebellion that shook our republic to its centre. It is only another oligarchy, another enslaving power, that is asserting itself against the interest of the whole people. There is fast forming in this country an aristocracy of wealth, the worst form of aristocracy that can curse the prosperity of any country. For such an aristocracy has no country—"absenteeism," living abroad, while they draw their incomes from this country, is one of its common characteristics. Such an aristocracy is without a soul and without patriotism. Let us save our country from this, its most potent, and, as I hope, its last enemy.

Jeffersonian egalitarianism, Jacksonian democracy, thus found their most telling voice in this era in the brave old man who, giving money lavishly to his charities, spending hours daily in the working-people's Institute he had founded, befriending every good cause, also turned himself in his last years into an unwearied fighter for social justice. His vision looked far ahead. He laid down a programme embracing State Socialism on a wide scale. He wished the government to build, own, and operate the Western railroads, instead of giving huge land grants to men who often stole their proceeds. He wished to see Washington exercise the most careful control of the national domain for the benefit of Western settlers. He wanted a postal savings bank system, to pay two and a half per cent on deposits. He called for government regulation of privately-owned railroads. He asked for "a complete civil service."[1] Speaking whenever occasion offered, sending open letters to conventions of bankers, scattering more than a million documents over the land, he made his voice heard. In 1883 he gathered up his numerous fugitive publications into an impressive, though decidedly repetitious, volume, *Ideas for a Science of Good Government,* which went into a second edition the same year.

In the first bleak weeks of 1876, Peter Cooper presided over a mass-meeting called in New York to urge that the State legislature and Congress take measures to assist the hundreds of thousands of

[1] He was also one of the first men to advocate unemployment relief by public works. He wrote during the great depression after the panic of 1873: "Let the government give immediate relief to unemployed labor, either through definite methods of help given to settlers of unemployed lands in the West, or by great and obvious public improvements, which are seen to be necessary to the prosperity and safety of a country—such as a Northwestern and a Southwestern Railroad." In this he was more than fifty years ahead of his time. *Ideas for a Science of Good Government,* 121.

unemployed. When the National Independent Party, or Green-backers, met in national convention at Indianapolis on May 17, with 240 delegates present from eighteen States and the Federal District, his name was in everybody's mind. The Western delegates wished to nominate David Davis of Illinois for President, but they were defeated. Peter Cooper was named instead, with Senator Newton Booth of California for Vice-President; on the withdrawal of the latter, Samuel F. Cary of Ohio took his place. The platform called for "financial reform and industrial emancipation." At first Peter Cooper positively declined to take the nomination; but on the solicitation of friends, he at last gave a conditional acceptance, expressing a hope that either the Republican or Democratic Convention would take a favorable attitude toward his financial tenets. When this hope failed, he addressed an open letter to Tilden and Hayes explaining his reasons for running. At his age his candidacy was but a gesture, and he polled only 81,737 votes in the entire country. But it was a gallant and long-remembered gesture. The chief practical success of the Greenbackers was in Illinois, where they chose five Independents to the upper chamber of the legislature—with results which, by the irony of fate, were to prove most unfortunate for Hewitt when these five men took a hand in the dispute between Tilden and Hayes.[1]

A fine, lovable, heroic figure—so Peter Cooper stands out against the murky background of the seventies. The overwhelming judgment of financial experts then and since has condemned his theory of the currency. It over-simplified the problem; it ignored the difficulties of detaching our monetary system from those of the other great Powers, all having a metallic base; it would have invited political manipulation; its immediate result would probably have been financial panic, its ultimate result disastrous inflation. Yet it offers some interesting resemblances to the systems of controlled currencies adopted by several nations after 1930. And for Peter Cooper's general attitude there can be little but praise. "An honest man with a sensitive social conscience," writes Vernon L. Parrington,[2] "he would have no hand in the great barbecue which

---

[1] The best treatment of this Greenback campaign remains that in Fred L. Haynes's *Third Party Movements Since the Civil War.*

[2] Parrington, *Main Currents in American Thought*, III, 276-282.

wasted more than it consumed; but the times were heedless of the counsels of honest men, and he was loved and laughed at and ignored. Like Franklin in the Constitutional Convention, he had outlived his generation and was thrust aside by the new economy that was taking over the custodianship of America."

CHAPTER XVI

The Tocsin of Reform

IN THE summer of 1874 it was evident that the nation which
had so long scorned the Democratic Party was turning back
to it as a means of punishing Grant and the Republican organization. The depression which followed the panic of 1873 was itself
grim enough to cause many voters to alter their allegiance. Yet it
was but the sable backdrop for a stage full of lurid and depressing
melodrama. Grant had generously been given his second chance,
and had already thrown it away. Nepotism, represented by such figures as his brother-in-law Casey in the New Orleans Custom House,
grinned at the spoils system, personified by such machine bosses as
Roscoe Conkling and Simon Cameron. Corruption infested the
executive departments as rats infest some slovenly warehouse;
after the Credit Mobilier scandal had come the Sanborn Contract
scandal, and sensational gossip about the Whiskey Ring was now
general. Favoritism seemed to rule the White House, and the bar
of the nation shuddered when Grant offered the Chief Justiceship
to Conkling, who discreetly refused it. The sickening waste, corruption, and violence in those Southern States which were still
under Carpetbag rule continued. As the year 1875 opened, General
Sheridan, overawing Louisiana with his Federal troops, asked Grant
to permit him to treat the hostile whites of that section as banditti,
a suggestion which Secretary Hamilton Fish justly pronounced
"atrocious."[1]

Nor was the expiring Forty-third Congress better liked than the
Administration. "Statesmanship in Congress," Thurlow Weed had
written in 1873, "is now so low that it will take many years to
build it up to a higher tone."

[1] James Schouler, *History of the United States*, VII, 246-252.

In State after State, plucking up hope, the Democrats were nominating their strongest candidates for the governorship. In the previous year Ohio had elected William Allen over Rutherford B. Hayes.
In Massachusetts, William Gaston, a capable, genial, and wealthy
Democrat, was selected for a run which proved brilliantly successful.
In New York the sentiment of the better Democrats for Tilden was
overwhelming. The City owed him a debt it could never pay for
his labors in completing the rout of the Tweed Ring. By sixteen
months of diligent labor, totally surrendering his private business,
he had given leadership to the reform movement begun by the
courageous exposures of the New York *Times*, and had accumulated the legal proofs which sent Tweed himself to jail.[1] He had
taken time to serve in the Assembly of 1872, and had there done
sterling work in reforming the State judiciary. As State Chairman,
he had ably marshalled his party, and the aged Horatio Seymour regarded him as his best possible successor in its leadership.
As we have seen, when the largest convention ever held by New
York Democrats met in Syracuse, and Horatio Seymour presented
his name, he was nominated for governor amid stormy cheers.[2] His
opponent on the Republican side was John A. Dix, the grand old
figure remembered for his telegraphic order, "If anyone attempts to
haul down the American flag, shoot him on the spot." He had carried New York by more than 55,000 majority two years earlier, and
had made a good governor. But with the Democratic undercurrent
running strongly, Tilden's victory was certain. Two years further
ahead, many Democrats saw the White House.

Of all this Hewitt was an interested spectator—the more interested because he himself was being urged to enter politics. In midsummer of 1874 the Democratic leaders of the Fifth New Jersey
District told him that they intended to nominate him for Congress.
He was not unwilling to add a new burden to his iron business and

[1] See the forthcoming life of Samuel J. Tilden by Alexander C. Flick (American Political Leaders Series) for the best account of Tilden's work in destroying the Tweed Ring.
[2] Professional politicians were in many instances astonished by Tilden's
strength. Theodore P. Cook, *Life of Samuel J. Tilden*, 138, 139. But as one of
the most experienced observers of New York affairs during two generations
states, Tilden had adroitly used the same implements that made Van Buren
irresistible. Without personal magnetism, he excelled in drawing men to him
by voluminous correspondence and in organizing them afterward. Elihu Root
to author, January 11, 1935.

Cooper Union, but he did not wish to represent that particular district in Washington. For one reason, it was normally Republican, and he could not hope for a long tenure. For another, the Republican who sat for it, William Walter Phelps, was a close friend; he had served two terms with ability and independence, and Hewitt thought he deserved reëlection. For still a third, since he had helped Tilden, Edward Cooper, and others reform Tammany, Hewitt's heart was in New York City. The ironmaster suspected that the district leaders were interested primarily in his pocketbook. He therefore declined. When they insisted, he took a decisive step. He changed his legal residence from Ringwood to New York City, where he occupied his own house half the year anyway, resigned his various honorary posts in New Jersey, and in a public letter to the governor announced that he was henceforth a New Yorker.

Appropriate steps had already been taken by Tilden and his other friends in New York. To Tilden's campaign for the governorship he was soon giving generously in time and money. In return, the shrewd, quiet leader of the State Democracy was anxious to thrust so efficient a colleague into a Congressional seat. Once there, Hewitt could be useful in two ways. He could be Tilden's principal lieutenant in Washington while Tilden himself, with his eye already on the Presidency, went to Albany; he could also stand against corruption in New York City and help keep the reform Democrats solidly in the saddle there. On October 5, 1874, the *Times* announced that "in the Tenth New York District the candidates for Congress are John Mullany and Abram S. Hewitt, Tammany Democrats, and James O'Brien, Independent Democrat." Mullany at once withdrew. O'Brien had been named by "the People's Liberal Democratic Convention," representing the Tweed men and other malcontents.[1] Tilden, apparently without much consultation of the ironmaster, had arranged for his nomination by the reformed Tammany and would hear of no refusal; it was necessary to wipe out the remnants of the Tweed gang which had put forward O'Brien. In this "gas-house district," comprehending the aristocratic little section around Gramercy Park, but populated chiefly by poor East Siders, no Republican was nominated. The contest was between the new Tammany and the old.

[1] New York *Times, Tribune,* October 4-28, 1874.

Hewitt was accepted by the lower East Side with surprising enthusiasm. He was Peter Cooper's son-in-law; his generous labor
policy at Trenton was well known; and the frequent misspelling of
his name as "Abraham" beguiled some Jewish voters into thinking
him of their race. Above all, hard times made the voters responsive
to an experienced business man who held lucid and positive views
on economic questions. Thousands were out of work, poverty was
general, discontent was spreading apace. When various delegations
called, he was touched by the fervent expression of their sufferings and fears.

"They told me," he later said in Congress, "that they were not
going to vote for me because I was a Democrat, or because I had
made them any contributions of money, or had demoralized them
with free liquor, or because I belonged to them and had to suffer
with them, but because they believed that the working classes had
been cursed with bad legislation, which interfered with a just distribution of the proceeds of labor; that every time a law was passed
affecting their interests it was sure to contain some provision which
in a covert way tended sooner or later to deprive them of their
just dues; and they came to me as a man who was accustomed to
study these questions and would have the courage to stand up in
this House and resist all legislation . . . which might tend to their
injury. . . . The simple confidence of these honest and trusting
souls went to my heart."

To Hewitt the principal needs of the country seemed clear;
economy, honest administration, sound money, and a low tariff.
Little speechmaking was needed. But one important address, entitled, "Tariff for Revenue Only: Gold and Silver for the Workingman as well as the Bondholder," he circulated in thousands of
copies. The previous session of Congress, stimulated by the popular
discontents, had naturally bloomed with wild inflationist schemes.
These panaceas for the current economic and financial ills had
been quite as popular among Republicans as Democrats. The
"paper money trinity" of the Senate, Oliver P. Morton of Indiana,
John A. Logan of Illinois, and T. W. Ferry of Michigan, were all
Republicans; and it was with pleased surprise that conservative
Easterners had seen Grant veto, in the spring of 1874, a bill to
permit the expansion of the greenback currency to $400,000,000.
Hewitt came out vigorously for the old Jacksonian principles of

hard money—gold or its equivalent—and no inflation, upon which he was in complete harmony with Seymour and Tilden, and of course much at odds with Peter Cooper. He also advocated a sharp tariff reduction, especially under the broad principle of free raw materials. He believed in levying duties just high enough to fill the Treasury; he wished them placed only upon manufactured goods which competed with our own wares; and he would keep them just high enough to cover the cost-differentials arising from our higher wage scales. Sound money and free raw materials were popular demands in a great financial and importing centre like New York.

Finally, he fired more than one shot at the vulnerable Grant. He even remarked that the poverty-stricken workers, reading of the President's fast trotters and fine equipages at Long Branch, must resent "the apparent indifference manifested by the chief officers of the government to the suffering which prevails throughout the land." The *Times* was grieved that a millionaire—an industrialist "for whom we have the highest respect personally"—should thus talk of the sufferings of the poor.[1] It forgot that Hewitt was in a real sense one of the poor himself. He lived in the plainest way, he worked harder than anybody in his employ, and he was carrying on the iron works, during the depression, at a cost of about $100,000 annually in deficits simply to furnish wages to his men. He sometimes remarked that he had hardly a dollar invested in luxuries; his whole capital was in productive enterprises which gave men employment at wages higher than he could really afford.

As fate would have it, the single piece of murderous violence in the campaign, the Croker shooting affray, touched Hewitt directly. Richard Croker was at this time a roistering, pugnacious blade of thirty, born in old Erin, from which he had come at the age of three, and trained in the notorious Fourth Avenue Tunnel Gang. His strong frame, fistic ability, bulldog courage, and quick brain had made him a leader of the East Side roughs and of the volunteer fire department. He was equally good at a wake, a stump speech, and a felonious assault. When Tweed was deposed, he had thrown his influence on Second and Third Avenues to Kelly and had been rewarded in 1873 with the office of coroner, worth about $15,000 a year in fees. Still posing as an adherent of reform, he was now

[1] October 23, 1874.

supporting Hewitt. On election day, November 3, 1874, John Mc-
Kenna, a political opponent aged about thirty, was murdered by a
bullet fired by someone in a group of toughs under Croker.[1]

The best evidence is that Croker's companion, George Hickey,
was the actual slayer. These men and two others had been wander-
ing about the tenth Congressional district since early morning
avowedly seeking to prevent the "intimidation" of voters. Such
patrol was needed, for O'Brien's more rowdy adherents, led by his
two brothers, had begun the day by going from poll to poll, creating disturbances and beating enemies. At Second Avenue and
Thirty-fourth Street, in front of a saloon, Croker's party met
O'Brien. Croker called him a dirty thief and bade him get out.
O'Brien retorted that Croker was a loafer and repeater, adding:
"You damned cur, I picked you out of the gutter and now you're
supporting a rich man like Hewitt against me for Congress." The
two exchanged blows; revolvers were drawn in Croker's party; and
a shot was fired. It struck McKenna, a supporter of O'Brien, who
was running up to interfere, in the head, and he fell mortally
wounded. Removed to a neighboring police station, the dying man,
whose impressions were obviously confused, made a direct charge
that Croker had first shot him. "When I fell," he added, "Hickey
fired two shots at me." Croker, after arrest, declared that "I never
carried a pistol in my life, and never will as long as I can use my
hands." Indeed, it was unlike him to bear a revolver, for not even
the pugilist Morrissey could knock a man out more quickly.[2]

When Croker was arraigned, John Kelly, Mayor-elect Wickham,
and Hewitt appeared, and Hewitt furnished the bail of $2,500 on
which he was released. He did this because he received confidential
information proving his innocence, because Croker had ostensibly
been acting in Hewitt's behalf, and because the savage outcry of
the Republican press seemed an attempt to lynch him. After a
Tammany coroner's jury brought in the expected verdict that

[1] The press gives highly partisan accounts of this episode; it is ably summed
up in Lothrop Stoddard's *Master of Manhattan: The Life of Richard Croker*,
53-60.

[2] Nevertheless, O'Brien's testimony was against Croker. He declared that
Croker had drawn a revolver and aimed it at O'Brien; that McKenna had
hastily stepped forward as if to make peace; and that Croker had then changed
his aim and fired. As McKenna lay on the ground, one of Croker's companions
fired at him again. N. Y. *Times*, November 10, 11, 12, 1874.

McKenna had been shot by some person unknown, Croker was re-arrested on a charge of murder and lodged in the Tombs, not far from Stokes, the wealthy young murderer of Jim Fisk. His trial began in December, under Judge George C. Barrett of the Court of Oyer and Terminer. Hewitt and Kelly had retained the best attorneys available, among them Henry L. Clinton, who had helped to prosecute Tweed, and General Charles Wingate, and Hewitt guaranteed their fees.

The trial, held amid popular excitement, finally resulted in a tied jury, six to six. Public opinion was acquiescent, for while the evidence was thin and conflicting, most of it tended to exonerate Croker. No effort was made to hold a second trial. Many years later facts came to light which indicate, as we have said, that the fatal shot was actually fired by Hickey. General Wingate stated just after Croker's death that during the trial the actual slayer had been in the courtroom, and intended, if the verdict were guilty, to confess. Croker, he added, had refused to let evidence be submitted that Hickey fired the shot. Judge Barrett also testified long afterward that he had ascertained that Croker was guiltless. Nevertheless, the young leader was temporarily disgraced, while the stigma of the affair clung to him through life. His position would have been even worse had not Hewitt's assistance impressed the law-abiding public.[1]

On election day the expected Democratic wave inundated the land. Of the thirty-five States which voted in the fall of 1874, twenty-three, including such Republican strongholds as Wisconsin, Ohio, Pennsylvania, and Massachusetts, went Democratic. The next House would contain only 106 Republicans against 178 Democrats. New York had given Tilden a larger majority than his most hopeful supporters had anticipated. Just before the polls closed a friend found him in his library on Gramercy Park. He was in one of the gay moods which rarely and briefly thawed his usual chill secretiveness. "What majority will you have?" Tilden asked. "Anything," was the reply. "How about fifteen thousand?" "Quite enough." "Twenty-five thousand?" "Still better." "The majority," said Tilden, "will be a little in excess of fifty thousand." This was not a guess, but an accurate estimate founded upon reports from the

[1] Cf. M. R. Werner, *Tammany Hall*, 308-310.

admirably organized army of party workers throughout the State who had conducted his campaign. His plurality was 50,317.

Hewitt was elected to Congress by a close margin, receiving 9,503 votes to O'Brien's 8,803. But he was glad that he had accepted the nomination, for a more favorable moment to enter the House of Representatives could hardly have been imagined. The Democratic majority in that chamber had a magnificent opportunity to distinguish itself by sound and conservative action, and to tear aside the veils which it believed to conceal a mass of corruption and mismanagement in the Grant Administration; and he and others meant to use that opportunity to the utmost.

On the opening day of the Forty-fourth Congress, December 6, 1875, Hewitt, taking his seat on the overflowing Democratic side, looked about him with curiosity. The House contained a few men whom he knew. From New York there were Fernando Wood, one-time mayor, and S. S. Cox, journalist and wit; from Pennsylvania, William D. Kelley, familiar to ironmasters for his devotion to their industry, and Samuel J. Randall, the well-tried captain of the protectionist Democrats; from Mississippi, Lucius Q. C. Lamar, friend of Thackeray, Confederate leader, and able educator and lawyer; and from Illinois, Carter H. Harrison, Sr., whom Hewitt had met in Chicago. Others he knew only by reputation: Blaine, Hoar, Reagan, Bland, Garfield and the famous Alexander H. Stephens of Georgia. It was the first House which the Democrats had controlled since Buchanan left the White House; and a thrill of elation ran through the majority as they looked up at the great bronze eagle poised over the Speaker's desk.

From the initial week the two parties glared at each other across the central aisle with unconcealed animosity. They knew that since the session just beginning would stretch well into the Presidential campaign of 1876, it would be occupied with politics rather than constructive legislation. With a Democratic majority of sixty-three in the House, and a Republican majority of eleven in the Senate, lawmaking was almost impossible. The Democrats exultantly announced that they would use the House committee to investigate the Administration in all its branches and all its suspected misdeeds; the Republicans nerved themselves to resist the assault and if possible to take the offensive. The session was to be a prolonged and desperate battle, with the Presidency at stake.

In his first days in Washington Hewitt underwent all the natural discomforts of a new member. "I do not yet feel at home in the House," he wrote on January 8, 1876. "The sensation is very like a bird beating its wings against the bars of a cage. The rules are very complicated, and the old members are so quick to detect small errors that a new man is oppressed with a sense of his nothingness. Perhaps I may get to like it better, but thus far the life does not suit me." Naturally this malaise was transient. He took a house at 1215 K Street, N. W., and soon felt sufficiently at home in Capitol society to lose his strangeness. More important was his discovery that he was after all to be one of the Congressional leaders. The Southern members, aware of Northern distrust, were willing to take a secondary position; the Northern Democrats were few. Hewitt was marked by his fifty-four years, his abilities, and his reputation as an industrialist, for a distinguished place in the little group which directed House affairs. This group included Speaker Michael C. Kerr of Indiana, William R. Morrison of Illinois, nominally majority leader, Hurd of Ohio, Randall of Pennsylvania, Cox of New York, and three or four more. They laid the strategic plans of the majority, held the Southerners back from rash mistakes, and shrewdly arranged the various investigations.

Early in the session James G. Blaine, in a sudden move designed to distract attention from the Democratic investigations and advance his own candidacy for the Republican nomination as President, suddenly made one of the most wicked appeals to sectional hatred ever heard in the House. On January 10, 1876, Randall had moved consideration of a bill to grant amnesty to all former Confederates still suffering under legal disabilities. Blaine proposed an amendment which excepted Jefferson Davis. He then launched into an arrogantly offensive speech, accusing the South of a long list of offences, and especially of the wanton abuse of Union prisoners during the war. After asserting that "Mr. Davis was the author, knowly, deliberately, guiltily, and wilfully, of the gigantic murder and crime at Andersonville," he added:

And I here, before God, measuring my words, knowing their full extent and import, declare that neither the deeds of the Duke of Alva in the Low Countries, nor the massacre of St. Bartholomew's Day, nor the thumb-screws and engines of torture of the Spanish Inquisition, begin to compare in atrocity with the hideous crime of Andersonville.

Instantly the Southern members, aflame with anger, sprang to answer Blaine's taunts. A partisan debate could produce no accurate judgment upon the abuses of Northern or Southern prisons; but reasonable men knew that the blame ought to be fairly divided between the two sections. The Southerners offered an effective reply. Blaine had mustered the effrontery to say that the Republican treatment of the South exhibited "an imperishable record of liberality, and large-mindedness, and magnanimity, and mercy." To this Benjamin H. Hill of Georgia made caustic rejoinder. "If, with masters enslaved, intelligence disfranchised, society disorganized, industry paralyzed, States subverted, Legislatures dispersed by the bayonet, the people can accord to that party the verdict of grace and magnanimity, may God save the future of our country from grace and magnanimity!" He recalled that the South had always wished to exchange war prisoners, but that the North, in 1863, had stopped the practise; that the South had vainly invited the North to send medicines and surgeons to the prisoners' camps; and that in August, 1864, the South had even asked the North to dispatch steamships to Savannah for its sick and wounded soldiers, to be released without equivalent, but that no ships had come until December. He then demolished Blaine's reckless assertions in a hundred words:

> Now I recall the attention of gentlemen to this fact, that the report of Mr. Stanton, the Secretary of War . . . on the 19th of July, 1866, exhibits the fact that of the Federal prisoners in Confederate hands during the war only 22,576 died, while of the Confederate prisoners in Federal hands 26,436 died. And Surgeon-General Barnes reports in an official report that in round numbers the Confederate prisoners in Federal hands amounted to 220,000, while the Federal prisoners in Confederate hands amounted to 270,000. . . . The ratio is this: More than 12 per cent of the Confederates in Federal hands died, and less than 9 per cent of the Federals in Confederate hands died. What is the logic of these facts according to the gentleman from Maine?

Yet it seemed for a time that Blaine had accomplished his purpose. Garfield, Seeley, Banks, and Randall all made speeches; recriminations were exchanged; Northern newspapers and Northern veterans responded enthusiastically to Civil War memories. Hewitt wrote Edward Cooper in discouragement: "We have got through with the Amnesty Bill, which was defeated after a ferocious debate. Blaine looked and acted like a tiger springing upon his prey. As a debater he is *facile princeps* in this House, but he is a demagogue and not a statesman."

Nevertheless, the Democratic counter-attack brought ample reparation; for when the majority launched their investigations they proved successful beyond the most sanguine expectations. The leaders had counted upon exposing a certain amount of laxity and extravagance. Actually, they brought to light scandal after scandal of a magnitude which shocked the whole nation.

Their cumulative effect can be indicated only by a compressed and consecutive recital. In January the full gravity of the Emma Mine scandal and the attendant misconduct of our Minister to England, Robert Schenck, broke upon the public. News came that John W. Forney, a lobbyist recently proved to have pocketed $25,000 of the corruption fund of the Pacific Mail Company, had been appointed to represent the Centennial Commission abroad. Our Minister to Peru was in trouble for disreputable operations as a money-lender. The trial of Grant's private secretary, Babcock, for complicity in the Whiskey Ring thefts, began in St. Louis. In February Babcock was acquitted, but not till after evidence had been presented which convinced most Americans of his complete guilt. Worst of all, a New York contractor, Caleb P. Marsh, testified that Secretary of War Belknap had for years taken bribes for allowing a friend of his wife to share in the profits of a rich Indian post-tradership.

March began with a Committee report giving proof of Belknap's guilt, and with his resignation—of which President Grant's hasty acceptance was itself a scandal. Schenck, leaving England for the United States, was served at the railway station in London with a civil writ, against which he pleaded diplomatic immunity. Senator Stewart of Nevada was exposed before the House committee on the Emma Mine affair as a sharper. The President's brother, Orville Grant, told the committee investigating the War Department that he had practised an unblushing jobbery with Indian post-traderships. A little later Schenck himself appeared before the Emma

Mine committee. He had now resigned and was a discredited man, but his testimony further disgraced him. A Congressional committee was meanwhile reporting on the Freedmen's Bank scandal; the Whiskey Ring trials in Chicago were developing the amazing extent of the revenue frauds; and the House Judiciary Committee commented caustically upon a circular letter which Attorney-General Pierrepont had sent to Western district attorneys, warning them against the grant of immunity to informers against the Ring Thieves. Improper expenditures to influence New York City elections were revealed in the Department of Justice, and frauds in the Custom House at New Orleans. Above all, in April the sensational Blaine scandal broke upon the nation.

This scandal, to Democrats a just retribution for Blaine's speech, originated in charges that in 1871 Blaine, whose extravagant life placed him under financial pressure, had unloaded upon the Union Pacific Railroad seventy-five almost worthless bonds of the Little Rock & Fort Smith Railroad for $64,000 in cash. This was presumably a virtual bribe to the Speaker for political protection which the Union Pacific needed. John C. S. Harrison, a government director of the Union Pacific, vouched for the charges. While Blaine and others were denying them and offering some queer explanations, there appeared before an investigating committee one James Mulligan, who had a packet of letters written by Blaine to men connected with the Little Rock. By a sharp trick, Blaine prevented the disclosure of their contents until he could arrange a theatrical situation favorable to himself. But when finally published, they gave substance to a new charge that he had prostituted the Speakership to benefit the Little Rock, and had later tried to wring financial favors from the railroad management on this score. His chances for the Republican nomination were shattered, and his reputation was left permanently besmirched.

Hewitt's share in the general work of exposure was an inquiry into the connection of Minister Schenck with the Emma Mine, and his report in May was one of the most effective documents issued that spring.[1] He proved that Minister Schenck had not gone into

[1] Speaker Kerr at the beginning of the session appointed Hewitt to the Committee on Public Buildings and Grounds. Since he had long sold iron beams for government buildings, he could not accept. He had himself transferred to the Committee on Foreign Affairs, where he showed a keen interest in helping Secretary of State Fish better our foreign service. Hewitt made two speeches in

the scheme innocently and credulously, but with unclean hands. The American sponsors of the Emma Silver-Mining Company had virtually bribed him for the use of his official position; they had offered him five hundred shares of stock, worth £10,000 at par, to be carried for a year without expense, and to be returnable at any time during the year without loss; they had guaranteed him dividends of 2 per cent (later 1.5 per cent) monthly; and they had agreed to pay him $2,500 a year as a director. In return, Schenck had publicly vouched for the "exceptional character" of the investment, a notoriously speculative Utah mine. When the British press first began to criticize him, he had cabled the State Department a flat misstatement: "Have no pecuniary interest except some shares, for which, after investigating fully, I paid dollar for dollar." Secretary Fish ordered him to withdraw from the management. But he delayed his resignation in the interest of speculators who were trying to maintain the value of the stock; and when he finally published it, he included a fresh endorsement of the "value and profitableness of the company." Moreover, he continued to speculate in the stock, buying it on margin. When, near the close of 1872, he received inside information that no more dividends could be paid, he hastily attempted through his second secretary of legation to sell two thousand shares short!

Hewitt summed up the evidence in his forcible report,[1] upon which E. L. Godkin of the *Nation* wrote him a warmly complimentary letter. It was the best document of the kind, said Godkin, that he had ever seen. Hewitt also drove its meaning home in a speech to the House on May 25, which had a broad application to all the disclosures of fraud and corruption under the Grant Administration. There were many evidences of public disgust with the government and of an overwhelming demand for change and reform. With this in mind, he did not despair of the future. Even

---

February, 1876, in favor of adequate appropriations for this service. He tried ineffectually to raise the pay of the consul-general at Cairo from $3,000 to $4,000, and insisted that the consulate at Beirut be retained as a protection to the Christians of Syria, including our missionaries.

[1] House Report No. 579, 44th Congress, 1st Session. This 16-page document is an admirable compression of all the evidence. It was republished together with Hewitt's speech of May 25 in the House, and circulated broadcast during 1876 by the Democratic National Committee. Yet both report and speech are strikingly devoid of any partisan tone.

in those corrupt times, he asserted, there were millions of Americans who demanded purity and character from their officials. The first century of the republic was drawing to a close; few were left who could remember the days of Jefferson, Madison, and J. Q. Adams; but the principles of honor and courage which these statesmen had inculcated were not forgotten. Men might well entertain the hope that a better day was near:

> The spirit abroad is the spirit of reformation. The people are determined to bring back that better era of the republic in which, when men consecrated themselves to the public service, they utterly abnegated all selfish purposes; when public officers rejected gifts as dishonoring alike the giver and the taker; when Presidents and great officers of state as a rule retired to honorable poverty; when Franklin with his modest income and uncourtly costume, even though he had a thrifty mind, rejecting all thought of gain while employed in the public service, was held in more honor than the proudest ambassador of the proudest empire; when John Quincy Adams sold his bank shares before he would take his seat in Congress, lest his vote might be called in question; when members of Congress knew not the mysteries of Crédit Mobilier; when members of the Cabinet were selected because they were statesmen, "honest, capable, faithful," and not because of their skill in managing party politics; when to be summoned into the public service was a priceless honor and not an opportunity for private gain. . . .

A fortnight after this speech the Republicans began gathering in Cincinnati for their national convention; and thus the curtain went up on the campaign of 1876.

CHAPTER XVII

The Campaign of 1876

BY MIDSUMMER of 1876, while Congress still sat discussing the scandals, the Presidential campaign was uproariously in swing. The Republican National Convention, after a brisk battle in which Conkling, Bristow, Blaine, Morton, and Hayes were the prominent aspirants, had made its choice on June 16. The Democratic Convention, meeting at St. Louis, had chosen its nominee less than a fortnight later. The governor of Ohio faced the governor of New York, each with a united party behind him.

The contrast between the two forces made this one of the most striking of all our Presidential battles. On the one side was Samuel J. Tilden, sixty-two, forty years of lucrative corporation law behind him, suave, cold, secretive, dilatory, without eloquence or personal magnetism, but with the most incisive intellect in public life—with sound ideas and brains and courage to execute them; Thomas A. Hendricks, bluff governor of Indiana, capable lawyer, and inflationist; a heterogeneous array of Southerners, Tammany men, old-time followers of Douglas and Seymour, Liberal Republicans led by Charles Francis Adams and Lyman Trumbull, and independents disgusted by "Grantism." On the other side was Rutherford B. Hayes, fifty-three, "one of the good brigadiers" in the Civil War, with ten years' experience in politics, a liberal of broad education, but with slight national reputation; William A. Wheeler, cultivated New York Congressman, one-time president of the State Constitutional Convention, and enemy of Conkling; a heterogeneous array of radicals, conservatives, spoilsmen, reformers, carpetbaggers, and Negroes. On one side was the cry for rescue from the depression, on the other the cry for rescue from the Rebel Southerners—the ragged shirt *versus* the bloody shirt. On the one side was a mass of desperate unemployed, desperate Louisianians and South Carolinians groaning under black rule, desperate battlers against national corruption; on the other men fearful of the South, of low tariffs, of cheap money, and of Democratic inexperience. The Solid South was taking its stand under the Democratic banner; the solid G. A. R. and a solid hundred-thousand of Federal office-holders under the Republican colors. Excitement, oratory, newspaper broadsides, and rallies were appearing as in no campaign since 1860.

To fervid party men of that day momentous issues seemed at stake—reform, the fate of the hard-beset whites of the South, the preservation of the Union; but actually none of them was involved. The issue of reform had been settled by the two conventions; Hayes and Tilden were equally committed to it. The question of white supremacy in the South was being inexorably settled by time. The Anglo-Saxon inhabitants had already reconquered all but three of the Southern States, and this year they convinced even Grant that they simply would not submit to continued Federal interference. The Union had never been in the slightest danger from the Southern "Rebels" or Democratic "disloyalty" since Appomattox. The only real question was whether Republicans or Democrats, Tilden or Hayes, should reform the national administration, withdraw the last Federal troops from the South, and attack some of the great new social and economic problems of the time. Neither party and neither man was equipped, as a matter of fact, to deal with these last-named problems as their complexity and gravity required.

Hewitt was in the very midst of this hard-fought campaign; for early in July Tilden selected him to be Democratic campaign manager,[1] and he at once took up the principal burden of organizing the party effort. The choice was logical. His wealth, his business experience, his restless enterprise and incessant energy, his ability to manage ten undertakings at once and manage them well, all recommended him. But quite apart from logic, it was dictated by Tilden's friendship and gratitude; for no one had done more to bring about the Cincinnati nomination.

Tilden had been a willing but laodicean aspirant for the Presidency. His lukewarm temper, the product of his cold disposition,

[1] That is, Tilden had him elected chairman of the Democratic National Committee.

scholarly tastes, and precarious health, is characteristically indicated by a letter which he had written a friend some time earlier.[1] After speaking in a deprecatory way of high ambitions, and saying that Silas Wright had once told him that "men who fix their eyes upon a distant object are apt to fail to see the sticks and stones in the path immediately before them," he went on: "Like yourself, I have seen everything. There are no illusions in my mind in respect to public life. I know that peace, content, and happiness are only in private station; and it is wholly exceptional in me to do what I am now doing." His associates, including Manton Marble and John Bigelow, had to stimulate his ambition for the White House at the same time that they cleared away innumerable local obstacles and defeated his national rivals, Hendricks, Hancock, Bayard, and Thurman; and none worked harder at both tasks than Hewitt.

Hewitt had labored with special vigor to familiarize the Democrats of the South and West with Tilden's name and to win delegates in those sections. He had written letters, helped to organize a Southern Committee in New York, and argued incessantly with Congressmen in Washington. Victory was not obtained without a vigorous effort, the nature of which he described many years later:[2]

> Governor Tilden was regarded by thoughtful politicians as the logical candidate of the Democratic Party for President . . . To make his nomination possible, however, required earnest and active preliminary work in the several States and especially in the South, where he was not as well known as statesmen like Thurman and Bayard.
>
> It was necessary, therefore, to organize a propaganda in behalf of Mr. Tilden, and to send out publications and missionaries in order to make his character and career known to the Democratic masses in the South, whose votes would necessarily be controlling in the coming Presidential Convention. This movement was the origin of what came to be known as the "Literary Bureau," afterwards so efficient in the President campaign of 1876. Whether the suggestion for the formation of this agency came originally from Mr. Tilden or not I do not know, but I do know that the cost of

[1] To A. Birdsall, September 19, 1874; Tilden Papers.

[2] Quoted from the secret history of the campaign of 1876 and disputed election of 1876-77 written by Hewitt in 1878 and revised and enlarged in 1895; Hewitt Papers. Hereafter this will be called "Secret History."

the enterprise was defrayed by Mr. Cooper, who was my partner in business and whose sister I married. The outlay was about $20,000.

When the convention met in St. Louis the results of this preliminary work became apparent. Mr. Tilden was in the lead from the outset, and on the second ballot was found to have more than two-thirds of all the votes, which finally were made unanimous.

At the convention itself Hewitt, though less in the public eye than Manton Marble, W. L. Dorsheimer, or Henry Watterson, had been quite as effective. William L. Scott, Montgomery Blair, and he talked little, moved energetically, and made sure of an overwhelming preponderance of delegates. On the first ballot Tilden had received 404½ votes, and his nearest rival, Hendricks, only 140½; on the second ballot he had 535 votes.

Hewitt knew when he accepted the executive chairmanship of the National Committee that the contest would be close. While Hayes aroused little popular enthusiasm, at least the Republicans could unite behind him as they could never have united behind Blaine, Conkling, or Bristow. Of all the independent Republicans who had attended the famous Fifth Avenue Conference of reformers held that spring, few prominent men save Charles Francis Adams and Parke Godwin refused to support him. William Cullen Bryant, for decades a friend of Tilden, allowed his business manager to keep the *Evening Post* Republican.[1] Carl Schurz was a tower of strength among German-Americans; Blaine, Conkling, Oliver P. Morton, and other party wheelhorses labored valiantly to keep the old organization in power. Zachariah Chandler of Michigan commanded abundant funds, speakers, and enthusiasm for a campaign organization. The recent scandals were ignored, impassioned rhetoric was concentrated upon Democratic "abuse" of the Southern negro, and Tilden's career was searched for flaws. Yet the Democratic party had certain manifest advantages. The economic depression, disgust with Grant, the desire of rational men to forget the war, the union of Northern and Southern elements in the party, the confidence bred by recent victories, were inestimable assets. If Tilden was not a statesman in the highest sense of the word, he was assuredly of greater natural abilities, keener mind,

---

[1] This interesting episode is described by the author in his *The Evening Post: A Century of Journalism*, 402-405.

and riper experience than Hayes, and worthy of the best traditions of Democracy. The party had rallied behind him as behind no man since Jackson.

Coming to New York in July, Hewitt supervised the opening of headquarters at the Everett House and a printing house at 59 Liberty Street; then, placing Colonel William T. Pelton, Tilden's nephew, in charge, he returned to Congress. He necessarily remained in Washington till the session ended in August, but made regular week-end trips to New York, and supervised the preparation of the most elaborate campaign textbook yet issued by any party, a volume of 750 pages dealing in detail with the Administration scandals and expounding Tilden's views and record. "For the first time in the history of Presidential campaigns," he wrote later, "the textbook became an arsenal from which ammunition was supplied for assault upon the enemy and for defence against his attacks. This book contained a summary of the results of the investigations instituted by the various Congressional Committees. It was generally regarded at the time as the most effective instrument which had ever been devised for supplying facts and arguments upon which the campaign might be successfully conducted. As a matter of fact, I believe that the preparation and publication of this book determined the result of the struggle." Tilden was not consulted upon it. Hewitt drew up an outline, hired the Washington correspondent of the New York *Sun*, A. M. Gibson, to help him, and wrote most of the arguments which accompanied the documentary materials.

In mid-August he was back in New York to face a mountain of work and one exigent political problem—the question of a nominee for governor. The Republicans had selected Edwin D. Morgan, one of the founders of their party, the able war governor in 1861-62, and a courageous man who had befriended Andrew Jackson and suffered for it. Could the Democrats do as well? Judge Sanford E. Church was vulnerable for his association with the Canal Ring; Andrew H. Green was hated by Tammany; William L. Dorsheimer of Buffalo was young and untried. By far the best man available was Hewitt, and the leaders almost unanimously turned to him. With the *World* and labor interests supporting his name, for a few days his choice seemed certain. Deeply reluctant, he wrote Tilden on August 25, 1876:[1]

[1] Tilden Papers.

My dear Governor:

I have been very much concerned at the suggestion of my name for Governor, because on the one hand I do not wish the nomination, and on the other I am so anxious to do the best thing to secure the election that I fear to refuse to do what your friends desire and deem best. I have given the most patient reflection to the matter and I have concluded that there is no well-founded objection to the nomination of Dorsheimer . . . While therefore I have been and am willing to make any necessary sacrifice of personal feeling to ensure success, I do not feel this sacrifice is either necessary or advantageous. I have therefore concluded to say positively that I cannot consent to be a candidate to the exclusion of Mr. Dorsheimer, who seems to me to be entitled to the nomination by every consideration of justice, good faith, and sound policy.

Governor Tilden and State Chairman Magone, however, prepared to overrule this protest. Charles S. Fairchild wrote urging the choice of Hewitt, for "his last speech, his whole conduct in Congress, have made him prominent and strong." And then the question was suddenly decided by reference to the State Constitution. "Hewitt," John Bigelow entered in his diary on August 31, "whom we all counted on for a candidate to succeed Tilden as governor, was found to be ineligible, not having resided in the State five years."[1] The man selected, after Horatio Seymour peremptorily declined, was Lucius Robinson, who added nothing to the party strength. Hewitt was renominated for Congress; his Republican opponent, one Babcock, was weak, and he was so certain of victory that he paid no attention to the district canvass.

All national campaigns are waged with three main armies: speakers, writers, and local organizers. To all three, but particularly the first two, Hewitt gave assiduous attention. Local canvassing had to be left chiefly to the State committees. The forces of publicity were mobilized as never before in any American election. Huge editions of the campaign textbook were ready before the end of August. At 59 Liberty Street, the "Literary Bureau" which had so effectively promoted the nomination of Tilden was reorganized and strengthened with a corps of writers to prepare editorials and news releases. Every day, circulars, containing matter ready to print

[1] John Bigelow, *Retrospections of an Active Life*, V, 280.

and suggestions for further arguments and news articles, were mailed to long lists of newspapers outside New York City. Simultaneously the campaign speeches of Democratic leaders were collected and published in bales. Most of them were issued in pocket-size leaflets resembling railroad time-tables, which could be easily circulated from hand to hand. "These leaflets became very popular and produced great results," Hewitt later testified. "It is estimated that at least one copy was published for every inhabitant of the United States, which would amount to about five for every voter. The effect was magical and the result upon the election was controlling."[1] The more important speeches were printed in large type on broadside sheets.

By September both sides had placed cohorts of speakers in the field. For the Republicans, Blaine, audacious as ever, led the host which swept across the doubtful states. As long as Congress had been in session he had been too ill to be re-examined by the Judiciary Committee. Within a week after its adjournment, however, his health was restored as miraculously as that of Jairus' daughter; in perfect vigor, he took the train and began travelling the length and breadth of the land delivering venomous attacks upon the Democrats. Upon the debatable soil of Ohio was concentrated the heavy Republican artillery—Schurz, Edmunds, John Sherman, Garfield, Ingersoll, J. D. Cox, Morton, and many more. Hewitt's speaking bureau was even more active. Senators Bayard and Thurman traversed the country. Samuel J. Randall, Lyman Trumbull, Charles Francis Adams, Cassius M. Clay, S. S. Cox, and Henry Watterson made up a second line of attack. In Indiana an unremitting battle for the Democratic ticket was maintained by Hendricks, Voorhees, McDonald, and two former Republicans, George W. Julian and Gustav Koerner, while there, and throughout the Middle West, German speakers were busy. Even colored orators were engaged in southern Illinois and Indiana to appeal to the negro vote, and Swedish, Bohemian, and French campaigners were sent out. Cyrus H. McCormick, the inventor, had been called upon by Hewitt to reinvigorate the party in the West, and as State Chairman in Illinois he threw all his business experience into the task.

Meanwhile New York was not forgotten. The Manhattan Club

[1] Secret History; the Hewitt Papers contain a number of specimens.

was a centre of Democratic activity. In September the State headquarters were removed from Albany to the Everett House, where
Chairman Magone and Hewitt could work together. The parlors
here presented a busy scene, with city leaders—Clarkson N. Potter,
Parke Godwin, Augustus Schell, John Kelly—rubbing elbows with
up-State men like Smith M. Weed and Daniel Manning. There was
much enthusiasm, much talk of "a Tilden wave," and much betting
by John Morrissey and his Tammany friends. The Democratic
nominee for mayor, Smith Ely, Jr., was so creditable that even the
Tribune praised him as "respectable, capable, experienced, and
honest." In up-State New York, Tilden was popular and the organization strong. Altogether, six hundred active Democratic clubs,
about three times as many as in any previous campaign, were
formed in New York.

The part which Tilden himself played in the campaign was
somewhat puzzling. Like Hayes, he made no speeches. During the
heat of summer he remained in Albany busy with official work
and a wide correspondence, but by October he spent much time at
the Liberty Street and Everett House headquarters. Yet he impressed both his party and the country at large as tardy, vacillating.
and excessively conservative.

While it was popularly supposed that his wealth gave the Democratic Party almost unlimited funds, actually he contributed little,
and Hewitt was grievously embarrassed for money. Edward Cooper
was treasurer of the National Committee. The amounts he received
and disbursed did not exceed $150,000. "The money was raised
with great difficulty," Hewitt later wrote,[1] "so that Mr. Cooper and
I, in addition to our personal subscriptions, *which were the largest ones made to the Committee,* were often in advance to a very
considerable amount. It is proper to add, however, that considerable
sums of money were handed directly to Mr. Tilden, and by him
were not handed over to the Treasurer. Out of the funds thus
placed under his personal control the expenses of the Literary Bureau were defrayed, and in the final settlement of accounts, more
than two years after the election, Mr. Tilden finally reimbursed
Mr. Cooper and myself for the excess of our disbursements beyond
the subscriptions we had made. This statement is made in order to
correct the impression that Mr. Tilden used a large private fortune

---

[1] Secret History.

in order to secure his election. From facts which are within my knowledge, I think the money received by him directly was nearly, if not quite, equal to the total amount of his expenditure, including the balance finally paid to Cooper and Hewitt."

Repeatedly, when funds were urgently needed, Hewitt had to refuse them. In the midst of the campaign a Florida leader, J. S. Boyd, of Jacksonville, came to national headquarters for aid. The State was trembling in the balance, but with very little money it could be made safe. "For ten thousand dollars," he exclaimed, "I will *insure* Florida for Tilden." After the battle, the National Committee was blamed for not sending more speakers, printed material, and workers into the doubtful Southern States. Hewitt would have been only too glad to do so. The keenness of his interest in the Southern battle comes out in repeated notes to Tilden—for example, one to Tilden asking him to talk with F. H. Alfriend of Georgia "on the state of the canvass in the South."[1] But almost the entire $150,000 which Edward Cooper collected was required in the North, and particularly in New York and Indiana. After the payment of speakers, printers, postage, and rents, little was left for the State Committees. It is safe to say that if Tilden, out of his superfluous wealth, had given $25,000 for legitimate campaign uses in Louisiana and Florida, his election would have been assured.

But Tilden was cautious, hesitant and though decisive enough when roused, too frequently limp; the chief reason being that he was a partial invalid. As a result of anxiety and overwork as governor, he had suffered a paralytic stroke in February, 1875, and its effects on both nerve and body were plainly evident. The New York *Tribune* justly charged that he was timid and halting.[2] "He postpones too much and waits too long . . . He rides a waiting race." And the historian of New York politics, D. S. Alexander, records: "In the larger field of action he had displayed a timid, vacillating character."

While Hayes issued a prompt letter of acceptance, dated July 8, Tilden waited until July 31. While Hayes's letter showed a vigor upon civil service reform and a sound currency which won general commendation, that of Tilden was disappointingly weak. Afraid of repelling the Western inflationists, he wrote with labored and

[1] August 24, 1876; Tilden Papers.
[2] N. Y. *Tribune*, September 19, 1876.

evasive verbosity.[1] The bad management of the gubernatorial nomination was laid at his door. When the Republicans accused him
of failure to make a fair income-tax return during the war, he was
curiously hesitant in meeting the attack. He kept silent until Hewitt himself applied to the Treasury for certified copies of the income
returns of both Hayes and Tilden. They were refused. Hewitt then
addressed a note to Judge James P. Sinnott, who had been Tilden's
confidential law clerk during the whole period when the income-
tax law was in force; and upon his insistence Sinnott made a detailed, though not wholly satisfying, statement. This was on September 21, only six weeks before election.

Throughout the summer, again, Tilden made no reply to Republican statements that his triumph would open the door to the
payment of tens of thousands of Confederate claims for wartime
damages. Blaine declared that "there is nothing in the world to
prevent" recompense by a Democratic Administration "for all the
articles that were destroyed down South during the war, all the
wild destruction that followed the war." These alarmist utterances
were accepted even by such calm observers as our Minister to England, Edwards Pierrepont, and required a calm contradiction, yet
Tilden made none. Hewitt finally went to his house on October 24
with a letter calling attention to the subject, and a prepared answer; he obtained Tilden's approval of these documents, and Tilden added one sentence to the reply: "Let the dead past bury its
dead." Taking them in hand, Hewitt hurried to headquarters to
give them to the press—for he feared Tilden would reconsider.
Just as he reached it Tilden's colored servant overtook him and
gasped out: "Mr. Tilden asks you to come back, sah." But Hewitt
curtly refused, and a few minutes later the letters were on the
wires.[2]

Unquestionably Tilden, maintaining a wide correspondence, seeing numerous party leaders, fingering many wires with sly adroit-
ness, gave some observers an impression that his was the guiding
hand of the campaign. But those at headquarters knew that he

[1] "He indulged in commonplaces and paltered with the financial question,"
says Rhodes; *History of the United States*, VII, 216. One phrase in this letter
led to the derisive term, "old usufruct Tilden."

[2] Hewitt told this story to Dr Nicholas Murray Butler, who gave it to the
author.

rather neglected it. He might keep closely in touch with trusted friends, but he almost ignored the official party organization. Hewitt later asserted that Tilden seldom conferred with him. In Albany he was busy; in New York City, "beset with visitors who occupied his time and diverted his attention from the work of the campaign. None of the manifestos of the Committee were prepared by him, although when opportunity offered they were submitted for his approval, which was never withheld. In fact, the Committee seemed to possess his confidence to such an extent that its members at times felt disposed to complain of Mr. Tilden's indifference. If he interfered at all it was usually to counsel economy in the expenditures."

Hewitt and his associates neglected little. The Republican press admitted that they far outstripped the Republican chairman, Zachariah Chandler. "A fresh instance of the sleepless vigilance with which Governor Tilden's canvass is conducted," said the *Tribune* on October 23, "is to be found in the circular issued from Democratic headquarters, urging Democrats to arrange their visits to Philadelphia [the Centennial] so as to be at home on election day." Every effort was made to get out a huge registration in New York City. It proved so large that the Republicans raised the usual cry of fraud and illegal naturalization. The one disregarded area was the South; the national headquarters did little, for it was financially helpless, in Louisiana, South Carolina, and Florida, the three States under carpet-bag rule; they were left for their own aroused whites to recapture.

Despite his office duties, Hewitt found time to make a few speeches. One vigorously defended Tilden's record at the outbreak of the war in 1861,[1] while another was provoked by Blaine. On October 16 Hewitt heard the former Speaker deliver an address in Cooper Union attacking Justice Clifford of the Supreme Court and other Democrats for certain entirely imaginary misdeeds connected with the war. The charges were so outrageously misleading that four nights later he mounted the same platform to reply. "The peculiarity of Blaine is," said Hewitt, "that he is perfectly reckless of assertion when he thinks the proof is not at hand to convict him of falsehood. I have carefully watched his mode of dealing with the House of Representatives, and I can produce many instances

[1] To be found in *Congressional Record*, Vol. IV, Pt. VI, pp. 5652-5655 (August 14, 1876).

to prove the justice of this criticism." This speech, published in pamphlet form under the title "Give Us Honest Men," is notable as the first thorough analysis of Blaine's railroad transactions.[1] Eight years later Carl Schurz, with the advantage of a fresh batch of Mulligan letters, furnished a more comprehensive and detailed examination; but Hewitt's biting review was sufficient to shatter Blaine's pretences to clear-eyed candor and a high code of honor.

Altogether, it was Hewitt and not Tilden who was the animating force of the Democratic campaign. His huge correspondence for the summer, the prominence given his efforts by the press while Tilden stayed in the background, are evidence of this; but we have other testimony. Years later Don M. Dickinson, at this time Democratic State Chairman of Michigan, wrote Theodore Roosevelt his impressions of the campaign. He described the fervor of the young men who enlisted under the reform banner and their tendency to idealize Tilden. Actually, he writes, they learned later that Tilden was but a marvelously skillful politician, while Hewitt was the true embodiment of the spirit of reform:[2]

> Mr. Tilden was at the head of the reform movement and was Mr. Hewitt's leader and mine. I know now that Mr. Tilden was

[1] This speech deserves close study by those who cling to a belief in Blaine's innocence. Hewitt was thoroughly convinced of his guilt. He pointed out that Blaine was accused of unloading his worthless Little Rock bonds on the Union Pacific; that somebody on December 16, 1871, *did* sell such bonds to the railroad for $64,000; and that in a letter of April 18, 1872, to Warren Fisher, Blaine admitted recently selling some bonds—and never explained to the Congressional Committee what these bonds were. Till he explained that transaction, he must be held suspect. Hewitt also pointed out in what a fearful position Blaine had stood just after his dramatic appearance in the House to read the Mulligan letters on June 5, 1876. The Congressional Committee was about to sit again. Mulligan was ready to appear before it and testify to additional facts and perhaps to missing letters. The trick of Blaine or his friends in sending a telegram to Josiah Caldwell in London, asking him to certify Blaine's innocence, was about to be exposed. "The great Republican leviathan was caught, and floundering in the very toils which he himself had constructed. Turn whichever way he might, there was no escape from the exposure and the disgrace which awaited him." It was at this juncture that he was stricken unconscious on the steps of the First Congregational Church in Washington and carried home to bed. His physicians asserted that any renewal of the inquiry would send him either to his grave or a lunatic asylum—and he remained an invalid till all danger of renewal was over, when his recovery was instantaneous. This speech, widely circulated in pamphlet form, did much to pave the way for the Mugwump movement of 1884. Copies are in the Hewitt Papers.

[2] March 15, 1902; Roosevelt Papers.

a very able, very adroit, and great politician of the school of Silas Wright and Van Buren. Hewitt was as true a patriot, as pure a man, as ever lived, in my opinion. His aims were exalted, and in his high purposes in political activity I do not believe he saw or considered himself at all. He was not a politician at all in the sense that Mr. Tilden was a politician. *He* was the ideal citizen, whom I as a boy and young man, had set up; but I did not realize it then. I know it now. I saw more of Hewitt than of Mr. Tilden. Tilden was silent on those things of which Mr. Hewitt talked most. Hewitt was Tilden's follower; and so, impressed by Hewitt, I idealized Tilden. I supposed I sat at Tilden's feet. I really sat at Hewitt's. My opinions of Mr. Tilden have changed as I have reflected upon the evidence. My opinions of Hewitt have only changed in that I now attribute to him, as I have for years, those qualities and characteristics that I most admire in a public man, and which I then credited to Mr. Tilden. I have used myself as an illustration, although in doing so there is palpably too much of the first person singular in this letter. But as *I* felt, the country was impressed; young men of force all over the country joined the Tilden standard, and went into the canvass of '76 with an energy and a *will* for success that of itself was so potent in winning votes that the organization of the party, which was practically crushed and dissolved in the Greeley campaign of but four years before, actually carried the country and elected a President for the first time since the Civil War.

I have no doubt whatever now that it was the Hewitt influence—the Hewitt impregnation of faith in, and his demands for purity and high patriotism in politics; *his* call upon young Americans for unselfish and aggressive civil battle for their country, and the tone and atmosphere that he gave the contest—the *timbre* of his battle-cries, that won the campaign, and not Mr. Tilden's "skill as an organizer." I was in that campaign a member of the National Committee *de facto* and chairman of my State Committee, and in touch with the campaign from first to last, and am very sure that I know. Mr. Hewitt knew it, too, though he never boasted of it, never claimed it.

The State elections of Ohio, Indiana, and West Virginia on October 10 were three encouraging straws. In Indiana James D. Williams, Democratic nominee for governor, had a plurality of 5,084 over Benjamin Harrison. In West Virginia the Democratic

candidate for governor ran up a plurality of 12,729. In Ohio the
Republicans elected their State tickets by a margin of only 6,636
for the highest post, the secretaryship of state. Hewitt issued a
triumphant address for the Democratic National Committee:

> Upon the three States of West Virginia, Ohio, and Indiana
> were concentrated all the influence of the Administration, all
> their efforts, and all the vast sums of money forced from the
> one hundred thousand officeholders of the party in power. These
> were heavy odds, not again to be encountered in such concentrated
> form; for in the November election the contest will be in every
> one of the thirty-eight States upon the same day. Nevertheless,
> against these odds the Democrats and Reformers of West Vir-
> ginia and Indiana have been victorious, and in Ohio they have
> all but rescued a State hitherto deemed hopeless, and have created
> an assurance of victory in November. . . .

In the closing weeks he threw himself into his work with sleepless
abandon. Men who wrote him on the iron business received word
later that he had been unable to read their letters. His assistant
Dr. R. W. Raymond informed an important customer that just once
he had "taken thirty seconds" from National Committee work to
make a crucial business decision. He had hoped to make a flying
trip in October to the Centennial Exposition, where his company
received a medal, but gave that up. When Sir William Siemens visited the country, he barely took time to give the great man a
dinner. Democratic lines were strengthened wherever funds permitted, and everywhere but in the lower South their condition was
satisfactory. But Hewitt had to write several such letters as that to
R. S. Tharis of Charleston on October 3, 1876:

> Your favor of the 25th instant with enclosure is received. I have
> read the proposed petition, and considered your request with
> every desire to meet your wishes. But as matters now stand, I
> find myself without means applicable to such purposes, and can-
> not therefore undertake to defray your expenses.

Election day, November 8, showed lowering skies in the East.
Rain shortly began in New York, and was hailed with elation at
Democratic headquarters as likely to reduce the Republican vote
up-State. As night fell the glare of numberless bonfires downtown
lit up the shining pavements, and calcium lights shone out over

acres of umbrellas gathered before the bulletin boards of the *Tribune, Herald,* and *World.* Hewitt, almost exhausted by his weeks of driving labor, was busy from early morning at the Everett House. Tilden arrived about noon and remained most of the afternoon; Colonel Pelton and John Bigelow were present most of the day; S. S. Cox, General McClellan, Clarkson N. Potter, and many more came and went. He drove home for dinner and then returned to headquarters. The place appointed for receiving Democratic returns was Irving Hall, which had a special telegraph, but he wished to avoid the heavy crush; and wires also ran to the Everett House.

The early returns, with an unusually heavy Democratic vote in the metropolis, indicated a landslide for Tilden. Later dispatches pointed to a closer race. But before the evening was far advanced it was clear that Tilden had swept New York State. A little later came proof that Indiana and New Jersey were carried by the Democrats, and that Connecticut inclined to their side. The flashing telegrams beat out a dramatic story of decisive popular majorities for Tilden in nearly every doubtful area of the North. By midnight the election seemed all but certain; Hayes had gone to bed in Ohio sure of defeat. Hewitt, tired out, left headquarters for his home. On the way he stopped a newsboy and bought a *Tribune.* There, in the principal Republican organ of the country, were the quiet headlines:

TILDEN ELECTED
HIS ELECTORAL MAJORITY SMALL

And below them was the news story:

> Tilden and Hendricks seem to be elected by a fair majority in the electoral college. They have probably carried the "Solid South" with the possible exception of South Carolina and Louisiana, have carried New York by from 25,000 to 30,000 majority, and New Jersey by a reduced majority. They have carried Indiana by 10,000 majority. Their total vote in the electoral college is likely to exceed 200. . . .

This seemed to place the result beyond doubt.

CHAPTER XVIII

Tilden: A Secret History

FOR some hours after midnight on November 7 almost everyone believed that Tilden had been elected. He had received, as the official returns later showed, 4,284,265 votes, against 4,033,295 cast for Hayes—a plurality of more than a quarter of a million.[1] He had carried New York by a plurality of more than 33,000; Indiana by more than 5,000; New Jersey by more than 12,000; and Connecticut by nearly 3,000. If the South were solidly his, as nearly everyone supposed, then he held twenty States with 203 electoral votes and Hayes eighteen States with 166 electoral votes. The Republican chairman, Zachariah Chandler, disconsolately closed the party headquarters in the Fifth Avenue Hotel and went to bed convinced of defeat. Nearly all the morning newspapers of the land were pounding off editions announcing a Democratic victory. For a brief interval Tilden was almost as much the President-elect, in one sense, as any party nominee has ever been. But for the intervention of a single journal, his triumph might have been quietly conceded.

That journal was the New York *Times*, then bitterest of Republican sheets. Hewitt at midnight had sent a messenger to inquire what majority it allowed Tilden, and had been met by the defiant reply, "None!" In the small hours of the morning the weary editors had gathered to consider the verdict of their first edition. There were four: John Foord, editor-in-chief, John C. Reid, managing editor, George Shepherd, and Edward Cary. Reid, who had been in Libby Prison during the war, and still more Cary, a strong

---

[1] Edward Stanwood, *A History of the Presidency* (1928 ed.), II, 383, gives the Republican count as Tilden, 4,285,992, and Hayes, 4,033,768; the Democratic count as Tilden, 4,300,590, and Hayes, 4,036,298.

partisan, were against any admission of defeat until the last ditch had been lost.[1] They perhaps knew that the *Herald* was refusing to follow the *Tribune* in conceding Tilden's election. Cary's resolute arguments persuaded the others. But as they still deliberated, shortly after three o'clock, there occurred one of those accidents upon which the fate of a government sometimes hinges. They received the following dispatch from Chairman Magone at the Democratic State—not national—headquarters.

Please give your estimate of electoral votes secured for Tilden. Answer at once. D. A. Magone.

This blundering message indicated that Magone felt uncertain of the result in the South. Before election day Zach Chandler had laid claim to Louisiana, South Carolina, North Carolina, and Florida; the *Tribune* had expressed certainty of Louisiana and the Carolinas; and now returns from these States were tardy. The *Times* editor knew that Republicans controlled the returning boards of Louisiana, South Carolina, and Florida, and that in a close-fought contest these men could manufacture majorities as Tweed had manufactured one in New York State in the Presidential election of 1868. There is evidence that early reports from the Republican chairmen in Louisiana and Florida conceded these States to Tilden, but that Chandler suppressed these reports. At this hour, the only authentic news the *Times* had from Louisiana was that the Republicans claimed it by 4,000 votes, the Democrats by 20,000. Already Cary had induced his fellow-editors to accept the verdict, "In doubt," and had written an editorial of that purport; but Magone's message added confidence to their stand. The first edition gave the news of a wavering result. Editorially, it asserted that either man might yet be found elected; that Florida, Oregon, and New Jersey were still undecided, while Louisiana and South Carolina were for Hayes; and that judgment must be suspended. The second edition, at 6:30, gave New Jersey to Tilden, making a total of 184 votes; Oregon to Hayes, making a total of 181; and declared that Florida with its four votes was doubtful. "If the Republicans have carried that State, as they claim, they will have 185 votes—a majority of one."

But between these two editions more history had been made.

---

[1] Cf. Elmer Davis, *History of the New York Times,* 117-155.

The audacity of the *Times* lay in its bold contention that Louisiana and South Carolina belonged in the Republican column. In the face of the preponderant returns, and without a scintilla of convincing evidence, it was filing claim to them as unquestionably for Hayes. The purpose of this claim was clear. It was to lay a foundation upon which the Republican returning boards could furnish the majority required. If this plan were to succeed the party managers must be induced to take control of the situation at the South without loss of an hour. At any moment some unwary Republican leader in New Orleans or Tallahassee might admit a Democratic victory. Hence, as dawn broke, the dramatic errand of the managing editor, Reid, through the hushed streets to warn Zach Chandler. The story of that trip has long been familiar: how, in the darkened hall of the Fifth Avenue Hotel, he ran upon W. E. Chandler, a national committeeman just arriving from New Hampshire; how, together, they roused Zach Chandler from his stupor of despairing exhaustion; how he authorized them to act; and how, as the sun rose, they sent telegrams to the responsible party heads in Louisiana, South Carolina, and Florida:

> Hayes is elected if we have carried South Carolina, Florida, and Louisiana. Can you hold your State? Answer at once.

Long afterwards, the men concerned indignantly denied that there had been any conspiracy to seize the needed electoral votes in the South. No, there was no conspiracy; there was simply an editor's bold and feasible plan, appreciated instantly by the party chieftains, and put into execution as rapidly as the telegraph could serve their ends. "Can you hold your State?"—and what Republican in Southern territory ruled for years by force, fraud, and corruption would not try to hold his State?[1] A few hours later that fateful day Zach Chandler defiantly announced the shibboleth of the united Republican cohorts:

> "Hayes has 185 electoral votes and is elected."

Thus, partly by accident, partly by bold design, partly by a flaw in the plans of the nation's founders, the means were supplied, in this centennial year of American democracy, for a clear frustration of the popular will. No one could deny that a preponderance of

---

[1] Cf. A. M. Gibson, *A Political Crime*, 55ff.

the American people preferred Tilden for the Presidency. His majority over all exceeded 157,000, his plurality over Hayes 250,-000; if we exclude the illiterate and ignorant negroes of the South, these margins would be increased by an additional quarter million and more. Yet the shining equities of the situation, the undeniable verdict of the electorate, received not the slightest consideration. This was political war, and in war all is fair. Any weapon was proper if it had the appearance of legality, and the great object was not to give the country the President it voted for, but to fight out the battle till every ruse, every technicality, every bluff, had been exhausted.

I

So long had the Democrats languished in outer darkness, so deep had been their humiliation in '64, in '68, and in '72, that in these brief hours of victory they must have felt that they were moving in a dream. If so, the newspapers of November 8 supplied a rude awakening. The *Tribune*, in its second edition, caught the note of the *Times* and trumpeted that the election was doubtful. Hewitt hurried to the Everett House. There he decided that certain steps must be taken instantly: observers must be hurried South, and preparations made to insure a fair scrutiny of the ballots in the three disputed States. At this point, part of the story can best be told in his own words. Two years later he wrote out a secret history of the disputed election, which in 1895 he rewrote and amplified. In this history, which he directed should never be published till all the men named therein were dead, he gave his own story of a contest in which, both as Congressional leader and Democratic national chairman, he played a vital role.[1] He begins:

> The struggle resulted in the triumphant election of Mr. Tilden not merely by a majority of all the votes cast, but by a majority of all the States in the Union. . . . . The country, however, was then astounded by the claim of the Republican National Committee that Hayes had secured 185 electoral votes and would therefore be declared President by a majority of one vote. As soon as this claim was made, based upon the votes of South Carolina, Florida, and Louisiana, I caused letters to be sent to the leading men of the North, Democrats and Republi-

[1] Copies of this history are in the Hewitt Papers.

cans alike, inviting them to proceed to South Carolina, Florida, and Louisiana for the purpose of seeing that a fair count was made, and the returns honestly canvassed. The next day President Grant, who was in Philadelphia, issued a similar request to leading Republicans only, and thus it happened that two sets of "visiting statesmen" repaired to the several States in doubt, one selected by General Grant acting as partisans, and the other selected by me for their standing and character without reference to their political affiliations.

The result is known to all men. The returning boards of the several States referred to gave the votes of these States to Hayes, although it was then known and is now universally admitted that the States of Florida and Louisiana were carried for Tilden. In this emergency the State of Oregon seemed to offer an antidote to the fraud thus perpetrated. Oregon had been carried by the Republicans, but one of the electors was disqualified from acting by a Constitutional provision forbidding Federal officeholders to act as electors. One of the Republican electors was a postmaster, and hence the Governor, who was a Democrat, refused his certificate and gave it to the highest candidate upon the Democratic ticket. Thus one vote was secured for Tilden, giving him 185 votes against 184 votes for Hayes, including all the votes from the three Southern States fraudulently secured through corrupt returning boards.

Feeling, however, that the vote secured in Oregon was not in accordance with the popular will, and ought only to be counted for Mr. Tilden in order to offset the palpable frauds in Florida and Louisiana, I prepared an address to the people of the United States setting forth the facts as they then appeared, and have since been demonstrated to have been true, and calling upon the people to assemble in their several places of meeting throughout the country to protest against the frauds which had been committed, and to express their determination that the people should not be robbed of their choice for President. This address as originally drafted is . . . evidence that I did not fall short in my duty as chairman of the Committee either in promptitude of action, or in submitting to my countrymen a plan of action for the prevention of the greatest wrong in the history of the Union. This address was submitted to Mr. Tilden on the 9th November [December], 1876. He made a few verbal alterations, and struck out the passage inviting public meetings on the ground that in the excited state of public feeling there would be violence.

Moreover, he added that it would be safe to trust to the sense of justice which sooner or later would show itself in the public mind and make the consummation of the fraud impossible. The address thus amended was then copied in a fair hand. . . .

Before, however, it could be given to the newspapers Mr. Tilden informed me that he preferred to delay action, and hence the address was never issued, and the Committee was left in the position of apparently acquiescing in the policy of inaction from which I absolutely dissented.

The remainder of the month of November was occupied in preparing the cases as far as possible for the consideration of Congress, which was to meet on the first Monday of December. In the meantime leading Democrats from all parts of the country were called into consultation, and at length a very brief address . . . was issued to the people practically referring the final decision to the two houses of Congress under the provisions of the Constitution.

We here break off his narrative, to which we shall return in a moment.

The elements of the situation in this great national crisis were simple. Every Democrat, high or low, believed fervently that Tilden had been elected and that the Republicans were attempting to steal the Presidency. Most Republicans were equally confident that Hayes was justly entitled to the Presidency, and that the Democratic claim to Louisiana, South Carolina, and Florida was based upon fraud, intimidation, and murder. Many Republicans, however, admitted that Tilden had been elected. They included such prominent men as Senator Roscoe Conkling and the editors of the *Nation*, New York *Evening Post*, and Springfield *Republican*. Other Republicans were doubtful, but held that national interest required the seating of Hayes. In all three Southern States the Republicans had an official machinery in the shape of returning boards which would enable them to claim the electoral votes on the face of the returns. The equivocal language of the Constitution upon the counting of the electoral votes—the statement that they should be opened by the president of the Senate in the presence of both houses of Congress, and should "then be counted"—made it possible for the Republicans to assert that the president of the Senate (which they controlled) should decide which electoral votes should be counted. The Democrats denied this and asserted that, when no candidate had a clear majority, the election, under another section of the Constitution, went to the House which they controlled. If the two parties should appeal to force, the Republican Administration obviously commanded the regular army. But the regular army was small, and in a number of Northern States, led by New York, the militia were under the command of Democratic governors.[1]

The statement of Hewitt given above, while essentially accurate, requires a certain amount of elucidation and expansion. On November 9 he issued his request that leading men of both parties proceed to the three disputed States to make certain of a fair count. Next day, November 10, President Grant called upon a number of prominent Republicans to go South and oversee the canvass of the returns. At the same time the President, through General Sherman, instructed General Augur, in Louisiana, and General Ruger, in Florida, to preserve order, and to see that the Republican Canvassing Boards "are unmolested in the performance of their duties" —instructions which were perhaps proper, but which evoked vigorous Democratic protests. At once leading Democrats and Republicans, commissioned by Chairmen Chandler and Hewitt, hastened southward. Upon New Orleans alone descended twenty-five Republicans, including John Sherman, Stanley Matthews, James A. Garfield, Matthew Quay, and Eugene Hale, and twenty-three Democrats, including Lyman Trumbull, William R. Morrison, John M. Palmer, Samuel J. Randall, Henry Watterson, and George W. Julian; "visiting statesmen," all eager to secure a party victory, and nearly all careless of strict justice. The Democratic visitors immediately began collecting information and preparing reports to Hewitt. On November 24 he published an encouraging manifesto to Democrats of the three States in a letter to Wade Hampton.

Hewitt's steps to secure the vote of one Democratic elector in Oregon, taken immediately after the election, should not be misconstrued. It was not a mere trick, but a maneuvre intended to place the Republicans between the horns of a dilemma. He knew that the Republican leaders intended first to throw out enough Democratic votes in Florida, Louisiana, and South Carolina, through the Returning Boards, to give them these States; and then

[1] An exhaustive study of the contest is furnished by Paul Leland Haworth's *The Disputed Presidential Election of 1876*; but it is marred by partisanship.

to maintain in Congress that no Federal authority had a right to go behind the official State returns. In Oregon, which the Republicans had clearly carried, one Republican elector was a postmaster. Thus holding a Federal office of trust and profit, he was disqualified under the Constitution from serving in the electoral college. The Democratic governor could maintain that the elector with the next highest number of votes, a Democrat, rightfully succeeded to the vacancy. To upset this contention, Hewitt believed that the Republicans in Washington would have to go behind the returns. If they went behind the returns in Oregon, how could they refuse to go behind them in South Carolina, Louisiana, and Florida? He made all this clear in a telegram of November 15 to Governor Grover of Oregon:[1]

> Upon careful investigation, the legal opinion is that votes cast for a Federal office-holders are void, and that the person receiving the next highest number of votes should receive the certificate of appointment. The canvassing officers should act upon this, and the governor's certificate of appointment be given to the elector accordingly, and the subsequent certificate of the votes of the electors be duly made specifying how they voted. This will force Congress to go behind the certificate, and open the same to get into merits of all cases, which is not only just, but which will relieve the embarrassment of the situation.

Meanwhile, the struggle in the Southern States had commenced. It is an old story, which will be retold only as new information can be contributed to it. By newspaper reports, letters, and telegrams from the "visiting statesmen," Hewitt was kept informed of whatever happened. We can summarize the background of events in a few brief phrases:[2]

Louisiana, the principal centre of contention:[3] Republican "statesmen" arrived November 12th, Democrats November 13th; a Returning Board of four—James Madison Wells, naval officer at the port of New Orleans and dishonest politician, Thomas C. Anderson, a corrupt local office-seeker, L. M. Kenner, once indicted

[1] Hewitt's reasons for intervening in the Oregon matter are given in full in the N. Y. *Tribune,* December 8, 1876.

[2] H. J. Eckenrode's study of the disputed election in *Rutherford B. Hayes, Statesman of Reunion* (American Political Leaders Series), is full, fair, and interesting.

[3] On Louisiana see Report 143, 44th Congress, 2d session, parts 1 and 2.

for larceny, and G. Casanave, a colored ignoramus;[1] canvass of returns begun November 20th; count in uncontested parishes finished November 27; canvass of parishes in which frauds, intimidation, or other irregularities were alleged continued till December 2; on the face of the returns, majorities for the Tilden electors ranging from 6300 to 8957; much evidence of Republic frauds in the over-registration of negro voters; much evidence of Democratic violence and intimidation in six parishes, and especially several bordering upon Mississippi and Arkansas; assumption by Republican visitors that all negroes would have voted for Hayes, despite proof that many had changed their allegiance in protest against carpet-bag misgovernment; tremendous Republican pressure on the Returning Board, with offers of Federal spoils; rejection by the Returning Board of approximately 13,250 Democratic votes and 2,040 Republican votes; resultant conversion of Democratic majorities of 6300-8900 into Republican majorities of 4600-4700.[2] Just before this result, a statement by the principal Episcopalian minister, two principal Catholic prelates, principal Presbyterian minister, and principal Jewish rabbi, with bank presidents and other prominent business men: "We believe with the people of the whole State that a large majority of the honest votes cast were in favor of the so-called Democratic Conservative candidates."

South Carolina, scene of a heated gubernatorial contest between D. H. Chamberlain, Republican, and Wade Hampton, Democrat:[3]

[1] General Sheridan had informed Secretary Stanton in 1867 that Wells was a "political trickster and a dishonest man"; Report of June 3, 1867. The Board had flagrantly violated the law by refusing to fill a vacancy with a Democratic member; in its count it now paid no attention to the law which required that charges of intimidation must accompany the returns and could not be added afterward; and its proceedings were conducted in secrecy and reported without details or explanation. *Nation*, December 14, 1876.

[2] John Sherman assured two leading Carpetbaggers, D. A. Weber and James E. Anderson, in writing, that he would reward them if the Returning Board made the proper decisions. "From a long and intimate acquaintance with Gov. Hayes I am justified in assuming responsibility for promises made and will guarantee that you shall be provided for as soon after the Fourth of March as may be practicable, and in such manner as to enable you both to leave Louisiana should you deem it necessary." November 20, 1877; W. E. Chandler Papers, Library of Congress. For a fuller list of similar promises made in various parts of the South see W. E. Chandler Papers, Nos. 8689-8692; W. B. Hesseltine, *Ulysses S. Grant, Politician*, 415, 416.

[3] On South Carolina see House Misc. Document 42, 44th Congress, 2d session, 131ff.; A. A. Taylor, *The Negro in South Carolina During the Reconstruction*, ch. XII.

a State Board of Canvassers—Henry E. Hayne, colored Secretary of State, F. L. Cardoza, colored State Treasurer, Thomas C. Dunn, white Controller-General, H. W. Purvis, colored Adjutant-General, and W. H. Stone, white Attorney-General, all Republicans; three of these men candidates for office in the very election upon which they sat as judges; election-day violence and repeating on both sides, armed negroes surrounding some polls, armed whites others; outrageous Democratic frauds in Edgefield and Laurens Counties; every indication of a close count on the surface of the returns; the final decision, November 21, giving the Democrats control of the legislature and consequently the governorship, but the Republicans the Presidential electors by a majority averaging 815; fruitless Democratic maneuvres to obtain one or more electors while retaining legislature; the general situation clouded by fraud and violence, but Hayes probably entitled to electors.

Florida: campaign less heated than in South Carolina; Republican "statesmen," including W. E. Chandler, E. F. Noyes, Lew Wallace, and Francis C. Barlow, arrived November 12th; Democratic "statesmen," including ex-Governor Joseph E. Brown of Georgia and Manton Marble, immediately following; much proof of Democratic violence and Republican fraud and repeating throughout the State; canvassing board of three—Samuel B. McLin, Secretary of State, Clayton A. Cowgill, Controller, and William A. Cocke, Attorney-General; first two avowed Republicans, third a Democrat serving in a Republican Administration; Board convened November 27 to consider local returns which on the surface gave Tilden a clear majority; returns canvassed with barefaced partisanship; many Democratic precincts and one whole county thrown out, sometimes on flimsiest pretexts; Republican precincts counted even when open to grave objections; the final result, proclaimed December 5, giving Hayes the electoral vote by majorities of which the lowest was 924. This partisan performance too much for one Republican observer, General Francis C. Barlow, who concludes that the Tilden electors have majorities of 30 to 55, and urges one of the Republican members of the Board to give Tilden the State;[1] careful later analysis proves almost conclusively that Tilden carried Florida.

[1] See Senate Report 611, 44th Congress, 2d session, pt. 4, pp. 12, 13; and W. W. Davis, *The Civil War and Reconstruction in Florida, passim,* which shows virtually beyond question that Tilden carried Florida.

II

By December 6, Hewitt knew that the canvassing boards had done the work assigned them by the Republican National Committee. Deeply outraged by the result, particularly in Louisiana and Florida, he had been helpless while the count was proceeding. On the day named, Palmer, Trumbull, and Julian mailed him a full report upon Louisiana, expatiating upon the dishonesty of the Returning Board, the secrecy of its final proceedings, and the false assumptions of the Republicans in throwing out Democratic votes. At this juncture Hewitt resolved to appeal to the voters of the land, 4,300,000 strong. The press reported Tilden "deep in lawbooks"; Democratic leaders said, "We shall do whatever Uncle Sammy tells us"; the *Tribune* aptly remarked that the party was "in the position of an army waiting for orders from its general"—but no orders came. Various men, notably August Belmont, had been urging that Tilden sanction a mass meeting and indignant denunciation of the "outrage." On December 7 and 8, Hewitt wrote out the brief, emphatic address mentioned above and on the 9th laid it before Tilden. Its opening paragraph read:

To the People of the United States:
Pursuant to the provisions of the Constitution, the electoral college met in the several States on the first Wednesday of December, and cast three hundred and sixty-nine votes for President and Vice-President. Of this number Samuel J. Tilden and Thomas A. Hendricks each received one hundred and eighty-five votes, while Rutherford B. Hayes and William A. Wheeler each received one hundred and eighty-four votes. On the face of the returns, therefore, already made public, but not yet officially counted by the two houses of Congress, Samuel J. Tilden is elected President and Thomas A. Hendricks Vice-President of the United States.
Included, however, in the one hundred and eighty-four votes counted for Hayes and Wheeler, are seven votes from South Carolina, four votes from Florida, and eight votes from Louisiana, which in our judgment belonged to and of right should have been cast for Tilden and Hendricks; and in the votes counted for Tilden and Hendricks is one vote from Oregon, cast by an elector who while he did not receive a majority of the votes of the people of that State, received the certificate of election from

the Governor in accordance with the law of Oregon, because the candidate who received the majority of the votes was ineligible by reason of the provisions of the Constitution of the United States. Assuming therefore that the intention of the people rather than the fraudulent returns in the Southern States and the provisions of the law in the Pacific State should be respected in the final count by the two houses of Congress, Tilden and Hendricks will be declared elected by two hundred and three votes cast for them, against one hundred and sixty-six cast for Hayes and Wheeler. . . .

But, Hewitt went on, the Democratic National Committee apprehended that an attempt would be made to pervert the final counting of the votes by the two houses of Congress in such fashion as to reject the one vote of Oregon cast for Tilden, on the ground that it did not express the will of the State, and to count for Hayes the votes of South Carolina, Florida, and Louisiana, on the ground that Congress was not competent to go behind the official returns. "The inconsistency of this position, however it may be disguised, is too obvious to deceive the people." He added:

We believe that the returns sent to the Vice-President can and should be enquired into. We believe that only genuine and not false or fraudulent votes should be counted, and to quote the words of President Lincoln, that "the two houses of Congress, convened under the twelfth article of the Constitution, have complete power to exclude from counting all electoral votes deemed by them to be illegal." We believe also that full effect should be given to the voice of the people, when expressed according to the laws of the State and of the United States, within the limits and under the restriction of the Constituion. If . . . these rules should be applied only when they enure to the benefit of the Republican candidates, and rejected when they work to their detriment, we have no hesitation in declaring our belief that the people of this country will never submit to such an act of injustice and usurpation.

Resistance should and undoubtedly will be made as heretofore in the courts, and by all the machinery known to the law, and by such powers as may be vested under the Constitution in the representatives of the people in Congress assembled. No assent will ever be given to the pernicious doctrine, that a single State or any number of States, can by the ingenious device of returning boards, expressly contrived for the commission of fraud, defeat the will of the people in the remaining States, where the vote is fairly cast and honestly returned. Unless this destructive invention, the infernal machine of recent politics, is promptly discarded, pretended intimidation supported by purchased affidavits will take the place of honest suffrage, popular elections become an expensive farce, and free government will destroy itself by deliberate suicide.

At this point Hewitt brought his appeal to the Democratic voters to a climax in the paragraph which, as he writes, Tilden struck out. He called for great party mass meetings on Jackson Day:

We utterly condemn therefore and boldly denounce all such fraudulent contrivances for the destruction of self-government, and we insist that when the votes shall be counted it will be the duty of the two houses of Congress to reject returns which on proper examination shall be found to be fictitious or fraudulent, and see to it that the real voice of the people, uttered in accordance with the provisions and the spirit of the Constitution, shall be expressed and not suppressed. . . .

We therefore call upon all lovers of their country, without distinction of party, to give free and frank expression to their opinions upon this question, which, in our judgment, is fundamental to the preservation of our national liberty, and to this end, while the people are yet free and independent, we invite them to assemble at their usual places of meeting in every city, town and hamlet in the country on the 8th day of January next to consider the dangers of the situation, and by calm, firm, and temperate resolutions, to enlighten their representatives in Congress now assembled as to their duties in this great crisis of our institutions, established by the virtue, wisdom, and sacrifice of our forefathers, and which we are bound by every consideration of duty and by every impulse of patriotism to transmit unimpaired to our children.

There still exists the original draft of this ringing address, with various minor corrections and the pencil marks by which Tilden cancelled the final decisive paragraph.[1] He then approved the document, but only for a day. Immediately afterward, as Hewitt writes, he issued orders to suppress the whole address, and thus left the Democratic party voiceless in the crisis. Why? Hewitt's proposed

[1] Tilden Papers, New York Public Library.

course commended itself to other Democrats. Leading Democratic Congressmen had approved it; David Dudley Field earnestly endorsed it. Henry Watterson wrote later:[1] "From New Orleans, on the Saturday night succeeding the Presidential election, I had telegraphed to Mr. Tilden, detailing the exact conditions there and urging active and immediate agitation. The chance had been lost. I thought then, and I still think, that the conspiracy of a few men to use the corrupt Returning Boards of Louisiana, South Carolina, and Florida to upset the election and make confusion in Congress, might, by prompt exposure and popular appeal, have been thwarted. Be this as it may, my spirit was depressed and my confidence discouraged by the tense quietude on our side, for I was sure that beneath the surface the Republicans, with resolute determination and multiplied resources, were as busy as bees." Blaine later told John Bigelow that the Republicans would have backed down if the Democrats had only been firm.[2] For this "quietude," this lack of firmness, Tilden alone was responsible.

Hewitt continued to think that every possible measure should have been taken to rally public sentiment. "I agree with you," he wrote an Illinois correspondent, "that meetings in every school district to protest . . . will do great good." And to a Florida Democrat he wrote: "Unless public opinion should make this revolution impossible, I think the Republican leaders are reckless enough to attempt it." On December 14 both he and Zach Chandler published short statements claiming the election, but nothing else was done.

The fact is that Tilden was again exhibiting marked indecision and timidity. He was spending whole days with John Bigelow on an examination of the laws and precedents for counting electoral votes! He was unwilling to issue a defiant statement to the country —such a statement as a Cleveland or Roosevelt would have lost no time in penning. He shortly proved unwilling, on the other hand, to coöperate with the Democratic leaders in Congress in finding a wise and fair method of adjudicating the question. Unquestionably his motives for inaction were elevated. Popular excitement was rising, angry talk was heard on every side, threats of force were growing numerous; the phrase "Tilden or blood" was on many Democratic lips. The *World*, edited by Manton Marble, wrote of the

[1] *"Marse Henry," An Autobiography*, I, 301.
[2] John Bigelow, *Life of Tilden*, II, 74, note.

mobilization of a Democratic army, and of many times forty thousand American men who would know the reason why if Tilden were counted out. By nature scholarly and philosophic, Tilden had none of the qualities of a rough-and-ready politician or a fighting man, and after four decades passed under the conservative influence of corporation law and finance, his whole instinct was for caution. The Young Men's Democratic Club sent a prominent member, Simon Sterne, to urge that he receive a group of serenaders and make a speech boldly asserting his title to the Presidency. Tilden was coldly hostile to the proposal. "It would not be decent," he curtly remarked.[1]

But however high his motives, they do not excuse the lack of vigor and energy which he displayed in this crisis. His course bears out the verdict of James Ford Rhodes that while in quiet times he would have made a good President, he lacked the physical courage, the nerve and decision, required of a leader in this period of sectional strife and partisan animosity. He was fearful of a recurrence of the paralytic attack of 1875, and a valetudinarian tendency had grown upon him; now, as during the campaign, he adhered to a strict regimen laid down by his physician. While Hewitt proposed and acted, the *Tribune* quoted other Democrats as coming out of Tilden's house with the words: "O, Tilden won't do anything; he's as cold as a damn clam."

III

We must now turn to the scene in Washington. Before Congress met on Monday, December 4, and before the final returns from the Southern Canvassing Boards had prompted him to write the address quoted above, Hewitt had taken another step. He had acted to bring about a conference between Tilden and the party leaders in the Senate. The result is described in his secret memorandum:

> In the Senate sat two Democrats who enjoyed the confidence of the Democratic Party to an extraordinary degree. They were Thomas F. Bayard of Delaware and Allen G. Thurman of Ohio. Both had been candidates for the nomination of President before the St. Louis Convention, and had only been put aside because of the superior availability of Mr. Tilden. Nevertheless their

[1] Sterne in the N. Y. *Times*, August 9, 1886; Sterne was an able lawyer, who repeatedly lectured in Cooper Union.

position in the party was one of controlling influence. Hence it was decided to request Judge Thurman on his way to Washington to pass through New York in order to consult with Mr. Tilden as to the course of action to be taken in the unprecedented controversy which was about to occupy the attention of Congress. Judge Thurman arrived in New York on Saturday prior to the meeting of Congress, and on Sunday at the house of Governor Tilden the conference took place, at which I alone was present with them.

The ground was carefully gone over, and the policy to be pursued was for several hours thoroughly discussed. The conclusion was thus briefly summed up by Judge Thurman, who stated the alternatives which presented themselves to his mind as follows: "We can fight; we can back down; or we can arbitrate."

To which propositions Mr. Tilden replied: "It will not do to fight. We have just emerged from one Civil War, and it will never do to engage in another Civil War; it would end in the destruction of free government. We cannot back down. We can, therefore, only arbitrate"—and thus the conference was brought to an end. Judge Thurman is still alive and can confirm this statement. He left for Washington with the determination to arbitrate, and I certainly understood that this was the determination of Judge Thurman and of Governor Tilden; and this conclusion governed me in the course which I subsequently pursued in Washington as a member of the House of Representatives. Whatever may have been my preference as Chairman of the National Committee, I felt as a member of the House that my superior duty was to my *country*, and I was greatly relieved that my sense of duty was not at war with the wishes of Mr. Tilden, who declared himself as desirous of a peaceful settlement of the controversy.

Senator Bayard also called upon Tilden, but not until the Christmas holidays. He spent an evening with him, and next day he and Lucius Q. C. Lamar four hours more. The interview was barren. "Mr. Tilden," writes Bayard's biographer,[1] "gave no intimation whatever of his intentions, nor any light upon the grave subjects under consideration. The compilation of Congressional precedents, then in course of preparation by Mr. Bigelow, was exhibited and referred to, but no plan of action was indicated."

As members of Congress arrived in Washington it became evi-

[1] Edward Spencer, *Life of Bayard*, 261.

dent that party feeling ran high. The angry Democratic cry of fraud was met by Republican retorts that the fraud was all on the Democratic side. If the Fifteenth Amendment had been fairly observed, they said, four or five Southern States would have given large majorities for Hayes. Representative Goode of Virginia shortly told the House that the country would soon reach the point where "one party or another must make an ignominious surrender, or we must fight. Are gentlemen prepared for the latter alternative?" The Republican members sent up a fierce shout of "Yes!"[1] A Republican came to Representative Payne of Ohio, and with tears in his eyes declared that men would be cutting each other's throats in the chamber before the fourth of March. That actual danger of civil war existed cannot be doubted. With the depression then at its bitterest, multitudes unemployed, and tens of thousands of men savage from want, it would be easy to find Northern material for riot and battle. At the South many whites, grown used to violence, were only too ready to take up arms. The governments of some of the most populous northern States, including New York, were in the hands of Democratic officers who felt scant regard for President Grant in Washington. Street affrays in two or three cities might supply the spark that would set off a terrible explosion.

In view of the certain futility of all debate upon the Constitutional provisions for the counting of votes, the position of President Grant was of great importance. The more men scrutinized the Constitutional rule, the more orphic it seemed: "The president of the Senate shall, in the presence of the Senate and House of Representatives, open all the certificates, and the votes shall then be counted." Counted by whom? By the president? By the two houses? Vice-President Wilson having died, the president of the Senate was Thomas W. Ferry of Michigan, a staunch Republican[2] who would be only too glad to make Hayes President if permitted. That would be grossly unfair—as unfair as to let the Democratic

---

[1] *Congressional Record*, January 25, 1877.

[2] Republican newspapers were confident that Ferry would count Hayes in if permitted. But Whitelaw Reid wrote Garfield that Evarts was doubtful of Ferry's staunchness; Royal Cortissoz, *Life of Whitelaw Reid*, I, 316. And a friend of Hayes, Mr. S. J. Cox, wrote him later that Ferry's nervous temperament made him a very uncertain quantity. "My belief is that if this [Electoral Commission] bill had been defeated, Mr. Ferry would either have resigned, or refused wholly to count any vote on his own responsibility." Cox to Hayes, January 31, 1877; Hayes Papers, Library of Congress.

House act alone in making Tilden President. But what if President Grant, as commander-in-chief, supported Ferry in counting the votes? Hewitt saw the importance of ascertaining Grant's views.

On Saturday night, December 2, immediately after the conference with Thurman, he left for Washington. Next day, December 3, he called at the White House by an appointment made through Secretary Fish. The newspapers as early as November 20 had published reports that Federal troops, with light artillery, were being concentrated in Washington, and some had hinted that Grant might use the dispute to prolong his term. With this in mind, Grant began by saying to Hewitt that he was tired of politics and public life:[1]

"I long for the day," he said, "when I shall be able to retire from office. I am counting the hours just as I did when I was completing my term at West Point, and longed for freedom from the everlasting routine and oversight. For sixteen years now I have devoted my life to the public service. I have had no interval of rest or possibility of escaping great responsibilities. During the war I was on the picket line, so to speak, for four years. If any of the principal battles where I gained the victory had been lost, the whole Union cause would have been lost. During Johnson's Administration, when I was general-in-chief, I was a buffer between Congress on the one hand and the President on the other, and I had to discharge more complicated duties than any other general-in-chief in times of peace. During the eight years of my Presidency the most difficult problems have been presented, and have had to be solved. I know," he concluded querulously, "that at times I have been misunderstood, but I believe that the great mass of the people are disposed to do my motives full justice."

Hewitt replied that he had no doubt whatever that they would; that Grant's career formed the most memorable part of American history; that his renown was the property of the American people; that all felt a jealous regard for his fame, and he could assure the President that the Democratic Party were disposed to do him full justice. Thoughtful citizens were confident now, he added, that at

[1] Hewitt's account of his conversation with Grant was dictated to a stenographer immediately after its close. Two copies were made. One was sent to Grant with a request that he make corrections if he saw any errors. He made none. The other copy is in the Hewitt Papers.

the close of his Administration he would do nothing to tarnish the glory of his past achievements.

"Well," said Grant, "the present House of Representatives has given no evidence of a desire to do me justice. They have raked up petty accusations against me. They have even brought back from Ireland a lunatic, who for a long time has followed me about, so that for six months I have had to carry a heavy cane for protection."

Hewitt, who knew nothing of this, begged the President not to attribute to the Democratic Party the malice or blunders of a few individuals. He added that Grant was recognized by both parties as the General who had brought the war to a victorious close, and who had assured the continuance of the Union. From this point the interview can best be described in a special memorandum which Hewitt dictated immediately upon returning to his house:

> I then remarked that the present crisis was one in which he could render to the country a greater service than any he had heretofore rendered, and that it seemed to me that it rested wholly with him whether the present complication should end in war, or in a peaceful solution.
>
> He replied that if there were to be any fighting he certainly would not begin it. That he would maintain order, as he was bound to do, but that he would not provoke any collision by the use of mere power, where it was not his duty to employ it.
>
> I then referred to the recent use of troops in South Carolina. He said that his orders to General Ruger directed him simply to preserve the peace, and that he had not been authorized to interfere in the organization of the legislature: That General Ruger's report showed he issued orders in accordance with these instructions, but that the orders had been misconstrued by a young officer, and that members had been refused admission to the hall, but as soon as this fact had been brought to the notice of General Ruger this obstruction was removed.
>
> Then, coming to the Presidential question, he said he thought he had sufficient information to justify him in forming a judgment as to the situation, and he repeated a remark previously made, that he did not think any man could afford to take the place of President, unless the general judgment concurred in the belief that he was fairly elected. That so far as South Carolina was concerned, he believed that the State had gone on the face of the returns, for Hayes and Wheeler, throwing out entirely the

counties there had been really no election; that they had been overriden by companies of armed men from Georgia, and that the black population had been deterred from voting, and although he, the President, had nothing officially to do with the matter, as it was confined to the returning board alone, he thought that these counties had been properly thrown out, and that the state of South Carolina should justly be counted for Hayes and Wheeler.

As to Florida, he said that the result was very close, but that on the face of the returns, he believed Hayes and Wheeler had a majority of about forty, and that this was independent of the question of frauds, which, if allowed a fair weight, would probably increase the majority, as he was credibly informed.

I asked him from whom he got his information, and he said from Mr. Kasson, who had gone South at his request.

Up to this point, the President had enjoined no confidence, but coming to Louisiana, he remarked that what he should say to me must be in confidence. He said that on face of the returns, Tilden and Hendricks unquestionably had a majority of six to eight thousand votes; that there were six parishes in which there had been intimidation to such an extent that he did not think there had been a fair election, and that they had to be thrown out; that he believed that when thrown out, there was still a majority for Tilden and Hendricks, to which I remarked that it was somewhere about two thousand, and that this majority could only be overcome by assuming that the votes of five thousand naturalized citizens of New Orleans were all Democratic, and that by throwing them out on account of some defect in the naturalization papers. The President remarked that the returning board in Louisiana was in very bad odor with the public; that the people had no confidence in it, and even if it did right, it would not be credited with honest intentions. He believed that there had been no honest election in Louisiana since Slidell got control of its politics.

I suggested to him that, as a matter of fact, it was not possible to have a fair election in that state, and that it was a most serious blow to Republican government that a state in which a fair election could not be had, should decide a Presidential contest.

The President replied that this was true, and that it would not be unreasonable that the vote of Louisiana should be thrown out, as it was in 1872, on account of irregularities of election, and the peculiar functions of the returning board. I remarked that this would give the election to Tilden; that he would then have a clear majority of all the electors appointed. He said "no"; that it had been held in Lincoln's time that the President must have a majority of all the votes to which the states are legally entitled.

I replied that it had been so asserted, but that no tribunal had ever considered the question. The President answered "certainly not, because Lincoln had the necessary majority." Whereupon I remarked that if a majority had belonged to the states in rebellion, it would not be held that the loyal states should go without a President, and he said: "Certainly not, they would have to do the best they could."

However, assuming that Louisiana were thrown out, and that it was still necessary to have one hundred and eighty-five votes, this would throw the election into the House, who would then elect the President, and the Senate would elect the Vice-President, which was one solution of the problem. However, he said he did not expect there would be any serious trouble; that a solution would be reached, that would, in the main, be satisfactory to the people. That if one of the doubtful states should cast all or any part of its votes for Tilden, that would settle the question. He would be inaugurated as quietly as he, General Grant, had been. It was not, however, for him to decide the question, but it was the duty of Congress under the Constitution: That his duty would be to see that their decision was carried into effect.

I asked the President whether in the event of the two houses getting into conflict, and coming to blows, he would feel it his duty to use the military force of Government to restore order. To which he replied: "Certainly not," but that if either side should call up an armed force or a mob, to its support, he would feel bound to protect the public property from its attack, and to repel them from the Capitol.

In conclusion, he said that his great desire was to retire from office with the country at peace, and generally satisfied with the conclusion which might be arrived at; and that he thought it rather hard that any one should suspect him, who had given his best years to preserve the country, of any design upon its liberties. I assured the President of the great gratification I experienced in hearing such sentiments expressed: That I was confirmed in my faith in his patriotism, and that it should not be long before the whole country, and both parties, would do him and his motives full justice.

I omitted to say, in the proper place above, that, speaking of the Presidential election, the President said that it was a matter of substance, and not of technicalities! That any attempt to appropriate a vote in Vermont, or Rhode Island or Oregon, which had given a Republican majority would be regarded only as a trick, just as any attempt to get a vote of Louisiana by fraud would be regarded as indefensible. I assured the President that I heartily concurred in this view, and that if a vote from Oregon was really certified to the Democrats, I did not believe that any other use would be made of it than to get a fair hearing in the case of the other States, which, in the judgment of the Democratic party, might be improperly certified to Hayes: That neither Governor Tilden or his friends desired to have him succeed to the Presidency unless he had been honestly elected, and that in the event of there being so much doubt in regard to the real result, as to make it difficult for fair-minded men to say who was elected, I felt justified in saying that Governor Tilden and his friends would cheerfully assent to a new election! That while he and they felt that they had a duty to perform, that they were not disposed to press an extreme issue in the face of a reasonable doubt.

Incidentally, I mentioned to the President that the House would probably appoint committees to investigate and report upon the facts developed in the elections of South Carolina, Florida and Louisiana. He replied that he expected that they would do so, and thought it very proper, and that it would be a very desirable thing to get reports from committees properly constituted.

Incidentally, the President said that Mr. Anderson on the Louisiana returning board, was a brother of Major Robert Anderson of Fort Sumter fame, and of Lars Anderson of Cincinnati; he must, therefore, be an honest man, and that he would be inclined to believe any certificate he might sign, and to discredit any certificate he did not sign. I since learn that the gentleman is not a brother of the gentlemen named.

As Hewitt descended the steps of the White House that night, he undoubtedly felt a thrill of relief. He had learned just what he had hoped for: that Grant believed Tilden to be elected; that he would not give Senator Ferry armed support in counting the votes; that he would not employ the army except as a last resort, and would use it then only to maintain order, protect public property, and execute the will of both houses—not one—of Congress.

IV

The House, with Speaker Randall in the chair, immediately took up the great issue before the country. Hewitt and the National Committee were anxious to have investigating committees appointed, and this was done. On the first day the House provided for three committees to visit Louisiana, Florida, and South Carolina respectively. Next day the Senate directed its Committee on Elections to scrutinize the recent contest in six Southern States and in Oregon. These inquiries, necessarily *ex parte*, in the end accomplished nothing except to accumulate a mass of material which has been of great use to historians. Democratic hotheads in the House, led by Fernando Wood, also attempted in these first days to institute impeachment proceedings against Grant for his alleged unconstitutional use of the army and other offenses. But a majority of the party, including Hewitt, were against any such folly and blocked it in the caucus.

At once, also, the question of rules for regulating the electoral count came up. The electoral votes for Lincoln in 1865 and Grant in 1869 and 1873 had been counted under the Twenty-second Joint Rule of the two houses; a rule providing that no ballot objected to by either house could be counted except by the concurrent vote of both chambers. This rule gave the Republicans manifest advantages as long as they controlled both Senate and House. But the Republicans having lost the House, the Senate in January, 1876, had scented danger, and while readopting all the other joint rules had expressly excluded this one. At first the House was disposed to argue—without any warrant in parliamentary law—that it remained in force until repealed by action of both chambers. "Mature reflection, however," writes Hewitt, "led to the conclusion that the Joint Rules only continued from Congress to Congress, and that in the absence of the specific action of both houses renewed by each Congress no Joint Rules existed for the government of their action." The House therefore reluctantly concurred in the omission of the Twenty-second Rule. It is obvious that if this rule had been re-adopted, it would have been competent for the House to have objected to the votes of South Carolina, Florida, and Louisiana.

Tilden would then have been inaugurated as President. "Some criticism," says Hewitt, "has been indulged in as to the action of the House of Representatives in assenting to any Joint Rules which did not include the Twenty-second, but such criticism is based upon the erroneous idea that the House, which was Democratic, could have coerced the Senate, which was Republican, into the adoption of any Joint Rule not acceptable to either house."

But then how should the obscure Constitutional clause be interpreted? A variety of extra-Constitutional solutions were being suggested. Many proposed another national election. It was universally agreed, however, that Tilden would carry the country, and the Republicans demurred. Others suggested a second election in the three contested Southern States. This would have been sensible; but again the Republicans saw that it would be sure to produce several Tilden electors, and objected. Most fair-minded men on both sides agreed that a plan of adjudication would have to be worked out. "Arbitration" was Hewitt's word. These conciliatory leaders were supported by public sentiment. Business men were alarmed by the prospect of riots or war; the moderate press demanded peace; petitions were flowing in for some means—any means—of orderly adjustment.

On December 7 George W. McCrary of Iowa, a Republican, introduced in the House a resolution calling upon the Speaker to appoint a committee of five to act in conjunction with any similar committee that might be appointed by the Senate; the two bodies to prepare without delay either a bill or a constitutional amendment for removing "all differences of opinion and all doubts and uncertainty" upon the result of the election.[1] This resolution had been submitted in rough form to leaders on both sides. Hewitt was one, and wrote into it a clause—"to the end that the votes should be counted and the results declared by a tribunal whose authority none can question and whose decision all will accept." He later wrote that he had framed this statement "for the purpose of calling public attention to the fact that the House of Representatives, controlled by Democrats largely from the South, desired to secure a peaceful result if possible to the controversy," and it was inserted in order to give effect to the conclusion to arbitrate

[1] *Congressional Record*, Vol. V, Pt. I, pp. 91, 92.

arrived at in the conference between Judge Thurman and Mr. Tilden.

The resolution went to the House Judiciary Committee, of which J. Proctor Knott of Kentucky was chairman. There is no ground whatever for John Bigelow's statement that Tilden was hostile to it. Indeed, a word from Tilden would have killed it. The committee, after enlarging the membership of the proposed Senate and House bodies from five to seven, favorably reported the resolution on December 14, and it passed the same day. On the 18th a similar resolution passed the Senate. Just before the Christmas recess, on December 21-22, Speaker Randall and Senator Ferry named the two committees. That of the House consisted of Henry B. Payne of Ohio (made chairman at Tilden's special request, a further indication of his partial acquiescence), Eppa Hunton, William M. Springer, and Hewitt, Democrats; with McCrary, George F. Hoar, and George Willard, Republicans. That of the Senate consisted of Allen G. Thurman, Thomas F. Bayard, and M. W. Ransom, Democrats; with George F. Edmunds (chairman), Oliver P. Morton, Frederick T. Frelinghuysen, and John A. Logan, Republicans. When Logan declined, his place was taken by Roscoe Conkling.[1]

Little could be done before the holidays. "The House Committee," writes Hewitt, "lost no time in holding a meeting at which Mr. Springer was appointed to collate the proceedings for counting the electoral votes in all the preceding elections of President and Vice-President in the United States. Singularly enough, this action was taken in ignorance of the fact that Mr. Tilden had already undertaken to prepare a similar compilation." Then the House broke up for Christmas. Though Congress reconvened before New Year's Day, the House Committee did not hold another meeting until January 3. When it did, the struggle for the Presidency entered upon a new phase.

A mysterious silence still enveloped Tilden. Nothing could better illustrate the secrecy of his movements than the fact that many members of Congress were at first unaware that he, John Bigelow, and Manton Marble were compiling a history of the electoral counts from the foundation of the government. To this task they devoted more than a month, the result being published in January under the title *Presidential Counts*. Most Democratic leaders in Congress

[1] *Congressional Record*, Vol. V, Pt. I, pp. 197, 198, 258, 766ff.

would have been incredulous if told that he was expending time and strength upon such an undertaking. It was a decidedly useful work for some lesser man, a lawyer like Charles O'Conor or an historian like George Bancroft; but it was absurd for the head of the party to labor on it to the neglect of more vital tasks. It abundantly proved one fact: that Ferry could not rightfully count the electoral votes—that all precedents were against the Republican theory that the president of the Senate had authority to do so. But it did not show who *did* have the right. In the past they had uniformly been counted by a group of tellers, one for the Senate and two for the House. But what if the tellers disagreed? On various occasions objection had been made to the vote of some State, as on the ground that it had still been a Territory at the time of the election, or that the electors had voted on another day than that prescribed by law. But never had the Presidency depended on the count; never had the issue been faced and a decision between the House and Senate tellers been made. Twice, indeed, a decision had been evaded by counting the votes both ways! Precedent, in short, offered no help. It left the deadlock as complete as ever, the necessity for arbitration as clear and unavoidable.[1]

Tilden accomplished little of value by this work, and still less by the long argument he wrote for the inaugural address of Governor Lucius Robinson of New York setting forth the Democratic contention of the right of the House to elect if a deadlock occurred. To no man in Congress, meanwhile, did he yield any large degree of confidence. His neighbor David Dudley Field, who had accepted a special election to the House to look after Tilden's legal interests there, was largely in the dark as to his leader's intention. So was his neighbor Hewitt. Henry Watterson spent the Christmas vacation at Tilden's house, and later boasted that he was Tilden's personal representative in Congress;[2] but the impetuous, flighty Ken-

---

[1] House Misc. Doc. No. 13, 44th Congress, 2d sess.

[2] *Century Magazine*, Vol. 86, p. 4; May, 1913. Mr. Elihu Root has given the author an illustration of Tilden's extreme secretiveness and caution. When Tilden's income tax case was pending in the courts, Mr. Root was called to his house to advise him. For a long afternoon the two went over documents in the case. Mr. Root could see that they were gradually approaching the core of the issue, but Tilden withheld a full explanation. Finally, seeing that the moment had come for a decisive statement, Tilden suddenly turned in his chair, beckoned to his secretary, and in the hoarse whisper that was left of his voice, asked for checkbook and pen. He painfully wrote out a check for a thousand dollars and

tuckian was one of the last men on earth in whom the cautious Tilden would fully have confided. Bayard, Thurman, and Samuel J. Randall were all uninformed as to Tilden's precise aims and all left to work on their own initiative.

Only two short months were now left before inauguration day. Business, the press, the pulpit, were demanding an end to the uncertainty. The contest swept rapidly toward a series of crucial decisions.

---

handed it to Mr. Root, who up to then had received no retainer. "Now," he said with a shrewd gleam, "You are my counsel and I can speak to you in confidence."

CHAPTER XIX

More Secret History

THE country passed a calmer Christmas than it had anticipated. The action of Congress in appointing committees to
devise "a tribunal whose authority none can question" had
reassured the nation. It was a heartening token that moderation
and patriotism were grappling with the crisis, and that the Anglo-
Saxon tradition of political compromise and of conformity to law
and order would again be vindicated.

Yet among the leaders of both parties, when Congress reconvened after New Year's, the uncertainty, tension, and apprehension
were extreme. The stakes seemed so great! If the Republicans, after
eight years of misgovernment and at the very depth of a terrible
depression, could hold the citadel of Washington, they might continue to hold it indefinitely; if the Democrats could now entrench
themselves in it under a President as able as Grant had proved
unfit, then they might begin a new period of Democratic ascendancy
as prolonged as that between Jackson and Buchanan. The South was
so eager to be free; vindictive Republicans were so anxious to
keep it partly chained. And how could the two sides be reconciled?
The Republicans had so much ground for believing that, in view
of the huge Negro vote at the South, they were honestly entitled
to some electors there; the Democrats had so much ground for
believing that Tilden, with his heavy popular majority, and need-
ing only one elector in four disputed States, was honestly entitled
to the Presidency.

Hewitt on January 3 gathered with other anxious members of
the House Committee in the Banking and Currency Committee
Room, in which John Quincy Adams had seen the last of earth.
He and others in brief speeches brought up a confusing variety of

questions. Should a new election be held? What would be the situation if on March 4th no person had been declared elected by Congress, and if the House had not elected one "as provided by the Constitution in case of failure to elect by the people?" Was it practicable to create an independent tribunal "to decide questions relating to the count upon which the two houses differ?" Was it practicable to set up a tribunal "which shall count the votes or determine any specific questions of law or fact which may be involved therein?" This meeting and those which followed it were secret. The details of the discussion are unknown. But at first, with most members doubtful and uncertain, it was futile, and not until January 10 was any really decisive action taken.

On this date Representative McCrary brought to the House Committee, and Senator Edmunds to the Senate Committee, plans for the creation of an Electoral Commission to settle all disputes growing out of the electoral count. Though McCrary's scheme was in the form of a printed bill, it was still rudimentary in character. The tribunal was to consist of Chief Justice Waite, and a number of associate justices, to be named in the order of their seniority on the bench; and its conclusions were to be binding unless both houses of Congress concurred in overruling them. "The origin of this bill," writes Hewitt, "has been attributed to various persons. It seems, however, to be probable that the suggestion came from President Grant, and the draft of the bill was prepared at his request by Senator Conkling." Senator Edmunds' very different plan was probably his own, for he later stated that he could not remember working with McCrary.[1]

The mere introduction of these two plans was of course tantamount to a surrender by the Republicans of their troublesome contention that the president of the Senate had the right to count the votes. The Democratic members, at an immediate night session of the House Committee in Chairman Payne's rooms in the Riggs House, tried to make this surrender explicit. Calling upon the Republicans to acquiesce in a resolution previously introduced by Chairman Payne, which declared that the president of the Senate was without power to count, they precipitated a fruitless debate. Representatives Hoar and McCrary stood adamant against any such resolution. A situation might present itself, Hoar argued, in which,

[1] Haworth, *The Disputed Election*, 198.

with no decisions made, with the nation facing imminent chaos and civil war, somebody might have to seize the bull by the horns and make the count. It would be wrong to tie the hands of the president of the Senate. Suppose new difficulties arose and the House, insisting there had been no election, refused to participate in the counting? In the emergency Senator Ferry might be forced to act. Hewitt rejoined by a tart question. "In case of such a conflict between the President of the Senate and the House of Representatives," he demanded, "would you sooner entrust the liberties of the people to a single Senator, who happened to be president of the Senate, than to the representatives of the entire American people?" This plainly staggered Hoar, who made no rejoinder; but the Payne resolution had to be laid aside.[1]

What should the Democrats do with the plan for an Electoral Commission? Obviously, it should be brought into a shape acceptable to the party leaders in Congress, and then laid before Tilden for his decision; and this is just what Hewitt saw was done.

Representative McCrary's bill was taken up section by section in the House Committee, and amended twice. One important Democratic change (later struck out) made the decisions of the Electoral Commission binding only when approved by both Houses of Congress; another debarred Chief Justice Waite from serving as head of the Commission on the ground that during the campaign he had shown personal hostility to Tilden. The Ohio jurist, a Republican friend of Hayes, was glad to be excused from a task in which his fairness would assuredly have been impugned. It was informally agreed that the five senior associate justices of the Supreme Court should constitute the Commission: to wit, Justices Clifford of Maine, Swayne of Ohio, David Davis of Illinois, Miller of Iowa, and Field of California. Two of these, Clifford and Field, were Democrats; Swayne and Miller were decided Republicans; and David Davis was an Independent. Any decision by this tribunal must be ratified by both Houses of Congress. The House plan for settling the dispute was thus whipped into satisfactory shape, though no formal vote of approval was given.

[1] Milton H. Northrup, "A Grave Crisis in American History," *Century Magazine,* October, 1901; Vol. 62, pp. 923-934. Northrup was secretary of the House Committee.

Meanwhile, members of the Senate Committee had been laboring upon the plan suggested by Judge Edmunds. This was radically divergent from the other in that it admitted select groups from both chambers of Congress to the tribunal; and when the House Committee learned its nature they at once agreed that it was superior in principle. It called for an Electoral Commission of thirteen. Five were to be named from the House, five from the Senate, four from the Supreme Court—the four senior associate justices; and one Congressional member was then to be eliminated by lot. Naturally, to all members of Congress it seemed that the legislative branch of the government ought to have a hand in the adjudication. But in retrospect we may well question whether the original House Committee plan of leaving the question to the five senior associate justices was not far better. The atmosphere surrounding this tribunal would have been cooler and more judicial, and the political pressure upon it much slighter.

Then ensued a series of hurried and fateful steps. The first joint meeting of the two committees was held on Friday, January 12, in the Senate Judiciary room. It was here that Senator Edmunds' plan was disclosed and discussed. Next day a second joint meeting took place. It was then fully agreed that the Electoral Commission should be made up from both houses of Congress as well as from the Supreme Court. But the House Committee strongly objected to the scheme for eliminating one of the Congressional members by lot, holding that if there were any such resort to the dice-box, it should be applied to the judges, leaving the political section of the tribunal equally balanced between the two parties. The discussion that Saturday lasted for hours. At its conclusion late in the afternoon it had been agreed by nearly all that the Electoral Commission should consist of fifteen men; that five should be taken from the Senate and five from the House; and that the names of the six senior associate justices should be shuffled in a hat, and one withdrawn by lot. The principal objector was a Democrat, Representative Springer of Illinois, who wished until Monday to think the matter over. Against heavy pressure, he kept insisting "Until Monday"—and he had his way.

Thus in the space of ten days just after New Year's—the ten days between January 3 and January 13—two plans for an Electoral Commission had been drawn up and threshed over, and one had been agreed to by most of the Democratic committeemen. But would it be equally acceptable to the general body of Democratic Representatives and Senators? Above all, would it be acceptable to Tilden?

The first question was easy to answer: for a large advisory committee of Democratic members had kept steadily in touch with the situation. This committee had been appointed by the House caucus early in December to help deal with the situation, and had consisted of eleven men—Lamar, Randall, Stevens, Wood, Payne, Holman, Warren, Atkins, Sparks, Watterson, and Hewitt. On the night of December 8, Hewitt had asked them to meet at his house. He presided, and they approved the address to the people which he had written and was about to lay before Tilden. Six Senators, Bayard, Thurman, Stevenson, Kernan, Bogy, and Eaton, were invited to join the committee, which on December 11 again met at Hewitt's house. A more systematic organization was now effected, with the wise and dignified Representative Lamar as chairman and Representative Warren as secretary. The advisory committee met repeatedly, sometimes at Hewitt's house, and sometimes in the Speaker's Room at the Capitol, and was fully consulted at every stage of the discussions of the Electoral Commission. There can be no doubt that it knew all about the plan finally agreed upon, and acquiesced in it.[1]

I

But what of Tilden? At this point we come to a highly controversial question, for several of Tilden's chagrined followers later asserted that he had not been adequately consulted. Hewitt's explicit statements, all susceptible of proof, fully dispel this charge. In his secret history he writes:

The Joint Committee adjourned (January 13) without final action, in order to enable the two Committees to consider the

[1] Representative W. W. Warren, secretary of this committee, describes its work in a long letter to Hewitt, dated Boston, July 19, 1878, in the Hewitt Papers. He states that at the meeting on December 11, which was the day after the McCrary Resolution was offered in the House, the committee held a long discussion of it. At two other meetings at Hewitt's residence, on December 12 and 17, this discussion was continued. The attitude toward the resolution was generally favorable. It was also discussed in the Democratic caucus. In both bodies Hewitt took the leading part; and he was in favor of the resolution.

position in which after the consultation they found themselves
to be placed. A resolution, however, was adopted imposing secrecy
upon the members of the Committees as to the nature of the bill
and the discussions which had taken place.

This obligation of secrecy led me to consult with the Democratic
members of the House Committee as to whether it applied to Mr.
Tilden. It was unanimously concluded that we had a superior
duty both to the Democratic Party and to him, and that he
should be consulted, and his approval secured before the House
Committee would commit itself to any action whatever. In accordance with this decision, I mailed to Mr. Tilden on Friday,
January 12th, 1877, a copy of the bill with the proposed amendments, and informed him that on the next day I would report
at his house on Gramercy Park for the purpose of getting his
counsel and decision thereon.

On Sunday morning, therefore, January 14th, I saw Mr. Tilden
and went over with him word by word the provisions of the bill
as amended. Various persons came and went during the day, but
as far as the consultation was concerned it was personal to Mr.
Tilden and myself. The only person to whom the bill was submitted, as far as I can remember, was the late Clarkson N. Potter,
who was the next-door neighbor of Mr. Tilden and possessed
his confidence so far as any person might be said to have had it.
The injunction of secrecy was violated in his case alone, but it
is certain that the bill was not during any conference with Mr.
Tilden shown to any other person whatever.

Mr. Tilden complained that action was premature, and of the
secrecy which had attended the preparation of the bill. I explained to him that the work was preliminary, and that the
Democratic members of the House had authorized and directed
me to say to him that they would not agree to have it reported
to the House in case he should disapprove its provisions or desire
it to be amended. I stated, however, that if the House Committee
should not report the bill I was sure that the Senate Committee
would do so, because the Democratic members of that Committee
had already agreed to the provisions of the bill. Mr. Tilden thereupon asked me whether it was not rather late to ask his counsel,
to which I replied: "The Senate Committee have not sent me
to consult with you, as the Democratic members are acting upon
their own responsibility in the performance of their duty. I am
directed, however, by the Democrats of the House Committee to

consult with you, and you may be sure that against your objection no bill will ever be reported to the House or can pass that body."

The question of approval or disapproval was thus distinctly presented to Mr. Tilden. On this point I did not get from him any definite opinion whatever. He objected to special features of the bill, and declared against choosing any one of the judges by lot, saying that he might lose the Presidency but he would never raffle for it. He asked for time to consider the matter, and finally before I left about nine o'clock on Saturday (Sunday) night to catch the train he said he would communicate further with me through Mr. Edward Cooper, who had a cipher which might safely be used. I remember perfectly well the remark with which I quitted his presence: "Now, Governor, understand that if you disapprove the bill it will be defeated; if you do not disapprove it it will be reported by the House Committee with such amendments as you may desire. I do not expect you to approve the bill as it stands, but we must take action of some sort, and I understand that if you do not disapprove, we are to make a report to the House with such amendments as you desire to have inserted." We parted, therefore, without any distinct approval or disapproval on the part of Mr. Tilden, but with the distinct understanding that I was to secure if possible the modification of the Six Judge Plan which provided for the elimination of one of the judges by lot, and for the substitution of some other mode of selecting the judges which might be satisfactory to Mr. Tilden.

That I was to make and did make this effort is proved by the very first telegram sent by me to Mr. Cooper in cipher on the day after my interview with Mr. Tilden: "Washington, January 15, 1877, to E. C. The Senate Committee will probably reject Five and report Six Judge Plan immediately. Our Senators feel committed to concur. House Committee will not concur and for the present will probably not report."

To this telegram Mr. Tilden sent the following reply:

"New York, January 15th, 1877. To A. S. H. Procrastinate to give days for information and consultation. The Six Judge proposition inadmissible. E. C."

It appears from this reply that Mr. Tilden did not utter a word against the principle of an Electoral Commission or against the Five Judge Plan, but rejected the Six Judge plan, leading me to infer as I had done in New York that the Five Judge Plan would be satisfactory.

Nothing can be more certain than that if Tilden had pronounced vigorously against the Electoral Commission plan, either at this interview or in the next few days, it would have been dropped instantly. Every Democrat in Washington was convinced that he had been elected President. He was the head of the party. His word at this moment was law. Whatever Bayard and Thurman did, the House Committee would rigidly obey his command. Tilden said so himself. During the tense days following this interview, he had a conversation with F. F. Marbury in his Gramercy Park library. They talked of the Electoral Commission. He paced the floor, discussing the measure with warmth. Then suddenly he said: "Why, if I were so disposed, I could kill this bill by the mere wave of my fingers"—snapping them in illustration.[1] When later the Electoral Commission gave the Presidency to Hayes, some of Tilden's friends (for reasons which we shall in due place discuss) tried to diffuse the impression that he had consistently opposed the bill. Henry Watterson so declared, and his story was repeated with adornments by Manton Marble and John Bigelow. But actually he did nothing of the kind. Like Hayes, he regarded the tribunal with apprehension and dislike, and refused to endorse it privately or publicly; but he never publicly condemned it or used his influence against it. He hesitated, and seemed to take the view that if the Electoral Commission were so shaped as to offer a substantial probability of victory he would accept it. He not only refused to say no, but by his discussion of amendments to the bill he appeared to acquiesce in it.[2]

On Sunday the 14th, after his second long conference of the day with Tilden and just before he caught the train to Washington, Hewitt talked with his lifelong friend Charles P. Daly, one of the State's ablest jurists. He laid before him the whole situation. He explained that Tilden had not taken any positive position, but had asked for more time to consider the bill. He explained also

[1] Marbury to Hewitt, March 24, 1888; Hewitt Papers.

[2] James Ford Rhodes comments that Tilden had two choices. One was to stand on the supposed right of the House to count the votes, and thus run the risk of war. "The other and nobler course for Tilden would have been to cooperate sympathetically with the leading men of his party in the Senate and the House in the endeavor to bring about a fair compromise so that the induction of the new President should be orderly and according to law. He took neither course, for he could come to no decision." Rhodes, VII, 246, 247.

that Bayard, Thurman, and other Democratic Senators felt that it would be dangerous to postpone some decided action to solve the national crisis, for they feared that further delay might precipitate a bloody conflict. Hewitt felt positive that if the House Committee hesitantly drew back, uncertain how to move, the impatient Senate Committee would unanimously report the pending plan as necessary to the preservation of peace. If it once did this, public opinion would rally vigorously behind its scheme. Perturbed by Tilden's indecision, and knowing that Daly was profoundly impressed by the gravity of the crisis, he asked for his advice. After reflection, Daly stated that he believed the Senate Committee would really be justified, if the House made no constructive proposal, in taking independent action. He added that he would recommend that the House Committee concur unless Tilden interposed an absolute veto. At Hewitt's anxious request, Daly then went to see Tilden himself. What ensued is best described in Daly's own letter to Hewitt a few years later:[1]

> I having told him of your visit, and of what had taken place between us, he suggested that we should walk out together and talk the matter over, as we might be interrupted if we remained in the house. We accordingly did so, and discussed the matter in all its aspects. I cannot recall all that took place in a conversation that lasted for more than two hours, but I write to say most distinctly that the result of the conversation was that he fully acquiesced in the course that was proposed to be taken, and that I so advised you. I recall distinctly the last words he said as we parted were: "I am afraid that we are giving up too much, but I do not see that we can do anything else."

And Hewitt himself writes:

> He took occasion on Sunday night after I had left for Washington to see Mr. Tilden on the subject and ascertain his decision. Judge Daly fortunately is still living, and has authorized me to say that Mr. Tilden, after expressing grave doubts as to the course which ought to be pursued in the emergency, told him that he was not willing to take the responsibility of disap-

[1] Daly to Hewitt, April 9, 1888; Hewitt Papers. Some impression of Daly's fine personality is given in William Allen Butler's *Retrospect of Forty Years, 1825-65*, p. 236; he was Chief Justice of the Court of Common Pleas for a number of years.

proving the plan proposed for arbitration, although he thought
that it should be modified as to the selection of judges. He did
not express any disapproval of the principle or the policy of the
bill, but confined his criticisms to the details of the . . .
Tribunal.

The charge that Hewitt did not sufficiently consult Tilden, and
that Tilden opposed the Electoral Commission plan which Hewitt
nevertheless supported, thus falls to the ground.

Hewitt therefore took the night train to Washington, arriving
early January 15, determined to obtain such a form of the Electoral
Commission as to render it acceptable to Tilden. Everyone realized
that the Supreme Court justices on the Commission would really
make the decision. There were good reasons why Tilden should
object to the so-called Six-Judge Plan. Under the Five-Judge Plan,
as hammered out in the House Committee, the five associate justices of senior appointment, Clifford, Swayne, David Davis, Miller,
and Field, would serve. That seemed fair to nearly all Democrats,
and Tilden had said nothing against it. But the Six-Judge Plan,
as drawn up in the Senate Committee—the plan of placing the
names of the six senior associate justices, Clifford, Swayne, David
Davis, Miller, Field and Strong, in a hat and then withdrawing one
—was open to several objections. The panel, consisting of three
Republicans, two Democrats, and one Independent, was one-sided;
the elimination of a name by lot might make it more so; and the
use of lots was "raffling for the Presidency." Hewitt's task was to
obtain the Five-Judge Plan, or one very like it; a tribunal fairly
balanced, and chosen without the use of lots.

The day that Hewitt returned to Washington, January 15, the
two committees held another joint session. He and his fellow-
Democrats once more tried to carry the Five-Judge Plan. Once more
the Republicans rejected it. To many of them, looking upon David
Davis as an enemy, it seemed certain to give the Democrats a majority of one on the Electoral Commission. They insisted instead
upon Senator Edmunds's original scheme for naming five Senators,
five Representatives, and four justices, one of the Congressional
members then to be eliminated by lot. For a time Hewitt hoped
that a conciliatory attitude would win them over. "Personally," he
said, "I am more in favor of some measure than of any particular
measure. As matters now stand, the Senate bill would not pass the

House. Therefore, I am very anxious that . . . the House put its ideas into the form of a bill." But as he measured the obduracy of the Republicans, he resolved that the Democrats must not yield —that they must insist on a true compromise. In reply to a question by Conkling, he made a significant statement. "My colleague," he said, "is aware of the disadvantages I labor under in making suggestions, and he has doubtless observed that I have had little to say in this discussion. Owing to my peculiar relations, I am unjustly supposed to speak for another. But my personal views are not always or necessarily in harmony with those of the person for whom I am supposed to speak." In other words, he recognized two duties: one, as Democratic national chairman, to Tilden and the party; the other, as Representative, to the nation. Both were very real and he expected to reconcile them, but he unflinchingly recognized his duty to the country as greater than to any party or any person. He went on: "I have great hopes of bringing our present plan to a point where both committees may agree . . . A plan has occurred to me which, at the proper time, I will submit."[1] That promise bore fruit two days later.

That afternoon, as we have seen, Hewitt telegraphed Tilden that the Senate Committee would probably reject the Five-Judge Plan and report the Six-Judge Plan immediately; that Bayard, Thurman, and the other Democratic Senators felt committed to join in this action; but that the House Committee would refuse to concur and would probably not report. He knew that this stubborn attitude on the part of the House Committee would please Tilden. And that same day Tilden sent his characteristic reply. The Six-Judge Plan was inadmissible, and he asked Hewitt to procrastinate for a few days.[2] "Procrastinate" was one of Tilden's favorite words and favorite ideas.

Next day, the 16th, brought another joint session and another wordy battle. But at last the Senate Committee, urged by Conkling and faced by Hewitt's immovable opposition, gave up its demand for use of the lot in making the Commission. Hewitt then telegraphed Tilden: "After protracted negotiations Senate Committee receded from Six Judges, declined Five Judges, and offered four senior associate justices, who are to choose the fifth judge excluding

[1] Milton H. Northrup, op. cit., p. 928, 929.
[2] Hewitt Papers.

Chief Justice. Our Senator friends earnestly favor acceptance because they do not believe it possible to pass over Field. The Democrats on the House Committee believe this is the last chance of agreement. We cannot postpone beyond eleven tomorrow, and if we decline Senate Committee will report their original plan, to which our friends are committed. Telegraph your advice." When this telegram was sent the situation was growing critical. A tremendous public demand was developing for immediate agreement. Bayard and Thurman were earnestly in favor of the Four-Judge Plan; that is, of letting the four senior justices, Clifford, Swayne, David Davis, and Miller, choose the fifth. How could the House Committee hold out if these powerful Democratic leaders joined the opposition?

Tilden's reply was delayed. That evening, while Hewitt waited for it, the Democratic leaders held an excited meeting. Hewitt summoned to the Speaker's Room the Democrats of the House and Senate Committees, the Democratic members of the House Committee appointed to investigate precedents in the electoral count, and the advisory committee. Of 23 men requested to attend, 22 responded. The best brains of the party in Congress were present: the Senatorial sages, Bayard, Thurman, and Lamar, together with such shrewd and practical Representatives as Randall, Holman of Indiana, Springer of Illinois, and Proctor Knott of Kentucky. The discussion was protracted and at times heated. All the Senators and some of the Representatives were for accepting the Four-Judge Plan. But several Representatives objected to it, and the explosive Henry Watterson was against creating any Electoral Commission whatever.[1]

In an address on Jackson Day Watterson had said that one hundred thousand Kentuckians would see that justice was done to Tilden, a threat which the press had roundly derided.[2] Now, declaring that the House should have stood fast on its right to count the votes, he denounced Hewitt, who presided, in offensive terms. He accused him of throwing everything away by his failure to call

[1] Representative W. W. Warren to Hewitt, July 19, 1878; Hewitt Papers. Warren based his letter on the minutes of the House Committee, which he had preserved.

[2] So he was generally quoted or misquoted; but see his own version in "The Hayes-Tilden Contest for the Presidency," *Century Magazine*, Vol. LXXXVI, 1-20; May, 1913.

out the people; he declared that nothing was left but to take the best terms they could get. "The only effect of the Electoral Commission Bill," he vociferated, "will be to put Mr. Hayes into office with a color of title, whereas otherwise he will have to be inducted by the Senate, General Grant, and the Army." Apparently it did not occur to him that it would be far better for the republic to put someone, whether Tilden or Hayes, into office with a fair legal title, than to let Grant and the Army put somebody in without it.

The meeting passed no resolution. But it was evident that some form of Electoral Commission bill was all but universally favored. Watterson himself, in the inaccurate account of this meeting which he later set down, is at least accurate in writing that there was "no other protestant."

Late that night, after the gathering had broken up, Hewitt received the expected reply from Tilden. He and General Richard C. Taylor, son of Zachary Taylor, who was staying at his house, required more than an hour to decipher it. It read: "Be firm and cool. Four Judge plan will not do perhaps worse than Six. Complaints likely to arise of haste and want of consultation with members and embarrassment in exercise of their judgment, after plan is disclosed, by premature committal of their representatives. There should be more opportunity for deliberation and consultation. Secrecy dangerous. Probably a mistake in itself and if it results in disaster would involve great blame and infinite mischiefs." After the evidence that evening that a majority of the Democratic leaders in Congress stood ready to accept the Four Judge Plan, this was a shock. But Hewitt told Taylor that he would never agree to any plan that Tilden opposed.

II

That night Hewitt never closed his eyes. He knew that he must do something to satisfy Tilden's objections; he also knew that if the negotiations now broke down and rioting and bloodshed followed, he would be held responsible. The only course was to offer his own special plan. On the following morning, January 17, the House and Senate Committees again met in joint session. After a few words by Representative Payne, who said that the Four Judge Plan was unacceptable, Hewitt brought forward this proposal.

"It has been said that any proposition which has the weight of a hair on one side or the other cannot pass," he remarked. "In this I concur. I was not surprised, therefore, that the House proposition to take the five senior justices was rejected, for it did lean a little to one side. The proposition for four judges, with Davis charged to the Democrats, is open to the same objections. I am satisfied that it would be defeated in the House. That conclusion I have arrived at with great reluctance. I could take it myself, but there are others who see in it an inequality that would prevent their giving it support. This matter has given me greater anxiety than I can tell. I have lain awake the whole night over it—have not closed my eyelids. I have felt that if an agreement failed, I would be charged with the responsibility. The proposition I have to submit, which has only this morning occurred to me, and which I have had no time to talk over with my committee, is this: that the two senior justices (Clifford and Swayne) each select another justice, and these four select a fifth. This plan seems to me absolutely just."[1]

The two committees then broke up to allow the Senate Committee time to consider Hewitt's proposal. When they met again shortly before three o'clock, Senator Edmunds stated that his group could not accept it. It was "built on the cob-house principle." But he offered a counter plan which, though based on geographical considerations, was very close to it. Let them take Clifford as representing New England, Strong the Middle Atlantic States, Miller the Middle West, and Field the Pacific Coast; and then let these four select a fifth judge. Hewitt instantly saw that this was merely his own plan in another form, and assented. "I can see," he said, "that that is less embarrassing than leaving the selection of the fifth judge between two senior justices, Swayne and Davis."[2] The House Committee then retired to consider this counter plan. The character of the discussion is unknown. But it was short, for at four o'clock the two committees again met and the House Committee signified its consent. Chairman Payne announced that one member only, Eppa Hunton of Virginia, still stood aloof, for he wished to consider the matter overnight. Felicitations were then exchanged. Hoar remarked that their friendly agreement would be considered one of the happiest events of American history; Thurman that it

[1] Milton H. Northrup, op. cit.
[2] Ibid.

would be hailed with joy from one ocean to the other; and Hewitt that it was "worth five hundred millions to the country at once."

Though nominally the fifth place in the judicial group was left undetermined, everyone assumed that it would be filled by David Davis. For this there were several reasons. He was the only avowed Independent in the Supreme Court; in all the debates he had been mentioned as the obvious choice; the Democratic justices, Clifford and Field, would certainly insist upon him; and Judge Strong among Republicans was known to favor him. Nobody knew what his political opinions now were. Appointed by Lincoln in Civil War days as an orthodox Republican, in 1872 he had sympathized with the Liberal Republic faction against Grant and had been willing to take its nomination. In the recent election many Green-backers had hoped he would be their nominee; he had not voted and had never said whether he preferred Tilden or Hayes. The fact was that he thirsted for the Presidency, however obtained, and was willing to flirt with either party to get it. But it was enough for the Democrats that he was an Independent. Tilden needed but one electoral vote, and any truly independent arbiter would insist upon going behind the grossly unfair returns from Louisiana and Florida boards. When that was done, Tilden would be President.

General Hunton had reserved his decision for twenty-four hours. The Democratic leaders naturally availed themselves of this inter-mission to place the new plan before Tilden. They had defeated the Six-Judge-and-a-lot scheme; they had got a variant of the Five Judge Plan; and they expected him to acquiesce. States Hewitt's secret history:

> The Democratic committee of eleven took advantage of this delay in order to communicate the result to Mr. Tilden, and for this purpose his nephew, who was understood to be his personal representative in Washington, was dispatched to New York with a copy of the bill as finally amended, to be submitted to Mr. Tilden for his approval or his rejection. Colonel Pelton returned to Washington on the morning of the 18th instant, and had a meeting of the House Committee. He reported that he had con-sulted with Mr. Tilden, who regarded the measure as a great improvement upon any previous proposition, and advised its adoption by the House Committee. Thereupon General Hunton,

who was present and who is still living to confirm this statement, signed the report, although with evident reluctance.

The general feeling, however, was that the victory was won, because no one doubted for a moment that Judge Davis would be selected as the fifth member of the Commission.

The report was made both to the Senate and the House at the regular session on the 18th of January, and the debate thereupon continued for several days in the Senate, where it was adopted on the 25th of January by a vote of 47 yeas to 17 nays, the Republicans voting 21 yeas to 16 nays; the Democrats 26 yeas to 1 nay; absent who were not voting; 9 Republicans and 1 Democrat.

In the House of Representatives the Bill was passed on the 26th January after a discussion which lasted two days, by a vote of 191 yeas to 86 nays, the Democrats giving 158 yeas to 18 nays and the Republicans 33 yeas to 68 nays; absent or not voting, 7 Republicans, and 7 Democrats.

An analysis of the vote proves that the bill was regarded as a Democratic measure, and that a large majority of the Republicans in Congress were opposed to its passage.

I thought at the time and I still think that the division of parties on this measure was largely controlled by the conviction that Judge Davis would have the casting vote, and that he could be relied upon to see that the will of the people as expressed in the election of Mr. Tilden should not be thwarted.

As to what passed between Tilden and his nephew Pelton at this interview in New York we have two pieces of evidence. Two and a half years later, in August, 1879, a friend of Hewitt's, Henry H. Smith, stayed at the Elberon Hotel in Long Branch with Pelton and Representative Blackburn. He asked the former, as he wrote Hewitt, whether Tilden had approved or disapproved the Electoral Commission Bill.[1] "In reply Colonel Pelton said that he made a trip to New York at the request of Mr. Hewitt, just prior to the vote in the House, expressly to ascertain Mr. Tilden's views and wishes in regard to the bill; that Mr. Tilden sent for two or three old and trusted friends with whom he had a long conference in regard to its details; and that finally, as the result of that conference and consideration of the subject, Mr. Tilden concluded that in view of the then existing situation and the serious trouble threatened

[1] Smith to Hewitt, February 16, 1888; Hewitt Papers.

by the failure to count the vote under existing law and rules, it was advisable to accept the bill, objectionable as it was in almost every respect. Mr. Tilden desired or suggested several amendments, but finally decided that it was inexpedient to make any formal suggestion to that effect. 'Thereupon,' said Colonel Pelton, 'I at once returned to Washington and advised Mr. Hewitt, Mr. Hunton, Mr. Springer, and other leading members of Mr. Tilden's conclusions, but for which the bill would not have passed the House.' "
Light is also thrown on Tilden's frame of mind by Simon Sterne.[1] They talked together repeatedly; Tilden showed great anxiety over the outcome; but he seemed at last to accept the Electoral Commission as unescapable. When Sterne voiced some objections to it, Tilden sharply replied, "What is left but war?" He was keenly alive to the fact that the Democratic Party had been regarded as disloyal during the war, and thought that it should make any sacrifice now to avoid civil conflict. "Let us not do anything," he told Sterne, "that will count against the reputation of the Democratic party; nothing that will enable enemies to charge us with lack of patriotism."

Beyond doubt, Tilden would have been happy to avoid any arbitration of the issue—any Electoral Commission or other tribunal. He would have liked to stand fast on what he called "the Constitution and the settled practise" of counting votes; to insist that the House must be allowed to seat him. In just the same way Hayes bitterly objected to the Electoral Commission.[2] Hayes would have liked to stand fast on the Constitution and the alleged right of the president of the Senate to count the vote. But Congress, in closer touch with public demands and feeling strongly the responsibility for a peaceful solution, found adjudication imperative. It having done so, Tilden and Hayes acquiesced—both reluctantly.

And this was really the only feasible course. The well-informed Washington correspondent of the *Nation* pointed out that the Democrats had no choice but to adjudicate. "The Democrats are much more disposed to treat or agree on some middle course or make concessions not because they have more grace, but because they are at a disadvantage and know it. Their opponents, in the first place, are in possession, which is nine points of the law. They

[1] Interview, N. Y. *Times*, August 9, 1886.
[2] John Sherman, *Recollections*, I, 561; Hayes Papers.

have the administrative machinery and the army in their hands, and are therefore able to do with impunity lawless things which if done by the other side would ruin it." Hewitt pointed out in a letter two years later that it would have been hopeless to take a stubborn stand on one interpretation of the Constitution while the Republicans stood stubbornly on another—each equally plausible. "After my interview with Grant on the 3rd of December I became satisfied that Tilden could not be inaugurated [in this way] without a resort to arms. After carefully considering the facts, I became satisfied that we could not wage war with any hope of success. I therefore directed my attention to a possible solution, and endeavored to provide a tribunal which would do justice."

When General Hunton signed the report approving the Electoral Commission bill, most of the Democratic Senators and Representatives were pleased and even jubilant. Only a few men, notably three Southern Representatives, Mills, Blackburn, and Watterson, attacked the measure. And the party might well believe that it had gained a victory. On the universal assumption that David Davis would be the fifth judge, numerous Republicans came to Hewitt and congratulated him warmly. "Senator Morton," he writes,[1] "said to me that it [the bill] was equivalent to the abandonment of the contest on the Republican side." The final vote showed how generally it was expected to give the Presidency to Tilden. In the House and Senate combined, the Democrats cast 186 yeas and only 18 nays; the Republicans cast 52 yeas and 84 nays.[2]

And the closing debate upon the Electoral Commission bill emphasized the fact that it was a Democratic victory. Morton and Garfield predicted that acceptance of the Tribunal would inevitably bring about the inauguration of Tilden. The former called the Commission bill "the contrivance for surrender." Among Republican Senators who took the same view and voted against the bill were Blaine, Hamlin, Ingalls, and John Sherman, the last-named obviously reflecting Hayes's own opinion. Among the dissenting Republicans in the House were Hale of Maine and Kasson of Iowa. Conkling called Morton's plan for letting the president of

---

[1] Secret history; Hewitt Papers.

[2] In these figures the author agrees with Haworth, p. 217; Rhodes (VII, 261) and Eckenrode (p. 210) give slightly different results. See *Congressional Record*, Vol. V, Pt. II, 913, 1050. Hewitt made an able and moderate speech for the bill; *Ibid*, 946-948.

the Senate count the vote "political Hell Gate, paved and honey-combed with dynamite"; but most Republicans were loath to abandon it. The New York *Tribune* opposed the bill as a capitulation. Some of the opponents, like Hayes, were against any adjudication whatever. Others felt that in drafting the plan for the Electoral Commission they had got the worst of it. Essentially, Congress had been faced with a choice between a Six-Judge Plan which assumed that David Davis was a Democrat, and a Five-Judge Plan which assumed that he was an Independent, and the Democrats under Hewitt had forced the adoption of the latter. Most Republicans believed that Davis would at any rate go behind the returns, and that for this reason alone the Democrats had won a great victory. It is far from certain that Davis, a slippery man with an eye on the main political chance, would have acted in this courageous way. But Hewitt himself believed that he would do so. For the second time, he felt that the Presidency was fairly within Tilden's grasp.

But if the party really held the cup of victory, it was rudely dashed from its hand. On January 26, the day on which the bill, under irresistible public pressure and "a perfect hurricane of petitions," passed the House and went to President Grant, news came that the Illinois Legislature had elected David Davis to the Senate!

"The writer," later declared Milton H. Northrup, secretary of the House Committee, "will never forget the drop in the countenance of the Hon. Abram S. Hewitt . . . when, meeting him in the hall of the House of Representatives, he informed him of Judge Davis's transfer from the Supreme Court to the Senate."

The full story of this calamity will probably never be known. Was Davis elected as the result of a sudden Republican plot to withdraw him from the Electoral Commission? Or was his election a mere piece of stupidity on the part of the Democrats in the Illinois Legislature? This Legislature had met on January 10, and a week later had begun balloting for a Senator to succeed John A. Logan. The Republicans and Democrats were closely divided, and the balance of power was held by five Independents. On the first ballot, 101 votes being necessary to elect, Logan received 98 Republican votes, John M. Palmer 88 Democratic votes, and David Davis 8 votes, with others scattering. The deadlock continued for more than thirty ballots without a break. Davis's vote never gained material importance, on a number of ballots his name never appeared at all, and everybody supposed he was out of the running. Then suddenly on January 24th his vote ran up to 97 on the thirty-fifth ballot and 98 on the two following. Most of the Democrats had broken away from their candidate and joined the Independents and a few Republicans behind Davis. Intelligence of this unexpected shift was printed as front-page news in Eastern journals on the 25th, and aroused the deepest interest and suspense. But before noon that day the decision was made. On the very first ballot, David Davis was elected Senator by 101 votes.

This sudden revival of his candidacy was curious. It was also curious that his election should have occurred on the very day that the Electoral Commission Bill (at "early breakfast time" after an all-night debate) passed the Senate, with passage in the House unavoidable. Possibly certain Republican leaders in Illinois, including Joseph Medill, had a fine Italian hand in the transaction; more probably it resulted from the blind Democratic eagerness to defeat Logan. In either event, the Democratic national leaders, and most of all Hewitt, were blameworthy for not taking precautions against it. A few astute observers had realized the importance of the Illinois contest. E. P. Mitchell, later editor of the New York *Sun*, happened to call on the strabismic Ben Butler just before the decisive ballot, and was asked the news. He began to explain the Senate debate. "No, no, I don't mean that," interrupted Butler. "I mean what's the news from Springfield?" And as Mitchell looked puzzled he added, "Springfield, Illinois—that's the place you want to watch!"[1]

But the Democratic leaders, who might have telegraphed Springfield the night of the 25th, let themselves be taken by surprise. Hewitt, after describing their astonishment and chagrin, says in his secret history:

> This surprise and disappointment were intensified by the immediate refusal of Judge Davis to be a nominee for the vacant position on the Commission, although his election as Senator in no respect disqualified him for the performance of the duty which he was expected to discharge. Whether rightly or wrongly, the conviction was general that a bargain had been made by the Republicans by which Judge Davis, in consideration of his being

[1] E. P. Mitchell, *Memoirs of an Editor*, 302, 303.

made Senator, should decline a position upon the Electoral Commission. Certainly if such an arrangement were made it was the last move by which, in the long game which had been played between the two parties, the final triumph was assured to the Republican Party. I can only say that Senator Morton, who had regarded the game as lost, showed as much surprise at this achievement as I felt, and could not restrain the expression of his satisfaction.

President Grant signed the Electoral Commission Bill on January 29. Next day the two houses each designated five members to sit upon the Commission; the Senate choosing three Republicans and two Democrats, and the House three Democrats and two Republicans. On the 30th the four justices, Clifford, Field, Strong, and Miller, met to select the fifth. They offered the place to David Davis. But the Republican press had hastened to declare him unavailable; in his ambition for the Presidency he was anxious to avoid a post which would almost certainly make his future candidacy impossible; and he insisted that his election to the Senate required him to step aside.

III

Yet the battle was by no means completely lost. Hewitt's hopes quickly revived. A fifth justice might be found who would be quite as fair as David Davis. Swayne, Hunt, and Bradley were the three remaining justices. Of these Swayne was unavailable because as a lifelong Republican from Hayes's own State he might be prejudiced, and because Tilden had personal objections to him. Should it be Hunt or Bradley? Hewitt consulted Senator Conkling, whose belief that Tilden had been elected made him a safe guide. He advised against Justice Hunt. He explained that Hunt and he were close friends; that Hunt knew Conkling's opinion that Tilden ought to be seated, and that to prove his independence, he might lean backward and thus unconsciously be unjust to Tilden. Hewitt adds:

> Practically, therefore, the choice was limited to Justice Bradley, whom I had personally known for many years in New Jersey as a very able lawyer and a man of the highest integrity. The confidence which I felt in him was shared by Mr. Tilden, but in order to make assurance doubly sure I requested a mutual friend of

Judge Bradley and myself, the late John G. Stevens of Trenton, N. J., to confer with Judge Bradley to ascertain whether he felt that he could decide the questions which would come before the Commission without prejudice or party feeling. The report of Mr. Stevens was entirely satisfactory. Judge Bradley was therefore selected with the distinct approval of the Democratic representatives, reinforced by the favorable judgment of Judge Clifford and Judge Field, who assured me that absolute reliance could be placed upon the radical fairness of Judge Bradley. In fact, they both stated that it was absurd to fear that any Justice of the Supreme Court would be governed by partisan feeling or influence, and this was in accordance with the general feeling in Congress and throughout the country.

Bradley was not a decided partisan. In some opinions, notably one against the constitutionality of the Enforcement Act, he had shown himself out of sympathy with the radical Republicans. He presided over the Southern circuit and was liked there. The Democratic *World* expressed pleasure in his selection, and declared that he was unsatisfactory to the Republicans.

It was therefore with rising confidence that Hewitt and the other Democratic leaders, on February 1, attended the joint session of the two houses which began the count of the electoral votes. At one o'clock the Senators filed into the House, where the Representatives awaited them. Senator Ferry took the chair. Speaker Randall was seated immediately on his left. The Senators were disposed on the left side of the hall, as viewed from the rostrum, and the Representatives on the right. In the galleries and in additional seats on the floor were foreign ministers, headed by Sir Edward Thornton, politicians and generals, and such distinguished observers as the historian George Bancroft. Ferry rapped for order, and the count began. The votes of half a dozen States were recorded without incident. Then Florida was reached, and a hush fell upon the hall. Objections were filed against both the Republican and the Democratic returns, and the vote of Florida was referred to the Electoral Commission.[1]

This body, which had already organized, did not include Hewitt. It would have been improper for the National Chairman to sit on

[1] See *The Proceedings of the Electoral Commission* in *Congressional Record*, Vol. V, Pt. IV, 1ff.

it, while he wished to help the Democratic counsel who appeared before it. Nor did it include Conkling, who notoriously questioned Hayes's title. The principal Democratic members were Senators Thurman and Bayard, and Representatives Hunton and Payne; the principal Republicans were Senators Frelinghuysen and Edmunds, and Representatives Garfield and Hoar. "The omission of Senator Conkling," writes Hewitt, "whose preferences were supposed to be for Mr. Tilden and who was the putative author of the bill creating the Commission, was remarked as tending to show the Republican animus in reference to the Commission. The choice by the House of General Garfield, who had opposed the bill, was also regarded as significant, but the feeling was general that substantial justice would be done by the Commission." The president of the Commission was Judge Clifford, and it met at three o'clock in the Supreme Court Room. But arguments did not begin till the next day, February 2.

Three Florida certificates were submitted, one Republican and two Democratic; the Republican return being signed by the former Governor and Secretary of State, one Democratic return by the Attorney-General, and the other Democratic return by the new Governor, under authority of the Circuit and Supreme Courts and the new Legislature. The first task of the Electoral Commission was to hear arguments for and against these Florida returns. On February 2 members of the House spoke, and at the next two sittings the counsel made extended appeals.

Hewitt and his associates had retained eminent attorneys: George Hoadly, Charles O'Conor, Jeremiah S. Black, Lyman Trumbull, and William C. Whitney. They faced an equally brilliant array of Republican lawyers, led by William M. Evarts and Stanley Matthews. The Democrats could not deny that the Republican return from Florida was perfectly regular and legal in form, for it had been certified by Governor Stearns and Secretary of State McLin. But they contended that the Electoral Commission should go behind this return, and examine the evidence of fraud and impropriety in the work of the State Returning Board. The Republicans, for their part, presented a set of strict-constructionist opinions, holding that no Federal authority possessed a right to review the method by which each State chose its electors; for the Constitution expressly declared that these electors should be appointed by each State "in such manner as the Legislature thereof may direct."

It may be asked why there was no understanding in advance whether the Electoral Commission should go behind the returns or not. The reason is simple: both parties completely disagreeing on the point, this was one of the primary questions to be adjudicated. Hewitt says in his secret memorandum that when the joint Committee first met, there was one subject upon which "all the members" seemed to be united. This was "that a Commission should be appointed which should and would be invested with power to go behind the returns so as to arrive at the true result of the election States. Judge Edmunds alone declined to commit himself as to the meaning of the words 'if any,' by virture of which the other members of the Committee seemed to think that the action of the Returning Boards must be inquired into and should be reversed, if substantial justice should seem to demand such action." But this was merely an impression and was incorrect. The Republicans utterly denied taking any such attitude, for they knew that the moment any tribunal went behind the returns, Tilden's inauguration was assured.

Nevertheless, for several reasons Hewitt and other Democratic leaders felt hopeful that any unbiased member of the Commission —Judge Bradley, if no other—would decide in favor of their contentions. One was that they had an important precedent on their side. In 1873 a Senate Committee *had* gone behind the return of electoral votes certified by the governor of Louisiana. It had found that the votes had never been counted by anyone possessing authority to count them, and Congress, on the footing of this report, had excluded the electoral vote of Louisiana.[1] Again, the Democrats believed that by their use of the Oregon return they had placed the Republicans in a hopeless dilemma. If the Electoral Commission refused to go behind the governor's certificate in Florida, how could it go behind his certificate in Oregon? And then there was the utter outrageousness of the counts in Florida and Louisiana. Was the Commission, on a mere disputed punctilio of State Rights, to let so disreputable and corrupt a body as the Louisiana Returning Board decide who should be President of the United States?

[1] House Misc. Doc. No. 13, 44th Cong., 2d sess., 358ff.

Thus the crucial date approached—the date of February 7. The arguments on the question of receiving detailed evidence as to the actual Florida vote, and of going behind the returns, were concluded late on Monday, February 5. The Commission withheld its decision until Wednesday. All day Tuesday, while it deliberated in secret from ten in the morning until nearly eight o'clock at night, the keenest anxiety prevailed among party leaders as to the stand which it would take. Everyone believed that the fourteen members first named would align themselves seven to seven, and that the decision would then rest with Judge Bradley. As it happened, Judge Bradley had not indicated to the secret session that day how he would vote. There was therefore a moment of extreme tension when, at three o'clock on Wednesday afternoon, Justice Miller offered a motion which in effect declared that the Commission would refuse to go behind the face of the official returns from Florida. Since these returns gave the electoral votes to Hayes, this was the crucial question. It brings us to Bradley's opinion and the most dramatic part of Hewitt's narrative:

The history of this opinion forms an important feature in the final outcome of the electoral count. As stated above, Mr. John G. Stevens was the intimate friend of Judge Bradley. He passed the night previous to the rendition of the judgment in the Florida case at my house. About midnight he returned from a visit to Judge Bradley, and reported to General Richard Taylor, who was also staying with me, and to Senator Gibson, who was awaiting his return, that he had just left Judge Bradley after reading his opinion in favor of counting the vote of the Democratic electors of the State of Florida. Such a judgment insured the election of Tilden to the Presidency with three votes to spare above the necessary majority. We parted, therefore, with the assurance that all further doubt as to the Presidency was at rest. I attended the delivery of the judgment the next day without the slightest intimation from any quarter that Judge Bradley had changed his mind. In fact, the reading of the opinion until the few concluding paragraphs were reached was strictly in accordance with the report of Mr. Stevens.

The change was made between midnight and sunrise. Mr. Stevens afterwards informed me that it was due to a visit to Judge Bradley by Senator Frelinghuysen and Secretary Robeson, made after his departure. Their appeals to Judge Bradley were said to have been reinforced by the persuasion of Mrs. Bradley. Whatever the fact may have been, Judge Bradley himself in a subsequent letter addressed to the Newark *Daily Advertiser* admitted that he had written a favorable opinion which on subsequent reflection he saw fit to modify.

This statement in all probability explains Bradley's mysterious vote. Rumors of what had happened that fateful night were soon bruited abroad, some very inaccurate and unfair. Judge Bradley later seized upon these reports, one of which included the harsh accusation that he had succumbed to pressure from Texas Pacific Railroad magnates, to issue a long statement.[1] He admitted that he had written a decision favorable to Tilden. But he explained that he had followed the alleged practice of some jurists in writing out two opinions, thus giving the arguments on both sides, and intending to accept in the end whichever seemed the stronger. In a world where anything is possible, this is possible. But it is certainly hard to believe. If the practise mentioned ever existed, it was excessively rare. There was no need to write out the arguments, for they lay in printed form before the judges.[2] Bradley's quick, clear mind was one of the last on the tribunal to require such aid. Moreover, the vital question of going behind the returns was not complex and did not require elaborate argument—it was a very simple issue of principle. Finally, Bradley's opinion did, as Hewitt writes, include various arguments suggesting an inclination to Tilden's side up to the last few paragraphs. And Stevens' accusation is strongly reenforced by a statement which his colleague on the Commission, Justice Field, shortly sent to Tilden in commenting upon the Newark *Advertiser* letter. "The language of the letter," he wrote, "justified some of the comments of the press upon *the change of views which the judge experienced shortly before the vote was taken in the Florida case*."[3]

[1] Newark *Daily Advertiser*, September 5, 1877.
[2] For an illustration of the way in which Bradley himself asked for printed briefs from the Democratic counsel, and at once received them, see *Proceedings of the Electoral Commission, Congressional Record*, Vol. V, Part IV, p. 40. Democratic briefs are printed in the *Proceedings*, pp. 729-774. Bradley's opinion is given there, pp. 259-261.
[3] Field to Tilden, December 11, 1877; Tilden Papers. The italics are the author's.

Stevens' statement indicates that up to midnight on February 7, Bradley accepted the Democratic view, but after midnight yielded to other influences. What were these influences? "During the whole sitting of the Commission," Bradley wrote late in 1877,[1] "I had no private discussion whatever on the subjects at issue with any person interested *on the Republican side,* and but very few words with any person. Indeed, I sedulously sought to avoid all discussion *outside of the Commission itself.*" But he does not deny here that he read his opinion to his old friend Stevens, for Stevens was on the Democratic side; nor does his statement carry a denial that he talked with Frelinghuysen after the departure of Stevens, for Frelinghuysen was on the Commission. For thirty years Bradley and Frelinghuysen had been the two leading attorneys at the New Jersey bar, and in perhaps a majority of the highly important cases during that period had been retained either as associates or opponents; there was a long intimacy between them. Hewitt was later told that after midnight Frelinghuysen had rung at Judge Bradley's door; that he had pleaded with Bradley to abandon the Democratic position; and that Mrs. Bradley, a highly religious woman and a strong partisan, had come downstairs in her dressing gown and prayed with her husband.[2] In the end, Bradley had yielded to their argument that, whatever the strict legal equities, it would be a national disaster if the government fell into Democratic hands. Perhaps still other influences were at work. Roscoe Conkling, in his famous assault on the Hayes Administration in the Senate on February 3, 1879, read a letter showing that the Administration had begged a lucrative job for Justice Bradley's son in the New York Custom House, alleging "manifest reasons."[3] The Texas Pacific Railroad lobby, which confessedly feared Tilden and hoped for favors from Hayes, may have instilled additional zeal into some of Bradley's friends. But as with David Davis and the Senatorship, the full truth will never be known.

[1] Charles Bradley, *Miscellaneous Writings of the Late Hon. Joseph P. Bradley* (1902). Note that O. O. Stealey says in *Forty Years in the Press Gallery,* p. 269: "George F. Edmunds . . . as a member of the Electoral Commission stiffened up Judge Bradley more than once when the latter was wavering."

[2] Mr. Erskine Hewitt and Mr. Edward R. Hewitt both had this story from their father. Mr. G. G. Frelinghuysen has kindly furnished the author information upon his father's intimacy with Justice Bradley.

[3] See *Nation,* February 6, 1879, for a summary of this speech.

IV

But even yet one chance remained. Hewitt clung to the expectation that Senator Conkling would still declare himself openly on Tilden's side, and would stay the tide. We recur to the secret narrative:

The decision in the Florida case produced a feeling of profound disappointment, but not of dismay. It was evident that the principles laid down in this case would necessarily secure one vote from Oregon—enough to secure the election of Mr. Tilden, even if the votes of Louisiana and South Carolina should be awarded to Hayes. Besides these States, there were cases of disqualified electors in other States, and particularly one in Illinois, a Republican elector who under the provisions of the Constitution was disqualified in consequence of holding the office of postmaster.

It was decided in view of the decision in the Florida case to object to the counting of this vote, although both sides conceded that Illinois had given a large majority for the Republican candidates. Before the two houses met, however, on the morning of the next day after the Florida decision was rendered, [I saw] Senator Conkling, with whom I had very intimate and confidential relations, leading me to suppose that as he had already taken ground against the claim of the President of the Senate to count the votes and declare the result, and had practically demolished this pretence in a speech of remarkable range and power, he would also when a contested case was reached in which the vote clearly belonged to Tilden, not hesitate to take responsibility of defeating the plans of the Republican leaders to count in Hayes at all hazards.

Senator Conkling asked me whether it was the intention of the Democrats to object to the vote of the Illinois postmaster. On receiving my reply in the affirmative, he said that he would advise us to refrain from this action, because it would be construed into a disposition on the part of the Democrats to claim a vote to which in justice they were not entitled, and that this would be quoted against us when the Oregon case should come up for decision. He added that there was a much stronger reason why we should make no claim in Illinois. He said that the Louisiana case, in which there could be no doubt as to the election having been in favor of Tilden by a large majority, would come up after the Illinois case, and that he would be met in the contention that Tilden was entitled to the electoral votes of Louisiana by the statement that the Democrats had not hesitated to claim a vote in Illinois to which they were not entitled.

I replied that I would submit his views to the Committee in charge of the objections, and accordingly proceeded at once to confer with J. Randolph Tucker of Virginia, who had the matter in charge. On full consideration by the Committee, Mr. Tucker informed me that in view of Mr. Conkling's position they had decided to pass over the State of Illinois without objection. It is proper here to state that no one on our side entertained a doubt of the Constitutional disqualification of this elector, but we all felt that our case would be weakened by the claim, and that the Electoral Commission would find some way to defeat it on account of its admitted want of equity.

The Louisiana case was reached on the same day and the returns were duly opened in the presence of both Houses; one return gave the vote of the State to Hayes, another return gave the vote to Tilden. To the surprise of everybody, a third return was presented giving the vote of the State to Peter Cooper. This last return was supposed to be the work of a crank, and was after some discussion omitted from the proceedings as having no validity whatever. Mr. Conkling was present at the joint meeting, but took no part in the discussions. It was expected, however, that at the meeting of the Senate on the next morning Mr. Conkling would take ground against counting the certificate of the Returning Board of Louisiana in favor of the Hayes electors. My conference with him in the Illinois case led me to this conclusion, and in the same evening Senator Barnum, who was in constant intercourse with Senator Conkling, assured me that the latter would on the following morning denounce the action of the Returning Board and show that the vote of Louisiana belonged to Tilden.

This was a forlorn hope—but it was a hope. Both chambers would have to act to keep the electoral vote of Louisiana out of the hands of the Electoral Commission, and cast it for Tilden. The House would gladly do so. If Conkling made a rousing speech, he might possibly carry the day in the Senate also.[1] The Springfield

[1] As early as December 7 an Albany dispatch to the N. Y. *Tribune* stated that Conkling was expected to speak forcibly in behalf of Tilden. He was a brother-in-law of Horatio Seymour; he disliked Hayes; and he had Presidential ambitions himself. "It is believed he will make so strong an argument against

Republican had reported on January 10 that if Conkling headed an open revolt against Hayes, Washington observers believed that enough Republican Senators "will follow him to make it successful." George Hoadly, later Governor of Ohio, was attorney in Washington for Tilden. He stated long afterward that he possessed full knowledge of Conkling's expected speech. He had gone "to bed that night in full confidence that Mr. Tilden would be placed on a legal basis for inauguration to the Presidency in the morning. Eight or nine [Republican] Senators had agreed with each other to cast their votes in the Senate to reverse the judgment of the Electoral Tribunal in the Louisiana case." Seven, with Conkling, would have been enough.

But this slender chance of retrieving the field was rudely shattered. Hewitt writes:

> But when the session of the Senate was opened on the next morning, Senator Conkling was not in his seat. On inquiry it was stated that he had been seen earlier in the day making his way to the railway station and had said that he was going to Baltimore. It is certain that he did not return until the next day, and in the interval the Louisiana case was, under the provisions of the law, sent to the Electoral Commission for decision, because the two Houses had disagreed as to the counting of the vote.
>
> I do not propose to give any account of the proceedings before the Commission in this case, but it is proper to state that the return actually approved by the Commission appears to have been the forged return, and that this fact was known not only to the President of the Senate, but to General Garfield, who was sitting as a member of the Electoral Commission. At this date, I can now understand why the Peter Cooper return was interjected when the certificates were opened. Attention was thus distracted from the discrepancy which undoubtedly existed between the two sets of the Republican returns, opened and submitted by the President of the Senate.

The absence of Conkling on the day set for his great speech has been variously explained. It has been said that some of his expected

---

the reception of the votes of the three Southern States that the Senate may consent to throwing them out. . . . The statement that Mr. Conkling is preparing a very strong speech upon the matter comes from so direct a source that its truth cannot be doubted."

followers failed him; that he became frightened by Republican threats; that he was notoriously unstable and fickle. Whatever the reason, his abstention destroyed the last Democratic hope of success. The Brooklyn *Eagle* declared two years later[1] that it possessed information that if he had denounced the Louisiana Returning Board, he would have been supported by a vote of 37 to 32. The Washington correspondent of the Philadelphia *Press* likewise asserted[2] that he knew the names of eight Republicans who, "disagreeing with the findings of the Commission, avowed their willingness to follow Mr. Conkling's lead, but who would not otherwise make the break." As for what Hewitt calls the "forged return," that is again a curious episode. The Constitution requires that certificates of the electoral vote of a State shall be presented in triplicate. When the Republican certificates from Louisiana were first brought to Washington, a supposed defect appeared in them. New certificates were hurriedly made out in Louisiana. But the time was then short, two of the electors were so far away that they could not reach New Orleans in season, and the State leaders calmly forged their names! Had the Democrats examined the Republican returns closely, they would undoubtedly have discovered this forgery, and they could have made the irregularity highly embarrassing to the Republicans. The accusation that Garfield and others used the Peter Cooper certificate as a trick to distract the attention of the Democrats was never answered and is doubtless true.[3]

But the battle was now over. By the familiar vote of 8 to 7, the Electoral Commission hastened to count the Louisiana electors for Hayes. Then on February 23, meeting at the home of Senator Thurman, who was ill and wished to participate, it counted the three electoral votes of Oregon in the same way. Hewitt always held that in going behind the returns certified by the Governor of Oregon it reversed the precedent created in the Florida case. Republicans asserted, however, and with reason, that there was a radical distinction: to go behind the returns in the South would require a recount of the whole popular vote, a scrutiny of innumerable questions of intimidation and fraud, and a broad substitu-

[1] February 22, 1879.
[2] February 20, 1879.
[3] House Report 140, 45th Cong., p. 58.

tion of Federal for State authority, whereas in the Oregon case it involved a mere rectification of the governor's action. Immediately afterwards the vote of South Carolina was also counted for Hayes. With these decisions, Hewitt wrote, "the greatest fraud in the history of the country was practically consummated."[1] While they were being made, the Democratic press was full of indignant protests; party leaders were angrily denouncing the tribunal; and among Democratic members of Congress a movement for a filibuster, to endure past March 4, was reaching proportions which threatened the peace of the country anew.

[1] Secret History; Hewitt Papers. It is of course clear that Bradley had a perfect legal and moral right to change his mind up to the last minute. But he had no moral right to swerve from his convictions at the last minute under political pressure. The author believes that Bradley failed utterly in the part of impartial umpire which he should have played. He believes also that precedent would have justified the Commission in going behind the returns (see Schouler, VII, 343-345): that an investigation in Florida, the first State, would have been quick and easy; and that it would immediately have given Tilden the Presidency.

CHAPTER XX

The Count Completed

WHEN the decision in the Oregon case, ensuring Tilden's defeat, was made on February 23, only nine days remained before a President must be inaugurated, and the electoral votes of nine States still had to be counted. "The indignation and excitement," writes Hewitt,[1] "were unbounded. Many Democrats declared their intention by dilatory proceedings to prevent further action; in this view many moderate members concurred, because the States of South Carolina and Louisiana were in the hands of carpetbag governments although at the late election the Democratic local ticket had been successful in both States. Personally I was anxious to have the count completed even though it should result as it must do, in the declaration on the part of the two houses of the election of Hayes and Wheeler." The imperative object, he believed, was to preserve the national peace; but in view of the violent anger of many Democrats, was this possible?

The proposed filibuster by Democratic Representatives to prevent the completion of the count offered the gravest danger; for if it were protracted until March 4, there would be no President, and once this happened, fighting would almost certainly begin. Many Democrats now looked toward such a result with rash eagerness. The would-be filibusterers fell into two groups. One, numbering about forty, consisted of irresponsible and hot-headed members of the Watterson type who swore they would never consent to "the fraud" that was making Hayes President. The others, chiefly Southerners, were unwilling to consent unless and until they received assurances that the last Southern States would be liberated from their thraldom. For the moment both groups filled the air

[1] Secret History; Hewitt Papers.

with threats. If they received the aid of Speaker Randall, and perhaps even if they did not, their filibuster would succeed.

In the country at large excitement and apprehension were
steadily mounting. Business was being arrested and the economic
depression deepened by the uncertainty. Newspapers of both parties carried inflammatory utterances. Hewitt knew that in numerous centres some of the Democrats were quietly preparing for hostilities. Democratic governors sat in Albany, Hartford, Indianapolis,
Trenton, and other capitals. Party leaders in all sections had written to Hewitt as Democratic Chairman of warlike preparations,
and had convinced him that civil conflict was close at hand. "To
this dread issue we were much nearer than was even at that time
supposed. The Democratic forces had been organized in fifteen
States, and were composed chiefly of the veterans of the war. . . .
Even the Commander in Chief had been selected, and the governors of many States had declared their willingness to act, in case
an emergency should arise, demanding the inauguration of Tilden,
by military force." In brief, when threats of a filibuster increased
on the 24th and 25th, fighting seemed little more than a week
away.[1]

Impressed with the danger, Hewitt called late one night on
William T. Sherman, commanding general of the army, and inquired what his course would be if the count were not duly finished. Some had suggested that President Grant ought to hold over
to prevent a vacancy, and Hewitt asked if, under such circumstances, Sherman would obey the orders of Grant. With characteristic incisiveness the general said he would not. "The term of President Grant ends at twelve o'clock on the 4th of March. He will
then be in no position to give orders to me, and I shall receive no
orders from him."

During these days the two most responsible Democratic leaders
in Washington, Hewitt and Randall, were in constant consultation
with each other. Meanwhile, Randall was in communication with
Tilden by telegraph and showed his telegrams to Hewitt. At first
it seemed difficult to obtain any decisive statement from him. "The
habit of Mr. Tilden's mind," Hewitt writes, "was to criticize and

[1] Senator Hoar bears this out; *Autobiography*, I, 369. A Democratic Veteran
Soldiers' Association was active, especially under Gen. J. M. Corse in the Middle
West; Haworth, *Disputed Election*, 188.

postpone, not to decide or approve." But when Tilden realized
that only two alternatives were left, acceptance of the result or
civil war, he never hesitated. He forthwith telegraphed Randall
that the verdict of the Electoral Commission must be accepted.
The best party leaders agreed that the count must at all costs be
completed; but how could this be assured?

It could be done only by inducing the Southern Representatives
to abandon the irreconcilable Northern leaders, and this could be
accomplished only by obtaining substantial Republican concessions. The story of these concessions—of the "Bargain", by which
unauthorized but authentic representatives of Hayes agreed that
he would discontinue Federal interference and permit the restoration of white government in South Carolina and Louisiana (the
Democrats having carried the State ticket in Florida) —is long since
familiar. Hewitt writes:

Finding that it would not be possible to complete the count
before the 4th of March in view of this [Southern and irrecon-
cilable] opposition, I addressed myself to President Grant in reference to the condition of affairs in South Carolina, and succeeded in arranging with him a course of action by which the
election of Wade Hampton was conceded as Governor and the
Democrats were recognized as having a majority of the Legislature.

Thus the case of Louisiana only remained to be considered
and arranged. As before stated, General Richard Taylor, the only
son of ex-President Taylor, and a resident of Louisiana, had
been a guest at my house from the beginning of the session of
Congress, and had been the means of a communication between
me and the representatives of the South, in and out of Congress.
A committee had come to Washington from Louisiana, at the
head of which was Major E. A. Burke, afterwards State Treasurer, but at that time the proprietor of the New Orleans *Times-
Democrat*. He bore full credentials from General Nichols, who
had received the majority as a Democratic candidate for Governor.

A conference was therefore arranged between the Louisiana
members and the personal representatives of Mr. Hayes, and
thus came into existence what was known as the Wormley Conference. Mr. Hayes was represented by General Garfield and Mr.
Charles Foster, both members of the House from the State of

Ohio. The communications and telegrams were all conveyed to Mr. Hayes through Lieutenant-Governor Young at Columbus, Ohio. This conference occupied the better part of two days, during which it was necessary to occupy the attention of the House so as to avoid the completion of the count until an agreement had been reached between the Wormley Conference as to the recognition of the Democratic Administration in Louisiana.

In South Carolina there were now two governments, one Democratic and one Republican; peace was being preserved only by Federal troops; and what Hewitt must have secured was not recognition of Wade Hampton and the Democratic government—for that did not come until Hayes had entered office—but a simple pledge of neutrality. But this neutrality obviously came close to recognition; for under it the Hampton government grew steadily stronger, and D. H. Chamberlain's Republican government steadily weaker.

The Wormley Conference, so named because held in part at Wormley's Hotel, marked the culminating phase of the intersectional negotiations. On February 26th and 27th a series of conferences was held between representatives of Hayes and the South; the former group including Garfield, John Sherman, and Stanley Matthews, and the latter General Taylor, John Brown Young of Kentucky, and E. J. Ellis of Louisiana. Late on the 27th Stanley Matthews and Charles Foster signed a letter to certain Southerners embodying promises as to Hayes's policy. They wrote that they would urge him to leave South Carolina and Louisiana to the control of their own people, and that "we have the most complete confidence that such will be the policy of his Administration."

On the surface this was acceptable, though some Southerners thought it too vague. But Hewitt knew the accompanying messages which passed between Hayes and his assumed agents. "It is proper to add," he writes, "that every telegram sent to and from the representatives of Mr. Hayes was promptly shown to me, and that I was familiar with the negotiation at every stage. How this information was secured I do not feel at liberty to mention." These messages, indicating that Hayes still felt uncommitted, were not satisfactory. Hewitt therefore took his last important step in this struggle—he deliberately delayed the count for one day to procure more satisfactory assurances. The delay also enabled the Democratic leaders to obtain Tilden's explicit approval of the abandonment of the contest.

The means by which he effected the delay were simple. On the 28th the count reached Vermont. The regular return having been read, Representative Poppleton asked whether it stood alone. Senator Ferry said it did. Then Hewitt arose and obtained the floor.

"I hold in my hand," he said, "a package which purports to contain electoral votes from the State of Vermont. This package was delivered to me by express about the middle of December last, and with it came a letter stating that a similar package had been forwarded by mail to the presiding officer of the Senate; I called upon him and . . . then tendered to him this package, the seals of which are unbroken and which is now as it came into my possession. He declined to receive it, upon the ground that he had no authority in law to do so. Under the circumstances, I now tender this package to the presiding officer of the Senate as purporting to contain electoral votes from the State of Vermont."

Before taking this step Hewitt had conferred with Tilden's counsel in Washington. Senator Ferry refused to accept the packet, which declared that a Democratic candidate for elector had been chosen because one of the Republican candidates was a postmaster. He said that the law prohibited him from receiving any return after the first Thursday in February, and waved aside Springer's angry assertion that he had accepted a return from the State of Florida on January 30th with the caustic comment: "The 30th of January is not the first Thursday in February." The joint session thereupon broke up without action. The Southerners had till next day, March 1, to extort fuller promises from the friends of Hayes. Meanwhile, Washington hummed with excitement. Few of the onlookers divined Hewitt's real motives; they were astonished that, after struggling so valiantly for an orderly adjudication, he seemed suddenly to go over to the obstructionists. It was only three days till March 4, and even those who knew Hewitt's motive feared that he had created a Frankenstein's monster that would overpower them.

Next day the public tension brought crowds flocking to the galleries and halls of the House. Nearly the entire Senate trooped across to watch the proceedings. It at once transpired that Hewitt's packet, after being presented to Senator Ferry, had disappeared.

An excited discussion was precipitated by a resolution demanding its restoration to the House. When Randall ruled that debate on the Vermont return should proceed whether the missing document were restored or not, obstructionists leaped to their feet, the galleries became disorderly, and for a few minutes the House was a mob. Some Representatives grasped their revolvers. Above the din came Randall's stentorian voice: "The Chair is determined that gentlemen shall take their seats. The Chair is not going to submit longer to this disorder. If gentlemen forget themselves, it is the duty of the Chair to remind them that they are members of the American Congress." As quiet was restored, the facts regarding the disappearance of the return came out. Senator Edmunds of Vermont and the secretary of the Senate, it appeared, were the last two who had handled it. Republican members of the House now saw that obstruction would continue until the package was restored; and immediately after Kasson of Iowa had forcibly pointed this out, the return was handed to Hewitt by a messenger from the Senate, who refused to reveal from whom he had received it.

Order being restored, under Randall's firm rulings the two-hour debate on the Vermont return was pushed to completion. The Democratic objections to the regular Republican return of course had no force. Delay only had been aimed at, and delay had been secured. That it had borne the expected fruit was made clear by Representative Levy of Louisiana in a dramatic appeal for completion of the count. "The people of Louisiana," he said, "have solemn, earnest and, I believe, truthful assurances from prominent members of the Republican party, high in the confidence of Mr. Hayes, that in the event of his elevation to the Presidency, he will be guided by a policy of conciliation toward the Southern States, that he will not use the Federal authority or the Army to force upon these States governments not of their choice, but in the case of these will leave their own people to settle the matter peaceably, of themselves. . . . I do not hesitate, for the reasons before stated, to declare that, actuated by a sense of duty to Louisiana, I shall throw no obstacle, by any action or vote of mine, in the way of the completion of the electoral count; but, relying upon the good faith, the integrity, and the truthfulness of the gentlemen who have given these assurances . . . I call upon those of my fellow-members who

40. Samuel Jones Tilden

39. Rutherford B. Hayes, 1869

41. Cartoon used in Peter Cooper's Greenback Campaign, 1876

42. SENATORS OF THE DEMOCRATIC ADVISORY COUNCIL, 1877: BAYARD,
McDONALD, THURMAN, KERNAN, AND STEVENSON

43. REPRESENTATIVES OF THE DEMOCRATIC ADVISORY COUNCIL, 1877:
GIBSON, WATTERSON, LAMAR, RANDALL, HOLMAN, HUNTON,
AND PAYNE

THOMAS F. BAYARD.   JOSIAH G. ABBOTT.   JOSEPH P. BRADLEY.

ALLEN G. THURMAN.   EPPA HUNTON.   STEPHEN J. FIELD.

FREDERICK T. FRELINGHUYSEN.   HENRY B. PAYNE.

OLIVER P. MORTON.   GEORGE F. HOAR.

NATHAN CLIFFORD.   SAMUEL F. MILLER.

GEORGE F. EDMUNDS.   JAMES A. GARFIELD.   WILLIAM STRONG.

THE MEMBERS OF THE ELECTORAL COMMISSION.—Photographed in Bust, Washington.—[See Page 154.]

44. THE ELECTORAL COMMISSION, 1887

45. Session of the Electoral Commission to Consider the Florida Returns, Supreme Court Room, February 5, 1877

46. DAVID DAVIS ELECTED TO THE SENATE, FEBRUARY, 1877

Naſt in Harper's Weekly

47. AFTER THE DISPUTED ELECTION, 1887
Harper's Weekly, March 24, 1877

have been influenced in their action upon this question by a desire to protect Louisiana and South Carolina to join me in the course which I feel called upon and justified in pursuing."

This was precisely what Hewitt had wished to bring about. Now entirely satisfied, he concurred with the other moderate Democrats in placing the Vermont electors in the Hayes column without a further struggle. The vote was 148 to 116.

The Senate thereupon re-entered the hall, and joint sittings were resumed. The votes of Virginia and West Virginia were counted. But when Wisconsin was reached, new objections came from the Democratic irreconcilables. The Senate once more retired, and another House debate ensued. Members from the two sides taunted each other. Blackburn of Kentucky, saying that the hour had now dragged past midnight into Friday, March 2, and that Friday was the day of Christ's death, remarked that it was fitting that it should also witness the crucifixion of "constitutional government, justice, honesty, fair dealings . . . amid a number of thieves." Williams of Kentucky rejoined that Friday was hangman's day, and that he rejoiced to see the strangling of "this bogus, pretentious, bastard brat of political reform, which for the last twelve months has affronted the eyes of gods and men." Speaker Randall, as Hewitt states, had finally received a telegram from Tilden assenting to the completion of the count. He therefore sent a messenger to the Senate to announce that the House would once more receive it.

It was now four a.m. on March 2nd. Members had been continuously at the Capitol for eighteen hours. In dazed exhaustion they heard Senator Ferry warn them and the galleries against any demonstration that might mar the dignity of the proceedings, and then solemnly conclude: "Wherefore, I do declare: That Rutherford B. Hayes, having received a majority of the whole number of electoral votes, is duly elected President of the United States for four years, commencing on the 4th of March, 1877." Hewitt writes:

I did not witness the completion of the count. After the last State had been called, my nervous system yielded to the strain of many days and nights of excessive anxiety passed without sleep. I was taken from the House by my friends in a state of collapse on the night of the second of March, from which I did not recover until after Hayes had taken the oath of office.

II

We must assign to Speaker Randall and Chairman Hewitt, among all the participants in Washington, the principal credit for the peaceful solution of the dispute. Hewitt's earnestness in pressing for arbitration, his firmness in supporting it, and his fidelity and bravery in abiding by its unhappy outcome, were all invaluable. Had Randall permitted dilatory motions, allowed the mass of testimony presented on Southern affairs to be read, or otherwise abetted the obstructionists, the regular induction of Hayes would have been frustrated. To his courageous course Hewitt has paid a just tribute:

> There was much excitement, and doubtless scenes of violence would have been witnessed but for the firmness of Speaker Randall, to whose patriotic action the country owes a debt of gratitude for the peaceful issue of this long, exciting, and humiliating controversy, upon which the attention of the country had been concentrated for many months with painful anxiety. In fact, on this late day, eighteen years after these occurrences, it is almost impossible to form any adequate idea of the excitement and apprehension which prevailed throughout the country. Business was arrested, the wheels of industry ceased to move, and it seemed as if the terrors of civil war were again to be renewed. Petitions from Chambers of Commerce and from all the centres of trade had deluged Congress in favor of a peaceful settlement of the controversy. Personally I was satisfied that it would be better for the country to have four years of Republican Administration based upon fraudulent returns, than to have four years of civil war. In this view I had the hearty concurrence of Speaker Randall, who was recognized as the firm friend of Mr. Tilden, and the unyielding upholder of his rights under the law. To his action in concurrence with my advice as Chairman of the National Democratic Committee was due in my opinion the escape from civil war.

Much credit also should be given to Tilden for his decision to avoid force and abide by law. As *Harper's Weekly* stated some years later, he could have precipitated a frightful civil war by a word; as Ambassador Gerard said when, in 1926, his statue was unveiled in New York, he merits the nation's lasting gratitude for following "the path of peace and self-abnegation." He had seen his candidacy carried to victory at the November elections by a heavy preponderance in the popular vote; he had seen this victory set at naught by the decisions of three irresponsible and in part corrupt boards, acting with brazen impudence in the interest of the Republican party; he had beheld the tribunal which Congress appointed to review the election as a whole refuse to investigate any of the wrongs suffered by the Democrats; and yet he never uttered a word that would arouse the passions of his followers. It was a rare example of self-restraint.

Yet we must not overlook the evidence—evidence from more than one source, and borne out by the general tone of his letters—that he found compensations for his disappointment. The protracted dispute had wearied him. Tired, half an invalid, by nature averse to political strife, he felt that he had gained as well as lost. Hewitt, writing from close subsequent observation, declares:

I have reason to think that although this result was a great disappointment to Mr. Tilden, he nevertheless felt a profound sense of relief from the dangers of the situation. If the count had not been completed, and Hayes had been declared President by the unconstitutional recognition of President Grant, or by the action of General Sherman in command of the military forces of the country, the position of Mr. Tilden would have been most embarrassing. He would either have been forced to take the oath of office under the constitutional choice of the House of Representatives which would undoubtedly have been made, or he would have been compelled to submit to the usurpation of the office to which he was legally entitled. No one doubted then, and no one can doubt now, that in the former event civil war would have resulted. To violence of any kind Mr. Tilden was by nature strongly opposed. He believed in peaceful methods, but also believed in giving effect to the will of the people. For such a conflict the state of his health entirely unfitted him, and moreover, his intimate connection with many great industrial and corporate enterprises would naturally lead him to a conservative course of action. It is enough to say that the emergency did not arise, but Mr. Bigelow seems to think that if it had arisen Mr. Tilden would have taken the oath of office and insisted upon his right to the Presidency.

At best it is a matter of speculation which I do not care to pursue further; but I believe that on the whole Mr. Tilden was satisfied by the result and consoled by the conviction that at the next Presidential election justice would be done by his triumphant reëlection to the great office of which he had been defrauded.

Tilden, remarking to H. K. Enos, of New York, and John C. New, of Indiana, early in December that he did not believe the Republicans would permit a fair settlement, had added a significant remark.[1] "However, I think I can retire to private life with the consciousness that I shall receive from posterity the credit of having been elected to the highest position in the gift of the people without any of the cares and responsibilities of the office."

The verdict of history upon the Hayes-Tilden election has long since been decisively registered. Without exception, all the principal historians of the period—Rhodes, Schouler, Dunning—have concluded that Tilden was certainly entitled to the electoral votes of Louisiana and probably of Florida; such is the view of the most careful historians of these States; and Hayes's most impartial biographer, Mr. H. J. Eckenrode, assigns Florida to the Democratic nominee. Grant, Conkling, Godkin, Samuel Bowles, Representatives Julius H. Seelye and Henry L. Pierce, and other distinguished Republicans, believed that Tilden had been rightfully elected. Charles A. Dana of the *Sun* and Conkling alike habitually referred to the new President as Rutherfraud B. Hayes.

Tilden, nearly ten years later, expressed his lasting resentment when, commenting upon a new book on the electoral system, he wrote[2] that the Democratic party "have beheld with indignation the chief agents in the frauds, perjuries and forgeries by which a pretext of documentary evidence was furnished on which to base a false count, rewarded by their appointment in numerous cases to most important civil trusts." But Hewitt felt more strongly still—particularly upon the scandalous activities of John Sherman, Garfield, and other Ohioans in Louisiana. When, in 1885, President Cleveland offered a government directorship of the Union Pacific to Ex-Governor Noyes of Ohio, he penned an angry protest:

I do not know who is responsible to you for the recommendation, but I wish to recall your attention to the fact that Governor

---

[1] H. K. Enos to Hewitt, February 15, 1888; Hewitt Papers.
[2] To George A. Jenks, October 21, 1885; Manton Marble Papers.

Noyes was one of the most prominent actors in the fraud which deprived Mr. Tilden of the Presidency in 1877. He went on a special mission to Florida, and by his unscrupulous action succeeded in stealing the vote of that State. He and William E. Chandler were the chief agents in the fraud. He received his reward in the shape of a commission to France; but no Democrat who had any self-respect ever called upon him, or had any intercourse with him. Personally, I refused to make his acquaintance, as I refused that of President Hayes. I am sorry that the appointment has been made, and I wish it could be withdrawn upon the ground, distinctly stated, that he was engaged in the Florida fraud. It seems to me that a black list ought to be made of the actors in the great outrage, and that no man among them ought ever to be entrusted with any place of power or of responsibility in which honesty is an element of availability. The knowledge which I possess of the transactions of that period, leaves no doubt in my mind of the entire want of integrity in the character of Governor Noyes. A man who would steal the Presidency would certainly sell his vote to a railroad company. What I now say to you I shall certainly not hesitate to say in public if that question ever comes up in Congress. In one of my speeches after the fraud was successfully perpetrated, I recited the names of the principal agents in the nefarious business. Governor Noyes is particularly mentioned, and I certainly regarded him as the most obnoxious of the whole crew of scoundrels. I have not written this letter without some reluctance; but I feel it to be my duty to put you on your guard against the selection of any of these malefactors for places of trust.

Yet such sentiments in no way lessened Hewitt's feeling of pride in his insistence upon a compromise. To the end of his life he believed that he had been more instrumental than any one else in securing acceptance of the Electoral Commission, and he regarded this as one of his chief public services. A fortnight after the inauguration he wrote an English friend that he had suffered "a great disappointment in regard to Mr. Tilden, but we have proven to the world that we are capable of self-government." Whether Tilden or Hayes became President was, in the long run, of little consequence to the republic. Hayes was honest, able, enlightened; as Hewitt often said, he did more to restore Southern self-government and sectional harmony than Tilden could have done. In any event, it was of paramount importance that the dispute should close without an interruption of orderly government, without—as the phrase went—Mexicanizing our political processes.

But this cool view was then impossible to embittered Democratic partisans. It was inevitable that, arbitration having lost them the Presidency, they should turn resentfully upon Bayard, Lamar, Randall, and others who had supported arbitration; it was inevitable that they should concentrate their hottest fire upon Hewitt. Watterson was foremost in this attack. He had told the House on January 26, 1877, that "if arbitration is our only recourse, as I believe it is, that proposed is both legal and just. Upon it, therefore, good men everywhere will rest the issue, trusting that the God from whom we received our fair, free system, building wiser than we knew, will bring it safely through our present danger." He would have done well to stick to this. But the moment the vote went against Tilden he veered back to a violent tone. On February 16 he published in the Louisville *Courier-Journal* a tirade against Hewitt, accusing him of saying, "with one hand upon his heart and the other in his pocket, 'I had rather see Hayes inaugurated than shed one drop of blood.'" Hewitt replied on March 3 that he had really said, in private conversation, "I would prefer four years of Hayes's Administration to four years of civil war." He still believed that as between anarchy and war on the one side, and peace, order, free speech, and the ballot box on the other, the moderate leaders had made the correct choice.

If any man had the right to criticize Hewitt, it was Tilden; yet he took pains at first to show that his confidence in the ironmaster was unimpaired. Hewitt, after recovering his strength, returned to New York. "I resumed my old relations of friendly intercourse with Mr. Tilden. He never made any complaint to me either in regard to my action or that of my associates. If he felt any dissatisfaction with our course he never expressed it, and there was nothing either in his manner or his conversation to indicate that my presence was less agreeable than it had been during the many years of our close and intimate friendship. My conclusion was that while he felt that the country had been defrauded of its rightful choice for President, he experienced a sense of relief, in view of the state of his health, from the burdens which the Presidency would have imposed. He seemed to think that his place in history was secure, and in the immediate circle of his friends, as well as by the public at large, he was treated with as much respect as if he had actually been inaugurated into the great office to which he had unquestionably been chosen by the people."

That summer, in London, Hewitt ran across Thomas A. Hendricks, and soon afterward they were joined by Tilden, accompanied by John Bigelow. The four repeatedly dined and walked together. Later in Paris, Hewitt, at Bigelow's request, took rooms in the same hotel used by Tilden, the Westminster. "We met daily as usual, and saw many interesting men and places in common. We decided to return home together, and did so, crossing the Channel in the stormy passage to which Mr. Bigelow refers so graphically; and finally together sailed upon the steamship *Scythia* for New York, where we arrived after a very stormy voyage." If Tilden felt any grievance, he concealed it marvelously. "It is simply incredible," concludes Hewitt,[1] "that he had any such feeling, and I think I am justified in assuming that while the issue of the great struggle in which we had been engaged was disastrous to his personal ambition, he felt that no proper effort and precaution had been omitted by me or those who coöperated with me in the establishment of the Electoral Tribunal. . . ." Other manifestations of Tilden's friendly confidence appeared when Hewitt resumed his Congressional duties; for Tilden both counselled and applauded Hewitt during the latter's earnest fight to repeal all Reconstruction legislation permitting Federal interference in elections.

But Watterson proved irrepressible. By the spring of 1878 the question of the next Presidential nomination began to seem important. The Democrats generally agreed that Tilden was the logical candidate, and that the campaign issue must be the great wrong perpetrated in 1876. Certain supporters felt that Tilden's position would be much stronger if he were presented as a leader who had never acquiesced in the Electoral Commission, for the cry of fraud could then be redoubled. Watterson, now out of Congress, came east to diffuse this view. In Washington he attended a Democratic Congressional caucus called to consider various topics; and the first topic considered, at Hewitt's suggestion, was that he had no business there. Breathing resentment, he took the New York train. He came with June, remarked the *Tribune*, and like June

[1] Secret History; Hewitt Papers.

"with a great gush of blossoms stormed the world." Some of these blossoms, dealing with the Electoral Commission, Tilden's supposed opposition, and the base conduct of Bayard, Thurman, Randall, and Hewitt, appeared in the press. Watterson wrought himself up, in fact, to describe Hewitt as "the red snake in the grass," "a falsifier and a charlatan," "a beggar on horseback," and even "a little bobolink whose clothes do not fit." This amused New Yorkers, who knew, as the *Sun* remarked,[1] that "a more painstaking and conscientious man than Mr. Hewitt does not live." Hewitt made a dignified reply, with which the subject might well have been dropped.

Unfortunately, the quarrel was entered by Manton Marble, onetime editor of the *World*. He published a long letter in the *Sun* of August 5, in which, trying to build up the legend that Tilden had been a strong, silent leader, betrayed by his followers, he levelled the gravest accusations against Hewitt. Marble declared that he himself had been present when on Sunday, January 14, Tilden received Hewitt and talked over the McCrary Bill for an Electoral Commission. He had heard Tilden express sharp disapproval—had heard him say: "There is time enough. It is a month before the count. It had best be used, all of it, in making the people and their agents fully acquainted with their rights and duties." He quoted Tilden as replying, when Hewitt said that the Democratic Senators would support the bill anyhow: "It is a panic of pacificators. They will act in haste and repent at leisure." He also quoted him as protesting, when Hewitt talked of the danger of civil war: "The fears of collision are exaggerated. And why surrender now? You can always surrender. That is all you have to do after being beaten. Why surrender before the battle, for fear of having to surrender after the battle is over?" He heard Tilden tell Hewitt that if arbitration were adopted, the membership of the tribunal ought to be fixed in the bill itself, and not left to chance and intrigue; and that the duty of the arbitrators to go behind the face of the returns should be expressly stated.

Finally, wrote Marble, Tilden on the night of January 16 had dictated a telegram for transmission in cipher to Washington through the National Committee. "Not having been sent to or seen by Mr. Hewitt, it is not pertinent to any controversy regarding

[1] N. Y. *Sun*, June 22, 1878.

him. . . ." But, he added, it showed Tilden's disapproval. It began: "No need of hot haste, but much danger in it. Some days' interval should be taken, the risk of publicity is harmless." It accused the Republicans of bullying tactics: "So long as we stand on the Constitution and settled practise, we know where we are." And it concluded: "Only way of getting accessions in the Senate is by House standing firm. And judicious friends believe in that case we will go safely through . . ." In a footnote to his letter, Marble added a specific request of Tilden's: "Please state that I have never questioned the good faith and patriotic purpose of Mr. Hewitt, or of any whose counsels and guidance he thought it his duty to follow." But Marble himself obviously accused the ironmaster of the worst kind of treachery.

This story was a tissue of falsehoods. Manton Marble, to begin with, had not been present when Tilden and Hewitt conferred as to the Electoral Commission. "Clarkson N. Potter," states Hewitt, "was the only person who overheard any portion of the conversation between Mr. Tilden and myself." In the second place, Tilden had never condemned the Electoral Commission, and had never uttered the speeches about a panic of pacificators and surrendering before the battle was fought. "Now I distinctly assert," writes Hewitt, "that no such remarks were addressed to me. They bear the internal evidence of having been carefully prepared afterwards, but whether they were dictated to Mr. Marble immediately after the conference or much later when he was preparing his letter, I do not know; but I do know that they were never expressed to me in my presence or hearing." If Tilden had felt so strongly that the Electoral Commission plan should be defeated, why did he not tell others? A single emphatic telegram to his legal agent David Dudley Field, to Henry Watterson, or to Eppa Hunton, *who in the end refused his approval until Tilden's nephew Pelton was sent North to consult him and brought back his assent,* would have wrecked the bill. And the explicit letter of Judge Daly's quoted above, confirming Hewitt's assertion that Tilden had merely suggested amendments, shows how false is Marble's story.

There remains Manton Marble's story of the long telegram beginning "no need of hot haste," which he declares Tilden dictated on the night of January 16 to send to Washington through the Na-

tional Committee rooms.[1] Marble admitted that it did not go to
Hewitt. Had it been sent to Hewitt, it would have been in Edward
Cooper's cipher. The only man in Washington who held the National Committee cipher was Pelton. Did he receive the telegram
and suppress it? On January 17 Pelton, after Eppa Hunton had
balked, went to New York to consult his uncle about the revised
Electoral Commission bill; on the 18th he returned with word of
Tilden's consent. It is evident, therefore, that this telegram referred to an *earlier form* of the Electoral Commission scheme; that
when Pelton explained the *new form,* the telegram was suppressed;
and that this suppression is actually an additional proof that Tilden had approved the new plan. Hewitt writes in his secret history:

> If the telegram were not suppressed with Mr. Tilden's con-
> currence, it might and would have been made public by him or
> his friends who had been assembled at his house, as stated by
> Mr. Marble, during the nine subsequent days of the debate, which
> took place in the Senate and in the House.
> During these nine days no syllable of dissent came from Mr.
> Tilden or his confidential friends, either to me or Speaker Ran-
> dall or Mr. Field or Mr. Watterson, all of whom except the
> Speaker made speeches in favor of the passage of the Electoral
> Commission Bill.
> It thus appears that Mr. Marble's attempt to use the suppressed
> telegram as the evidence of Mr. Tilden's disapproval of the Bill
> as finally reported, utterly fails, for the simple reason that the
> telegram referred to different arrangements, and not to the Bill
> as finally agreed to by the House Committee and reported on the
> 12th of January. It is in fact a boomerang, clearly showing that
> the new arrangement must have been satisfactory to Mr. Tilden,
> or else the telegram would not have been suppressed. For its
> publication in accordance with Mr. Tilden's demand for pub-
> licity would undoubtedly have prevented the Committee from
> reporting the Bill, and if it had been reported before the publi-
> cation of the telegram, there was abundant time during the nine
> days of debate which ensued in the Senate and in the House for
> Mr. Tilden to have made his objections known, if he felt any,
> and for Mr. Pelton to have made known to the Committee any
> change of mind on the part of Mr. Tilden of which he had
> notice, either by telegram or otherwise. As a matter of fact, not

[1] Actually this telegram, in the Tilden Papers, is dated "Jany 17, 1877, Midnight"—which raises the question whether it was sent on the 16th or 17th.

the slightest intimation was given by Mr. Tilden or by Colonel Pelton to any Democratic members of the House that the Bill as reported was not regarded as satisfactory. On the contrary, Pelton was indefatigable in his efforts to secure votes for the Bill.

It is probable that Tilden wrote this long telegram when he first heard the details of the revised Electoral Commission Bill, just before Pelton visited him on January 17; that having no other means at hand, he sent it through the National Committee cipher while Pelton was en route; that Pelton talked to him, and explained the bill; that Tilden then asked Pelton to suppress the telegram; and that when a year and a half later Manton Marble undertook to write a defense, and called upon Tilden for documents, this document was unearthed with the telegrams that had been sent in the Cooper cipher. Marble then unscrupulously used it without reference to its true character. Possibly Tilden's remarks about not surrendering in advance, and the panic of pacificators, had likewise been heard by Marble at some earlier stage of the dispute, and he deliberately transferred them to the Tilden-Hewitt conversation which he had never heard at all!

Within a short time Tilden badly needed all the defensive art of his friends, while Manton Marble was beyond defense. The publication of the "cipher telegrams" late in 1878 utterly discredited both Pelton and Marble, and greatly impaired Tilden's chances of success in another election. The story of these telegrams is too familiar to need detailed rehearsal. It is sufficient to recall that in the spring of 1878 the Democratic leaders in the House appointed a committee under Clarkson N. Potter to inquire into the canvass of votes in the late Presidential election in Louisiana and Florida. Visiting the South, the committee found witnesses who gave sensational testimony. In Florida Samuel B. McLin declared that in helping to give the electors to Hayes he had been influenced by heavy Republican pressure, by excitation of his partisan zeal, and by a promise of rewards if Hayes were seated. He also asserted that various Republican election officials had since testified to wholesale ballot-box stuffing. In Louisiana more than a dozen negro witnesses retracted their affidavits of 1876 concerning violence and intimidation. One local officer swore that John Sherman had made him a written promise of lucrative Federal appointment. In both States the committee found that almost every one of the dozens of persons concerned in turning the electoral votes over to Hayes had received Federal office. Some of the appointments were plainly a reward for corrupt acts.

The effect of all this on public sentiment was tremendous. It enforced Tilden's statement, made from the steps of his Gramercy Park mansion on returning from Europe, that he had been robbed of the Presidency by a "political crime" which the people should never condone. Hewitt closed the House debate on the report of the Potter Committee. The party press was enthusiastic over his address, which more than fulfilled all the Democratic expectations. He received from John Bigelow a letter, written by request of Tilden, conveying the warm thanks of the latter for the effectiveness with which he had riddled the Republican position and vindicated Tilden's claims before the country. This letter was fresh evidence of Tilden's amity.

But then came the unexpected Republican inning. Early in 1877, the Western Union Company had delivered to Congressional committees some 30,000 telegrams sent by Republican and Democratic leaders during the campaign and the dispute over the election. Many were in cipher. By one of the tricks too common in those times, all the Republican dispatches were returned to the Western Union and burned, but Republican leaders secretly retained about 750 Democratic dispatches. By another trick, these were conveyed to the New York *Tribune*; and by methods recalling Poe's *Gold Bug*, its staff deciphered them. They put a searing flame to several reputations. For example, the *Tribune* published with much beating of tom-toms the telegrams exchanged between Manton Marble in Tallahassee, and Colonel Pelton at Tilden's residence. On December 2, 1876, Marble telegraphed that he had just received "a proposition to hand over at any hour required Tilden decision of canvassing board and certificate of Governor Stearns for two hundred thousand." Pelton telegraphed back that the price was too high. Marble then obtained a revised quotation—one electoral vote for $50,000. And Pelton joyously replied:

Telegram here. Proposition accepted if done only once. Better consult with Wooley [a Democratic agent who had also offered an electoral vote for $50,000] and act in concert. You can trust him. Time very important and there should be no divided counsels.

The *Tribune* also published dispatches showing that a Tilden agent sent to South Carolina, Smith M. Weed, had telegraphed Pelton that he could secure the electoral vote of that State for $80,000, and that Pelton had then eagerly gone to Baltimore to close the transaction. But it, like the Florida purchase, had fallen through.

Of all these negotiations Hewitt, as the testimony showed, was completely ignorant. "It is certain," he wrote Bigelow at the time, "that none of these dispatches were ever shown to me."[1] The negotiators had been too wise to approach him. He knew, as he says in his secret history, that votes could be bought, but refused to touch them.

It has been stated that the vote of Louisiana prior to the final count of the Returning Board was offered for sale. The price named to me was $200,000, and it was stated that the larger portion of the money would go to Wells and Anderson, and a lesser amount to their colleagues on the Returning Board. I declined to make the purchase and notified Mr. Tilden personally of the fact on the Sabbath Day when the offer was made. Long after the completion of the count I was informed that other Democrats, less scrupulous than I was, actually completed the arrangements for the purchase, and provided the amount of money required to be paid in New Orleans. This transaction fortunately came to the knowledge of Governor Tilden before the money had been paid over, and was arrested by his prompt intervention . . .

Subsequent events, however, made it clear to me that the Republican managers were not governed by the same standard of rectitude. I had it from the mouth of Governor Wells himself that the offer rejected by the Democrats had been accepted by the Republican managers, and that they had agreed after the inauguration of President Hayes to raise the money to pay the amount in cash. In consequence of the failure to redeem this promise, Governor Wells subsequently came to Washington and threatened to expose the whole transaction. Whereupon, as I was informed on good authority, a considerable portion of the money was raised and paid over to Wells in Washington in order to quiet the immediate clamour, with the promise that the remainder should be paid in time. Whether it was paid or not I do

[1] February 9, 1879; Bigelow, *Retrospections*, V, 400.

not know. Possibly Wells was quieted by his appointment to the office of Collector of Customs for the Port of New Orleans; his confederates were also provided for, some by offices and some by money.

Hewitt was present when Tilden was examined at his own request by the Potter Committee. The parlors of the Fifth Avenue Hotel, where it sat, were crowded by people anxious to hear the distinguished witness. Tilden entered at half-past eleven with his brother Henry and John Bigelow. A compassionate whisper ran through the room as men caught sight of the thin, slight figure, garbed in black, who had aged so sadly in the past two years. He was a painful spectacle as with slow, halting walk he shuffled past the table and reached his seat. His limbs seemed stiff and rigid, as though he were suffering from a paralytic contraction of the muscles. Without animation or expression he extended his hand to Thomas B. Reed and Frank Hiscock, his two examiners. Then, after saluting the Democratic members, he stiffly and slowly removed his fine silk-lined overcoat, cautiously turned around, and sank into a chair, while he adjusted a large handkerchief in his breast pocket. For two and a half hours he was mercilessly questioned. Without losing for a moment his composure and suavity, he repelled the attack at every point, insisting that he had been privy to none of the negotiations described, and that when he had heard of any of them he had at once interposed a veto.

But for Pelton and Marble defense was impossible. They could only plead the end against the means, and say that they were "ransoming stolen goods from thieves."

Until these disclosures Hewitt had confidently looked forward to the renomination and reëlection of Tilden. He had regarded his candidacy as essential to party success and to the vindication of the national honor. "I had never ceased to urge upon Mr. Tilden the duty which he owed in this emergency to his country, and I used to say to him, when he spoke of his failing health, that even if he had to be carried into the White House in his coffin, he owed it to himself and to the country to face even death rather than the great fraud should be condoned." But the publication of Marble's mendacious letter, which Tilden could have forbidden had he chosen, had chilled his feeling toward the party leader. Now Marble was irretrievably disgraced, and the exposure of Pelton's intrigues had gravely injured Tilden. A millionaire, could he have been completely ignorant of these machinations conducted from his own home by a penniless nephew? Hewitt's view was that Tilden had seen none of the cipher telegraphs sent to and from Gramercy Park, his nephew managing the business alone, but that he had intentionally refrained from knowing anything about them and could have found out a great deal had he tried. At any rate, a number of Democratic newspapers at once pronounced Tilden unavailable. Hewitt was no longer national chairman, having resigned that post on March 3, 1877. But he and other Democratic leaders now looked toward the campaign of 1880 with dark forebodings.

CHAPTER XXI

"No Other Had Done So Much"

IN *The Education of Henry Adams* the autobiographer writes that "Adams knew, more or less, all the men in any way prominent at Washington, or knew all about them. Among them, in his opinion, the best-equipped, the most active-minded, and most industrious was Abram Hewitt, who sat in Congress for a dozen years, between 1874 and 1886, sometimes leading the House and always wielding influence second to none. With nobody did Adams form closer or longer relations than with Mr. Hewitt, whom he regarded as the most useful public man in Washington; and he was the more struck by Hewitt's saying, at the end of his laborious career as legislator, that he left behind him no permanent result except the Act consolidating the Surveys. Adams knew no other man who had done so much, unless Mr. Sherman's legislation is accepted as an instance of success."[1]

Though many observers found fault with the membership of Congress in this period, actually the principal defects lay rather in the machinery. The House in the seventies and eighties was abler than those who sneered at it supposed. James Bryce was surprised to find so much character, shrewdness, and keen though limited intelligence among the members.[2] It lacked the great lights which adorned the British Parliament, but it also lacked the rich dull parvenus and ignorant sporting squires who clambered into British politics; most of the men had made their own way by energy and smartness, and their practical sagacity merited respect. To be sure, perhaps five-sixths of the Representatives were politicians, while members of long professional or business training, like Hew-

---

[1] *The Education of Henry Adams*, 294.
[2] Bryce, *The American Commonwealth*, I, 142ff.

itt, were rare. But a body which included such keen minds as John G. Carlisle and Tom Reed, such able parliamentary managers as Garfield and Samuel J. Randall, such scholars as L. Q. C. Lamar, was far from despicable.

Hewitt felt keenly the frustration which Henry Adams attributed to him, but as a special Senate report in 1881—the Pendleton Report—indicated, this frustration was largely inherent in our governmental mechanism. He often reflected that the British political system had points of manifest superiority over ours. Under such a system, the election of 1874 would have placed the Democrats in complete control of the government, he and other leaders would have taken full legislative charge, and salutary reforms with respect to the South, finance, civil service, and the tariff would have been hurried through. As it was, the mechanical rigidity of our government kept a minority in partial power for years after the popular vote had pronounced against it; only at rare intervals could one party control House, Senate, and Presidency together, and so act freely. During his whole period of service the Senate was Republican, the House Democratic, and party feeling in both ran high.

Moreover, the House was a Laocoön struggling against the serpentine constriction of bad rules, organized obstruction, and lack of responsible leadership. Hewitt was shocked when he first entered it by the noise, hurry, confusion, and inattention, like a street-corner mass-meeting. A huge chamber, twice the necessary size, desk-lids clapping, pens scratching, pages scampering about, groups talking and laughing, galleries humming, while the Speaker rapped a tattoo; the few who listened to a debater gathered about him with strained ears. He was shocked still more by the waste, literally of weeks, in roll-calls on motions to adjourn and other dilatory tactics, and by the inefficiency of the leaders. The whole government, in fact, with the two chambers politically opposed, neither well led, and neither responsive to the Executive, was nearly at a standstill. The tariff question, the currency question, railroad regulation, international copyright, a general bankruptcy law, a dozen other urgent problems, were simply evaded.

With his insatiable passion for efficiency, Hewitt shortly proposed reforms in the House procedure. The *Nation* and other organs were soon commending some suggestions which he made for removing the worst physical obstacles to debate and bettering the style of speaking.[1] His plan was to partition the hall of the House in two. One half of it should be arranged with benches facing each other on the two sides of the House, as in the British Commons. This half should be sacred to debate; no conversation, no writing, nothing but the discussion of legislation permitted. The other half should be fitted with desks or similar conveniences for writing and with sofas for talk or general business. A gong would notify the members when a vote was about to be taken. The alteration would permit better thinking, better oratory, and better progress in every way. At the same time Hewitt suggested changes in the House rules to prevent the worst types of obstruction and hasten the pace of legislation. But both types of reforms were delayed for years—even that in rules till Tom Reed took the gavel in 1890.

Yet, despite his impatience, Hewitt found happiness in Washington and did useful work; for he achieved enjoyment and usefulness by versatile endeavor. Seeing that men who tied themselves to one object, like W. R. Morrison with tariff reform and John A. Reagan with railway regulation, were doomed to heartache and disappointment, he identified himself with many. This required immense and unremitting labor, but it brought compensations.

I

He did not keep his house at 1215 K Street, N. W., beyond one term. His wife, burdened with a large family and anxious to remain near Peter Cooper, found it necessary to live in New York. He stayed at various addresses—the Arlington, Wormley's, or some private house.[2] At one time (1881) he and Roscoe Conkling were under the same roof at 1500 J Street;[3] at another he was on I Street, where, to ensure quiet, he took two floors, though he lived on only one. Among his friends, John Sherman at first took a prominent place. "He is the ablest man, in my judgment, in the Republican party," Hewitt said in 1880;[4] "and they owe what power they have got to the brains and energy of John Sherman more than of any other man in this community." But this growing intimacy was chilled by the events of 1876. Henry Adams, Clarence

[1] *Nation*, April 4, 1878.
[2] Congressional Directories, 1875-79.
[3] Hewitt to Mrs. Cake, September 27, 1881.
[4] Speech at Terrace Garden, New York, October 29, 1880.

King, Randolph Tucker, Conkling, Lamar, and Hoar were also good friends.[1] Social life in Washington was distinctly more enjoyable under the Grant Administration than under President Hayes, for after 1876 political acerbities were greatly heightened. Hewitt and many other Democratic leaders never spoke to President Hayes, never set foot within the White House grounds.

In asking a place on the Appropriations Committee in 1877, Hewitt intended to appeal to the power of the purse to abolish the use of military force in civil affairs. Reconstruction legislation had endowed the Executive with wide authority to employ Federal troops in preserving order at the polls, and in the South this power had been grossly abused. He and other Democratic leaders determined that they would give the Republicans the choice of seeing the worst features of this legislation repealed, or the funds for the army cut off.[2] The fight which ensued filled most of Hewitt's time between the disputed election and a two-years' vacation from Congress which Boss Kelly gave him in 1879-80 by refusing to permit his renomination by the New York Democracy.

The House first showed its grim temper when, in the session ending March, 1877, it declined to pass the Army Appropriation Bill except with provisions which would make it impossible to use the troops in sustaining Republican claimants in South Carolina and Louisiana. The bill failed. The army was maintained for months without lawful appropriations.[3] When, in October, 1877, President Hayes called an extra session to meet the situation, Federal troops had been withdrawn from the South, and the Demo under Hewitt made a temporary concession. An appropriation passed without any restriction; but Hewitt served notice that at the regular session in December the House would act to repeal the obnoxious general legislation. When this session began he again took charge of the Army Bill. Acting with Proctor Knott, Chairman of the Judiciary Committee, he drew up an amendment prohibiting the use of the army as a *posse comitatus* in civil proceedings, except as expressly authorized by the Constitution or an act of Congress. This passed the House, but the Senate rejected it. Another deadlock loomed up. Some important provisions looking toward an economi-

---

[1] Hewitt in the *Nation*, December 2, 1880.
[2] S. S. Cox, *Three Decades*, 630ff.
[3] *Annual Cyclopaedia*, 1877, p. 661.

cal reorganization of the army, which Hewitt had framed after prolonged study and conference with army officers, were also involved. But his Democratic colleagues agreed to sacrifice everything else rather than the *posse comitatus* clause, which would restrain a Federal marshal from ordering out troops in petty disturbances that the ordinary peace officers of a State were competent to handle, including election disturbances. Finally the Senate yielded, and President Hayes signed the bill with the clause included. The first victory had thus been won.

The next great object of the House Democrats was to repeal or modify the Act of February 25, 1865, which empowered the Federal authorities to employ troops "to repel the armed enemies of the United States, or to keep the peace at the polls."[1] Hewitt proposed to strike out the last eight words we have quoted. When Congress met again in 1878, the House caucus rallied solidly behind him, and although Senators Bayard, Morgan, and Lamar doubted the propriety of attaching legislative riders to appropriation bills, the Senators fell into line. Hewitt then (February 1, 1879) introduced an Army Bill with a drastic repealing clause, which not merely forbade the use of Federal troops at the polls, but laid restraints upon Federal civil officers in elections within the States. In his speech supporting the bill,[2] he pointed out that the law of 1865 had been passed in the atmosphere of war, when passion reigned supreme, and should long since have given way to more moderate principles. He read the British statute of George II which prohibited soldiery from coming within two miles of any polling-place on election day, and other British laws bulwarking the processes of civil government against the slightest military interference. "They are not in England willing to have the power of the army compounded even for a day with the machinery by which civil process is enforced."

But the Senate deadlocked with the House, and would not recede. It became clear that the bill would fail. Just before it did so, on March 3, Hewitt made another speech explaining the great principle which he wished to vindicate:

Mr. Speaker, this presents an issue which involves the very

[1] Revised Statutes of the United States, Sections 2002, 5528.
[2] *Congressional Record*, February 2, 1879.

essence of free government. The difference between a despotic government and a free government is this: that in a despotism the military power is superior to the civil; in a free government the civil dominates the military power. And this principle is one which we never fought for; it came to us as an inheritance from our fathers. It was so well recognized that when the Constitution was formed it was not even deemed necessary to insert an article to that effect. . . . No English-speaking man for two hundred years has questioned the principle that soldiers should never be present at the polls; and the question could never have been raised in this country, the demand could never have been made in our land, but for the unhappy calamity of a civil war. In time of civil war all political rights must be surrendered to the exigencies of the conflict. And so it was here . . . A convertible currency, specie payments, almost every traditional right, disappeared in the presence of the great danger with which we were confronted. Now for fifteen long years we have been striving to recover that lost ground.

We have made gigantic efforts, sacrifices such as the world never saw, to get back to the resumption of specie payments; and yet we have done nothing for the resumption of our political rights, the rights which lie at the very foundation of this government. The time has come to recover this lost ground, and I think it is a reproach to our patriotism that the resumption of specie payments should have preceded the resumption of the rights necessary for the preservation of free government.

When the Army Bill failed, Congress again had to be called in extra session to provide the necessary appropriations. Hewitt, who had just been dropped for two years because of Boss Kelly's war on all of Tilden's friends, was absent when this took place. Yet from his home in New York he could rejoice in the partial victory then won. President Hayes, in summoning the extra session, protested against the attempt of the House to force legislation upon the President and Senate by refusing to pass indispensable appropriations unless such legislation were attached. With this position, broadly speaking, Hewitt sympathized. He had explicitly declared that "as a rule general legislation upon appropriation bills ought to be avoided." But he believed that, in the light of numerous Anglo-American precedents, the popular chamber had a right to insist upon a redress of painful grievances before it voted supplies.

And the upshot of the whole dispute was a compromise.[1] The House receded from its drastic amendment to the Army Bill, applicable to civil as well as military action in maintaining order at the polls. Instead, it inserted the following clause, which the Senate and President accepted:

That no money appropriated in this act is appropriated or shall be paid for the subsistence, equipment, transportation, or compensation of any portion of the army of the United States to be used as a police force to keep the peace at the polls at any election held within any State.

With this Hewitt was well satisfied. It reëmphasized the fundamental principle which he held in mind, and together with his *posse comitatus* clause rendered the use of national troops to overawe Southern voters substantially impossible.

On the currency question he spoke frequently, for he was an earnest supporter of specie resumption and the gold standard. "I almost got down on my knees to my fellow Democrats," he said later, "appealing to them not to depart from the old time-honored platform of hard money and specie payments."[2] He of course resisted at every step the movement for the free and unlimited coinage of silver at 16 to 1 which had begun in 1874, which in 1878 forced the passage of the Bland-Allison Act for the coinage of at least $2,000,000 worth of silver every month, and which thereafter made itself felt as a grim threat whenever times became hard. Perhaps his most notable speech on the money question was that of August 5, 1876, against Bland's free coinage bill. Already Western members of Congress had begun to elaborate their charge of "the crime of '73"—of a dark and sinister conspiracy of plutocratic interests to raise the value of the dollar, and hence of all debts. Hewitt was one of the first to present a complete analysis of the events leading up to the demonetization of silver in 1873, showing that the statute then passed had merely ratified, by general consent, the previous decree of economic forces. So conspicuous did he make himself as an opponent of free silver that H. S. Bolles dedicated his *History of Currency in the United States* to him.

But it was labors for governmental efficiency that were most char-

[1] *Annual Cyclopaedia*, 1878, pp. 268, 269.
[2] Terrace Garden speech, October 29, 1880.

acteristic of Hewitt; and even in the half-paralyzed Congress of those days he was able to do a little. He gave careful attention to the diplomatic and consular service, having an eye in especial to the maintenance of sufficient consulates for the promotion of trade. Another object of his concern was the army. When he entered Congress it had fallen, as usual in time of prolonged peace, into an unhappy state. General Sheridan and other officers with whom he talked were emphatic upon the need for a reorganization. Small as it was, it suffered from too many units of skeleton character. One company, Hewitt found, had eight privates, one musician, and ten commissioned and non-commissioned officers; another had nine privates and six officers; a third consisted of four privates and a captain! The bill which Hewitt tried to carry through Congress in the first weeks of 1879 reduced the number of regiments, companies, and officers, but provided for filling up the cadres. A company was to be a real company; a regiment, a real regiment.

This bill, as we have seen, failed. But meanwhile Hewitt had taken steps which he hoped would bring about the needed reform at a later date. He had first had a joint Congressional committee appointed to report on army reorganization (1878), and immediately afterward an expert commission. "This provision," he had said, "will secure a reorganization of the army, whether in this Congress or the next I do not know, and I frankly say I care but little." And at the same time he scored a genuine achievement in legislation for reorganizing the Western surveys.

Here was a subject of broad importance, with the appeal to the imagination that he always relished. A few years earlier the great mountain region of the Far West had been a savage, ill-explored, and almost inaccessible wilderness. It was roamed over by only a few scouts and hunters; the agents of the fur companies and daring pathmarkers like Frémont had furnished an outline view of its structure, but nothing more. But by the centennial year all this was fast being changed. Railroads were being carried across the mountains; mining camps had been scattered through them; patches of green farms were to be found; organized settlements were supplanting the Indian and buffalo. Yet the work of reducing the vast trans-Missouri West to the uses of civilization was still in its infancy. Hence the government showed great zeal in pushing forward a number of enterprises for exploring, surveying, and mapping the region. In 1867, when Nebraska was admitted to the Union, Congress had provided for a complete survey of that State, and for a thorough geological exploration of a broad belt along the fortieth parallel. Other undertakings had been added to the list, until four distinct enterprises were on foot. They were Dr. F. V. Hayden's work as head of the first division of the Geological and Geographical Survey of the Territories; Major J. W. Powell's work as director of the second division of that survey, with special attention to the Rockies; Lieutenant George M. Wheeler's geographical survey of the territories west of the 100th meridian; and Clarence King's geological survey along the fortieth parallel. In addition, the Coast and Geodetic Survey was far from idle.

Here was a glaring field for consolidation of effort. The four or five separate undertakings had little relationship and no harmony. They were controlled by different governmental agencies: the Coast Survey by the Treasury, the Hayden and Powell surveys by the Interior Department, and the King and Wheeler surveys by the War Department—all jealous of one another. At the outset, the War Department had been the natural agency for exploring the West. The savagery of the tribes, the necessity for basing the work on scattered army posts, and the fact that West Point gave the best topographical training in the country, had all pointed to the military arm. But these conditions no longer existed. The Indians had been pacified, settlements offered many bases, and several schools of science had far outstripped West Point. Civilian scientists, in fact, had come vigorously to the front. Professor J. D. Whitney had done admirable work in exploring and mapping the Western mountains; in his school of practise had been trained the brilliant Clarence King; Major Powell had commenced as a private explorer; and Professor O. C. Marsh of Yale had made daring paleontological raids into the wilds. As it became evident that consolidation was needed, the War Department demanded that it be given exclusive charge of the work; but the scientists of the nation rallied to resist the demand. The time had come, they said, for it to be written *arma cedunt togae*.

When Hewitt first studied the question he inclined to the War Department's side of the controversy. But Clarence King and other scientists expostulated with him, while he was completely converted by a report by the National Academy of Sciences. This body, after an inquiry, reported that all geographical and topographical work ought in general to be conducted by the Coast and Geodetic Survey, while all geological and economic exploration should be consolidated under a single Geological Survey—both to be subordinate to the Interior Department and organized on a coöperative basis. Hewitt wrote the appropriate legislation into the general appropriation bill of 1879. In this same bill he incorporated a provision for study and codification of the land laws by an expert commission.

This legislation met with much opposition. There were jealousies regarding the headship of the new Geological Survey, for Hayden had his champions as against King and Powell, who actually became the first and second heads respectively. There was the old jealousy in the War Department of civilian encroachments. There were powerful Western interests which fought to the last against any measure designed to strengthen the land laws. All Hewitt's skill and force were needed to carry the legislation in the House. He answered every objection, struck out vigorously at the "grasping corporations and overpowering capitalists" who were trying to seize our great Western heritage, and showed that the Engineering Corps of the army would be kept quite busy enough in making needed military surveys.[1] As he said, eminent scientists would not care to place themselves under young officers of the army. Above all, he explained the incalculable importance of the Western domain, the vast potentialities of wealth and growth locked up in it. In the end, he triumphantly carried the bill. Years later, when the Geological Survey hung the portraits of King and Powell in its office, it was asking for that of Hewitt as well.

II

The destructive railroad riots during the great strike of 1877, a fierce protest against repeated and unjustifiable wage-cuts, gave many complacent Americans a severe shock. Most people had comfortably assumed that equal laws and the equal ballot, with the opportunities of the half-empty West and of our fast-expanding industrialism, would prevent any class warfare. But the savage outbreaks from Baltimore to San Francisco, with Pittsburgh dominated

[1] For his principal speech, see *Congressional Record*, February 11, 1879. It was published in pamphlet form under the title, "Our National Inheritance and How to Enjoy It."

for a day and a night by a wild mob and Federal troops called out
in many parts of the East, blew away these illusions as a cold gale
rends a fog. Men suddenly realized that the statistics which proved
that labor had been badly off even in the seven boom years after
the war, and that wages had lagged far behind the cost of living,
had meant cruel human suffering.[1] They realized that after years
of wage-reductions, unemployment, soup-houses, destitution, and the
other sad phenomena of depression, workingmen might grow desperate with want. Were the riots a portent of class conflict? What
was to be the future of labor in our democracy? A number of men
asked these questions with a conscientious anxiety for human
values; others were stung to an angry defense of Property. The
latter group talked, like John Hay in *The Breadwinners*, of the
"dangerous classes," of the devil getting into the workingmen.[2]

When Hewitt read of the riots he instantly took sides with the
men and against the railroads. His relations with the Camden &
Amboy, and its successor the Pennsylvania Railroad, had shown
him how they squeezed industrial towns in an extortionate grip,
until explosions like that in Pittsburgh were all too natural. He
had seen enough of the stock-watering, speculation, and costly rate-
wars on lines like the Erie to know what executive mismanagement
constantly cost the workers. And while he condemned violence, he
condemned still more the hasty use of Federal troops. He said in
the House:[3]

> We are told that we ought to have a large Army, and a very
> large Army, to put down impending strikes. I take issue with
> that proposition. It is not in accordance with the theory of this
> government that the United States is to maintain an army for the
> purpose of restraining any portion of its citizens in their just
> rights. The right to strike is a just right. No man can coerce
> another to work against his will. It is just as sacred a right as
> the right to employ, if you can find anyone willing to hire him-
> self to you. The wisdom of strikes is another matter. . . .
> But I will be told that strikes result in disorder. So, unhappily,
> they have heretofore; so they will again. But it forms no part of

[1] Cf. Norman J. Ware, *The Labor Movement in the United States, 1860-95*,
pp. 1-55; John R. Commons and Others, *History of Labour in the United
States*, II, 13-85.
[2] W. R. Thayer, *John Hay*, II, 5ff.
[3] *Congressional Record*, May 18, 1878.

the duty of the national government to repress or to check such disorders. In the first place, it is the duty of the police, where there is one; where there is no police, it is the duty of the sheriff; and where the sheriff is unable to check disorder, it is the duty of the State to do it. . . . The provision of the Constitution which gives authority to the General Government to furnish troops and give assistance in case of insurrection was intended only as a last resort, where the State had done its full duty in maintaining a police and a citizen soldiery, and had found itself overpowered.

The riots resulted in an inquiry into labor problems by a House Committee, of which Hewitt was by general consent appointed chairman. There being no appropriation to defray the expenses of witnesses, he paid large sums for this purpose from his own pocket. Since the field was vague he took great pains to lay down a definite programme, and after correspondence with Edward Atkinson and other experts drafted a careful questionnaire.[1] He intended to elicit exact information upon the profits of shops and factories in the years 1860-78; upon wage-rates during that period; upon changes in living costs in different localities; and upon fluctuations in employment. Some of the best economists of the day, including David A. Wells, William Graham Sumner, and Francis A. Walker, promised him assistance and advice. Open hearings began in the New York postoffice building on August 1, 1878, were continued in Pittsburgh and Chicago, and finally ended in New York again. A wide range of witnesses was heard. Hewitt took pains in Pittsburgh to summon the labor union leaders, including the head of the Iron Association; elsewhere he called economists;[2] he brought together much data on prices, such as that gathered by Carroll D. Wright in Massachusetts; and he examined Charles Frederick Adams upon governmental schemes of social insurance. He also set an example to other employers by having Superintendent Slade of the Trenton mills give elaborate testimony upon wages, profits, and losses. The complete evidence filled more than a thousand printed pages.

This was valuable in itself, but for a time Hewitt also contemplated an interpretive report with elaborate recommendations. "I find it the most difficult piece of work I have ever undertaken,"

---

[1] Circular sent to witnesses; Hewitt Papers.
[2] Hewitt to Edward Atkinson, July 18, 1878; Hewitt Papers.

he wrote Arthur L. Perry of Williams College.[1] For several reasons it was never completed. He lacked the time; and when the long depression gave way in 1879 to prosperity, popular interest in the subject died out. Most important of all, he knew that the committee as a whole would never endorse the ideas upon the need for a true partnership of labor and capital, for a rapid spread of profit-sharing plans, and for a system of social insurance, which he wished to propose.

For a decade he had been alarmed by the growing hostility between employers and employed. "I should say that the feeling of mutual respect and confidence and good will was rapidly diminishing in America," he told the Royal Commission in 1867. "Within the last five years there has been a very great diminution of it." He had thought then that the two best remedies would be the growth of labor unions and a fairer division of profits. Upon the latter remedy—upon profit-sharing schemes in particular—he had spent much thought. At first he had believed that the States ought to pass laws encouraging employers to sell their workingmen participation-certificates, yielding an annual share of the profits. These might be paid for in either money or labor. They would give the worker no control whatever over the property, but would assure him a part of any annual surplus, and would thus stimulate his exertions while satisfying his sense of justice. Hewitt had also believed that some factories might be owned and run coöperatively by workmen and employers. "I tried to persuade myself," he later wrote Mrs. Josephine Shaw Lowell, "that in the work of production it would be possible to utilize the coöperative principle successfully, but I have been compelled by observation and experience to abandon any such hope."

As he had pondered the question, his views had undergone a rapid development. He had read many books, chiefly English, on the labor question—Sir William Erle's treatise on the legal status of trade unions; the writings of Thorold Rogers; Henry Crompton's *Industrial Conciliation*; and various histories of the labor movement. He had discussed the subject of labor at length with Edward Atkinson, A. J. Mundella, and others. Atkinson, the liberal-minded manager of various profitable business enterprises in New England, was a prolific writer upon industrial topics; Mundella, a hosiery-

[1] January 3, 1880; Hewitt Papers.

manufacturer of Nottingham and long a member of Parliament, was the principal framer of the Factories Act of 1874, and much interested in labor conciliation and arbitration. He corresponded with Hewitt, and stayed at the latter's house on his visits to America. Above all, Hewitt was guided by the writings of John Stuart Mill, whom he quoted incessantly.

In the end, the ironmaster had concluded that the growth of great corporations which raised their capital by the sale of stock was making the profit-sharing principle feasible by a new and simpler road. Let the employees go in for stock-ownership as fast as they could save money; let the employers distribute stock among their workers. "If you will think of it a moment," he wrote Mrs. Lowell,[1] "you will see that corporations consolidate management, but properly regulated, diffuse ownership. When extended so as to cover all the productive operations of society so far as may be possible, each person engaging in the work of production may, and probably will, be interested directly in the profits of the corporation as a stockholder."

When Hewitt failed to complete his interpretive report on labor for Congress, he did the next best thing by presenting his long-pondered ideas on the labor question in an elaborate address to the Church Congress held in Cincinnati in October, 1878. This address was then published as a twenty-page pamphlet, of which he distributed 250,000 copies within the next few years.[2] It provoked much editorial comment in the press and much general discussion. Its readers found it almost sensational, not for any belligerency of ideas or luridity of phrase, but because it ran directly counter to the dominant opinion of the period. Most employers still held that labor unions were a pernicious and even an anti-social growth; nearly all of them held that wages should be regulated solely by labor supply and demand, without reference to the profits of employers. Hewitt argued, on the contrary, that the rapid expansion of labor unions would benefit the country, and that employers must consent to a fairer division of industrial gains as a mere matter of social justice.

He began by saying that the conflict of labor with capital had a natural origin in men's desire to correct the gross inequalities of

[1] May 29, 1885; Hewitt Papers.
[2] Its full title is: "The Mutual Relations of Capital and Labor."

distribution; "and so far from being a subject of regret, is to be welcomed as evidence of a healthy and growing vital force in the organization of society." He reviewed the impressive expansion of trade unions in Great Britain since 1850 as a most encouraging token of changing ideas. While in the United States the depression had crushed most labor organizations, in England many had flourished. In twenty-five years the Amalgamated Society of Engineers had accumulated a fund of £275,000; the Society of Carpenters and Joiners in sixteen years a fund of £74,000. At the General Trades Union Congress held at Leicester in 1877, no fewer than 112 unions, with nearly 700,000 loyal members, were represented. Hewitt hoped and believed that the American trade unions would revive with good times and rising employment. "A new power," said he, "has entered into the industrial world, which must be recognized. It is also apparent that this power cannot be destroyed by force or violence unless society be destroyed with it. It must be heard. Its just demands must be heeded." To be sure, some unfortunate and destructive strikes had been waged along with others that were just and beneficial:

> But one good result has been achieved. Labor is thoroughly organized and marshalled on the one side, while capital is combined on the other; each powerful to destroy the other if they engage in conflict, but equally powerful to assist each other if they work together in harmony. The contending forces are thus in a condition to treat. The great result achieved is that capital is ready to discuss. It is not to be disguised that till labor presented itself in such an attitude as to compel a hearing capital was unwilling to listen, but now it does listen. The results already attained are full of encouragement.

In conciliation and arbitration, as tried by his friend Mundella at Nottingham, he placed but limited faith. While valuable in mitigating the rigors of industrial conflict, he believed that they did not strike at the heart of the problem; at best they merely brought a little nearer that mutual confidence between capital and labor which must precede a concerted attack upon the ugly evils of modern industrialism. The sole ultimate appeasement of the workers' sense of injustice must be found in a more equitable distribution of wealth, and this meant almost revolutionary changes in the ownership of capital. Its control must pass from the few to the many. The States, he said, should hasten to pass laws facilitating part-ownership by employees; the new corporations which were rising in such numbers and power should take steps to sell shares to their workers; and labor leaders should encourage the men to buy them. Thus gradually a genuine association in the ownership and control of great industries would be built up. Such a partnership he believed almost essential both to industrial peace and to continuous efficiency or high production. It would increase the output of goods, and at the same time enlarge the scale of popular consumption and raise the standard of living.

It is evident that Hewitt over-estimated the altruism which American capitalists could then be persuaded to show; while he indulged in a number of generalizations which time has proved erroneous. Declaring that most great fortunes had been amassed through some form of monopoly or unfair advantage, he remarked that "the days of monopoly are now numbered"—though only a few years later the first trust was born! He also asserted that the spread of stock-ownership by employees would facilitate agreements between competing corporations which would "place checks upon reckless production involving sales at a loss." This showed a shrewd perception of the fact, now so evident, that competitive price-slashing injures labor more than it does any other element; but employee-ownership, when tried, has had no such restraining effect, and industry and government have had to try other means of checking sporadic over-production and ruinous price-cutting— the NRA being the latest. He took too optimistic a view of the time required to bring about extensive employee-ownership. Pointing to the rapidity with which great numbers of petty investors had built up the Schulze-Delitzsch system of coöperative institutions in Germany, he asserted: "It is easy to see that in a single year a large fund could be accumulated for investment in business enterprises, and that in a generation the whole capital invested in industrial undertakings might be transferred to the wage-earning classes."

But what was really important in his address was the prevision which he displayed on many other aspects of the industrial and labor problem; for he caught a clear glimpse of several of the great lines of future development in America. In his speech we may find a prophecy of the policy of working with, and not against, capital which the A. F. of L. and other conservative unions have actually followed; of the immense extension of stock-ownership among workers which actually came a generation later; of the increase in both production and consumption which accompanied it, and which led exuberant observers in 1928 to talk of a new economic era; and of the vast recent growth of social insurance and "welfare" legislation. He laid down a number of striking conclusions:

The points which I have sought to enforce are, that the great question now pending is the equitable ownership of property, and that no ownership which does not conform to the principles of justice will be tolerated by society.

That the present distribution of wealth does not conform to the principles of justice.

That distribution has been undergoing a change during the whole Christian era, and that this change has been to distribute the ownership more and more over the great mass of society. . . .

That this progress towards a more equitable distribution must result in the diminution of great fortunes, the improved condition of the poorer classes, and the consequent extinction of pauperism.

That the conflict between capital and labor which has assumed such prominence in our day, resulting in strikes, conciliation, and arbitration, is a healthful but transitional stage towards a more intimate and beneficent association of capital and labor through the corporative principle.

That in the nature of things it would seem that corporations must continue to grow and absorb the great bulk of the business of the world, but that these corporations will be organized upon a distribution of ownership among those who are engaged in them, so that in the end the business of the world will be conducted by men in association with each other, each being directly interested in the ownership of the enterprise in which he is engaged.

That the result of the better understanding thus produced will be such an economy in the work of production as to cheapen commodities and extend their consumption, whereby the condition of mankind will be greatly benefited, and the resources which are now utterly wasted in the strife between capital and labor, resulting in strikes and lockouts, may be appropriated towards the creation and maintenance of funds to insure the working classes against the temporary evils which are necessarily produced by the introduction of machinery and the dislocation of labor from causes over which they have no control; that society owes indemnity in such cases to the industrious poor, and that the principle of life-insurance, adopted already by the British Government, points out the method by which such indemnity may be provided, not only without imposing additional burthens upon the producing classes, but making such provision a measure of positive economy, extinguishing pauperism and largely reducing the necessity for public charity.

These utterances were made near the close of the seventies, when capitalistic conservatism and aggressiveness were the supreme economic force in America; when Eastern employers brought Chinese hands across the continent to break a strike; when E. L. Godkin wrote of workingmen as "a large, passionate, ignorant, and, through their ignorance, very discontented and uncomfortable constituency." They were made not by an academic theorist, but by a practical ironmaker and lawmaker, and one of the largest American employers. However crude in certain respects, in others they displayed a remarkable penetration. The whole programme of the railroad brotherhoods and A. F. of L. as these organizations developed in the next quarter century was to make labor and capital equal partners, to link them in that beneficent association of which Gompers often spoke. A whole school of latter-day economists was to restate and amplify Hewitt's ideas upon industrial efficiency, mass production, and enlarged consumption. The doctrine that the state should insure the worker against hazard was destined to shape legislation in half of Europe before his death, and in America soon after.

To most Americans in the autumn of 1878 the times seemed gloomy indeed. A fortnight after Hewitt spoke in Cincinnati the Greenback-Labor Party exhibited a strength in the Congressional elections which shocked Eastern observers. Polling more than a million votes in the nation as a whole, and more than 100,000 in Pennsylvania alone, it elected fourteen Congressmen. But Hewitt's address was thoroughly optimistic. The growth of great corporations seemed to him to offer a means of diffusing wealth as well as improving production. He pointed out that it was the dazzling growth of property which had made the recent inequalities in its distribution so glaring; that it was the striking rise in the living-standards of the people which had made the recent relapse to a lower level during the depression so painful. "The standard of conscience has been raised with the level of comfort. Privilege slowly but surely recedes before the advance of knowledge. The question, 'By what right?' penetrates the very heart of power, and is no longer answered by the plea of tradition." He did not expect a revolution—he believed that evolution would solve the problem. But he warned the more conservative and hidebound economists of the day to stand out of the way of this evolution; for, he said, it "is not to be resisted and objected to because the abstract thinkers of the world would prefer some other method."

Thereafter he lost few opportunities, in Congress or outside, to expound the principles which he had laid down in Cincinnati. In the years 1880-85, before the labor question received general attention, he continued to repeat his leading ideas upon the distribution of wealth, the need for strong labor unions, the possibilities inherent in widespread stock-buying by employees, and the importance of social insurance. Nor did he refrain from enunciating still more radical doctrines. The swollen fortunes which were built upon mere population-increase seemed to him to need lancing. In a speech in Brooklyn in 1880,[1] which the *Times* roundly denounced, he echoed some of the views of Henry George's *Progress and Poverty*:

> What right have the workingmen—the poor men—in the unearned increment in the property of the country? By unearned increment I mean the property which is accumulated without effort by its possessor. For instance, I have in my mind's eye a man who inherited some real estate in this city which in the lapse of years has grown to enormous value. . . . [He meant William B. Astor.] By no act of his has he accumulated his wealth. He is allowed to retain possession of it because we do not know how to arrange it better. But is not the workingman, who, by his productive labor, made the land rich, entitled to a share of it? Not in the communistic sense that has lately received attention—but has he not some rights in that property which is the result of his skilled and industrious labor, and not of the man who holds possession? Every intelligent person knows that John Stuart Mill has discussed the question of increment, and has arrived at the conclusion that in some way it should belong to the people, and not to the individual who happens to get hold of it. I think the sub-

[1] Brooklyn *Eagle*, November 18, 1880.

ject will bear a more exhaustive discussion before the people than it has yet received.

Throughout this period the chief instrumentality in the maldistribution of wealth—an instrumentality even more viciously effective than the bad currency and banking system—was the high protective tariff. Hewitt was interested in the relations of the tariff to labor, to the consumer, to industry, and to the Treasury; and in Congress after Congress he vehemently attacked it. His views had changed with changing times. While the nation was under the extremely low tariffs of 1846 and 1857 he had favored some moderate —very moderate—increases. But the high tariffs of 1862 and 1864, to which marked additions were made in the next half dozen years, his study of the British and American economists who so eloquently advocated free trade, and his general allegiance to the Democratic Party, now led him to demand lower duties. As an ironmaster, his interests were exceedingly mixed. He had reason to desire high duties on iron, but low duties on certain foreign ores. Yet there is little evidence that at any time after the war his attitude was affected by pocket considerations. As the depression of 1873-79 ended, the tariff issue grew acute, and he threw himself into the struggle for downward revision.

III

It was a gallant battle that he and others fought, first under the leadership of William R. Morrison of Illinois, then under Roger Q. Mills of Texas, and finally under the stalwart Grover Cleveland. It cut sharply across party lines. A considerable group of Democrats from industrial areas, led by Samuel J. Randall, were for high protection, as a smaller group of Northwestern Republicans were against it. Hewitt was necessarily conspicuous in the struggle, for no one spoke with so much authority on economic questions.

Most tariff speeches are dull, but his possessed originality in two respects—their emphasis on free raw materials, and on the true relation of the tariff to labor. Other men in and out of Congress showed that the war tariffs were ill-adapted to an era of peace, and that in diminishing our foreign trade they had hit the farmer hard and contributed to the long depression. But he alone argued at length the need for cheap raw or unfinished materials. Among these he enumerated copper and iron ores, jute, carpet wools, and certain chemicals and textiles, declaring that if they were let in duty-free no interests would suffer and many would benefit. Certain plain facts of the depression emphasized his arguments. "My own personal observation during the summer of 1877 in France, Germany, and England," he told the House in 1878,[1] "satisfies me that the condition of the working classes in England was then less grievous and more comfortable than in either of the other countries or in the United States." Except in one industry, iron and steel-making, free-trade England then had sufficient employment for all her operatives; and though wages had been reduced, they remained adequate to support the working population "in better case than here or elsewhere abroad." Why? England, with her untaxed raw materials to feed her busy mills, her ability to supply her own wants at low prices and to carry on a huge export trade as well, enjoyed manifest advantages over America; for our tariffs were not only unwarrantably high, but were ill-adjusted as between different industries. In Hewitt's opinion, free raw materials would do as much to make America a workshop for the world as they had done for England.

Upon the relation of the tariff to the steel industry Hewitt could speak with undisputed authority. By 1880 the United States was producing almost a million tons of steel rails each year, or more than even Great Britain. Thirty-two Bessemer converters had been built or were building by that year.[1] The converters of the Edgar Thomson plant alone turned out for Carnegie and his partners in two months of 1880 some 125,000 tons of steel ingots, or about twice as much as the largest British plant. The age of steel, after the long depression, was bursting into full bloom. Steel railroads, bridges, fences for the Western plains, ships, buildings, pipelines, tools, and a thousand other articles called for fast-increasing quantities of the metal. During the depressed years, consumption had been small and the new plants had made only moderate profits. But when prosperity returned in 1879 the country demanded steel with greedy eagerness, and the makers had a golden harvest ripe to their hands.[2]

[1] *Congressional Record*, February 21, 1878.
[2] Their capacity was about 1,750,000 tons a year; J. M. Swank's *Report*, 1880.

In reaping this harvest, the manufacturers of steel rails were aided by a tariff of $28 a ton, imposed in 1870; a virtual subsidy that was almost as superfluous, as misplaced, as costly, as if the government had voted $28,000,000 a year into the pockets of the mill-owners. The cost of making steel rails had dropped enormously. In England, in 1880, the average price was about $36 a ton and, in 1881, about $31 a ton. In America, where the whole duty and more was clapped on to this, the price in the same two years averaged $67 and $61 a ton. That is, in the years during which we were breaking all the world's records for railroad-construction, we had to pay about twice as much for rails as England; a tax which was of course ultimately footed by the people, and most of all by the overburdened farmers of the West. Carnegie, already wealthy in 1878, had become a few years later one of the very richest men in the world. His steel works made money in dazzling sums. Even in the dark years 1877 and 1878 the profits were approximately $190,-000 and $250,000 respectively; while in 1879 they were $402,000, and in 1880 they leaped to more than $1,625,000. Since he held 59 per cent of the capital stock of the Edgar Thomson Company, most of these profits flowed into his private fortune.[1]

Carnegie was able to enrich his partners as well as himself; he was able to pay Captain Bill Jones, the despotic manager of the Edgar Thomson working force and the greatest American expert on the Bessemer process, a salary exceeding that of the President of the United States. But he and his partners showed no inclination to share with labor by giving it unusual wages, shorter hours, better housing, or unemployment benefits; they were interested only in their own millions. Travelling widely, and often conducting his business from distant points in Europe and America, Carnegie heard in 1880, as he was setting out to climb Vesuvius, of the mighty forward surge which his profits were taking, and gave a wild hurrah. He valued the money, and he also valued the proof that his works had beaten the Cambria Company. As for his total gains from all his holdings—the Union Iron Mills, the Lucy Furnaces, the Keystone Bridge Company, and the rest—his biographer reveals almost nothing. But one significant fact is allowed to escape.[2] Before de-

[1] Burton J. Hendrick, *Life of Carnegie*, I, 200ff.
[2] Ibid., I, 298.

parting on his world tour in 1878 Carnegie took a sheet and wrote down his estimate of net returns for the ensuing year. They came to two millions. When the books were finally balanced, the net earnings proved to be $2,100,000—and 1879 was poor compared with the years that immediately followed. No wonder that one of his partners exclaimed, "Surely this cannot last!" But no such expressions of gratified surprise came from Carnegie's workmen, whose pay was kept at a low level.

Other steel mills were doing as well; their profits between 1879 and 1883 surpassed the wildest dreams of the owners, and startled European observers. Since the Bessemer patents were controlled by a small number of companies, the richest of the returns were enjoyed by a semi-monopolistic group. It could be said for the steelmakers that most of their profits were converted into extensions of plant which ultimately made steel unexpectedly plentiful and cheap; but that did not excuse the tariff.

The debate in 1882 upon the bill for entrusting tariff revision to a commission, a Republican measure which held no promise of true reform and which Hewitt opposed, gave him an opportunity to tell some home truths about the tariff schedules, the corporation earnings, and the pay of steel workers. On March 30th he delivered a long speech on "Wages and the Tariff." He showed the exorbitance of the $28-a-ton schedule, its utter lack of relation to realities. Carnegie about this time, in fact, informed the other members of the Bessemer Steel Association, as a threat to support his demand for a larger share in their pool, that he could roll steel rails at $9 a ton![1] Such men as Carnegie, Daniel Morrell of the Cambria Works, Samuel Felton of the Pennsylvania Works, and Joseph Wharton of the Bethlehem Company, were making enormous fortunes; yet they paid their workingmen no more than unprofitable industries did. Moreover, they were consistently hostile to labor unions, and they were already bringing in large numbers of ignorant immigrants—for the importation of contract labor was not forbidden until 1885—in order to keep wages low and conditions unfavorable for organization. Nothing could better illustrate the emptiness of the protectionist boast that high tariffs meant high pay. Said Hewitt:

[1] Ibid., I, 213.

Last year the production of steel rails in this country was in round numbers a million of tons. Inasmuch as the demand exceeded the supply, the whole, or nearly the whole duty, $28 per ton, was added to the price. I think I am justified in saying from my knowledge of the business that the profits of last year were between fifteen and twenty millions of dollars, on an original investment of not more than the same amount. Now, if this vast profit had been divided between the owners of the works and the labor employed in operating them, the community at large, though still paying an extravagant price for the steel rails which they require, might perhaps look with some complacency upon the exactions to which they have been subjected by the operation of the law . . .

But what were the true facts as to this "division"?

According to the census returns, the workmen employed in the Bessemer steel works in 1890 were 10,835 in number and were paid $4,930,340, being at the rate of $460 per head, while in the iron works 80,133 workmen received $34,047,099, being at the rate of about $450 per head. As a matter of fact, I presume they were paid at exactly the same rate on the average. But there was this remarkable difference between the two branches of the business: In the steel works, $5,000,000 paid out in wages produced a profit of from fifteen to twenty millions to the proprietors, while in the iron works, $5,000,000 paid out in wages did not produce more than $1,000,000 profit to the owners. At least in my experience the profits on the manufacture of iron do not exceed in the average of years 20 per cent of the amount paid out in wages.

The operation of the tariff, therefore, so far as steel rails is concerned, is not to benefit the working classes, who are not paid at any higher rate than they would be paid in any other branch of business, but to take from the community at large at least fifteen times, if not twenty times, as much profit as the general average business of the country will warrant. It is thus that the rich grow richer and the poor poorer . . .

What should be done? In general, Hewitt desired no drastic revision of the tariff, for sharp and wholesale reductions would ruin him and many others. As for years past, he believed that free raw materials, with moderate cuts elsewhere, offered a solution for the problem. Cheap materials would lead to a rapid expansion in many lines of business; they would work no injury to producers for our home market, for ocean charges were always sufficient to compensate for lower wages abroad. Free raw materials, he added, would make possible a corresponding reduction in the duties imposed on numerous manufactured products of which they were a component part. "This reduction of duty on the manufactured product will lead to lower prices, which in their turn will produce a larger consumption, whereby the area of employment will again be enlarged. Notably in this class of reductions will be placed the manufactures of cotton, wool, iron, steel, and many chemical products." He declared that he could and would produce the testimony of the most intelligent manufacturers engaged in all these industries that carefully planned reductions of 25, 35, and occasionally even 40 per cent would be beneficial.[1]

Unquestionably a moderate tariff reduction was needed for at least four principal reasons: the existing rates actually injured many lines of manufacture, they bore heavily on consumers, they cut down our export trade and lowered farm prices, and above all, they were piling up a most embarrassing annual surplus of nearly $150,000,000 in the Treasury. Yet Congress evaded its duty. The Tariff Commission, after travelling about the country and hearing many witnesses, made a report which was surprisingly sensible in view of the high-protection views of its members; a bill was drawn up, embodying many healthful changes and slightly reducing the general level of the tariff; and President Arthur gave it his support. But in Congress, and particularly in the Senate, the special interests fell upon it ferociously. In the spring of 1883 a bill was passed which actually raised the average duties! Meanwhile, such Republican leaders as Speaker Keifer of Ohio and Representative Robeson of New Jersey were trying to convert the Treasury surplus into a porkbarrel. They succeeded in appropriating $80,000,000 for local and special purposes, largely useless, over Arthur's veto—rivers and harbors improvements, unnecessary public buildings, and the "repair" of worthless warships.

Hewitt was ill when the tariff bill of 1883 came up for final passage. He sorely regretted that he was not there to denounce it. Samuel J. Randall and a little group of other Democrats had voted against their party on the bill. The next time Hewitt met Randall

[1] Cf. *Nation*, April 6, 1882, for warm editorial praise of the speech.

he said just what he thought of him, "in friendship," ending: "I consider that you have broken from the Democratic Party. You had better join the Republicans and be done with it!" The fall elections had given the Democrats control of the next House, and Randall hoped to be made Speaker again. But Hewitt wrote Carlisle, a low-tariff man, that he would support him and oppose Randall to the last ditch, and he was much pleased when the Speakership went to the clear-headed Kentuckian.

Early in 1884 he made himself heard once more upon the tariff. The House Democrats had brought forward the Morrison Bill for a horizontal reduction of twenty per cent on most duties;[1] and on April 30 he delivered a long speech upon "The Emancipation of Labor." Once more, addressing himself particularly to workingmen, he showed how the great industrial interests, subsidized by the tariff, cheated and abused them. But this speech was novel in its emphasis upon the need for strong labor organizations, and upon the connection between the tariff and trade unions.

He pointed out that when the high-protectionist tariff of 1883 became law, more than half the iron furnaces of the country had been in blast. In 1884, after it had been in operation twelve months, nearly two-thirds of the furnaces were idle—432 were cold and only 269 in blast. Before the Act of 1883 raised the duty on iron ore from 40-45 cents a ton to 75 cents, workers in the iron mines received $1.25 a day; a year later many were getting 75 cents a day. For twenty-five years the country had crouched behind the highest tariffs in Christendom; and what was the result? The Senate Committee on Labor and Education had just conducted an exhaustive inquiry among our workingmen. The testimony given was stamped by almost complete unanimity. A great majority of witnesses agreed, first, that the earnings of workingmen in the United States were insufficient to afford a decent maintenance for their families; and second, that on the whole the condition of the working people of the United States in the past twenty-five years had deteriorated. They were worse off in housing, in clothing, in food, than in 1860. Only the progress of invention had offered them a partial compensation for the lost ground.

Hewitt, not content with studying this testimony, had travelled widely in the East during 1883-84. In the coal fields of Pennsyl-

[1] To Howard Potter, March 3, 1884; Hewitt Papers.

vania he had been shocked by the wretchedness and misery that
he beheld. "When I saw that men who worked a whole day away
from the light of heaven, and who took their lives in their hands
every time they entered a pit, are housed in hovels such as the
lordly owners of the mines would refuse to stable their cattle in,
then I felt that something was wrong in the condition of the American laborer."

He thus opened his speech with a biting indictment of high-pro-
tection as a device by which, under pretence of aiding the workingman, rich corporations and individuals too often wrung from the
public the means of making themselves still richer. He then turned
to an uncompromising indictment of contemporaneous American
capitalism for its hostility to labor unions. Whenever the demand
for goods was high, the manufacturer in many fields found the tariff
nothing less than a lump subsidy; he took it all, and added it to
his normal competitive profit:

> And this he did, and was doing, when I spoke in this House
> two years ago, in one great department of our industry, the
> manufacture of steel rails, which were then subject to a duty of
> $28 a ton. The price of the foreign rails had advanced to a point
> where it would have paid him to make rails without any duty;
> but of the duty of $28 a ton he added $27 to his price, and trans-
> ferred from the great mass of the people $50,000,000 in a few
> years to the pockets of a few owners, who thus indemnified them-
> selves, in a very short time, nearly twice over for the total outlay
> which they had made in the establishment of the business.

Nor did the manufacturers—the Fricks, the Morrells, the Mc-
Cormicks, even Carnegie, just embarking on his career of decidedly
well-advertised philanthropy—feel that their wealth should be shared
with the workmen:

> Did they divide any portion of that magnificent bounty with
> the men they employed? Were not these men subjected to the
> rigorous law of supply and demand? And how inexorable that
> law is, when applied to labor, cannot be understood until you
> recollect those vast regions of the world which the gentleman
> from Pennsylvania (Mr. Kelley) tells us are filled with pauper
> labor, open to be brought here in competition with American
> labor.

Wages were advanced a trifle, and something was doled out

from the great mass of this legislated wealth to the workingman; but any attempts of the trade unions to get a fair share of this great profit would have been met, as it is met today, by the importation of foreign labor. Aye, in the State of Pennsylvania today the Hungarian and Polish immigrants are fighting for the crust of bread which is denied to the American workingman. The trade union, therefore, in an overstocked market, with the doors open for foreign immigration, is absolutely powerless.

Moreover, argued Hewitt, the tariff, which cut down our exports as well as imports, and so deprived us of natural outlets for manufactured goods, had done much to accentuate the alternations of glut and overproduction; and these injured the workingman most.

> How often are we confronted with the spectacle of workmen striking to resist the reduction of wages made in consequence of an overstock of goods, and failing utterly, as they must do, in the object which they have in view. At the great strike in Pittsburgh last year, which lasted four months, the owners rejoiced at the stoppage, because they had a large surplus of goods on hand. The stoppage was a benefaction to the masters, and of course the trade unions failed.
>
> I want the workmen of this country to comprehend this great fact. They have no means of bringing owners to terms except through their labor associations, and their labor associations fail every time when you have an overstocked market.

Free trade, he believed, was favorable to labor unions. Such unions had flourished mightily in Great Britain since the adoption of the free trade principle, and for quite evident reasons. Low tariffs had opened the markets of the world to England; overproduction had been lessened, and the demand for labor increased; and the union leaders had been able to build up strong organizations and wage successful strikes. He quoted a brochure by Robert Giffen, of the British Board of Trade, which showed that in fifty years the real income of the masses in the United Kingdom had been approximately doubled. How? Partly through the free trade policy which had made Britain the principal workshop of the world, partly through the progress of invention and technology, partly through the stubborn efforts of the trade unions. Free trade made it possible for the unions to go to the masters and say, "Your contribution is capital, which is worth 5 or 10 per cent, as may be agreed;

your other contribution is management and administration, which is worth a certain percentage easily determined by the experience of the nation. The rest belongs to us, and we intend to have it." They should have it, said Hewitt. In defiance of most American employers, he declared that if their workers wished to advance they must become as well organized as in England, and as ready to strike for their rights:

> In a strike which I witnessed on the Brighton Railway in England I had an interview with one of the chief officers of the great Association of Amalgamated Engineers. I asked him what was the limit of the wages which they expected to get from the railway. He said: "There is no limit; we intend to have all the net earnings of these railways, except a fair remuneration for the capital actually invested, and fair salaries for those who administer them; and the only question with us is to find out what the amount is, and we intend to have it." That great association contained as its members all the engineers of Great Britain, numbering many thousands. It has a great fund in its treasury of nearly a million of dollars, and it has had as much as a million and a half at one time.
>
> It selects one concern at a time, and puts the men there employed upon a strike until their demands have been acceded to. The hours of labor have been cut down by this process to fifty-five hours per week, and the wages of labor have been largely increased, for no man can say them nay within the limits of right and justice which they strive to observe.

He spoke admiringly of the Trade Union Congress, representing a half million workers, which had met while he was last in London. "Their deliberations were conducted with a calmness, with a courage, with an intelligence that would do honor to this House, or any other deliberative body in the world. They did not seek to attack capital. They have learned that capital is their best friend, but they intend to make it their servant, and they can make it their servant." When a naïve Congressman asked if he would repeal the conspiracy laws of various States, as England had done, he replied that they were a disgrace to the statute books. And in the spirit of his Church Congress address, he went on to hail the coming association of the workers with the capitalists in the ownership and management of property. "That process is only at the beginning, but thank God, the day is at hand . . . when workmen themselves will be the owners of all the machinery upon which they expend their daily toil, and shall themselves have whatever profits the God of Nature intended them to have as the fruit of their labor."

The Morrison Tariff Bill was blocked in the House on May 6, 1884, by a vote of 159 to 155, with 41 Democrats aligned under Randall against the measure. Another hope had been lost; not even the Democratic House could be held in line for tariff reform. As a gesture and a foundation for future labor, Hewitt immediately introduced his own bill, which was carefully planned to meet the objections to a crude horizontal cut, and which the *Nation* pronounced "very meritorious."[1] But there was no time to consider it. Congress adjourned with no substantial progress made. But Hewitt had after all accomplished a little. He had reëmphasized the principle of free raw materials, first energetically advanced by David A. Wells just after the Civil War, and then almost forgotten until he took it up. He had asserted once more the rights of labor before a House in which unions and strikes were frequently denounced, and seldom and feebly defended. He had laid down as irrefutable the thesis that "for the welfare and improvement in the condition of workers for wages, the principle of association in labor partnerships or trade unions is indispensable." Let men extend the power of labor unions, he had said, and at one stroke much would be done to put bounds to "legalized robbery" and to break down special privilege; the country would be a little less of "a pandemonium in which men are struggling with each other like demons for the possession of property."

Men knew that, as a practical employer, Hewitt practised what he preached. The two Trenton companies were both family properties, and stock-distribution was therefore impracticable. Profit-sharing on any other plan would have been almost impossible, for the revenues of the iron business after 1873 seldom if ever amounted to more than a moderate interest on the investment, and often fell below it. At least once Hewitt told the workers that Edward Cooper and he would be glad to turn the mills over to them if they would guarantee five per cent on the capital—which of course they could not do. But the wages were good; during the eighties and nineties heaters and rollers in the rolling mill made $5 to $10

[1] *Nation*, May 15, 1884.

a day for piece-work, and puddlers in the puddling-mill $5 to $8, while foremen in the shops received $75 to $100 a month. Carpenters, machinists, and blacksmiths received $1.50 to $1.75 a day. The standard shift was ten hours, and there was no driving. Since Trenton remained little more than an overgrown town, the costs of living were low and the conditions of life pleasant. House-rent in the two decades named ranged from $10 to $15 or $20 a month for very comfortable, if not at all points convenient, quarters. Lots could be bought for $100 up, and houses for $750 up, while a fair house, without plumbing, could be purchased for $1,000 up. The percentage of homeowners among the workingmen was high. The employees' cottages made up an attractive district, with shade-trees, lawns, fruit, and kitchen-gardens; in fact, it had at one time been the best part of Trenton. Tin buckets were few, for most workers went home for their meals.[1] Three holidays were granted—Christmas, the Fourth, and picnic-day; this last being a day in midsummer when the entire works were closed, and the employees and their families went to Morrisville Grove across the river in Pennsylvania. This festival Edward Cooper or Hewitt always tried to attend.

Till 1885 most of the working force were Germans, British, Irish, and native Americans, with a few Swedes; later came Hungarians, Slavs, and Italians, but the policy of the owners was hostile to any large use of South Europeans. The tenure of employees was remarkably long; men came as boys, and stayed till old age. The strong community spirit of the employees' neighborhood had much to do with this. While unions were rather encouraged than the opposite, they never struck sturdy root. About 1884 a number of workers joined the Knights of Labor; later, a majority of those in the rolling mill entered the Amalgamated Association. Though the newspapers sometimes credited Cooper and Hewitt with never having a strike, this was inaccurate; the Amalgamated called one strike in the later eighties, which ended when, after six weeks, the employees came back without ill feeling. Both Cooper and Hewitt were at pains to allow no interference with the political opinions of the workers. They refused to permit any political polls of the employees, or to let politics be discussed in the mills. Injuries to the men were fairly rare. If a worker was crippled, he was given

---

[1] In Trenton and elsewhere the author interviewed former employees whose memories went back to the eighties.

employment in some easy capacity at full pay; if he was killed, his family was helped.

Altogether, Hewitt had a right to say, in his speech on "the emancipation of labor":

This is no dream of an enthusiast, for I am a plain man of business, nor is it an excursion into the realms of Utopia, for I have been trained to weigh and measure the results of human action. It is a sober deduction from the study of the operation of the principle of association, which has crowned this age with material achievements of stupendous grandeur and beneficence, and which is invading and taking possession of every domain of human affairs. It has already begun to organize labor for emancipation from the bondage of ages, and it will be found as easy of application, and as fruitful of benefit, in this final field of action, as it has been triumphant and beneficent in other spheres of social development.

CHAPTER XXII

"In Peace and Charity"

THE Democratic Party, until the renascence of 1884, remained an ailing party in State and nation. But particularly was it sick in New York City, where it suffered from the long disease called Tammany. Boss Kelly, a narrow-minded martinet, suspicious and vindictive, had no sooner fully established himself on the ruins of Tweedism than he displayed an arrogant hostility toward every reform element. In 1876 the Tilden forces, as we have seen, had elected Lucius Robinson governor for three years. In 1878 the same Tilden reformers, under the aegis of the old Irving Hall Democracy, elected Edward Cooper mayor by a decisive majority over the Tammany candidate, Augustus Schell. Both were able and courageous men, who set to work vigorously upon reform programmes.

Kelly, realizing that they were too intent upon their duties to give much time to politics, assailed them furiously.[1] Cooper was the first to feel his strength. As Godkin wrote, he was a mayor of conspicuously good intentions but conspicuously bad success in executing them.[2] When he began removing corrupt and incompetent department heads in summary fashion, Kelly saw his opening. Though the Charter provided that such removal must be preceded by categorical charges and a public hearing, the exasperated Cooper ejected certain officials without observing all the formalities. Kelly had one of them, Police Commissioner Sidney P. Nichols, apply for reinstatement by a judicial writ; and after prolonged litigation and much conflict of legal opinion, the highest tribunal of the State handed down an opinion which upheld Nichols and constituted a

[1] D. S. Alexander, *Political History of New York*, III, 378ff.
[2] *Nation*, October 21, 1880.

virtual reprimand to Mayor Cooper. The mayor was instructed that he could dismiss men only after inquiry and public hearing—which meant that his hands were tied.

The boss rubbed his hands. And that fall Tammany also took the field against Governor Robinson. When the State Convention met, Kelly was on hand with insolent air to resist his nomination. He demanded General H. W. Slocum instead; he angrily declared that he stood ready to bolt the party. When the convention gave Robinson the honor he had richly earned, the Tammany delegation marched out of the hall. Groans and hisses followed its footsteps. But that very evening it showed that it meant business by holding a separate convention and nominating John Kelly himself for governor! He stumped the State, attacking Tilden as "the old humbug of Cipher Alley," and jeering at Robinson as too "sore-eyed" to recognize the bills or officeseekers of New York City. It was a disgusting performance, but it accomplished its object. On election day the Republican nominee, Alonzo B. Cornell, received a plurality of some 42,000 over Robinson, while almost the whole Democratic ticket went down in defeat. Kelly was revenged.

Hewitt at first watched the party schism with dismayed regret. He did not approve of Mayor Cooper's more extreme policies, and especially of his abrupt dismissals from office. When a friend inquired why he had not interposed, he replied that he had taken no part in Cooper's nomination or election, and until March 4, 1879, had been so absorbed in his duties in Washington "that there was no opportunity for him to advise with me, or for me to give him advice if it had been asked." He added: "The mayor is a man who usually acts on his own judgment, and we never interfere with each other's duties."[1] When Tammany left the convention, he still wrote in regretful terms.[2] "If, by any personal sacrifice, I could save the State, you may be sure that I would make it. But both sides distrust me, or rather regard me as not in sympathy with them. In this they are right, but it leaves me without influence with the extreme men, and I have not been able to see that I could intervene with any hope of success." But as Kelly persisted in his efforts to destroy Governor Robinson, Hewitt shared the anger of all self-respecting Democrats. He felt that something must be done

[1] To George N. Herman, May 20, 1879; Hewitt Papers.
[2] To Alexander Thain, September 17, 1879; Hewitt Papers.

to make a repetition of such treachery impossible, and the day after election burst out that Kelly should be disciplined at once.[1] "There can be but one opinion in regard to the conduct of Tammany Hall. It has been infamous; and whatever may be the result to Mr. Tilden personally, the men who have wrought this mischief should never be allowed to rule the Democratic Party." This feeling was accentuated by the events of the next eight months.

As the campaign of 1880 drew near, the desire of most Democrats for Tilden's renomination remained strong. Despite the cipher telegrams, other candidates were hardly considered, and the press in general took his selection as a matter of course. The great issue of the Republican frauds of 1876-77 simply could not be given up. Tilden himself reëmphasized it in various public utterances, declaring that the supreme question was whether "this shall be a government of the sovereign people through elections, or a government by discarded servants holding over through force and fraud." He had taken up his residence in 1879 at the beautiful estate of Greystone-on-the-Hudson, where in the seclusion of his fine library, or pacing the lawns high above the river, he talked with visitors from all parts of the country. When the State Convention met in April, Tilden's forces swept all before them, emphatically endorsed him, and bound the New York delegates by the most drastic unit-rule in the history of the party. Once more Kelly bolted. He called a Tammany convention in Shakespeare Hall in New York City; he dictated its resolutions, denouncing Tilden as a cunning multi-millionaire whose career "has been marked with selfishness, treachery, and dishonor," and who was trying "to force himself upon the party to its ruin"; and he chose a group of dissenting delegates to hammer at the door of the Cincinnati Convention.

These threatening gestures had their effect. Many delegates who had been for Tilden hesitated and drew back. Two days before the convention organized, Tilden addressed the New York delegates a letter which was not intended as a complete withdrawal, and which in other circumstances would have been ignored. After reviewing his services, he said that he desired nothing so much as an honorable discharge, and wished to lay down even his quasi-leadership and seek the repose of private life; but he did not say that

[1] To Andrew I. Sanford, November 7, 1879; Hewitt Papers.

he could not be drafted, and there is good evidence that he hoped to be. Nevertheless, the combination of the letter, the cipher telegrams, the rumors of Tilden's bad health, and above all, Tammany's menaces, was too much. On the third ballot, June 24, Winfield S. Hancock was nominated. Kelly had triumphed again, and this time over the titular head of the Democratic Party.

Once more Hewitt felt outraged. It is true that he no longer admired his old leader, while he also questioned Tilden's physical fitness. "His intellect is unimpaired," he had written in April,[1] "but his body is afflicted with infirmity which may compel him to decline to be a candidate." But while Hewitt was not sorry that Hancock displaced Tilden, he felt it unendurable to let Tammany dictate to the party—that something must be done to teach Kelly a memorable lesson. He and others were willing to postpone this lesson till after the election; but they would then visit their wrath upon the boss in a way he would never forget.

Hewitt played an active but inconspicuous part in the Garfield-Hancock campaign. Though refusing to be considered for the campaign chairmanship, he served as a member of the national committee. In midsummer he went to Europe, and for a time was ill in London. Returning, he accepted the "united Democratic" nomination for Congress in his old district. He had indignantly severed all connection with Tammany Hall and temporarily joined the Irving Hall Democracy, but Tammany dared not refuse him support. He spent much time at national headquarters and made several speeches.

Late in the campaign, he committed the most unfortunate error of his political career by lending his name to the circulation of the famous Morey letter. Two weeks before election,[2] the obscure New York journal *Truth* published in facsimile a letter dated January 23, 1880, signed J. A. Garfield, and addressed to H. L. Morey of the Employers' Union in Lynn, Mass. This letter declared that Chinese immigration should not be halted until the interests of American employers had been fully conserved. It produced a sensation. Somebody brought the supposed original to national headquarters that day and showed it to Randall, Barnum, and Fox, who had all served in Congress with Garfield, and who all

[1] To A. D. Pridemore, April 22, 1880; Hewitt Papers.
[2] *Truth,* October 20, 1880.

pronounced the signature genuine. Hewitt also looked at it. It was written on regular Congressional stationery, and the signature seemed correct, while its views harmonized with those Hewitt had long attributed to Garfield. For greater safety, Hewitt went to his business office, took from the files three letters that Garfield had sent him earlier that year, and compared them with the facsimile of the Morey letter. His last doubts vanished, and he made a categorical statement which had wide influence: "Some people may incline to pronounce this letter a forgery. I have seen it; I am familiar with General Garfield's signature; I have compared it with his letters in my possession, and I have no doubt it is genuine."

Garfield, of course, denied the letter, a thorough search revealed no such man as Morey, and the Democrats were thrown on the defensive. Hewitt should have admitted the lack of proof. But long observation had led him to regard Garfield's word as untrustworthy. In a speech at Chickering Hall on October 27, he therefore said that he still accepted the letter—"I believed it then, I believe it now" —and went on to criticize Garfield as slippery. "He is a most attractive man, and I have never seen his superior in point of intellect. But there is one thing which every man who ever served with him, I think, on the floor of Congress, must have discovered, that he has not the courage of his convictions; that he very often takes positions which command the respect of his adversaries, and when the voting comes to be done he votes the other way. That is his character."[1]

But in this instance Garfield spoke the truth. The roorback was fully exposed before election day, and instead of helping Hancock it injured him. A Republican judge of the Supreme Court in New York shortly seized an opportunity to deliver a fierce and quite gratuitous attack upon Hewitt. The latter had no choice as regarded Garfield but to apologize, which he did with manful completeness. In a letter to the *Nation* he admitted making a hasty judgment, and bowed to "the censure due to an unintentional indiscretion." He also made every effort to ascertain the true authorship of the letter, giving a considerable sum to Chairman Jewell of the Republican National Committee for this purpose. Actually, the pincipal responsibility for the hasty Democratic action lay with Barnum, the national chairman. But Hewitt did not try to shift

[1] N. Y. *Times, World,* October 28, 1880.

even part of the burden to other shoulders. Late one night he was accosted in the streets by the publisher of *Truth*, who had also been deceived, and who thought that other men at national head-quarters should have taken more of the blame. "It strikes me that Randall has acted shabbily," he told Hewitt. "He abandoned you to Republican abuse when he was as much responsible as anybody." Hewitt was offended. "That is not true," he replied. "Randall has been quite willing to bear his share of the blame. He wrote me a letter containing a frank statement on the subject. I didn't publish it because I felt no need of backing in the matter."

The election of 1880 proved a heavy blow to Democratic hopes. Garfield received a slight plurality of the popular votes, and 214 electoral votes against 155 for Hancock. Once more John Kelly earned the resentment of his party. Had he rallied to the national ticket and labored for party harmony in both State and city, Hancock might well have carried New York; in which event he would have been President with 190 electoral votes against Garfield's 179. Instead, Kelly disregarded Hancock completely, and offended the reform Democrats by an exhibition of arrogance not equalled since Tweed's day. He forced the nomination of an undesirable man for chief judge of the Court of Appeals. When the city ticket was drawn up he overrode those who again demanded Edward Cooper, and by devious maneuvering brought about the nomination of William R. Grace. Personally, Grace was unexceptionable; a man of character, brains, and large business experience as shipper and merchant. But if elected, he would be the first Catholic mayor of the city, and the first foreign-born mayor since colonial days; he was a close friend of Cardinal McCloskey; and many voters honestly feared that if Catholics controlled the Board of Apportionment, which distributed the School Fund, part of it would be diverted to the parochial schools. The result was that many German Democrats voted a straight Republican ticket.

Hewitt was profoundly depressed. "If we fail this time," he had written,[1] "we may as well abandon the attempt." After the contest he wrote A. L. Perry of Williams College that Democracy seemed without leadership or principle. Imperatively, the time had come to strike at Boss Kelly. In the fall of 1879 Kelly had defeated Governor Robinson, in the summer of 1880 the nomination of

[1] To T. O'Brien, April 26, 1880; Hewitt Papers.

Tilden, in the fall of 1880 Hancock; Hewitt had helped to root out the Tammany cancer in 1871, and now he and other reform leaders resumed the same task.

The result was the formation of the County Democracy. A determined mass-meeting of anti-Tammany Democrats was held at Cooper Union as the year 1880 closed. Resolutions calling for the regeneration of the New York Democracy were adopted, and a committee of fifty, shortly increased to one hundred, was chosen to launch the undertaking. Hewitt was chairman. When a sub-committee of twenty-one was appointed to draw up definite plans, he again headed it. Among his associates were William C. Whitney, of New England birth and Harvard training, not yet forty, who had been corporation counsel for the past five years, and had successfully contested claims-suits for some twenty million dollars against the city dating from the Tweed days; Oswald Ottendorfer, owner of the *Staats-Zeitung*; Robert B. Roosevelt; E. Ellery Anderson; and Edward Cooper. A number of plans, already prepared, were at once laid before the committee. One came from the Young Men's Democratic Club, one from Irving Hall, and one from a special "committee of ten."

After much discussion, in August, 1881, the committee of one hundred, dominated by Hewitt and Whitney, gave its approval to a final program for remodelling the party.[1] The distinctive feature of the new organization was to be its broad democracy. In Tammany Hall, a small cohort of district leaders under their despotic boss had controlled the whole organization. The Republican organization was similarly dominated by a little clique. But the governing committee of the new County Democracy—the Organization Committee—was to have no fewer than 678 members. It was to be chosen by the enlisted party voters in each Assembly district, who at the same time were to select the local committees. The "halls" would cease to hold sway over the politics of New York City, and plain party members would take charge. With rapidity and enthusiasm the voters were enrolled. On October 7 Hewitt announced that the County Democracy had 26,500 signed members, and that its delegates in the impending State Convention would claim to speak for the entire city.

[1] The printed constitution is in the Hewitt Papers, as are the various tentative plans.

And so they did. When the convention met in Albany, the editor-banker Daniel Manning, sturdy protégé of Tilden and a heavy-fisted leader in State politics, was in control. The County Democracy men were cordially assigned to seats, while the Tammany delegation was sternly debarred. Rufus W. Peckham, presenting a committee report on the subject, implied the harshest condemnation of Tammany's treachery; and Kelly, who was on the scene, found the atmosphere of the hotel lobbies freezingly hostile.

That fall, demonstrating its pristine energy and alertness, the County Democracy carried the city elections with a belligerent whoop. Many Tammany district leaders deserted to it. A majority of several thousand votes was run up. Of the Assemblymen from New York County, Tammany Hall was left with but eight against the County Democracy's twelve; of the State Senators, Tammany held only three, the County Democracy four. One of Mayor Cooper's last acts before leaving office had been to deprive Kelly of his place as Comptroller. Mayor Grace showed equally little inclination to befriend Tammany, and for the moment the Hall was almost completely stripped of patronage and power. Many predicted that Kelly, growing aged and infirm, would abruptly disappear from public life.

But in local, as in national, affairs the reform Democrats found this a period of lost causes, of defeated hopes. Hewitt, re-entering Congress in 1881, shortly had to transfer all his energies to national affairs, and ceased to give more than passing attention to the city. The year 1882 afforded Tammany a shining opportunity, and Tammany never missed its opportunities. A governor was to be elected. Two men, Roswell P. Flower and General Slocum, were eager for the nomination and hence willing to bid high for any group of delegates. Kelly could offer votes, and both rivals smiled upon him. When the State Convention met in September, Tammany was on hand. This time the County Democracy failed to hold the door against its rival. Instead, the seats for New York City were divided, thirty-eight going to the County Democracy, twenty-four to Tammany, and ten to Irving Hall. As it turned out, Tammany's candidate, Slocum, was not nominated for governor. Neither was the favorite of the County Democracy, Allan Campbell. Hewitt himself might have been chosen had not Tilden been chilly and Kelly hostile. The prize went instead to the mayor of Buffalo, a tall, strongly-built man with Saxon hair and blue eyes, frank and kindly though sometimes brusque in manner, who had visited the convention city for a few hours before the balloting began—Grover Cleveland.

As events soon showed, Cleveland's nomination was to prove a fearful disaster to Tammany. But no one knew that at the time, and the important fact seemed to be that Tammany had once more regained its place in State councils. Moreover, that autumn the County Democracy weakly compromised with Tammany in city affairs. It abandoned its proper choice for mayor, Allan Campbell, and joined hands with Kelly in nominating Franklin Edson, who was duly elected on the great Cleveland tidal wave.

It is difficult to ascertain from Hewitt's papers just how much hope he had pinned to the County Democracy. He was too shrewd and experienced not to be realistic about the movement; he always knew what immense powers of recuperation the Tiger had. Nevertheless, from his Washington office, he must have felt sorely disheartened in watching the organization which he had done so much to create as it merely marched up the hill and down again. In 1880 the leaders had denounced Kelly unsparingly; in 1881 had tried to strike him a mortal blow; and in 1882 had shaken hands with him! Such was the force of expediency in politics. The day was certain to come when Tammany, biding its time, would finish its antagonist with a sudden pounce and a stroke of its iron paw.

I

But from the unsatisfactory world of politics Hewitt could always turn to other spheres of activity—spheres that, as we have said, were really more important. He was ill-equipped for the political hurly-burly; he was too impatient of disorder and inefficiency, too hot-tempered and hasty, too intolerant of less capable men. But he was admirably fitted for many other fields of endeavor. The short, nervous, intense ironmaster, with his quick walk and gestures, his air of command, his incisive speech, could do as much work as a half dozen ordinary men. Never quite well, constantly suffering from dyspepsia, headaches, and insomnia, his ailments were of a kind that stimulated his nervous energy, that did not depress him but keyed him to higher exertion, more restless activity. For years he slept at best four or five hours a night, and sometimes hardly at all; but, as he lay awake, he planned the next day's work in minute detail, and with the dawn was up and laboring at top speed. "My engine," he would say with a rueful smile, "is too powerful for my boiler capacity."[1] But this racing engine enabled him to manage a half dozen businesses, to do at Cooper Union the work of an ordinary college president, and to make contributions to the study of social and economic questions, all while keeping his seat in Congress.

The iron and steel plants ran smoothly because Edward Cooper and he had able subordinates. Charles Hewitt had died in 1879, and was difficult to replace. But eight or nine capable men helped to administer the properties controlled by Cooper & Hewitt—E. F. Bedell, F. J. Slade, and Joseph Stokes, respectively secretary, treasurer, and superintendent of the New Jersey Steel & Iron Company; Charles E. Hewitt and William Hewitt, treasurer and vice-president of the Trenton Iron Company; B. F. Fackenthal, Jr., superintendent of the Durham and Ringwood works and of the Pequest furnace which had been built at Oxford, N. J., in 1874; and Dr. Rossiter W. Raymond, who had a marked gift for secretarial and administrative work and who, with the title of consulting engineer, 1875-1895, was invaluable in the Burling Slip office. The principal products of the Trenton Iron Company after 1880 were merchant rods and steel and iron wire; those of the New Jersey Steel & Iron Company were beams, bridges—it spanned some important rivers—chains, and shapes. The furnaces supplied forge-iron and pig-iron not merely to the Trenton plant but to Bessemer mills elsewhere, while at Ringwood magnetite ore was now mined in large quantities. Although by 1880 huge iron and steel works farther west had eclipsed the Trenton-Durham establishments, the latter remained important in the iron trade, and gave work to about 2,000 men.

Patent affairs very properly occupied much of Hewitt's time. The manufacture of open hearth steel expanded steadily during the seventies and eighties, and he tried to convince all its makers that the Martin patents, which he controlled, were indispensable. Year by year Cooper & Hewitt sold rights to various users, sometimes on a royalty basis, but more frequently for lump sums. By 1877 the purchasers included ten important firms scattered from Boston to

[1] Quoted to the author by President Nicholas Murray Butler of Columbia University.

Cleveland, and thereafter the list steadily lengthened.[1] Considerable sums were remitted to the Martin family, for the ordinary charge was $7,000 for the first furnace, and $3,500 each for the second and third. Unfortunately, some users contested the bills for payment. Cooper & Hewitt retained the services of two experts. Alexander L. Holley, the foremost engineer in the steel industry, was of great assistance to them in recommending, installing, and perfecting the process, while P. H. Watson, now the best patent attorney available, dealt with legal problems—both on a commission basis. Even with their aid, increasing difficulties were encountered. Late in 1879 five additional corporations, including the Cambria and Bethlehem works, and the Roane Company, were granted licenses.[2] But at this very moment Hewitt complained of "very serious embarrassments" resulting from patent litigation, and of at least $200,000 involved in pending suits. The Midvale and the Pennsylvania Steel Companies were especially stubborn. Finally, in 1885, the latter won its case, the courts deciding that the Martin patent had really expired some three years earlier, and that nothing more could be collected upon it.[3]

At the same time, Hewitt tried to make something of the patents for the Post-Pernot furnace, which he regarded as in some respects better than those of Sir William Siemens. He had obtained the rights to this furnace on his visit to Europe in 1875. For a time he had hoped to form a "Steel Patent Trust Association," absolutely controlling the various patents of Siemens, Martin, Post, and Pernot, and thus the making of open hearth steel; his design being to charge moderate royalties on a consolidated and perfected process. But the Post-Pernot patents never really won American favor.

II

Peter Cooper celebrated his ninety-second birthday on February 12, 1883, in his usual good health. He invited some old friends to dinner. When one, the eminent merchant and philanthropist William E. Dodge, died a few days before the date set, Hewitt wrote Dodge's son: "There is something grand in the spectacle of a man whose life has been one long record of goodness coming bravely

---

[1] Rossiter W. Raymond to Pierre E. Martin, February 5, 177; Hewitt Papers.
[2] Rossiter W. Raymond to Otis Iron & Steel Co., October 28, 1879; Hewitt Papers.
[3] Rossiter W. Raymond to Pierre E. Martin, June 8, 1885; Hewitt Papers.

up to the portals of death, and entering at once without pain into the blessed life beyond the grave. Mr. Cooper was greatly shocked, and at first we thought we would give up the dinner; but on second thought it seemed to us that this event rather emphasized the occasion of Mr. Cooper's continued health and usefulness." With his faculties hardly impaired, Peter Cooper still frequently appeared in public. As late as February 1, 1883, he spoke briefly before the New York Association for the Protection of American Industry.[1] He read Henry George's *Progress and Poverty* and J. B. Dixwell's *Premises of Free Trade,* and published comments on them. For some years he had followed a fixed daily routine. After an early breakfast with his grandchildren he would drive to Cooper Union and transact business. In the afternoon he usually spent an hour at the Burling Slip office, and later received visitors in the parlor of the Lexington Avenue house. On Saturday evenings he seldom failed to attend the special lecture at the Union, slipping quietly to his armchair, the same that Lincoln had used, on the platform. Hewitt had urged him to write an autobiography, and during 1882 he began dictating portions of it.

To the very end he was full of anecdote, of eager interest in men and events, and of enthusiasm for all his ventures. As he had himself remarked at ninety-one, length of days had not resulted in the slightest weariness of spirit. When young men came to visit the Hewitt daughters, they would say, "Mrs. Hewitt, mayn't we go across the hall to see Mr. Cooper?"—and he was always glad to chat with them.[2] Elihu Root helped him draw up one of his last legal papers. It closed with a few lines at the top of a sheet of foolscap. He always remembered the cautious gesture with which Peter Cooper, in signing it, drew the tail of the "P" down to the bottom of the page and up again; he was not going to risk the forging of a postscript![3] In the family circle on Lexington Avenue he occupied a unique place. The children delighted in his kindly ways, his stories of New York in Jeffersonian and Jacksonian times, his little gifts. They liked to see him place his walking-stick under his easy chair to rock across it, for he thought the roughened motion good for his health. Sometimes they played pranks on him. Once, taking advantage of his short-sightedness, Cooper Hewitt and Sally, who

---

[1] Published in his *Ideas for a Science of Good Government,* 393ff.
[2] Erskine Hewitt to author, February 2, 1934.
[3] Elihu Root to author, January 12, 1935.

wanted a small sum of money, disguised themselves as beggars, rang the bell, poured out a pitiable tale of woe in trembling voices, and carried away $2. They later told him of the imposture and offered to return the money, but he laughed in great enjoyment of the joke. Mrs. Hewitt never went to bed without knocking softly at his door and asking if he wanted anything.

Late in March, 1883, he contracted a slight cold. It seemed trifling, and on Saturday morning, March 31, he drove as usual to the Union. That evening his cold grew worse, and next day pneumonia set in. By Tuesday morning it was evident that he had little chance of surviving. He spoke freely of what should be done after his death, gave his last instructions respecting Cooper Union, and took a calm farewell of friends and family. At three o'clock on Wednesday morning his long and stainless life came to an end. Seldom has the city felt a greater sense of loss. Flags were placed at half-staff, long and feeling articles were published by the press,[1] and preparations were made for the most impressive funeral that New York had seen in many years.

Early on Saturday, April 7, the coffin was placed in front of the pulpit of All Souls' Church, and the upper half of the lid removed, disclosing the strong aquiline features and snowy hair of the philanthropist. On his breast lay a single lily-of-the-valley, but the pulpit and platform about were lost under masses of flowers sent by hundreds of citizens. At nine o'clock eighteen students of the Union marched in as a guard of honor, and the doors were thrown open. Till mid-afternoon an endless throng of spectators rolled by. Among them were nearly four thousand students and alumni of the Union, and delegations from all the civic and charitable organizations of the city. The funeral address was delivered by the Rev. Dr. Robert Collyer. Then the coffin was lifted to the hearse; and a spontaneous procession that none could number, that resembled the immense outpouring of the London masses which two years later so impressed the world at the funeral of the great social reformer, Lord Shaftesbury, fell into line behind the carriages.[2]

The interminable procession, in passing to the ferry, moved along what were ordinarily the busiest streets of New York. The shops

---

[1] Joaquin Miller's poem in the *Herald* was a typical tribute; *Poetical Works*, edited by Stuart P. Sherman, 440.

[2] The press printed long descriptions; see also Hughes, *Peter Cooper*, Ch. I.

were closed, and many were draped in black. When it reached Broadway, far as the eye could reach that thoroughfare was stilled and empty save for banks of onlookers filling the pavements. The bells of scores of churches tolled as the procession moved forward. In Brooklyn, through which the body was taken to Greenwood Cemetery, the scene was the same. Next day a thousand American pulpits dwelt upon the obvious lesson of Peter Cooper's career, the lesson that E. L. Godkin effectively presented the following week in the leading editorial of the *Nation*:[1]

No one can have seen or read of the funeral of Peter Cooper on Saturday without being struck by the impression which his career has made on the minds of the younger generation. There has been no such funeral in the city in our time. No such tribute has been paid to a man who never held high political office, and never made his mark in war, or in literature, or in science. Nor did he owe this to the fact that he was a successful business man, shrewd, enterprising, inventive, prudent, who never made a great mistake, never failed to meet all his liabilities, tried many things and succeeded in all, and, while never speculating, was never left behind in the race for industrial progress. This and other cities have produced many men as skilful in making money as he was—men, too, who owed as little to fortune or extraneous advantage as he did, but who, when they died, got no honor from anybody but their own family and personal dependents or old business associates.

What made his death a public event, and his funeral a great public occasion, was not only the fact that he devoted so much of his fortune and his energy to the service of his fellow-men, but also the other fact, of so much importance in our time, which Mr. Collyer described in his admirable address by saying, "Here lies a man who never owned a dollar he could not take up to the Great White Throne." In other words, Peter Cooper was honored because he was a man who contrived, not for a brief season, but through a very long life, not in one enterprise, but many, to unite the highest integrity with the highest success, and who had at every stage used his success, so far as it went, to make the world a happier and easier abode for such of his fellow-men as he could reach.

"He died as he had lived," wrote Hewitt, "absolutely in peace and charity towards all mankind." And he remarked that he doubted

[1] N. Y. *Nation*, April 12, 1883.

whether any other man had ever passed his closing years with such a serene sense that his aims in life had been fulfilled. His work, in fact, had been completely done. He had sometimes remarked that his life had fallen into three periods of thirty years each. The first was spent in getting a start; the second in accumulating means for the benevolent plans which he had formulated; and the third in executing these plans. With his labors finished, since the age of ninety he had been ready to go.

Hewitt, discontented with New York politics, discouraged by the dark prospect for any notable accomplishment in Congress, could always turn to Cooper Union with a feeling that here was a field of scope and importance. Now, more than ever, its responsibilities were thrown upon his shoulders. Up to Peter Cooper's death the gifts of the founder, with some slight additions by Edward Cooper and Hewitt, had aggregated $1,550,000. In addition to the $660,000 which the building and original equipment had cost, Peter Cooper had given largely to current expenses, and on his eightieth birthday had furnished $100,000 for endowment. When the will was read, it was found that he had bequeathed the Union $155,350. To this Edward Cooper, Hewitt, and Mrs. Hewitt at once added $100,000 more. The resources of the school were still very straitened. Happily, within a few years some generous legacies came from an unexpected quarter. A succession of deaths in the family of Peter Cooper's young brother William, the ne'er-do-well sailor whom he had enabled to make a fortune in managing the glue factory, furnished a series of bequests. In all, $340,000 was received from William Cooper's estate, a sum which permitted a considerable expansion of classroom facilities.[1]

Hewitt was full of plans for the Union. Within a fortnight after Peter Cooper's funeral he was appealing to Thomas A. Edison to assist in establishing a school of electrical engineering there. Edward Cooper and he soon made important changes in policy. Volunteer teaching was discontinued, for the trustees decided that there must be no instruction outside their control. Hewitt's daughters, now grown, began giving fuller and fuller attention to the needs of the women's art school.

But he was not through with public life yet; for just ahead lay the stormiest and most spectacular services of his political career.

[1] Annual Reports, Trustees of Cooper Union, 1883-87.

CHAPTER XXIII

A Quarrel with Cleveland:
The Henry George Campaign

O N MAY 24, 1883, with ceremonies graced by President Arthur, Governor Cleveland, and other dignitaries, Brooklyn
Bridge was opened. After fifteen years of labor and the
expenditure of $10,000,000, Brooklyn and Manhattan were joined
by a structure both immense and beautiful. With its great free span
of 1,595 feet, capable of sustaining seven times its own weight of
6,740 tons, it was one of the signal feats of modern engineering.
When Stephenson had built his tubular bridge over the Menai
Straits, he declared the suspension principle impracticable for
heavy traffic over such distances; yet the Roeblings had now erected
a suspension bridge that dwarfed his, but was far less expensive,
far lighter, and far stronger.[1] It was also a work of art. From the
Gothic arches of the thirteenth century cathedrals of Europe to this
highly utilitarian structure seemed a far cry. Yet as man looked
at these glistening catenaries of steel, this smooth and symmetrical
roadway slung between magnificent towers of stone, they felt that
it was almost as satisfying aesthetically as a great mediaeval church.[2]

The address on this occasion was made by Hewitt. It was to him
that John A. Roebling had addressed the letter (June 19, 1857) first
proposing the Brooklyn Bridge, and he had inserted it in the *Journal of Commerce* to call public attention to the project. When the
Tweed Ring, which had begun the bridge, broke up, Mayor Havemeyer had appointed him a trustee to investigate the expenditures
and report on the advisability of proceeding. Finding that while

[1] Cf. Hamilton Schuyler, *The Roeblings.*
[2] Irving Fineman, "An Engineering Family," *Saturday Review of Literature,*
January 2, 1932.

the Ring intended to steal large sums, they had not yet reimbursed themselves for their preliminary outlay, he made a favorable report. No other public man had followed the undertaking so sympathetically. The elder Roebling, a titanic figure who had founded a town, built up a huge manufactory, and strewn the East with bridges and canal aqueducts, had died in 1869, after finishing his design for the bridge, from an accident in a preliminary survey. His son Washington, taking up the task, had been gravely injured in a caisson accident and had conducted the work with a telescope from his bed. Hewitt, knowing both intimately, had always admired in particular the unique genius, the fiery spirit, of the father.

In his address[1] he paid fitting tribute to both. Engineers, he said, are of two kinds, the creative and constructive, and the creative engineer, like the poet, is born and not made. "If to the power to conceive is added the ability to execute, then we have one of those rare geniuses who not only give a decided impulse to civilization, but add new glory to humanity. Such men are Michael Angelo, Leonardo da Vinci, Watt, Wedgwood, Brunel, Stephenson, and Bessemer; and such a man was John A. Roebling. It was his striking peculiarity that, while his conceptions were bold and original, his execution was always exact." After a reference to the unexpected engineering difficulties encountered after the elder Roebling's death, and the malicious rumors of graft and mismanagement, he spoke of the younger man. "During all these years of trial and false report, a great soul lay in the shadow of death, praying only to stay long enough for the completion of the work to which he had devoted his life. I say a great soul, for in the springtime of youth, with friends and fortune at his command, he gave himself to his country, and for her sake braved death on many a well-fought battlefield. When restored to civil life, his health was sacrificed to the duties which had devolved upon him, as the inheritor of his father's fame and the executor of his father's plans."

Hewitt then turned to a fact all too painfully prominent in American consciousness—the municipal corruption which Bryce shortly called the chief defect in the American political system. The oppidan age had now fully begun; population was rapidly concentrating in the cities, where comforts, conveniences, and facili-

[1] Published as a 26-page pamphlet, 1883.

ties for recreation and culture abounded. In 1840 our urban population had been only 8.5 per cent of the whole, but in 1880, 22.5 per cent. This swift growth had been accompanied by increasing complaints of dishonest administration, nowhere louder than in the city of Kelly and Croker. Said Hewitt:

> I am here by your favor to speak for the city of New York, and I should be the last person to throw any discredit on its fair fame; but I think I only give voice to the general feeling, when I say that the citizens of New York are satisfied neither with the structure of its government, nor with its actual administration, even when it is in the hands of intelligent and honest officials. Dissatisfied as we are, no man has been able to devise a system which commends itself to the general approval, and it may be asserted that the remedy is not to be found in devices for any special machinery of government. Experiments without number have been tried, and suggestions in infinite variety have been offered, but today no man can say that we have approached any nearer to the ideal of good government which is demanded by the intelligence and the wants of the community.

What should be done? He bade the city find an answer in the imposing new bridge, which represented a triumph of two principles: the organization of expert knowledge, and the establishment of a fixed and centralized responsibility for results. It was more difficult to govern a community than to build a bridge; yet the people of New York had deliberately allowed the *ignorance* of the city to be organized for government, and by diffusing responsibility had allowed ignorance and greed to escape any penalty for their misdeeds. When utterly outraged, the community would arise in a brief spasm of wrath to punish the culprits of the hour, and then relapse into grumbling inertia. New York needed, above everything else, changes in the mechanism of government to make its public servants accountable beyond any chance of evasion. Then the voters might gradually be educated to insist upon sound administration:

> Is there intelligence enough in these cities, if thus organized within the parties, to produce the result which we desire? Why, the overthrow of the Tweed Ring was conclusive evidence of the preponderance of public virtue in the city of New York. In no other country in the world, and in no other political system than

one which provides for and secures universal suffrage, would such a sudden and peaceful revolution have been possible. The demonstration of this fact was richly worth the twenty-five or thirty millions of dollars which the thieves had stolen. Thereafter, and thenceforth, there could be no doubt whether our city population, heterogeneous as it is, contains within itself sufficient virtue for its own preservation. Let it never be forgotten that the remedy is complete; that it is ever-present; that no man ought to be deprived of the opportunity of its exercise; and that, if it be exercised, the will of the community can never be paralyzed. . . .

If the lesson of the bridge, which I have thus sought to enforce, shall revive the confidence of the people in their own power, and induce them to use it practically for the election to office of good men, clothed, as were the engineers, with sufficient authority, held, as they were, to corresponding responsibility for results, then indeed will its completion be a public blessing, worthy of the new era of industrial development in which it is our fortunate lot to live.

In the summer of 1883 Hewitt made a Mediterranean trip, going part of the way with the Scotchman who did so much to mesh the world with cables, Sir John Pender, on his ship *Volta*, and being joined in Greece by his family. The Peloponnesian scenery and monuments vividly recalled the classical reading of his youth. All studious undergraduates at Columbia in the forties learned Greek and Latin thoroughly. In Athens he amused himself by trying bits of ancient Greek upon cabmen and shopkeepers, and though he had not opened a Greek book for forty years was able to make some ideas clearly understood.

But it was his visit to Turkey that was most diverting. The infamous Abdul Hamid—"Abdul the Damned"—had then been Sultan for only eight years, and was an object of intense curiosity to the western world. As soon as he had mounted the throne he had begun to exile the liberal entourage of his predecessors; treacherously breaking the promises he had given to his ministers, he had suppressed the constitution that they had made him publish, dissolved the parliament, and crushed every liberty; and had constructed at Yildiz an immense fortress-palace, a city in itself, where he surrounded himself with a regular army chosen from antagonistic Mohammedan races, Albanians, Kurds, and Arabs, so that he could count on their devotion. Many were the stories told of his cruelty and sensuality. The world still recalled with bated breath the atrocities with which he had stamped out the Bulgarian rebellion. Turkey, yet reeling from the heavy blows of the disastrous war with Russia in 1877, hopelessly misgoverned, and the prey of endless official corruption, was on the verge of bankruptcy—indeed, two years earlier the sultan had had to consent to a foreign control over the debt. In Constantinople Hewitt showed a keen interest as he went sightseeing under the guidance of the delightful American Minister, Lew Wallace.

Through some curious circumstances, Abdul Hamid heard of his visit and sent for him at Yildiz, overlooking the Bosporus. The monarch, a dyspeptic, harsh, suspicious recluse, the victim of nervous disease, was notoriously lonely, and liked to talk with foreign visitors of prominence. Someone had told him that Hewitt might be President; others that he could give useful advice on American investments. Hewitt was warned before the audience not to put his hand into his pocket or reach for a handkerchief, for Abdul Hamid, fearful of everybody, fully armed, and an unerring marksman, might shoot him. He was received in a closely-guarded room lined with mirrors. Abdul, as was his custom, asked the visitor his views on Turkish Government, and took a liking to Hewitt's quick, frank speech. At the end he remarked that the American should see Brusa, in Asia Minor, once the Turkish capital, which he thought might regain that dignity if, as he feared, the Turks were driven from Europe. He would provide a military escort as protection against brigands, and wished Hewitt to report his impression of the administration and the economic possibilities of the region.

Hewitt and his party therefore crossed the Sea of Marmora to Mudania, where 150 cavalrymen were supposed to be waiting. Only fifty appeared, and when he asked where the others were the commander replied: "The others are in the barracks. You see, it is not their turn to wear the uniforms!" On every hand were evidences of oppression and poverty. They saw a railroad which French concessionaires had built, but which was now disused, a locomotive lying on its side, because the rolling-stock ordered for it did not fit the gauge. They lunched at a monastery surrounded by an olive grove of enormous gnarled trees (tradition stated that Pericles himself had halted for refreshment under olives on the spot), but which was now being cut down because of the excessive taxes. On returning to Constantinople, Hewitt candidly described to the Sultan the abuses which he had witnessed, declaring the taxes unbearable and urging immediate reforms in administration and justice. Abdul, in defending his government, remarked that his judges must be good because they served without pay. To this Hewitt, who knew that they thrived on *baksheesh* and corruption, courteously replied: "Has it occurred to your majesty that they must live, and that he who pays the most will get the favorable decision?" The Sultan did not offer Hewitt, as on a similar occasion he did M. de Blowitz, the Order of the Medjidie; but he suggested that he would be glad to have him remain as a government adviser.

Hewitt was back in the United States to attend to much miscellaneous business before the Congressional session, including a new venture in Western cattle-ranching, and the collection of materials for a life of Peter Cooper by Thomas Hughes. This biography, a labor of love, was completed two years later and published by Macmillans, in England, in 1886. It made a slender green volume of 245 pages, written with enthusiasm in the graphic style of which the author of *Tom Brown at Rugby* was master. But it had many defects. It began with a description of Cooper's funeral and closed with a misprinted Greek quotation! It showed little research, was badly arranged, inadequate, and marred by frequent inaccuracies. Worst of all, since Hughes lacked the background to understand Cooper and his environment, it gave the rugged industrial pioneer the flavor of a Dr. Arnold hero. Mrs. Hewitt purchased the entire edition, brought it to America, and stored it all in boxes in the Lexington Avenue basement, so that no library in the world possesses a copy. Though Hughes had good reason for protest, there is no record that he ever complained.

As the presidential contest of 1884 drew near, Hewitt gave Grover Cleveland cordial support for the Democratic nomination. He and Edward Cooper joined with William C. Whitney in rallying the County Democracy behind the governor, and assisted in sending a solid State delegation, bound to Cleveland by the unit rule, to the Chicago convention. He went to Chicago on the same train with Whitney and Smith M. Weed, and aided in lobbying for Cleveland. For a time there was a movement to make him a candidate, but he resolutely opposed it. Weeks before the convention rumors had been circulated that Tammany, which hated Cleveland, would use Hewitt to head off the governor. Cleveland himself warned one of his aides of this possibility.[1] Hewitt was of Presidential size; he would satisfy the demand for a reformer; and while Tammany feared him, he would be a less bitter dose than the man from Buffalo. But there were two reasons why this maneuver could not succeed. One was that Kelly lacked the strength to accomplish it—for, detested by Southern and Western delegates, his opposition to Cleveland simply made that rugged leader more attractive; the other was that Hewitt would not lend himself to it. He did not want the nomination, saying that he was too frail in health and too rich in pocket to make a good candidate, and that he had committed himself to the governor.[2]

At Chicago the Tammany men first supported Ben Butler. When they perceived that he was an object of derision, Kelly came to Hewitt on the floor, drew him aside, and proposed that he let Tammany make a desperate effort to throw the New York delegation to him. Perhaps by acting together, Tammany, the County Democracy, and a few others could have made Hewitt a formidable contestant. But he cut off the boss with an abrupt sentence: "Mr. Kelly, I am pledged to Cleveland."[3]

His principal concern at the Convention was that the Democratic party should make the tariff a genuine issue. Months earlier he had implored numerous party leaders not to let it be evaded. "Your views and mine," he wrote John G. Carlisle,[4] "do not differ in regard to the tariff and the policy to be pursued by the Democratic Party. We are for protection where protection is needed, and we are in favor of affording it by the removal of obstructions rather than by the creating of new obstacles to trade. We believe in revenue reform, leading steadily towards commercial freedom and ultimate free trade, which in another generation will be the policy of this country by universal consent." In this endeavor he succeeded. He was a member of the platform committee, and himself wrote the tariff plank—a plank which, while promising to protect wage rates,

[1] Allan Nevins, ed., *Cleveland Letters*, 29.
[2] To A. M. Waddell, June 4, 1883; Hewitt Papers.
[3] Erskine Hewitt to author, October 26, 1932.
[4] June 1, 1883.

denounced the abuses of the existing schedules, and pledged revision on the general basis of a tariff for revenue only.

In the campaign which followed he felt intensely the importance of electing Cleveland over Blaine as a candidate of suspect integrity. "No one here believes," he wrote a California friend,[1] "that the people of this country are so hopelessly ignorant or indifferent as to the character of men as to elect Mr. Blaine to the Presidency." And a little later:[2] "I am quite clear in my own mind that Blaine must be defeated at all hazards, and I cannot help but feel that Cleveland has been raised from obscurity to prominence in order to accomplish a work which was too difficult for ordinary methods. I have never thought that justice had been done to the stone in the sling of David." In the last fortnight of the campaign he was constantly on the stump, speaking three or four times a night. Near the end of the fight Democratic funds gave out; we have seen that one reason why Tilden lost in 1876 lay in the lack of money, and no one knows how near Cleveland came to losing in 1884 for the same reason. Hewitt labored hard to obtain funds from his rich acquaintances. "The National Committee is utterly without money," he wrote on October 28,[3] "and we are now making frantic struggles to get some means to go on with the work until the day of election." His own campaign contribution was exceeded only by that of William H. Barnum, for he and the firm of Cooper & Hewitt gave $25,300.

The press talked of a Cabinet position for Hewitt, and his friends believed that Cleveland should offer him the Secretaryship of the Treasury. He thought otherwise. "I do not imagine for a moment that any position will be offered me," he wrote, "and if offered, I shall not be inclined to accept it. But I shall be in the House, ready to serve."[4] The Treasury went to Daniel Manning, an eminently sound choice. Political necessities also dictated the appointment of William C. Whitney as Secretary of the Navy, and there was no room for a third New Yorker in the Cabinet. Hewitt was offered his choice of several secondary diplomatic positions—Spain, Italy, or Austria. But he preferred the House, and indeed felt re-

[1] To W. R. Selkirk, October 2, 1884; Hewitt Papers.
[2] To President Seelye, October 16, 1884; Hewitt Papers.
[3] To J. D. Duffield; Hewitt Papers.
[4] To A. M. Waddell, November 15, 1884; Hewitt Papers.

sentful that Cleveland had robbed Congress of so many strong members: Bayard, Garland, Lamar, S. S. Cox, and others. The only place he would have taken was the ministership to Great Britain.

At first Hewitt's relationships with the new President were harmonious. He called at Cleveland's hotel when the latter visited New York in November. "I find," he wrote a friend,[1] "that he is resolute to have an honest and patriotic Administration. He is of course very inexperienced, and must rely upon the Cabinet with which he must surround himself. In this respect I have no doubt he will exercise sound judgment." He was delighted by the appointment of the courtly Bayard, whom he had long admired, as Secretary of State, and pleased also by Cleveland's early indication of policies. The President-elect at once made it clear that he was in favor of sound money, a just and cautious foreign policy, and civil service reform, taking a firm stand on three of the most contentious issues of the day. To a professor at Robert College, Hewitt wrote:[2] "I have seen Governor Cleveland, and find that his head is level and that he means to do the work which is expected of him."

But a marked coolness gradually grew up between the two men. Hewitt was irritated by the appointment of Edward F. Noyes of Ohio as government director of the Union Pacific Railroad. A little later he urged the President to appoint General N. J. T. Dana, a Union soldier who had been an officer of various Middle Western railroads, to a government position in connection with the construction of the Northern Pacific. Cleveland refused on grounds which Hewitt regarded as an aspersion upon Dana's probity. Another minor irritant was the treatment given the postmaster of Amherst, Mass., Mr. John Jameson, father of the distinguished historical scholar John Franklin Jameson. A Republican, he had turned Mugwump and supported Cleveland, while he was a most efficient public officer. Learning that he was likely to lose his place to a Democrat, President Seelye of Amherst asked Hewitt to intervene, and the latter sent a vigorous protest to Postmaster-General Vilas.[3] Nevertheless, John Jameson lost his place.

But the fundamental cause of the coolness lay much deeper. Cleveland and Hewitt held precisely the same political tenets, but

[1] To Howard Potter, November 28, 1884; Hewitt Papers.
[2] To E. A. Grosvenor, November 15, 1884; Hewitt Papers.
[3] To Postmaster-General Vilas, March 20, 1885; Hewitt Papers.

temperamentally and intellectually they were at opposite poles. Hewitt's quick mind, his kinetic character, his desire to carry reform and efficiency into a dozen fields at once, his belief in strong executive leadership, made him impatient of Cleveland's slow albeit thorough mental processes, his caution, his inability to deal with more than two or three questions at once; impatient above all with his limited or "constitutional" view of the functions of the Presidency. In his first two years, particularly, Cleveland clung to the Pierce-Buchanan theory of his office, holding that he was not to lead but merely to execute; while Hewitt believed that the time was ripe for a President like Theodore Roosevelt or Woodrow Wilson, who would act instantly and aggressively to carry the nation into new paths. He thought also that Cleveland was too inflexible and unimaginative.

The first and lesser of their two chief disputes grew out of Cleveland's summary and destructive revocation of the "grass leases" in Indian Territory. In 1883 Hewitt had taken the leading part in organizing a million-dollar corporation to conduct a ranching business on 1,100,000 acres of land leased for ten years in the Indian Territory. Three groups had united in this enterprise: some Easterners headed by himself and Edward Cooper, some Westerners headed by Edward Fenlon of Fort Leavenworth, and Sir John Pender and other wealthy Britons. When Hewitt was in London in 1883 he had helped to sell many shares. The land in question belonged to various Indian tribes, principally the Cherokees. But their chiefs had formally leased it at two cents an acre to Western men, from whom the cattle company sublet it, Hewitt having no leases in his own name. The rent paid was small, but the Indians could themselves make no profitable use of most of the area, and outside the Territory vast tracts of public land were used by cattlemen rent-free. During 1883-84 the range was stocked, the company paying $20 a head for well-bred Texas yearlings. To avoid friction with other cattle companies, a great part of the land was fenced in. "I believe it to be the very best cattle enterprise that ever has been, or ever can be, organized in this country," Hewitt had written to Pender.

Hewitt's associates—for he kept entirely out of the leasing lest he be accused of using his Congressional influence—had taken special pains to consult the Interior Department. Secretary Henry M.

Teller pronounced the transaction entirely legal and fair, and stated that the Arthur Administration, regarding it as decidedly beneficial to the Indians, would protect the company against intruders.[1] But the Cleveland Administration took a different view. When it entered office some of the Indians were angrily complaining that their chiefs had sold the tribal heritage for a mess of pottage. Several other cattle companies had encroached unwarrantably on Indian lands and had given rough treatment to some braves accused of killing steers. An outbreak threatened in the Indian Territory, and Eastern sympathizers took up the outcry. Cleveland first dispatched General Sheridan to the region to report. He then issued an order giving the cattle companies just forty days to remove their stock from the Indian Territory, and another order requiring the demolition of all fencing on Indian lands or public lands as illegal. Hewitt was then in Europe, having been ordered abroad by his physician. Edward Cooper protested, but in vain. The summary order may possibly have averted Indian disorders—though the result was that the tribes got no revenue from the land; but it was certainly inhumane to the cattle. In midsummer of 1885, when the plains were baking under the August sun, vast droves had to be hurried by fuming, protesting ranchers out of the Territory upon surrounding areas that were already overcrowded—for the cattle business had now been overdone. It was impossible to arrange for adequate pasturage or water. Many died on the drive or just afterward. No proper winter quarters were available; a season of exceptional severity came on early, bitter northers smiting the plains; and before spring huge numbers had perished.

It is not certain that Cleveland did well to abrogate the grass leases, and at all events more time should have been granted for evacuating the herds.[2] Hewitt's company suffered as badly as others. His manager estimated that the direct losses from the President's order amounted to $76,000, and indirect losses came to much more.

---

[1] Quoted by Hewitt in a letter to W. H. Barneby, England, December 29, 1885; Hewitt Papers. In a long letter to George R. Peck of Topeka, Kan., March 4, 1884, Secretary Teller explained and defended the leases of the Cheyenne and Arapahoe lands. He stated that the leases were clearly authorized by Section 2117, Revised Statutes, and were for the benefit of the Indians—indeed, were "highly beneficial." Department of Interior Papers, No. 1040, Indian Division, 1884.

[2] Cf. Osgood, *Day of the Cattleman.*

Believing that British investors ought not to be penalized by the action of the American Government, Hewitt took steps to reimburse them. "I am prepared of my own free will, and not from any legal or moral obligation, to make good . . . so much of the loss as has arisen from the action of the government." He paid a number of British stockholders, telling them that the Administration's course had been "most unjustifiable." Various Westerners besought him to introduce an indemnity bill in Congress. He wrote them that while an indemnity ought to be paid, for "the order was uncalled for and I believe illegal except from the point of view that the President took that it was necessary in order to prevent Indian hostilities," he did not believe that Congress would take any action; and of course it never did.

Much more severely did Hewitt condemn Cleveland's early inaction on the tariff. He believed that his own tariff bill of May, 1884, which the *Nation* had praised and which embodied the principle of free raw materials, offered a basis for further effort. He thought that Cleveland should treat the campaign plank as a solemn pledge,[1] and when Congress met in December, 1885, should throw himself vigorously into the fight for a reduction of excessive schedules. To be sure, Randall's little battalion of protectionist Democrats threatened to bar the way in the House, while the Senate was still Republican. But Cleveland's prestige was so high, his power over the patronage so great, that he could thrust Randall to one side. A moderate bill, cutting down the huge Treasury surplus that was now becoming a national menace, and benefiting many manufacturers by cheaper raw materials, would find Republican adherents in the Senate. Even if it failed there, it would give the party an impregnable issue upon which to go before the country. All that was necessary was for the President to bring the issue squarely before Congress in his annual message, act with Speaker Carlisle in placing a proper man at the head of the Ways and Means Committee, use pressure on Congressmen, and, together with Secretary Manning, put effective arguments before the country.

Not one of these steps was taken. Cleveland dealt only casually with the subject in his voluminous annual message. He brought no pressure upon Congress. He allowed Speaker Carlisle to make Mor-

---

[1] Hewitt had written this plank; cf. his letter to W. L. Wilson, October 31, 1893.

rison head of the Ways and Means Committee; an estimable man, but without ability as an orator, without parliamentary skill, distrusted by the East as a free-silverite, and best known for the unworkable horizontal bill defeated in 1884. On December 23, 1885, Hewitt wrote a friend:[1] "The President has not yet taken the proper means to strengthen himself with his party; and you must have noticed, with a sense of humiliation, that there was not a Senator to make answer to Mr. Beck's tirade against the Administration." The second Morrison Tariff Bill was ignominiously defeated in the House in the spring of 1886, with Cleveland an almost passive spectator. Randall, as a gesture, brought in an opposition bill. In an effort to extricate some gain from the melée, Hewitt prepared a measure to correct numerous evils in the administration of the tariff, and in particular to create a better system of bonded warehouses.[2] This bill was favored by both high-protectionists and tariff-reformers, and a great meeting of New York merchants and shippers called for its passage. But Morrison selfishly insisted on attaching it to his own measure, so did Randall, and it failed with both. When the session ended Hewitt resolved, in disgust, to retire from Congress. As he wrote Representative Springer of Illinois:[3]

> The fact is that I am utterly discouraged in striving to secure the reformation of the tariff. After years of labor I succeeded in getting the Democratic Party to adopt a sensible platform upon this subject. This is not a free trade platform, but it pledged the party to revenue reform, and to the removal of obstructions to the conduct of business. It would have been easy to execute this policy but for the fact that Mr. Carlisle saw fit to put Mr. Morrison at the head of the Committee on Ways and Means. So far as I can see he is the chief obstacle, innocently, of course, to the reformation of the tariff. . . . If I thought that there would be any better chance in the next Congress to secure action than there has been in the present, I would not decline reëlection, although the state of my health admonishes me to avoid mental labor.
>
> But I see no prospect of any better position. If we carry the next Congress, Mr. Carlisle will be the Speaker, and Mr. Morrison will be the chairman of the Committee on Ways and

[1] To A. H. Buckner of Missouri; Hewitt Papers.
[2] H. R. 5010.
[3] October 4, 1886.

Means; we shall have a repetition of the policy of "how not to do it," and the Democratic Party will enter upon the next Presidential contest with the stigma of having violated its pledges.

When his decision became known, great pressure was brought upon him to modify it. He was told that tariff-revision could not be postponed much longer. By the end of the fiscal year 1886-87 all the public debt subject to call would have been paid off; the Treasury would be accumulating a surplus of more than $100,-000,000 annually, for which there was no use unless the government embarked upon unnecessary and injudicious public works; and the only way out would be to cut down the schedules. No one knew so much as he about the tariff, and it was his duty to stay. As late as October 8, 1886, he had not made up his mind whether to run again. The County Democracy was anxious to renominate him. Tammany, semi-hostile and reluctant as ever, was also prepared to do so rather than face a storm of condemnation and a possible Republican victory. "I have been very much embarrassed," Hewitt wrote Richard Croker, who had now succeeded Kelly as chief of the Hall, "by the reflection that my retirement might be productive of injury to the public interest . . . I have gradually come to the conclusion, therefore, that if the people of my district are unanimous or practically so in asking me to go back I would not be justified in refusing reëlection. . . ." He asked a few more days for consideration, and then the question was suddenly taken out of his hands.

On the night of October 11 Hewitt and his family were at the home of Edward Cooper, their own house just across the street being under repair. He was talking after dinner in the library with Cooper and former Police Commissioner McLean when the doorbell was rung by newspapermen. They announced that at the Tammany Convention an hour earlier one of Croker's lieutenants had taken the floor and nominated Hewitt for mayor, and the nomination had been carried with a rush. Hewitt was incredulous. "This is such an astonishing piece of information that I cannot help thinking there is some mistake about it," he said. He refused to say whether he would accept, and next day was still noncommittal.

Back of this unexpected maneuver lay a chain of extraordinary circumstances. Tammany was suffering from a severe fright. That year, a great wave of labor unrest had rolled across the land. An angry strike had occurred on Jay Gould's railroads in the Southwest, a wage dispute at the McCormick Reaper Works in Chicago had culminated early in May in the bloody Haymarket Riot, and altogether nearly 1,500 strikes had occurred, crippling or closing about 10,000 establishments. In New York City, labor troubles on the street-car lines and a boycott of the Thiess Brewery had both resulted in violence and arrests. The Knights of Labor were at the height of their power, and many discontented workingmen were eager to resort to political action. Particularly in New York did they have good reason for doing so. The street railway strikes were embittered by the fact that the venal Board of Aldermen had granted franchises which gave the rapid transit interests enormous profits, while their employees worked twelve, fourteen, and even sixteen hours a day for a pittance. In April, almost the entire Board of Aldermen had been indicted for taking bribes, and labor leaders perceived an opportunity to capitalize the public indignation.[1] They prepared to run a labor candidate for mayor.

In midsummer a labor committee called upon Henry George to offer him their nomination. His *Progress and Poverty*, published seven years before, had brought him international fame and made him the idol of the poor and oppressed. To workers he seemed the shining apostle of a better social order. George at first demurred.[2] Fearing that he would humiliate himself and his cause by an ignominiously small poll, he said, when the committee made a second call, that he would not run unless pledged at least thirty thousand votes. The response to this demand surprised even the labor leaders. Pledges rolled in like a flood till 34,000 had been received. Tammany saw with alarm that fully half of its vote would probably be swept away by the Henry George movement. Indeed, the New York *Tribune* estimated that three fourths of the labor vote would come from Tammany's ranks.[3] In consternation, Boss Croker and the County Democracy despatched an emissary, William M. Ivins, to tell George that if he would keep out, the County Democracy and Tammany would join in sending him to Congress. Ivins also said: "You cannot be elected mayor, but your running

[1] Gustavus Myers, *History of Tammany Hall*, 269.

[2] Henry George, Jr., *Life of Henry George*, 459ff.

[3] September 24, 1886.

will raise hell, and we don't want that." George leaped to his feet. "You end my uncertainty," he said. "I do not want the labor and responsibility of the mayor's office, but I do want to raise hell. I will run!"

Late in September the County Democracy indicated its intention of renominating Mayor Grace, who had made a courageous stand against waste and corruption. Tammany at once served notice that it would put a rival ticket in the field. Such a Democratic split would ensure Henry George's election. On October 5, at a great labor meeting, George formally accepted the nomination. The size, enthusiasm, and confidence of this gathering struck dismay to the regular Democratic leaders. At Albany Governor Hill was alarmed, and in Washington President Cleveland's political advisers showed apprehension, for it was important to both that the metropolis remain in Democratic hands. Let a labor revolt of political character get well started, and no one knew how hard it would hit the party that had always made a special appeal to workingmen. Governor Hill came to New York in person; so did Secretary Manning, and Cleveland's private secretary, Daniel Lamont.[1] Hurried conferences were held. There was talking of uniting the various Democratic factions about Edward Cooper. Administration organs appealed to Tammany to be magnanimous and accept him. Then, on the 10th, as if inspired, the New York *World* declared that many believed Hewitt the best possible candidate, and next evening Croker dramatically swung Tammany to him. Bourke Cockran made a characteristic speech to the convention. "The name of our candidate places this nomination beyond all desire for office or spoils. It comes from our desire for the supremacy of the Democratic party. The name in itself is a tower of strength. . . . It means Democratic control to the city of New York, and a broad pathway to Presidential success in 1888."

It was a beautiful bit of strategy. The County Democracy had no choice but to drop Grace and fall into line. "We might as well admit," said one of their leaders, "that we are euchred."

This action placed before the city a candidate who appealed strongly to all independents and many Republicans, and who would be sure of not a few labor votes. Godkin remarked that the nomi-

[1] *Times*, October 7, 1886.

nation was the pleasantest surprise to which Tammany had ever treated the city.[1] "Mr. Hewitt is just the kind of man New York should always have for mayor. . . . He is an eminent business man, one of the largest and most successful employers of labor we have, an authority on most of the economic questions of the day, and has a character on which, although he has been for long years in politics, nobody has ever been able to inflict the slightest damage." The County Democracy, hastening to accept the nomination, divided the minor nominations with Tammany. Irving Hall was left out in the cold, and in a fit of pique endorsed Henry George for mayor.[2] It was a small faction of dubious reputation, but it gave George the assistance of a political machine of the conventional type.

The Republicans on October 15, while Hewitt still hesitated, offered their nomination to Theodore Roosevelt. Though not twenty-eight, Roosevelt had gained an enviable reputation in the State Assembly as a reformer. He had just promised Hewitt to "take off his coat and work for him"; and as he wrote Henry Cabot Lodge, he stood no chance of winning. But he had nothing else at the moment to do, and as he explained to Hewitt, "It is too good a chance for a young man to advertise himself!" The Republican bosses, who hoped to bleed him for a large political fund and then sell him out,[3] were taken aback when he began running his own campaign with characteristic fire. On hearing of Roosevelt's nomination and the growing impetus of the Henry George movement, Hewitt yielded to pleas that he alone could avert a single-tax victory. After insisting that Croker should give him a private pledge never to ask any office for himself or his friends, he published his letter of acceptance on October 17. Thus began the most stirring campaign of the city's history, for never before or since have men of such ability contended for the prize.

It was inevitable that the battle should swiftly develop into a fierce attack upon Henry George as an incendiary theorist and agitator. "We believe," said the *Nation*, "that nothing has occurred in the history of New York threatening its welfare so seriously as

[1] *Nation*, October 14, 1886.
[2] Irving Hall had been represented in the Grace Administration by the president of the Board of Aldermen; he was not renominated.
[3] New York *Sun*, October 21, 1886.

the George movement." In other words, Godkin asserted that Henry
George was more dangerous than Fernando Wood or the Tweed
Ring. This was nonsense; yet Curtis and *Harper's Weekly*, Pulitzer
and the *World*, Whitelaw Reid and the *Tribune*, all denounced
George as a wild revolutionary, while Carl Schurz assailed him as
an apostle of class warfare. It was not merely his essential doctrine,
that land monopoly and unearned increment are the chief sources
of social injustice, which deeply alarmed property-holders in a city
distinguished by high land values and immense fortunes built
upon unearned increment. There was also the fact that in his writings Henry George had denounced monopoly and plutocracy with
flaming eloquence, and had pictured the wretchedness of the East
Side, the misery of our submerged tenth, in a way which conservatives might well call violent. In doing so he had performed a national service. But all passionate reformers arouse antagonism, and
many sober men feared that George, with his assaults upon the
exploiting class, would disrupt the peace of the city.[1] The workers
might act too hastily upon his theories.

George was unfortunate, too, in many of his supporters. Radicals,
cranks, windbags, and even revolutionaries flocked to his standard.
The Anarchist leader, Johann Most, in durance on Blackwell's
Island, gave out an interview applauding him and prophesying
that the labor movement would divide the voters of the nation
into two hostile bodies, capitalist and proletarian, and would cul-
minate in civil war. George himself was betrayed into indiscreet
utterances. The *World*[2] shortly quoted him as saying that "the
great epoch of the French Revolution" was "about to repeat itself
here," and though he declared that this was a garbled quotation,
the press kept reiterating it. He also said that the city ought to
furnish free transit just as it furnished free schools and water, and
the *Nation* quoted him as actually promising this to the voters.
Even his admirers had to admit that he was in a decidedly equivocal
position. He was running for office to "raise hell," to give greater
currency to his single tax theory and other radical doctrines, and
yet he expressly disclaimed any intention, if elected, of trying to

[1] Vernon L. Parrington remarks of Henry George that "in him the French
Revolutionary doctrine came to its most original expression in America"; *Main
Currents*. III, 136.
[2] October 22, 1886.

put the single tax into execution. Herein lay an implicit contradiction which might well puzzle impartial men.

Hewitt from the outset disregarded Roosevelt, and concentrated his fire upon Henry George and the less tenable of the ideas he represented. Few men in the country had spoken as frequently and forcibly as Hewitt in favor of labor. But he believed that labor in the eighties could best advance its interests by forming strong unions, and would only injure its cause by turning aside to establish a special labor party. Henry George was doing labor a disservice by heading such a party, just as he was doing it a disservice by commixing the single tax with its legitimate demands. Hewitt was willing to go as far as John Stuart Mill on the appropriation of unearned increment by the state, but like all economists of standing then and since, he was unwilling to go as far as George. Moreover, Hewitt thought of the city and people of New York as a whole—not in terms of a rich-man's party or a laboring-man's party. For economic aims let labor create economic organizations —that is, vigorous and aggressive unions; but for political aims let the workers act through the ordinary parties which cut across group lines and special interests. As Hewitt said, the Henry George campaign was based on class issues and not political issues; his organization had thrust aside the true question of efficient and honest government, and at least indirectly, had made the question one between employer and employee, between landowner and landless. In his letter of acceptance he expressed this idea sharply:

A new issue has been suddenly sprung upon this community. An attempt is being made to organize one class of our citizens against all other classes, and to place the government of the city in the hands of men willing to represent the special interests of this class to the exclusion of the just rights of the other classes. The idea which underlies this movement is at war with the fundamental principle upon which our government was organized. . . . The injurious effects arising from the conclusion that any considerable portion of our people desire to establish the ideas of Anarchists, Nihilists, Communists, and mere theories for the democratic principle which involves the right to private property, would react with the greatest severity upon those who depend upon their daily labor for their daily bread . . . The horrors of the French Revolution and the atrocities of the Commune offer conclusive testimony against the dreadful doctrines which can only be enforced by revolution and bloodshed, even when reduced to practise by men of good intentions and blameless private life.

He protested against class-war ideas drawn from Karl Marx, for "between capital and labor there never is and never can be any antagonism. They are natural and inseparable allies." But he objected, above all, to the very idea of a labor party in America; it was as bad as a capitalist party; parties should represent governmental aims and not economic antagonisms. "The issue," he wrote, "is between the democratic ideas of the founders of the republic, and the Socialistic views of mere theorists." It had first been presented in New York City, and it should there receive a decisive answer.

Henry George made an immediate and effective reply,[1] which led to a heated exchange of letters. Denying that his candidacy represented a movement of class against class, he described it as a movement of the masses against the classes, and in particular a mass revolt against the corrupt class of politicians who led Tammany Hall and the County Democracy. The great body of plain New Yorkers, he continued, were on his side, while the spoilsmen of two disreputable Democratic factions were against him. He asked Hewitt to explain why his letter of acceptance contained "no references whatever to the crying evils which mark the administration of our municipal government, nor any word of censure for the corrupt political system which has made Democratic institutions in New York a byword and reproach." He also suggested that the two debate the single-tax theory, even though the mayoralty would give neither an opportunity to put it into practise. Hewitt found it easy to answer this. He refused to discuss the single tax, which he characterized as confiscatory, and he declared that he would be a reformer in spite of Tammany:[2]

I perceive that you object to my nomination because it was made by politicians. My experience has taught me not to fear them. For ten years I have been nominated for Congress by men whom you condemn as politicians, and I have not found this fact to be any bar to the conscientious and independent per-

[1] N. Y. *World*, October 19, 1886.
[2] Ibid., October 21, 1886.

formance of my public duties. I am not so impracticable as to reject the methods by which society at any given time is governed, and to decline to do my part as a citizen because the machinery of politics is not to my liking. . . . I do not deem it necessary to give any specific pledge or promises to people among whom I have lived for sixty years and whom I have already served to the best of my ability, and, if I may judge by my repeated re-election to office, to their satisfaction.

When George, losing his temper, charged that Hewitt had bought his seat in Congress, the ironmaster rejoined that he had never spent a dollar directly or indirectly for a nomination. And when George told a brass-workers' meeting in Irving Hall that "hereafter in politics the millionaires will be on one side and the working-men on the other," Hewitt urged the voters to read Taine's *French Revolution* to see whither such doctrines led.

Though George had not a single newspaper, his party organized a brilliantly effective canvass. In almost every precinct Henry George Clubs were established. A small army of speakers, led by Samuel Gompers and Daniel De Leon, took the field. While it included so many of the lunatic fringe that Godkin remarked that nothing like it had been seen since Greeley's campaign in 1872, it won votes. George himself, from cart-tails at noon and platforms at night, spoke indefatigably. Undersized, bald save for a fringe of reddish hair, his strong jaw emphasized by a sandy beard, when speaking he was the very picture of a fighter. Reporters called him "the little red rooster" or "the little game cock"; phrases he did not like, for he was vain and lacking in humor, but which did him no harm. Crowds followed him everywhere, and at huge rallies hats were passed to pay the hall-rent.

On the Saturday night before election there was a great parade of George's followers. No fewer than 30,000 men and women, and some believed 70,000, in a cold drenching rain, without music and with few torches, passed the reviewing stand in Union Square, cheering as they went. "That night," Gompers wrote,[1] "we felt confident of the election of George." No such parade had ever been seen before in a city campaign. Yet the canvass closed, as it had begun, with the betting 10 to 3 on Hewitt. An extraordinary registration had been announced; approximately 230,000 voters had

[1] Gompers, *Seventy Years of Life and Labor*, I, 318.

enrolled, or 10,300 more than had voted for mayor in 1884, when the Presidential campaign had swelled the total. It was certain that many Republicans had swung to Hewitt. "If the panic grows," Roosevelt had written Lodge, "thousands of my supporters will go to Hewitt for fear George may be elected—a perfectly groundless emotion." The newspapers exhorted them to do so, while Carl Schurz appealed especially to the German Republicans. In the last hours of the contest it was whispered that Platt had promised Croker to swing his followers to the Democratic candidate, but this was mere rumor. Hewitt himself made numerous appeals to Republicans. "As for Mr. Roosevelt," he told a meeting of merchants, "I trust that at some future time he will receive the reward due to his energy, his ability, and his character, but he has made a mistake. He has allowed himself to be made the tool of designing men."

Early on election day reports came in to headquarters that the Republican machine was making district deals at the expense of Roosevelt. There is evidence that about 2 p.m. Platt's lieutenants actually sent out word that since Roosevelt could not succeed, Republicans should all vote to assure Hewitt's triumph over Henry George. These votes were needed, for Hewitt himself predicted that the labor ticket would poll between 70,000 and 80,000 votes. "The race between Mr. George and myself," he added, "will be closer than my friends think."

By ten o'clock that night it was evident that Hewitt had been elected, and by midnight that his plurality over Henry George exceeded 20,000, while Roosevelt had run a bad third. At an informal reception at the New Amsterdam Club, Hewitt said that his election was not a personal triumph: "It is the people's victory." That same night George, addressing an enthusiastic crowd at the Central Labor Union Hall, told it that if the election had been completely fair he would have been chosen. Bribery and intimidation had defeated an honest verdict of the people, but he had nevertheless demonstrated the political power of labor in a way that politicians would never forget—so he asserted. The official totals later gave Hewitt 90,552 votes; George 68,110; and Roosevelt 60,435.[1]

The charge that the election had been decided by fraud and

[1] Myers, *Tammany Hall*, 270.

bribery, so hastily made by Henry George, was never sustained and is beyond question untrue. The excitement of the campaign resulted in more careful scrutiny of the polls and the count than usual. Newspapers of the day, Republican and Democratic, united in declaring that frauds had been very few. It is conceivable that several thousand votes might have been added to Hewitt's total by illegal registration, bribery, and manipulation of the count, but it was impossible to give him a margin of 22,400 ballots in that fashion. Unquestionably the Republican desertions to him were the decisive factor. By his own estimate he received about 10,000 Republican votes, and by Roosevelt's about 15,000; some given him by the machine, but a majority cast voluntarily.

Hewitt was willing to admit the striking import of the vote which Henry George, without real political organization, without newspapers, and without money, had polled. "The significant fact standing out as the result of the election," he generously said,[1] "is that 68,000 people have deliberately declared that they have grievances which ought to be redressed, and that they have no expectation that the existing parties will give them the relief they desire." Much as he admired some of Henry George's writings, he felt that he had done a public service in preventing what George himself would have hailed as a victory for the single tax, and in rebuking the formation of a class party or labor party. It is a significant fact that never since has a labor party gained any footing in municipal politics, and it shows the artificiality of George's incursion into political affairs. Hewitt also felt, and justly, that his experience would permit him to be a better mayor than George, who would have been fettered from the outset by the intense suspicion of half of the city. But he meant to govern the city primarily for just the plain, discontented people who had voted for George. He had said during the campaign that he would act in the interest of the masses; in the moment of victory he said so again, adding: "I will make no promises or professions. I know that it is the fashion for men elected to high office to make them, but I prefer to act as my conscience dictates. Let me be judged by my acts."

[1] N. Y. *World*, November 4, 1886.

CHAPTER XXIV

A Reform Mayor

H EWITT'S inauguration as mayor on New Year's Day in
1887 was everywhere hailed as offering the hope of a new
era in the city's history. "It is expected," said the *World*,[1]
"that it will mark the beginning of better government, of more
honest methods, in our municipal affairs." At a reception in City
Hall the new mayor, quick, vital, alert as ever, bubbled over with
good spirits. There is some reason for saying that the mayoralty
of New York is, next to the Presidency, the most important executive position in the land; and at last he was to have an opportunity
to show his hatred of disorder in a large sphere. He congratulated
Mayor Grace upon his achievements. He smiled reproachfully at
Fire Commissioner Purroy—"The last time I saw you, you were
getting me into all this trouble." He had a jocular word for the
head of the Civil Service Board: "Go on with your examinations,
Mr. Professor, but don't, I pray you, examine the mayor." He
was cordial to School Commissioner Schmidt. "You received your
education at Cooper Union. I approve of your work in favor of
the establishment of evening high schools—there ought to be one
in every ward. The Cooper Union was intended to be a model
for such work. I know of one man who got all his education at
Cooper Union and is today worth $800,000." As he was leaving, a
cablegram was handed him from Scotland:

To Mayor Hewitt, New York.

Provost Donald, Dunfermline, sends greetings from the town
of Robert the Bruce and Ralph Erskine.[2]

[1] January 2, 1887.
[2] N. Y. *World, Times,* January 2, 1887.

That night the mayor took to his bed with an attack of sciatic rheumatism. The seizure proved severe and long-continued. Once a rumor even flew about the city that he had died; but, with mind as keen as ever and energy undiminished, he soon turned his sickroom into an efficient mayor's office. On January 3 he sent the aldermen a message of broad scope, outlining his hopes and intentions.[1] He pointed out, as William R. Grace had often done, that the mayor's powers for reform in this rich city of 1,650,000 people were lamentably restricted; but he meant to do all that was possible.

The chief limitation upon his powers lay in the total want of municipal home rule. Legally the city was a creation of the State; the State Legislature could and did constantly interfere in all of its affairs; and as it was a bi-partisan interference for purposes of plunder, the results were almost invariably bad. Not until the adoption of the State Constitution of 1894 did New York begin to have a really substantial protection against State meddling. The legislature "makes and unmakes mayor, commissioners, and common councils at its constitutional pleasure," wrote Hewitt. Another heavy limitation upon any mayor's usefulness lay in the wretched decentralization of power under the existing city charter. His authority over departmental heads was slight. Most of them had a tenure long outlasting the mayor's—the Police Commissioners, for example, served six years against the mayor's two; he could make no removals save for serious offences, and then only after public hearings (which might be protracted by legal quibbling) and with the approval of the governor. Once he appointed the head of a department, his executive functions therein ceased, for the commissioners were responsible for all subordinate appointments, and for the conduct of all departmental affairs. Still another handicap was the low character of the board of aldermen. The Broadway franchise scandal had shown that in 1884 twenty out of twenty-two members had shared a bribe of $500,000, and there had been too little improvement since.

Hewitt could not make a clean sweep of the chief executive offices; at the outset, in fact, he had few places to fill. On May 1, however, a half dozen offices would become vacant—a Park Commissionership, one of the four Police Commissionerships, and Com-

[1] Ibid., Jan. 4, 1887.

missionerships of Health, Charities, and Taxes. Little by little he hoped to weed out incompetent men. He expected also to accomplish something in other directions.

He proposed, as a beginning, that the city debt be refunded at a lower rate of interest, for it was costing the taxpayers an unjustifiable sum. The bonded indebtedness, after making allowance for the moneys in the sinking-fund, was then about $93,300,000. Of this more than $31,000,000 bore interest at six per cent, and more than $35,000,000 at seven per cent! He also announced that through the two Commissioners of Accounts he would investigate all city departments "to the utmost extent of the power" they possessed, and deal severely with any delinquencies. He described the need for more parks, better street lighting, and tenement house reform. He announced that he would organize a "Cabinet" in the city government by calling the departmental heads and the President of the Board of Aldermen together from time to time for consultation. He was determined that the executive departments should act in harmony, and show vigilance against unwise or malicious legislation in Albany.

All this sounded hopeful to reform elements. But it gave little indication of the cyclonic energy Hewitt was about to apply to city affairs, or of the degree to which the mayor's office was shortly to become a storm-centre.

The first indication of the dynamic new treatment of city affairs was a summons to the Superintendent of Police, William Murray, to come to the mayor's house.[1] Hewitt had not lived in New York most of his life without realizing that it was usually "wide open," and that the first test of a reform government was its attitude toward the countless resorts of vice. New York in the preceding few years had been almost as much the paradise of thieves, thugs, pimps, prostitutes, confidence men, gamblers, and panhandlers as Dr. Parkhurst and the Lexow Investigation later proved it to be in the early nineties. The same triple alliance of crooked underworld, crooked politics, and crooked business that Lincoln Steffens later described with such startling vigor already existed. Hewitt had given much time just after the election to quiet personal investigation. He had covered all parts of the city, often late at night; had

[1] Hewitt told the story of this meeting to Everett P. Wheeler; see Wheeler, *Sixty Years of American Life*, 334-336.

found the closing laws for saloons almost a dead letter on Sundays and weekdays alike; had learned that gambling-dens, bawdy-houses, and other illegal establishments were running without concealment. The police force, though raised to nearly 3,500 in Mayor Grace's last year, was making little real effort to enforce the law. A system of political protection was obviously in effect.

Wrapped in blankets in an easy chair, Hewitt sternly called Superintendent Murray's attention to the fact that the city was running wide-open, that conditions in some districts were scandalous, and that police-graft was obviously general. "All you say is true," Murray admitted. "Well," demanded the mayor belligerently, "can these places be closed up?" "Certainly; it is only necessary to give the orders." "Then why do they exist at all?" "As to that," said Murray impudently, "you had better ask some of your political friends." Hewitt vigorously disclaimed any friendship for the powers in Tammany. "But," he said, "are they interested in such places?" "Many of them," rejoined Murray, "and if the order goes out, you will be attacking the men who were your best supporters in the last election and who put you in the mayor's chair." "Well, that is a revelation," said Hewitt, sarcastically. "But it makes no difference who the interested men are. The places have got to be closed."

He also inquired as to the amount of graft. "What are *you* worth, Murray?" he demanded. Murray, a New Yorker by birth, had been a private in the Civil War and had joined the police in 1866; a rough, ignorant, hard-hitting fellow, he had never held a better-paid office than inspector at $3500 a year until he was made Superintendent shortly before Hewitt came in. But he admitted that he was now worth $300,000. "Did you ever have any business but that of policeman and police captain?" Murray admitted that he never had. "How about the captains?—do many make fortunes?" Murray thought that most of them did. "You can understand," he explained, "that as long as this condition of things goes on, there are plenty of opportunities." "Well," concluded the mayor, "you have told me frankly the state of affairs. All I ask is that from this day you do your duty. If you are worth $300,000 you can afford to be honest."

Hewitt also called in the president of the Police Board, Stephen B. French, who had been a Commissioner since 1879. He was a man with an adventurous past; he had served on a whaler, dug gold in California, and after the war combined politics and mercantile pursuits in New York. It was impossible to try police officers for neglect of duty until he had approved the charges against them. He and one or two of the other Commissioners were frequently accused of making a very good thing out of the appointments they controlled. When Hewitt told French what had passed between him and Murray, and declared that he expected the Police Board to help suppress the dives, he received a very grudging consent. The Commissioner thought he could deter the mayor by telling him that he was stirring up a hornet's nest, and ruining all his chances for reëlection. He was good enough to add, no doubt jocularly, that if the system of political protection were left undisturbed the mayor could get his share of its benefits—that is, "a portion from each one of the appointments."[1] But he left the house ready to act.

The police at once began to suppress the worst dives. By the beginning of March Hewitt, his health recovered, was in City Hall and pushing his disinfection with energy. "We have made a good beginning in closing the disreputable resorts," he announced. "It will be followed up. The law must be obeyed, no matter whom it hits or who is behind these resorts."[2] He had hired a private detective to explore the underworld. When, in response to his demand that the Police Department furnish him a list of all the disreputable resorts, Murray sent in a brief roster, he returned it with copious additions, and sent a copy of the whole to the press. "I am informed," he wrote ten days later, "that there are many places in which theatrical performances, accompanied by the sale of liquor, are carried on without license. Among the illegal places of resort are the following"—and he gave another long set of addresses. His first additions to the police list comprised addresses of gaminghouses, fences, green-goods swindlers, roulette houses, panel houses, and the like. The second list included unlicensed concert-saloons and cheap burlesque halls. Both constituted a direct challenge to Superintendent Murray and the police captains. They had been trying to hoodwink the mayor, and in a letter accompanying the second list Hewitt remarked with an ominous suavity:[3]

[1] Wheeler, *Sixty Years*, 335.
[2] N. Y. *World, Times*, March 5, 1887.
[3] N. Y. *World*, March 24, 1887.

These places I do not find upon any list which has been sent to me by the Superintendent of Police. Hence I conclude that they have not been reported to him by the captains of the police districts in which they are situated. If I am correct in that assumption it indicates a want of knowledge on the part of the police authorities, which is possessed by citizens who choose to use ordinary observation in regard to the disreputable places of resort, commonly called dives, kept open in this city. I respectfully request you will cause an examination to be made . . .

When police captains denied the existence of some of the places mentioned,[1] the mayor furnished specific information; for example, he identified a Bowery resort where an obscene dance was performed nightly, and asked why Captain Allaire had ignored it.

With surprising rapidity, the illegal and vicious resorts were closed or at least went into hiding. Police Commissioner John R. Voorhis and President Beekman of the Board of Aldermen inspected the worst districts late in April, and found a marked improvement. "The city is being attended to by the police," they stated. Newspapermen found curious changes. One of the worst resorts of thugs and gamblers, Harry Hill's saloon, had become a dairy restaurant; the "Plymouth" at 27 Bowery, a meeting-place for prostitutes and yeggs, had been turned into a shooting-gallery; and all the notorious dives in the Bowery-Chatham Street region were being transformed or closed.[2] Encouraged by the mayor's activity, churches, newspapers, and civic organizations began to attack their pet antipathies in the underworld. The *Times* and *Tribune* charged the police with failure to enforce the Ives' Pool Law, and supplied the names and addresses of pool-halls where gambling went on unchecked. Hewitt ordered the Police Commission to keep these places closed "as tight as a drum," and this was done. The most notorious poolroom, De Lacy's at 33 Park Row, after taking legal advice, went out of business.[3] Panhandlers and other types of swindlers, long denounced by the *World*, trod more warily or went elsewhere. The redoubtable Anthony Comstock took up afresh his campaign against pornographic literature, photographs, and exhibitions, and the mayor supported him. New York in six months

[1] Ibid., March 31, 1887.
[2] New York newspapers, April, May, 1887.
[3] N. Y. *World*, June 2, 1887.

became a cleaner, brighter, more decent city, and remained so throughout Hewitt's term.

"A public officer who has put his hand to the plow cannot go back," said Hewitt.[1] He knew well that virtue in any great city acts spasmodically, but he hoped that the particular spasm which he directed would have some lasting effects. If anything permanent were to be accomplished, the more corrupt police captains must be ousted. He wished to make examples of the two most conspicuously unfit men, Captains Anthony J. Allaire and Alexander Williams. Four years earlier a grand jury presentment (May, 1883) had charged them with protecting gambling dens in their precincts. Three months earlier Anthony Comstock had sent Williams the names of saloons where roulette and faro games were running and had called on him to close them, but without result. After Hewitt's election the pair evinced a sudden zeal in law-enforcement, and Williams in particular began to deal harshly with houses of prostitution in Thirty-first Street.[2] But the mayor collected evidence and had formal charges filed against them. Early in July they were tried before the Police Commission, but, as everyone expected, were acquitted. The mayor could not remove them—he could not even threaten Superintendent Murray with removal, for the governor had to concur and everyone knew that Governor Hill would not; and all the elements of future corruption remained in the police force.

One law in particular was broken flagrantly, universally, and constantly all over the city—the Sunday closing law for saloons. Like Roosevelt when the latter became a Police Commissioner, Hewitt felt that he could not wink at this violation. All his life he detested the saloon. As he frequently said, it was the chief source of poverty and crime. The city's crowded prisons, its overcrowded hospitals, its charitable institutions, were kept filled by the excessive use of intoxicants.[3] Yet he never believed in prohibition. At this very time a vigorous debate was raging between the advocates of high-license for saloons and the advocates of total prohibition, and he emphatically sided with the former. He wrote a great meeting of high-license men, who were organizing under Dr. Howard Crosby

[1] N. Y. *World*, May 3, 1887.
[2] N. Y. *World*, June 10, 1887, reviews this subject.
[3] See his statement in N. Y. *World*, January 8, 1887.

for new State laws, that the available evidence was all in favor of their contentions. Nevertheless, he was determined that something should be done about the open and corrupting disobedience of the Sunday-closing law. The two alternatives were strict enforcement of the existing statute followed by a popular revolt, or modification of the statute; and he heartily favored the latter.

"In view of the fact," he wrote the high license meeting in February, 1887,[1] "that a very large portion of our population come from countries in which the Sabbath afternoon is used for recreation as well as rest, and that the privilege of taking light refreshment in social gatherings is rarely abused by them, it would, in my judgment, contribute very much to the ease with which we could prevent violations of the law if this concession to the habits and wishes of a portion of our people could be made. With this obstacle out of the way, I believe that the evils of the Sunday traffic in strong drinks could be altogether abated." He had a bill embodying this concession introduced at Albany by Assemblyman L. A. Giegerich, and when the prohibitionists attacked it, he sent Giegerich an unanswerable argument.[2]

He had found the Sunday-closing law unenforced, he wrote. The Police Department had told him that it was unenforceable; others had told him that even partial enforcement would require a far larger body of patrolmen. New York's foreign-born citizens would rise in angry opposition. What remedy was available save a milder law? "This bill does not provide for opening the saloons on Sundays. On the contrary, they will all remain closed, as they now ought to be but are not, under the terms of the law. . . . Special licenses will be granted to a moderate number of reputable places of entertainment where beer and light wines may be procured." The proposed measure, he concluded, was in the true interests of temperance reform.

But when it became evident that the fanatical prohibitionists, led by the Manhattan Temperance Association, would not permit the bill to pass, he felt that his course was clear. He would attempt a rigorous execution of the law and let the resulting storm show the utter impossibility of enforcement. The result might be saner legislation.

[1] N. Y. *World, Times,* February 26, 1887.
[2] See letter to Giegerich, *World, Times,* March 24, 1887.

To the public he announced that he would carry out the law to the limit; "it may drive a good many of us into political retirement, but we shall do our duty." He warned the police[1] that they would be held strictly accountable for further violations, and they at once took the war-path. On April 10 hundreds of timid saloon-keepers closed their places, but hundreds more admitted customers by side-doors, even while policemen stood in front of the building. That day 107 saloon-keepers were arrested.[2] The German-Americans, Irish-Americans, and Italian-Americans were loud in complaint. The firm of Koster & Biel's managed a big saloon-restaurant in Twenty-third Street which had become a notorious rendezvous for prostitutes. When the mayor served notice on them to obey the law, they showed defiance. They were owned by big brewery interests, and they reminded Hewitt how much the brewers had contributed to his campaign fund. But he made them toe the mark with celerity. On April 17 some 150 additional saloon-keepers were arrested, while the police reached into precincts never before invaded—the best hotels. Even claret in a teacup was forbidden.

A howl of protest went up from owners and patrons of the exclusive hostelries of the city—Delmonico's, the Hoffman House, the Brunswick, the St. James, the Sinclair, and others. "The excise law of New York," wrote Godkin,[3] "which prohibits even the serving of liquor by hotel proprietors to their guests on Sunday, had not been enforced in this city for a great many years, until last Sunday. . . . It is the almost universal expectation that Mayor Hewitt's enforcement of the law will cause its modification, at least so as to make the serving of liquor at hotels lawful." The mayor and police, fortified by an opinion on hotel liquor from the Corporation Counsel, were obviously determined to make the law as irritating to everybody as possible.

The result was precisely what Hewitt had anticipated. Organized protests grew swiftly to impressive proportions. The Bohemians held a meeting, and the Irish another. Representatives of seventy-six German singing societies gathered in Arion Hall on May 1 to discuss the situation and ask for a reconsideration of the law. On the first Sunday in May temperance enthusiasts were treated to

---

[1] His orders to Commissioner French are in the *World*, April 5, 1884.
[2] N. Y. *Times, Tribune*, April 11, 18, 1887.
[3] *Nation*, May 12, 1887.

the sight of throngs filling the ferries to Brooklyn and New Jersey, and coming home in joyous inebriety.[1] The press assailed the statute which virtuous rural statesmen had fastened upon the city. Hotel managers appealed to their Assemblymen, and the Hotel Men's Association, meeting at the Ashland House, sent a committee of five to ask the mayor if his enforcement could not be relaxed.

In response to this uproar the legislature yielded. When foreign-born citizens held a meeting at Cooper Union on May 5 to demand beer with their Sunday entertainment, a suitable measure had already been introduced. "I have asked the legislature," Hewitt announced the day before,[2] "to change the law so that beer may be sold in respectable places where music is performed. I see no harm in that." This bill—the Cantor-Giegerich Bill—immediately passed, and was signed by Governor Hill on May 11. It vested in the mayor the power of licensing concert saloons or beer-gardens, and Hewitt at once gave notice that he would issue permits only to applicants of good character. When a leader of the County Democracy, James McCartney, requested a license for "The" Allen, who was running a place of dubious repute at Oak Point, Hewitt lost his temper. "No, sir," he rapped out,[3] "and I'm astonished that you should ask a license for such a man. No such person can get a license in this office." He kept a vigilant eye upon beer-halls and beer-gardens, and was quick to revoke licenses for cause. He ordered all such places to close not later than midnight, and refused to listen to the Aldermen when they pleaded for longer hours.

As for the hotels, he suggested an appeal to the courts. "I cannot give you any permission to go on and violate the law," he told a plaintive delegation of managers, "but I will give you every facility to make a test case." On June 11, by pre-arranged plan, the owners of the Gilsey House and the Fifth Avenue Hotel were arrested for selling liquor on Sunday. The lower court held that their licenses did not permit the serving of liquor in any form on that day or on election day. They at once appealed, and on June 24 the Supreme Court reversed the decision, holding that while hotels must not open their bars on Sundays they might serve liquor to their guests with meals. Corporation Counsel Lacombe planned

---

[1] N. Y. *World, Times,* May 2, 1887.
[2] Ibid., May 5, 1887.
[3] N. Y. *World,* May 24, 1887.

to carry the question to the Court of Appeals, but he left office before doing so and the hotels remained victorious.[1]

If Hewitt had possessed the power, he would have reorganized the Police Department altogether. Mayor Grace's frequent statement that a divided executive authority was "executive office paralyzed" was true of most city departments, but truest of all of the police.[2] There should have been but one head, easily removable by the mayor on charges. "The police is essentially a military organization," remarked Hewitt. "Divided counsels in its management can only be injurious." What would London have thought of putting its force under four heads, stamped by the law itself as partisans, and all practically non-removable? In practise there was some apportionment of duties; one Commissioner looked after discipline, one after supplies and repairs, and one after police pensions. But each man thought himself empowered to give orders to the Superintendent, conflicts of authority were frequent, and nobody was fully responsible for the work of the department.

Equally deplorable was the condition into which the police courts had fallen. The city had eleven police magistrates, mostly Dogberries, who presided over these courts and (in panels of three) over the court of Special Sessions. They had made a record of scandalous delinquency and neglect. More courts were sadly needed, for even efficient and honest officers would have found the burden excessive. When Hewitt took office some six thousand unprosecuted cases of alleged offenders out on bail had piled up, many of them two or three years old. The district attorneys and magistrates were so occupied with unbailable cases, in fact, as to have little time for bailable felonies and misdemeanors. A criminal court for the special trial of excise cases was particularly needed. But the worst evils sprang from the bad character of the magistrates. A majority of them were ignorant politicians, subservient to the bosses of Tammany and the other machines, and anxious to give no offence to the saloon-keepers who furnished votes and money. They were usually blundering and prejudiced, and several were corrupt. When accused men had a pull, the plainest evidence of assault, larceny, prostitution, or disorderly conduct was ignored; flagrant offenders

[1] N. Y. *World, Times,* June 12, 25, 26, 1887.
[2] See Citizens Union Campaign Book, 1897, for material on defects of the government, 495ff.

who "knew" somebody were dismissed unpunished. The magistrates often atoned for this favoritism by fits of gross brutality to those who had no protectors.[1] One or two were more than suspected of conniving at blackmail by the police.

Hewitt not only joined the Grand Jury in recommending a special court for excise cases, but tried to teach the magistrates their duty. In June, 1887, he wrote Magistrate Murray, one of those most noted for subservience to politicians, bluster, and uneven justice, in sharp terms.[2] Why, he asked, had Murray failed, after receiving clear evidence that a Democratic politician named Patterson had violated the Sunday-closing law and had rented the upper part of his saloon-building to prostitutes, to convict the man? The mayor had called Patterson before him, and the saloonkeeper had admitted his guilt. "There is no doubt that the law has been shamelessly and openly violated by Patterson. You seem to regard the evidence as insufficient. I shall feel it my duty to exercise the most careful supervision over this saloon, and I trust that you will do your part, when complaints are made, to secure the punishment due to this offence." Everybody knew that it was an instance of political protection, but Murray tried to brazen it out. Writing that he had not been convinced of Patterson's guilt, he impudently added: "If he admitted it to you, as a good citizen you were bound to bring it to the attention of the proper authorities not by letters in newspapers, but by testimony in court."

This insolence aroused the mayor's anger. "I am much obliged to you," he replied,[3] "for informing me as to my duty as a good citizen. I have endeavored to perform it by conveying information which I received from Patterson to the police authorities, but when you gave me this advice you knew that you had already discharged Patterson prior to his interview with me. If he should again be arrested and appear before you, I shall be found quite ready to give such evidence as I possess. If you had been as anxious to get at the truth of the case as you have been to suppress it, neither of these parties would have been discharged. . . . I advise you to get at the truth, the whole truth, and nothing but the truth."

The police magistrates continued to turn loose men who were

[1] *Harper's Magazine*, March, 1887.
[2] N. Y. *World, Times*, June 9, 1887.
[3] N. Y. *World, Times*, June 10, 1887.

plainly guilty, but who had powerful friends, or who, as saloon-keepers, controlled votes. Again and again Hewitt expressed his resentment, but he was helpless. Early in 1888 he told reporters[1] that he had a list of fourteen prisoners who, after being sentenced to a month in jail apiece, had all been discharged by one police magistrate within five days after sentence was passed. "These discharges were made to oblige politicians, friends of the prisoners. What sort of justice is that?" In his message to the Board of Aldermen in January, 1888, he referred to the hundreds of cases dismissed with no real hearing. "I know no language in which to express the feeling of indignation which the dismissal of these cases has excited in my mind. The remedy is to be found in the appointment of justices trained in the law, of considerable repute in the profession, and divorced as far as possible from contact with party politicians." He recommended[2] that the law be changed so that no one could be appointed until he had served at least ten years at the bar, and nobody given the oath of office until a majority of the Supreme Court justices in the metropolitan district had certified that his standing was good, and that he was competent to fill the office. Till the end of his term he constantly tried to excite public concern on the subject, and with some success.

Hewitt made a stand, in fact, against crooked and incompetent officials all along the line. When he took office the Health Department was demoralized. Its head, a war veteran named Shaler, had shown inefficiency, subserviency to politicians, and downright corruption; and Mayor Grace had removed him in the summer of 1886. But, for political reasons, Governor Hill failed to acquiesce, and he was still holding over. The new Mayor remonstrated so vigorously that Hill completed the removal early in March. Hewitt then surprised politicians by appointing an experienced engineer, who had never been in politics and never held office, but was editor of the *Iron Age* and the *Metal Worker*, and had written much on sanitation. This new official at once ordered the bureau heads to prepare reports on the work they were doing, and to submit plans for improvements. He notified medical employees that their whole time was required—that "the Health Department was not organized for the purpose of increasing the income of physicians while build-

---

[1] N. Y. *Evening Post*, January 18, 1888.
[2] Mayor's Annual Message, January, 1888.

ing up their practise, and where private interests conflict with the public service the alternatives presented are resignation or removal for neglect of duty."[1] The department was soon doing twice its old work.

Another notoriously unfit officer was J. J. O'Brien, chief of the Bureau of Elections—a Republican district leader, who had often been denounced by the press. After the election of 1886 his own party had investigated his conduct and condemned him for improper practises. He was a subordinate of the Police Department, and his three-year term expired on August 13, 1887. On the first of that month Hewitt issued an order bringing his office into the classified civil service. O'Brien, knowing that he could not risk the competitive examination, defiantly asserted that as an elective officer he was exempt from civil service rules. "I am beyond the reach of the mayor," he snorted to reporters. "Not even his most devoted friends," said the *Nation*,[2] "pretend that he could pass an examination for the place. His own party will no longer trust him with its campaign funds, yet it asks to have the city trust him with its election returns." The day O'Brien's term expired, the Corporation Counsel warned the Police Commission that the offce must be opened to competition under Mayor Hewitt's orders. An examination was duly held by the Civil Service Board, the three topmost names were sent to the Commission, and they were requested to choose one. They refused. O'Brien was still in office as a holdover. and they meant to keep him there. Then, in his second annual message, Hewitt called attention to their dereliction with characteristic tartness.

"They have failed to obey the law," he wrote,[3] "and there is no power which can compel them to obedience. Meanwhile, the holder of this important office has been the subject of investigation by his own party. . . . We are presented with the spectacle of an officer charged with supervising the elections, who has been guilty of conducting an election in a manner so reprehensible as to call down upon him the condemnation of his own political associates. How long the self-respect of the Police Board will allow this scandal to continue I cannot predict, but it is sufficient reason why

[1] N. Y. *World*, March 31, 1887.
[2] *Nation*, August 11, 1887.
[3] January, 1887.

there should be a change in the constitution of the Commission which allows it to exist."

Early in his term Hewitt called the ambulance service to account. On the morning of June 8, 1887, a house-painter fell off a roof at Lexington Avenue and Twenty-second Street, just across from the mayor's house. Mrs. Hewitt saw the accident. The mayor ran across and found the man unconscious on the sidewalk with a young doctor attending him. A policeman telephoned the New York Hospital for an ambulance, but was told that the accident was out of their territory. The mayor then commandeered a wagon, had servants put a mattress in it, and hurried the painter to the hospital. Later the Bellevue authorities said that they would have sent an ambulance if the mayor had turned in a hurry call. "Maybe I was stupid," said Hewitt, "anyhow no one seemed to know about hurry calls; I know I was doing all the hurrying." The painter died soon after reaching the hospital, and the mayor wrote an indignant letter to President Simmons of the Department of Charities and Correction, saying that nobody who had witnessed the poor fellow's sufferings could forget the inhumanity of his treatment. His statements to the press were scorching. The coroner's jury censured the poor ambulance service, and improvements duly followed.

Meanwhile, the mayor had turned to the condition of the streets. Though no longer foot-deep in many places with encrusted dirt, as they had been in the sixties, they were bad enough. Hewitt agreed with the *World* that they were dirtier than the streets of any other civilized metropolis on the globe. "There is no other city in the world," he burst out,[1] "which presents such a spectacle as is to be found every day in the main thoroughfare of this city, encumbered as they are by ash-barrels, vessels containing garbage, and obstructions of almost every kind." To be sure, the annual appropriation for street cleaning, a million dollars, was inadequate. But, in addition, the departmental methods were poor. The hours for collecting ashes and garbage on the main thoroughfares, even Fifth Avenue, were eight to ten in the morning, when they were crowded with well-dressed people.

"I observe," Hewitt wrote Commissioner Coleman on March 23, 1887,[2] "that the ash-barrel nuisance is being intensified. The high

[1] Quoted in *Nation*, March 31, 1887.
[2] N. Y. *World*, March 24, 1887.

winds which prevail at this season of the year carry the fine ashes into the faces of passers-by, and the time selected for emptying these barrels is most inopportune. I respectfully request that you will explain to me, in writing, the necessity for carrying on this work in the middle of the day, and in the irregular manner in which it appears to be done." Of course there was no such necessity. Commissioner Coleman responded by trying the removal of ashes and garbage between midnight and seven in the morning, and found the new plan excellent. The mayor praised it a few weeks later. "I have taken particular pains to investigate the matter, and I find that the system is a success."

The critical-minded mayor also took up the needless obstruction of traffic by wagons left in the streets all night long. Numerous teamsters from Brooklyn and New Jersey were in the habit at nightfall, when they went home, of leaving their drays and carts in the side-streets of Manhattan and thus paying toll only on their horses. It was in such wagons that penniless Joseph Pulitzer had slept when he first came to New York. Hewitt, remarking that it was illegal to use the streets for storage, directed the Bureau of Encumbrances to impound wagons which thus became a nuisance. By the middle of May no fewer than five hundred vehicles had thus been temporarily seized. The teamsters mended their ways—though, as the mayor later wrote, the police remained slow to realize that the streets were not properly a place of deposit for waste materials, shop-goods, and carts, or a place for carrying on business. At the same time Hewitt occasioned some amusement by forbidding street-organists to carry monkeys about the thoroughfares.

The next object of his indignation was the street-car companies, and the immediate provocation was their practise of covering their tracks with sand. In a sharp letter on April 22 he called this "an intolerable evil." It was the real source of many of the complaints against the Street-Cleaning Department, he said, and "in windy weather fills the eyes and nostrils of passers-by with powdered sand and clouds the air with dust." At his instance, an ordinance on the subject was introduced in the Board of Aldermen. The traction companies protested that sand was needed to keep the horses from slipping. "The trouble is," Hewitt bitingly replied,[1] "that the railroad companies try to make one horse do the work of two, but I

[1] N. Y. *World*, May 24, 1887.

am determined that the streets shall not be made dirty to accom-
modate the street-railway companies, if I can prevent it." They
should roughen the pavement between the tracks for the horses, he
added. "You are making money enough. Your roads are bonded
for five times their value, and yet you make 20 per cent a year;
but you shall not defile the streets while I am mayor." The companies, however, adroitly enlisted Henry Bergh and the Society
for the Prevention of Cruelty to Animals, talked eloquently of
crippled horses, and in the end defeated any aldermanic action.[1]

The high rails used by the traction companies, designed by
Hewitt himself many years earlier and rolled in part at the Trenton
mills, had now become antiquated. Better models, flush with the
pavement, were being made in Europe, and the mayor obtained
one from Paris. He pointed out that the jutting rails in use im-
peded traffic and made mechanical street-cleaning difficult, while
it was impossible to replace worn-out rails without much destruction of the pavement. In the spring of 1888 he had a bill introduced at Albany to prohibit the laying of any more of the old
rails, but it encountered stubborn opposition from the companies.
They demanded compensation for even a gradual change. Hewitt
made an indignant speech to representatives of the Chamber of
Commerce, the street railways, and the Truckmen's Association
who appeared before him.[2] "After the city has granted the railroads the most valuable of franchises, for which no adequate or
just return is made," he said, "the plea for compensation for an
improved change in their rails is too much. I will guarantee that
any road in the city can substitute an improved rail for those now
in use and then pay ten per cent upon its stock. The condition of
our streets resulting from the abominable manner in which the
car companies break up the pavements and then lay the high centre-
bearing rails is disgraceful. . . . At least nine-tenths of the grievances are due to the high centre-bearing rail, and arise from not
keeping the pavement clean." He was not advocating any particular make of rail, he added, but simply a new type.

But the legislature failed to pass the bill, and the traction officials would not act. Till near the close of Hewitt's administration
nothing was done. Then the Harlem Railroad, controlled by the

[1] N. Y. *Evening Post*, December 31, 1888.
[2] N. Y. *World*, February 15, 1888.

William H. Vanderbilt Estate, asked permission to replace its horse-cars on Fourth Avenue with electric cars, and the mayor seized the opportunity to exact a promise that the old rails would be replaced with new ones of better design. The substitution of electrical power for horses would in itself, he believed, do away with much of the filth that had accumulated between and beside the rails.[1]

Still another corporate imposition had meanwhile felt the mayor's lash. The rapid growth of the city northward and the progress of invention had led to a constant tearing-up of the streets by electrical, gas, and steam-heating companies. In the fall of 1887 Hewitt complained to Commissioner Coleman.[2] "Notwithstanding the efforts you have made to keep the streets clean, I think I have never seen them in a worse condition than they are in at present. This is due to the innumerable excavations going on in every part of the city, not only covering the streets with dirt, but leaving an accumulation from the trenches when they are repaved." Was no remedy available? He asked for an inspection and a detailed report, that the Department of Public Works might enforce the law. When a steam-heating company ripped up Broadway in six different places at once, with a copious litter in every spot, he was thoroughly annoyed. "That must not happen again," he told the manager,[3] "and if there is any law in this community to stay it, I will see that it is stopped." The Board of Trade supported him, calling upon the legislature to take some action.[4] After Hewitt's first months as mayor, the public service corporations showed more caution in their excavations.

For shams of every kind the mayor had a healthy intolerance. One of these shams was the pretence that heavy taxes could be levied upon the personal property of all wealthy New Yorkers. Early in his term formal charges of negligence and dereliction were brought by the vice-president of the Taxpayers' Central Association against two tax commissioners. They were accused, specifically, of failing to levy assessments on personal property worth fifty million dollars, and of undervaluing various street-railway properties and other possessions of the estate of William H. Vander-

[1] N. Y. *Evening Post*, December 31, 1888.
[2] N. Y. *World*, September 22, 1887.
[3] N. Y. *World*, September 23, 1887.
[4] N. Y. *World*, October 13, 1887.

bilt and of the New York Central. This complaint obviously represented an effort by the large realty interests of the city to lighten
their own tax-burden. As Hewitt knew, fiscal experts found much
fault with the whole theory and practise of personal property assessments; they were constantly being evaded, and they produced
the grossest inequalities. For thirty years, while favoring an income
tax, he had held that all personal property except bank shares
ought to be tax-exempt, and he believed now that it would not be
necessary to add more than one-sixth to the realty taxes to compensate for the loss. This doctrine approached so close to that of
the single-taxers that once, when the mayor gave utterance to it,
Henry George uttered the gleeful comment that he had "become
one of us"; to which Hewitt replied that he had held these views
for almost a generation, and had obtained some of them from his
study of Malthus.[1]

The moment the attack on the tax commissioners began, Hewitt
announced that he disapproved of any sudden, formidable, and
greedy drive to collect on every penny of personal property; for it
would encounter fierce legal opposition, and if pressed too far,
would drive capital from the city.[2] Moreover, he did not believe
that the commissioners had been unduly negligent. Being a large
holder of realty himself, and having little personal property, he
would obviously suffer as much as anyone from restricted collections
on personalty; nor could he be accused of regarding his friends'
interests. The Corporation Counsel on May 2, 1887, advised him
that there was no real case against the commissioners. Nothing in
the law required them to assess the stock of street railways at its
market quotations, while they had apparently followed a just and
sensible course in dealing with the Vanderbilt Estate.[3] It was true
that the personalty in this estate, really worth perhaps $40,000,000,
had been assessed at only $8,000,000; but it was also true that the
executors and trustees had threatened that if the assessment were
raised, they would take themselves and their holdings completely
out of reach by a change of residence. The vice-president of the
Taxpayers' Central Association still professed to be dissatisfied. But

[1] See N. Y. *World*, January 11-13, 1888, for the discussion between Hewitt and
George.
[2] N. Y. *World*, April 30, 1887.
[3] N. Y. *World*, May 4, 1887.

no one came to his assistance, and after Hewitt had asked the two tax commissioners for written explanations, the case rested as it stood. A full reform of the State and city tax system was as yet impossible for anybody to accomplish.

Hewitt exhibited the same independence in his appointments. In general, Tammany fared ill at his hands, and the County Democracy fared well, but simply because the latter had the best personnel. Petty grafting having been proved in the Dock Department, he let the Tammany Commissioner go when his term expired, and named a business man belonging to the County Democracy, Charles W. Marshall, in his stead. On the same day, May 9, 1887, he named three other County Democrats and one Independent Democrat to important commissionerships.[1] He remarked that he had "endeavored to look solely to the interests of the city without regard to political divisions; but I have not considered it to be to the disadvantage of a Democrat that he has been recommended by the organization whose nominee the mayor was in the late election." Yet he reappointed an efficient Tammany man, Coleman, as Street-Cleaning Commissioner, though the County Democracy opposed it. He also did a favor to Richard Croker, whom he knew to possess brains and energy. Croker's term as a Fire Commissioner having only two more years to run, Hewitt in May, 1887, renominated him in place of Edward Smith, an outgoing County Democrat, to serve the full six-year term. This astonished his reform friends, but the *World* admitted that Croker was well qualified.

In all these labors for reform Hewitt knew what a terrific dead weight of inertia and indifference he was pushing against. He knew well that when he tried to reform the police, critics would say he was attempting the impossible; that when he tried to abolish dirt, litter, and slovenliness, they would say he was dealing with trifles. It was, indeed, impossible to get rid of graft and corruption when they were entrenched behind the abominable charter which the legislature had fastened upon the city. To issue orders upon street excavations and organ-grinders' monkeys might indeed seem to be taking trifles seriously. Yet the mayor, with all his nervous hurry, his sleepless vigilance, his peppery outbursts, had one underlying purpose in mind. He meant to set up a standard of vigilance by which future mayors could be measured; he meant to show that

[1] On these appointments see N. Y. *World, Times,* May 10, 11, June 11, 1887.

an efficient public officer was one who fought all along the line, who was good-natured about nothing, who was dead in earnest about everything; he meant, in short, to set an example that the city would not forget.

Often he amused the city by the brusque informality of his acts. When he inspected the city hospital for insane women on Blackwell's Island he lay down on a cot to try it, remarking as he rose: "Well, I suppose I could get used to it."[1] When a Staten Island ferry company forced its passengers to travel one Sunday in company with six elephants and a dromedary, he sent it a pungent letter of rebuke. Once he returned from New Jersey in a pouring rain, and contrary to his custom, took a cab from the slip to his house. "How much?" he asked the driver, who did not recognize him. "Five dollars," was the reply. "What!" exclaimed the mayor. "You heard me—five dollars!" repeated the man insolently. "Here it is," said Hewitt, "and you will report to me at the mayor's office at nine o'clock tomorrow." The startled driver looked up, saw the two lamps which the city places before the mayor's house, glanced at Hewitt sharply, whipped his horse, and drove off without waiting for a cent.[2] Not infrequently a workingman in overalls was seen stating his grievances to the mayor, who always showed keen concern. At that time fraudulent employment agencies were numerous. Whenever a poor man or woman complained of being victimized the mayor called policemen, made them make an investigation, and if necessary himself revoked the license. Once a young man reported that he had been swindled by William Gay & Company of 27 Warren Street, self-styled publishers who advertised for book salesmen and took "deposits" for applicants. Hewitt sent a patrolman for Gay, and when he appeared jerked out: "I know you and all about you. You are a swindler. I shall have an officer stationed in front of your premises with instructions to refer all inquirers to the mayor's office hereafter. Pay that man his money." And Gay paid it.[3]

"No other mayor," said the *World* when he had been in office for six months, "has ever introduced so many important reforms in so short a time. His fight against the dives and in favor of

---

[1] N. Y. *World*, December 18, 1887.
[2] Mr. Erskine Hewitt to author, February 3, 1933.
[3] N. Y. *World*, February 12, 1888.

clean streets, his constant surveillance over the heads of departments, and his efforts to secure good and defeat bad legislation at Albany, are all well known." And Godkin also wrote: "We doubt if the people of this city realize fully the importance of the experiment which Mayor Hewitt is making in City Hall. He is trying with great sagacity and pluck to give us local government conducted upon sound principles."[1]

[1] N. Y. *World*, July 3, 1887, *Nation*, June 23, 1887.

CHAPTER XXV

Parks, Electricity, and Subways

B Y THE middle eighties the new electrical age showed a re-
fulgent dawn in our largest American cities. Edison, establishing in 1883 his Pearl Street station to distribute current
for incandescent lamps, was soon lighting a large part of downtown
New York. In 1884 an electric trolley was successfully operated by
an open-slot conduit in Cleveland; experiments were shortly being
made in other cities; and by 1887, when Frank J. Sprague completed his thirteen-mile trolley-line with overhead wires in Richmond, Va., everyone knew that electricity was destined to become
one of our principal agencies of transportation. The telephone was
spreading its network throughout urban communities. Every novel
application of electricity in our cities meant some change in their
general economy, some fresh problem to be solved, some entrenched
interest to be cleared out of the way; and Hewitt became mayor
just when these readjustments were most pressing.

It was evident, to begin with, that more and more of New
York's street lighting must be done by electricity. Gas lamps were
dim, expensive, and troublesome by comparison with either arc or
incandescent lights. Unfortunately, the corrupt Board of Aldermen
had given three electric-lighting corporations, the United States,
the Brush, and the East River Companies, a practical monopoly of
the field.[1] They were allied with powerful politicians, and the
Board blocked all competition by other companies. Hewitt found
that costs might be reduced nearly a third if contracts were honestly
let to the lowest bidder; and early in 1887 he took up the fight
against the "electrical combine."[2] He confronted a division of

[1] See N. Y. *World*, January 7, 8, 1887, for articles on the lighting situation.
[2] N. Y. *World, Times*, May 18, 19, 1887.

authority. Contracts for street lighting were let by a Gas Commission, of which the mayor was head; but the erection of standards and wires was controlled by the Board of Aldermen. Various companies were ready to offer low rates in different sections if assured of the right to string their wires. But when they submitted bids to the Gas Commission embodying this stipulation, the Commission had to reject such bids as beyond its powers.

The obvious way out was suggested by Hewitt. He drafted a resolution declaring that any company which received a contract from the Gas Commission would automatically be empowered to erect the necessary poles and wires. Having done this, on May 17, 1887, he called in Dowling, an East Broadway saloonkeeper who was Aldermanic leader in the arrangement with the "electrical combine," and delivered an ultimatum. "It is your duty to do your part toward getting cheaper lighting for the city and I want you to do it. If you don't vote for this resolution I will know why. I don't propose to let the Aldermen act in the way they have been acting without making my most emphatic protest. I am told that you are the head of this business and I want to tell you what a mistake you are making." Dowling protested that he had a right to his own opinion. "I don't care what your opinions are," retorted the mayor. "It is your duty to pass this resolution, and if you don't do it I will know the reason."[1]

The Board met to take action on May 20. Hewitt had already addressed to them—and the public—an indignant letter which summarized the situation and concluded:

It is now evident that the city can be supplied with electric lights at a cost not greater than that which heretofore has been paid for lighting with gas. The preference of the public for the electric light is pronounced, and the advantages in the prevention of crime, the good order of the city, and the general comfort of the inhabitants is so marked that the Commission feel it their bounden duty to extend the lighting system as far as the means at their command will permit.

This cannot be done without the cooperation of your honorable body in giving the necessary consent. On what principle this should be denied, I cannot see.

For the moment, the aldermen showed their teeth. After two

[1] See the N. Y. *World, Times, Tribune,* May 18-24, 1887, for this controversy.

hours of wrangling, they defeated the mayor's resolution by amending it to impose on the new companies conditions which had never been imposed on the old, and which could not be complied with. Hewitt immediately announced that he would never countenance such discriminatory conditions, and asked the District Attorney to inquire into the relations between the aldermen and the "electrical combine." The press supported him; and, confronted with public hostility and the threat of an awkward investigation, the aldermen gave way. At their next sitting they passed the resolution which Hewitt wished. It thus became possible for a half-dozen new companies—the American, the Waterhouse, the Ball, the Mount Morris, the Harlem, and the North New York—to submit bids. The aldermen also appointed a committee to confer with the Gas Commission upon districting the city in order to facilitate its general illumination by electricity;[1] and to meet the charge of corruption, one member introduced a resolution for an inquiry by the Board itself. This resolution was of course tabled as soon as public indignation abated.[2] But on the essential point the mayor had won a complete victory.

A more spectacular controversy quickly arose over the burial of the unsightly wires which then festooned New York streets like some enormous spider-web. They and the supporting poles were ugly, obstructive, and dangerous. The telephone and telegraph wires carried low voltages, but above them were now being strung electric-light wires, sometimes singly and sometimes in heavy cables, for high-tension currents. Whenever they fell into the streets or across pre-existing wires, to which they transferred their high charges, they became a menace to a score of lives. New York had for some years lagged behind other States and cities in requiring wires to be placed underground. Finally, in 1885, the legislature had created a Board to deal with the problem in the metropolis. It was empowered to build conduits, and to compel electrical companies to use them. At first it was essentially a local body and did good work. But the politicians and their selfish allies in the electrical business had designs on this as on all other agencies of government. A bill was introduced in the spring of 1887 to reorganize the Board, converting it into a State rather than local body,

---

[1] See N. Y. *World*, January 1, 1888, for a review of all this.
[2] N. Y. *World, Times,* June 8, 1887.

under the full control of Governor Hill as to both appointments and removals.

Hewitt and his city "Cabinet" protested;[1] they pointed out that this was a problem which the city could best handle for itself, and that State interference merely created trouble. When the politicians at Albany persisted, they asked that at the very least *ex-officio* places be given the mayor, controller, and commissioner of public works. But the bill, as Governor Hill signed it, created a new Board of Electrical Control of three men appointed by the governor, with only the mayor added in *ex-officio* capacity.[2]

The worst fears of the city were soon realized. Three cheap politicians were reappointed, who showed themselves far more eager to serve the interests of the public-utility corporations than those of the city.[3] In fact, the whole intent of the law was perverted; the work of putting wires underground almost stopped; and by the end of 1888 contracts were actually being carried out for erecting 150 miles of new overhead wires in densely populated areas! The three politicians on the Board held that the whole labor and expense of removing existing poles and wires should be borne by the city, while Hewitt insisted that the companies ought to stand the cost. He also contended that even if the city wished to deal with the problem it had no money available for the purpose. In the resulting deadlock each side accused the other of delaying the removal of the wires by stubborn behavior.

During the latter half of 1887 about 250 miles of electrical ducts were built underground by the Board, acting through the Phoenix Construction Company, and were rented to the corporations.[4] But that fall Hewitt refused to vote for an extension of the conduits until he was assured that existing poles and wires would be removed without expense to the city. He also annoyed the other members of the Board by extending the civil service system to all employees above the grade of laborers.[5] The following spring he came to a complete rupture with them, and on May 10 left a Board meeting with the defiant announcement that he would attend no

[1] N. Y. *World*, April 21, 1887.
[2] Ibid., June 28, 1887.
[3] See editorial review, N. Y. *Evening Post*, Dec. 31, 1888.
[4] *Harper's Weekly*, Dec. 10, 1887.
[5] N. Y. *World*, August 2, 1887.

future sessions.[1] He directed the Corporation Counsel to obtain a
writ of mandamus requiring the companies to take down the wires,
but the Board refused to support any such step. During 1888 the
quarrel waxed acrimonious. A careless linesman was killed, and
when the coroner's jury summoned the mayor to testify, he told it
that the Board was trying "to put the mayor instead of the wires
into a hole."[2] The dispute gave obvious point to his utterances
upon the folly of the continual State interference with city affairs.

Ever since Hewitt had known New York City its most troublesome problem had been rapid transit. Horse-cars had been introduced in 1832 on Fourth Avenue, and had gradually spread to
other thoroughfares. By the close of the Civil War there were a
dozen car-lines, which carried more than sixty million passengers
annually. Their principal competitors were light horse-omnibuses,
which thronged Broadway in particular. These omnibuses charged
passengers ten cents a ride, ran down many pedestrians, were
crowded to bursting at rush hours, and in general might be called
an indispensable nuisance. Two years after the war, plans for an
elevated railroad, drawn by Charles T. Harvey, were approved by
the city and State authorities; construction was soon begun by
private capital; and by 1870 a single-track line had been completed
up Ninth Avenue to Thirtieth Street. After some initial vicissitudes,
the elevated system proved brilliantly successful.[3] Before 1881 the
lines along Ninth and Third Avenues had reached Harlem, while
one on Second Avenue had progressed to Sixty-ninth Street; and
traffic and profits were large. The progress of the elevated roads
was due largely to Cyrus W. Field, who late in the seventies had
used most of his fortune to purchase control of the system, and
whose talents and energy gave a marked stimulus to the whole
undertaking.[4]

But while the elevated lines thus helped enormously in developing upper Manhattan, they furnished only a temporary solution.
By 1886 passenger traffic had again outstripped all means of conveyance. The elevated roads were then carrying a million people
a day, and could hold no more. At rush hours the overcrowded

[1] N. Y. *World*, May 11, 1888.
[2] N. Y. *World*, May 30, June 1, 1888.
[3] J. B. Walker, *Fifty Years of Rapid Transit*, passim.
[4] Walker, *Rapid Transit*, 122.

48. Peter Cooper and Thomas Hughes

49. PETER COOPER

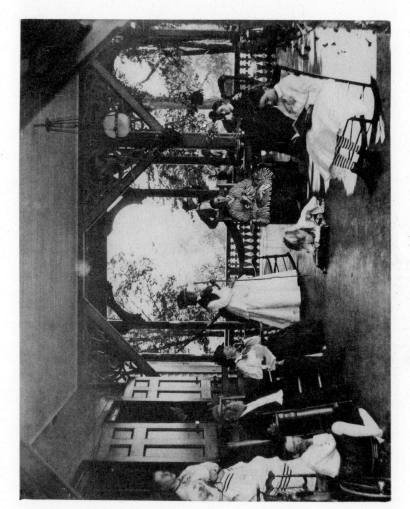

50. Piazza at Ringwood and family group about 1873

51. Sketch by Daniel Huntington of Peter Cooper for his
group picture, The Cable Projectors

53. HENRY GEORGE

52 HEWITT, DRAWN FROM LIFE BY V. GRIBAYEDOFF

NOW LET MAYOR HEWITT PROVE THE POWER OF MAN OVER BEAST.

54. After Hewitt's Election as Mayor, 1886
Nast in Harper's Weekly

55. Brooklyn Bridge after Hewitt's Dedicatory Speech, 1883

56. FELLING THE OVERHEAD WIRES IN UNION SQUARE
W. A. Rogers in Harper's Weekly

trains travelled so slowly that the phrase rapid transit seemed a
jest. Every seat was occupied, every strap was seized, and a triple
row of men and women swayed and stewed in the aisles. The press
declared that the congestion was inhuman and indecent. If Henry
Bergh had the right to stop an overloaded dray in the interest of
the horses, when would somebody gain the right to stop an overloaded train in the interest of the passengers? A multitude of plans
were suggested. "Who," asked the *World*, "will be the Moses to
lead us through this wilderness of uncertainty?"[1]

Additional elevated lines, to be sure, might be built. The Metropolitan Rapid Transit Company, now partly controlled by Jay
Gould, was eager to construct a road above Broadway, and maintained a well-endowed lobby in Albany to battle for a franchise.
Hewitt had always opposed the lax grant of great public franchises
for nothing. At a mass-meeting in Cooper Union in February, 1873,
he had made an address in favor of city-owned rapid transit lines;
and the meeting had adopted resolutions and appointed a Committee of One Hundred to go to Albany and support the requisite
bill—a bill which, of course, failed.[2] Now, as mayor, he hastened to
take up arms against the threatened grab by the Metropolitan
Company. Passage of its franchise bill would give away a right
worth millions, and would ruin the most important street of the
city.[3] If property-owners along Broadway actually yielded to Gould's
proposal, the city ought to receive at least ten per cent of the gross
proceeds of the line in return for the franchise; but he was against
it under any circumstances. He sent the legislature an appeal for
further study of the problem—an appeal which effectually killed
the bill:[4]

> The existing railroads have practically reached the limit of
> their capacity. Besides, though operated with great care and abil-
> ity, they are not in reality satisfactory to any class of the com-
> munity. They do not in effect provide rapid transit, which is the
> chief requirement of that portion of our population who night
> and morning pass from one end of the island to the other. No
> legislation can or will be satisfactory that does not make ade-

[1] N. Y. *World*, January 23, 1887.
[2] Walker, *Rapid Transit*, 126.
[3] N. Y. *World*, April 6, 7, 1887.
[4] N. Y. *World*, April 21, 1887.

quate provision for the rapid growth of our population. . . .
Certainly any new structure should be absolutely free from the
objections developed by that now in operation. The legislature
is in no condition to study and solve this great problem at its
present session . . . We earnestly protest against any action at
this time turning over the main highway of the city to private
ownership.

And ten months later, in a message to the Board of Aldermen,[1]
Hewitt offered his most striking plan for the public welfare—the
plan which fully justifies the subsequent bestowal upon him of the
title of "father of modern rapid transit."[2] His basic proposals were
substantially identical with those incorporated in the Rapid Transit
Act of 1894, under which the city's first subways were finally built.
He suggested that the city should refuse to permit the erection of
any more of the lines; that it should plan its own system of underground transit; that the construction of the system should be done
with city money but by a private corporation; that the same corporation should then lease the road for operation during a limited
term of years, paying for the equipment; and that it should pledge
itself to pay the city not only interest on the bonds issued for construction, but at least one per cent annually for a sinking fund.
At the end of a definite period the city would thus come into possession of a fully equipped subway system, free of any debt. In the
course of his career Hewitt devised many schemes, but none showed
to better advantage his fusion of practicality and imagination, the
hallmark of constructive talent.

"The time has come," he wrote,[3] "when the growth of the city
is seriously retarded by the want of proper means of access to and
from the upper and lower portions of the city. Unless additional
facilities are provided, the population which ought to increase at
the upper end of the city will be driven to Long Island and New
Jersey. Our rate of taxation depends upon the growth of the unoc-
cupied portions of the city, particularly north of the Harlem River.
This year $55,000,000 is added to the assessed values of real estate.
The result is that the rate of taxation will not be materially in-

---

[1] The date of the message was January 29, 1888; see N. Y. *Times, Tribune,
World,* January 30, Feb. 1.
[2] For this title see Walker, *Rapid Transit,* 129.
[3] N. Y. *World, Evening Post,* February 1, 1888.

creased, although the appropriations are nearly $4,000,000 greater than the year before. This increase in value cannot go on unless the upper part of the island is provided with increased facilities of transport. . . . It therefore concerns the citizens as a whole to see that these increased facilities are provided, and it will be proper for the city itself to make the provision, because the citizens as a body will thus get the benefit of the increase in the value of property which these facilities will create."

Any adequate system, he added, must satisfy a number of requirements: Its trains must offer really *rapid* transit, running forty to fifty miles an hour; its rails must be laid on an absolutely solid foundation, which meant either underground or on a solid embankment; it should follow the lines of the city's natural growth; and its facilities should be adequate for not only the present but the early future.

Proceeding to details, he stated that it would be wise to recognize that access to central Manhattan by rail was practically controlled by the New York Central, which owned four tracks from the Harlem River to Forty-second Street, two of them being used for through trains and two for local traffic. He proposed that a bargain be struck with this railroad.

It should be asked to surrender its two local lines for the city's rapid transit needs, to be extended to the tip of the island. At present they were of little use to the railroad.[1] "These two tracks, however, when properly lighted, ventilated, and shut off from the other tracks, would be available for a system of transit which passes under the station and is continued to the City Hall." The city should build its continuation below Forty-second Street station down through the Fourth Avenue tunnel to Thirty-second Street, then along Fourth Avenue to Lafayette Place, and thence in an open cut to City Hall. This continuation would provide four tracks in all, two for local trains and two for expresses; the latter stopping only once between Grand Central and City Hall, and the locals at Grand Street, Bleecker Street, Astor Place, 14th, 23rd, and 33rd.[2] *Above* Forty-second Street there should be two arteries, one for the east side and the other for the west. That is:

[1] The Grand Central station was then too small for the rapidly-growing crowds.

[2] All these are now used for local subway stations.

Two of the tracks [above Forty-second] will then proceed to
Harlem River, and thence passing under the Harlem River will
furnish frequent traffic for the eastern portion of the city and
the annexed district. The other two tracks will turn to the left
under Forty-sixth Street to Broadway, under which they will
pass to Fifty-ninth Street, at which point the boulevard [Central
Park West] is reached. Here four tracks should be laid in an
open cut, extending in time as far as may be desirable.

The execution of this comprehensive plan, it was clear, would
furnish rapid transit to all of upper Manhattan and what is now
The Bronx; would avoid any addition to the unsightly elevated
structures; and would also avoid any marring of Broadway below
46th Street. Nevertheless, the mayor was not sure but that Broadway ought to be touched. The plan would be much simpler if the
West Side tracks, instead of branching to Grand Central, ran
straight down Broadway from Central Park West to the Battery.
This would avoid a detour, and would restrict the East Side line
below Grand Central to two tracks instead of four. Of course all
trackage on Broadway should be kept out of sight and sound in
a subway. Business interests along that great thoroughfare would
not be endangered, and would even stand to gain from the improved accessibility of shops and offices. If a Broadway subway
were combined with a four-track open-cut along Central Park
West, Hewitt wrote, "I shall feel that the very best possible solution of the difficult problem of rapid transit for this city had been
reached."

Hewitt insisted that the subway system should be planned and
owned by the city; but he would have the municipality contract with
the New York Central for its construction, and then lease it to
the Central for operation. At the end of thirty-five years, the annual
rental would have wiped out the entire cost—that is, it and the sinking fund would have amortized the three per cent bonds with
which he expected the city to pay for construction. The road
would then revert to the city, and become a source of revenue "for
all time." To ensure economy, construction should be supervised
by a board comprising the mayor, comptroller, and commissioner
of public works.

As he outlined the whole plan, it seemed both simple and
feasible; yet it naturally provoked a spirited discussion. Members

of the Real Estate Board were enthusiastic, declaring that Hewitt had offered the boldest and most farsighted scheme ever devised for the city's growth.[1] The Chamber of Commerce adopted resolutions of approval.[2] The *World* struck a suspicious note, intimating that he had simply revived an old scheme of Commodore Vanderbilt's "to construct an underground road as a feeder for the Harlem and the Hudson River Railroads."[3] But the mayor quietly explained that he had written his proposal without consulting any officers of the New York Central, while the Central itself took a distinctly chilly attitude. President Chauncey M. Depew told reporters that he would be willing to build the rapid-transit system "under certain conditions," but that he would have to be convinced that it "would pay." Moreover, he objected to a thirty-five-year lease at a rental sufficient to amortize the construction bonds, saying that the city would then own a railroad for which the New York Central had paid. He suggested that his own engineers and the city engineers make separate investigations, and then discuss and develop plans together. On the whole, however, the plan was well received, the press commending it as an admirable basis for constructive discussion.

For a time it also seemed likely to have political support. The County Democracy, meeting in Cooper Union on February 10, endorsed it. President Foster of the Board of Aldermen, a Tammany man, pronounced it excellent, and expressed a hope that the legislature would grant the necessary authority. A Committee of the Chamber of Commerce, under Seth Low, appeared before the Board of Aldermen in its behalf. Late in February even the aldermen endorsed Hewitt's proposals in general terms. Unfortunately, they sent the legislature a draft bill which was full of improper features. It assigned to the Board of Aldermen itself the principal responsibility for constructing the subway, and complete control of it afterwards. Hewitt, with some emphatic words upon the folly of entrusting an elective assembly with the direct expenditure of large sums for public works, pointed out that the bill was unconstitutional, and announced that he would prepare one of his own.[4]

[1] N. Y. *World*, February 2, 1888.
[2] N. Y. *Evening Post*, February 1, 1888.
[3] N. Y. *World*, February 11, 1888.
[4] N. Y. *World*, March 1, 1888.

With the aid of Corporation Counsel Beekman, he immediately did so, and sent it to Albany on March 10. It provided for a Rapid Transit Board consisting of the mayor, comptroller, and commissioner of public works, which was to meet, hold public hearings, draft a plan for a road or series of roads, and determine upon the mode of construction, the equipment, the motive power, and the rates of fare.[1] The Common Council was to have power to suggest amendments, and also the power of final approval or disapproval. The mayor's bill provided that the contractor was to pay an annual rental equal to the bond-interest plus two per cent for amortization. The legislature at once prepared to take up the subject.

At this juncture occurred a dramatic and long-remembered event —the great blizzard of Monday, March 12, 1888. A rainstorm on Sunday turned at twilight into snow, which fell with increasing fierceness during the night. Next morning the air was still thick, howling winds piled the snow into high drifts, and the transportation facilities of the city were almost at a standstill. Horses could not draw their cars a few blocks without exhaustion. Passengers had to be rescued from elevated trains by high ladders. Few and hardy were those who reached downtown New York. By mid-afternoon, with the storm still raging, all business was suspended. The Stock Exchange was closed, the postoffice paralyzed. Electric wires and poles fell, and much of the city was in darkness. That night, with many business men stranded downtown in their offices, the cold grew intense, dropping to five above zero.

Some who struggled homeward through the drifts experienced genuine peril. Roscoe Conkling, most famous of the victims of the storm, set forth from his Wall Street office to his suite in the Hoffman House. Later he described his struggle.[2] "There wasn't a cab or carriage of any kind to be had. Once during the day I had declined an offer to ride uptown in a carriage because the man wanted $50, and I started up Broadway on my pins. It was dark and it was useless to try to pick out a path, so I went magnificently along, shouldering through drifts and headed for the north. I was pretty well exhausted when I got to Union Square, and wiping the snow from my eyes, tried to make out the triangle there. But it was impossible. When I reached the New York Club at 25th Street, I

---

[1] N. Y. *World*, March 17, 1888, gives its provisions.
[2] Quoted in the N. Y. *World*, March 14, 1888.

was covered all over with ice and packed snow, and they would scarcely believe that I had walked from Wall Street. It took three hours to make the journey." A month later he was dead.

The lesson of the storm grinned at the paralyzed town. It was clear that as the city's distances lengthened an underground transit system would become absolutely necessary. As late as Friday no cars were running on Broadway below Fourteenth Street. Hewitt hastened to point out the moral, and he was echoed by the Board of Trade and Transportation, which computed that the loss from the passenger tie-up alone reached several million dollars.[1]

Late in March, after the Board of Aldermen voted its expected condemnation of his bill, Hewitt left for Albany to speak in its behalf. For an hour and a half on March 29 he addressed the Railway Committees of the Senate and Assembly. The metropolis, he said, had exhausted the capacity of its existing transit lines. Its predicament was so serious that as soon as he took office he had begun to study the question. He had finally reached three conclusions. First, the new system should be constructed and owned by the city, to which all profits should eventually come; second, some arrangement should be made to build it without placing a heavy burden upon the taxpayers; and third, while the construction should be a municipal enterprise, the money should not be disbursed by any city official.[2] He added that he had suggested the New York Central as a possible agent for two good reasons: It was a responsible corporation, and it was already in possession of part of the proposed routes. "I do not, unfortunately for myself, own a cent of the stocks or bonds of that company, nor does any member of my family."

His bill, though supported by the Chamber of Commerce, of course failed. With Tammany and the Platt machine both against it, it was never even reported from committee. But its principles had taken hold upon the public mind, and the small seed was destined to grow into a mighty oak. Six years later legislation was passed embodying all its essential principles. Six years later still, construction was under way for a system that was to be publicly owned and that after an initial period of private operation might

[1] N. Y. *World*, March 15, 16, 1888.
[2] N. Y. *Evening Post*, *World*, March 30, 1888.

even be publicly managed.[1] On October 3, 1901, Hewitt received
from the Chamber of Commerce a gold medal commemorating the
initiative and vision which he had displayed in devising a plan for
true rapid transit, and bearing the words: "By his genius benefactor of the city and conservator of the commonwealth." He said
in accepting it that he regarded it as the crowning honor of a long
career, and that his children would treasure it among their most
precious inheritances.[2]

He met hardly greater immediate success in his equally farsighted attempt to establish a system of small parks. His interest
had been awakened in the subject by Joseph Chamberlain's work
of slum-clearance in Birmingham, and by Jacob Riis's eloquent
activities in New York. For several years now this able Danish-
American journalist, a stocky, cheerful, persistent worker whose
blue eyes shone with earnestness and kindliness, had been trying to
let more air and light into the city's slums. In particular, he had
been urging that the noisome, disease-ridden tangle of alleys, pas-
sage-ways, and courts, with 609 congested tenement-houses, called
Mulberry Bend, far down on the East Side, be given drastic treatment. It was an Italian area, full of filth, banditry, and hopeless
poverty, with an infant mortality which reached appalling figures.
In a single block in 1862, a typical year, 155 children under five
years of age had died—a funeral every other day.[3] Riis wished to
transform the section and save hundreds of lives by driving a wide
street through the "bend." He, like Hewitt, also wished to establish
small parks here and there in crowded parts of the town; parks not
for the rich but the poor.

Till Hewitt entered office all the proposals for new streets and
parks had come to nothing. But he took the keenest interest in
Riis's work, and in the recommendations made in 1884 by the first
Tenement House Commission. In the spring of 1887 he had a bill
introduced at Albany authorizing the expenditure of a million dollars annually by the city for additional small parks. "This measure
we regard as one of imperative necessity for the health, comfort,
and decency of our people," he wrote;[4] "as one not merely of hu-

---

[1] See N. Y. *Times*, July 4, 1900, for an article tracing Hewitt's influence on
the new system.
[2] Proceedings, Oct. 3, 1901.
[3] See particularly Jacob Riis's *How the Other Half Lives*, Chs. 5 and 6.
[4] N. Y. *World*, April 21, 1887.

manity but of justice." It passed. Meanwhile he had asked the Health Department to designate the localities in which congestion and infant-mortality were worst,[1] and taken other steps to use the new authority. He ordered the Park Commission to see that seven small parks which had been closed for lack of money were repaired, provided with benches, and opened to the public—Abingdon Square, Jackson Square, and others.[2] Before he left office steps had been taken to establish three entirely new parks; one at the foot of East Eighty-sixth Street, one at Mulberry and Bayard (Columbus Park), and one at Corlear's Hook. With a vigorous beginning thus made, he entertained high hopes that pleasant green squares would shortly appear in all the slum areas. Some years later he wrote Richard Watson Gilder:[3]

In drawing the Act I had in mind what was done in Birmingham, Manchester, and other English cities. It was my idea in the Mulberry Bend Park to erect a building of considerable size, containing baths, laundries, and comfortable sitting rooms warmed properly for the poor people of the neighborhood. My idea was that the bath itself should be free, but a small fee be charged for towels, soap, etc. . . . So, in regard to rapid transit, my main idea was to get these people into purer air, with better surroundings, at a low cost. My trouble was that I did not take the public into my confidence, mainly because I did not wish to pose as a benefactor or philanthropist. I regarded it as my official duty to improve the conditions of urban life. Of course, my term was too brief to permit me to see the fruition, but if I had had the people behind me instead of ignorance, folly, and corruption ahead of me, I might have hoped at least to inaugurate a better state of things than we now witness.

He was eager also to have playgrounds established to keep boys out of mischief. "On the east side of the city there are boys between seventeen and eighteen who amuse themselves by shooting policemen," he said. "I sympathize with the small boy who is driven off the streets by tyrannical policemen." A dozen youngsters wrote him that whenever they tried to play ball in Duane Park the patrolman chased them away. He intervened, procured them a special

[1] N. Y. *Herald*, June 23, 1887.
[2] Hewitt to President Borden, June 22, 1887; Hewitt Papers.
[3] Hewitt to Richard Watson Gilder, January 31, 1895.

permit, and received a grateful letter. "We respect your answer," they wrote, "and are very thankful to you, sir, and we shall be as careful as we possibly can be of the park. Goodbye, James Rennery and chums."[1]

Unfortunately, slum-clearance is costly. The million-dollar appropriation each year was not enough in itself to create even a small park; and though Hewitt expected the fund to be cumulative, his Tammany successors, for selfish reasons, decided that all money not used within a given twelvemonth lapsed to the treasury. A change in the law had to be obtained. The fight was vigorously renewed, till finally in the middle nineties an effective new Act was passed.

"Everything takes just ten years," said Hewitt in 1896, a decade after he had helped secure the Small Parks Act, as he took his seat as chairman of the Advisory Committee on Small Parks under the new law.[2] In his two years as mayor he had not been able to clear the streets of dangerous wires, to obtain the adoption of a rapid-transit plan, or even to open a fair road for the small parks movement. But ten years later the wires were down, the subway plan had been adopted, the small parks were actually being created. He had done something after all.

[1] N. Y. *Herald*, December 8, 9, 1887.
[2] Riis, *The Battle with the Slum*, 287.

CHAPTER XXVI

A Good Man in Sodom

BEFORE Hewitt had been in office a half year, his honesty and fearlessness had of course raised up a host of enemies. Tammany, which he treated with unexpected roughness, began counting the months until it could elect a more tractable mayor, and the politicians in the County Democracy were equally hostile. Every inefficient or corrupt officeholder in City Hall cursed as he saw Hewitt enter its doors. Saloonkeepers, gamblers, and other denizens of the half-world and underworld found no epithet too harsh to apply to him. But he went his own brusque way.

From the outset, behaving precisely as if he had no thought of reelection, he felt little expectation of another term. It was obviously a misfortune that his tenure was only two years instead of four. It was equally unfortunate that no organization then existed which could rally all the independent voters of New York to his support. The County Democracy had degenerated into a semi-corrupt machine interested chiefly in spoils; the Citizens Union, the City Club, the Good Government Clubs, and the idea of Fusion still lay in the womb of the future. With defeat practically certain, Hewitt thought it better to hew to the line of his convictions, to conciliate nobody, to say just what he thought, than to play the game of politics as even reformers must sometimes do.

His blunt, uncompromising temper was sometimes given a harsh edge by his inveterate irritability. He did not mean to be rude or cutting, but he was, and often apologized for it both to individuals and to the general public. "The fact is," he wrote a friend,[1] "I have not had as much sleep as three or four hours per night for the last forty years, and should think myself very well off indeed if I could

[1] To J. W. Bouton, May 2, 1892; Hewitt Papers.

count upon any such average. . . . Looking back, I am surprised
at the amount of suffering which a man can endure without breaking down. The misfortune is that the want of sleep makes people
irritable and impatient, and they are often condemned when they
ought to have sympathy. This I find the severest punishment to
which I have been subjected, but people who suffer from want of
sleep must learn to bear with misconstruction as well as with the
loss of most of the pleasures of life." Sometimes he had three or
four sleepless nights in succession, and his sharp speeches must be
judged with this in mind. He combated his insomnia as best he
could; he never drank coffee or wine, though sometimes a little tea.
Sulphonal enabled him to sleep, but was followed by such intense
depression that he employed it only in emergencies. In general, he
used quinine, finding that two grains would put him to sleep for
at least one or two hours. But whether he had no sleep at all, or
broken sleep obtained by mild drugs, the result was inevitable;
his optimism was not dimmed, he still loved action, society, labor;
but he became sharp in retort. And even when he was in good
humor the swift and brutal candor of his speech offended many.
He refused to swerve an inch to please the press, the labor organizations, the varied racial strains of the metropolis, or the national
and State Democracy—and in some degree he displeased them all.

The newspapers in general remained his staunch friends and supported his policies, but they would have been much more cordial
had he treated them with a little tact. He was particularly ruffled
at times by the omniscient and admonitory tone of Pulitzer's *World*
and Dana's *Sun*. Late in 1888 John A. Cockerill, the impulsive
Southwesterner who was then managing editor of the *World*,
charged him with compelling the Commissioner of Accounts to
"whitewash" a certain derelict officeholder. Hewitt was testifying
before a State Committee. "I say that Colonel Cockerill, if he so
states, is an unconscionable liar," he remarked. One of the attorneys
begged the committee to restrain the mayor, but he replied that
he had ample justification for his language, and repeated the
statement.

Again, in the autumn of 1887 New York witnessed a spirited
contest for the district attorneyship. Many independents and reform
Democrats favored DeLancey Nicoll, the scion of a distinguished
family, who as assistant district attorney had won his spurs in the

prosecution of the "boodle aldermen" of 1884. Though he was a Democrat, the Republicans on October 26 formally nominated him. But organization men in Tammany Hall and the County Democracy, including many of high character, supported Colonel John R. Fellows, a capable politician who had done good service for Tilden, Cleveland, and Hewitt. The mayor preferred Fellows on the score of long experience and mature ability. So did President Cleveland, who unhesitatingly gave out a statement of support. The result was a violent outcry from the *Times, World,* and *Sun.*[1] President Cleveland revoked his statement, and remarked that he had been a fool for making it. His opinion of Fellows had not changed in the least, but he realized that a President has no business meddling in city politics.[2] Hewitt, however, stood by his guns. He wrote a letter to the Harlem Democratic Club predicting that Fellows would destroy the power of certain politicians to control voters through fear of indictment. He also bade defiance to the newspapers:[3]

The present campaign has developed an old issue in a new and aggravated form. After the Presidential election of 1876 this community became tired of what was denominated boss rule. It determined to put an end to personal politics. I took an active part in the movement, and was punished by a refusal on the part of the Democratic machine to renominate me for Congress. . . .

But I have encountered another and a new kind of boss, who has given me a great deal of unsought advice and a large amount of unnecessary bulldozing. I refer to the newspaper boss. Sitting in his editorial sanctum like a brooding Buddha, he does not hesitate to claim omniscience and to endow himself with omnipotence. The political boss was responsible to his party, the newspaper boss is responsible only to his own pocket. He is as dangerous as he is despotic. He must be suppressed.

Hewitt was obviously referring to Dana and Pulitzer. They were men of brilliant abilities, but also of imperious temper and at times capricious judgment. Dana was often cynical toward reform, and Pulitzer was dictatorial. "The Nicoll movement," he went on, "is in its inception a newspaper dodge and in its conclusion a disgrace-

---

[1] See these Journals, November 1 to 10, 1887.
[2] Allan Nevins, *Grover Cleveland,* 427.
[3] N. Y. *Times, Tribune,* November 2, 1887.

ful stratagem of the Republican managers to demoralize the Democratic Party." The *World* retorted vigorously: "There is just a faint suspicion that Abram Sufficiency Hewitt would like to be the boss of this town himself." Fellows was elected, and made a respectable official.[1]

Equal brusqueness characterized the mayor's attitude toward the Knights of Labor, then at the very height of its short-lived power. Friendly though he was toward labor organization, it was the craft unionism of the A. F. of L., not the one-big-union principle of the Knights, that he approved. Several other characteristics of the Knights displeased him: the demagogic leadership of Terence V. Powderly, their ready acceptance of numerous radicals and cranks, the excessive frequency with which they called strikes, their use of the boycott, and above all, their basic assumption that the interests of capital and labor were opposed. Early in his term he wrote a letter to be read at a Democratic dinner, protesting against secret labor organizations (the Knights having originally been secret), and arguing for the open shop.[2] Workingmen, he declared, should be allowed to decide for themselves whether they would join a union; nothing was more unjust than to call decent non-union men "scabs," to hunt them from factory to factory, and to demand, under threat of ruinous strikes, that they be denied employment. Later, at the opening of the clubhouse of Bricklayers' Union No. 7, a strong and prosperous craft union of the type which he liked, he made a speech which was generally interpreted as a direct attack upon the policies of the Knights of Labor, and especially upon their fatal readiness to call strikes.[3]

But his most dramatic quarrel was with the largest and most powerful of the racial elements then found in New York, the Irish-Americans. They had been wont to celebrate St. Patrick's Day with a gay parade; and on March 6, 1888, a committee of the united Irish societies called at City Hall to ask the mayor to review them. Hewitt, busy at his desk, received them affably. He smiled pleasantly until Chairman E. L. Corey remarked: "The majority of Irishmen

---

[1] N. Y. *World*, January 3, 1888.

[2] *Nation*, March 3, 1887.

[3] *Nation*, March 20, 1887. He remarked that continual striking was a token of the rawest period of trade-unionism. "The unions, like children, go through a dental period, and the first thing they do is to show their teeth." He praised British unions for devoting most of their funds to social work and mutual aid.

vote the Democratic ticket, and your vote came largely from Irishmen, a considerable portion of whom belong to the societies who
will parade on St. Patrick's Day." At that his face stiffened and a
sudden chill dropped upon the room.

"Now let us understand each other," he said deliberately. "I am
mayor of this city. You ask me to leave my duties to review this
parade—" "But Mr. Mayor, St. Patrick's Day is a holiday," broke
in one member. "It is not a legal holiday," said Hewitt. "You ask
me to leave my duties and review your parade, and you speak of
the vote cast by the Irish in your societies for the Democratic candidates. I may be a candidate for mayor or for President next fall
and may want all the votes I can get. The Irish votes cast for any
particular candidate in this city would elect him. But for the purpose of getting this vote, I will not come down to the level of reviewing any parade because of the votes of the nationality represented. I will review no parades, whether Irish, German, or Italian,
as a Democrat. I will review parades only as mayor of the whole
city and irrespective of party considerations."

"Mr. Mayor," Chairman Corey broke in, "we do not ask you
to review the Irish societies as a Democrat, but as mayor." But the
others murmured resentfully. And Hewitt replied emphatically:
"Gentlemen, you have my answer. I shall not review your parade
on St. Patrick's Day."[1]

This was a sensation. No previous mayor had refused to review
the marchers on Erin's great day. Hewitt had clearly uttered his
mind without thought of the consequences. The *World* spoke of
his "momentary whims and chronic prejudices," and recalled that
he had reviewed a parade of Italian societies the previous fall in
commemoration of Garibaldi's defense of Rome. But many citizens
felt greatly refreshed. "We presume," wrote Godkin,[2] "Mayor
Hewitt has done nothing to give more genuine pleasure to a large
body of people than his blunt refusal to review the Irish procession
on St. Patrick's Day. The courage of it is so novel that it both delights and amuses, in these days when politicians pass so much of
their time looking around to find clubs, or societies, or brotherhoods before which to abase themselves." Godkin, himself born in
Ireland, was aware that the old American stock in New York re-

[1] N. Y. *World, Tribune, Evening Post,* March 7, 8, 9, 1888.
[2] *Nation,* March 15, 1888.

sented the anti-British character of the parade and the importation of European quarrels into our country. "The pretense in which mayors have always hitherto been in the habit of indulging, that they considered it something very fine, has been one of the most pitiful episodes in municipal politics."[1]

But the cup of Irish grievances was to receive some additional drops. The previous autumn, when reviewing the Italian societies, Hewitt had refused to allow them to hoist their flag over City Hall, saying that nothing but the stars and stripes would be displayed there during his term.[2] The Irish societies now feared a similar rebuff. Alderman Patrick Divver offered a resolution providing that the Irish flag should float over City Hall on March 17, and his associates passed it unanimously. Another resolution was passed requesting the mayor to place the American flag at half-staff on the day of the funeral of Kaiser William I.[3]

When reporters carried the news to Hewitt, he quietly remarked that he was "unalterably opposed to having any foreign flags displayed on the City Hall." On Friday, March 16, the American flag floated at half-staff in sympathy for mourning Germany. On the 17th, Hewitt ordered the national, State, and city flags all hoisted over City Hall in honor of Ireland, but forbade use of the green banner.[4] That evening he attended the dinner of the Friendly Sons of St. Patrick. In his speech, awaited expectantly, he made but one reference to the incident: "The day will come when you will see the flag of Ireland floating where it ought to float, over a free nation in a free Ireland."[5] Three days later he returned the Irish flag resolution to the aldermen with a courteous and carefully reasoned message.[6]

He had obeyed the resolution regarding the Kaiser's funeral, he wrote, because no objection could be brought against such a salute to German grief with our own banner; he had disregarded the other resolution because he could permit none but the American ensign to fly over the building. On previous occasions he had de-

---

[1] Hewitt added that "this reviewing business" was a rather childish survival from old monarchical days anyway; *World*, March 9, 1888.
[2] N. Y. *World*, September 3, 1887.
[3] N. Y. *World*, March 14, 1888.
[4] N. Y. *World, Tribune*, March 18, 1888.
[5] Ibid.
[6] N. Y. *World, Times*, March 21, 1888.

clined to allow the British, German, French, and Italian flags to be flown there, and could make no exceptions to the rule. He was certain, he added, that this rule was based upon sound public policy. On grounds of principle, the country should recognize no difference between its native and its foreign-born citizens. They were all one; they had but one flag. It was the duty of public officers to regard them as a unit, and not to consent to any such demarcation into groups as the use of alien flags would indicate. On grounds of expediency, the heavy immigration of the past seventy years, which had taxed our powers of assimilation to the utmost, made it important to emphasize every symbol of Americanism. "Of these, nothing is more potential than the flag of the country which is associated with memories altogether American. Its supremacy should never be diluted by any suggestion of divided allegiance. . . . If it be right that Ireland should be governed by Irishmen, as France is governed by Frenchmen and Germany by Germans, then it is equally true that America should be governed by Americans, and that so far as the flag is the symbol of Home Rule, it, and it alone, should float from the seat of sovereignty."

But ten days later the Irish-American aldermen, too much irritated to drop the matter, amended the city ordinances to permit themselves to direct, by special vote, which flags should thereafter be displayed. Hewitt vetoed the bill. The amendment was very clumsy, he wrote;[1] for by a veto of each special resolution the mayor could always delay the flying of a foreign flag for at least twenty-five days. Why didn't the aldermen act honestly and pass an ordinance requiring the mayor to hoist the Irish flag over City Hall on St. Patrick's Day forever? That would present the issue squarely. The German, Italian, Jewish, English, and other foreign-born groups in the metropolis could then express themselves upon it in direct terms. Did the Irish-Americans think they were being unfairly treated in New York?[2]

I have pointed out that of the population of this city the Irish-born amount to 16.4 per cent. . . . And yet of the members of the Board of Aldermen seven out of twenty-six are of Irish birth, which is equal to 27 per cent. . . . The same rule of representation prevails in nearly all of the departments of the city gov-

[1] N. Y. *Tribune*, April 11, 1888.
[2] N. Y. *Tribune*, April 11, 1888.

ernment, except in the police, where the returns show that the
force contains 28.1 per cent of Irishmen born, which is nearly
double the normal percentage. This excess is at the expense of
the German element which . . . actually has only 4.14 per cent
of the appointments. But when we come to examine the nationality of the inmates of the institutions under the care of the
Commissioners of Charities and Correction we find that a larger
ratio appears. From the report of 1886 . . . the Irish furnish
more than double the number of inmates which would naturally
belong to their percentage of population, while the Germans
and the native-born are below the percentage due to their proportion of the total population. . . .

The facts above stated, when properly considered, should impose a modest restraint in claiming new privileges, which are
not known to the law, and not desired by the more conservative
portions of the nationality in whose favor the exception is demanded.

When the clerk reading this message reached the statistics upon
prison and asylum inmates, Alderman Divver called upon him to
stop. "We have been insulted enough by Mayor Hewitt," he
shouted.[1] One of his colleagues invented the story that Hewitt's
father had placed the British royal arms over the door of his furniture shop![2] The legislation was passed over the mayor's veto.[3]
But on May 4 a mass meeting of professional men, merchants, and
plain citizens at Cooper Union tendered the mayor its warm commendation.[4] The whole episode received from E. L. Godkin a characteristically pungent comment:[5]

Nothing can better illustrate the oddities and anomalies of
our city government than that a paper as interesting and important as Mayor Hewitt's message on the composition of the population of New York should have been addressed to a body as
ignorant and unlettered, and probably as corrupt, as the Board
of Aldermen. We elect as municipal representatives of a great
commercial capital men of no standing, either social, financial,
moral, or intellectual, in the community in which they live, and
then, to prevent their doing mischief, we deprive them of all

[1] Ibid.
[2] This was Alderman Dowling; N. Y. *Times*, April 25, 1888.
[3] Ibid.; the vote was 20 to 3.
[4] N. Y. *World*, May 5, 1888.
[5] N. Y. *Evening Post*, March 21, 1882.

power. But, as if with the view of making their absurdity conspicuous, we put into the Mayoral chair a man fit to be the chief minister of a great state, and oblige him to explain his acts to this little knot of nondescripts who have barely mastered the arts of reading and writing. There is nothing like this in the civilized world, we repeat; there has been nothing like it in Christendom since the barbarians descended on the Roman Empire. We dare say, in some of the Roman towns, small bands of Frankish or Gothic ruffians may have masqueraded as municipal councillors, but no eminent Roman wrote state papers to them. When it was necessary to persuade or placate them, the citizens probably made up a load of raw meat for them or sent them a barrel of wine.

The fact was that Hewitt had no use for those groups which later came to be called "hyphenates." New York City was notoriously cursed with them. Tammany at times was a hyphenate organization, for while its first object was always patronage and plunder, hostility to Great Britain was usually a good second. Many Tammany voters had supported Blaine against Cleveland in 1884 simply on the ground that Blaine had repeatedly showed his dislike of England. This very year, 1888, the uproar over the Sackville-West affair showed how insistent the Irish-Americans were upon bedevilling American politics with a European question. Hewitt had resented for years the way in which the Pennsylvania steel interests and other great employers imported cheap European labor to keep down wages and compel submission to long hours and other abuses. It was therefore natural for him in 1888 to make a speech upon the dangers of unrestricted immigration—dangers recognized by all a generation later, when the doors of the nation were swung to with a bang.

"I think the feeling is very general in this country," he said on July 5, "that the time has come when this country of ours, which has cost so much in sacrifices of every kind, should be the country of Americans. It does not belong to the rest of the world. It belongs to our own people." American labor, he added, lost most from the swollen tide of immigration, for it could not compete with a horde of European workers; American politics lost nearly as much, for the masses of ignorant foreigners in our large cities were manipulated by machine bosses. He proposed two reforms: that a literacy test should be applied to all immigrants who sought our shores;

and that, except in unusual instances, aliens should not receive full citizenship for at least fourteen years. Nothing, to his mind, was more scandalous than the wholesale manufacture of voters in New York out of newcomers who knew nothing of American political ideas, nothing of the Constitution, nothing of current political issues.[1] In subsequent utterances, while asserting that nobody in Washington had shown greater zeal to protect the foreign-born than himself, he pressed the point.[2]

It was of course easy to misrepresent the mayor's position, and even without this it would have been unpopular. Just after the Irish flag episode, a meeting was held at the Skating-Rink at Lexington Avenue and 104th Street to discuss the subject; and many asserted that the mayor would not have the courage to attend. He and a son entered the hall surrounded by a police escort. The short little mayor was half-way down the centre aisle before he was recognized, and the Irish audience rose with a startled uproar to attack him. The knot of policemen, with Hewitt and his son in the centre, desperately fought their way to the end of the hall and out the rear door, where more police awaited them. Speaking was out of the question.[3] At a Tammany meeting at this time one of the men loudest in denunciation of Hewitt was Bourke Cockran. Soon afterward, he called on Sunday afternoon at the mayor's house for tea, and coolly remarked: "You were quite right. I attacked you only under orders from the Hall, and I hope there will be no personal feeling." But he added that after what Hewitt had done, the idea of his reëlection was preposterous.

But it was not the press, the Knights of Labor, and racial groups alone that Hewitt irritated; he also offended the Democratic machine headed by Governor David B. Hill. Construction of the great new Croton Aqueduct for increasing New York's water supply had begun in 1885. More than thirty-three miles in length, and destined to require almost a decade of work, it was the most expensive undertaking upon which the city had yet embarked. The State Commission which controlled it, and which enjoyed a wide power over the contracts and engineering details, originally included three city officials—the mayor, comptroller, and commissioner of public works.

[1] N. Y. *Sun*, July 5, has a full report of the speech.
[2] N. Y. *Herald*, October 23, 1888.
[3] Erskine Hewitt to author, October 25, 1933.

But in 1886 the legislature passed a bill by which the mayor and comptroller were to be replaced by three members selected by the governor. Mayor Grace and the press protested, but in vain. The result was that Governor Hill appointed three worthless men; a majority of the Commission blindly followed the orders of Rollin M. Squire, the characterless Commissioner of Public Works; and there began a veritable orgy of corruption, extravagance, and loose practices.[1]

The Commission dismissed its secretary to make room for a political hack, and then reëmployed him, nominally in another capacity, when the new appointee proved unable to do his work. It showed the grossest favoritism in letting contracts. The law governing these contracts was then frequently violated by sub-letting them to cheaper contractors, who would have been glad to do the work for the city in the first place. Some $800,000 was paid for excavations that were never made; expensive rubble masonry was put in where dry filling would have sufficed, at an unnecessary cost of $1,000,000; and when one of the contractors did defective work, three of the commissioners consented to overlook it for $150,000. A contract was let on highly improper terms to the former chairman of the Democratic State Committee, John O'Brien, and part of his dishonest profits were then used to pay a note for campaign expenditures which Governor Hill and his law-partner had signed.[2] All this was at first kept strictly secret, but it was shortly discovered in an interesting fashion.

There was a cholera scare in New York City in the fall of 1887. At Hewitt's request the quarantine establishment, controlled by the State, was investigated by two committees, one from the College of Physicians in Philadelphia, the other from the New York Academy of Medicine. Their reports disclosed appalling defects and shortcomings, and he called upon the governor to have remedial legislation passed.[3] Instead, Governor Hill seized the opportunity to satisfy a personal grudge by ousting Thomas Collier Platt from the presidency of the Quarantine Commission.[4] Boss Platt struck back. He controlled the Senate; it appointed a special committee

[1] D. S. Alexander, *Four Great New Yorkers*, 128, 129.

[2] See *Harper's Weekly, Nation*, September, 1888, for a review.

[3] Articles in the N. Y. *World*, January 3, 4, 1888, cover this subject fully.

[4] See Platt, *Autobiography*, Ch. XI.

under J. Sloat Fassett of Elmira to investigate the Hill Administration; and Fassett at once began an inquiry into Aqueduct affairs.[1] Within a few weeks it had pried off the lid, and the shocking
stench threatened to play havoc with Hill's political career. By
the end of June much of the extravagance and dishonesty had been
exposed, Hill's law partner had fled to Connecticut to escape a sub-
poena, and Hill himself was alarmed by the storm of public wrath.

At this juncture Hewitt resolved to make the most of Hill's desperate situation and coerce him into granting the city some much-
needed concessions. When, early in July, the governor called a special session of the Legislature to appropriate money for the State
prisons, Hewitt sat down and wrote him a peremptory letter:[2]

I appeal to you for an act of justice to the City of New
York, which you alone are in a position to render. A special
session of the Legislature has been convened, which can consider such subjects as you see fit to submit to it. I ask you to
recommend the repeal of Chapter 337 of the Laws of New York,
passed May 13, 1886, by which the Commission for building the
new Aqueduct was reconstituted. This law was enacted by the
Legislature and approved by you against the protest of the municipal authorities of this city, made in accordance with the
general demand of public opinion. It has needlessly increased
the expenses of the Commission, and has excluded the Mayor and
Comptroller from its deliberations because they were not acceptable to the contractors . . . The contracts for the construction of the work have been confessedly violated by under-letting
. . . and in many ways, too numerous to mention, the interests
of the city have been sacrificed to the demands of the contractors
and the requirements of party politics. . . . The people of the
city are astounded at these revelations. The opinion is universal
that such changes in the law should be promptly made as may
be required to free this great public work from further entangle-
ments with political and personal interests.

The situation is not without embarrassment; but it presents a
plain duty to which neither you nor I can shut our eyes. We are
Democrats, while the Legislature is Republican. This is a fortunate conjuncture, as it will enable both political parties to clear
themselves from further responsibility for this unfortunate legislation.

[1] N. Y. World, Times, April 22, 1888.
[2] Printed in N. Y. World, August 21, 1888.

This letter, dated July 13, was not immediately made public; that was not necessary. Hill was only too glad to follow Hewitt's suggestions, for they opened a way of retreat. In a special message to the legislature, he proposed that the Aqueduct Commission be reorganized to include the mayor, comptroller, commissioner of public works, president of the aldermanic board, and three other men appointed by the mayor![1] He even threw in some resounding generalizations upon the propriety of giving New York a healthy amount of home rule, admitting that he had sometimes yielded to vicious legislation affecting the metropolis, but asserting that at other times he had saved it from great wrongs. Hewitt sent him a congratulatory letter of subtly ironic quality.[2] "This city has for a long time stood like a sheep dumb before the shearers," he wrote, and added that he expected the valiant Hill thereafter to protect it.

The legislature passed the Fassett Bill, which provided that the Aqueduct Commission should consist of the mayor, comptroller, commissioner of public works, and four others appointed by the mayor. Hill meekly signed it. Thereupon Hewitt, announcing that these were the most important appointments of his administration, named four men who had nothing whatever to do with politics. One was General James C. Duane, just retired as Chief of Engineers of the Army; one was Francis M. Scott, well known as an attorney; the two others were equally well qualified. "It is safe to say," remarked the *Evening Post*,[3] "that within the memory of living politicians no such commission as this has ever been named by a mayor of New York." Two were Republicans, and two were County Democrats.[4] The new Aqueduct Commission was completely trustworthy, and it rapidly cleared up the mess left by its predecessors, ensuring the completion of an economically-built water system.

Governor Hill, after this humiliation, hoped that the investigation would be dropped, and Platt was willing. But the mayor vigorously demanded that the Fassett Committee continue its inquiry, and the press of course seconded him.[5] Immediately after it resumed

---

[1] N. Y. *Times, World,* July 20, 1888.
[2] Published in N. Y. *World,* August 21, 1888.
[3] September 26, 1888.
[4] See Hewitt's description of these men, N. Y. *World,* August 1, 1888.
[5] N. Y. *World,* July 30, 31, August 1, 1888.

its hearings on August 9, John O'Brien, the former Democratic State Chairman who had become one of the contractors, gave his testimony implicating Hill in the use of dishonest Aqueduct profits to pay off campaign notes.[1] Ex-Mayor Grace also testified that Hill had signed such notes for $30,000; that various politicians had induced the former Aqueduct Commission to give O'Brien the contract for a certain section at a price of $54,000 in excess of the lowest bid; and that after this award was made, O'Brien and his partner had sold the contract for exactly $30,000![2] Altogether, the final hearings were damaging in the extreme to Hill. And Mayor Hewitt appeared in person, making public the letter he had written to prod Hill into calling for the reorganization of the Commission.[3] It is easy to understand why Hill, facing a hard campaign for reëlection, was eager by 1888 to see Hewitt dropped from politics. He would feel much safer with a good Tammany man in City Hall, ready to play the game according to the accepted Queensberry rules.

Nor did relations between the Cleveland Administration and the mayor improve at all during the early months of 1888. Hewitt could at times behave in an exceedingly tactless, not to say ungracious, way; and he felt that it was impossible to overlook the slights that he had received. On Memorial Day Cleveland, accompanied by Secretaries Fairchild and Whitney, visited New York to review a joint parade of the G.A.R. and the Richmond Grays. Everyone expected the mayor to welcome him and stand at his side during the review; it would have been the generous and courteous course, whatever their past differences. Instead, Hewitt failed to call on Cleveland, and on May 29 announced through his private secretary that he would take no part in the review, for he had received no invitation to do so. The G.A.R. at once protested that there had been some misunderstanding—that it had sent him a cordial invitation both to the review and to commemoration services in the new Metropolitan Opera House; but Hewitt did not appear.

While this was of slight importance, Hewitt made the incident worse by his excessive readiness to criticize Cleveland for lack of

[1] N. Y. World, August 30, 1888.
[2] N. Y. Tribune, August 24, 1888; Nation, August 30, 1888.
[3] He appeared August 20, 1888; see N. Y. Times, World, August 21.

constructive qualities. On the morrow of Memorial Day, the mayor happened to talk with a visitor from Buffalo. He was in one of his most irritable moods. The visitor asked if, having written the Democratic tariff plank in 1884—having given the party one of its most telling slogans, "Unnecessary taxation is unjust taxation"—he would not perform a similar service at the approaching St. Louis convention. Hewitt rather snappishly replied that he would take no part in the canvass, and would not make a speech or contribute a dollar. The Buffalo man, whose identity was not revealed by the press, but who was evidently a friend of Cleveland, asked why he would not assist the President. "Because he is no statesman, and I don't believe in his reëlection," replied Hewitt. Asked if he thought Cleveland would be reëlected, he answered: "He may, but not by my help." This was an indiscreet outburst. The *Tribune* got hold of it and published it in full, while other Republican organs gleefully took it up.[1] Nor did Hewitt make his position any better when, Cleveland having been renominated on June 6, he commented on the event in the most frigid terms. The party had possessed no real alternative, he said, but he would play no part in the campaign. "I do not intend to meddle with politics as long as I occupy the office of mayor."[2]

Repeatedly, during the first half of 1888, he declared that he would not be a candidate for reëlection. When the press discussed the possibility that he might seek the nomination for governor in opposition to Hill, he said that he wanted no office whatever. "Promotion for a man of my years means only weariness of the flesh. I am already counting the months to the end of my term." He called on good citizens to "cast your eyes about this community, and find the man who will take up this work when I shall lay it down." At this the best newspapers protested as with one voice. The *Commercial Advertiser* declared that the city simply could not spare a mayor who had resisted corruption so effectively, and proposed a citizens' movement to renominate him. The *Times* and *Herald* concurred, and even the *World* declared that he should be compelled to run.[3] The *Evening Post* was emphatic: "There ought to be no doubt about the action of the people. Mr. Hewitt has

[1] N. Y. *Tribune*, June 6, 1888.
[2] N. Y. *World*, June 7, 1888.
[3] June 11, 1888.

his weaknesses and infirmities, but the average of his official action is exceedingly high, and the city will be blind to its own interest if it does not command his services for another term . . ."[1] Hewitt was moved by these utterances, and spoke feelingly of his unfinished tasks.

But while a host of independent voters could be counted upon, it soon became clear that many of the County Democrats and Republicans could not. The baser elements in the County Democracy had been hostile to the mayor from the outset. Henry D. Purroy, one of their leaders, had long been in close relations with Croker and Tammany, and was eager to foment an insurrection. When the mayor delivered his strictures upon hyphenated voters, Purroy saw his chance. A fortnight later he ostentatiously withdrew from the County Democracy, alleging that the organization, "in the person of many of its chiefs, is deeply tainted with the same Know-Nothingism which the people of the United States, irrespective of party, crushed nearly one-half century ago." The secession soon became formidable. On July 22 the chairman of the finance committee resigned. On July 24, at the Morton House, Purroy launched his "Democratic Central Campaign Organization," with seventy-five men, representing every assembly district, present. These bolters had two primary aims, to support Governor Hill for renomination and reëlection, and to join Tammany in crushing Hewitt;[2] that is, they meant to strike a blow for machine politics and spoils in both State and city. Hill and Croker were with them at every step. On July 28 the governor had a long and confidential talk with Purroy and Kearny in Saratoga, and made it clear that he thoroughly approved of their endeavors to destroy the County Democracy.[3]

As Tammany, the "Hoy Purroy," and Hill leagued themselves against him, Hewitt's fighting spirit rose and he showed tokens of a changing mind. On August 6 he told newspapermen that if his supporters insisted upon a renomination he would "not run away from it." A few days later he took steps to dispel the foolish charge that he looked intolerantly upon all foreign-born citizens. In a tart letter to the American Party, a little anti-alien group which had held a convention in Baltimore and nominated him for President,

[1] August 9, 1888.
[2] N. Y. *World, Times*, July 23, 24, 25, 1888.
[3] N. Y. *World*, July 30, 1888.

he declared that he disagreed with their tenets, that the sole issue of the campaign was tariff reform, that he was a loyal Democrat, and that they must not use his name.[1] When Hill was renominated on September 12, he took a further step into the open. This renomination showed that the governor's alliance with Tammany was complete; and the prospect of three years more of Hill at Albany and at least two of Tammany in New York revolted all decent voters. "Many of the papers persist in saying that I am seeking a renomination," said Hewitt.[2] "That is not true. I have no desire to assume the responsibilities of the office for another two years. . . . However, should Tammany nominate a candidate simply on the ground that he would distribute all his patronage among the members of that organization because he had been named by them, I might feel it my duty to allow the use of my name as a candidate against him." This was clearly an invitation, and it brought an immediate response.

It quickly became evident that there would be a three-cornered contest for the mayoralty. At a long conference with President Cleveland in Washington, Croker, on September 21, obtained a promise that he would keep his hands off city affairs. Tammany forthwith announced that it would rather be beaten than win with Hewitt, and would bring out its own man. As for the Republicans, Platt and the National Committee were eager to put up a candidate to use for trading purposes, if nothing else, in behalf of Benjamin Harrison.

Hewitt was the first to be named. On October 4 a great meeting of the best men of the city, including Carl Schurz, J. Pierpont Morgan, William E. Dodge, Jr., James A. Roosevelt, Benjamin H. Bristow, James C. Carter, and Morris K. Jessup, was held in Cooper Union. "No body of citizens more fairly representing the intelligence and character of the community," wrote Godkin,[3] "was ever gathered in that hall." They offered Hewitt an independent nomination. He refused an immediate acceptance, asking them to wait and see if all the regular Democratic organizations, including Tammany, would not coalesce behind some thoroughly able candidate —for "there are some good men in Sodom." Next day Tammany

[1] N. Y. *World*, August 18, 1888.
[2] Ibid., September 14, 1888.
[3] N. Y. *Nation*, October 11, 1888.

presented its answer by selecting Sheriff Hugh J. Grant, a representative of its spoils element. The secessionists from the County
Democracy at once lined up behind him. And Hewitt thereupon
announced that he would take the independent nomination. Five
business men pledged him $25,000 for expenses, but in the end only
one, H. O. Havemeyer, actually paid his $5000.

Alarmed by the threat of a Democratic schism in New York City,
Administration leaders tardily attempted to patch up a union. Im-
mediately after the Cooper Union meeting Secretary Whitney and
Daniel Lamont hastened to the city, where they sent a delegation
to wait on the mayor. It comprised Senator Arthur Pue Gorman,
National Chairman W. H. Barnum, and Representative W. L.
Scott.[1] Though it pleaded for "Democratic harmony," it really
wanted Hewitt's withdrawal. He recognized as much in his reply.
"If you gentlemen had called on me a week ago," he said,[2] "I
might have retired, but I intend to run now; nothing can prevent
me." Next day, October 7, the County Democracy nominated him
by acclamation, and the battle was on.

It was a contest between Tammany on one side, Hewitt, the independents, and the County Democracy on the other. The Republican
ticket, headed by the lawyer Joel B. Erhardt, and the Labor ticket,
headed by one Coogan, were merely complicating factors. Yet many
regular Republicans, led by Theodore Roosevelt, swung behind
Erhardt.

Having no taste for personalities, Hewitt refused to assail Hugh
J. Grant's character. Grant was of Scottish, not Irish, blood; he
was comparatively honest, and had been distinguished as one of
the two men on the boodle Board of Aldermen who were clearly
unpurchased. Barely thirty, vigorous, good-looking, and of genial
manners, he made a strong candidate.[3] He had stood for mayor in
1884, but had been defeated by Grace. Hewitt wished to conduct
his canvass on the ground of broad principle, and in his acceptance
speech on October 8 he said that Tammany had nominated a gentleman against whom he had not a single personal objection.[4] "It is
not the man, but what he represents. He represents the spoils prin-

[1] N. Y. *World*, October 6, 1888.
[2] N. Y. *Herald*, October 6, 1888.
[3] John L. Heaton, *Story of a Page*, 72.
[4] N. Y. *World*, October 9, 1888.

ciple and nothing else." Why, Hewitt inquired a little later, did Tammany declare that the mayor must be defeated at all costs? This great spoils organization, when he entered office, had expected a plentiful helping of jobs, perquisites, and contracts. It had got none, and within five months was violently attacking him. Now it was looking ahead. Croker and its other chieftains were aware that the incoming mayor would have the appointment of twenty-three commissioners and heads of departments, whose terms would be long and who, if named by Tammany, would make possible its control of the city for many years. They were eager to gain access to the vast expenditures of the city for this period, and to renew the old system of political protection of vice and crime.

Had the best elements in the Republican ranks joined the County Democracy in supporting him, Hewitt's chances of victory would have been excellent. But Erhardt made an active campaign on the ground that his party had been slighted by Mayors Grace and Hewitt, pointing out that of the twenty-five heads of city departments only three were Republicans. Roosevelt was assuring Republican voters that they had their finest opportunity since the Civil War to elect a mayor.[1] Nothing aroused Hewitt's resentment so much as this failure of the reform Republicans to play a truly independent part. Just before election day he addressed a large bi-partisan meeting in Chickering Hall. Recalling that he had defended the city gates against the forty thousand job-hunters of Tammany, he rebuked the numerous prominent Republicans who, after beseeching him to run, had broken their promises of support.[2] "What kind of Pharisees congregate on the corner of Thirty-ninth Street and Fifth Avenue? Mr. Chauncey Depew, in his speech to the Union League Club, urged them by every consideration of honor, of interest, of intelligence, to vote for the Republican candidate and to vote against me. And yet no man in this community has more frequently come into my office and congratulated me upon the manner in which I have administered it." He went on:

Besides Mr. Depew, my old adversary, Mr. Roosevelt, also paid his respects to the Union League Club and to me. I think it is a pity that this young gentleman, who was used as a catspaw two years ago by men with whom he would not then or now con-

[1] See N. Y. *World*, October 20, 1888, for Roosevelt's position.
[2] N. Y. *Evening Post*, November 2, 1888.

descend to associate socially, did not remember that when he returned from Europe after the protracted period of rest which was required to solace him for his defeat, he came into my office and said to me, "Mr. Hewitt, I feel it my bounden duty to come and say to you how much I admire and respect you for the manner in which you are discharging your duties." This was a generous act on the part of Mr. Roosevelt. I know he felt it. He is an ingenious young man with a future before him of good for himself and the city.

Above everything else, Tammany relied for success in the election upon a bargain with the Republican machine controlled by Platt. In essentials, this was a deal by which potential Cleveland votes were traded for potential Erhardt votes; Tammany knifed the Democratic national ticket, and Platt knifed the Republican city ticket. Late in October the *Tribune* was frantically pleading with the three principal Republican officeholders in the city government, French, Smith, and Patterson, not to sell Erhardt out to Grant for pledges of reappointment and other favors. "This is the sort of politics," commented Godkin, "which the Union League Pharisees consent to make pleasant and profitable at the expense of the city." Just before election day it was an open secret in political quarters that great blocks of Erhardt votes had been "traded off." A number of local Republican and Tammany leaders shared in the transaction, and the Labor nominee, Coogan, was believed to have played a part in it. Not only did Tammany wish to elect a mayor, but it distinctly wished to see Cleveland defeated. A few weeks later one Republican newspaper published a circumstantial account of the use by the Republican National Committee of $150,000 for the purchase of three great blocks of voters involved in the bargain.[1]

In the nation, Cleveland went down in defeat. So, in the city, did Hewitt. The final result stood: Grant, 114,111; Erhardt, 73,137; and Hewitt, 71,979. As more than once since, the Tiger had slipped in between two opponents. Mayor Grant, supported by Hill at Albany, and with a long list of appointments at his disposal, would enjoy more power than any of his predecessors since the Tweed Ring days. Tammany again held a helpless victim under its claws.

[1] N. Y. *Mail and Express*, November 22, 1888; N. Y. *Evening Post*, December 6, 1888.

What use it made of its quarry, the Lexow Investigation a half dozen years later revealed.

Hewitt accepted the verdict gracefully.[1] A few weeks later he was pleased to receive an invitation, signed by more than four hundred of the most distinguished citizens, to a public dinner at Delmonico's "as a testimonial to your efficient administration of the duties of your office." No such banquet had ever before been proposed for a departing mayor. Though he declined the invitation, he regarded it as an evidence that he had by no means failed in his purposes. In one sense, to be sure, he *had* failed. Reform had broken down in New York City after only two years. But reform always breaks down in the metropolis within a short time. And even had he been more tactful, even had he compromised and played the political game, he would almost certainly have been defeated. By his unyielding adherence to conviction he had set an example that would shine like a beacon for years to come.

[1] Hewitt published a cheerful review of his administration in the press on December 31, 1888.

CHAPTER XXVII

The Pattern in the Loom

IN HIS last weeks as mayor, Hewitt accomplished a few more useful results. He selected a new Board of Education, the press commending his nine appointees;[1] in helping to prepare the city budget for 1889 he repelled a number of forays upon the treasury; and he induced the Metropolitan Museum of Art and the American Museum of Natural History, in return for increased grants of city funds, to open their doors to the public without charge on either two evenings each week or on Saturday afternoons—a happy innovation for working-people.[2] On the last day of the year he submitted to the Board of Estimate a detailed summary of his stewardship, in which he pointed out that the city's credit had never been so good, and that its securities now commanded higher prices than those of London itself.[3] Then, on New Year's Day, 1889, he surrendered his control of affairs to the pliable "Hughie" Grant, the corrupt Purroy, and the ruthless and grasping Croker. It was a turning point in city affairs; it was equally a turning point in Hewitt's life, for now, approaching his seventieth birthday, he quit office forever.

There awaited him not only the iron business, the glue business, two Western cattle companies, his Southern ventures, and the direction of Cooper Union, but above all, a new range of municipal, charitable, and educational activities. New York always overtasks a few unofficial civic leaders, and now he was one of these willing few. While he had more leisure than before, his friends still thought his life one of excessive labor. Unlike most hardworking men, he

[1] N. Y. *Evening Post*, Nov. 22, 1888.
[2] Ibid., Dec. 26, 1888.
[3] Ibid., Dec. 31, 1888.

had never sighed, even in tired moments, for complete freedom—had never talked of rural ease or a lodge in some vast wilderness. Retirement would, in fact, have been irksome to his active, restless temperament, and he meant to wear out rather than rust out. We may well pause at this point, nevertheless, to describe his salient personal characteristics as exhibited in business and civic affairs, in his home, and in larger social circles.

Beyond question, Hewitt's fundamental characteristic was his intense dislike of disorder and inefficiency, his constant uneasiness in their presence, his eagerness to do something to abate or correct them. American life was full of both confusion and stupidity. A country that had grown too fast, a population that had become too heterogeneous, an individualism that was often riotous and irresponsible, spread about him a scene of waste and selfishness. Love of system was part of his English heritage, but it was something more than mere cold system that he craved. Deeply innate in his nature was an instinct for efficiency and intelligent management. Faced with the chaos, extravagance, and blundering so evident in American society, he felt impelled year after year to do battle with them. Most business men of his generation were willing participants in the Great Barbecue, but to him the barbecue of a continent seemed criminal and intolerable.

In business, he had been able to exert his love of order and efficiency to the utmost. He had been the first in America to experiment with efficient new processes in the iron industry—the Bessemer process, the open-hearth process, the Post-Pernot process. He had been one of the pioneer writers upon a planned and progressive relationship between employers and labor. When he went into politics and was chosen campaign chairman of the Democratic party, he had striven to introduce into its management an orderliness and efficiency like those of his mills on the Delaware. In Congress, again, he had attempted to correct the errors of our financial system and tariff system, the wasteful management of our western resources, and our want of foresight in dealing with defense. Elected mayor of the nation's largest city, he had been appalled by the disorderliness and dishonesty which faced him on all sides, and had struggled against them valiantly. His political ideas all had a fundamental relationship to his devoted belief in plan and efficiency. He was against unrestricted immigration because, in addition to being unfair to American labor, it conduced to social disorderliness. He opposed the prohibition of all railroad pools by the first Interstate Commerce Act because he believed that some pools brought order into chaotically over-competitive business.

It was from this unrelenting hatred of waste and clutter that his constant overwork and sense of strain chiefly sprang. Observers were impressed not by his incessant industry, which is common enough in America, but by the high tension of his industry. He was always keyed to a pitch superior to that of men about him. It was systematic, carefully planned work, it avoided mere fuss and fury, but it was work that crammed sixty seconds of effort into fifty-five seconds of time. Though one of his principal defects was incapacity to make the best use of subordinates, he knew how to make the best use of himself. After leaving the mayoralty, he usually spent the early morning at home; from 11 to 3:00 he was at the Burling Slip office; he gave the late afternoon to business conferences, Cooper Union, or meetings of the Barnard College or Burke Foundation Trustees; and in the evening he was at home again, rigidly declining most dinner invitations. To the last he seldom took a real vacation. On his frequent trips abroad he restlessly dealt with business papers, wrote, or talked energetically with shipmates; and he was no sooner in Europe that he was off inspecting iron mills.

The result was to accentuate some of the peculiar traits—anfractuosities, as Dr. Johnson called them—of a personality that, while usually winning, was often marked by abrupt demeanor, harsh words, and stern action. Everyone could see in later years that he was a man of frail physique. In a letter of 1896 he described himself as five feet eight inches in height, and weighing but 140 pounds; and after middle life his health grew more and more precarious. Even while mayor his hair was gray, his frame stooped, his face deeply lined. He suffered not merely from insomnia but sciatica, headaches, and nervous indigestion. To be sure, his children sometimes thought that he exaggerated his sleeplessness. Once, at Ringwood, there was a brief, violent rainstorm in the middle of the night. He came down to breakfast complaining that he had not slept a wink, but it turned out that he had not heard the rainstorm. At this Peter Cooper Hewitt remarked: "Father goes to bed, and then dreams he is lying awake!" But there can be no question that the affliction was heavy.

At best, he was "a hard man to work with"—unless the worker was nearly as efficient as Hewitt himself. He had little patience with blunders, loose ends, lack of punctuality, or other evidences of laxity; and while it was one of his particular traits that he always accepted large trials philosophically, small difficulties and errors often provoked him to an outburst. When a careless officer sank a valuable ore-barge in New York harbor and turned up white with apprehension, Hewitt to his astonishment was gentleness itself; but a misplaced letter might cause an upflare. Under his sharp rebukes for incompetence, a certain type of employee was likely to leave his office resentfully. One result was that his business was always exceptionally efficient; but another was that he never commanded, as men like Mark Hanna and James J. Hill did, the affectionate personal loyalty of a large body of employees. He was regarded with too much fear. His exhibitions of testiness were not confined to his own associates, for when preoccupied he was often rude to total strangers—rapping out a sharp sentence at some interrupter without knowing later that he had spoken at all! We find him, for example, writing George L. Miller in 1878 to explain his brusqueness to an army officer who had brought a letter of introduction. "I remember that he called upon me at a time when I was overwhelmed with business, and had been without sleep for a long time. My manner is never very affable, but when I have lost sleep I am told that it is very objectionable. Of course Major Nickerson knew nothing of my peculiarities, and so set down to rudeness what was simply an earnest expression of inability to be of use to him." Newspaper men used to say when they went to interview him as mayor: "Come on, let's work the growler!" Yet gradually people learned to take his sharp utterances, which really meant little, humorously. A vivacious young woman who was often at the Lexington Avenue House and loved to talk with him was accustomed to begin their conversations by saying: "Now don't bite me!" His family took the same amused attitude. A standing household joke was the remark a woman had been heard to make one night when, as mayor, he entered a theatre and was applauded. "I don't like him. I think he is a fine mayor, but they say he is dreadfully cross to his family!"

Yet ordinarily his frank, buoyant personality was attractive; and all of his intimates knew that his irritability cloaked a very kindly nature. He was particularly eager to help young men. His combination of irascible tongue and kind heart is well illustrated by an incident which General Charles H. Sherrill records of a visit to Ringwood about 1896. He writes:[1]

> One evening while spending a week-end at his country place in Ringwood, I had come down early to dinner and found no one in the drawing room but Mr. Hewitt. He sat there in absolute silence, so presently, feeling that a man so young as I should attempt to make conversation, I asked him where the gas came from which illuminated the house. He snapped out at me in reply, "Don't be a damn fool. Give a little thought to matters before you commence to ask questions. Of course, it came from near by and not from a great distance." I was both surprised and vexed, and said nothing more to him. In fact, I consulted his two daughters that evening, fearing that he had taken a dislike to me and therefore I had better withdraw from the house party, but they assured me he meant nothing by his outburst, but that he had been suffering from an attack of indigestion that day.
>
> I thought that he had forgotten the whole circumstance, but a couple of days afterward his secretary telephoned me a request to come down to his office. I had just started up a law firm with two friends of mine and we had only opened our office the week before. It is easy to imagine their and my delight when I returned from a really charming interview with Mr. Hewitt charged by him with drawing some papers concerning real estate and the Cooper Union. The first bill that the new firm sent out went to Mr. Hewitt for these services. We made it a modest one in the hope that it would encourage the receipt of more business from so important a client. The bill came back with an endorsement written and signed by Mr. Hewitt to the following effect: "Don't be a damn fool," and enclosed was a check for double the amount of our bill.

A trait almost as prominent as his hatred of disorder, and one which contributed to his seeming irascibility, was his independence. He often said that his early poverty had made him prize independence above everything but rectitude. He had seen in his father's misfortunes and his mother's hardships what it was to be without money; his struggles for an education had made him envious of the freedom of other boys. He realized that financial independence is

[1] To author, Jan. 15, 1932.

almost a *sine qua non* of moral independence, and his first great aim in life was to achieve it. Yet he set no exaggerated valuation on wealth. He wrote:[1] "The most unhappy men I have ever known have been those who are blessed with large means." No small part of his rise in the world was due to the air of rugged intrepidity which he always carried with him, and no small part of his failure to rise further was due to an excess of it. Godkin once remarked that he had a little too much iron in his constitution. Without being combative, he always did and said just what he thought was right. He might have gone much further in politics with more tact; for he could never, to use Holmes's metaphor, round off the sharp-cornered cubes of Truth into balls in order to make them roll about easily.

We have seen this trait exhibited in large matters, but it was even better illustrated in small ones. He was stern about little abuses and meannesses. In 1871 he learned that Tweed, soon after removing from Oliver Street to Fifth Avenue, had taken two Indian effigies from the old Tammany Hall (replaced in 1868 by a new building) and had used them in his house as hatracks. Hewitt, as a member of the Hall, at once hired a hack and drove to the house to reclaim them. He was always ready to stand up for what he deemed his rights at the cost of personal unpleasantness. One April morning in 1891, passing through Water Street, he found that a truckman of the Perth Amboy Terracotta Company had blocked the sidewalk with a large box. He waited with an angry frown. The clerk of a neighboring store civilly asked the truckman to get the box out of the way. The latter, without provocation, responded with an insulting remark to Hewitt. "Thereupon," wrote Hewitt to the terracotta company, "I took the number of his truck, which is 4130, and as a good citizen I feel bound to report to you the fact that your employee not only violates the law, but insults those who suffer by his neglect. Of course on complaint to the City Marshal I could have his license revoked, but I think it more courteous to inform you of the facts so that you may deal with them as you see fit." Any infraction of the city ordinances which came under his eye was at once reported; any violation of State law provoked his wrath.

But if he insisted on his own rights, he was equally solicitous of

[1] To J. W. Leavitt, June 22, 1883; Hewitt Papers.

those of others. He hated special privilege, and his papers contain many indignant rejections of it when offered to himself. It is sufficient to quote a letter which he wrote while Congressman to the superintendent of the railway mail service:[1]

Dear Sir:
I have received a card instructing the employees in charge of the distribution of mails to extend to me the privilege of riding in the offices of the postal cars of railways. This ticket is given to me as a member of the House of Representatives. I do not understand that any such privilege is conferred by law upon members of the House of Representatives, nor that you have the right to confer it by law, and I see no reason why Representatives should have any privileges not possessed and enjoyed by other citizens. I protest, therefore, against the issue of such tickets, and I would return mine to you but for the reason that I shall take occasion to confer with the Postmaster-General as to the propriety of this unusual proceeding, which is open to the construction of an attempt to conciliate Representatives by the offer of courtesies unknown to the law. I have the honor to be, yours truly, Abram S. Hewitt.

A man of this type, vigilant against all abuses, was particularly useful in the United States of a generation ago, where our general prosperity had induced a complacent good-nature about many small evils. Hewitt detested this good-nature. He never expected to be handled good-naturedly himself when he made errors, and seldom handled others so. He believed in calling a spade a spade, a theft a theft, a scoundrel a scoundrel. When he thought President Cleveland had acted improperly, he wrote him a plain letter about it. While he liked William C. Whitney personally, he always believed him one of the most sinister figures of his time, for no other man had done so much to teach big business how to make a corrupt use of politics. In 1891 he and his son Erskine were in London. They entered the Bristol Hotel just as Whitney came down the steps. "Hello, Hewitt," said Whitney, "are you going back to the States soon?" "No," said Hewitt, shortly. "Well," replied Whitney, "you ought to go back and take the nomination for the Presidency. You deserve to get it." Hewitt flushed angrily. "You ought to go back and stand trial for the Metropolitan Street Railway operations," he

[1] September 29, 1881; Hewitt Papers.

retorted. "You deserve to get a jail term." And Whitney broke off his laugh when he saw that Hewitt meant just what he said.[1]

He always felt that Croker had treated him treacherously, both because he had broken his solemn promise not to ask for office by demanding one for H. D. Purroy, and because he had opposed Hewitt's renomination; while the ironmaster was horrified by the corruption of the boss's regime after 1889. Sometime early in the nineties they were at a reception at the Waldorf. An officious friend came up with the boss, saying, "Here is Mr. Croker, Mr. Hewitt." "I once knew a man named Croker," said Hewitt contemptuously. "I helped pay a lawyer to defend him for murder." And he squarely turned his back.

Yet if asperity was prominent in his makeup, it was always controlled by his love of justice, and frequently banished altogether by his innate kindliness. While it was characteristic of him to think in terms of general principles, and to brush from his path any one who stood between him and a large objective, he could make allowance for human nature. Sometimes he was surprisingly considerate of others. For example, a bookkeeper at the Burling Slip office whose personal habits were so notoriously bad that he had never dared to ask for a raise in salary, was once discovered stealing from the petty cash account. Hewitt taxed him with theft. "Yes, Mr. Hewittt," said the man. "I have been working for you for twenty years. My children are growing up and need education. You are still paying me only $2000 a year and I need $2400. I have taken enough from the petty cash each year to make up that sum; not a cent more. Now send me to jail." Hewitt read him a severe lecture—and kept him on with slightly increased pay! The man was not worth it, but the ironmaster thought that his family, in which were several devoted daughters, merited generosity.

All his life Hewitt was an unrelenting enemy of the liquor traffic; and in New Jersey he tried to prevent the sale of intoxicants not merely on his own property, but near it. All the more striking is a letter to his agent at Ringwood in 1894.[2] "Vreeland, who keeps the drinking shop on the road from Hewitt to Erskine, applied to me on Sunday for permission to take the water from a spring on my land back of his house. I told him that I had no ob-

[1] Erskine Hewitt to author, Oct. 24, 1932.
[2] To C. S. Stites, June 2, 1894.

jection to his having the water, but that he had behaved so badly in reference to the sale of liquor that I wanted to have no business with him, and I refused to give him any authority to take the water. I wish you to see Vreeland and say to him that on reflection I am not willing to return evil for evil, and hence he can take the water, provided he can sign the stipulation herewith enclosed."

Edward M. Shepard, to whom Hewitt was almost a father, once recalled that early in the eighties, "at a time when he was overwhelmed with work," he became interested in the desolate grief of a poor cobbler in the upper part of the city whose son was under criminal prosecution. Hewitt asked young Shepard to help him with the legal technicalities of the case. For his own part, during several weeks he gave time and effort without stint, climbing long flights of stairs, meeting ignorant and importunate people, and gathering evidence in every possible corner. He was determined that the cobbler and his son should get their full rights; and, wrote Shepard,[1] "the world will never know the thousand things like this in his career." He might have added that the world would never know of the innumerable instances in which Hewitt exhibited his abiding sense of trusteeship. One was in his treatment of railroad passes. Being himself president of the Greenwood Lake Railroad, he was presented with a great many; but he always insisted on paying full fare, even on his own road, unless he was travelling on railway business.

In nothing was Hewitt's readiness to live for objects outside and larger than his own more evident than in the scope of his later public interests. On leaving office, he threw himself without reserve into a score of undertakings. He had always tended to scatter his energies over even too wide a field; and now in old age he enlisted in philanthropic, educational, and civic activities without thought of ill-health, weight of years, or the burden of his mills and mines.[2]

He became a faithful trustee of the American Museum of Natural History, and the Metropolitan Museum of Art. He had been a member of the State Charities Aid Association from its establishment; as the managers said,[3] he "gave to it freely of his time, his

[1] *Review of Reviews*, February, 1903, "Abram S. Hewitt, A Great Citizen."
[2] Cf. N. Y. *Evening Post*, Feb. 27, 1903.
[3] See minutes of the Board of Managers at the annual meeting in 1903, and Brooklyn *Citizen*, Jan. 28, 1903.

wisdom, and his strength." One of his last public appeals was in opposition to some legislation which menaced its interests. Throughout the nineties he took a lively interest in the work of the Small Parks Association; and as we have seen, when Mayor Strong's reform administration in 1897 appointed a Small Parks Committee to select park sites under the new legislation, he gladly accepted the chairmanship. It was he who insisted that Jacob Riis be made its secretary, and who urged that the heavy-fisted, courageous Dr. Joseph D. Bryant, now best remembered as Grover Cleveland's friend, be placed on the committee for his knowledge of public sanitation and his burly energy.[1] Of this Small Parks Committee, which did such valiant work to let light into the city's crowded districts, Jacob Riis and he were always the two principal members. The Charity Organization Society had no better friend, and he made generous gifts of money to it.

He always took a special pride in his work in helping to plan the Burke Foundation. In old age, John Masterson Burke came to Hewitt for advice. He had a large fortune, and no one to inherit it. His had been a striking career; his father was a drunken scamp, his mother often penniless, and he sometimes said that his own first recollection was of being kicked out of home and later awaking in a snowdrift, with his houseless mother beside him! Hewitt suggested to him several worthy objects of charity. Burke, he said, might endow a new hospital; he might establish a group of dental clinics, for they were much needed; or he might set up a convalescent home for the poor. This last proposal appealed to Burke, who adopted it, and left money in his will for it—the home to be named after his mother. He asked Hewitt to help him draw up the plan; and the latter not only did this, but shrewdly suggested that Burke make complete legal arrangements with his cousins and other relatives, binding them not to fight the will. This was done, and, following Burke's death in 1909, the Foundation in 1915 opened an exceptionally successful institution.

In addition to these labors, two old loyalties laid strong claims upon Hewitt. One was professional. Though he had never received any formal training in technology, he felt a fraternal regard for the guild of engineers; and twice, in 1876 and 1890, he acted as president of the American Institute of Mining Engineers. In the

[1] To Mayor Strong, June 3, 1897; Hewitt Papers.

former year the Centennial Exhibition brought numerous foreign engineers to our shores; while in the latter both the British Iron and Steel Institute and the German Ironmasters' Association visited the United States. On both important occasions he played the rôle of host with dignity and distinction.[1] For nearly twenty years he was also vice-president of the American Iron and Steel Association. But this was a more perfunctory service, for he strongly disapproved of the high tariff activities of the body and especially of its secretary, James M. Swank of Pennsylvania.

The second strong tie of loyalty was to Columbia College, or as it became officially styled in 1896, Columbia University. He had a warm regard for Dr. Barnard, whose twenty-five years of service as president ended in 1889; for his profound scholarship, his progressive aims, his eagerness to liberalize and broaden the institution. But he had felt impatient over the conservatism of some trustees and the failure to obtain financial support from the wealthy metropolis.

When, in 1890, the merchant Seth Low was installed as president, Hewitt's hopes quickened. He wrote President Low that "I anticipate the very best results from the union of business experience with scholarship in the work of education."[2] The ensuing decade was in fact a period of greatly accelerated growth, with numerous large gifts, a new and more spacious site, and a renovated curriculum. Hewitt helped to raise funds, made suggestions for strengthening various departments, and even recommended men for professorships; in 1893 proposing Clarence King for a chair in geology.[3] Wishing Columbia to be the greatest university in America, he was jealous of her competitors. "I have never," he wrote Chancellor McCracken of New York University in 1892, "been able to come to the conclusion that two universities should exist in this city. Columbia College has got the start and will keep it. I wish very much that an understanding could be reached by which your university could be made part of a general association with one governing body which should represent the university idea, and distribute the work to be done among the several component elements so as to be most effectual and economical." When Colum-

---

[1] See *Transactions* of the Institute, Vol. XXXV, February, 1903.
[2] To President-elect Seth Low, Oct. 16, 1889; Hewitt Papers.
[3] To the same, May 3, 1893; Hewitt Papers.

bia removed to Morningside Heights, and the handsome buildings designed by Charles F. McKim were dedicated on May 2, 1896, Hewitt made the formal address of the occasion. A few years later, in 1901, he became a trustee, and till his death remained a valued adviser of President Butler.

But his most assiduous labors for the University were given to Barnard College. As we have noted, he believed firmly in higher education for women and in coeducation. When lectures at Columbia were first thrown open to women early in the eighties, two of his daughters attended. Barnard was founded in 1889; and especially after Emily J. Smith (later Mrs. George Haven Putnam) became dean in 1894, he lent it cordial support. He was proud to be one of the early trustees, and within a short time was made chairman of the board. Its meetings were frequently held at his house, and he became familiar with all sides of Barnard's work. His labors have been commemorated by Hewitt Hall, the largest residential building of the college.

The year before the Civil War Hewitt had become a member of that useful and already venerable body, the Chamber of Commerce of the State of New York. When first nominated by James G. Cannon, president of the Fourth National Bank, whom he regarded as an unprincipled financier, he declined with characteristic asperity. William E. Dodge then stood sponsor for him, and he accepted. After his mayoralty he was called upon by the Chamber for hard labor in several fields. His influence in the body, said the *Nation*, was unrivalled. "Every topic that he saw fit to discuss was handled in a masterly manner. He marshalled his facts in faultless English and with logical precision. In public speech he was never at a loss for a word, and when he finished one of his impromptu addresses in the Chamber or out of it, the listeners were always charmed and generally convinced."

In particular, the Chamber relied upon him for counsel on the difficult problem of rapid transit. The seeds he had sown during 1888 soon began to take root. An Act was passed in 1891 establishing a Rapid Transit Commission, with power to lay out subway routes, adopt methods of construction, and offer the franchise in perpetuity to the highest bidder; but bidders did not come forward. In 1894, therefore, the Chamber, feeling that grave dangers lurked in any further delay, appointed a committee to report upon the

problem of rapid transit. It offered the chairmanship to Hewitt.
The position was one of great toil and difficulty, requiring the
mastery of a mass of intricate and technical details; but he unhesitatingly accepted the thankless task, and guided the Chamber in
preparing and urging effective new legislation. Later he performed
still another signal labor for the Chamber. In 1902 the old project
of a Hudson River tunnel was revived by the New York and New
Jersey Railroad Company, organized by William G. McAdoo. It
took over the tunnel which had already been bored 3,900 feet out
from Jersey City, and applied to the Board of Rapid Transit Commissioners for a perpetual franchise. The Board duly granted this
franchise on July 10, 1902, but approval by the aldermen and
mayor was delayed. Though the Hudson River tubes were now a
crying need, the aldermen haggled over details. Observers suspected that Tammany Hall was trying to hold up the McAdoo
Company for a huge sum in graft. The Chamber of Commerce deputed Hewitt to approach the heads of the tunnel company and
the city administration, and expedite action, and his appointment
did much to break the jam. He bade the tunnel officials not to pay
a cent in graft, he served notice on Tammany that the Chamber
would speak out bluntly if there were needless delay, and in December, 1910, the tunnel plan went through.

He was a member of the City Club from its foundation in
April, 1892, and later gave cordial support to the Citizens Union.
When a fire devastated Jacksonville, Fla., in 1901, he was chairman
of the New York relief committee. When, after the panic of 1893,
the Association for Improving the Condition of the Poor appointed
a group to encourage the migration of impoverished city people to
farms, he was again chairman. Every worthy cause tried to enlist
him for, as the *Nation* said, "all things that bore his stamp were
recognized as golden." He was even one of the incorporators, under
Federal enactment, of the National Conservatory of Music. All his
labors were undertaken without fuss or publicity, and he rather
shrank from the public gaze. He meant simply to be a good citizen;
he was carrying out the resolution made when he landed penniless
from the wreck of the *Alabamian* in 1844. It should be added that
while never ostentatiously religious he was a faithful member and
vestryman of the Calvary Episcopal Church at Fourth Avenue and
Twentieth Street.

Hewitt's social tastes, like most of his other traits, were highly individual. A reticent man outside his own circles, he disliked leaving his house for entertainment. He had little tolerance for "society" in the narrow sense, for the idea of exclusiveness irritated him, and he was scornful of pretensions to rank based on wealth or title. Yet he was never a democrat in the way in which Lincoln or Peter Cooper were democrats; he was never a citizen of that ideal country of Burns or Wordsworth in which the plowman is equal to the great leader. He felt that men who had risen high in worldly place from obscure station, displaying brains and character in the process, had reason to feel pride and to regard themselves as above ordinary folk. Peter Cooper, believing that some of the finest of men might be ambitionless or unlucky, recognized no gradations but those of virtue; Hewitt recognized social gradations based on personal achievement. He therefore took pleasure in associating with men of affairs, in having about him people of known accomplishment. If they had risen against obstacles of poverty and hardship, so much the better. He admired Carnegie (with reservations) as an industrial leader sprung from the cottage of a Dunfermline weaver; Sir John Pender as the greatest cable-layer of the world sprung from equally humble Scottish origins; Tilden as the leader of the American bar sprung from a Hudson Valley hamlet. A family anecdote illustrates this feeling. Edward Cooper's daughter Edith married Lloyd S. Bryce, the son of a successful New York lawyer, an Oxford graduate who was well-educated, well-connected, and by inherited wealth very well off. He was a brilliant conversationalist, a writer of amusing novels, and from 1889 to 1896 a capable editor of the *North American Review*, which dropped into his hands as an inheritance from a friend. Once at dinner Bryce, who had a touch of snobbery, spoke condescendingly of Peter Cooper's humble origins. To Hewitt this was treason. Swift as a flash he rebuked Bryce with the remark that he ought to be proud to recall that his own grandfather, in Peter Cooper's early days, had been "so poor he carried his lunch in a newspaper." Hewitt's distaste for the inner circle of New York society was shown in 1883, when the glittering fancy-dress ball of the William K. Vanderbilts on March 24 advertised the fact that at last the Vanderbilt clan was really inside the gilded portals. Mrs. Hewitt accompanied a son and daughter of Sir John Pender to the ball. But when the press re-

ported that Hewitt himself was present as King Lear he was resentful, and took no little pains to deny the report to his friends.
He was equally contemptuous of British titles whenever they were
unearned. Once, as mayor, he performed the civil ceremony which
united an English nobleman with a New York girl, and the girl
kissed him. On returning home he remarked, in well-founded anticipation of a subsequent request for some financial favor: "I suspect that will prove the most expensive kiss I ever got."

It was characteristic of him and Mrs. Hewitt that they never
thought of Fifth Avenue, but kept to the plain, roomy Peter Cooper
house in the middle-class district above Gramercy Park. The note
of this house, as of Ringwood, was liveliness. While he disliked to
go out, he loved to have a constant flow of people coming in; he
loved witty, informative conversation, and loved to dominate it.
In its singularly catholic fashion, the 9 Lexington Avenue mansion
was for years one of the social centres of New York. It was remodelled in 1883. Peter Cooper had built it as a high-stooped
house; Mrs. Hewitt altered it to an English basement house. Stan-
ford White, then only thirty and but recently made a partner in
McKim, Mead & White, took the plans in hand. It was a difficult
task, and his studies under H. H. Richardson had not especially
fitted him for interior designing. Mrs. Hewitt purchased some fine
old oak panelling in England, and a beautifully carved fireplace
and mantel, which White did not use quite as she wished. Nevertheless, the remodelled structure, with a fine staircase of Italian
marble, a dining-room of noble proportions, large drawing rooms,
and a ballroom which occupied the space once given to Peter
Cooper's stable-loft, made the interior of the house as delightful
as its exterior was homely. The family could entertain on an ambitious scale; as the six sons and daughters grew up there were
occasional large dances and musicales, and a steady succession of
dinners and teas.

In the nineties a witty coterie, including Mrs. Stuyvesant Fish,
Mrs. John La Farge, Robert Hargous (famous as an inventor of
funny stories), Lloyd S. Bryce, his close friend Bourke Cockran,
and John C. Van Dyke made the house notable for entertainment.
On every Sunday afternoon an amusing group could be found
there. Few distinguished Britons came to New York without a letter
to the Hewitts. Friends of the family understood that a place

would always be waiting at dinner if they dropped in. If they telephoned ahead that they had a guest who had done something, who was interesting, he was equally welcome. The result was that within limits almost everybody might be there: a distinguished European, a Tammany leader, a Senator, a man just acquitted of embezzlement, a Columbia professor, Mme. Calvé. The artistic tastes of the daughters (for Sally made a specialty of eighteenth century art) brought in painters like J. C. Beckwith and W. L. Metcalfe, and architects like McKim. The talk was always about events and ideas, never about persons. Hewitt delighted in swift-paced, sparkling, allusive conversation, and was usually the genial autocrat of the table. He was a master of repartee and badinage, he had a huge fund of illuminating facts, and, drawing upon a rich stock of experience, he was an admirable story-teller.

Those who had seen him only outside his house, where he often seemed reticent or even shy, were surprised at his animation. His eyes would sparkle, the domelike forehead which gave him the look of a Greek sage would flush, and his features would glow with animation. As the years passed, in telling his stories he sometimes indulged in a pardonable tinge of dramatization or exaggeration, a product of his enkindling imagination. Like Sir Walter Scott, he liked to dress up an old anecdote with cocked hat and walking stick. This exaggeration, late in life, sometimes crept into even a public speech. Once in particular, shortly before his death, some overdrawn statements about his "secret mission" from Minister Dayton to Minister Adams in 1862, which Charles Francis Adams, Jr., at once disproved, caused him much vexation. But in conversation allowance could be made for it, and it merely added to the charm of his abounding vitality.

The contrast between the master and mistress of the house was one of its delights. Hewitt was intense, nervous, unresting, testy; his wife was mild, kindly, and gracious, radiating a calm benignity as he radiated energy. While the one stimulated, the other soothed. Mrs. Hewitt, wise and gentle in everything, inheriting all the amiability and tolerance of Peter Cooper, knew perfectly how to manage her husband. There was more petticoat rule in the house, particularly when she and her daughters joined forces, than one would have supposed, but they ruled Hewitt without his knowing it. At Ringwood, for example, he would gladly have sold off much of the ground in order to surround himself with brilliant, active people; but she wanted room for her precious gardens and for long quiet vistas, and Ringwood was left untouched. Once, while he was in Washington, she showed a friend some extensive alterations she was making in the Ringwood house. "Have you told Mr. Hewitt?" asked the friend. "No," said Mrs. Hewitt with placid wisdom. "I would rather have one scolding when it is all ended than two, one at the beginning and the other at the end. And in no time he will think he did it himself anyway." Sure enough, when the friend returned to Ringwood some months later, Hewitt was proudly showing the changes to some guests as improvements which he had made himself!

Hewitt's closest friends were Clarkson N. Potter, Samuel Barlow, Randolph Tucker, "Dick" Taylor, R. Fulton Cutting, Morris K. Jesup, and the brilliant Clarence King. The last-named became a great favorite, as Hewitt admitted when he wrote: "My intimate connection with him for many years in public and private matters has produced an admiration for his attainments and his character that may possibly warp my judgment." In his later years he was fond of the cultivated and vivacious Richard Watson Gilder. Several churchmen should be named, particularly Bishop Potter of the Episcopal Church, and Robert Collyer, the eloquent Unitarian clergyman who was pastor of the Church of the Messiah, 1879-1903. When Collyer paid a visit to his native Yorkshire in 1883, Hewitt, with his wife and Edward Cooper, sent him a purse on the eve of his sailing.[1] Even Bolton Abbey, Hewitt wrote, might look lovelier if the minister did not feel worried by money matters. "I am not without hope of finding you some day lying on the grass under the shade of the tree near the stepping stones which lead from Ilkley over to the old manorhouse of the Fairfaxes." A few Englishmen should be added to this list. The most important, besides Thomas Hughes and Sir John Pender, were Sir William Cunard and J. Lothian Bell, the latter an ironmaster of North Allerton who had been a most affectionate friend of Peter Cooper.

Dr. Rainsford, the robust Anglo-Irish clergyman who became vicar of St. George's on Stuyvesant Square in 1883 and soon made it a notable example of the institutional church, was introduced to Hewitt at a dinner at Mr. Peter Barlow's. "That first night of

[1] Hewitt to Collyer, June 11, 1883; Hewitt Papers.

our meeting," he writes,[1] "Hewitt was so kind as to let me feel that he would like to see more of me. 'I am a rather lonely old man,' he said; 'if you are ever free of an evening and could come and spend an hour in my library, I would be glad.' So rejoicingly I went and sat at his feet, and learned more from him about New York, its needs and its dangers, than any other man in its two and a half millions could have taught me." Dr. Rainsford adds: "Excepting Theodore Roosevelt, I think Mr. Hewitt was the ablest, most cultured, and certainly most honest politician I ever knew." The vicar could not understand why his capacity and character had never been recognized by higher office. "All he had and was, he ever placed at his country's service. And when he chose to exercise it, his personal charm was as remarkable as his erudition. He knew New York from the Battery to the Harlem. . . . He knew Washington. He was extraordinarily acute and brilliant in his judgment of men." At large semi-public gatherings, Dr. Rainsford usually found him silent. But "when alone with him, or in a small and congenial party, he was, with the sole exception of Clarence King, the most brilliant conversationalist I ever listened to."

Sometimes Hewitt's wit carried a slight barb. Once his son Erskine, coming home from Princeton, found standing before the fire in the drawing-room a short, rotund man with a keen, humorous face. "Where do you come from, young man?" demanded the stranger. Erskine furnished some information about Princeton. The visitor, who plainly thought that the youth should know him, stuck his thumbs in the armholes of his waistcoat, threw out his chest, and said complacently: "Look at me. I've never been to college, and see what I am." At that moment Hewitt entered. "Ah, but Mr. Carnegie," he remarked, "just think what you might have been if you had only gone to college!" On another occasion he played a neat joke as mayor on some Tammany officeholders. In March, 1888, occurred the great Sullivan-Mitchell prize-fight in New Orleans. A number of politicians, including some heads of city departments, planned a trip thither, to be prolonged by fishing and junketing. Hewitt, hearing of the special train and other preparations, dug up a provision of the charter which made officeholders removable if absent from the city without leave for a certain period of time. He was kind enough to place a copy of this, with an announcement

[1] William S. Rainsford. *Story of a Varied Life*, 343, 344.

of his intention to act upon it, on the desk of the would-be excursionists—and it instantly broke up the party!

Usually, however, his fun was quite devoid of malice. He could appreciate a joke on himself. No less a person than the Sultan of Turkey once quite unconsciously played one on him. After Hewitt's visit to Constantinople he sent the ironmaster a number of handsome gifts—rugs, an elegantly fitted desk, with gold-dust for blotting powder, and other objects. Hewitt responded by sending the Sultan various mementos, among them a large number of specially-monogrammed cigarettes from the Allen & Ginter factory in Richmond—for Abdul Hamid preferred Virginia tobacco to Turkish. But the bulkiest of the Sultan's presents was a consignment of beautifully bound editions of Arabic classics; and Hewitt was staggered when the Custom House sent him a bill for duty on these books. He hastily avoided payment by giving them to the Congressional Library; and when he informed the Sultan of this, Abdul courteously sent him another set! They also had to be given away. Once, at a dinner, a jurist of the city twitted William M. Evarts about the prodigious length of his sentences. Newspapers then frequently carried sesquipedalian utterances, some genuine, some invented, which they attributed to Evarts; and extracting one from his pocket, the judge read it. The company laughed. But Hewitt, leaning forward, said sternly: "That is certainly an astonishing sentence, but in view of what today's papers say of you, Mr. Smyth, it ill becomes you to criticize it." "How is that?" exclaimed the judge. "Because," with his characteristic grim smile, "you are quoted there as uttering a sentence that was to last the whole life of the prisoner." One specimen of Hewitt's humor even got into *Punch*. In the eighties he was visiting the annual exhibition of the Royal Academy in London when the then heir to the throne, the Duke of Clarence, entered. Hewitt hastily moved out of the way to an open window. Much to his consternation the Duke wandered over, wiped his brow, and remarked that it was a warm day. "Yes," said Hewitt, "but there is more heir apparent than there was." An equerry sent the unblushing pun to the weekly.

Ringwood during the summers was a very gay place. Every weekend brought its quota of guests; often twenty or thirty people sat down to dinner on Saturday night and Sunday. The amusements were walking, riding, driving, tennis, croquet, fishing and shooting in season—for Hewitt had stocked Shepherd's Pond and the brooks with trout and the woods with game—and, above all, talk. He had a marked taste for objects of historical value; old books, prints, portraits, weapons, and the like. In 1889, for example, he bought from the Hagerman family 41 pewter dishes which, with six others in the National Museum at Washington, had formed the camp service of General Washington. With its relics of Colonial and Revolutionary days, and the beautiful furniture made by John Hewitt and Peter Cooper, the house gradually became a veritable museum. It was never pretentious, like the great country houses then being built on Long Island and in Westchester, but it was one of the most interesting seats in the metropolitan area.

Notable Americans and foreigners could be found chatting on the lawn flanked by the chain and mortar, and the place provided a combination of gaiety and intellectual interests more characteristic of English country places than American. J. St. Loe Strachey, editor of the London *Spectator*, came more than once. He has recorded his pleasure in the "delightful house amid a kind of Scottish scenery of lakes and hills, a highland estate with some forty or fifty miles of private drives," and in Hewitt's reminiscences.[1] Henry Adams was also there repeatedly, and was sufficiently intimate to ask presents of Ringwood butter for such mutual friends as L. Q. C. Lamar. Hewitt was one of the few men to whom he sent instalments of his unpublished history of the United States under Jefferson and Madison, and the one who did most in encouraging him to complete it. Indeed, for some years during and after his Washington service, Hewitt was close to the Adams-Clarence King group, and corresponded irregularly with both men. We may quote two of Adams's letters to him as indicative of their friendship, and as interesting in their allusions to King's attack of insanity:

1603 H Street, Washington
April 25, 1894

My dear Mr. Hewitt:

I reached my house two days ago, after four months' absence, and a few hours afterwards the express brought a huge case, which could be nothing but a bomb, and which I, being a bit of anarchist myself—under your education—told my man William to open with precaution. He soon brought me your magnificent

[1] London *Spectator*, March 15, 1924.

volume. I looked into the index to see what I was doing there, and found that I was the owner of some pictures. Someone had senile decay bad. Perhaps it's I, for I notice that I get everything wrong; but I think it is my brother Charles. Anyway, I firmly believe that I am not the owner of those pictures, but that they belong to my brother John. Not that it matters. The pictures will stay at the old house in Quincy all the same. The volume shall go there too, when I am done with it; and shall sleep in the dust of our family diaries. A century or two will ripen the whole batch, and by that time America will not feel so tired of us as it does now—nor shall we feel so tired of it.

I suppose you and I shall meet again in the next world, provided Grover Cleveland does not administer it; but I notice that while he administers this one, my friends here are few and very far between. I am sorry, and take refuge in the most remote islands and mountains I can reach; but my friends, for choice, go to Bloomingdale in the interval. I have brought Clarence King back, well and gay; but I think this is only because I am so much loonier than he, that he felt relatively like Solon and Solomon. He will be in New York next week. We have had a really youthful three months in the tropics, and got back a good twenty years; but I've lost more than that in the last two days, and already feel like old Tom Jefferson and John Adams rolled into one, on July 4, 1826. I hope King will not find New York as depressing as I find Washington. He ought to get out of it at once, and stay out of it. To be sure, I have said the same thing to so many people that New York would be depopulated if they followed my advice; but as the choice seems to lie between living at Bloomingdale or living outside of civilization, I feel bound to state it clearly.

As soon as possible I shall start off again, but where and for how long I know not. The chief difficulty is to find a tolerable companion, for, as one grows older and sillier, one grows more exacting in the matter of companions, and finds it hard to discover youth, energy, humor, intelligence, and enthusiasm all in one. I have to put up with apologies like La Farge and King; but revenge myself with the consoling reflection that they have to put up with me. On the whole, however, even they are better off than they would be in Wall Street, or even in that Via Sacra of my native city—State Street. At least, I hope so.

When you have succeeded in getting the world settled down into some condition that I can understand, or that understands itself, please write me a line, wherever I am, and I will return, hoping to see you again in my house in Washington. Trusting for a day not too far off, I am

Ever truly yours,
Henry Adams.

1603 H Street, Washington,
April 27, 1894

My dear Mr. Hewitt:

My house will be full of girls for the next month, and I can't well leave them without a matron. Nieces are a more serious duty than daughters, and I have a round dozen, more or less, who are a great pleasure as well as a responsibility. I have succeeded in seeing, at last, all my brothers—John, Charles, Brooks, and Edward Hooper—clear out for Europe, where I heartily hope they will stay, for they are all tired and worn out, and ought to be shut up in Bloomingdale with the rest of my friends; but their children are sprinkled over creation, and won't go to Bloomingdale for several years. Meanwhile, at this season, they like Washington, which is a chief reason why I am here. So, for the next month or six weeks I shall probably run a girl's boarding-house at this address, which will prevent my availing myself of your kind invitation.

As for King, he seems to me at this moment more steady, quiet and sane than I ever knew him; but he has still to face the intense depression which New York never fails to excite in every sane mind. The healthier one is, the more depressing New York becomes. I regard myself as fairly average, but I can't stand New York. If I were in King's place, I would keep as far from it as my credit would permit. He had better geologize the negro with me in eastern Cuba.

Ever truly yrs,
Henry Adams.

Ringwood gained much in social attractiveness from the transformation of the neighboring community of Tuxedo. When Hewitt first acquired the estate, Tuxedo Lake and some 6,000 acres of adjacent country were owned by the Lorillard family. Old Pierre Lorillard, the noted tobacconist, had taken it for debt in 1814, built a shooting-lodge, and sold timber from the land. It remained essentially wild until long after the Civil War. But the second Pierre Lorillard, who was about ten years younger than Hewitt, determined in the seventies to develop part of the tract, and formed the Tuxedo Park Association. In 1886 Tuxedo Park and the Tuxedo Club were opened. Within the next decade numerous wealthy New Jersey and New York families removed to the district, until it was fairly covered by fine estates. Many of the residents were good friends of the Hewitts, and Pierre Lorillard, R. Fulton Cutting, Henry Holt, and Francis Lynde Stetson frequently visited at Ringwood. Before the end of the century Tuxedo had become one of the recognized centres of American society.

Hewitt was too busy a man to read omnivorously, and Mrs. Hewitt hardly read at all beyond the newspapers and some gardening magazines. Their house impressed people as a house of talk, not of books. Nevertheless, in certain fields Hewitt did read with the intensity of a student. He had time for this because his range of amusements was narrow. He rarely went to the theatre or opera, cared nothing for cards, never hunted (though he liked walking and riding), and seldom visited any club except the Century. What interested him most in his reading, as we should expect, were *problems*, historical, governmental, and economic. He never tired of discussing constitutional questions, of comparing British and American political practise. This interest in problems took him to history, where he admired Lecky, Macaulay, Henry Adams, Rhodes, and above all, John Richard Green. It took him to treatises like Woodrow Wilson's *Congressional Government* and Bagehot's writings. He read much biography, and at least once sent an appreciative letter to an author. When William C. Martyn's *Wendell Phillips* appeared in 1890, he wrote: "The style is peculiar, but very attractive, and you manage to make the life of that great orator almost as real as if the reader were actually a looker-on in the scenes in which he figures." But above all, Hewitt delighted in economics, upon which alone he owned a valuable collection of books—for he sent other volumes to Cooper Union as fast as he finished them. He knew all the classical British economists from Adam Smith on; was familiar with such Americans as David A. Wells, Francis A. Walker, and Arthur L. Perry; and knew Marx from the Sonnenschein edition of 1887. He was a lifelong admirer of John Stuart Mill, and regarded his *Principles of Political Economy* as an incomparable treatise.

He had a strong taste for statistics, and performed mental operations with the lightning accuracy for which George W. Perkins was later notable. Unfortunately, he possessed no literary impulse; and this deficiency explains why he published so little on economic topics. In 1890, in congratulating Edward A. Atkinson on his productions, he earnestly lamented this. "If I had the same facility and love for composition which you possess, I am afraid that in some respects I would have anticipated your labors. But nature denied me the taste for composition. Hence I never do anything in that direction except upon compulsion." When he did write it was very painfully, but also very well.

His chief pleasures, apart from his work, were naturally found in his family. He would have smiled at Andrew Carnegie's statement, after his death, that his home was "much of a heaven upon earth," but there was truth in it. When his children grew up they were not free from dissension; but they were at least all united in an intense devotion to their father. He carefully supervised their education. The sons, Peter Cooper, Edward R., and Erskine, had the curious fortune of attending a girls' school; that of Miss Eliza Torrey, daughter of the botanist John Torrey. Hewitt was an old friend of the family, the school was close by in Forty-fourth Street, and its discipline was commendably rigid. Pupils could read their lessons but once before reciting, and that the day before, a rule which compelled them to concentrate. Moreover, Hewitt felt that coeducation had a refining influence upon boys. The oldest son, Peter Cooper, had talents of which we shall say more later. Edward, after leaving Princeton, went in the autumn of 1890 to the University of Berlin. Erskine, after graduating from Princeton, studied law at the Down-Town Law School and in the office of Parsons, Shepard, Ogden, & Closson. Clarence King took a warm interest in Erskine, and once, when the family physician thought that the youth needed a summer in the mountains, insisted that he accompany a party of the Geological Survey which was going to the Yellowstone under Arnold Hague. Hewitt sent Dr. Hague a note which contained an interesting phrase about himself. "He is a quiet, unpretentious boy of considerable ability and irreproachable habits," he wrote. "He does not lose his temper, in which respect he is in marked contrast to his father."

It is natural for fathers to delight most in their daughters, and Hewitt found greater pleasure in his girls than in his sons. For one

reason, the boys gradually left the parental hearth, while two of
the girls stayed. The oldest, Amelia Bowman, or "Amy," had a
hare-lip and was shy and retiring, but she united strong practical
sense with charm and sweetness of temper. She was married during
the eighties to Dr. J. O. Green, a Kentuckian by birth, and a
strikingly handsome man of versatile abilities, who had studied
medicine in Paris. Just before Christmas in 1891 Hewitt's first
grandson was born, but died a few days later. The other daughters,
Sarah Cooper and Eleanor Gurnee, affectionately called "Miss
Sally" and "Miss Nelly," became the life of the household. Sally
was educated at Miss Porter's school at Farmington, Conn., noted
for its conservatism and thoroughness, and Nelly at Miss Torrey's,
while both were also carefully tutored abroad. Nelly was the
harder-working; Sally the more brilliant socially, with a whimsical
humor and a gift for repartee like her father's. Both girls were
original and full of resource, and they gave entertainments that
had a flavor all their own. Both had several opportunities to marry,
but preferred to make careers for themselves, and their pursuits
were precisely of the sort that pleased their father. They were
interested in everything: they loved company, they helped manage
the Ringwood estate, they were good horsewomen, and they enjoyed travel. They had their father's efficiency and his independent
temper. They set up a cooking-school in the city where the products
of Ringwood were sold; they founded the Ladies' Amateur Orchestra, and both played violins in it; they were energetic anti-suf-
fragists. Sally wrote a book on roadmaking, an art which she practised by building many miles of fine highway at Ringwood. It was
no uncommon thing for her to walk into the blacksmith shop at
Ringwood with her mount, help to make the horseshoe, and lift
the horse's hoof to her knee to see that it fitted. Both poured most
of their spare energy and cash into the improvement of Cooper
Union, doing work of great permanent value for its courses in art
and design.

Altogether, Hewitt had reason to count himself, in his private life,
a fortunate man. And yet those who saw him in his daily habit knew
that his life was always laborious, was full not only of burden but
frequently of pain, and was strikingly devoid of ease and luxury.
He was not even a rich man in the generally accepted sense. He
gave so largely, he made such repeated sacrifices to maintain em-

ployment at Trenton and Durham, that he was often pinched for funds. The sons were kept on rigid allowances; such avoidable expenditures as cab-hire were held to a minimum; the table was plain, and waste in any form was sternly rebuked. His family long remembered the half-humorous consternation he displayed one night when he returned from a public meeting held to raise a fixed sum for the Charity Organization Society. Russell Sage had been present, and a group had told Hewitt that if he would make a speech they thought Sage would contribute. Hewitt had taken the floor, declaimed earnestly upon the work of the C.O.S., and had finally been so carried away that he had promised $5,000 from his own pocket. Russell Sage was manifestly touched. At the close of the meeting he rushed up and said, "Yes, Mr. Hewitt, somebody ought to give that money!" But he did not subscribe a cent, and as Hewitt walked home he realized he did not have $5,000 on hand and hardly knew where he could get it!

Many a man, after so active a life, would have felt justified in relapsing into *otium cum dignitate*; but he preferred to continue his activities to the end.

CHAPTER XXVIII

The Fight for the Gold Standard

WHEN Hewitt left the mayoralty, the paramount questions of the day were the tariff and the monetary issue; and of the two the latter produced the most uneasiness. Could and would the gold standard be maintained? No one knew. The demand for the free and unlimited coinage of silver was gaining formidable strength in the West and South; the Republican plank on money in the recent campaign was interpreted there as a promise to "do something for silver." It soon became clear that President Harrison lacked the unwavering courage of Grover Cleveland; and under the Sherman Act of 1890 the government began buying nearly fifty million ounces of silver a year, almost the total American production, for coinage. Simultaneously the gold reserve in the Treasury began to fall to a dangerously low point. It was evident that if another depression smote the country, with large gold withdrawals by Europe, we should be in imminent danger of going to a silver basis. Much of the West desired such a consummation as fervently as the richer East dreaded it.

Hewitt had his own contacts with the West and South, and particularly the latter. In 1889 he seriously considered transferring the Trenton iron works to the South. Twenty years earlier, when he had wished to carry them to Pittsburgh or the Great Lakes, he had been estopped by his responsibilities to Peter Cooper and the Cooper Union. At Cooper's death he had been immersed in politics. Now for the first time his hands were free. Southern iron was already underselling most of the Northern mills; the basic process, by which iron ore was fluxed with limestone, promised to make Birmingham one of our great steel centres. His operations at Trenton were still greatly hampered by high freight rates (the Northern railroads charging more than the Southern), and by the tariff of 75 cents a ton on imported ores. Why should he not follow up his successful venture with the Roane Iron Company and embark on a new industrial career with the South as his stage?

Early in 1889 he joined a party of Northern capitalists who went to spy out the land.[1] Among them were Andrew Carnegie, Edward Cooper, Frederic Taylor, H. B. Pierce, Secretary of State in Massachusetts, and Governor D. H. Goodell of New Hampshire. A fanfare of Southern editorials, newspaper stories, and speeches greeted the group. Reception committees waited upon it as it travelled through Chattanooga, Knoxville, Birmingham, Atlanta, and Columbia. A boom in Southern real-estate was beginning, and the visit of the deputation lent it impetus. The Northerners were genuinely struck by the potential wealth of the section and the energy with which the business men were building up foundries, textile-mills, tobacco factories, and cottonseed oil plants. Carnegie spoke in glowing phrases, and Taylor said that he would amend Horace Greeley's advice to read, "Go South, young man, go South." Hewitt on his return wrote the owner of some iron furnaces at Sheffield, Ala., that he and Edward Cooper were "filled with admiration at the perfection of the plants which have been established in many places in the South," and only wished that they could exchange their works at Trenton and Durham for some which they had seen below Mason and Dixon's line.[2]

For a time Hewitt believed that it might be feasible to merge a number of small plants near Birmingham into one powerful corporation similar to the Tennessee Coal and Iron Company. He employed two agents to make the necessary inquiry into the finances of the small plants, and discussed the matter thoroughly with various Southern industrialists, notably Patrick Calhoun (a son of John C. Calhoun), and Enoch Ensley of Memphis, the principal organizer of the Tennessee Coal and Iron Company. His intention was to go to England, make fuller inquiries into the basic steel process, and if these proved satisfactory, to raise money in London and New York for the venture. In a letter to Ensley he expressed mingled enthusiasm and caution. "Of one thing I am entirely satis-

[1] See the account of his interesting trip in Richard H. Edmond's, *The South's Redemption*, published by the Manufacturers' Record Company in 1890.
[2] To William Brockie, March 28, 1889; Hewitt Papers.

fied, and that is the practicability of organizing an association which would be able to defy the world in the manufacture of pig-iron and ultimately in working it into useful forms. Of course the temptation is very strong to be concerned in such a company; but Mr. Cooper and I are determined not to enlarge our present operations unless upon a basis which will be enduring and will satisfy the most intelligent and exacting judgment." Early in April he sailed for Europe.

Yet this tentative plan came to nothing. For one reason, he found Englishmen uninterested in Southern development. Great Britain was just experiencing the first reaction after a brisk company-promoting boom which had lasted several years; business was uneasy, and the Baring disaster, the great thunderclap which preceded the worldwide financial troubles of the nineties, was just ahead.[1] For another reason, Hewitt found that the speculative era which had set in at the South had induced owners of mines and furnaces to ask impossible prices. He wrote a Richmond friend that many Southerners apparently thought New York a financial milch-cow which would give money at the lightest touch, and that the offers laid before him were so high that nobody could make simple interest on the investment.[2] The advice of Calhoun and Ensley was to go slow. Hewitt knew something of the astonishing possibilities of the Minnesota ore-fields, where the great Mesaba Range was now being tapped, and he knew that to tear up the Trenton plant by the roots would be costly. On his return from England he contented himself with a reorganization and simplification of the Roane establishment which restored it to full prosperity.

He also turned his attention to railways, and temporarily became concerned in that consolidation of small lines which ultimately, after J. P. Morgan had become the dominant figure, produced the great Southern Railroad. He found certain acquaintances, chiefly Southerners, trying to unite various routes into a system of about 9,000 miles which would cover much of the richest cotton and mineral areas. He was tempted to put money of his own into it. He also offered to try to obtain British capital, and wrote Sir John Pender:[3] "In a general way the scheme would require about ten

---

[1] R. H. Gretton, *Modern History of the English People*, I, 264.
[2] To Gen. Joseph R. Anderson, March 28, 1889; Hewitt Papers.
[3] March 7, 1890; Hewitt Papers.

millions of dollars now, and probably as much more in the course of the next three or four years. I think it will be shown that this amount can be made to earn four or five per cent interest at the outset."

Hewitt made a new tour of the South in the spring of 1890 to inspect railway properties. He then asked Patrick Calhoun to go to England, and when Sir John Pender cabled encouragingly, dispatched him on a fast steamer. Calhoun bore letters to British friends extolling the resources of the South, and pointing out the possibilities of a great consolidation under the aegis of the Richmond & Terminal road. But this undertaking also, for various reasons, came to naught. Calhoun was in England for several weeks, returning in June. He talked with a number of British financiers, finding them still hesitant to invest in Southern properties. In his absence, moreover, a group in the key railway, the Richmond & Terminal, spoiled all his plans. This line was in the hands of two factions. One, to which Calhoun belonged, was conservative and trustworthy; the other was speculative and irresponsible. The latter group, gaining control, forced the price of the stock up to 28, a figure much higher than the British investors would pay, persuaded the head of the company that it would be a mistake to seek foreign capital, and took measures to raise funds from the stockholders.[1] Nothing could be done until, following the panic of 1893, the house of Morgan came into practical possession of the lines of the Southern Railroad, and knit them together with a strong hand.

In the West, Cooper & Hewitt were now the principal stockholders in the Bronson Cattle Company, a Texas corporation managed by E. B. Bronson. Its herds, bought in 1883 during the flush period of Western ranching, had been established on the Pecos Ranch in northwestern Texas; a strip some fifteen miles long and of indefinite width on the east bank of the Pecos River. The headquarters were a few miles south of Monahan on the Texas Pacific Railroad. Part of the grazing land was owned by the railway, but most of it by the State. During its first few years the company paid dividends. Then came lean times—droughts in summer, storms in winter, heavy mortality, and low meat prices. Though the herd had a strength of nearly 12,000, which should have made it possible to sell 1,500 to 2,000 beeves yearly, that number never reached

[1] June 6, 1890; Hewitt Papers.

market. By 1890 transfer to a new area in Texas, farther back from
Pecos, became necessary, and heavy losses were taken.[1] Hewitt was
also the principal owner of the Dacotah Company ranch in Mon-
tana, which was equally unprofitable. He held a large area of wheat
land in Todd County, Minn., where the town of Hewitt was named
after him, and still owned farms in Illinois and Iowa.

Altogether, Hewitt knew much at first hand of the South and
West. He had travelled there; he had extensive investments there;
he kept informed of their problems and sentiments; more than
once he refused to foreclose his Minnesota mortgages. The South
regarded him as one of the most helpful of Northern business men.
As the silver tide rose he took an attitude of stern opposition, but
it was a comprehending opposition which lacked the arrogance so
common among Eastern capitalists.

The situation grew critical in 1893. Close on the heels of Cleveland's second inauguration one of our worst financial panics suddenly burst and brought an appalling business depression. Hewitt
had foreseen that hard times were coming. In 1890 he had regarded
the Sherman Silver-Purchase Act and the McKinley Tariff as
grievous errors, for which the nation must pay; while in 1891 he
had written Sir Lowthian Bell that the great Southern land boom
had ended disastrously, and that the future had many dark elements.[2] He wished to have both the high-tariff folly and the silver-
purchase folly undone, and he held strong views of his own as to
the proper method.

President Cleveland, in calling a special session of Congress for
August 7, 1893, determined to concentrate all his efforts upon a
repeal of the silver-purchase clauses of the Sherman Act. Hewitt
would have preferred a more elaborate programme. He wrote the
editor of the Social Economist early in July[3] suggesting that Congress be asked to take three steps. First, it should pass a joint resolution empowering the President to suspend the further purchase
of silver at his discretion. Second, the House should instruct the
Ways and Means Committee, the Banking and Currency Committee, and the Coinage Committee to report at an adjourned session
in October the measures required for reform of the tariff, for a

[1] Letters of Fenlon to Hewitt, May-August, 1890; Hewitt Papers.
[2] Hewitt to Sir Lowthian Bell, December 26, 1891; Hewitt Papers.
[3] To George Gunther, July 8, 1893; Hewitt Papers.

more elastic currency system, and for a more effective banking system. Third, Congress might well promise some measure of relief for the Western silver miners, so long as it clearly recognized the fact that "the present unit of value, which is the gold dollar containing 23.22 grains of gold nine-tenths fine," should be preserved.[1] Hewitt believed that Congress could carry out this programme in a few days and adjourn to allow the relieved business world to recover, taking up more complex legislation in the autumn. Cleveland's procedure was at once narrower, clumsier, and more uncompromising.

On October 30 the repeal of the silver-purchase legislation was at last effected. Congress, meeting in December in regular session, then took up the tariff. The Ways and Means Committee—under William L. Wilson—had been preparing a measure; and Hewitt, delighted by the prospect of victory, had hastened to lend his aid. At an early stage he had offered Wilson his advice.[2] The chairman asked him to prepare the iron and steel schedule, which he did, and he furnished general counsel upon other provisions.[3] He urged that both coal and iron ore go on the free list. "I say this notwithstanding the fact that I am very largely interested in iron ore mines and in coal mines, both anthracite and bituminous, upon the Atlantic slope. They have nothing to fear from foreign competition. The ores are kept low in price by the competition from Lake Superior, for which there can be no protection and no remedy. We can mine ores in New Jersey and along the coast generally for less money than the freight from any foreign country."

But all the hopes attached to the new Wilson Tariff bill were doomed to frustration. No sooner had it passed the House than a small group of protectionist Democrats allied themselves with the Republicans in the Senate and mutilated it beyond recognition. Hewitt's principle of free raw materials was completely defeated; free coal and free iron ore were both lost. Like others, he was now convinced that Congress was largely a body of fools and knaves.

[1] The letter indicates that Hewitt would have favored a generous coinage of silver under two conditions: that it should be redeemable in gold only at its bullion value, and should be tender for debts only by special contract. Neither condition was acceptable to the free silver forces.

[2] October 4, 1893; Hewitt Papers.

[3] See Hewitt's letters to William L. Wilson, October 27, October 31, 1893; Hewitt Papers.

His indignation would have been less intense if, while the Wilson Bill was being destroyed, the silverite storm had died away. Instead, the inflationist agitation quickly revived; and the first days of 1894 witnessed a vehement demand for' coining the silver seigniorage in the Treasury. A bill for this purpose passed both houses; Cleveland vetoed it; and the anger of the free-silver men rose higher than ever. They would be satisfied with nothing less than the destruction of the gold standard.

While the Seigniorage Bill was pending Hewitt seized an opportunity to express his opinion of Congress in a memorable way. He knew that the South attached weight to his words. When asked to speak at the dinner of the Southern Society on Washington's birthday, 1894, he decided that the time for polite platitudes had passed. He began with a feeling tribute to John G. Carlisle, his strong character, lucid intellect, and sound judgment. He referred to the high standards of Southern statesmanship in the days of the Virginia Presidents, of Jackson, Clay, and Benton. But, he continued, what a sad decline in recent years!

One Southern man is battling today in Congress for something in which he profoundly believes and has absolute faith. He wants to coin the seigniorage. He might as well try to coin a vacuum. The silver dollar was not made to represent the market value of the dollar, but less than the proper weight was put in it and it was called a dollar. The difference between the true value and the current value—I might say the sham value at which the dollar was coined—is what is called the seigniorage. Now, this sham and fraud is proposed to be coined into more money. More than that, every dollar of silver that is in the Treasury is represented by a certificate by which the owner has a right to demand a dollar as good as a gold dollar. That is the law as well as the foundation of public credit. Now, if all the silver in the Treasury today were sold at its market value, there would be a shortage of $100,000,000 in gold to redeem the silver dollar. I said we might as well try to coin a vacuum. It is worse than that: it is like trying to coin a negative quantity on the other side of the vacuum.

Some Southern Senators had lately joined David B. Hill in defeating, on political grounds, two excellent nominations made by Cleveland to the Supreme Court. Hewitt expressed his scorn for Hill, and went on:

Gentlemen, public credit cannot be maintained unless you teach your fellow-citizens of the South that there is no royal road to value. Get your Southern representatives to rise to the standard of those great men who, from the foundation of the government down to 1860, stood in the Congress of the United States, not only as statesmen representing the whole country, but as men who understood that the fundamental principles of value and property were the creation of higher power, which no man, by act of Congress, can undo or overturn.

Go and tell your Southern Senators that Calhoun and Benton and Crawford and Reeves, and the other great men who for so many years represented them in the Senate of the United States, would have abandoned even the high position of Senator and gone home in sackcloth and ashes rather than to have degraded the great commission which they held from their States into the mere servitude of a politician without reputation, without character, without right to speak for the State of New York.

The Representatives who sit in Congress from the South are not up to the standard either of the great men who formerly sat there, or the demands of the situation. How do you account for it? I account for it in this way: At the close of the war everybody in the South was ruined. Every man who had any ability immediately betook himself to some kind of business by which he could support himself and his family.

The speech was warmly applauded, for most members of the Southern Society felt as Hewitt did. But at the South it excited indignation. *The Tribune, Times,* and *World* of February 24 carried long dispatches from Washington quoting the resentful Southern leaders. "Ill-timed, untrue, and unjust," said Cobb of Alabama; "he looks at matters through the eyes of a millionaire and a recluse," declared Call of Florida; "the spleen of a dyspeptic old man," asserted Champ Clark of Missouri. Under the circumstances, the speech could have little effect at the South. The people there believed, as Enloe of Tennessee said, that New York loved to insult and traduce the Southern people.

As 1896 opened, Hewitt was well aware of the rising strength of the silver tide in the Democratic Party. Southern friends wrote that it was impossible to dam it back. He welcomed the imminent crisis, for he thought recovery in business impossible until the standard of value had been decisively fixed at one point or another. Nor did he hesitate for a moment over the prospect of deserting his party if it pronounced for silver; he wrote his friends that he would instantly abandon Democracy if it adopted an unsound platform. "You are quite right," he informed a Texas firm,[1] "in thinking that important transactions cannot be made until this question is settled, and you are also right in your view that if we were to pass upon a silver basis there would be an era of bankruptcy and ruin such as this country has never witnessed. The ultimate result is, however, certain. This country will never consent to remain on any other than a gold standard of value."

The action of the Republican Convention delighted him. He had long known the Vice Presidential nominee, Garrett A. Hobart, of New Jersey. "When you see Hobart," he wrote John W. Griggs of Paterson, later McKinley's Attorney-General,[2] "tell him that he will get a good many Democratic votes unless the Chicago platform and candidate shall be very different from what I expect." When the Democrats met in Chicago he believed that the battle was already lost. "Unless an independent ticket is put in nomination by the sound money Democrats, I shall feel constrained to vote for the Republican nominee, although I could wish he were less of a wobbler on the currency question." But the result of the convention was even worse than he had anticipated. The moment he heard of Bryan's nomination he felt that only McKinley's election could avert a national disaster.

"There is but one course to be taken," he wrote a returning delegate.[3] "The sham Democrats must be crushed out; and the heresy which they have incorporated into the platform expurgated as a national pest. Personally, I shall vote for McKinley; and I sincerely hope there will be no third party. The battle should be fought for the issue of sound money and the honest payment of debts. If we then fail, we may regard universal suffrage as a failure."

Like other capitalists, he let it be known that he regarded all investments as unsafe unless McKinley were elected. He informed an Alabama firm that he was acquainted with nobody who would buy Southern property until it was decided whether the nation

[1] To Matlock, Cowan, & Burney, Fort Worth, Tex., June 12, 1896; Hewitt Papers.
[2] June 19, 1896; Hewitt Papers.
[3] To John E. Hurst, Baltimore, July 15, 1896; Hewitt Papers.

was to have fiat money or not. He hesitated to carry through the pending purchase of some West Virginia coal lands. If Bryan were elected, he wrote,[1] "we shall see a panic such as we have never had in this country, and it will not be pleasant to be in debt, because it will be impossible to sell property or to raise money." His chief resentment, like Cleveland's, was directed against the Southern Democrats, and he declared to an old friend that he doubted whether he would ever live to see Democratic principles reintegrated in an effective organization:[2]

In truth there has been no Democratic Party since the war. The Southern people have simply acted with the remains of the Democratic Party in the North, because by their aid repressive measures could be prevented. The Force Bill was thus defeated. On the other hand, the Northern Democrats were in a position to compel support for sound money and for tariff reform whenever the emergency became sufficiently marked, but there has never been any real sympathy between the two sections, and the Northern Democrats have in reality been hated more than the Republican politicians who have been trying to capture the South. I have long foreseen the collapse which has taken place. . . . The old-fashioned Democratic representatives, trained in the school of Jefferson and Seymour and Tilden, have no choice but to vote the Republican ticket.

As the most exciting political campaign since 1860 roared into full activity, with Bryan touring the country, McKinley speaking to noisy delegations from his front porch in Canton, parades and rallies enlivening every city, and the silverites denouncing Wall Street while the gold-standard men denounced repudiation, Hewitt threw himself into the battle. He temporarily forgot the Trenton and Burling Slip offices. He accepted the vice-presidency of the Democratic Honest Money League. At its Fifth Avenue Headquarters, a half-dozen blocks from his house, he was the dominant figure, and when he left it was usually to go to the Republican headquarters nearby. Governor Hill's adherence to Bryan made it necessary for conservative Democrats like Charles S. Fairchild, former-Governor Roswell P. Flower, and Hewitt to exert themselves vigorously to help carry New York for the gold standard.

[1] To C. H. Parker & Co., July 20, 1896; Hewitt Papers.
[2] To G. L. Miller, July 20, 1896; Hewitt Papers.

Though he had at first believed that all Democrats should unite behind McKinley, he soon saw that the organization of a Gold Democratic Party with its own ticket was a political necessity. It would help McKinley in many Western and Border States. While determined not to vote with it, he was glad to assist it. He watched with approval the steps taken for a Gold Democratic Convention in Indianapolis, in which his young protegé Edward M. Shepard was prominent. Representative W. D. Bynum of Indiana, who was in charge of drafting the platform, wrote Hewitt for advice. The ironmaster urged him to make the principal issue the preservation of the Constitution; for, he said, Bryan wished to place a fictitious value on silver, and this was a violation of the spirit if not the letter of the Constitutional provisions regarding money and the sanctity of contracts.[1] At Bynum's request, he even sent him a draft platform emphasizing this constitutional issue; but the convention wisely preferred a platform which appealed to the voters on grounds of principle and of practical economics.

As tens of thousands of Democratic business men in New York State, fearful of the effects of free silver on trade and property, rallied behind Flower, Fairchild, August Belmont, and Hewitt, the ironmaster became the chief Eastern intermediary between the Gold Democrats and the Republicans. He was officially on the Finance Committee of the former party, unofficially on that of the latter. His letters show how largely the Gold Democratic campaign was financed and guided by the Republican managers. Leaders of the new party knew that their nominees, Palmer and Buckner, were unlikely to carry a single State, but they hoped to wrest doubtful States, like Kentucky, from the Bryan column to McKinley's. After the middle of August Hewitt was in constant communication with Cornelius N. Bliss, Republican Treasurer. Within a few weeks the entire task of collecting Gold Democratic funds in New York City had been handed over to him, for the treasurer of the new party, Charles J. Canda, was busy elsewhere. He wrote scores of letters appealing to his wealthy friends on the ground that there was entire harmony of action between Chairman Bynum and Chairman Mark Hanna.[2] Early in September he arranged with Bliss to raise, in addition to the general Gold Democratic collections, a special

[1] To W. D. Bynum, August 21, 1896; Hewitt Papers.
[2] For example, to H. L. Pierce of Boston, October 6, 1896; Hewitt Papers.

fund for the Palmer and Buckner campaign in the critical States of Michigan, Indiana, and Kentucky, on condition that the Republicans contribute half as much more. This special fund proved a great success, quickly rising to almost $100,000.[1]

The wide correspondence which he carried on shows just how effectively the partnership between the Republicans and Gold Democrats was maintained. He knew the principal men in charge of the State campaigns for both parties, and kept in close touch with them. In West Virginia, for example, the Republicans had placed Senator Henry Gassaway Davis in control of their arrangements, and were sure—as Hewitt wrote a friend—"of a successful issue." Hewitt worked closely with the Republican National Committee in supplying speakers. He answered an application from Congressman W. P. C. Breckinridge of Kentucky, for instance, by saying that he was doing his best to get Schurz to go. He saw that the two parties coöperated in supplying material to the press. Whenever appeals came from the Gold Democratic workers for help in a particular locality, he went at once to Bliss if the Gold Democratic funds proved insufficient. Thus we find him writing one Western leader, F. R. Pemberton, on September 18, that he had had two interviews with Bliss in one day; that as a result Bliss had already sent the man a check for $4,000; and that "we are to meet again next Wednesday, when the whole subject of the Democratic movement in the West will be considered." A few extracts from his letters will demonstrate better than paragraphs of exposition how rapidly his special fund grew once he put his shoulder to the work:

(Hewitt to Cornelius N. Bliss, September 23, 1896)

We had a meeting of our finance committee yesterday, and started the subscription list, to which Mr. Whitney and I each subscribed $5,000. I explained the willingness of your Committee to assist, and we hope to raise $50,000 immediately and probably $50,000 additional. The Committee wish to coöperate with your Committee as to the expenditure, and the $5,000 sent to Kentucky will be put down to your contribution toward the combined effort.

(Hewitt to J. B. Baines, Charleston, W. Va., September 25, 1896)

I have been drafted for the purpose of raising money to put

[1] To Cornelius N. Bliss, October 19, 1896; Hewitt Papers.

and keep the third ticket in the field. This task is extremely difficult, because contributors as a rule, knowing that the fight is between McKinley and Bryan, prefer to send their money directly to the treasurer of the Republican Committee. I am met on every hand by polite refusals to do anything for the third ticket, on the ground that however important it may be in the West, it is a damage in the East. It is extremely difficult, therefore, to get money to meet the current expense of keeping open the headquarters in this city and in Chicago, and the burden has been imposed upon a very few men who feel with you that the present crisis really means the death of the Republican Party and the new birth of the Democratic Party.

(Hewitt to Don M. Dickinson, Detroit, October 8, 1896)

I enclose herewith my check for $20,000 in your favor, being the quota assigned to the State of Michigan. You will of course let Mr. Bynum and Mr. Hanna know that you have received this amount. Mr. Foster does not mention any additional subscription secured by you, but if there be any it should be paid over to me, because it will form the basis of a renewed application to the Republican Committee for additional aid.

(Hewitt to George Foster Peabody, New York, October 8, 1896)

In accordance with the request contained in your letter of this date I have mailed to Don M. Dickinson my check for $20,000. In my note to Mr. Canda last evening I told him that I had secured $6,000, making the total amount in my possession actually $65,000, with a promise of $1,000 additional. Today I have received no reply from Mr. Pierce or from Mr. Ottendorfer, from whom I expected to get a subscription. In regard to Major Byrne, it is perfectly true that I had a conversation with him yesterday. He seemed to know of the fund, and wished to learn whether any of it could be applied to the Honest Money League. I told him that it had been raised for Michigan, Indiana, and Kentucky, and that not a dollar of it could be turned over to him, but that the Republican Committee had promised to take care of his arrangements.

Thus, while there were two gold-standard parties and tickets in the field, the managers of both had but a single thought, to elect McKinley. Never before had money been raised in millions for a Presidential campaign as Hanna, Bliss, and Charles G. Dawes raised it that year. There has been much controversy ever since over the exact amounts expended by the Republican National Committee, the estimates running all the way from two to five millions. The former figure is much too small; and the Gold Democratic Party and the Honest Money League should unquestionably be added to the agencies which disbursed large sums taken from Republican sources. Among the subscribers to Hewitt's special fund, it should be noted, were men long eminent in the Democratic Party—August Belmont, James J. Van Alen, Oswald Ottendorfer, and Oscar and Isidor Straus. Some of them gave generously to the Republicans as well.[1]

Had the election been held a week after the cross-of-gold speech, Bryan would probably have swept the country. Yet from the outset Hewitt felt confident of final victory. It seemed to him fortunate that the movement for free and unlimited coinage came to a head at a time when the silver dollar was worth, as bullion, almost precisely fifty cents in gold. To bring the country to a silver standard would obviously mean cutting the value of the dollar squarely in half. This fact made it easy to present the subject graphically to the man in the street. When a wage-earner was asked whether he would rather be paid in a cheap dollar or a dear one, he invariably asked for the most valuable dollar he could get, for he knew that wages would be advanced only by slow stages to meet any new standard of value. It was also easy to present an effective argument to the host of poor men who had put their dollars into savings banks or insurance policies. "I conclude, therefore," Hewitt wrote on September 10, "that upon a fair discussion, which is now inevitable, Bryan will have no chance of being elected, but on the contrary I think the condemnation of the Chicago platform will be so emphatic as to lay the spectre of repudiation at rest for a generation at least."

Yet while he was glad to see Bryan repulsed—while four years later he again voted against Bryan and the resuscitated issue of free silver—he had little faith in McKinley and still less in the Republican Party. He was apprehensive of its tariff policy, and of the many selfish and plutocratic interests allied with it. "In the first moments of their success," he wrote, "the Republicans profess to be very patriotic and magnanimous, but I suppose that when they

[1] See Canda's list of the chief contributors in a letter to Hewitt, October 27, 1896; Hewitt Papers.

get into power they will follow the same greedy and selfish policy they have always pursued. I have never known Republican politicians to make any sacrifices, either for patriotism or justice. . . . What concerns me most is the evidence of antagonism between the rich and the poor in this city." Again the prophetic elements in his statement proved all too well grounded. A few years later men could see that some highly pernicious forces had triumphed along with McKinley, Hanna, and the gold standard.

CHAPTER XXIX

A Citizen of New York

WHEN Elihu Root called Hewitt the first citizen of New York, when Carnegie said that if the metropolis was asked to name its foremost representative "there would be substantial agreement in its response, Abram Hewitt," they were not uttering conventional eulogies. But Hewitt would have disliked the term "first citizen," and would have thought it a sufficiently proud appellation to be called simply a good citizen of New York. Such a citizen, in the fullest meaning of the term, he always strove to be.

In 1894, when the subject of rapid transit finally came to a head, he was enabled to complete one of his principal services to the city. By that time all thoughtful citizens agreed that something must be done at once to bring about the construction of subways. The legislation passed three years previously, creating a Board of Rapid Transit Commissioners which was foolishly empowered to sell a franchise for a privately-owned line, had failed to achieve any useful result. The new body, the Steinway Commission, was under Tammany control. The opposition of Jay Gould, who did not wish a new system competing with his elevated roads, was too powerful both politically and financially.[1] A Constitutional Convention was about to meet, and many believed that the situation demanded some change in the fundamental law of the State. Mr. R. T. Wilson, a banker, at this moment published a plan proposing that the city, under a constitutional amendment, should lend its credit to a private corporation to build and own the subways.

This plan ran counter to Hewitt's firmest beliefs. The legislature

[1] J. B. Walker, *Fifty Years of Rapid Transit,* 123-138, describes the failure of the Steinway Commission.

looked to the Chamber of Commerce to give it leadership, and the Chamber at its meeting on February 15 was on the point of adopting Wilson's plan. A small committee, of which Cornelius N. Bliss was the most prominent member, recommended that the city lend money to private owners for two-thirds of the cost of constructing subways. Jacob H. Schiff and other influential men supported the recommendation; most members plainly favored it. But at this point Hewitt rose and performed the remarkable feat of swinging the Chamber, by a single extemporaneous speech, in an entirely different direction.[1]

He began by saying that the measure proposed to the Chamber was unprecedented in the history of the city, State, or nation. The city was asked to lend its money to build a great public utility which would then be owned and administered by private individuals under virtually no legal restrictions:

When the State of New York was confronted by a greater problem than this, the greatest that has ever presented itself to a civilized community on this side of the Atlantic, the construction of the Erie Canal . . . the State took it in hand, became the owner, borrowed the money, paid for the work, and perhaps unfortunately, retained the administration of the property after it was constructed. The City of New York has pursued the same system. The Croton Aqueduct was constructed by the public at its own cost and administered by its officers. In no instance has the city of New York ever gone into partnership with a private company. In no instance has the government of the United States ever done such a thing. The loaning of the public credit, to which the committee has referred in the case of the Union Pacific and the Central Pacific Railroads, is a most unfortunate illustration of the danger of any connection between the State or National Government and private enterprises. It is true that great enterprise has added to the value of the property of this country and its revenues infinitely more than the entire cost, but it is also true that every dollar of the money advanced by the government of the United States in aid of that enterprise was stolen by the people who had charge of the enterprise. It is notorious that when the first mortgage bonds of that company were issued, by act of Congress taking precedence of the loan of the United States Government, the whole $30,000,000 of Union Pacific Bonds

[1] The fullest report is in the N. Y. *Times*, February 16, 1894.

was divided by the Credit Mobilier among the stockholders and put into their private pockets. The whole of that money was simply a free gift. . . .

In the only departure which I have ever known the City of New York to make from the sound principle of having no connection whatever with private enterprises, the scandal was equally great. The Brooklyn Bridge was originally a private corporation, with private stockholders. The City of New York never loaned its credit to the Brooklyn Bridge—not a penny—but what it did was to subscribe for a portion of the stock. The City of Brooklyn did the same thing. The administration of the work was in the hands of private stockholders, and it culminated in a scandal of the worst kind; and the result was that the City of New York and the City of Brooklyn were compelled to do—what they ought to have done in the first place, or to have done nothing—they were compelled to buy out the private stockholders, and become the sole owners of the work.

The precedent, he added, would lead speculators of all kinds to try to obtain the city's money for their own private schemes. He then laid down what he considered the fundamental principles of a sound settlement, four in number. The city should be authorized by the legislature to construct the subways. It should borrow the money and provide the capital at a cost not exceeding three per cent. It should plan the routes and supervise the work, but avoid the danger of graft in construction and initial operation by making a lease to a responsible corporation, under careful restrictions. Finally, it should require this corporation to pay an annual rental of not less than five per cent, sufficient to meet the interest and amortize the bonds in thirty-three years; thus leaving the city sole owner.

The Chamber of Commerce tabled the subject for two weeks. When it met again on March 1 Hewitt took the floor before an unusually heavy attendance. The result was told in newspaper headlines the next day.[1] Said the *World*: "Hewitt's Pepper Tells. The Chamber of Commerce Deserts The Wilson Rapid-Transit Plan. New York Should Build The Road." The *Herald's* headlines ran: "Let The City Build The Road. Construction To Be Leased. Hewitt's Able Arguments." The ironmaster, after another vigorous speech, had offered a resolution which was carried by practically

[1] N. Y. *World, Herald, Times,* March 2, 1894.

unanimous vote. Its essence was that the city should lend the money and be the full owner of the subways, but should entrust their construction and operation to a corporation on terms that would provide a sinking-fund for gradual extinguishment of the debt. Even Wilson had yielded to his clear-cut arguments. "I'm not sure that I do not almost prefer Mr. Hewitt's plan to mine," he told the Chamber. "It would be much easier to finance it." Most of the newspapers strongly supported his ideas, as did sentiment among business and professional men, and though Mayor Gilroy and other Tammany politicians protested, the Chamber drafted a suitable bill and sent it to Albany with general public backing. The result was a new law, signed by Governor Flower on May 22, 1894, which put into effect (subject to a referendum) precisely the scheme which Hewitt had urged.

This new law, as the historian of rapid transit in New York says, accomplished what previous enactments had failed to achieve; it did so through the provision for public ownership, which made the city's credit available for construction at low interest rates; and it was passed primarily because of the leadership of Hewitt and the Chamber of Commerce. Hewitt had achieved one of the clearest-cut victories of his career.[1]

In 1890 the British Iron and Steel Institute, partly as a courteous recognition of the fact that the United States had now surpassed Great Britain in the production of both pig-iron and steel, held its annual meeting in New York City. The American Institute of Mining Engineers, as we have noted, elected Hewitt its president and deputed him to welcome the British guests. They reached New York in September. Since the British Institute, founded in 1869, had been the parent of the American Institute and of the Verein Deutscher Eisenheuttenleute, both had large delegations present. Indeed, the meeting was virtually an international convention of the iron and steel industrialists of the three foremost nations of the world. Earlier in the year the council of the British Institute had unanimously voted to confer the Bessemer Gold Medal upon Hew-

---

[1] "The Act passed in accordance with the plan of Mayor Hewitt, May 22, 1894, accomplished what previous Acts had failed to achieve mainly if not entirely because of the provision for public ownership. This made possible the use of the city's credit in providing the millions needed to bring the great project to fruition." Walker, op. cit., 139. Hewitt did much to persuade August Belmont to go into the enterprise, which the latter at first regarded with suspicion.

itt. He protested vigorously, arguing that the medal had already been given to Peter Cooper, thus sufficiently honoring all of Cooper's associates; and that he would be sufficiently in the limelight as president of the American Institute, and did not wish to appropriate all the honors of the occasion. The medal was forced upon him, but not until after he had protested again to Sir Lowthian Bell:[1]

> As you know, my relations with the British iron trade have been exceedingly close, and I have been almost the only American ironmaster who has uniformly and persistently advocated a liberal revenue policy in reference to British products. For me to take the medal under such circumstances will lay me open to the charge of receiving compensation for services rendered. There is a narrow spirit in some quarters which would be sure to criticize your action, and to reproach me for having taken advantage of the situation to appropriate the honors which belong to others. I am quite sure that if you see fit to give the medal to John Fritz, who is now an old man, it would give great gratification to the iron and steel industry of this country.

Hewitt had to make the presidential address. He determined that as in 1872 he had exhibited his boldness by making a prophecy as to iron production in 1900 which then seemed fantastic, so now he would predict an early end to *laissez faire* in the whole domain of iron and steel. He foresaw two coming transformations. The workers, within a few generations, would insist on a larger and larger share of control, until the time would come when the industry would be run primarily for them and the consuming public, and not for the capitalists. Again, the process of consolidation would go forward as in other industries; trusts were springing up on every hand, and greater and greater aggregations of capital would appear. They should not be regarded with hostility, for they were a logical development, and they should be regulated instead of exterminated. How? His answer was simple: by complete publicity—pitiless publicity—upon hours, wages, prices, working conditions, and everything else.

The result of his reflections was that the austere individualists of the American, British, and German iron industry who gathered in Chickering Hall on September 8 received a shock. Most of them were two-fisted believers in the old economic order. The Americans,

[1] April 23, 1890; Hewitt Papers.

in particular, were nearly all rugged conservatives like Frick, Carnegie, and Gary. They were rejoicing over the imminent passage of the McKinley Tariff, were hostile to labor unions, and believed that government had no right whatever to interfere with business except occasionally to subsidize it. They complacently expected to hear from Hewitt a tribute to the magnitude of their industry, its wealth and power. Instead, he launched into a prolonged discussion of its human relationships.[1] The United States, he said, had raw materials, money, skill, and ample man-power: but one prerequisite of healthy national growth still remained to be secured. It was harmony between capital and labor. "The final answer to our inquiry as to the ability of the United States to supply the iron required by the continued progress of the country and the march of civilization throughout the world depends therefore upon the establishment and maintenance of friendly relations between the employers and the employed." This, he added, raised the most serious problem of the age. Throughout the world the relations between capital and labor were highly unsatisfactory. "They are undoubtedly undergoing a process of readjustment not unlike that which followed the abolition of serfdom at the close of the Middle Ages."

He thereupon proceeded to lay down a series of axioms which he called incontrovertible. The first was that workers and employers had an equal right to combine "to advance or to reduce wages, or to establish or resist legislation which either or both may regard as essential, desirable, or objectionable." To men like Frick this seemed outrageous; it was a cardinal axiom with them that steelworkers did *not* have a right to form unions. Hewitt's second axiom was that neither party had the right to coerce the other into submission except through the action of the courts, or of tribunals duly constituted by joint agreement. Many ironmasters never hesitated to coerce their employees, doing it by blacklists, spy-systems, evictions, and the use of deputies and coal-and-iron police or Pinkerton men in time of trouble. The third axiom was that workmen had a perfect right to strike at will, and employers to discharge workingmen, unless bound by an agreement not to do so; but no man had the right to compel other workmen to cease from labor,

[1] Published in a 48-page pamphlet under the title of "Iron and Labor"; New York, 1890.

"nor has the employer any right to lock out his workmen in order to compel submission to obnoxious rules." No right to use the lockout at will! Hewitt's final axioms possessed equal trenchancy. He believed in the open shop, but in the same breath he condemned the employers' blacklist as an outrage. He denounced the boycott, but he reiterated that labor unions were a blessing to society, and said that so long as they abstained from violence they were to be commended and encouraged by all thoughtful citizens.

What, then, was to be done when capital and labor came into conflict, and how was the settlement of disputes by force and coercion to be avoided? If strong aggregations of capital were faced by truly strong unions, he said, both sides would shrink from a destructive battle. He did not believe in compulsory arbitration, but on the basis of British experience since 1869, he thought that a system of voluntary arbitration would yield valuable results. Yet to arbitrate labor controversies properly, authoritative information was needed. Workingmen could not be satisfied that they were getting a fair wage until they knew something about the profits and losses of their employers, and they had a right to know:

> It is manifest that this method of settlement involves publicity as to the profits of business. There is undoubtedly great reluctance and some ground of objection to the disclosure of cost and profits; but as a matter of fact, the transfer of business to great corporations has really made this information public property, and in the iron business there is no longer any pretence of concealment either from stockholders or competitors. Surely, then, there remains no valid reason for denying to the workmen the information necessary to enable them to formulate reasonable demands; and it is to the interest of the owners to give this information, inasmuch as the margin of profit on manufacturing operations is now narrowed down to the smallest limits consistent with a moderate return on the profit employed.

Full and constant publicity, he argued, would also offer the best means of controlling the activities of trust and monopolies, which many shortsighted reformers wished to destroy entirely. Industrial consolidations or combinations were inevitable, they offered great economies, and they would curb the excesses of competition; but they must be kept within strict bounds. The government would never be properly armed for this task until it required all great corporations to furnish complete information as to wages, prices, and profits. They should also be compelled to open their books "to the inspection and scrutiny of public officers appointed for the purpose." This principle of public inspection was already recognized and enforced with respect to banks, insurance and trust companies, and railroad corporations. It should be extended to all industrial corporations. Punitive legislation could then be reduced to a minimum; for "no real abuses can survive the criticism of the press when they have been fully investigated by an impartial tribunal."

The basic principle of this recommendation was written a dozen years later into President Theodore Roosevelt's law creating a Federal Bureau of Corporations;[1] while later still the Recovery Act of 1933 demanded uniform accounting systems and open books for industries under trade association control. But in 1890 Hewitt's ideas met with chill hostility from industrialists, who had no intention of letting their profits or policies be canvassed by the public. They listened unresponsively as he concluded: "The present century, now nearing its close, has been preëminently an era of invention and of development in the forces of nature, enriching society and opening possibilities of general culture beyond the dreams of enthusiasm. Industrial peace is, however, necessary to the fruition of the hopes of a better adjustment of social relations, and of progress which will remove all privileges and all impediments to the final establishment of equal rights." The business baronage of the day was not interested in the removal of privilege and unequal rights.

In similar spirit, Hewitt in 1896 employed the dedication of the new buildings of Columbia University on Morningside Heights for a sharp reminder to wealth of its neglected social duties. The bright May day witnessed an impressive scene. Beside President Seth Low stood Governor Levi P. Morton, Mayor Strong, Bishop Potter, and many distinguished alumni; a huge concourse stretched in front. Hewitt's oration, which contained some unusual touches of sonorous eloquence, was entitled "Liberty, Learning, and Property." He rehearsed the many public services of King's College and Columbia, recalling the work of Hamilton and Gouverneur Morris, of Jay,

---

[1] Hewitt's idea was taken up, with due credit to him, by Arthur Twining Hadley, the *Nation*, and others.

Kent, and DeWitt Clinton. Then, turning to issues of the day, he dealt with both the rights and the responsibilities of property.[1]

Most of the speeches heard in Academe in that year of the great free silver battle, like President Cleveland's at the Princeton sesquicentennial, dealt with the defence of property against confiscatory measures. Hewitt attempted a more balanced discussion. Taking note of the vehement denunciation of wealth heard in many quarters, the widening fissure between rich and poor, and the fact that never before in American history had men seen "such general discontent among the working classes as there is today in the presence of superfluous wealth controlled by a small number of individuals," he asked whether our moneyed men were making proper use of their holdings. Did a fair share of it go to satisfy the social and spiritual needs of the country? He felt bound to answer no; too much energy in America had gone into money-getting and far too little in money-distribution; while wealth had grown fat intellectual endeavor had starved.

He had a forcible illustration for his remarks in the history of Columbia itself, for up to that time the richest city in America had done singularly little for its own university. For dreary decades Columbia College had lain in a state of comparative stagnation. The effort to revive and enlarge it in 1854, when the old college site became available for revenue, and a committee under Dr. H. J. Anderson presented a scheme for a true university, had failed. The efforts of such able men as Hamilton Fish and President Barnard to obtain adequate funds had likewise come to little. Meanwhile, many other colleges had fared as badly. From 1800 to 1865 there was an actual decline in the number of college graduates in the United States in proportion to the whole population. "In other words," said Hewitt, "while the country was growing in wealth, the conservative influence of sound learning was steadily diminishing, with the depressing results which are seen today in every department of public life, in the halls of legislation, and in the sensational character of the public press." Only recently had a healthy change become manifest:

[1] The oration was published by the University in handsome format; see also the New York press, May 3, 4, 1896. Dean Van Amringe speaks of Hewitt's "noble oration, distinguished for learning, wisdom, and eloquence." Brander Matthews *et al.*, *A History of Columbia University*, 164.

The feeling is rapidly spreading that the time has come for a new and nobler civilization. A spiritual wave like that which produced the crusades, erected the cathedrals and the universities in the Middle Ages, or the later movement which culminated in the Renaissance and the Reformation, is plainly in sight and ready to usher in the advent of the next century, when the question will be, not as in the eighteenth century, "What are the rights of man?" or in the nineteenth century, "How are these rights to be made available for the production of wealth?" but rather what is the duty of society in regard to the use of the wealth which has thus been created. Already we can see the effect of the coming movement. In the present generation there has been a sudden and wonderful outbreak among rich men to endow higher institutions of learning, which they instinctively recognize as the true saviours of society . . .

The masses of the people have never demanded equality of fortune, and indeed understand it to be impossible; but they have always insisted, and will always insist, upon equality of opportunity. With free schools and universal education, with opportunities for the youth of exceptional ability in the ranks of the rich or the poor to secure the benefits of the highest instruction, the approaches of communism need never be feared. Equality of opportunity insures the ultimate distribution of wealth upon just conditions and within reasonable periods of time.

In short, instead of using his address to assert that education is the bulwark of property, he used it to point out that property should be the bulwark of education—and that one great object of education is to distribute and level property. And he ended by saying again that the nation needed vigorous reform. "Social reforms never come from below. They originate in the trained intellect of scholars, and in the inspirations of genius in an atmosphere favorable to their reception. Slowly but surely great ideas descend and penetrate the mass of the people." The restraint with which his conservative audience naturally received the address led Hewitt to feel disappointed with it. Driving home, he said sadly to his son Edward that it was inferior to his Brooklyn Bridge address and that he was losing his powers; but actually, he had never uttered a more salutary or forcible message.

In still other ways in these years he expressed his inherent liberalism. In 1890 Andrew Carnegie wrote a somewhat foolish article for the *Tribune* on "How to Win a Fortune." Youthful years, he stated, are the most valuable for gaining knowledge; while the college man is wasting his time upon "the barbarous and petty squabbles of a far-distant past," or mastering dead languages, the young business man is "hotly engaged in the school of experience." A college training was of course essential for the professions, but the almost total absence of college men from the upper circles of business seemed to justify the conclusion that higher education "is fatal to success in that domain." This irritated Hewitt. Asked to give his opinion, he said that he did not suppose the value of higher education was open to question, and assuredly did not believe that the chief end of man was success in money-making. He suggested tartly that Carnegie define his terms.[1]

"What do you mean by success? Certainly I will not admit that mere wealth is success. In my own case I have tried all my life to do my duty. If in the course of that I made money I rejoiced; if I lost, and I lost money as frequently as I made it, I bore that with equanimity. I have given my children the best possible educational advantages. I am not trying to leave them wealth, nor do I care whether their education has aided or injured their ability to make money. I am satisfied to leave them thoroughly educated. Others may regard money-making as success; I do not, nor will I discuss this matter upon that low plane." He concluded with an emphatic sentence—"If I were offered a fortune without education, or an education without fortune, I would unhesitatingly accept the education."

The event of the nineties which, apart from the money question, aroused his feelings most strongly, was Cleveland's belligerent message to Congress on the Venezuelan question. It seemed to him so needless, arrogant, and dangerous that at first he could not believe that Cleveland had been in sober possession of his faculties. He at once gave the press an interview,[2] declaring that the Monroe Doctrine had no application to the dispute, that there was nothing in international law which required nations to submit disputed boundaries to arbitration, and that it was outrageous for Cleveland to hint that the United States would, if necessary, enforce its own

[1] N. Y. *Tribune*, May 4, 1890.
[2] N. Y. *Tribune, World,* December 19, 1895.

decision as to the line between Venezuela and British Guiana. We had many powerful economic reasons for not rushing into war with Great Britain. Back of them lay "the greater question whether two peoples, allied by ties of blood and language and history, shall be plunged into a bloody conflict because they happen to differ in regard to the location of an arbitrary line through a wilderness in a country farther away from the United States in time and access than the centre of Africa."[1]

With jingoes eager to thrust the United States toward war, Hewitt was anxious lest the British Ministry do something that would make it impossible for either government to recede. He immediately cabled a request to Salisbury's secretary to take no action for the moment, and through Sir John Pender sent him two letters.[2] In these he proposed that the British Government meet Cleveland halfway by offering to coöperate with the American Commission that was to investigate the boundary. England should appoint a similar body to go to the disputed region. Such an offer would quiet all the popular antagonism in the United States, and disarm our bellicose Secretary of State, Richard Olney; while time in itself would exert a sobering influence.

Of more direct utility were his steps to see that the Chamber of Commerce exerted its influence effectively. He foresaw that the next regular meeting, on January 2, 1896, might easily divide it into two parties, one approving and one assailing the President's message, thus rendering it helpless to guide public opinion. A constructive report, avoiding praise or censure, must be put before it. He prepared appropriate resolutions. Their gist was that the American Government should request Great Britain to appoint an equal number of commissioners to act with ours; that the two nations should agree upon a presiding officer of the highest ability; and that the joint committee, after a careful inquiry, should present an advisory report to the two governments. On the day set for the meeting Hewitt was ill with a cold. He asked Carl Schurz to take his place, and the latter made an impassioned speech. The resolutions were carried with enthusiasm, and an eminent committee,

[1] Hewitt published another emphatic statement in the *Outlook*, December 26, 1895.

[2] Pender to Hewitt, December 28, 1895; "I have sent on to Lord Salisbury your letter and enclosures." Hewitt Papers.

which included Hewitt, Schurz, John Bigelow, Oscar S. Straus, and Seth Low, was appointed to urge adoption of the plan. The American press gave the action of the Chamber much publicity and commendation. "The whole effect of the meeting," Hewitt wrote Sir John Pender,[1] "was the production of a much better state of feeling, not only here but throughout the country."

But as we should expect, Hewitt's principal service to the community after his mayoralty lay in the fostering oversight which he gave to Cooper Union. During all the years after Peter Cooper's death, Edward Cooper continued to be president of the board of trustees, and Hewitt the secretary or chief administrative officer. The staff by the beginning of the nineties consisted of nearly forty devoted men and women, some of them persons of distinction. George W. Plympton, an able civil engineer, had become director of the night schools; J. C. Zachos, who was growing old in the service of the institution, continued his work as curator of the library and professor of English literature; and among the teachers in the women's art school were R. Swain Gifford, N.A., and J. Alden Weir, N.A. While his political cares were greatest, Hewitt had been relieved of much detail in the conduct of the Union by one of his chief business lieutenants in these years, Dr. Rossiter W. Raymond. He could have found no better aide. Raymond was a graduate of Freiberg in Germany. Along with Raphael Pumpelly, he was one of the pioneers in American mining and mineralogy on a scientific basis. No less an authority than John Hays Hammond has written of his "brilliant career of nearly sixty years, which . . . spread his fame as mining engineer, professor, author, linguist, lawyer, editor, poet, and musician wherever science and literature were esteemed."[2]

Because of the very brilliancy of its success, Cooper Union always seemed poverty-stricken and overburdened. With an annual budget in 1890 of about fifty thousand dollars, the trustees could easily have spent thrice that much to advantage. Year after year the applications for admission to the women's art school were at least double its capacity, while the applicants for entry into the men's five-year course were four or five times as numerous as the Union could

[1] January 6, 1896; Hewitt Papers.
[2] John Hays Hammond, *Autobiography*, 63.

admit. A few New Yorkers, such as Percy R. Pyne, Wilson G. Hunt, and Robert C. Goodhue, had given small sums to the institution, but the only gifts of substantial size were from the Cooper-Hewitt households. Hewitt could truthfully write in 1896 that "Mr. Peter Cooper's family have appropriated his entire estate to the work thus far accomplished"—that is, the entire estate not tied up in trust funds. Edward Cooper and he year after year made up the deficits and paid for special expenses, but could do no more. The receipts from rented stores and offices furnished four-fifths of the Union's assured income, and so long as dependence on this source of income continued it could not expand even within its own building.

At the beginning of the nineties steps were taken to enlarge the art school. The Cooper and Hewitt families furnished $50,000 in cash, the building was heightened to accommodate about 250 additional women students, and more teachers were employed. Though Mrs. Susan N. Carter, the principal, urged that these additional students be required to pay a small tuition fee, Hewitt refused to hear of it, saying that Peter Cooper had always insisted that his school be free in every department.[1] But it was not so easy to enlarge the facilities for technological instruction for men. Though Hewitt appealed for funds in every likely quarter, he long met with nothing but deaf ears.

Meanwhile he tried various expedients for placing the Union on a broader foundation, with ampler resources. During 1895 he visited Hamburg. Here he inspected the flourishing commercial school maintained by the city's board of trade. At once he conceived the idea of interesting New York business men in a similar venture. On his return, he wrote J. Pierpont Morgan, who had recently given a handsome endowment to the free trade schools planned by Colonel Auchmuty; for he believed that if Morgan broached the project to the Chamber of Commerce, it might be adopted.[2] The Germans, he argued, were gradually but steadily shouldering other nations, including the Americans, out of many overseas markets; one reason for their success lay in the thorough training afforded by their commercial high schools; and the time had come when the United States should rear up a body of young men thoroughly pro-

[1] To Mrs. Carter, March 14, 1890; Hewitt Papers.
[2] To J. Pierpont Morgan, Sr., August 23, 1895.

ficient in commercial pursuits. This was long before the day of university schools of commerce and business administration, and Hewitt's proposal showed his characteristic vision. If the Chamber of Commerce would furnish even $10,000 a year to pay instructors, he wrote, Cooper Union would supply free quarters and open well-planned courses. But the Chamber regarded educational work as entirely outside its province.

Some months later the removal of Columbia University from its midtown quarters to Morningside Heights seemed to Hewitt to open up another possibility. As early as 1893, indeed, while helping President Low to raise money for the uptown buildings, he had written Low that it would be a misfortune if the Madison Avenue site were abandoned for educational purposes.[1] "It seems to me that if you and I were to make an effort, we could raise money sufficient, certainly with the aid of the city, to make a great technological institution which would complete the work now begun by the Cooper Union and the Auchmuty Trade Schools." The idea soon aroused his enthusiasm. During 1895 he spoke and wrote to a number of wealthy men regarding it; and early in 1896 he included in the annual report of Cooper Union a plan for vastly enlarging the scope of the school by the use of the former Columbia buildings. Some three million dollars, he estimated, would suffice. In various letters he elaborated the project in detail.[2]

For thirty-seven years, he wrote, the Cooper Union had been feeling its way and ascertaining the requirements of the working classes. It had done much solid practical good. But its main success had been exploratory, in showing the direction in which efforts should be made to improve the condition of the ambitious workers of the city. They hungered for education in numbers far surpassing any existing provision for their needs:

There are over 1,100 young men on our waiting list, seeking admission to the full course of the Cooper Union . . . To this course we can only admit 180 pupils per annum. There are therefore over five years' supply of pupils. The institution is entirely inadequate to deal with this demand, which would be tenfold at least if it were not generally understood that it is idle to apply for admission in the hope of being received in less than three or

[1] To Seth Low, January 3, 1893; Hewitt Papers.
[2] For example, to Seth Low, July 28, 1896; Hewitt Papers.

four years. I am very deeply moved by this state of things, and if I had the means, I would at once efface the stigma which rests upon the community in not providing education for these young men, who otherwise are relegated to the streets. I do not know how I can make my fellow citizens understand how necessary it is to deal with this condition of affairs. I only know that the old buildings of Columbia College, if appropriated to this service, would—for the present at least—provide accommodations for the great mass of intelligent young men who are clamoring for an education . . .

The same necessity exists for the young women . . . If we would appropriate all the space in the Cooper Union now devoted to the night classes, to day classes for the young women of New York, we should at least be able to make a beginning in the direction which appeals to our judgment and our sympathy. There are thousands of girls in this city who would be glad to take advantage of such instruction, which would make them self-supporting and self-respecting. At least a million dollars can be wisely used at once in making the provision for these young women.

To transfer the technological classes for men at Cooper Union to the buildings on Madison Avenue, to use the released space at the Union for larger women's classes, to spend two millions uptown and one million downtown for all this expansion—such was Hewitt's dream. But it proved unrealizable. "There has been no response to my suggestion and I do not expect to have any," he wrote sadly. Had he been able to sell his properties in Trenton he might have used his own fortune for the purpose, but a sale was then quite impossible.

Nevertheless, within a few years he had the satisfaction of seeing the financial position of Cooper Union abruptly and completely transformed. The annual report for 1901 showed an endowment of $958,000; that for 1902 showed an endowment of $2,113,350. This represented a veritable revolution, a change from poverty to affluence; it crowned all the labor of Hewitt's lifetime, of "forty-three blessed years," as he put it, in the service of the institution.

The story of this financial transformation was dramatic, and to friends of Cooper Union thrilling. Hewitt told it with characteristic vividness in the last address he ever delivered at a Union commencement, on May 31, 1902.[1] It was Andrew Carnegie who had taken the first step to lift the school to higher ground. As the old century closed, he had written Hewitt saying that in testimony of his admiration for Peter Cooper, his high esteem for Hewitt himself, and his sympathy for the work of the Union, he wished to give it $100,000. Hewitt accepted this gratefully. Meeting Carnegie soon afterward, he said that the gift would furnish the beginnings of a fund to free the Union from the necessity of renting out part of its space, and that he hoped to obtain more money from others. Carnegie replied: "I did not understand the case. Let me give $300,000." And so he did. At a second meeting not long afterward, Hewitt told the benevolent Scotchman that if he could get still another $300,000 he could greatly widen the scope of Cooper Union's work. Carnegie thereupon gave this additional sum on condition that the Cooper-Hewitt families match his two gifts. They were only too glad to do so. "It had previously been arranged by Peter Cooper's descendants," said Hewitt, "that a trust fund of $350,000 created by him for the benefit of his grandchildren, and the residuary interest of his children of $250,000 in the property subject to trust, should come to the institution on the deaths of the members of the families, as they occurred. It was now arranged that the whole property should be transferred to the institution at once to meet Mr. Carnegie's gifts." This involved breaking the trust fund and selling, at a heavy disadvantage, the properties comprising the site of the present Chrysler Building. The transaction was completed in January, 1902.

Again, one day early in 1902, H. H. Rogers came to 9 Lexington Avenue for a chat. He had a cup of tea with Hewitt. On leaving, he remarked: "I have enjoyed myself so much that I would like to leave a little gift for the Union. I want it recorded as anonymous." He handed Hewitt an envelope. Not until fifteen minutes later did the ironmaster think to open it—and the check inside was for $250,000!

"Old men dream dreams," said Hewitt in this last commencement address[2]—and he still had some dreams for Cooper Union. It had never been a trade school. But there was great need for a school to teach the finer handicrafts, the highest types of mechani-

[1] Published in full in the annual report of Cooper Union, 1903.
[2] *Ibid.*

cal work. The United States had still to import artists from Europe
to execute such work. The Sixty-Ninth Regiment Armory, near
Cooper Union, was soon to be vacated. Why should it not be turned
over to the Union for a trade school of the most artistic type? The
Astor Library in the neighborhood was also, thanks to the new
Public Library on the Astor, Tilden, and Lenox foundations, soon
to become vacant. The students needed a special library building;
why should not some rich man give this one to the Union? Thus
Hewitt's last speech in the familiar basement hall was devoted half
to thanks for past blessings, and half to far-reaching plans for the
future. "In conclusion," he said, "let me again quote Scripture, and
say for the trustees, that we have 'fought the good fight—we have
finished our course with joy.' As for myself, I think I am quite prepared to say: 'Lord, now lettest thou thy servant depart in peace,
for mine eyes have seen thy salvation.' "

The new gifts to Cooper Union at last made it possible to stop
renting shops and offices, and use every part of the building. They
enabled the trustees to enlarge the course of night study, to open
day classes for men in technology and science, and to reëquip the
chemical and physical laboratories. The admission requirements
were also raised. Notwithstanding the larger facilities, and in spite
of the stricter tests, both the day and night classes were soon full
to overflowing again. "The demand for this kind of instruction
appears to be practically unlimited," wrote Hewitt.

Hewitt's three daughters, Nelly, Sally, and Amy, had opened
in May, 1895, a museum of decorative arts modelled upon the
famous Musée in Paris, which had aroused Nelly's enthusiasm. The
trustees, recalling that Peter Cooper had designed one floor in his
original plan for a museum, were glad to assist. The idea shortly
proved an inspiration. No such institution existed in New York,
and a collection was glaringly needed. The enthusiasm of the young
women appealed to their friends, and gifts came pouring in. The
merchant George A. Hearn, whose wife had been a schoolmate of
Mrs. Hewitt, was generous in his donations; so was Mrs. William T.
Blodgett, whose husband's art collection had once been the finest
in the city; so was Jacob H. Schiff. J. Pierpont Morgan, meeting
Hewitt at dinner, asked in his abrupt, impulsive way what the
daughters were just then doing. When told that they were bargaining for the unique Badia collection of textiles, on sale in Bar-

celona, he requested that all the papers be sent him that night, as he was sailing for Europe next day. A few weeks later he wrote that he had purchased not only the Badia collection, but the Vives collection in Madrid, and the Stanislas Baron collection in Paris. This princely gesture placed the Cooper Union Museum at one bound almost abreast of the South Kensington Museum in its textile treasures. A friend, despite many protests, insisted upon organizing a council to furnish financial assistance, and this body showed great munificence. Gradually a rich collection in all the varied examples of decorative art was built up. Sally, with the advice of her sisters, made a fine collection of art books, which went to the museum after her death.[1]

Cooper Union was not so imposing an institution as it might have been if, as Hewitt proposed after the Civil War, it had become affiliated with Columbia, or if it had taken over Columbia's abandoned buildings. But it was a school in which the city took pride. Since Lincoln's famous address in 1860, it had become associated with some of the most historic memories of the metropolis. It had blazed a broad new path in the education of the hardworking mechanic and struggling youth. It had combined, far better than more pretentious institutions, a practical training in science and mechanics with an inspiring instruction in art; it had illustrated Ruskin's doctrine of the identification of the highest utility with the highest beauty. Its free reading room and lecture hall had been instruments for broad popular education. In its early history it was the embodiment of Peter Cooper's benevolent impulse and Hewitt's directing brain; but Hewitt hoped that in its later history it would gain many new supporters and far transcend the early designs.

[1] See the pamphlet by Eleanor G. Hewitt, *The Making of a Modern Museum* (1919).

CHAPTER XXX

"The General Outcome"

IN HEWITT'S last years it became evident that the inventive genius of Peter Cooper burned again in the brain of the oldest grandson, named after him. If anything had interested Peter Cooper it was the intellectual development of young people. Discerning the mechanical bent of little Peter Cooper Hewitt, he had encouraged it by placing in a small greenhouse behind the Lexington Avenue house a workshop containing carpenter's and blacksmith's tools, other handicraft implements, a forge, a turning lathe, and a small steam engine for power. When Hewitt's children asked for toys he would say: "I won't buy them, but I'll give you material to make them." He and Hewitt provided for occasional lessons by a master mechanic. Cooper Hewitt thus grew up with tools for his games and scientific magazines for his early reading. As a mere lad he could forge and temper a piece of iron, convert it into steel, sharpen or weld it. The old colored blacksmith at Ringwood taught him to mend machinery. When his mother put new plumbing into the Ringwood house he stayed with the workmen until he had learned to fit joints, install valves, and solder pipes with the best of them.[1]

As Cooper Hewitt grew older he put an impetuous energy into more ambitious diversions. He assembled in the greenhouse the parts of a toy locomotive, bought by his father, which generated steam and pulled small cars. At Ringwood he installed an engine in a rowboat, with an effective screw propeller made of the blades of an old water-wheel. Later he built another engine into a fishing-launch on Greenwood Lake, using it for picnics, and playing havoc with the fishermen's trawls. When he first crossed the ocean in the

[1] Memorandum by Miss Sarah Hewitt; Hewitt Papers.

Scythia he made friends with the chief engineer and haunted the engine-room. He also delighted in electrical experiments. His father gave him Faraday's books, and, beginning with Leyden jars and wet batteries made from preserve jars, he soon built more elaborate apparatus. His sister Nelly has described how she was "made to stand on glass plates and hold firmly to the brass knob of an electrical generator, as her brother turned the glass wheel, until she became a human storage battery, her long golden hair rising until each strand, quivering with the current, stood stiffly out at full length and she looked like the wild woman of Borneo. The onlookers were always tempted as with one impulse to draw the long spark from her, while like a cornered hare she fled in every direction to escape the shock and dissipate the electricity gradually. It was better than tag." Under Cooper Hewitt's leadership the children installed a telegraph system from their sunny first-floor playroom to the basement and third story, the wires passing through the staircase well. He made sending and receiving instruments, attached batteries, and mastered the Morse alphabet. Later he constructed a primitive but usable telephone, with a wire across the street to Edward Cooper's house.

As a young man he developed certain foppish qualities; outwardly he fitted the term "dude," and was sometimes laughed at. But in games, in outdoor sports, in everything that required manual dexterity and quick coördination of mind, eye, and muscle, he always excelled. Michael Pupin writes that his expertness was so uncanny that his friends felt that "a part of his thinking apparatus was in his hands."[1] For some years he was the champion fly-caster of the country, winning many prizes at tournaments. As a young man he set jewels, made musical instruments—an exquisite lute is still preserved—and produced beautiful stained glass, which he flowed, colored, cut, and leaded in designs that attracted the admiring attention of Tiffany's. He was a remarkable dancer. Always skilful, always eccentric, he insisted upon others taking daring risks along with him. His friends long remembered how, on a New Haven hill, he once swept his loaded bobsled, with unerring nerve, under the legs of a horse that had suddenly turned into the road. Another pastime was braking the cars at Ringwood down the gravity road from the mines to the ore-dump. Thrusting young people, and

[1] Michael Pupin, *Peter Cooper Hewitt.*

even their elders, into the car, he would take it down at a speed that raised shrieks of fear. Sometimes distinguished men—Samuel J. Tilden was one—would be heard demanding vigorously that he slow down and let them off. The guests at Ringwood numbered not a few scientists. With these visitors, Raphael Pumpelly, Clarence King, Professor Chandler of Columbia, and above all Hiram Maxim, Cooper Hewitt made warm friends. When Maxim brought an early model of his rapid-fire gun to Ringwood to be tested, Cooper was the only one with a touch sufficiently light to fire one shot only.

During the nineties, with a workshop in Madison Square Tower, the young man gradually became famous; and Hewitt took a natural pride in his inventions. The greatest of them, the mercury vapor lamp, was patented the year Hewitt died. Among others were a static converter or rectifier (to transform alternating into direct current, and vice versa), an electrical interrupter, and a wireless receiver; while he discovered the fundamental principle of the vacuum tube amplifier, so important in wireless telephony. In the field of electrical conduction through gases and vapors he was a daring pioneer. His methods were always unacademic and unorthodox. Usually he designed and constructed his own instruments, which might be bizarre but were successful. He possessed an intuitive foreknowledge of how a given device would operate. When he finished building his static converter, for example, he mentioned to his brother Edward that it was complete and would meet his highest expectations. "Have you tried it?—Does it work?" demanded the brother. "No, I haven't tested it," said Cooper impatiently, "but of course it works; it's got to work." They went to the laboratory, he started the mechanism, and it acted to perfection.[1]

Hewitt had other reasons for happiness in these years. His health actually improved as he grew older. In 1897, the year he was seventy-five, the physician Robin in Paris succeeded in greatly lessening his ailments by treatments of sulphate of soda; he slept better, his digestion was stronger, and till the last weeks of his life he had strength for every task.

Moreover, in the years at the turn of the century, troubled by wars, imperialistic expansion, the trust problem, and the evils exposed by the muckrakers, he felt little of that unhappiness about America and the world which many old-school liberals expressed. He refused to deplore our acquisition of Puerto Rico and the

[1] Edward Cooper to author, March 10, 1934.

Philippines. On the contrary, he thought American control of the dependencies likely to do this country no harm and the islanders much good. In this attitude his admiration for British colonial administration was influential; but what counted most was his inveterate hatred of slovenliness, backwardness, and inefficiency, for he believed that American rule would mean order and progress. Before peace had been made with Spain in 1898 he wrote President McKinley in favor of accepting our share of the white man's burden, and called his attention to the tenth chapter of Benjamin Kidd's recent *Social Evolution*, saying that Kidd's views as to the development of the tropics were very suggestive. "I fully agree with him that our people can never colonize these regions, but we may furnish the control which they require, using domestic agencies as far as possible, as England now does in India and Egypt."[1]

Nor, though he deplored the exactions of the trusts, did he regard the growth of large business units as in general injurious to society.[2] In 1899, asked to appear before the Federal Industrial Commission, he had testified to the contrary. "Corporations have continued to grow, and at the present moment they threaten to absorb the entire industrial business of the country which is capable of being administered by centralized management. This is precisely the direction which I anticipate, and seems to me to be in accordance with the evolution which has taken place within the half-century, and which may be in accordance with a natural law, if there be natural laws involved in the progress of modern civilization. My own view is that when industry has been sufficiently centralized and the ownership widely diffused through the distribution of shares, the workmen will gradually acquire these shares and control the property which they represent . . . The corporate movement, however, seems to me to be altogether advantageous to society. I do not doubt that with time, spread of knowledge through technical education, and the general improvement in the intelligence of men, who under our modern conditions of industrial life have ceased to be machines and have become operators of machines, the standard of self-respect, of comfort, and of happiness will be permanently raised."[3] He always thought the Sherman Act the

[1] Hewitt to McKinley, Sept. 12, 1898; Hewitt Papers.
[2] N. Y. *Tribune*, April 14, 1899.
[3] Statement to the Industrial Commission; see also Hewitt to John E. Parsons, Oct. 19, 1897; Hewitt Papers.

wrong way to deal with the trusts. "Competition can be the death of trade as much as the life of trade," he used to say.

To the last he continued incessantly busy. "I am striving to close up such private interests as still require attention," he wrote in 1899; but he never really wished to withdraw from business. He and Edward Cooper disposed of their cattle companies in the West, selling the Texas herds at a large loss in 1893 and the Lakotah Company holdings at a small one in 1897.[1] In 1900 the New Jersey Steel & Iron Company was sold to the American Bridge Company, which was formed that year. But in all his other enterprises he remained active, and even added new ones to the list. He was still part owner of the glue works, over the management of which in the nineties he and Edward Cooper had the only serious dispute of their lives. They still had the Trenton Iron Company. Shortly after leaving the mayoralty he had made large investments in coal lands in West Virginia, which he extended as his means permitted. He was the principal owner of the Gauley Mountain Coal Company, in which Levi P. Morton, George T. Bliss, and other New York capitalists also held shares. The largest holdings were at Anstead, just southeast of Charleston, near the point where the Gauley River pours into the Kanawha. Actual management was vested in W. N. Page, a man of experience, but Hewitt maintained general supervision and made many trips to the district. He was still part owner of the Roane Iron Company, now profitable again.[2]

What he refused to do was to enter any business which merely wanted his name, or to which he could not give proper attention. This was an old rule of his. Early in the nineties one of the partners of the North American Trust Company, then not in the best of order, had called on him. Dilating on the prospects of the company, he had offered Hewitt the presidency at $50,000 a year. Hewitt quietly refused. The caller suggested $75,000–$100,000. Then, as Hewitt still refused: "Name your own salary." At this Hewitt turned upon him with some heat. "Do you wish me for my knowledge of banking, or for my name?" he demanded. "If it's for my knowledge of banking, I am not worth $10,000 a year. If you want my name, it is not for sale at any price." For similar reasons he later refused a directorship in the Equitable Life. "I can't be a

[1] The Lakotah Company realized $100 a share.
[2] To P. D. Pollock, April 30, 1898; Hewitt Papers.

57. MR. A. S. HEWITT FROM A PORTRAIT BY BONNAT

58. MRS. HEWITT AND HER THREE DAUGHTERS

59. Mrs. Hewitt In Later Life. From a Portrait by Porter

60. Hewitt's Three Daughters: Sarah, Amy, and Eleanor Hewitt

61. Dinner at 9 Lexington Avenue before the Vanderbilt Fancy Dress Ball

62. PETER COOPER HEWITT, THOMAS A. EDISON, HUDSON MAXIM, AND OTHER
AMERICAN INVENTORS, 1917

63. HEWITT SPEAKING AT COLUMBIA UNIVERSITY

64. FATHER KNICKERBOCKER SHOWS HIS APPRECIATION OF HIS BEST
ALL-AROUND CITIZEN.   *Reproduced from Puck, 1901*

director without knowing what is going on," he told James Hazen Hyde, "and to know what was going on in your great company would take all my time."[1] Had others taken a similar position, the great insurance scandals of 1905 would have been prevented.

An enterprise which displayed his continued zest for business adventure was the development of the Louisiana sulphur deposits. During the eighties a German mining engineer, shambling and guttural, had come to Hewitt's office with a scheme for tapping the rich sulphur beds known to exist near Lake Charles, not far from the Gulf and the Texas line. Here, ages past, during the Eocene or Miocene age, a vast geyser had spouted away, leaving the sulphur encrusted within and about its crater.[2] Now the ore was covered with thick strata of clay, limestone, and worst of all, gas and quicksand. Ordinary mining operations had always ended in disaster. But the old German believed that he could sink caissons, and then within them put down shafts of reinforced steel. Hewitt, after investigation, plunged into the enterprise, and formed a company in which William R. Grace, H. McK. Twombly, and other wealthy New Yorkers also became interested.

It is impossible to go fully into the dramatic tale of what followed. For years one costly failure followed another. Then a striking new figure appeared—Herman Frasch, already well known for his process of de-sulphurizing the highly offensive Ohio and Canadian petroleum, which had enormously increased its value.[3] He entered Hewitt's office one day in 1894, a volatile, headstrong, rushing German with a touch of dynamic genius. Hewitt forthwith became his chief supporter in his plans for getting the sulphur up through the hitherto impenetrable gas and quicksand. At first Frasch offered little beyond a general scheme for forcing down superheated steam through one pipe to melt the sulphur, and pumping it up through another. But after a long sequence of heartbreaking losses, his plans were finally made workable. A narrow shaft was bored, as for petroleum. A series of concentric pipes was inserted. Through one pipe live steam was forced down, through another compressed air to render the melted sulphur volatile, and

[1] Erskine Hewitt to author, April 14, 1932.

[2] *Scientific American*, June 1, 1907.

[3] For Frasch see *World's Work*, July, 1914; *Journal Society of Chemical Industry*, May 30, 1914.

through another sand to hold it in place. It bubbled to the surface, and was run into settling tanks. At one time all the backers of the scheme but Hewitt had been utterly disheartened. He himself had wavered. But Frasch had secured a chance to talk to Mrs. Hewitt at Ringwood; she, like her father, sometimes loved to take a chance; and she insisted on sticking—adding money of her own. Then overnight the losses were converted into truly dazzling profits.[1]

His purchase of large coal holdings gave Hewitt a new interest in labor questions. As always, he encouraged unions, but he also insisted on the open shop. At the same time, he paid careful attention to working conditions. His manager, Page, was instructed under no conditions to hire Slav or Polish miners, but to confine the force to those who had an American standard of living. "One reason why I was led to engage in this enterprise was the assurance that Anstead was so situated as to make a desirable place of residence. I hope, therefore, in the improvements which you make, that you will always bear in mind the general plan of having comfortable residences for our employees, and that you will so arrange the location of the houses as to ensure good drainage, and if possible, garden spots for each house. I should like, if the property will warrant, as it seems it will do, to have Anstead regarded as a model mining town, and I am quite sure that Mr. Bliss sympathizes with me . . . I cannot too strongly impress you with the idea that we are very averse to making profits or dividends at the expense of the comfort, morality, and happiness of the employee."

Doubtless Hewitt's experience with labor problems in West Virginia colored his views upon the great anthracite strike of 1902, in which President Roosevelt ultimately compelled a settlement by arbitration. He thought that the strike ought to have been averted. The country blamed the pig-headed mine operators most for the trouble. Hewitt blamed both sides. He had talked with John Mitchell, head of the United Mine Workers, shortly before the strike, and advised him against it. "Use the money that the strike would cost to buy the common stock of the coal companies," he said, "and then pay yourself the wages you deserve." This was not very practical advice, and Mitchell said so. "Well, don't get into an impasse," said Hewitt. "What is that?" asked Mitchell, who

[1] Erskine Hewitt to author, June 24, 1932; *Scientific American*, August 4, 1906; June 1, 1907.

was not well educated; and Hewitt replied, with a humorous gleam, "It's a blind alley that you can't get out of without turning around."

The fact was that Hewitt disliked the United Mine Workers as an organization which stood for the closed shop, while he gave insufficient attention to the sins of the anthracite operators.[1] Their arrogance was unquestionably the chief cause of the strike; yet several weeks before Roosevelt acted, Hewitt issued a statement which took the operators' side completely. It was one of the most unfortunate utterances of his career. "You ask," he told a *Tribune* reporter,[2] "whether the time has not arrived for arbitration in order to end the coal strike in the anthracite region. I think the time has arrived when the plain truth should be told, as well to the striking miners as to the public. . . . For a quarter century I have uniformly maintained the right and duty of association, both on the part of employers and employees. Such organizations, however, must be for lawful purposes." And he went on:

> The unhappy controversy now existing is not based upon any reasonable claim which labor can make for shorter hours or better wages. It is true that Mr. Mitchell alleges this to be the object of the strike, but as a matter of fact it is notorious that the real object is to secure recognition of his national organization as an authority entitled to decide upon the rates of wages and the conditions of labor in the coal fields wherever situated. If this demand be conceded it will not be possible for any man not having a union card to secure employment in the coal fields. This will amount to a denial of the right of every man to sell his labor in a free market. The concession of this demand will make Mr. Mitchell the dictator of the coal business and put him in control of votes enough to decide the next Presidential election . . .
>
> It would be far better to abandon the business of mining anthracite coal than to concede the demand of any man or set of men to deny the right of employment and of labor upon which the whole structure of free government is founded, and to which this country owes its phenomenal progress. In my judgment, therefore, the operators are only doing their plain duty in declining to arbitrate a question which is in the domain of con-

[1] A. E. Suffern, *Conciliation and Arbitration in the Coal Industry*, 240-252.
[2] N. Y. *Tribune*, August 26, 1902.

science and involves the personal liberty of the individual. The only solution for the trouble is for Mr. Mitchell to order the strike off without delay.

Had the strike been solely for the closed shop under the United Mine Workers, Hewitt's stand would have been as strong as it was courageous. But the miners insisted that the strike was primarily for better hours and wages, and offered to let a Federal commission pass on the issues. In the end, when Roosevelt's commission awarded a ten per cent wage increase but denied recognition of the United Mine Workers, Hewitt approved of both parts of the decision.

But his liberalism never really flagged. Against this utterance should be set his passionate denunciation, at a meeting of the Pro-Cathedral in Stanton Street, in 1900, to raise funds for slum work, of the indifference of many rich people to social misery. Since 1840, he said, our national wealth had increased five times as fast as population. Means existed in abundance to remove all the misery which the East Side typified. "The rich have not even begun to do what they ought to do." He knew many who were not giving half of what their fathers gave before them. How could they accept all the wealth which modern industry had built up and do nothing to correct the evils which industry created? "Good God! Can this be the end for which we have been working all these centuries? For Heaven's sake, is this the result of our industrial development, and must our prosperity be purchased at such a staggering price? If these terrible tenements, these overcrowded districts, these dark and foul dwelling-places, and all the attending misery must go with industry, then I would to God that every industrial centre could be destroyed as were Sodom and Gomorrah of old!"

As Hewitt attained fulness of years, there also came fulness of public esteem. He had outlived the enmities of his busiest years. Old controversies had been mellowed by time. He resolutely declined to embark upon new ones, and even when John Bigelow's *Tilden* appeared in 1895 with a distorted account of his part in the disputed election, he contented himself with revising his own narrative written in 1878, and quietly laying it away in his safe. He found many tokens that no one in New York now counted for more in civic and philanthropic enterprises. He sat on the Palisades Interstate Park Commission,[1] and in 1902 was a member of the municipal committee to welcome Prince Henry of Prussia. When J. Pierpont Morgan organized the United States Steel Corporation, which combined the Carnegie holdings with other gigantic properties, he pressed Hewitt to become a director. It was important to inspire confidence in Great Britain, where the corporation hoped to sell much stock, and Morgan knew that Hewitt was highly regarded in London. When the time came to present the first report to the stockholders, Morgan and Gary desired to make it public at once. H. H. Rogers and others demurred. Since Morgan could never make a speech, he asked Hewitt to plead the case for publicity in board meeting, and the latter did so with such effect that the opposition was silenced.

Late that same year, 1902, the United States Steel Corporation announced a great stock-distribution scheme which took the industrial world by surprise. Nothing quite like it had hitherto been known. Every employee, from those earning $800 or less a year to those earning $25,000 a year or more, was given an opportunity to buy the 7 per cent preferred stock of the corporation. It was offered them at less than market value, and they might pay for it in modest monthly instalments. In the first year, 26,399 men subscribed for stock. Everyone recognized the source of this plan. As Ida M. Tarbell says in her life of Gary, "Abram S. Hewitt, upon whom Mr. Morgan had long relied for advice . . . had no doubt strongly influenced Mr. Morgan in these matters."[2]

On Hewitt's eightieth birthday Carnegie sent him "cordial greetings upon ten octaves, every note truly struck and grandly sung," while President Roosevelt telegraphed his "congratulations to New York in having in you one of the best possible object-lessons in good citizenship." Various men had awakened to a realization that his career as a political and civic leader possessed more significance than they had previously grasped. A striking expression of this feeling came from Don M. Dickinson. Except in the Gold Democratic campaign there had been no close association between him and Hewitt. But in a long reminiscent letter of 1902 to President Roose-

---

[1] Gov. Voorhees of N. J. to Hewitt, May 11, 1900; Gov. Roosevelt to Hewitt, June 25, 1900; Hewitt Papers.

[2] Ida M. Tarbell, *Life of Elbert H. Gary*, 162, 163.

velt, he explained that Hewitt, not Tilden, had really revitalized the Democratic party in the seventies.[1] We have already quoted the passage in which he wrote that Hewitt's "demands for purity and high patriotism in politics" had been the essential element in the party's rebirth; that Hewitt had labored without selfishness and without reward whereas Tilden had labored in large part for himself. He suggested that President Roosevelt should "notice" Hewitt; that the ironmaster be summoned occasionally to give his advice, or that some conspicuous governmental position be offered as a testimonial of the President's admiration:

> I think you will agree that Mr. Hewitt possesses the trust of the people of this country in a remarkable degree. It is a universal belief among all sorts and conditions of men that on all current and very momentous questions between capital and labor, the rich and poor, he is a careful and comprehensive student, and that in his judgments upon them he stands absolutely impartial as between these classes, and would solve the issues according to the best lights of an honest and very able man. The respect for him, the belief in his honesty, the great weight attached to his views on all economic and all public questions, is practically universal; and when it is considered that very few men in public life, and probably not one in private life like his own, are so widely known among the people at large, he is a remarkable, a unique figure of our time. His occasional touch of nerves, manifested in a sort of fretfulness occasionally in his public utterances, are taken as humorous rather than ill-humored. Taking him by and large, I doubt whether there is a man in the country whom the people would be more pleased to see honored.

To this the President replied:[2]

> My dear Mr. Dickinson:
> I can say with all sincerity that I shall feel more than contented with my public life if some day in the future my children have the chance to see a letter written about me, by one of my friends who knows the facts, like this letter of yours about Abram S. Hewitt. I thought very, very highly of Mr. Hewitt already. If possible, his letter makes me think even more highly of him.

---

[1] Don M. Dickinson to Roosevelt, March 15, 1902; Roosevelt Papers.
[2] Roosevelt to Dickinson, March 26, 1902; Roosevelt Papers.

Do you mind my saying that it also adds to the great respect and admiration I already felt for you?

Now, if an opportunity comes, I shall be more than glad to do as you suggest about Mr. Hewitt. I say "if an opportunity comes," because, as you with your great experience of public life know, it is not possible to foretell just how the chance will shape itself. It may be that when an opportunity to give Mr. Hewitt what he deserves arises there will be some imperative necessity to recognize the claim of someone else. I say this only because I do not want even impliedly to promise more than I am able to perform. But I want to add that I would particularly like, for my own sake, to satisfy my own feeling as to the recognition of the highest quality of citizenship, to pay the compliment, to give the acknowledgment, to Mr. Hewitt.

Now can you indicate at all specifically the kind of thing you would suggest? I do not believe I ought to offer him a position in the Cabinet, even though an opportunity arose. Short of that there is nothing I would not gladly offer him; and as far as I am personally concerned, I should be only too delighted to have him in the Cabinet. But from the political standpoint, both as regards him and myself, I should doubt the wisdom of so doing.

Faithfully yours, Theodore Roosevelt.

But it was too late for such honors.

As 1902 closed it was evident to Hewitt's family that his health was dangerously frail. On January 8, 1903, he was attacked by obstructive jaundice. His physicians, Dr. E. L. Keyes and Dr. E. L. Keyes, Jr., realized there was little hope for his recovery. On Sunday the 11th it was thought that he could not live out the night, and members of the family were summoned to his bedside. But he rallied with astonishing vitality, and by Thursday it was even believed that he might pull through. That night, however, a relapse made it plain that the end was near. Oxygen was used, his mind remained lucid, and he chatted with those at his bedside. On Saturday afternoon he began to sink, and his three sons and three daughters, with their mother, waited in hourly expectation of his death.

The end was characteristic of the man. As morning began to dawn on Sunday the 18th, those dearest to him were gathered about the bed where physicians strove to keep the vital spark alive. Though his strength was ebbing he remained perfectly conscious, and made repeated efforts to comfort his children and wife. He knew that only the administration of oxygen sustained him. Suddenly, with the decision he had always shown, he reached out, grasped the little tube firmly, and removed it from his mouth. A faint smile flickered across his face. "And now," he whispered, "I am officially dead." His eyes lighted up for an instant, and he was gone.

His very simple funeral in Calvary Church on January 21 was a memorable occasion. The fifteen hundred people who filled the building were, the *Times* declared, "the most distinguished company ever assembled in New York to do honor to the memory of its foremost citizen." The city government, the universities, and nearly all the civic and philanthropic institutions of the metropolis were represented. The pall-bearers included Andrew Carnegie, Seth Low, J. Pierpont Morgan, Senator John Kean, Jacob H. Schiff, and Lord Charles Beresford. Bishop Potter departed from the commitment service to read Richard Watson Gilder's poem, "The Great Citizen—Abram S. Hewitt":

> Mourn for his death, but for his life rejoice,
> Who was the city's heart, the city's voice.
>
> Dauntless in youth, impetuous in age,
> Keen in debate, in civic counsel sage.
>
> Talents and wealth to him were but a trust
> To lift his hapless brother from the dust.
>
> Because he followed truth, he led all men,
> Through years and virtues, the great citizen.
>
> By being great he made the city great;
> Serving the city he upheld the state.
>
> So shall the city win a purer flame,
> Led by the living splendor of his fame.

Nor was this all. After his burial in the Peter Cooper plot in Greenwood Cemetery in Brooklyn, a series of memorial meetings provided an expression of genuine grief as well as admiration.

Ex-President Cleveland[1] spoke at the City Club on January 27, recalling how unselfishly Hewitt had turned from business "to place his wonderful mental endowments and his astonishing knowledge and information at the service of the city." Carl Schurz declared that Hewitt was one of those rare men whose life-story, if truthfully told, would be a sustained eulogy. "I wish," wrote President Roosevelt, "there was some way in which I could express my profound sense of personal bereavement in the death of Abram S. Hewitt, and above all my feeling as a citizen of what we all owe him. His presence has been in the literal sense of the word an inspiration to the decent performance of duty by all who wish well to the state, and the memory of his life is a heritage of honor for the city." At the next monthly meeting of the Chamber of Commerce, after speeches by Carnegie, Schurz, and William E. Dodge, Jr., Morris K. Jesup made a suggestion which was immediately acted upon. The grand stairway of marble in the new building of the Chamber, he recalled, contained niches which were to be filled, as time passed, with statues of the most influential leaders of the metropolis. "Let us honor ourselves, as we seek to honor the long and useful life of him who is gone, by placing in the first space a statue of the purest marble, representing . . . the purity, sincerity, and unselfish devotion to duty of Mr. Hewitt." And Ex-Mayor Low spoke for all when he said:

"New York seems lonely without Mr. Hewitt."

Finally, as the most fitting of all memorials, a group of leading citizens, meeting in City Hall, opened subscriptions for a special endowment fund to extend the work of Cooper Union. Before the month ended Carnegie had given $50,000, and William E. Dodge, Jr. and J. Pierpont Morgan $25,000 each; and within a short time the treasurer of the fund was able to present Cooper Union with a check for almost $250,000.

For mere eulogy Hewitt would have cared nothing, for throughout his life he disliked praise; but for this gift to enlarge the educational work which had so long been nearest his heart he would have cared a great deal. Once a publisher had suggested that he

[1] It is pleasant to record that all animosity between Cleveland and Hewitt had long since disappeared. Cleveland once paid Hewitt a notable tribute by remarking: "If I only knew as much as Abram S. Hewitt, I might amount to something!" Richard Watson Gilder, *Grover Cleveland, A Record of Friendship*, 45.

write his autobiography. He at once returned a decided refusal, protesting against the idea that his acts were worthy of any special notice, and stating what he believed to be the great aim and justification, humanly considered, of life. "I try," he wrote, "to keep myself free from the vanity which would be implied in my case in preparing for the public an account of my life. Lives are not to be measured by what people think of them. The results are registered from day to day, and for all time, in the progress and constitution of society. I am content to play my little part on the stage, and have it forgotten as soon as possible by the public. If I have done any good, insignificant as it may be, it will appear in the general outcome of society."

APPENDIX I

A Note upon Sources

THE principal manuscript sources used in the preparation of this volume have been as follows: (1) The John Hewitt Papers, a small body of letters and accounts now in the possession of Mr. Erskine Hewitt; (2) the Peter Cooper Papers, a somewhat larger collection in the same custody, which are supplemented by papers and relics in the possession of Cooper Union; (3) the Abram S. Hewitt Papers, consisting of a wide range of materials (though many were unfortunately destroyed by fire), also in Mr. Erskine Hewitt's possession, but intended ultimately for the Library of Congress; (4) papers of Cooper & Hewitt, or as the firm was for a time known, Cooper, Hewitt & Company, part of which are in the Library of Congress, and part held by Mr. Erskine Hewitt; (5) the Samuel J. Tilden Papers in the New York Public Library; (6) the Manton Marble Papers, some of which the author consulted in the University of London, for Mr. Marble spent his last years in England, but most of which are in the Library of Congress; (7) the Bourke Cockran Papers, consisting almost altogether of clippings, in the New York Public Library; (8) the Grover Cleveland Papers in the Library of Congress, the author having also a large private collection of Cleveland transcripts; and (9) the Carnegie Papers in the Library of Congress, which contain a number of Hewitt's letters. It would be impossible to list here all the books and pamphlets consulted, of which only the most important are mentioned in the footnotes. The Eglinton Library of the Columbia University School of Mines has been especially valuable in its resources upon the technological and business developments of the iron and steel industries.

APPENDIX II

The Growth of Peter Cooper's Fortune

PETER COOPER'S little brown notebook of accounts contains a series of tables showing the steady growth of his fortune. The first page, dated March 1, 1833, is headed, "Statement of property ownded by Peter Cooper." This statement runs as follows:

4—Houses in front and one in rear of lott together with feed hous and stables and thirteen lotts on the Third Avenue and Thirty-third Street Valued at—	$25,000—
One lease on 60 feet fronting on 33 Street 170 deep Valued at	500—
One hous stable and two lotts corner of 28th Street and fourt Avenue—Valued at—	8,000—
Glue Factory and Lease of ground Valued at—	10,000—
Stock now in factory	15,000—
Four houses and stables on lease in the Bowery—	1,000—
Nine lotts Forge Steam engine works shop and tools—	10,000—
10 Shares of Canton Stock $44 paid—	1,000—
20 Shares of Susquehannah Rail road Stock with $50 paid in	1,000
Ten hundred and fifty dolars lent to J Cooper	1,050
	$72,550

And on the next page the list continues thus, no date being given. The time is evidently the later thirties:

Mortgage held against Daniel Smith and Lucius Lockwood—dated June 22, 1835—	3,000.00
47 Shares of Camden Rail road stock	7,000.00
One store and lot in Bowery	9,000.00
One house and lot Bowery	7,000.00
433 acres of land in Pensilvania	500.00
One house and 2 acres of land City Island	500.00
Cash lent to S. Bedell	700.00
Cash lent to Margaret Baker	1,177.84
Cash lent Wm. Henry and S. Bedell Paid	
Cash lent to James Cooper Paid	
13 lots in Baltimore	2,000.00
One hous do in Alisanna St	2,750.00

8 Lotts on 12 Avenue	1,600.00
1 Lott on Bloomingdale Road	250.00
Money on interest to Peter Palmer	6,600.00
2 Houses and lotts on Third Avenue	5,000.00
6 Lotts on Fourt Avenue	2,931.00
	50,909.00
	72,550.00
	$123,459.00

A statement of a few "Book Debts dew Peter Cooper" follows. Then comes a page exhibiting his property as of February 21, 1846. It shows holdings in New York and Williamsburg valued at $157,-500, the most important being the "Eight lotts on 3 Avenue 7th St & Bowery," worth $33,000, and the glue factory, with twelve acres of land, worth $30,000. He also had at Trenton property valued at $183,000, and a number of notes and mortgages, the total being no less than $383,500. Then comes still another tabulation dated July 10, 1856. It shows that Peter Cooper then had property worth no less than $1,106,000, exclusive of paper. The glue factory, with seventeen acres of land and the stock on hand, is listed at $300,000, while the Trenton holdings came to $480,000 more. Cooper wrote at the bottom of the page, "I make no account of Block of ground and holding on Astor Place worth $500,000"— he had devoted that to public uses. And he added: "I have at this time notes and debts dew me. This $150,000 is more than sufficient to finish building on Astor and pay all that I owe." Thus the book ends. In little more than twenty years his fortune had grown from less than $75,000 to more than $1,100,000, without counting the gift to education which he conservatively estimated at $500,000, and which really came to more than $600,000.

Index

121. Ogden, Col. Joseph, } St Did Saley
     "   David Sr. }

~~Hewitt~~
149   Amelia Bowman, 1856
       Sarah Cooper   1858
       Peter Cooper   1861
       Eleanor Gurnee   1864
267   Edward Ringwood   1866
       Erskine   1871